THE AMERICAN PAST: A SOCIAL RECORD

1607–PRESENT

EDITED BY

IRWIN UNGER
New York University

DAVID BRODY
University of California, Davis

PAUL GOODMAN
University of California, Davis

XEROX COLLEGE PUBLISHING

Waltham, Massachusetts / Toronto

The American Past: A Social Record

1607–Present

ACKNOWLEDGMENTS

Footnotes have been omitted except where they are
necessary for an understanding of the text.

DANIEL BELL, "Crime as an American Way of Life." Reprinted from *The Antioch Review,* vol. 13, no. 2, by permission of the editors.

RAY ALLEN BILLINGTON, "Frontier Democracy: Social Aspects" from *America's Frontier Heritage* by Ray Allen Billington. Copyright © 1966 by Ray Allen Billington. Reprinted by permission of Holt, Rinehart and Winston, Inc.

MILDRED CAMPBELL, "Social Origins of Some Early Americans" from *Seventeenth-Century America* by James Smith. Reprinted by permission of the University of North Carolina Press. Copyright © 1959 by the Institute of Early American History and Culture.

STOKELY CARMICHAEL, "Toward Black Liberation." Reprinted by permission of the University of Massachusetts Press.

CARL N. DEGLER, "Revolution Without Ideology: The Changing Place of Women in America." Reprinted by permission of *Daedalus,* Journal of the American Academy of Arts and Sciences, Boston, Massachusetts.

OSCAR HANDLIN, "Old Immigrants and New." Reprinted by permission of Collins-Knowlton-Wing, Inc. Copyright © 1956 Oscar Handlin. "The Significance of the Seventeenth Century" from *Seventeenth-Century America* by James Smith. Reprinted by permission of the University of North Carolina Press. Copyright © 1959 by the Institute of Early American History and Culture.

JAMES A. HENRETTA, "Economic Development and Social Structure in Colonial Boston." First published in the *William and Mary Quarterly,* 3rd ser., vol. 22 (1965). Reprinted by permission of the author.

WILL HERBERG, "Religion and Culture in Present-Day America." Reprinted by permission of the University of Notre Dame Press.

"THE INDUSTRIAL WAR." Reprinted from the November 1937 issue of *Fortune* magazine by special permission; © 1937 Time, Inc.

KENNETH KENISTON, "You Have to Grow Up in Scarsdale to Know How Bad It Is." Copyright © 1969 by The New York Times Company. Reprinted by permission.

AUBREY C. LAND, "Economic Base and Social Structure: The Northern Chesapeake in the Eighteenth Century." Reprinted by permission of *The Journal of Economic History.*

SAMUEL LUBELL, from pp. 28–50 of *The Future of American Politics* by Samuel Lubell. Copyright, 1952, by Samuel Lubell. Reprinted by permission of Harper & Row, Publishers, Inc.

ROY LUBOVE, "The Tenement Comes of Age" from *The Progressives and the Slums: Tenement House Reform in New York City, 1890–1917.* Reprinted by permission of the University of Pittsburgh Press. Copyright © 1962 by the University of Pittsburgh Press.

MILTON MAYER, "By Power Possessed." Reprinted by permission of the University of Massachusetts Press.

PERRY MILLER, "The Contribution of the Protestant Churches to Religious Liberty in Colonial America." Reprinted by permission of the estate of Perry Miller and *Church History.*

ROBERT MOATS MILLER, "The Ku Klux Klan." Those portions reprinted herein were originally published in *Change and Continuity in Twentieth-Century America: The 1920's,* edited by John Braeman, Robert H. Bremmer, and David Brody. Copyright © by the Ohio State University Press. All rights reserved.

DAVID MONTGOMERY, "The Working Classes of the Pre-Industrial American City, 1780–1830." Reprinted by permission of *Labor History.*

WILLIAM L. O'NEILL, "Divorce in the Progressive Era." Reprinted by permission of the author and the *American Quarterly* of the University of Pennsylvania. Copyright, 1965, Trustees of the University of Pennsylvania.

Contents

PART 3
Recent America 1914–Present

Introduction

It has been said recently that American students have lost their taste for history. This is true in a limited way. Young people are tired of the sort of history — and particularly American history — that they have generally been taught. This is history that continues to emphasize the political surface of things without regard for the changing underlying patterns of life that have characterized our nation in earlier eras. Although historians have long since asserted their independence from "past politics" as a framework for their portraits of the past, all too often they cannot avoid the traditional approaches rooted in political administrations.

The alternative to the political approach is the social one, broadly conceived. But what is social history? Is it simply the narrative with the politics left out? How does it differ from intellectual history? Does it include economic history? These questions are not easy to answer. There is clearly a historical thread that is primarily sociological. The history of the family, of the relations between the sexes, of population changes, of social classes, of racial contacts — these and other examinations through time of the institutions and the interactions studied by sociologists represent social history strictly conceived. Many of the articles in this volume are of this sort.

But social history may also be said to include the development of ideas, especially the ideas that percolate down to ordinary men and govern the way they see the world. Though a study of such ideas as they change and develop may be conceived of as intellectual history, it may also be said to belong to the realm of social history. And the same is true of the vitally important aspect of social life concerned with the way men have earned a living and organized the economic institutions that surround them. This is certainly economic history, but it is also social history in an important sense. While the intellectual currents of an era may be separated from the purely social, this separation process, surely, is apt to be more difficult in the case of the economic impulses that make themselves felt in a given epoch.

In our conception of what constitutes social history we have taken all of these themes, and more, to be our proper sphere. We hope that the social history we have chosen to reprint here will provide the student with a vivid glimpse of the way life was led by men and women in America's past. By now, the number of really fine articles in American social history is large. Due to space limitations in this volume, we can only include a very small proportion of these excellent essays. Nevertheless, we believe the reader will find here some of the best of the recent writings. We do not always agree with the points the various authors of the following selections make, but we do believe that they have made them well and interestingly. We trust our readers will agree.

IRWIN UNGER
DAVID BRODY
PAUL GOODMAN

PART 1

The Early Years
1607-1815

The Transit of Civilization from the Old World to the New

Englishmen crossing the ocean to America expected to transfer to the new colonies the familiar institutions and arrangements under which men lived in the Old World. The forms of government, religious worship, economic activity, and family relationships that people knew at home became the basis for establishing new societies in a wilderness. But according to Oscar Handlin in the following selection, Englishmen failed to transfer intact the structure of society they left behind.

Establishing settlements proved to be full of surprises. The migration of people and institutions was selective. Few English aristocrats, for instance, were willing to migrate to an empty wilderness. Hence, the class structure in America lacked a hereditary aristocracy, such as occupied the top of the social pyramid in England. Similarly, colonists did not reproduce English political patterns. The Crown, which played a dominant role in English politics during the seventeenth century and was still a major force in the eighteenth century, was a remote and much weaker institution in the colonies. At a time when the tendency in England was for political authority to gravitate to London, in the colonies power became fragmented, dispersed among the gentry of dozens of towns and counties. Nor did Englishmen plant in America a productive system like that in England. There, most arable land was under cultivation and falling into the hands of fewer and fewer landowners as the wealthier, more progressive landlords pushed unneeded peasants off their estates. In America, a virgin continent awaited the axmen to clear the trees, and abundant lands made possible an ever-growing army of small freeholders who chiefly populated British North America. Religious institutions, no less than political and economic institutions, underwent alteration in America. Instead of supporting a state church, embodiment of the one true faith, the colonists spawned a dozen competing churches, none of which enjoyed the monopoly possessed by the Church of England. The result was that, though few came to America with the purpose of creating a new society, well before the American Revolution discerning observers realized a new society was emerging in the colonies inhabited by what one Frenchman described as "a new race of men."

FOR FURTHER READING:

BOORSTIN, DANIEL. *The Americans: The Colonial Experience.* New York: Random House, Vintage Books, 1958.*

HANDLIN, OSCAR. *The Americans: A History of the People of the United States.* Boston : Little, Brown & Company, 1963.*

VER STEEG, CLARENCE. *The Formative Years.* New York: Hill & Wang, Making of America Series, 1964.*

Asterisk denotes paperback edition.

The Significance of the Seventeenth Century OSCAR HANDLIN

The historian is trained to see the past in its own terms. He studies the seventeenth century as the product of that which had gone before it, and he attempts to reconstruct the culture and society of the American colonies as those might have seemed to the men who lived in them.

This is the necessary perspective for an understanding of the period. An impressive body of recent studies has shown that the settlements along the coast of North America were elements of imperial systems that had their counterparts in many other regions of the world. We have learned that the institutional life of the colonies can only be understood against a background that reaches back to the medieval past. The labor system, the forms of government, even the modes of thought of the seventeenth century extended patterns that had long before been developing in Europe. To see in them the forerunners or prototypes of what would emerge in the eighteenth or nineteenth century is grievously to misinterpret them.

But our purpose in celebrating the 350th anniversary of the settlement of the Jamestown colony must be somewhat different. The seventeenth century should have general meaning, for we — and the historians along with the rest of us — live, after all, in the twentieth century; and we expect somehow that the experiences of the men who began to come off the ships at Jamestown have also a meaning for us in the twentieth century. A commemorative occasion is a time for retrospection — for looking backward from the present to take account of the way we have come. It has its picturesque and interesting aspects, of course. But its true value arises from the opportunity it offers us to acquire perspective on the present and the future. From that point of view, it is our obligation to look back to the seventeenth century for what it can reveal of the antecedents of our own culture.

In that respect the seventeenth century was immensely significant. In the decades after the settlement at Jamestown, three generations of Americans — the first Americans — began to shape the social order, the way of life, and an interpretation of their own experience that would influence much of subsequent American history. Pick up the story where you will — in the eighteenth or nineteenth century or in our own times — and invariably in these matters the threads lead back to the seventeenth century. It will be worth while to discuss each of these developments briefly.

The colonists who settled at Jamestown and elsewhere along the coast after 1607 brought with them fixed conceptions of what a social order should be like. Their whole effort thereafter was devoted to recreating the forms they had known at home. Yet in practice their experience persistently led them away from the patterns they judged desirable. The American social order that finally emerged was abnormal. That is, it not only diverged from the experience of the European society from which the newcomers emigrated, but it was also contrary to their own expectations of what a social order should be.

The settlers were loyal to the governments from which they emigrated, and they were conservative in their attitudes toward existing institutions. Repeatedly they ex-

---

Source: Oscar Handlin, "The Significance of the Seventeenth Century," in *Seventeenth-Century America*, ed. James M. Smith (Chapel Hill: University of North Carolina Press, 1959), pp. 3–12.

---

plained that their emigration was not intended to disrupt but rather to preserve and improve the society they left. Nevertheless they were constantly moving off on tangents through the force of circumstance and the pressure of the environment. A number of examples will clarify this point.

The forms of colonial government developed slowly and erratically. The first settlers transplanted two forms commonplace in the practice of Europeans in this period. The chartered commercial companies, as in Virginia and Plymouth, carried across to their plantations institutions that went back to the medieval boroughs. The proprietary colonies rested on old feudal precedents. Both efforts at imitation quickly proved unstable, however, and the colonies of either sort passed through a period of rapid change.

The problem of changing political forms was, of course, also troubling Europe in the seventeenth century. But in the Old World this era witnessed the emergence of the centralized bureaucratic state. Theory and practice moved in the same direction, toward the derivation of all authority from a single source, such as the Crown, however defined.

The colonies accepted the theory. Their most prominent men were surprisingly legalistic and had no inclination to dispute the authority under which their government functioned. But practice took another direction. Power tended to devolve to its local sources. Whether that involved the town, as in New England, or the local powers sitting in the vestry, as in Virginia, the characteristic political organization was decentralized. Whatever acknowledgment might be given to the authority of the Crown, political institutions were decisively shaped by the necessity of defining connections to local power. Significantly, the most stable colonies of this period were Connecticut and Rhode Island, where the organization of local government in the towns preceded and remained basic to the organization of central political institutions.

The dispersal of power to local sources was, however, characteristic of other, nonpolitical institutions also. The churches developed a *de facto* congregational form, despite the fact that their communicants theoretically held to a belief in centralized authority. Apart from the Plymouth Separatists, there was no disposition to challenge the traditional hierarchical and centralized structure of the church. Yet, the New England Puritans, once here, found themselves closer to the Separatists than to the Church of England of which they had expected to remain adherents. Most strikingly, the members of the Church of England throughout the colonies continued to acknowledge that a bishop was essential to the full practice of their religious duties. Yet in practice, delays, obstructions, and evasions prevented the emergence of an episcopate before the Revolution. Religious functions too seemed to devolve to their local sources.

These developments were related to the structure of the population, which was also anomalous in the sense that it ran contrary to the expectations of those who planted the colonies. The founders expected that their societies would consist of functionaries and peasants. The companies anticipated plantations populated by servants, that is, by soldiers and clerks, who would carry forth the business of trade and defense. The proprietors looked forward to a population of native or imported peasants who would reconstruct some sort of manorial system in the New World. This was evident, even toward the end of the seventeenth century, in the plans of the Carolina proprietors.

Instead, surprisingly, all the colonies developed a society of yeomen and artisans

— not by plan, and often, it seemed, simply through the want of an alternative. Yet the consequences were radical. There developed in the mainland colonies of the seventeenth century a wide variety of social types, a microcosm of the Old World as it were, ranging from slaves and servants at the bottom through yeoman farmers and artisans, to a gentry at the top. Within this variety of types there were both the recognition of actual stratification and a high degree of mobility. The fact that a servant was different from a yeoman and yet that a servant could become a yeoman led to the definition of a new concept of freedom and to the development of distinctive social institutions.

In the structure of the population, therefore, as in the evolution of governmental and other institutions, the seventeenth-century colonies followed an abnormal path, one which was different from the experience of Europeans at home or in other parts of the world and one which was contrary to their own expectations. The causes of this abnormality were complex. In part it was due to the extensive quality of the land to which these settlers came. They had pitched upon the edge of an almost empty continent; and the existence of open space to which men could withdraw remained a constant condition of their life. That in itself was an element tending toward looseness of social structure.

Furthermore, they encountered no going society with fixed institutions of its own. The Indians who inhabited the region had a culture, of course. But they were so few in number and so little prepared to resist as to have relatively little effect upon the whites. The Europeans of the same period in India or even in Africa were significantly influenced by the institutions they encountered there; those in America, hardly at all. Indeed the American colonists were often disappointed in their natives. The continued inclination to refer to the Indian kings, queens, and nobility reflected an eagerness to discover in the red men a fixity of forms that did not exist. Its absence was a further source of instability.

But most important, the institutional looseness of the seventeenth century was related to the way of life that developed in the colonies. The American seventeenth-century social order was disorderly by the expectations of normal men. But the settlers were not normal men. The terms of American existence compelled frequent and serious deviations from the norms of behavior accepted by the men who peopled the colonies. Every aspect of their existence combined to produce disorder.

The century was occupied by a succession of waves of immigration, so that the experience of transplantation was not limited to one group or to one moment, but was repeated again and again. And that experience caused enormous shocks in the personal and social relationships of those involved in it. The circumstances of the crossing at once threw these men and women into disorder. It takes an effort of the imagination to conceive of the conditions of life on the three ships which came to Jamestown in 1607. These vessels of 100, 40, and 20 tons, respectively, were laden with the gear and the supplies and provisions for the voyage and also with all that the plantations would at first require. Yet, there was also room on these tiny craft for 140 people. The settlers were almost five months in transit, at the mercy of the winds and weather and of the unknown sea. Later voyages involved larger ships — but not much larger; and the time spent in crossing shrank, although not dependably. But accommodations were never commodious and the experience was never pleasant. Few immigrants recovered quickly from the difficulties of crowded and uncomfortable weeks at sea in tiny ships that carried them to their strange destinations.

Many of those who made the crossing were people whose life was already in disorder. Often, they had already been displaced and compelled to move once; their stamina had already been tried. The residents of London who came to the colonies had, as likely as not, been born in the country and had drifted to the city. Others among the newcomers, like the Pilgrims, like the Finns who settled on the Delaware, like the German sectarians, were already uprooted and had already deviated from the settled life of stable societies.

Hard conditions of life compounded the disorder for a greater or lesser time in each of the colonies. Everywhere the settlers who survived could look back upon a starving time, a period when the margin between life and death narrowed perilously and when the very existence of the feeble societies hung by a thread. So, in retrospect, the Virginia burgesses looked back to the administration of Sir Thomas Smith and recalled:

The allowance in those tymes for a man was only eight ounces of meale and half a pinte of pease for a daye the one & the other mouldy, rotten, full of Cobwebs and Maggots loathsome to man and not fytt for beasts; which forced many to flee for reliefe to the Savage Enemy, who being taken againe were putt to sundry deaths as by hanginge, shootinge and breakinge upon the wheele; & others were forced by famine to filch for their bellies, of whom one for steelinge 2 or 3 pints of oatmeale had a bodkinge thrust through his tongue and was tyed with a chaine to a tree untill he starved. Yf a man through his sickness had not been able tow worke, he had no allowance at all, and so consequently perished. Many through these extremities, being weery of life digged holes in the earth and hidd themselues till they famished. . . . So lamentable was our scarsitie that we were constrained to eat Doggs, Catts, ratts, Snakes, Toad-Stooles, horsehides and wt nott; one man out of the mysery he endured, killinge his wiefe powdered her upp to eate here, for wch he was burned. Many besides fedd on the Corps of dead men, and one who had gotten unsatiable, out of custome to that foode could not be restrayned, until such tyme as he was executed for it, and indeed soe miserable was our estate that the happyest day that eyer some of them hoped to see, was when the Indyands had killed a mare they wishing whilst she was boyling that St *Tho: Smith* [the Governor] was uppon her backe in the kettle.

Later prosperity never dimmed the memory of the early difficulties; and there remained always areas where the trying experience of survival was being repeated. As settlement spread, there was always at its edge a brutal and disorderly struggle for existence.

Some of the harsh features of pioneer life disappeared with the development of settled communities. But others endured for a long time. A high death rate remained constant and throughout the century embittered the personal relationships of the colonists. In the first winter at Plymouth, one-half the Pilgrims died. Between 1606 and 1623 about five thousand immigrants came to Virginia. They had children and raised families. Yet at the end of that period there were only one thousand left.

Nor was this cruel mortality simply a condition of initial settlement. It remained characteristic of seventeenth-century life. Infant mortality was murderous; and although many children were born, the number of survivors was distressingly low. It was rare in this century that a husband and wife should live into old age together. The frequency of remarriages by widowers and widows showed how familiar a factor in life was death.

More generally, constant nagging difficulties intruded in the management of the details of home or farm or shop. Old habits did not apply to new circumstances; and it was hard for individuals to fulfill the personal, family, religious, or communal roles they were expected to play. This, perhaps, explains the harsh judgments that the colonists were always making of one another. The lack of stability or orderliness even in the home was particularly troublesome. In the tight quarters of the seventeenth-century houses, large families had to learn to live with one another, and also with the Negroes and other strange servants. Emotional strains were inevitable and weak community discipline sometimes led to violence, desertion, or criminality. The lack of permanence, the constant mobility that shifted individuals and families about through the continent exacerbated all these tensions. By contrast, the old homes of the Old World in retrospect came to embody orderliness. Often, in thinking of what they had left in Europe, the colonists expressed a poignant sense of separation from the source of stability and culture.

Finally, their life was rendered harsh by the apparent hostility of the elements. The wilderness itself created problems for men accustomed to open spaces. In the folk literature of Europe the forests were peopled by wild, inhuman creatures often hostile to man. In America even the climate and the changes of the seasons were unfamiliar. Most important, the denizens of the wilderness were a constant threat to the flimsy structure of civilization. The Indians grew more and more fearsome as the century advanced; and on the borders French and Spanish Papists were a continuing threat. In the face of all these dangers, there was no security in the settlements. The precariousness of existence was at the root of the disorder that overwhelmed them. Everywhere from the moment they boarded ship the first Americans found risks of the greatest order inseparable from the conduct of their lives.

The native-born, that is, the second and third generations, were more at home in the wilderness and, never having known Europe, were less pressed by the necessity of making comparisons with that which had been left across the ocean. They had sources of instability of their own, in their heightened rootlessness and mobility. But they were likely to accept the disorder and precariousness that troubled their immigrant parents or grandparents as a way of life and to adjust to its conditions.

The men subject to so many elements of abnormality and disorder necessarily interpreted their own experiences in a distinctive way. They were constantly driven to ask questions that other men had no need to raise. People whose families had lived generations without end in the same village had no cause to wonder why they were where they were or to speculate on the significance of having been placed where they were. But the immigrants whose conditions of life and whose institutions had been driven so far from every ordinary course necessarily had to seek answers to such questions.

The necessity was particularly urgent in the seventeenth century when men ascribed to every event a deep meaning. Nothing that occurred was taken as simply random. Everything was the product of the intent of some mover. A tree did not fall; it was felled. If a monstrous child was born or a school of porpoises seen, that was a sign of something. In the same way, there was necessarily a significance to the painful shift of population that created colonial society. In an era in which men believed literally in signs, portents, curses, spells, and imprecations, to say nothing of witches, they had to seek a meaning to their own unusual experiences.

The first Americans continued the habit of explaining every occurrence in terms of a familiar dichotomy. On the one hand, they could see in some events good impulses, derived from God and reflecting a divine intent. But they also found abundant evidence of evil impulses or dark desires emanating from satanic intentions. The fearful men who lived with risk and disorder were constantly on the lookout for the means of identifying and interpreting what happened to them. As a simple matter of a guide to personal life, it was essential to know whether an incident was the product of divine or devilish interference.

The same confrontation of good and evil could be seen in the social world that surrounded the individual. There in the external wilderness, in the savagery of life without reliable guides, were the sources of corruption. Were not the Indians imps of Satan, and the Papists, creatures of the Devil, and was not therefore the whole American experience one which endangered man's salvation? On the other hand, was it not possible to identify that which lay across the ocean with that which was good and conducive to man's salvation? Europe, from the American perspective, was the source of morality, of law, of order, and of Christianity. But in that event, how was the colonist to explain his migration, away from order to disorder, away from law to savagery, away from Christianity to the spiritual perils of the New World?

The question thus raised could be answered on both the personal and the social level; and the answer on the one offers an analogy to the answer on the other. The character of this response may be discerned in the poem that a grieving grandmother wrote in the 1660's to explain to herself the death of three grandchildren within four years. All were under the age of four. Surely these tender innocents had been stricken down through no fault, no evil deed, of their own. There was, however, a reason. Anne Bradstreet explained:

> By nature Trees do rot when they are grown.
> And Plumbs and Apples thoroughly ripe do fall,
> And corn and grass are in their season mown,
> And time brings down what is both strong and tall.
> But plants new set to be eradicate,
> And buds new blown, to have so short a date,
> Is by his hand alone that guides nature and fate.

An unnatural misfortune of this sort was thus in itself evidence of a particular divine concern. While the nature of God's intentions might be inscrutable to men and closed to fallible human understanding, the event itself nevertheless was a sure indication of some particular purpose. It could even supply a kind of assurance of divine interest and oversight.

It was also true that a way of life out of the usual course was evidence of some particular design. The whole character of the plantation of these settlements, by its very abnormality, indicated that there had been some special purpose to the coming to America. The fact that this whole area had been withheld from previous human habitation indicated that there was some special intention for its use. The fact that their institutions and their course of life did not follow any usual pattern was itself a sign that these settlements had an unusual destiny.

As the immigrants examined their own coming, they could see evidence of a larger will in their own careers. Their migration was largely the product of their own helplessness, of social forces over which they had no control — persecution by the Established Church, changes in agriculture and the unavailability of land, the disruption of the wool trade and the growth in the number of men without employment. But on the other hand, the migration was also the product of their own choice. Not all those who were persecuted or displaced or unemployed had come. Migration stemmed from a compulsion that forced the emigrant to leave and also the positive act of will by which he decided to go. The emigrant might thus be compared to a legate dispatched on a mission by a potentate, a legate who accepted the errand voluntarily. The fact, too, that not all those who went arrived reflected a process of survival and seemed to imply a kind of selection of some from among the rest.

In no other way could these people account for the experience but by the conclusion that somehow they had been chosen to depart from the ways of ordinary men and to become in their own lives extraordinary for some special purpose.

Among some of the colonists this intention was spelled out with considerable sophistication. New England Puritans thought of themselves as led by Divine Providence to a new Canaan where they were to create a new kind of society that would be a model for the whole world. Their city upon a hill would ultimately be emulated by all other men. It was a part of the scheme of divine redemption, occupying the stage at a critical turn in the cosmic drama that had begun with the Creation, that had been continued in the Reformation, and that would end in the Second Coming.

Elsewhere the explanation was less sophisticated, less explicit, and less literate. But there nonetheless emerged again and again expressions of conviction in a sense of mission — to convert the Indians or to civilize the wilderness. The newness of a New World reserved for some ultimate purpose and waiting for those who would bring it under cultivation or use it as the setting for their own experiments in salvation confirmed the successive groups of immigrants, in the seventeenth century and later, in the belief that there was a profound importance to their coming.

The second and third generations were different in this respect also. They were natives, not subject to the strains of the decisions that had burdened their parents or grandparents. Indeed, in the eyes of the immigrants, the second generation seemed a ruder, less cultivated, and wilder people. That accounts for the complaints about declension and about the loss of the sense of mission that began to be sounded in the last quarter of the century.

But the second generation had actually not lost the sense of mission so much as transformed it beyond the recognition of their predecessors. The very fact that they were a wilderness people, at home in the New World, gave them a sense of power. They could deal with the forest and the savage as their parents could not. Out of contact with the standards of the Old World, they developed their own, and their ability to do so generated confidence in their own capacity for achievement.

Therefore they too, although in a different form, were moved by a conviction of the grandeur of their destiny; and they could link that conviction to the potentialities of the land, which was not alien to them as it had been to their parents. Pride in their own power and in the future greatness of their homes created for them a picture of themselves as a people destined to conquer, an idea to be eloquently expressed just after the turn of the century by Robert Beverley.

In a variety of forms, the sense of mission has remained a continuing theme in American life. In the eighteenth century Jefferson's generation gave it secularized liberal expression. The nineteenth century imbued it with the spirit of liberal reform. And at the opening of the twentieth century, it was woven into the ideology of imperialism. So, too, social disorder, the acceptance of risk, and the precariousness of life that developed in the seventeenth century long remained characteristic of America. It was the significance of the seventeenth century to bring into being peculiarities of character and institutions, the influence of which was long thereafter felt in the history of the United States.

The Red Man as the White Man's Burden

From a population of between 1 and 2 million, when white men first encountered them in North America, the Indians steadily declined for almost three centuries until there were only little more than 200,000 left in 1900. This tragic event had its roots in the pattern of relationships between the natives and the Europeans that took shape in the colonial period. In the following essay, Roy Harvey Pearce describes how New England Puritans regarded Indians either as their instruments or as an obstacle to achieving their goals.

The grim choice facing the Indians was "civilization or death." By "civilization," however, Americans meant *their* version; but even the most receptive Indians, subject to untiring missionary efforts, proved unable to adjust. "For, take a young Indian lad," a French traveler in the colonies observed, "give him the best education you possibly can, load him with your bounty, with presents, nay with riches; yet he will secretly long for his native woods . . . and on the first opportunity he can possibly find, you will see him voluntarily leave behind him all you have given him, and return with expressible joy to lie on the mats of his fathers."

At first, Europeans and Indians lived in peace. Indians welcomed the artifacts whites brought and had little fear of such fledgling settlements as those at Jamestown, Virginia, or at Plymouth, Massachusetts. And whites patronizingly regarded Indians as "noble savages," or one of the ten lost tribes of Israel, or primitive but brave and resourceful people. Being outnumbered, whites could not risk conflict until they had grown stronger. As the European population grew and spread more deeply into the forests, Indians became alarmed. Warfare followed until the Europeans subdued the Indians and restored peace temporarily. A thousand times on a thousand frontiers this process repeated itself. For though the Indians never stood much chance against the whites in the long run, the Americans had to subdue each tribe they encountered separately, because the Indians were divided into a hundred innumerable tribes and the defeat of one did not reduce the others. Though warfare killed many Indians, the white man's disease, against which the red man had little or no immunity, killed many more.

Troubled by the Indians' tragic fate, Americans rationalized it as the just reward of a race many regarded as "a set of miserable, dirty, lousy, blanketed, thieving, lying, sneaking, murdering, graceless, faithless, gut-eating skunks whose immediate and final extermination all men . . . should pray for." Those whose troubled consciences could not be stilled by dehumanizing the Indians found comfort in the thought that the Indians' decline was the price one had to pay for the advance of civilization. Two centuries after the Puritans defined the Indians in terms of their own needs, an American novelist updated their explanation of the red man's historic role: "He hath a pioneer mission, to prepare the wilds for the superior race; and, this done, he departs; and, even as one growth of the forest, when hewn down, makes way for quite another growth of trees, so will he give place to another people. Verily, the mysteries of Providence are passing wonderful."

FOR FURTHER READING:

HAGAN, WILLIAM T. *American Indians.* Chicago: University of Chicago Press, 1961.*
PEARCE, ROY H. *Savagism and Civilization.* Original title: *Savages and America: A Study of the Indian and the Idea of Civilization.* Baltimore: The Johns Hopkins Press, 1967.*
VAUGHAN, ALDEN T. *New England Frontier: Indians and Puritanism.* Boston: Little, Brown & Company, 1965.*

Asterisk denotes paperback edition.

The "Ruines of Mankind": The Indian and the Puritan Mind ROY HARVEY PEARCE

The Indian whom colonial Americans everywhere encountered was, above all, an obstacle to civilization. And he was an obstacle not only to overcome, but also to understand and then perhaps to civilize in the overcoming. For in his very nature, in what was taken to be his essential humanity, the Indian seemed to be capable of that civil state which the colonizers had achieved, yet seemed somehow not to be inclined toward that state. The problem for those Americans who wanted to understand him was to define the nature of his savage society — what in the eighteenth century came to be called his "savagism" — in such a way as to relate it to the nature of the high civilization which they were bringing to the new world. Thus, in the perspective of our cultural history, a colonial understanding of savagism is really a colonial understanding of civilization — of the good life as the Indian did and did not share in it. And colonial definitions of savage life are really re-definitions of civilized life, *apologia* for that life, expressions and applications of theories of civilization.

So it is that we may comprehend our colonial civilization concretely and particularly as it realizes itself in working out its ideas of the savage. So it is that the New England Puritan obsession with the savage is a significant aspect of the New England Puritan obsession with the civilized. This essay, then, is offered as a study in the history of colonial New England civilization — a history in terms of the Puritan idea of the savage, as that idea came to be worked out in the context of Puritan experience with the Indian and his society.

For the Englishman going to New England in the 1620's and 30's, the destiny of the Indians could be understood only as it related to the destiny of the whole colonial enterprise. In Plymouth the Pilgrim rejoiced to find that it had pleased God so to possess the Indians with a fear and love of the English that they would forthwith submit themselves as loyal and dutiful subjects. Moreover, it was to be observed that God had lately sent a "wonderful plague" among the savages and had so destroyed them and left most of their lands free for civilized occupation. The Indians whom the Pilgrims found were amenable enough; watched closely, dealt with fairly,

Source: Roy Harvey Pearce, "The 'Ruines of Mankind': The Indian and the Puritan Mind," *Journal of the History of Ideas,* vol. 13 (1952), pp. 200–217.

punished occasionally, they gave little trouble. But then, God had already shown them the way with His plague.

For Puritans in the Massachusetts Bay Colony and what came to be Connecticut, matters were somewhat more difficult. Although in 1634 John Winthrop could write to an English friend, "[the natives] are neere all dead of the small Poxe, so as the Lord hathe cleared our title to what we possess," yet Indians to the south and north, who were plagued mainly by the English themselves, were relatively strong and independent. Twice in the century formal frontier war was waged: in 1637, against the Pequots, who were easily slaughtered at Mystic by Mason's expedition; and in 1675–1676, against the Wampanoags and their leader King Philip, who were destroyed in their turn, though not quite so easily as had been the Pequots. And continually there was trouble on a small scale; the problem was to keep various tribal groups split up and thus weak in striking power, to protect frontier settlements from marauding bands of Indians, somehow to combat papist French influence on the northern Indians, and gradually to take over lands as the proper time came. Steadily, as the colonies developed in holdings and in power, the English moved further inland from their coastal settlements and took over more Indian land. Warfare resulted. But this too was part of God's Way with New England.

For, and Puritans took this as the meaning of their own history, God had meant the savage Indians' land for the civilized English, and, moreover, had meant the savage state itself as a sign of Satan's power and savage warfare as a sign of earthly struggle and sin. The colonial enterprise was in all ways a religious enterprise. Demonstrating land tenure from theology had been simple even for Pilgrim precursors of the Puritans. Robert Cushman, if it was he who in 1622 contributed the concluding section to the Pilgrim *Mourt's Relation,* argued merely that the Indians were heathens and thus in need of conversion; that Indians' lands were empty, English lands full, and the English therefore bound to go to the Indians and fill their lands:

> Their land is spacious and void, and there are few, and do but run over the grass, as do also the foxes and the wild beasts. They are not industrious, neither have art, science, skill or faculty to use either the land or the commodities of it; but all spoils, rots, and is marred for want of manuring, gathering, ordering, &c. As the ancient patriarchs, therefore, removed from straiter places into more roomy, where the land lay idle and waste, and none used it, though there dwelt inhabitants by them, as Gen. xiii, 6, 11, 12, and xxxiv, 21, and xli, 20, so it is lawful now to take a land which none useth, and make use of it.

This argument was at the center of the New England understanding of the Indian in the seventeenth century as, in fact, it was in some version to be at the center of American understanding of the Indian until the middle of the nineteenth century. For the Pilgrim as for the Puritan, religion and empire, christianization and civilization, divine order and natural order, were known to be one. So Cushman concluded,

> Yea, and as the enterprise is weighty and difficult, so the honor is more worthy, to plant a rude wilderness, to enlarge the honor and fame of our dread sovereign, but chiefly to display the efficacy and power of the Gospel, both in zealous preaching, professing, and wise walking under it, before the faces of these poor blind infidels.

Such statements on this problem of land tenure as came some seven years later from Massachusetts authorities were characteristically more legal in tone and concern than Cushman's but were pointed towards the same conclusions. Indian lands were to be bought if local savages should pretend to ownership, but to be bought only as a means of keeping peace with those savages. For, in truth, the Indians possessed their lands only as a natural right, since that possession existed anterior to and outside of a properly civilized state and since that possession was not in accordance with God's commandment to men to occupy the earth, increase, and multiply; what followed, then, was that the land was technically *vacuum domicilium,* and that the English, who would farm the land and make it fructify, who would give it order, were obliged to take over. If the Indians were ever to be civilized, if they were ever to know the true God, they would be obliged to let God's chosen people lead them to God's chosen civilization; specifically, the way to God was through His chosen civilization. This is perhaps essentially what we call the Protestant-capitalistic ethic; but it is also, and more particularly, a late Renaissance ethic — a solemn and brave, even desperate, determination to hold on to the idea of a received, assured order which would give meaning and direction to all life. For John Winthrop, in 1629, it was a matter of such divine logic:

> . . . the whole earth is the Lord's garden, and he hath given it to the sons of Adam to be tilled and improved by them. Why then should we stand starving here for the places of habitation, (many men spending as much labor and cost to recover or keep sometimes an acre or two of lands as would procure him many many hundreds of acres, as good or better, in another place), and in the mean time suffer whole countries, as profitable for the use of man, to lie waste without any improvement.

Convinced thus of his divine right to Indian lands, the Puritan discovered in the Indians themselves evidence of a satanic opposition to the very principle of divinity. In a world in which the divine plan was so clear, in a world through which the Bible would guide all men in all things, in a world in which civilization and the divinely illuminated human reason had to count for everything, the Indian might well be a terrifying anomaly, at best a symbol of what men might become if they lived far from God's Word. Yet these savages were essentially men; and so they had to be brought to manhood and the civilized responsibilities of manhood. And this was to be achieved through bringing them eventually to God. As the wild lands of New England were to be improved, so were the wild men. For the Puritan there could be no half-way measures in his own life or in the lives of the savages about him. It was never a question of understanding the savage as he was, of knowing him in his low state. Rather it was a question — a driving necessity, really — first, of finding the savage's place in a Puritan world, and then, of making the savage over into a Puritan. If one looked closely at the savage, it was to look closely at a similitude to God's Way with the world — as one would look closely at a storm, or an illness, or a death, or a birth, or a quarrel among one's children — and so to discover evidence of that Way.

Wherever the Indian opposed the Puritan, there Satan opposed God. Satan had possessed the Indian until he had become virtually a beast. Indian worship was devil worship. The faintly optimistic (and propagandistic?) reports about Indian religion which were published in London early in the seventeenth century soon were drowned out in the general recounting of the evil religious state of the savages. Typically, when Dr. John Stoughton, Rector of St. Mary Aldermanbury, London, wanted to encourage the erection of a college in which Indians, among others, should be trained, he felt constrained to argue the great necessity for the college from the fact that ". . . the Divell is not unlike to stire them up to[o] for the disturbance of this worke intended for the overthrow of his Kingdome in them. . . ." Satanism, it was abundantly evident, was at the very core of savage life. And it was not hard to associate the physical state of the Indian, his living a cold hard life, with his spiritual state; hence, everywhere one might see in the flesh what it meant to be a devil-worshipper. So racial and cultural tension mounted throughout the century, until, in the 1690's, the very presence of evil Indian devil-worshippers was taken as part of the evidence of that great visitation of witches to New England, which we call the Witchcraft Craze. Indian witch doctors clearly were sharing diabolically in the wonders of the invisible world. At the end of the century, when Cotton Mather interpreted the continuing (now French-inspired) Indian skirmishes after King Philip's War as the direct result of God's harrowing sinful and weakening New England through Satan, he too was sure that New England witchcraft and Indian witchcraft were all of a piece:

> The Story of the Prodigious War, made by the Spirits of the Invisible World upon the People of New-England, in the year, 1692, hath Entertain'd a great part of the English World, with a just Astonishment: and I have met with some Strange Things, not here to be mentioned, which have made me often think, that this inexplicable War might have some of its Original among the Indians, whose chief Sagamores are well known unto some of our Captives, to have been horrid Sorcerers, and hellish Conjurers and such as conversed with Daemons.

Practical experience seemed to bear all this out. Fighting to hold on to their lands and their culture, the Indians would properly be savage. Inevitably New Englanders living on the frontier settlements suffered raids, destruction, sometimes captivity, and inevitably they interpreted each as God's warning to New England through Satan. Of the hard captivity of Mary Rowlandson in 1676, the contemporary editor of her narrative concluded:

> I must say, that as none knows what it is to fight and pursue such an enemy as this, but they that have fought and pursued them: so none can imagine what it is to be captivated, and enslaved to such atheisticall, proud, wild, cruel, barbarous, brutish (in one word) diabolicall creatures as these, the worst of the heathen. . . .

In the frontier settlements to the west and south and to the north in Maine, it was destroy or be destroyed. And it seemed everywhere continuingly evident that this frontier fight for survival was but another skirmish in man's Holy War against Satan, now on a new-world battlefield. When, as late as 1703, Solomon Stoddard recommended to Governor Joseph Dudley that troublesome Indians be hunted down with dogs, he was arguing as John Underhill (second in command to Mason at the proceedings at Mystic) had argued some sixty-five years before in defense of the massacre of the Pequots:

> It may be demanded, Why should you be so furious? (as some have said). Should not Christians have more mercy and compassion? But I would refer you to David's war. When a people is grown to such a height of blood, and sin against God and man, and all confederates in the action, then he hath no respect to persons, but harrows them, and saws them, and puts them to the sword, and the most terribelest death that may be. Sometimes the Scripture declareth women and children must perish with their parents. Sometimes the case alters; but we will not dispute it now. We had sufficient light from the Word of God for our proceedings.

Thus it was that the whole history of the relations with the Indians, which was part of the whole history of the Puritan enterprise, was read in light from the Word of God. Edward Johnson's *Wonder-Working Providence of Sion's Saviour in New England* (1654) deals characteristically with that history. Now, Johnson's account is generally concerned with the whole history of New England seen properly *sub specie aeternitatis;* as a result, he is able to find the right place and the right amount of space for each of the important events in the course of colonial relations with the Indians. Devoting large parts of some seven of his eighty-three chapters to the discussion of Indian affairs, he tells how God had sent a plague in 1619 (the correct date is, of course, 1616–1617) to clear the way for the settlers at Plymouth and how the Indians had been thus disposed to receive those settlers peacefully; he tells how a plague among the Massachusetts Indians likewise saved the Bay Colony in 1631 ("Thus did the Lord allay their quarrelsome spirits, and made roome for the following part of his army."); he recounts the history of the Pequot War in some detail, pointing out, as had many another, how this war and the Antinomian troubles of the 1630's were equally Satanic trials for men establishing a Holy Commonwealth; he recounts further God's intervention in a possible Indian war in 1645; and finally, he insists that by the 1650's missionary work to the Satanic heathen is going well. In every event he can find evidence that God, through Satan, has been showing the colonists at once their own sinfulness and the promise of their great undertaking.

Later Puritan historians deal more specifically with Indian troubles, and, of course, they recount later troubles — King Philip's War and the continuing skirmishes in the northeast throughout the seventeenth century and into the eighteenth. Yet in tone and orientation their work simply duplicates Johnson's *Wonder-Working Providence* and reflects equally the integrative orthodoxy of Puritan culture. Often writing more in detail and from broader and more immediate experience than does Johnson, they emphasize even more than he the brutish, diabolical quality of the Indian enemy. To this end, Captain John Mason appends to his *Brief History of the Pequot War* (first printed separately in 1736) a list of "special providences" by means of which the English have won their victory. In his three-part report (1675–1676) of King Philip's War, Nathaniel Saltonstall insists that however heavily the hand of the Lord lies upon his Puritan sinners, still He "hath Commission to the Sword" to destroy the crafty, bestial, diabolical creatures who oppose those sinners. William Hubbard, in his *Narrative of the Indian Wars in New England* (1677), is sure that King Philip's War in particular is nothing less than a Satanic plot against God's Chosen People: The war could not possibly have occurred because of anything the English have done to the Indians.

> What can be imagined, therefore, [he says] besides the instigation of Satan, that envied at the prosperity of the church of God here seated, or else fearing lest the power of the Lord Jesus, that had overthrown his kingdom in other parts of the world, should do the like here, and so the stone taken out of the mountain without hands, should become a great mountain itself, and fill the whole earth: no cause of provocation being given by the English.

Thus through the century and beyond, the Puritans wrote down their history and discovered and rediscovered the Indians' place in that history. In such a vein, in such a manner — to note only the full-fledged histories — Increase Mather wrote his *Brief History of the Warr with the Indians* [*i.e.,* King Philip's War] (1676) and his *Relation of the Troubles which have hapned in New England, By reason of the Indians there: From the Year 1614 to the Year 1675* (1677); his son Cotton wrote his *Decennium Luctuosum* (1699), which was included, somewhat expanded, in the *Magnalia Christi Americana* (1702); and Samuel Penhallow wrote his survey of troubles with the northeast Indians early in the seventeenth century, *The History of the Wars of New-England with the Eastern Indians, or a Narrative of their continued Perfidy and Cruelty* (1726). History was everywhere cosmically and eternally meaningful. A Satanic principle was part of that meaningfulness; and the New England Indians somehow embodied that principle. The Indian was significant precisely as history was significant.

Out of such an understanding of the nature and destiny of civilized man in New England, here rose the Puritan understanding of the nature and destiny of savage man. There was, at the outset, no difficulty in accounting for the origin and genesis of the savage: Universally it was agreed that the Indians were of the race of men — descendants, in order, of Adam, Noah, and those Asiatic Tartars who had come to America by a land-bridge from northern Asia. This was orthodox seventeenth-century opinion. And it allowed Puritans to account simply for the savage, heathenish state of the Indian. Was he not perhaps the farthest of all God's human creatures from God Himself? Descended from wanderers, had he not lost his sense of civilization and law and order? Had he not lost — except for a dim recollection — God Himself? And wasn't he, as a direct result of this loss, in the power of Satan? Seen thus — and only thus — as one item in a God-centered course of experience, the Indian took on an awful meaning for the Puritan mind.

The Puritan writer on the Indian was, therefore, less interested in the Indian's culture than in the Indian's fallen spiritual condition as it was to be seen everywhere about him. Such early accounts of the Indians as those contained in Edward Winslow's *Good Newes from New England* (1624), Francis Higginson's *New-England's Plantation* (1630), and William Wood's *New England's Prospect* (1634) describe the appearance, social organization, and customs of the local Indians sketchily and, considering the tone of later accounts, somewhat optimistically: The heathen Indians, almost wiped out by the plague, living without the benefits of civilization, fearing their enemies, will certainly welcome the English; and it will be, presumably, no great task to civilize them and so to bring them to Christianity. But as the century wore on, as more distant Indians became better known, and as all the Indians seemed more and more to be setting themselves against civilization and Christianity, as disputes and warfare broke out, it seemed clearer and clearer that all Indians were inextricably involved in their low state and so not worth discussing in great detail. By the 1680's even Daniel Gookin, in charge of Christian Indian settlements for the United Colonies and so known to be soft toward the savages, could give only a despairing account of Indian culture. His account of the Indians in his "Of the Language, Customs, Manners, and Religion of the Indians" is straightforward and gloomy. The Indians have been and continue to be — with a few Christianized exceptions — brutish and barbarous; they indulge in polygamy; they are revengeful; the men only hunt and fish and fight while the women cook and do a little planting; they are all thieves and liars and by now they have virtually all become drunkards. True enough, they are hospitable and have some faintly systematic way of government. Yet their worship of the sun, moon, and the earth and of both a supreme doer of good and a supreme doer of evil and their submitting to their powwows, who are nothing but witches and wizards holding familiarity with Satan, damn them forever. Gookin might have held out a hope for missionary efforts with the Indians; but his evidence is not far from that which caused William Hubbard, in 1677, fiercely to denounce an Englishman who had turned Indian during King Philip's War, married a squaw, "renounced his religion, nation, and natural parents, all at once fighting against them." Captured, this man had been examined and condemned to die. And Hubbard had been obliged to comment:

> As to his religion he was found as ignorant as an heathen, which no doubt caused the fewer tears to be shed at his funeral, by, being unwilling to lavish pity upon him that had divested himself of nature itself, as well as religion, in a time when so much pity was needed elsewhere.

Savage life, then, could be only a life against nature and against religion.

What mattered, therefore, was not the intrinsic character of the New England Indians, but rather the meaning that that character might have the whole of New England life. Thus we must note in passing that the account of tarnished noble savages in Thomas Morton's *New English Canaan* (1632), of hypercholeric warriors in Philip Vincent's *True Relation* (1638), of natural men in Thomas Lechford's *Plain Dealing* (1643) and in John Josselyn's *Account of Two Voyages* (1674) — each of these attempts by non-Puritans to describe New England Indians "disinterestedly" would have seemed to Puritans mistaken in its very disinterestedness. Precisely because the Puritan was so deeply concerned with the meaning of the Indian for the whole of his culture, he hardly could conceive of describing that Indian disinterestedly. The Puritan understanding of the nature and destiny of savage man is to be found, as we have seen, in the record of Puritan-Indian relations, in Puritan accounts of God's Way with New England, and finally, as we shall see, in the history of the bitter failure of Puritans to bring the Indians to civilization and to God.

From the first, the Puritans, like most other seventeenth-century colonizers, firmly intended to convert the heathen. This indeed was an essential part of their mission on earth as they understood it. They were justified in taking Indian lands because they could use those lands as God had intended them to be used; yet God had also intended that His colonizers give civil and spiritual form to aboriginal dwellers in those lands. Practically, then, Indians were to be made into Puritans. Now, this was to be merely the peculiarly Puritan form of the Renaissance obsession with order and rationality; the Puritan mind, however, was to be so intense, so very fierce in its seizing upon ultimately supernaturalistic and absolutistic sanctions for a particular and local notion of order and rationality, that, unable to face the fact of cultural change and human variance, it was virtually blind to such alien forms of order and rationality as existed in aboriginal New England cultures. Equally, there is little evidence that Puritan order and Puritan reason, with their special scriptural ground, ever meant very much to the New England aborigines who were to be saved by that order and that reason.

". . . the glory of God, the propagation of the Gospel of Christ, the conversion of the Indians, and the enlargement of the King's Majesty's dominions in America . . ." — so go the expressed aims of the Massachusetts Bay enterprise. And chiefest of these aims was to be conversion. Yet the record of individual New England missionary efforts is relatively scattered, involving, as it does, almost as many organizations as men. Apparently money was first sent to New England for missionary work in the 1630's. During the 1630's, too, Roger Williams and perhaps John Eliot were active among the Indians. In 1636 Plymouth Colony enacted laws to provide for the preaching of the Gospel among the Indians, and in 1643 Thomas Mayhew began to carry on missionary work on Martha's Vineyard and Nantucket. Little or nothing was achieved, however, until November 1644 when the Massachusetts General Court asked the ministers to recommend measures for converting the Indians; two years later the General Court directed the ministers to elect two of their number every year to engage in gospel work among the heathen; and in 1646 John Eliot, having learned a local Indian dialect, began systematically to preach to them. Then, in 1649, Edward Winslow, acting as London agent for the United Colonies, managed to get Parliament to authorize the incorporation of "The President and Society for the Propagation of the Gospel in New England." It was this organization, poorly administered, which financed missionary work in New England until the Restoration. When, with the Restoration, the charter of "The President and Society" was declared legally invalid, a royal Charter was granted, in February 1662, to the "Company for Propagacion of the Gospell in New England, and parts adjacent, in America." It was this Company which carried on most of the financing of missionary work in New England until 1779, when the Revolutionary War caused remittances to America to be cut off. A "Society for Promotion of Christian Knowledge," formed in England in 1698, the "Society in Scotland for Propagating Christian Knowledge," formed in 1709, and an abortive "Society for Propagating Christian Knowledge," incorporated in Massachusetts in 1762, also variously contributed to the holy cause. (The "Society for the Propagation of the Gospel in Foreign Parts" was an Anglican corporation founded in 1701, which sent its missionaries mainly to the Indians in the middle colonies and which gave up work with the Indians late in the eighteenth century.) All these organizations issued, finally, in "The Society for Propagating the Gospel among the Indians, and Others, in North America," founded in 1787. A great number of intentions and organizations certainly — but few practical results. Only with such self-consciously dedicated souls as Eliot and the Mayhews in the later seventeenth century and with various evangelical missionaries such as Sargeant and Brainerd in the earlier eighteeenth century, did the Gospel reach the heathen. There were, it seemed, only a few workers for this vast, wild vineyard.

For all his assurances that it was his holy mission to convert the heathen, to the Puritan in the middle of the seventeenth century, the business seemed to be proceeding with agonizing delay. Why, he wondered. And, as always, he had answers from scripture and from reasoned interpretation of scripture. As we have seen, Indian troubles, Indian opposition, and Indian recalcitrance were taken to be God-ordained reminders to the Puritan that his way on this earth was a hard way; and so the Indian was to be literally and continually the devil's advocate for a people who needed such to remind them of their own sinfulness and the agonizing hope of regeneration and election. Moreover, in the 1640's it seemed that there was specific scriptural authority for the delay in Indian conversion. The wild prophecy of Revelation 15 was interpreted as meaning that there could be no large-scale conversion of the heathen until the Jews themselves had been converted and until the Anti-Christ had been destroyed. The notion still persisted in the 1670's, during King Philip's War, when Increase Mather — in a history of that war — tried to erase it by pointing out that, in spite of the troubles which had resulted in the war, there nevertheless was a "glorious Sprinkling" of Indian converts in New England.

It was indeed a "Sprinkling," and as such the result of work carried on by a few men who felt a deep personal need to go to the Indians directly — yet the great majority of whom were so sure of their Puritan way that they could not see the Indians as anything but imperfect copies of themselves. John Eliot, for example, worked for the Indians from 1634 on, was able in the 1640's to preach to them in their own language, translated the Old and the New Testaments into the local Massachusetts dialect, founded a Christian Indian town in 1651 and saw thirteen others founded by 1674, even ventured in 1659 to suggest that it would be possible to form the purest of Christian Commonwealths on the basis of his experiments in organizing Indian towns. Yet the evidence of the various accounts of his work he sent to the Society for the Propagation of the Gospel shows that he viewed savage life as one of satanic degradation and that he knew the Indians to be, as Cotton Mather pointed out in his biography of Eliot, "doleful creatures who were the veriest *ruines of mankind,* which were to be found any where on the face of the earth." Even a man like Roger Williams, who strove for savage as well as for civilized rights, was appalled by the Indians in their "hideous *worships* of *creatures* and *devils.*" The Indians needed a Christian God; and the missionaries devoted themselves to bringing that God to the Indians. Their faith was simple: If they could go to the Indians, first organize their living into some civil pattern, and then teach them the Word, they might be pulled from the embrace of Satan. An ordered civil life was the basic condition of an holy life; civilization was properly a means to holiness. The Civil and the Holy Covenants of man with God were parts of a cosmically great principle of order. And civil order was a prerequisite of holy order.

Yet for all their faith in themselves, their society, and savage potentialities for civilization and God, the few missionaries who worked with the Indians were bound to fail. The Indian wars of the 1630's and 70's, the expansion of New England, the very clash of civilized and primitive cultures — these spelled the doom of the New England Indian, in spite of the effort of a "Sprinkling" of missionaries; for, as we know now, the missionaries themselves carried an alien and destructive culture to the Indians. Actually, by the end of the seventeenth century, it seemed very clear to all concerned that the New England missionary enterprise was likely to fail. The trials of King Philip's War had hardened Puritan hearts; even the Christian Indians, well on the way to salvation, were mistreated. A list drawn up in 1698 gives 2500 as the number of converts in the Indian towns, and points out that most of these are dying off rapidly. For this Cotton Mather blamed not the citizens of the Holy Commonwealth but the English traders who were bringing liquor and vice to the Indians. His father, seeing the Puritan faith weakening everywhere about him went further and instanced both the failure of the missions and the successes of the corrupt traders as partial proof of that weakening. Instead of being converted, he sermonized, the Indians are being perverted; for there are no more goodly Eliots among us; and now God has sent disease among the Indians as a final warning to us to mend our ways before he withdraws his Glory from us as he has from the Jews and from the Spanish and even from those in old England. Indian drunkenness, which had been sadly remarked before, came regularly to be denounced in a kind of ritualistic Puritan breastbeating. Yet we can see that the cause of failure went deeper than the introduction of disease and drunkenness and vice. It stemmed from the very quality of Puritan understanding of the Indian, necessarily from high Puritanism itself —

from the desperate need of those who had settled New England to hold on to their special beliefs about the nature and destiny of man if they were to hold on to their God-ordained way of life. They had to assume that the Indian's nature was essentially and absolutely one and the same with their nature; for the very integrative orthodoxy of their society demanded such an absolute. Herein they might very well fool themselves. Or so a Royal Commission noted in 1665 — reporting first that in Rhode Island "is the greatest number of Indians yet they never had any thing allowed towards the civilizing and converting of the Indians," and then that in Massachusetts:

> They convert Indians by hiring them to come & heare Sermons: by teaching them not to obey their Heathen Sachims, & by appointing Rulers amongst them over tenns, twenties, fifties, &c. The lives, Manners, & habits of those, whom they say are converted, cannot be distinguished from those who are not, except it be by being hyred to heare Sermons, which the more generous natives scorne.

This is perhaps unfair, certainly antagonistic. Yet it points, however obliquely, to the essential fact: that the seventeenth-century Puritan, in trying to recover for the Indian a civil and religious purity which he was sure he had already recovered for himself, was simply defining one reality in terms of another, the primitive in terms of the civilized, the Indian in terms of the Puritan. And, in the nature of things, he was bound to be wrong — and so to fail in his holy enterprise.

However, there was yet, and anticlimactically, to be hope. It was to be essentially an evangelical hope, a hope of saving the Indian not so much for civilization but for God, and this just before he should die. It was a hope which rose as part of the last ditch efforts of Puritans to hold on to their covenant theology and polity in the face of the rationalistic theology, material prosperity, and general enlightenment which had been making men discount the sense of sin since the last quarter of the seventeenth century.

During the first quarter of the eighteenth century, reports to the English missionary societies which were financing missionary work recounted, proposed, and promised great things — increased use of native missionaries, a kind of reservation system, some thirty congregations newly established in southern New England, more attempts to get to the eastern Indians whom the French papists had debauched, coöperation with Dutch missionaries working among the Five Nations, and attempts to combat the effects of liquor, dishonest traders, and disease. Yet God was angry with New England for her failure to Christianize the heathen when He had clearly indicated in Scripture that it was to be done. Thus Solomon Stoddard, he who had recommended in 1703 that Indians be hunted down with dogs, could conclude by 1723:

> And as we dread to go to Hell our selves, it should be awful to us to consider their Damnation. Love and Pity calls for it, that we should help them out of their Danger. We should pity *Beasts* in Misery, much more *Men:* Tho, they be Brutish Persons; yet, they are of Mankind, and so objects of Compassion. It is an act of Love to our own nature to seek their Salvation. . . .

Who were the Indians who were thus to be saved? There was, for example, Joseph Quasson who had been bound to a white man when his father died in debt, who in his servitude had learned how to read and had come to know God. Freed, however, he had become a roisterer and a drunkard, and so by 1726 a condemned murderer. The account of Quasson which we have was written from his death-cell by a friendly minister. And the point that the minister makes is this: the fact that Quasson had been bound to a white man; that his trial was delayed three years after the murder; that he was given seven weeks to live after being condemned; that liquor was taken away from him — all this shows how hard the Lord has been working for his salvation. And there was Sarah Coomes, the dying six-year-old of whom Experience Mayhew wrote in 1727:

> She lay sick a considerable while before she died; and in that time continued to crave Instructions in things of God and the eternal World, and to express her Assent to, and acquiesce in them. She in particular expressed her steadfast Belief of the Doctrines of Christ's Person, Suffering, and Intercession for Sinners; and when she prayed, she called upon God to have Mercy upon her for his sake.

This is the Puritan sense of sin *in extremis.*

And in the context of the general failure of the sense of sin, there is to be understood, along with the neo-Calvinism of the Great Awakening, the final revivalistic interest in Indian conversion. The work of New-England born and trained Congregationalist missionaries had shifted by 1725 to the western parts of the middle colonies, where they were joined by and so worked with Scotch-Irish Presbyterian missionaries from the middle colonies. Here began that union of Congregationalist and Presbyterian missionary efforts which was to become official at the end of the century. The infusion of Presbyterian Calvinism must have done much to hearten the Congregationalist ministers. For the ministers herein involved, John Sargeant, David Brainerd, Charles Beatty, and Jonathan Edwards chief among them, conversion was everything and civilization nothing; the high Puritan faith in the uses of civilization as a means to conversion had gone almost entirely. So, in a report prepared for the Society in Scotland for the Propagation of Christian Knowledge, Brainerd is primarily concerned with "experimental [*i.e.,* experiential] religion" — which is to say, religious conversion as it relates to overt emotional tension and crisis. He tells, for example, of his violent preaching to Indians, 8 August 1745, in Crosweeksung, New Jersey; he was pleased that the Indians were not able to "withstand the shock of this surprising operation. . . . They were almost universally praying and crying for mercy in every part of the house, and many out of doors, and numbers could neither go nor stand." He was thus living up to the precepts of Ebenezer Pemberton who had preached at his ordination, insisting that conversion was to be achieved only by powerful preaching: "They [the preachers] are to 'compel sinners to come in' by a living representation of the power and grace of an almighty Redeemer. And in his own short life, so his editor, biographer, and intended father-in-law, Jonathan Edwards, was pleased to note, the desperately consumptive Brainerd showed evidence, above all, of those authentic religious affections only through which men are surely and truly saved. In an edition of the *Life of Brainerd,* published after Edwards' death, there was included further contemporary evidence of the need for violent conversion of the heathen — this in Charles Beatty's "Further remarks respecting Indian affairs." Beatty argues in so many words that the conversion of the Indians must precede their being civilized; for the Indians hate civilization and Christianity equally and must be convinced of the misery of their spiritual state before they can realize the misery of their civil state. Only "gospellizing" will succeed where civilizing has failed. Thus the continuing miserable state of the savage heathen was taken as additional evidence not only of the failure of earlier missionary methods but also of the need of direct and violent religious experience as an absolute prerequisite to civil and social improvement. Having virtually destroyed the Indian by trying to bring a new, civil life to him, the New England missionaries, encouraged by their Scotch-Irish Presbyterian brethren, were now to call the Holy Spirit directly to the Indian in order that they might give him that new life immediately. Certainly, a miracle was needed.

Always deriving its meaning from the Puritan view of man and his nature, inevitably the Puritan understanding of the Indian issued, towards the middle of the eighteenth century, into a particular form of the revivalism and anti-rationalism into which the Puritan view in general had issued. And so, this final Puritan understanding of the Indian is to be comprehended essentially as it relates to the Edwardean neo-Calvinism of the Great Awakening. Always the Puritan mind had worked from the inside out, from God and Scripture and reason to man and nature. Whatever he saw outside, the Puritan had somehow already seen inside. Understanding the Indian as he was related to man and nature, the Puritan thus succeeded — if he did succeed — only in knowing a little more about God and Scripture and reason, and in understanding himself. There is a simple explanation, perhaps: In order to make his new society in a new world, the Puritan could not afford to understand anyone but himself.

Peopling the Colonies

Except for sparse numbers of intractable Indians, the English found an uninhabited continent with which nothing could be done without a sizable labor force with the right skills. Recruiting people, therefore, became one of the principal problems facing colony-builders. For 300 years, a steady stream of Europeans migrated to America, pushed by poverty and oppressed at home, pulled by freedom and opportunity in America. In all, some 60 million people left Europe in the years following 1700, most headed for America. This movement was one of the great folk migrations in history. In the following selection, Mildred Campbell closely examines groups of seventeenth-century immigrants to illuminate who they were and what forces propelled them.

Though North America drew on all parts of the world for its population, England supplied most of those who came during the first two centuries. At that time, England was unable to fully employ willing workers on the farms and in the towns. An agricultural revolution forced tens of thousands off the land, as enterprising large landholders discovered that it was more profitable to consolidate many fragmented plots into large, but well-managed estates. The displaced peasantry, however, had no place to go in this preindustrial era. Many became public charges and drifted into the towns, especially London which was fast becoming a metropolis. At the same time, many urban craft guilds encountered tough competition from new, more efficient modes of production, and they, too, suffered eclipse. The result was large-scale technological unemployment, until the Industrial Revolution in the latter half of the eighteenth century created new jobs.

Until then, however, those people who could no longer continue at old jobs, either accepted inferior ones, sank into pauperdom, or migrated. According to Mildred Campbell, the migration was a highly selective process that appealed more to the young than to the old, and to the not-so-poor more than to the impoverished. Young people, hoping to inherit a family plot or trade, experienced the pangs of economic dislocation most acutely, and were most prone to seek alternatives. And those who descended from yeoman farming and skilled artisan families, in contrast to the poorer peasantry and unskilled laborers, had more to lose by staying in England where opportunities were shrinking. Rather than suffer a decline in status, some came to America where they could become landowning farmers and prosperous craftsmen as their forebears had been.

The breakup of medieval patterns of agricultural and industrial organization, a process that occurred first and most extensively in England, later spread to the rest of Europe, and in the nineteenth century sent millions of Europe's landless and homeless to the New World.

FOR FURTHER READING:

HANDLIN, OSCAR. *The Uprooted.* New York: Grosset & Dunlap, 1957.*
HANSEN, MARCUS LEE. *The Atlantic Migration.* Magnolia, Mass.: Peter Smith, 1940.*
SMITH, ABBOTT E. *Colonists in Bondage*: *White Servitude and Convict Labor in America.* Magnolia, Mass.: Peter Smith, 1947.*

Asterisk denotes paperback edition.

Social Origins of Some Early Americans   MILDRED CAMPBELL

A study of American origins must eventually lead to the structure and functioning of many Old World societies, for the national fabric is woven of many threads. But the people who came first in their sturdy ships of fifty to a hundred tons, who kept coming throughout the seventeenth century until the small seaboard settlements had moved out of their first precarious existence to a more certain future — these have a special claim upon us. Indeed, one wonders whether individuals ever meant as much to any enterprise as did those who filled the emigrant ships in that first century of colonization. Emigration across the Atlantic has never ceased from their day to ours, but only then did actual survival depend on the arrival of a relatively few people.

It was also only in the first century that those who came were a fairly homogeneous group in terms of national origins. For despite the Dutch on the Hudson, and small groups of Swiss, Swedes, Finns, and French Huguenots pocketed along the coast, the small vessels which set out on the American voyage were chiefly English built and English manned. Their cargoes, moreover, consisted largely of Englishmen and, later and in smaller numbers, Englishwomen. Even the Scots and Irish, who in the next century would crowd the harbors of the New World, were a minority in the first century.

We have long been accumulating a vast amount of information about these early settlers, and able historians have exploited the material with skill and insight. Only in more recent years, however, have serious attempts been made to push the story further back. We now try to discover their social origins. We want to know more about what they brought with them; not their material possessions — the *Susan Constant* and her sister ships provided space for only the barest minimum of necessities — but that other luggage which every individual perforce carries about with him, his heritage. That heritage was the sum total of his own experiences and the environment in which he grew up; it had made him what he was and determined, to an extent, what he would become. The impact of the New World might, and we know often did, produce marked changes in a settler which, for good or ill, would affect his whole future. It could never entirely obliterate his past.

Let us admit at the outset that we shall never know the past of these first Americans, still English in their own eyes and in the eyes of others, as well as we should like to know it; nor shall we be able to answer half the questions about them that can be asked. An appallingly large number of them never lived to play their part in

Source: Mildred Campbell, "Social Origins of Some Early Americans," in *Seventeenth-Century America*, ed. James M. Smith (Chapel Hill: University of North Carolina Press, 1959), pp. 63–89.

the enterprise to which they were so important. Thousands either died on the voyage or during the first year after their arrival. Most of those who came never kept personal records and no records were kept about them. Except for the concern of a ship captain or his agent that there be a profitable cargo for the outgoing voyage, their homeland in most cases took little note of their leaving. And the New World soon made it clear that their past mattered less than what they could do in the "needful" present. But the search is worth while if one can know even a little more about the lives of these people in their native England: the social strata from which they sprang, the fabric of life in their home communities, the reasons why the New World made its appeal — all matters about which we have thus far little concrete information.

The scene of the search is England under the Stuarts and in the Cromwellian interlude. Recent decades have taught us much about the entire social background of this period. Professors Trevelyan and Rowse paint the larger canvas in the bold strokes they use so effectively. Wallace Notestein perhaps comes nearer than anyone else to taking up residence among seventeenth-century Englishmen and learns from his close acquaintance both big and little things about them that are revealing. Others have dealt more narrowly with special segments of society, or have done what the English scholars do so well — shown what life was like in specific localities. The Tawney-Trevor Roper controversy over the gentry has also added light as well as heat. Such studies have enabled us to read a broadside addressed to "earls, lords, knights, gentlemen, and yeomen," with a better knowledge of what those terms mean. There remains, however, a multitude of shadings to vex us, especially in the lower groups and in the more mobile and intricate relationships of urban society.

In searching for the origins of American settlers we shall not be concerned equally with all of the social strata. Yet two basic aspects of seventeenth-century social philosophy which affected everyone must be kept in mind: first, the universal acceptance of the concept of social gradation and a complete belief in its rightness; and second, the belief, held simultaneously, that differences in rank, although normally to be observed, were not unalterable. One will not, of course, forget that the period of the Civil Wars produced a handful of Diggers on St. George's Hill who espoused a doctrine of communistic living, or that John Lilburne and his fellow-soldiers turned a part of the Cromwellian army into a debating society on political democracy. The issues of these debates would one day assume great importance; but they are probably remembered more for their later significance than because of any immediate effect they had on social structure. Degree, priority, and place, as Shakespeare described it, as the clergy taught and preached it, and as the people of all ranks lived it, was the accepted social philosophy of the day. "For that infinite wisdom of God which hath distinguished his angels by degrees . . . hath also ordained kings, dukes . . . and other degrees among men."

The normal expectation of the members of every class was to see their children settled and married within their own social group. On the other hand, if a man came to a position of substance and outlook more in keeping with another class above or below him, he eventually moved into its ranks. This practice had long lent a freshness and toughness to the fiber of English society. Now in the fast changing and more competitive conditions of the Tudor and Stuart era, social fluidity was greater than it had ever been. Some deplored the current development in which "Joan is as good as My Lady," where "Citizen's wives have of late growne Gallants," and "the yeoman doth gentilize it." But most people considered it a source of national strength that "in England the temple of honour is bolted against none."

It worked both ways though. A man could go down as well as up. Inflationary prices, a fluctuating land market, defective land titles, precarious investments, and bad debts created a milieu which gave some men their opportunity and brought dismal failure to others. Every social category had its crop of new men. Increased competition placed a higher premium on personal initiative than had been known in an earlier England. In emphasizing the manner in which pioneer colonial life developed individual initiative, it may be that we have not sufficiently recognized that much initiative was already present in the society from which the early settlers came, that indeed this may partially explain their coming.

In England tales of discovery and exploration had enlisted the interest and stretched the imagination of people of every class. But those at the top of the social hierarchy rarely were concerned with actual settlement. In terms of patronage and investment, however, many of them were active. Lord Baltimore had able friends among his own associates to aid in the Maryland enterprise; and no fewer than eight earls, one viscount, and a bishop helped to launch the Virginia Company under its second charter in 1609. Interest in colonial schemes became a favorite hobby, more than a hobby in some cases, with noblemen at the court of Charles II. But in answer to the query, "Who would venture their persons and who their purses?" the noblemen usually answered in favor of the latter, and few members of the nobility actually emigrated with the intention of remaining in the colonies.

Below the nobility came the knights and country gentry: "gentlemen of the blood," of ancient lineage. But with them also were newly landed men, office holders, members of the professions, university men, and many with business and mercantile interests — these too were known as "gentlemen." Dozens of such men became involved in colonial activities. Indeed, one wonders if seventeenth-century America would have advanced much beyond the trading-post stage had it not been for their money, vision, and perseverance. They were the men who instituted, to a great extent financed, and almost wholly ran the great companies under which the first colonies were started. The wealthier and more important men like Sir Ferdinand Gorges, Sir John Popham, Matthew Cradock, Sir Thomas Smith, carried on their work from England. But others came in person to lead the new plantations: younger sons of the financial backers, gentry of lesser pretensions, clergymen, and merchants. This was especially true in the earlier years, partly because leadership from below had not yet had time to develop, and partly because it seems to have been the original intent that the colonies should be led by individuals of the upper classes, a policy in keeping with the philosophy of the time. It is also apparent that in the beginning such men had little idea that the demands made upon them by the New World would be so different from those to which they had been accustomed at home.

More is known about these leaders than about any of the other settlers and for obvious reasons. They were the articulate ones. They themselves wrote and kept records, though not perhaps as many records as we should like, and others wrote about them. They were the clergymen about whom Perry Miller, Alan Simpson, and a host of writers tell us, those who preached *Puritanism in Old and New England* and made frequent journeys back and forth. Among them are some of Louis Wright's *First Gentlemen of Virginia* and some of John Pomfret's proprietors of *The Province of West New Jersey*. They wander through the pages of Bernard Bailyn's *New England Merchants in the Seventeenth Century*. In terms of social origins, less illustrious people also belong in this group: bankrupt businessmen; ill-starred younger sons and brothers of the gentry; proverbial ne'er-do-wells whose families hoped that a change of scene would set them on a better path, youths like Lady Finch's unruly son, "whom she sent to Virginia to be tamed." Sometimes family hopes for reformation were realized. Often enough, however, parents had to face the fact that the voyage across the Atlantic was not sufficient to bring about the moral transformation desired. Despite this unpromising contingent, men of the rank of knight or gentleman (whether that rank came by birth or acquisition) played a role in colonial society out of proportion to their numbers. And the more we know about them, the better off we shall be. They are recognized by the title "Sir" if they were knights, or merely by "Mr.," a term not applied below the gentry. In many colonial narratives they are spoken of as "the better sort" and in lists of ships' passengers are usually identified as the "men of quality." Thus one ship carried "eighteen men of quality and eighty-seven others." Another speaks of "seven gentlemen and sixty-four others." And again, we read of "about a score of men of quality and a hundred and four others." One becomes familiar with the pattern.

But who were "the others"? Practically nothing is known about them, although the passenger lists make it perfectly clear that they account for the overwhelming numbers in the emigrant ships. "How to people His Majesty's dominions with people?" becomes a kind of recurrent refrain in the plantation literature of the seventeenth century. It was "the others" who chiefly furnished the answer to that query. Because there were so many of them and because our information about them is so woefully scant they have perhaps a special claim to attention. Who actually were they? Did they belong chiefly to the "middling people" — yeomen and artisans? Were they largely the poor agricultural laborers whose sorry plight in this period is well known? Or were they mostly riffraff from the streets of London and Bristol, the poor who had so increased under the Tudors as to demand state action; or beggars, and condemned persons who filled the prisons? We know that all of these were represented among the early colonists. But beyond that we have had little concrete information about them, and slight knowledge of the relative degree with which the various groups responded to the appeals from the New World for settlers.

Two sets of seventeenth-century manuscripts merit attention for what they have to offer about the identity of "the others." They record the departure of slightly more than 11,000 emigrants from Bristol and London in the second half of the seventeenth century. The Bristol record, the more important of the two, contains the names of some 10,000 people who shipped from that port between 1654 and 1685. It provides a small amount of data for the entire group over the whole period; but the fuller part of the record, and that part which contains information pertinent to the subject of social origins, covers approximately the first 7 years and deals with upwards of 3,000 people. The London record includes approximately 750 men and women who left for the New World in the year 1683–84. Although a smaller sample, it contains the same type of information (including several additional items) as found in the Bristol record, thus providing comparative material from another area. The London and Bristol records list only a few of the many thousands of men and women who made their beginning in the New World as indentured servants before the American Revolution. But they originated in a period for which data are scarce; hence, though neither record is statistically perfect, both deserve careful consideration.

The first significant fact about both records is that they deal entirely with people who were coming to America as indentured servants. This is perhaps fortunate; for studies made in the last two decades have demonstrated that a far larger percentage of our colonial population entered the country under indenture than was formerly thought. One-half of the total is held to be a conservative estimate. On the question of their social origins, moreover, almost no concrete information is available.

The plan of indenture has been so fully treated by scholars that only a brief definition is required here. Under the indenture terms, a prospective settler agreed to serve a master in one of the colonies for a period of years (usually four or five), in return for free passage across the Atlantic and certain "Freedom dues" when his term of service was over. One aspect of indenture, however, has not been sufficiently considered: the fact that within the framework of English society, as it actually functioned in the seventeenth century, such a practice would be considered not only natural but salutary. This is of great importance if we look at the New World from the point of view of the prospective emigrant still in England, or of the family of a young person contemplating settlement. The whole idea of service and services in return for land, training, protection — in short, for social and economic security — was an idea basic to medieval thinking and practice and one that had by no means disappeared. The practice of apprenticeship, for example, was not legalized and specifically defined until 1563, but it had been the general practice for generations.

The same mental and social outlook that found positive values in the seven-year apprenticeship for young children would see social values in a four- or five-year indenture for a young man — and even more for a young woman — who was preparing to set out on a journey of three thousand miles in the hope of eventually establishing himself. Promotion literature advised young single men — particularly those with small means — to go into service for a few years and especially recommended indenture for young women. Some tales that came back across the water about the life of an indentured servant in the American colonies made it clear that it was often very different from the version presented in the promotion literature. But stories of those settlers who had been fortunate circulated in England as well; and the practice of indenture, which was based on the long-accepted principle of service, could weather reports of abuse and failure.

Historians have long been interested in the social status of the colonists who came under indenture; but throughout the first third of the twentieth century it remained a subject of the widest conjecture, despite the tremendous amount of excellent work done in the colonial field. Professor Andrews, who often deplored our lack of sufficient knowledge on the subject, said of the indentured servants in Virginia: "Some of them, perhaps many, seem to have been in origin above the level of menials, to have good family connections in England, and in a few instances to have been even of gentle birth." Marcus Jernegan believed they came chiefly from the undesirables and the agricultural class who under conditions in England had no chance to better themselves. In his *First Americans,* Professor Wertenbaker shared this view. The bulk of the indentured servants were, he said, "poor laborers who were no longer content to work in misery and rags in England while opportunity beckoned them across the Atlantic." Fifteen years later he had accepted what Abbot Smith, Richard Morris, and others were saying, namely, that "all kinds came." An analysis of the Bristol and London records helps to define that phrase and to show in what proportions different social groups were represented.

It is a matter of considerable interest that approximately twenty-five percent of the Bristol group are women. We shall have something more to say of them later. Among the men, yeomen and husbandmen are in the majority; they account for about thirty-six percent, with the yeomen outnumbering the husbandmen. Artisans and tradesmen number approximately twenty-two percent; laborers account for about ten percent; gentlemen and professional men make up a little less than one percent. Thus the farmers outnumber the skilled workers almost two to one, and the combined farmers and skilled workers outnumber the laborers more than five to one.

In the smaller London sampling, the women are somewhat under the twenty-five percent of the Bristol records. The skilled workers outnumber the yeomen and husbandmen in almost the reverse proportion to the Bristol record: approximately two to one. This difference is, of course, to be expected in the records of an urban center. The husbandmen are also more numerous than the yeomen. But as in the case of the Bristol servants, the number of farmers and skilled workers in comparison with the laborers is in a ratio of about five to one.

A question may be raised concerning the authenticity of the status terms. Would not an ordinary laborer, knowing that masons, bricklayers, and carpenters were in great demand in the colonies at high wages, possibly try to assume a skill for which he had no training? Some may have tried this deception, and it is possible that the number of artisans should be slightly lowered to take care of self-styled craftsmen. But two factors weigh in favor of the general validity of the terms. First, the number and variety of the skills listed in the records suggest accuracy: there are ninety-eight trades, many of which, such as the tuckers, fullers, and button makers, were not those most sought after by the colonial agents. Secondly, men in the seventeenth century were still accustomed to being recorded in terms of their status or occupation. They were so listed in court records, wills, deeds, leases, and business transactions of all kinds. It would have seemed natural and prudent to give the same information for this record as for all others. Hence, allowing for a certain margin of error and even some false reporting, the evidence still points to a large majority of farmers and tradesmen over laborers.

The relatively low number of laborers was at first puzzling. According to writers of the period, the laborers' status was the lowest in the social hierarchy. They were the most numerous and poorest members of England's working population. Although their wages rose slightly during the first half of the century, they tended to remain constant, even in some places to drop a little, from then until the end of the century. Those who worked by the year for an annual wage ranging from three to five pounds were perhaps the most fortunate. They had a roof over their heads and something to eat. We think it a hardship that the medieval serf could not escape the land, but neither, it may be well to remember, could the land get away from him. His life was meager, often harsh, but economically it was more secure than that of his successor, the landless laborer.

In the comments of some of their contemporaries may lie a partial explanation of the laborers' lack of enthusiasm for emigration. Thomas Ludwell, a Somerset man, received a request for servants from his brother in Virginia. He answered that there were workmen in his neighborhood to spare, but "they will live meanly and send their families to the parish to be relieved rather than hear of such a long journey to mend their condition." Robert Southwell, who had had poor luck in his attempt to recruit laborers in 1669, said of them: "They are loth to leave the smoke of their own cabin if they can but beg neere it." There are other comments in the same vein. The laborers were accustomed to little; they could do with little. In times of dearth they would be hungry; but they had rarely had full stomachs, and while they might come close to starvation, the parish would not let them die. In addition, they were a superstitious lot and quite possibly would have been frightened by the tales about the dangers of the long voyage over strange waters.

If the London and Bristol records can be taken as a fair sample (and they are in accord with other recent studies), it is clearly a mistaken assumption to think that the laborers formed the large part of those who came to America as indentured servants. The majority were farmers and skilled workers.

Most of the women in the list were not classified according to status except as "singlewoman" or "spinster," the latter term being used at this period to describe either a married or an unmarried woman. A number of "widows" were listed, and a few women were classified according to the skill or occupation which they hoped to have in the homes of their new masters — "dairy maid," "lady's maid," and the like. Young women often went in twos and threes from the same village, and now and then the lists show members of the same family. It is quite possible that a larger percentage of women than men came from among the laborers. Country folk had their own measuring rods in terms of social codes and behavior patterns; a yeoman or tradesman of some standing would feel more reluctant to see his daughter set off on such a journey than would a laborer. Yeomen and husbandmen worked alongside farm laborers getting in the crops and mingled with them in the village alehouse. Yet it was not considered the proper thing for the daughters of yeomen to work in the fields, although the wives and daughters of laborers did so as a matter of course. Daughters of yeomen and tradesmen, however, often went into the service of families in their neighborhoods, and in certain industries such as lacemaking, girls were apprenticed in the usual way.

There are women listed in both these records who were going in answer to personal requests from planters in Maryland and Virginia for servants of various skills. Charles Peck of London was sending one to his brother Tom in Virginia at the latter's request. She was to serve in his own home, and "not be soulde unless to some planter for a wife." It was commonly accepted that a husband was the chief inducement the New World had to offer a young girl. Nor would she have much trouble getting one, although the match was not always with the wealthy planter that the promotion literature promised. It is interesting that promoters were becoming a bit more discriminating in their advice respecting the women who were wanted. They were somewhat on the defensive about the women who had been sent over from the houses of correction: "But if they come of honest stock, and have good repute they may pick their husbands out of the better sort of people." Three months, one of them thought, was as long as one could hope to keep a good maid before "some proper young fellow" would come after her.

Servants sought as wives were purchased either in pounds sterling or tobacco. This businesslike way of approaching marriage strikes a wrong note in our generation. But it would have seemed quite normal to the seventeenth century, where every girl (except those of the very lowest groups, who were not too particular about such things) was accustomed to a marriage that was largely a business arrangement. Women who went to the colonies, however, may not always have accepted husbands immediately, even if they were not under indenture; there was plenty of work at good pay for them until such time as they did marry. Later in the century when many servants were going to Pennsylvania, Gabriel Thomas lamented about the exorbitant wages women could command: "They are not as yet very numerous which makes them stand on high terms for their several services." He added, however, "They are usually marry'd before they are twenty years of age."

Practically all of the servants were young. Indeed, it is clear that the whole plan for indentured service was designed for the young unmarried man and woman. It is easier for the young to be uprooted, and a new-found land across the sea would beckon to twenty-one as it would not to fifty. The Bristol record does not give ages, but they are given in the London group. The majority were between the ages of eighteen and twenty-four, with twenty-one and twenty-two predominating — just the age when the young tradesmen were finishing their apprenticeship. The large number of farmers and skilled workers going under indenture demonstrates the appeal which this method of emigration made to single young men of small means and even to those whose parents could perhaps have managed the passage money.

A young man just out of his apprenticeship would not, if he remained in England, set up for himself at once. Likewise, a yeoman's son, unless he were the eldest or his father were able to buy land for him, would work at home or for a neighboring yeoman or gentleman through his earlier years while he accumulated piecemeal holdings of his own. English yeomen were a canny lot. Perhaps farmers everywhere are. To be able to get to America without any expense to himself or his family would appeal to a lad brought up as these had been. Besides if a young man went to America alone without enough money to buy labor, reputed to be both high and scarce, what could he do with the fifty or a hundred acres of land that he hoped to get? Nobody knew better than a farmer's son that it took more than one pair of hands to get crops in the ground and to harvest them. These were some of the facts that would have been in the minds of the yeomen and husbandmen, carpenters, tilemakers, and weavers whose names are enrolled in the Bristol and London lists.

A few married men went without their wives, leaving them sometimes provided for, sometimes not. And there were a few married couples going together, but not many, for this practice was discouraged because of complications likely to arise on the other side. Finally in 1682 an order prohibiting a married man from going as an indentured servant went into effect. But it is doubtful if recruiting agents looked into the matter too closely. There are examples in other records of groups of married people who paid their own passage, but were apparently somewhat older and better established. They took along with them single young men and women under indenture — their neighbors, friends, and kinspeople. They would thereby get the "headright" lands for having brought them over, and the young people coming as servants were with friends and kinsfolk during their early years in a strange country. Hundreds who were not so fortunate left it to chance to place them in the hands of a good master or a poor one when the ship docked.

It is significant that the married people referred to above who took their families and paid their own passage were for the most part farmers and tradesmen of the same social rank as the servants they took with them. This was, I believe, generally the case. For one of the gratifying by-products of the information concerning status that comes from these records is that through them we are also able indirectly to determine the status of the remainder of "the others" who filled the emigrant ships. If the laborers at the bottom of the economic scale account for a relatively small number of those coming under indenture, it is certain that they were not widely represented among those who paid their own passage. The reluctance of the laborers to go as servants has already been shown. If one adds to that the crucial fact that they simply would not have had the five or six pounds required to pay their own passage, it is clear that there would be few of them in that group. Individuals or small groups sometimes came over in the personal service of men of better substance, but this would not account for many. If, therefore, the laborers at the bottom of the social and economic hierarchy were a minority, as were also the "men of quality" at the other extreme, we can but conclude that "the others," both those who came under indenture and those who paid their own fare, were drawn from the middling classes: farmers and skilled workers, the productive groups in England's working population. The difference between those who came as servants and those who paid their own fare was partly economic, with the poorer farmers and "decayed" tradesmen coming under indenture; and partly, as we have seen, it was a matter of age, experience, and marital position.

Status is basic to the quest for social origins. But before attempting further to spell out its meaning in terms of actual living conditions, we must pay our respects to one other relatively small group among the Bristol servants, the children. The term of service set down in the indenture provides the key for determining their numbers. The vast majority of adult terms are for four or five years, the four-year term slightly predominating, although now and then a servant went for two or three years, or more rarely, even for one. Children, however, were sent for longer terms in order that they should reach adulthood by the time their service was over. Their average term was seven years, as was that of the ordinary apprentice in England; but in both cases it might be as high as ten or twelve years, depending on the child's age.

About eight percent of the Bristol group went for a term of six years or more, chiefly seven. But seven years or longer is also the term assigned to those recalcitrants whom the justices of the peace sent to the colonies for the punishment of minor crimes. How can we know that the emigrants with terms of seven years or more were not these delinquents rather than minors? It is likely that some of them were, for delinquents of this type were sent along with other servants and we know of some who were in this group. Fortunately, the London indentures containing the actual ages for everyone are of assistance in this problem. For they show that almost all of the indentures for long terms (about six percent in this record) apply to children under fifteen. Only occasionally is an older person given a longer term. An examination of Quarter Sessions court records, where instances of forced emigration for minor crimes were documented, offers supporting evidence during the years in question that this type of punishment was apparently used sparingly by the county officials. Hence, unless there was a larger percentage of delinquents in the Bristol group than among those going from London, which hardly seems likely, we may assume that the majority of Bristol's eight percent assigned to long terms were also minors.

Not infrequently, of course, some of the individuals deported for misdemeanors were likewise minors; often the children who went as servants were orphans or problem children whom someone wished to dispose of. We glimpse them now and again in the records. John Morgan, a Bristol upholsterer, appeared in July, 1659, with an uncancelled indenture that had been made out for David Thomas, a Glamorgan boy who was bound to him. He should have been registered earlier: "But in regard he was on shipboard, and could not be brought up for fear of his running away, he was not enrolled in the middle of the book." A fourteen-year-old girl in

London was taken out of White Chapel jail to which she had been committed for "pilfering lace" and with the consent of her father and mother was indentured for service in America. A stray letter among the London indentures tells the story of Robert Redman. An uncle in Cambridge had sent him up to London to be put aboard *The Hopewell*. He writes that in the boy's trunk "is his best and worst cloathes, an extra shirt, 2 pr. stockins, 6 neck cloathes, 6 handkerchers, 2 caps, 1 hatt, 1 pr. shoes." Instructions are given that anything else needful is to be provided. "If 9 years or tenn yeares service be required," the uncle writes, "I am contented provided he have his bellefull of food, with cloathes to keep him warm and warm lodgin at night." He asks to be told when the boy is "disposed of" and to whom and "how to rit a letter to his master and to him." It is apparent that things have not gone well. Young Redman is not to be given the keys to his trunk for fear he will either sell or give away his belongings. "I could keep him no longer," the uncle says; yet he hopes he will have a good voyage, and has sent along "Balsome and salve" for the ship's surgeon to use in treating an injury on the boy's leg. After a somewhat formal ending according to the fashion of the day, a postscript adds that "Thers a Rage to dress his wounded leg with."

Aside from the delinquents, both minor and adult, sent by the justices, two groups of indentured servants entered into their contracts under compulsion: convicts and, during both the Commonwealth and Restoration period, political prisoners. Neither group will be considered here; for with the few possible exceptions which have been considered among those holding long terms, it seems clear that these records deal with the ordinary men and women who went to America under indenture of their own volition. Therefore, we turn again to the two basic records for additional clues which will make possible at least a fragmentary reconstruction of the environment they were leaving behind them.

Next in importance to the status term is that part of the record which gives the emigrant's place of origin; for without this information, it would be impossible to enlarge our understanding of the American settler's background. Both records show how widely the New World ventures were known in England. The Bristol names include representatives from every English county except Rutland, and many from Wales. An overwhelming majority are from the West, with Somerset, Gloucestershire, and Wiltshire taking the lead among the English counties and Monmouthshire first among the Welsh. Proximity to Bristol undoubtedly accounts partly for this concentration; but it is significant that some western counties are much more sparsely represented. Outside the heavy concentration in London and Middlesex, Yorkshire furnished the largest number to the London group.

The place of origin carries significance beyond the servant group; for if large numbers of servants were coming from certain centers, it is almost certain that there were also large numbers from these same centers who paid their own passage. The largest number of servants recorded in the Bristol group, slightly more than half, booked for Virginia. One is therefore not surprised to come upon the following passage from James Southall's sketch of a Virginia family, in which he discusses the section in England that was the source of so many of Virginia's early settlers. He describes an area

> about thirty miles north of Bristol in the west of England, running due north and south for a distance of about ten miles and with an average breadth of three miles, where a . . . ridge of the Malvern Hills divides the county of Hereford from the county of Worcester and on the southeast of these, on the south bank of the upper Severn, with yet ampler di-

mensions stretches the county of Gloucester, all three counties touching each other at a common point near the city of Gloucester.

It was in this district, the author says,

> and from Somersetshire, and the neighboring counties of Wales . . . from Warwick on the north, Devon in the southwest, Herts and the Isle of Wight in the south, and across the Bristol Channel from the coast of Ireland, that in Virginia, the counties of Henrico, James City, Charles City, Isle of Wight, Gloucester, Surrey, and Prince George were largely settled.

Except for including Ireland and the Isle of Wight, he has described almost exactly the area chiefly represented by the Bristol record. Along with East Anglia, and Lincolnshire and Yorkshire in the north, the West Country was the homeland of thousands of the early settlers. From the beginning there was in the West a strong tradition for the American adventure. The New World would not seem so far away to West Country boys, many of whose fathers and brothers earned their living as mariners and seamen on ships that plied between Plymouth, Bristol, and lesser ports to the New World. They were not, said a contemporary, of "the In-land sort," who were "wedded to their native soils like a Snaile to his shell, or . . . a mouse to his chest." Their grandfathers would have sailed or known people who sailed with Drake and Raleigh — and grandfathers are all alike. It was natural that Hugh Peter, telling the House of Lords in 1665 about his departure to New England, should say that he "by birth in Cornwall was not altogether ignorant of that place." It is then to the West Country that we must turn. For here lay the farm lands and villages from which almost eighty-five percent of the Bristol emigrants came.

Three centuries have inevitably changed the West Country. The most conspicuous difference is the growth of modern urban centers; yet there has been less change than in some parts of England, and one can drive through miles of rural Gloucestershire, Wiltshire, and Somerset, where the country must look much the same as it did three centuries and a half ago when many of its humbler people were preparing to leave. There are evidences now of more intensive agriculture, but the contours of hills and green sloping meadows remain the same. It is a good land to look upon. So also they must have thought who were departing from it. For it is a great mistake to assume that emigration, for whatever purpose, meant that people left home and familiar surroundings with no regrets. Even the most rabid of the New England Puritan clergy, full of spleen and invective, frequently expressed devotion to old England and the "mistaken ones" who stayed behind. These folk who left the West Country were not very articulate; they could not have said what they felt as did a later West Country man:

> 'Tis time, I think, by Wenlock town
> The golden broom should blow.

But chance words and phrases that appear in prosaic colonial records betray the same nostalgia. It was probably sheer homesickness that overcame the boy from a Gloucestershire village who went to Bristol with a friend intent on shipping to Virginia — he let the other boy go on without him, the record says, and "came back home."

The houses they lived in, especially the homes of the lesser folk, were made of whatever natural building materials the locality afforded. Some of the small stone houses that can be seen today in Cotswold villages were there then, some newly built, some already old — all evidence of the prosperity that Cotswold wool had brought to the locality. Beyond the Cotswolds to the west in the Severn Valley, a redder sandstone furnished excellent building material, but it was hard to quarry and in general was reserved for churches and the houses of great men. Farmers and tradesmen built their houses mostly of a combination of wood and some kind of plaster spread often over a wattle framework. "Cob," as it was called, used largely in Devon farmhouses, was a mixture of mud, straw, gravel, and chalk. These houses were small, varying from the two to three rooms of the less well-to-do to as many as eight or nine in the houses of wealthy yeomen, small clothiers, and tradespeople of some substance. The homes of the laborers have not survived; they were probably little more than hovels and, except for some very newly built, were almost certainly without much light. John Aubrey, himself a West Country man, wrote of Wiltshire in 1671 and remarked that within his remembrance the use of glass had been restricted: "Copyholders and ordinary poor people had none." The inventories attached to wills supply details of the interiors of these crude homes. Trestled furniture was still being used, although sometimes "joined" tables are mentioned. Pewter dishes were by now a commonplace in the cupboards of the middling people, but wooden trenches were still in everyday use. Occasionally there were a few prized silver teaspoons. Their standards of both comfort and cleanliness would, of course, be scorned by people of like position in modern society.

It is understandable that promoters found these middling people of the West Country satisfactory settlers and made special efforts to induce them to go to the colonies. It was not merely their skills that were wanted. They had other qualities born of the kind of lives they had lived that would stand them in good stead. They were not, it is true, accustomed to the peculiar type of pioneer hardship that prevailed in America, but their lives in England had known little comfort or ease. The craftsmen were accustomed to working from five in the morning until seven or eight at night. Farmers labored outside from daylight until dark and carried on indoor tasks by fire and candlelight. A man could not be idle and hold his own in the demanding world in which they lived. Idlers there were, of course, but lower and middle class families did not have the means to care for loafers.

Men of the West Country like those elsewhere were forced to adapt themselves to the competitive and acquisitive society common to their age. Those with a greater margin of wealth could weather the crises better. Because of their fairly simple standard of living and the fact that they were practically self-supporting, the farmers were less affected by the high prices of outside products than almost any other group. Despite market fluctuations, they could usually sell their sheep and grain at a very good profit.

Wealthy yeomen of the West Country not only had glass and chimneys in their houses, but were now installing wainscoting in their "halls" and "parlours." The members of this class were aggressive, and if they held their land in a good tenure — that is, if it were freehold or of that particular kind of copyhold which carried similar security — they were most probably affluent. But circumstances which brought success to many meant failure for others. Land hunger was rife among all classes. Wealthy clothiers, drapers, and merchants who had done well and wished to set themselves up in land were avidly watching the market, ready to pay almost any price for what was offered. Even prosperous yeomen often could not get the land they desired for their younger sons; and indeed those who did not hold their own land in a good tenure ran the risk of losing it.

The West Country was good farming country, especially for sheep raising. Somerset in particular also had excellent land for tillage, and its farmers were noted for their skill. Yet even if the title to his land were clear, a West Country farmer could fare badly compared with farmers in some sections of England. For the West was a conservative part of the country. Change came slowly there, and only a beginning had been made with inclosures. More than a century later George Turner, writing of farming conditions in the vale of Gloucestershire, could still say: "I know one acre which is divided into eight lands, and spread over a large common field, so that a man must travel two or three miles to visit it all. . . . But this is not the worst. . . ." And he continued to recite the woes that West Country farmers were still enduring.

A great deal of the land was still copyhold, and large landholders kept the village economy almost on a feudal basis. The farmers from Tetbury, Chipping Sodbury, and other Gloucestershire villages were still performing services that had long since been discarded in many parts of England. The tendency, moreover, to retain long leases (ninety-nine years was the most common), once an advantage to the leaseholders, was now catching up with western farmers. Many leases which had been made out in Elizabeth's reign were now "falling in," leaving the tenant to face increased fines and rents or the likelihood of seeing his land go to someone else. It is not surprising if farmers facing these and similar conditions lent a sympathetic ear to the tales of ship captains and their agents, colonial promoters, and returned travellers — tales of a country where land was to be had for the asking, or nearly so, where leases did not "fall in," nor rents come due, where, in short, a man was his own landlord. That these promises were often highly exaggerated, that there was not land in many places, at any rate, suitable land, to be had for the asking did not alter the landlord dream. It is a commonplace to say that land was the greatest inducement the New World had to offer; but it is difficult to overestimate its psychological and social importance to people in whose minds land had always been identified with security, success, and the good things of life. "Now we can get few English servants," said a member of the Barbados Assembly in 1665, "having no lands to give them at the end of their time which formerly was their main allurement." Tradesmen as well as yeomen and husbandmen looked forward to becoming landholders. Richard Norton was a Bristol millwright and John Hatten a watchmaker, but they, no less than John Rose, a Wiltshire husbandman, and Morgan Jones, son of a Monmouthshire yeoman, carried with them indentures that called for fifty acres of land in Virginia or Maryland. This was in 1655. In later years the Carolinas and Pennsylvania would make even more attractive land offers.

With the bulk of the family land going to the eldest son, it had been the traditional pattern for farmers in every section of England to apprentice one or more of their other sons to trade. This was especially true in the West Country, where the cloth trade had for generations been a source of employment. Hard times among the East Anglian clothworkers made it easier for Winthrop and the other Puritan leaders to gain recruits for New England. The exodus of West Country clothworkers to America in the second half of the century is less well known but merits equal attention. The plight of the West Country was made considerably worse by economic disruption during and after the Civil Wars. No part of the nation was unaffected by this conflict, but the West was especially hard hit. As a key city Bristol early became a major objective and was successively under the control of both armies. The neighboring countryside suffered accordingly. "This England," said one, "is merely the ghost of that England which it was lately." Ships rotted in Bristol harbor; Gloucestershire woolen mills were plundered; clothworkers in Somerset were left without employment for months.

Nor did matters improve when the wars were over. Returned soldiers found themselves without work. Slack periods in the cloth business came in close succession. Prices fluctuated. Problems growing out of the plight of war widows, disabled soldiers, and an increasing number of poor rose to plague local officials and cast a pall of gloom over village communities. "I wish I could hear what condition you live in," an Essex tradesman had written a few years earlier to his Virginia kinsman, "for I fear if these times hold long amongst us we must be all faine come to Virginia." If the emigrant records can be taken as a key, many West Country men and women were now thinking the same thing. The annual exodus of servants shipping from Bristol rose from slightly less than 300 in 1655 to almost 800 in 1659, and hundreds more emigrants were going with their families and paying their own fare.

Discontent in the West Country cloth towns was not new. The trade had suffered somewhat earlier in the century, but it was not until after the Civil Wars that the complaints so increased in volume and bitterness. Modern scholars are inclined to think that the depression in the cloth trade traditionally assigned to the late Commonwealth and early Restoration years was not as damaging to the industry as was earlier thought. They tend to see the complaints from clothiers as disgruntlement over a shift to new men and new methods rather than a decline in the industry itself. But they all agree on the bad effects of the situation for the workers. The local records at Taunton and Trowbridge and Gloucester are filled with the hardships of the clothworkers: those who "toiled in their cottages from Castle Colne and Malmsbury on the edge of the Cotswold country" and in the industrial towns on the Avon, "to Westbury, Edington and the other villages under the plain." And it was from Castle Colne, Malmsbury, Westbury, and other villages under the plain that John Niblett, the clothmaker, Thomas Allen, the worsted comber, Edward Webb, the feltmaker, and John Davis, the tailor, with dozens of their friends and neighbors, made their way to Bristol during the late fifties and early sixties, to sign the indentures which assured their free passage to America. Other tradesmen and farmers in the nearby countryside were likewise affected, for hard times cannot come to a basic industry in a rural area without affecting auxiliary trades and the whole working population.

Tradesmen, like farmers, were worried not merely by present uncertainties but by the lack of future opportunity. It had once been the expectation of journeymen that they would advance their status three or four years after apprenticeship. Many were beginning now to find that they would have to be wage earners all their lives. Skilled workers of certain kinds much needed in the colonies could sometimes get special favors written into their agreements. John Walker and Samuel Minor, both carpenters, had made such arrangements. Walker's term was only three years, with a wage of forty pounds per annum while he was still in service. Minor, probably younger, was bound for five years, to receive twenty pounds the first three years and twenty-five the last two. Most of the servants, however, were either not that forehanded or their skills were not such as would be so much needed in America. Land and high wages were counted on to make up for that.

Despite the fact that industry and the land had each its peculiar character and concerns, their interaction in the general economy was very marked. What each could offer or failed to offer to the individual was of paramount importance. Together they provided the economic framework within which West Country farmers and tradesmen shaped the course of their lives. The laborers, whether agricultural or urban, were perhaps most immediately affected by the current fluctuations common to both Cromwellian and Restoration years. They eked out a meager living on their daily wage if there was work for them. If the cloth works were "still" or harvests were thin, they became a public charge; the local records bear eloquent testimony to the efforts of harassed parish officials to look after their poor. For such among them as were ambitious there was little or no opportunity. Emigration offered it and, as we know, there were some who took advantage of the offer. But most of them were not ambitious. Their niche in the social and economic scale was not threatened as was often that of small landed men or craftsmen.

It would, however, be a great error to assume that these West Country people thought only of economic matters. It should also be remembered that numerous though the emigrants were from any region, far more people stayed at home than left. To think otherwise would be to distort the view of the background of American immigration. There had long been a good deal of mobility among England's working population, particularly among young single men who moved around in search of work when times were bad in their own communities. In some cases families whose sons emigrated to America were already accustomed to having them away from home. The life of country communities would not be markedly changed because here and there a young person or a few families left. Those at home would carry on with the normal pursuits of daily life as dictated by their rank and position in the community and by individual and group interests.

Aside from the demands of daily occupations, perhaps the central focus of their activities was religion. Their scale of values was in large part determined by it, and it profoundly affected the shape and substance of their mental and social outlook. To the middling people of the West Country, as to many of their kind elsewhere, religion meant non-conformity. It was not, of course, all of one brand — that is the essence of non-conformity. "How many ways do you make it to heaven in this place?" a royalist chaplain had asked in 1647 as he deplored the "rabble of heresies" around Bristol. The years under Cromwell had not eased their troubles as much as many had hoped for. There was probably not much actual religious persecution, although it was not wholly absent; Quakers were cruelly treated at Bristol in 1654–56 and hundreds of them went to America in the following years. A comparison of the Bristol list with Besse's "Sufferers" shows an identity of almost five hundred names. Granting the error which may originate in the prolific repetition among West Country names, these figures cannot be entirely without significance. And not only Quakers were troubled. The West was indeed as the royalist chaplain had found, a hotbed of activity of the various sects. The rise in the Bristol emigration for 1659 has already been indicated. It is significant that the largest annual exodus came in 1662, when the first Restoration statutes against dissenters went into effect. Between eight and nine hundred servants went to America in that year from this one port. If the non-comformists of the West Country had not fared too well in the Commonwealth, they certainly did not expect the return of the Stuarts to help matters. Nor did it.

George Herbert, earlier tracing the cycle through which he thought religion ran her course, startled some of his friends by saying:

Religion stands on tiptoe in our land
Readie to pass to the American strand.

Nor had he been unaware of the social and economic implications:

Then shall Religion to America flee;
. . . .
My God, Thou dost prepare for them a way,
By carrying first their gold from them away,
For gold and grace did never yet agree
Religion alwaies sides with povertie.

Josiah Child was only the best known of various writers in the second half of the century who pointed out the "great swarms of new inhabitants" whom the New World received because of the restrictions placed on dissenters in England.

Nowhere were non-conformity and the ferment which it bred more deeply rooted than in the clothmaking centers. Richard Baxter, a Puritan clergyman of yeoman origins, pointed out this relationship as he looked back upon the part played by the various classes in the Civil Wars. Writing in 1683, he said,

> On the side of Parliament were the smaller part (as some thought) of the gentry in most of the countries and the greatest part of the Tradesmen and Freeholders, and the Middle sort of men; especially in those corporations and countries [counties] which depend on Cloathing and such Manufactures.

The preoccupation of the middling classes with non-conformity has often been noted. It was, says Alan Simpson, "weavers at their looms, tradesmen in their shops, and yeoman farmers in their homes" among whom Puritanism chiefly took root. Certainly non-conformity, clothmaking, and emigration were active influences in East Anglia in the first half of the century. It was also a combination that was active in the West Country in the second half. Restrictions on non-conformity and the impoverishment of the clothmaking industry gave the New World a double appeal. By no means, of course, were all of these Somerset farmers and Wiltshire and Gloucestershire clothworkers deeply religious people. Far from it. But most of them had been brought up in non-conformist groups which had, to a great extent, shaped the pattern of their lives. As Oscar Handlin has said about the effect of the church on later comers to America, it was not so much that they "rationally accepted doctrines" as that their beliefs were "closely wrapped in the day-to-day events of their existence." And as was true of most people in seventeenth-century England, whatever their religious persuasion they accorded it intense loyalty and were ready to defend it with all of the energy — to say nothing of the invective — at their disposal. Religious controversy was in the very air they breathed; and it inevitably colored personal and neighborhood activities which often had nothing to do with religion.

With certain Puritan clergymen, religious conviction may well have been the primary motive for emigration. It may have motivated some other people, but this would not, I think, have been true of most. Among the farmers and tradesmen who left their native villages, religion was a kind of cement which gave unity and security to those who were thinking of moving to a new life in strange surroundings. Families would be readier to permit their young people to make the voyage if they went with neighbors of the same religious persuasion as their own. Threats and discrimination, moreover, were no balm to people already disgruntled; hence one more factor was added to the existing restiveness, one that provided the emotional and psychological stimulus sometimes needed to translate economic wants and needs into action.

The New World was the beneficiary of this state of mind. For many it seemed to provide the best answer to their needs and hopes. "They say there's bread and work for all, and the sun shines always there." The gospel of this line from an emigrant song of a later period was at the heart of the movement from its beginning. For West Country men and women Bristol was the nearest port from which ships went almost weekly during the summer months. For others it was London or one of the lesser ports. Laborers went if they could be persuaded. Convicts and, on several occasions, political prisoners were forced to go. But over the course of the years, the majority of "the others" who found shipping in the trading vessels that regularly plied the western waters were England's middling people — the most valuable cargo that any captain carried on his westbound voyage.

The Beginnings of Slavery

For over three centuries, the international slave trade transported millions of Africans to America, denuding one continent of precious human resources to enable whites to exploit another. Finding the Indians in Central and South America ill-suited to enslavement, the Spaniards turned for labor to the "Dark Continent," a source on which it was especially dependent, because relatively few people migrated from Spain to the colonies. The English sent abroad many of their own people and, therefore, relied less on blacks. Yet, even in British North America on the eve of the Revolution, slaves formed some 20 percent of the population. The "peculiar institution" had put down deep roots in the American Plantation colonies as the following selection by Thad W. Tate, Jr., makes clear.

The precise origins of slavery in America are clouded in uncertainty. Of this, however, we can be sure: the Spanish example, the drive for profits from large-scale plantation agriculture and white racism resulted in the debasement of the black man.

The first Africans arrived in Virginia about a decade after the first settlement, yet the legal status of Negroes remained unclear for almost a half century. Since slavery was a status that had long disappeared in Britain and was unrecognized in English law, the colonists had no familiar precedents with which to fix the black man's position. Some, in fact, were treated as indentured servants — those Englishmen who bound themselves to work for several years to pay for the cost of passage to America. Yet unlike indentured servants, from the outset, blacks could not count on being free after a term of service. Until the end of the seventeenth century, the number of blacks in the colonies was few, and they could be adequately managed by informal means. But as their numbers grew, problems of discipline, ownership, and descent became more vexing. As Negroes came to play an indispensable role in the emerging plantation economies of the southern colonies, their white masters felt the need to codify the black man's position into law. The results were the black codes which permanently and clearly fixed the Negro's future as a bondsman until the Civil War.

Facilitating the emergence of slavery in the British colonies were English attitudes toward black people. Commonly regarded as inferior creatures, not far removed from the beasts of the jungle, blacks — like Indians — were the victims of a dehumanization process that enabled whites to live with those qualms of conscience that few could entirely subdue. Yet as much as Europeans wished to believe that Africans were subhuman, they were never wholly convinced. Not even a slave trader such as Captain Thomas Phillips, commander of the ship *Hannibal*, 1693–1694, could escape doubts. "Nor can I imagine," the captain confessed, "why they should be despis'd for their color, being what they cannot help, and the effect of the climate it has pleas'd God to appoint them. I can't think there is an intrinsic value to one colour more than another, nor that white is better than black, only we think so because we are so. . . ."

FOR FURTHER READING:

DAVIS, DAVID B. *The Problem of Slavery in Western Culture*. Ithaca, N.Y.: Cornell University Press, 1969.*

JORDAN, WINTHROP D. *White Over Black*. Baltimore: Penguin Books, 1969.*

STAMPP, KENNETH. *The Peculiar Institution*. New York: Random House, Vintage Books, 1956.*

Asterisk denotes paperback edition.

From *The Negro in Eighteenth-Century Williamsburg*   THAD W. TATE, JR.

The Eighteenth Century: The Growth of Slavery

The 16,390 Negroes residing in Virginia in 1700 had grown to 26,559 by 1720, to 30,000 by 1730, or almost double the 1700 figure. In the next decade — the 1730's — the Negro population doubled once again, reaching an estimated 60,000. It was not long until annual importations of Negroes had climbed to a peak of three or four thousand a year, while the number of Virginia-born Negroes increased correspondingly.

By mid-century the estimates of population varied widely, but Governor Dinwiddie's 1756 figures were perhaps as reliable as any. Estimating from the count of tithables, he arrived at a total population in Virginia of 293,472, of which 173,316 were white and 120,156 Negro. By the 1760's the proportion of white to Negro was not quite half and half, a ratio which remained more or less constant to the end of the eighteenth century. As was to be expected, the highest density of Negroes occurred in the Tidewater, but slaves were also numerous in the Piedmont. Only in the Valley and in the mountain areas was the Negro population really small.

This rapid increase did not depend alone on the willingness of the colonial planters to employ Negro labor. It also demanded the evolution of an efficient, large-scale slave trade. Through much of the seventeenth century sporadic Dutch trading activity was responsible for most of the importations of Negroes. The Virginia Assembly attempted to encourage this trade in 1659 by exempting Dutch merchants from paying ten shillings per hogshead duty on tobacco received for Negroes, permitting them to pay instead the two shillings English duty.

English mercantile interests did not become actively involved in the African slave trade until the Restoration. In 1662 The Company of Royal Adventurers Trading to Africa received a monopoly of the slave trade. This company, however, survived for only ten difficult years and never recorded a contract for supplying Virginia with Negroes. In 1672 a new company, the Royal African Company, received a charter which passed along to it the monopoly of the slave trade to the English colonies. There has been a tendency to assume too easily that the company was able to take full advantage of its favored position. In reality, the Royal African Company found it difficult to protect itself against interlopers from both England and the colonies. Not even the support of the Crown, which consistently instructed royal governors to

---

Source: Thad W. Tate, Jr., *The Negro in Eighteenth-Century Williamsburg* (Williamsburg, Va.: Colonial Williamsburg, 1965), pp. 23–42, 101–113, 164–170, 176–181, 200–208.

give all possible encouragement to the company, could help. The Royal African Company contracted on several occasions in the 1670's for shipments of Negroes to Virginia and made some deliveries. But, even though Governor Culpeper's statement that the company had never sold slaves in the colony was obviously an exaggeration, the Royal African Company was unsuccessful in dominating the Virginia market.

Some of the challengers of the company monopoly seemed to have established good local connections in Virginia through men like the first William Byrd and William Fitzhugh. In the 1680's Byrd was interested in a number of transactions that involved bringing in small shipments of Negroes from the West Indies. About the same time Fitzhugh was in correspondence with a New England merchant about the details of trading tobacco for slaves.

Ultimately, in 1698, the Royal African Company lost its monopoly, being forced to give way to an arrangement which permitted "separate traders" to carry slaves by paying certain duties to the company. Other merchants could now openly compete, sending their vessels, among other places, to the landings and ports which dotted the Virginia rivers. The figures for 1699–1708, which show that the separate traders carried 5,692 Negroes to Virginia and the Royal African Company 679, are a clear indication of the weak position of the Company in the trade. After these years shipments of slaves by the Company became increasingly intermittent, though there were still a few to Virginia in the 1720's. Then, after 1730, it no longer shipped Negroes from the African coast. The flow of slaves continued, however, with Bristol and Liverpool merchants dominating the trade. A sprinkling of New England vessels also brought slave cargoes from Africa, and a number of Virginia ships were employed to bring small groups of Negroes from the West Indies into the colony.

As the century progressed, new Negroes were sold farther and farther up the rivers, until settlements on the Fall Line like Rocky Ridge, across the James from Richmond, became the most important slave markets in the colony. There was also a domestic trade in Virginia-born Negroes, prized for their greater skill and adjustment to white civilization and therefore commanding higher prices.

As much as they had come to value slave labor, Virginians viewed these large-scale importations of Negroes with misgivings. No one has yet managed a completely satisfactory explanation of why the colonists began to wish they could put some limit on the number of slaves to be introduced into the colony. An older generation of Virginia historians claimed to find evidence of moral and humanitarian objections to the trade in human beings. Some of them have even charged that slaves were forced on the Southern colonies by the pressure of greedy British and New England mercantile groups. Any close reading of the evidence quickly suggests how little support there is for this point of view, whether it be the prevailing attitudes of most of the planters toward the Negro or in the fact that no cargo of healthy slaves ever lacked for purchasers. It is clear that much less idealistic reasons were responsible for the planters' objections.

For one thing, social control of the Negro played a large part in the increasing uneasiness of the whites. Fear of slave insurrection became a daily fact of life in Virginia, and ultimately the slave owners came to feel that there must be a limit beyond which the proportion of Negroes in the population could not safely go. An economic factor was also involved. Often the explanation has been that owners of Negroes already in Virginia had a speculative interest in keeping additional African

Negroes out in order to assure a steady increase in the value of their own human property. What seems more convincing, however, is the fact that many planters opposed the further drain of money and increase in colonial indebtedness that the purchase of African slaves necessarily imposed. Prosperity in the slave trade was directly related to economic conditions of the tobacco market with the result that it suffered some of the same consequences of overextended credit. The more perceptive colonists were fully aware of the connection.

The principal stratagem which the leaders of the colony evolved for discouraging too rapid an increase in the number of slaves was an import duty on African slaves that could be disguised as a revenue measure. The long series of laws which enacted these duties began as early as 1699, and, for the first few years, were honestly intended to raise funds rather than discourage trade. The initial act, for example, levied a charge of twenty shillings for each Negro imported specifically for the construction of the new Capitol at Williamsburg. With one renewal this duty continued in force until late 1703. After a three month interval in early 1704 during which no duty was in effect, the impost was revived in April, 1704. From then until 1718 some form of duty was in force without an important break. The tendency to make the duties prohibitory in character also began to appear, for during these years the amount climbed as high as £5 per Negro.

From 1718 to 1723 the Assembly made no attempt to continue the duty. Then, in 1723 an attempt to restore it at the rate of 40 shillings touched off the first organized opposition from English traders. The flood of petitions and representations by these men carried enough political weight to persuade the King to disallow the 1723 law and all subsequent attempts of the Assembly to pass a duty over the next nine years.

By a change of tactics that made a 5% ad valorem duty payable by the prospective buyer rather than by the importer the General Assembly broke the deadlock in 1732. Thereafter and until the outbreak of the Revolution an ad valorem duty on slaves was in effect in Virginia, except for six months during 1751. The 5% rate of 1732 was gradually increased, until it stood at 20% during part of the French and Indian War. The whole effort to discourage the foreign slave trade led ultimately to the unsuccessful petition of the Assembly in 1772 for a complete end to further importations and to the successful prohibition of the trade by the new state government in 1778. But these events are more logically a part of the American Revolution in Virginia. Down to the outbreak of that struggle African slavers and West Indian traders continued to land their human cargoes in the colony with but little discouragement.

The role which the African Negroes and their American-born descendants assumed in plantation society possesses a certain familiarity. The fact that most histories of slavery leap so quickly to the nineteenth century, where the details of plantation life survive so much more abundantly, does place difficulties in the way of a full picture of the eighteenth. However, the general outlines of the work of the Negro slaves, of their daily existence, and of their immovable position at the bottom of a stratified colonial society seem clear enough.

The largest proportion of Negroes — men, women, and children — were field hands, assigned to growing tobacco and the other marketable crops the colony produced. This was the real purpose for which slavery had evolved, and it represented the institution in its most impersonal, burdensome, and typical form. The account of the field slave's lot by J. F. D. Smyth, an English traveler in Virginia just before the Revolution, is admittedly an unflattering one and no more to be accepted uncritically than any other single observation; but it is probably accurate enough in its description of the working day:

> . . . He [the slave] is called up in the morning at day break, and is seldom allowed time enough to swallow three mouthfuls of homminy, or hoecake, but is driven out immediately to the field to hard labour, at which he continues, without intermission, until noon. . . . About noon is the time he eats his dinner, and he is seldom allowed an hour for that purpose. . . .
>
> They [*i.e.*, the slaves] then return to severe labour, which continues in the field until dusk in the evening, when they repair to the tobaccohouses, where each has his task in stripping alotted him, that employs him for some hours.

A smaller, but still significant number, of slaves fared somewhat better as household workers and personal servants of the master's family. Almost invariably accounts of slaves who enjoyed especially lenient treatment or some bond of affection from their masters refer to Negroes from the household staff. Even so, there has been an easy tendency to view this group of slaves in a romantic light, and there is much we really do not know about their life.

A third segment of the slave labor force was composed of skilled and semi-skilled craftsmen. In time Negroes performed substantially all of the work on plantations in certain trades, especially carpentry and cooperage. Frequently, they were also proficient millers, tanners, shoemakers, wheelwrights, spinners, and weavers. Not only did these slave artisans perform tasks necessary for individual plantations; they were also instrumental in the commercial development of the Southern colonies, especially in tanning, in the rudimentary iron industry which was developing, and in the preparation of lumber and staves for export.

There are not many extant lists of slaves which provide a specific breakdown of the division of labor on the plantation from which they came. There is one, however, for Green Spring Plantation in 1770, when the estate of its deceased owner, Philip Ludwell, was being settled. At that time Ludwell's son-in-law, William Lee, described the slaves at Green Spring as including 59 "crop Negroes," a figure which was "exclusive of boys"; 12 house servants; 4 carpenters; 1 wheelwright; 2 shoemakers; and 3 gardeners and hostlers.

It is easy to overestimate the number of slaves owned by an individual planter and even easier to miscalculate the number used to operate a single plantation or quarter. The eighty-odd Negroes at Green Spring were the largest single group from a combined total of 164 on all the lands belonging to Philip Ludwell's estate. This total was more than enough to mark Ludwell as one of the more substantial members of the planter aristocracy, as his membership on the Governor's Council also testified.

If we were to judge Ludwell by the pattern of slave ownership revealed in the tax records of the 1780's, he would belong very nearly at the middle of the hundred leading families of the colony. These tax records, which have been most effectively analyzed by Professor Jackson T. Main, furnish the only comprehensive records on how widely slave ownership was distributed in Virginia before the nineteenth century. While the position of the leading families had begun to decline somewhat by the 1780's, the change was as yet so slight that the statistics are generally reliable for the entire later colonial period.

What becomes immediately clear from these tax records is the error of regarding even most of the wealthiest planters as having owned "hundreds" of Negroes. One man, Charles Carter, owned 785. He was followed in turn by William Allen with 700, Robert Beverley of Essex County with 592, Robert Carter of Nomini Hall with 445, and David Ross, the Richmond merchant-planter, with 400. Aside from these top five there were only eighteen other men in the entire colony who owned more than 200 slaves. The average for the hundred leading families was about 180 slaves, eighty on the home plantation and about a hundred elsewhere. A number of families who fell within this top group owned far less than a hundred Negroes.

If there were relatively few large-scale slaveholders in Virginia, the vast majority of families in the average Tidewater or Piedmont county nonetheless owned at least a small number of Negroes. In a sampling of eight of these counties the records indicated that three-fourths of the heads of families held slaves. Forty per cent of them, however, owned fewer than five Negroes. In the light of these statistics a true picture of slavery in colonial Virginia must take into account the humbler man who owned no more than two or three slaves as well as the more substantial planter.

Until the rationale of the American Revolution had begun to work its logic on the minds of Virginians, any doubt which the average colonist ever had about the wisdom of slavery stemmed either from the unpleasant prospect that the slaves would one day rise up and butcher the master class or else from suspicion that, as a business proposition, slavery simply did not pay its way. The threat of insurrection was in part dealt with through the tightening of the black codes, as well as by the attempt to discourage new importations of Negroes; but it was less easy to deal so directly with the economics of slavery.

The relative advantages and disadvantages of slave labor was, however, a subject often on the mind of the planter. Philip Fithian's account of a conversation with the wife of Robert Carter adequately sums up the reaction in theory of many planters to a situation with which they were unable to deal in fact:

> After Supper I had a long conversation with Mrs Carter concerning Negroes in Virginia, & find that She esteems their value at no higher rate than I do. We both concluded, (& I am pretty certain that the conclusion is just) that if in Mr Carters, or in any Gentleman Estate, all the Negroes should be sold, & the Money put to Interest in safe hands, & let the Lands which these Negroes now work lie wholly uncultivated, the bare Interest of the Price of the Negroes would be a much greater yearly income than what is now received from their working the Lands, making no allowance at all for the trouble & Risk of the Masters as to the Crops, & Negroes. — How much greater then must be the value of an Estate here if these poor enslaved Africans were all in their native desired Country, & in their Room industrious Tenants, who being born in freedom, by a laudable care, would not onlyly inrich their Landlords, but would raise a hardy Offspring to be the Strength & honour of the Colony.

One reason the planters questioned the profit in slave labor was the high cost of investment in slaves. In more pessimistic moments they also criticized their Negroes as wasteful and unproductive workers, either from lack of skill or deliberate resistance to forced labor.

To a large degree, the planters were inclined to rationalize other deficiencies in the agricultural methods of the colony at the expense of their Negroes. If there was one way in which slavery succeeded, it was as an economic system. Any problems of debt or credit arising from large investment in slaves was in reality a by-product of the uncertainties of tobacco cultivation. The supposed inefficiency and ineptitude of slave labor was more likely to be the fault of the wasteful methods of farming common to almost everyone who tilled the Virginia soil. Moreover, the cheapness of a slave's maintenance easily outweighed high purchase price, lack of training or skill, and even the prospect of his unproductive old age.

Whatever doubts the Virginia planter may have felt about the wisdom of enslaving an alien people, it must have seemed in the mid-eighteenth century that slavery was certainly here to stay. The rapid growth of the Negro population, the size of the slaveowners' investment, the usefulness of the labor, and outright fear combined to make the replacement of slavery unthinkable.

The Social Life of the Negro in Williamsburg

An oppressed community nearly always has a furtive quality about its life that conceals what its members really think and do and feel among themselves. This is simply a matter of self-preservation, of protecting whatever degree of independence its members still possess. Negro neighborhoods in the South have as often as not retained to the present day vestiges of such a barrier against white intrusions. As slaves the Negroes had even more need of this defense, and there are occasional evidences of the resourcefulness of the slave inhabitants of eighteenth-century Williamsburg in this regard.

No better example exists of the way in which the Negroes who lived here were both an integral part of the busy life of the capital and yet a society that could not be completely comprehended by their masters than the ability of the local Negro community to hide runaways. It is perfectly clear that the Negroes who had lived here any length of time were well known to most of the white residents in the way of all small towns. Advertisers in the *Gazette* often felt it unnecessary to tell more about a Williamsburg slave than the executors of Josiah Royle's estate did about a mulatto girl, Jenny, of whom they stated, "As she is well known in the Neighbourhood of this City, a more particular Description is unnecessary. . . ."

Yet Jenny and other Negroes just as well known were runaways who were thought to have remained in hiding in or around Williamsburg. In some cases a master only suspected that his slave had remained here secretly. But there were other instances where slaves had been seen in Williamsburg since their "elopement" and still could not be recaptured. Many of these fugitives had relatives or acquaintances in town whom the owners realized were probably hiding the fugitives. William Carter, for instance, stated of his mulatto girl, Venus, who had run away in December of 1766, "I imagine she is either harboured by other slaves in kitchens and quarters in and about town, or else gone for *Nansemond* county, from whence she was purchased a few years ago."

There was also difficulty with slaves who had once lived in Williamsburg and returned as runaways. Edward Cary, Jr. owned an 18-year old female slave raised in York County and leased to Philip Moody in Williamsburg in 1774. The next year Cary hired her out to John Thruston in King and Queen County; but Kate — this was the girl's name — had acquired attachments in Williamsburg that led her to flee Thruston's plantation. As Cary announced, "She has got a husband in *Williamsburg*, and probably may pass for a free person, as she is well acquainted in that city, and I have repeatedly heard of her being there." It hardly seems possible that this slave girl could have been a fugitive almost two years, have been recognized frequently in Williamsburg during that time, and yet not have been recaptured and returned to either Cary or Thruston. Above all, she could hardly have succeeded, unless the slave community had ways and means of shielding its members that the slaveowner could not readily penetrate.

Kate's experiences illustrate another feature of the life of the Negro under slavery. She had run away to Williamsburg in the first place because she had a husband here, an important point for a number of reasons. The customs and practices of eighteenth-century slavery did not usually permit the marriage of slaves, even baptised ones, in any legal or religious sense. Yet for every slave who took advantage of, or was unable to resist, the open invitation to promiscuity inherent in such a situation, there were many others who tried under the most difficult conditions to pursue a normal family life. The slaveowners gave a certain recognition to these "marriages," although they often did not hesitate to destroy a slave marriage by selling one mate.

There are even accounts of a sort of marriage ceremony known as "jumping the broomstick," in which the Negro couple stepped across a broomstick together as a symbol of the fact that they considered each other husband and wife. One slave has left a personal recollection of her mother's broomstick marriage. As the mother recounted it to her daughter, the young couple simply decided on a Sunday that they would like to be married. Thereupon they went up to the kitchen and asked to see their master by sending word through the cook. After determining they were old enough — both the boy and the girl were 16 in this instance — the owner readily assented and sent them off to one of the Negro women, Aunt Lucy, who was probably either the midwife or the oldest woman; and she performed the broomstick ceremony. Since it was Sunday and all the Negroes were around their quarters, the old woman called them together immediately. They formed a circle around the couple, while Aunt Lucy recited a few verses from the Bible and laid a broomstick on the floor. The couple locked arms, jumped over the stick, and were then husband and wife in the eyes of the other slaves in the quarter.

The slaveowners understandably preferred to have their Negroes marry on the home plantation to lessen the chance of runaways and to insure that children born to the couple would belong to him. Permission to marry on a neighboring plantation was sometimes granted, though it usually restricted the couple to a single visit a week.

It is only possible to speculate about the problem slave marriages might create in a town such as Williamsburg, where a large number of slaves belonging to many different owners lived in close contact. The number of unions of slaves belonging to different owners undoubtedly increased, and the master's consent was probably much less vital than on an isolated plantation. He was also likely to be able to do far less about destroying a marriage made against his will. These slave marriages may well have been the occasion of a lot of trouble in Williamsburg. Certainly this is the source to which a large number of fugitive slaves can be traced. Edmund Cary's Kate, whose flight from King and Queen to Williamsburg has already provided so much by way of illustration, had lived in Williamsburg only a year and yet found a slave to whom she considered herself wed. Gaby, a male slave belonging to James Burwell at King's Creek, was listed twice in three years as a runaway. Both times he had fled into Williamsburg where his wife worked. Slaves brought into Williamsburg from some distance and thereby separated from a wife frequently ran off, too — in this case not into hiding around town but back to their original home.

The frustrations that slaveowners experienced in trying to recover slaves in hiding around town seems all the more surprising in the view of the living arrangements for slaves. While our exact knowledge about where slaves lived in Williamsburg is sketchy, we can be reasonably certain they lived on the master's property, perhaps close to the main house where surveillance should have been relatively easy.

The conventional arrangement on the large plantations with one or two rows of crude slave cabins, possibly at some little distance from the plantation house, was more extensive than even the larger town households required. There were Williamsburg properties on which undoubtedly an outbuilding or two was used specifically for slave quarters. When a house that had belonged to Peter Randolph was offered for sale, the description pointed out that it included five major outbuildings — two stables, a coach house, a kitchen, and a servant's house of the same dimension as the kitchen. One of the advertisements on runaways refers to "kitchens and quarters in and about town," as if there might have been a fairly large number of slave quarters scattered through Williamsburg. In other cases the living space for slaves seems not to have been a separate building but only the second-floor rooms over the kitchens. Eliza Baker remembered slaves living over the kitchen at the Garrett House in the nineteenth century. Household servants sometimes had no quarters of their own but simply spread pallets in the hall, on the staircase, or somewhere else in the house after the family had retired.

Whatever the arrangement of living quarters for the slaves, they never were provided with much furniture. At best there can hardly have been more than a bed or a cot and maybe a few discarded pieces from the main house. In the specific instance of Williamsburg not a single inventory has appeared that suggests anything definite about the furnishings of slave quarters. The inventory of the William Prentis estate did include a room-by-room listing of furnishings that also included outbuildings. It contains one or two entries of possible value. Described as being "In out House, Yard, &C" were a number of tools, some scrap metal, and a few chairs and chests. These last few pieces of furniture could have been used by the slaves, although no beds at all were included. Also, several items were "*At old Nann*[y's?]," one of Prentis's slaves being called old Nanny. This included only a frying pan, a pot, a grindstone, and a few tools, however, and no furniture at all.

The Negro slave had little time to spend as he wished — usually Saturday nights and Sundays plus additional time at one or two major holidays like Christmas and Whitsunday. Descriptions of plantation life substantially agree about the way in which the slaves spent their spare time. On Saturday nights they usually gathered in the slave quarters for dancing, which was as much their favorite recreation as it was that of most other Virginians. Philip Fithian has described how by five o'clock on Saturday at Nomini Hall "every Face (especially the Negroes) looks festive & cheerful — " Sundays the Negroes might tend their garden plots or spend as much time as possible sleeping and resting.

The slaves in Williamsburg probably enjoyed a social life that cannot have been much different, especially in amount of free time. Despite laws forbidding it, the Negroes here seemed able to procure and consume alcohol in some quantity. The Negro girl described as "fond of Liquor, and apt to sing indecent and Sailors Songs when so" is a good case in point. So is the series of charges and countercharges involving the merchants Daniel Fisher, John Holt, and John Greenhow. Fisher was charged by the other two with selling liquor to Negroes without the written permission of their masters. When the case came into court, Fisher turned on his accusers and claimed that Holt had "without the least scruple whatever" served two Negroes whom Fisher himself had turned away. The aggrieved Fisher also claimed that John

Greenow was "infamously remarkable for trafficking with Negroes in wine, or any other commodity, Sunday not excepted." These accusations involve so much personal bickering and name-calling that acceptance of them at face value is impossible; but their general tenor suggests that a certain amount of dealing with slaves in liquor went on in Williamsburg. Many of the masters may, for one thing, have been lenient at times about issuing permission for their slaves to have intoxicants. William Byrd recounted the well-known instance in which Governor Spotswood could not get his servants to remain sober for a large holiday entertainment at the Palace until they were promised the privilege of getting drunk the next day.

Most of the aspects of life discussed above would have been the private concern of a free person. The slave, of course, had no such right. Where he lived, whom he married, and sometimes even what he did for amusement were no more his to decide than the work he would do or the master he would serve. Yet by a combination of evasion and defiance the slaves were often able to achieve some degree of independence in their social life. Town life, if anything, seemed to increase this degree of freedom and to create a slave community with its own thoughts and pleasures and with the means of protecting its fugitives.

The Law and the Negro

The evolution of the Negro's legal status from ordinary indentured servant to servant for life to slave was followed by the development of a separate legal code, distinct trial procedures, and harsher punishments for Negroes accused of criminal acts. Inevitably the slave's lack of personal freedom would have necessitated some revision in the English legal system that had been transported to Virginia. But it was unrelenting fear of the Negro as a potential insurrectionist and constant determination to police his conduct rigidly that instigated most of the early laws affecting Negro slaves.

Only in the last two decades of the seventeenth century did anything more than the faintest beginning of a separate criminal law for Negroes begin to appear. An act of 1680 for preventing Negro insurrections was the first real "black code" in Virginia, providing specific punishments for the three crimes of leaving the master's property without permission; lifting a hand against a "Christian," that is, a white man; and for hiding or resisting capture after running away. Conviction on the last charge required the death penalty. A 1691 statute that was of the greatest importance as the first legal restriction on manumission of slaves in Virginia also provided a systematic plan for raising a force of men to recapture "outlying slaves," or runaways who were in hiding. Then in 1692 the legislature provided the first trial procedures, in particular the denial of jury trial, which applied specifically to Negro slaves.

There were three more or less comprehensive pieces of legislation in the eighteenth century covering the trial, punishment, and regulation of slaves. The first passed in 1705 to be replaced in 1723 by one which was in turn superseded by the act of 1748. These were the basic codes for the later colonial period, and most of the other legislation affecting Negro crimes, with the exception of laws dealing with runaways, was not much more than a minor modification of these two measures.

As has already been suggested, the first law aimed at a crime by Negroes other than running away was the 1680 statute designed to prevent insurrections by punishing slaves who kept their master's property without permission or resisted a white man in any way. On the supposition that this act went unnoticed the Assembly required two years later that it be read twice a year in every church. The more comprehensive statute of 1723 sought new safeguards against an armed rising by withdrawing the privilege of benefit of clergy from Negroes convicted of plotting or attempting such rebellion and by forbidding all assemblies of slaves that were not licensed by the masters and held for public worship. It also denied all Negroes free or slave the right to possess weapons, except that free Negroes who were householders or militiamen might keep a single gun and Negroes residing on the frontier might be licensed by the justice of the peace to carry arms. All of these restrictions continued in force under the law of 1748.

Most crimes other than running away or rising in rebellion that a Negro might commit were actions defined in laws that applied equally to all persons in the colony. It is revealing, however, that two felonies, hog stealing and the administration of poisonous medicines, were the occasion of special provisions dealing exclusively with slaves. Hog stealing reached the point that on the third conviction it became a capital offense without benefit of clergy. Such were the risks involved in the temptations of the delicate flavor of roast pig.

The restriction of poisonous medicines obviously arose out of the belief of the whites that a great many Negroes continued to practice the witchcraft and tribal medicine they had brought from Africa both in honest, if primitive, attempts to cure ailing slaves but also in malicious attempts to destroy an enemy. One section of the 1748 code provided capital punishment for Negroes who prepared and administered medicine of any sort, unless their owner had consented. Benefit of clergy was allowable only where the slave could prove there had been no evil intent. In the wave of Negro crimes which David Mays described in Caroline County from 1761–1764 there were no less than three trials under this law in a three months period during 1762 with convictions in two of them.

Beginning with the legislation of 1692 a separate court procedure developed for the trial of Negroes differing markedly in its rapid movement to trial and lack of constitutional guarantees from that accorded the free man. In capital cases the core of this process was (1) the immediate imprisonment of the slave, (2) issuance by the governor of a commission of oyer and terminer to persons in the county involved to arraign and indict the offender and to take for evidence the confession of the accused or the oaths of two witnesses, or one in some cases, and (3) "without the sollemnitie of jury" to pass such judgment as the law allowed. Throughout the colonial era there was but one modification in this method of trial. In 1765 the governor was permitted to issue general commissions of oyer and terminer to four or more justices of the peace in each county, including one of the quorum, thereby eliminating the necessity of a special commission for each trial.

Initially the procedure for trying slaves did not provide for testimony by other Negroes. In 1723, however, it became permissible in capital cases involving Negroes to take such testimony from Negroes, Indians, or mulattoes "as shall seem convincing," wording which clearly implied that they were not to be accepted as sworn witnesses nor to be questioned at all, except when absolutely necessary. However, this provision for the use of slave testimony in 1723 may have been an opening wedge for employing Negro witnesses far more widely than the law intended. For a new law of 1732 stated that no Negro, mulatto, or Indian should be admitted in court, be sworn as a witness, or give evidence in a case — practices which the law complained had been allowed, even in the General Court — except in the trial of a slave for a capital offense. One subsequent modification occurred in 1748 when free Christian Negroes, Indians, and mulattoes were allowed to appear in any case involving another Negro, Indian, or mulatto. In brief, however, all these technicalities come down to the fact that the slaves normally could testify only in a capital case involving another Negro. . . .

Just as the very nature of slave status had demanded trial procedures that to some extent abridged the traditional English and colonial guarantees of individual right, it just as logically required a system of punishment that was exclusively corporal. The courts might fine a master whose neglect contributed in some way to a criminal act of one of his Negroes, but the slave could not normally make satisfaction in this way. For minor offenses or when the slave was able to avail himself of benefit of clergy, whipping became the prescribed penalty — 10 lashes for coming on a plantation without permission, 39 lashes for attending an unlawful meeting, or 39 for possessing weapons illegally, to cite a few examples.

More serious crimes which did not warrant capital punishment, even in the harsh criminal codes of the day, required what may have been a more unpleasant fate than death itself. That penalty was mutilation or dismemberment. A slave giving false evidence would, for instance, receive his 39 lashes and then have his ears nailed to the pillory for half an hour, after which they would be cut off. Under the law of 1748 his ears would have been nailed to the pillory and then cut off one at a time rather than simultaneously. Dismemberment was a favorite punishment for the slave who continually ran away, went abroad at night, or lay in hiding. Both the 1723 and 1748 acts specify its use for these offenses. Since the dismemberment usually took the form of cutting off a foot, it was a practical, if cruel, way of curbing the sort of ungovernable Negro who really constituted the greatest threat of all against slavery as a police institution. That dismemberment sometimes reached proportions which struck even slaveowners as barbarous is, however, evidenced by a 1769 statute which in the future forbade the castration of a slave for continually lying out and reserved that punishment solely for Negroes guilty of the attempted rape of a white woman.

Finally there were the whole series of crimes for which conviction carried the death penalty, the felonies for which white persons would also have been executed plus offenses such as rebellion or the administering of medicines that applied only to slaves. According to the customary practice of colonial Virginia slaves were ordinarily hanged, but a slave named Eve who was convicted in Orange County of poisoning her master was drawn upon a hurdle to the place of execution and there burned at the stake. Then there are also instances in which the head of a slave who had been hanged was cut off and put on public exhibition.

One economic problem arose with capital punishment of a slave. The owner was apt to view the execution as costing him the loss of a valuable piece of property, no matter how serious the slave's crime had been. In the 1705 statute affecting trial procedure for capital offenses, the justices were impowered to put a reasonable valuation upon any slave they condemned. When this valuation had been certified to the Assembly, the owner would be reimbursed from public funds. This method of compensation remained in force throughout the colonial period with the result that few sessions of the Assembly fail to record favorable action on the request of some owner to be paid for an executed slave.

The punishment which the courts meted out to slaves for crimes against public order in no way interfered with the disciplining of slaves by their owners and overseers. In fact, the law protected to extreme limits the master's privilege of punishing his slaves. One of the earliest pieces of legislation affecting slavery was the 1669 statute exempting a master from indictment for felony if a slave were killed while under punishment. The law reasoned that there could be no felony without malicious intent and that no one could be presumed to destroy his own property deliberately and maliciously. The Assembly made some dent in this line of reasoning in 1723, by providing that the master might be indicted if there were at least one lawful witness to testify that the killing of the slave had been a willful act. But with this one unlikely exception owners remained exempt from prosecution for the death of a slave under correction, even though new royal governors were often instructed to work for laws to punish masters who deliberately killed or maimed a slave.

The dissection of a long list of laws is a tedious business at best; and once their contents have been outlined, there is not much more to be said. One significant development in the eighteenth century, however, was the collection of most of the criminal law affecting Negroes into the two comprehensive statutes of 1723 and 1748. They provided the colony with a "black code" nearly as well-defined and systematic as those of a later day.

This much can be said for the justice administered under these laws — it was often harsh, but it was uniform and not arbitrary. And it was rapid, for the slave did not often languish in jail awaiting trial. To that extent the slaves of colonial Virginia could have fared worse, as indeed they did in parts of the New World.

The net effect of these statutes, however, was to make the law for the Negro slave almost exclusively a police instrument for maintaining the stability of society and largely to demolish that more attractive side of law, the safeguarding of the individual from unnecessary invasions of his person. Perhaps only the uncomfortable fact that the slave was not fully a person in the eyes of the law saved this one-sidedness from seriously damaging, for free men even, the traditional guarantees to the individual that Virginia had inherited from English law.

* * *

There has already been occasion, in connection with the movement for high import duties on slaves, to comment on the lurking fear of insurrection which haunted every slaveowner. As the number of slaves mounted steadily toward half the population of the colony — and, of course, more than half in areas where the slaves were really concentrated — it became possible to conceive of the destruction of society itself, if a Negro uprising were really to take hold. Newspapers all over the colonies were quick to publish every available detail of a real or rumored attempt of slaves to rebel; and much of the restrictive legislation against Negroes in the colony was admittedly aimed at this unwelcome possibility.

To what extent was the alarm of the whites exaggerated? One count of uprisings or threats of uprisings during the entire course of slavery in Virginia lists 72 of which only 9 occurred before 1776. The truth is difficult to measure; for instead of specific, brief episodes more often there were periods of general unrest lasting several years at a time. Judged on this basis, about a fourth of the years from 1700 to 1775 were marred by an abnormal degree of this uneasiness. The fact remains, however, that no white person was killed in an organized slave insurrection in Virginia before the Nat Turner rising of 1831.

The first recorded attempt at a slave uprising in Virginia occurred in the Northern Neck 1687. As so often happened, one of the men involved confessed and the attempt was checked. The slave who had been leader was not executed but was whipped around Jamestown from the prison to the gallows and back, forced to wear an iron collar for the rest of his life, and forbidden ever to leave his master's plantation.

A more serious plot, which centered in Surry and Isle of Wight Counties but also involved James City, was uncovered in March, 1709. Once again it was a slave who betrayed the plan to the whites — a Negro named Will, the property of Robert Ruffin of Surry. It fell to the Governor's Council to direct an investigation of the whole matter and issue instructions for the trial and punishment of the Negroes involved. The way in which they proceeded provides a good picture of the operation of all levels of government in the colony in the face of what, to these men, presented a serious crisis. First of all, the Council apparently issued warrants for the arrest of all suspects, similar to one issued for four Negroes in Bruton Parish, Angola Peter, Bumbara Peter, Mingo, and Robin. Then the county justices of Surry and Isle of Wight were ordered to examine all suspected slaves, releasing those only slightly involved with appropriate punishment and holding the leaders in the county jail, until the record of their examination could be examined by the President of the Council, Edmund Jenings. James City Negroes were not considered to be so deeply involved. Here, with a single exception, the slaves, who had been rounded up and held under guard, were to be tried at the next county court, punished, and released. There is an account of the close cross examination of several of these slaves in a letter from Philip Ludwell to Jenings. The questioning by Ludwell and three others had cleared Commissary Blair's slaves and a number of others of complicity, but it had also turned up the evidence against John Brodnax's Jamy, the one James City slave ordered held in prison.

About a month later the Council ordered the principal culprits, those still held in jail, to be tried before the General Court, where three of them were presumably convicted and hanged. One of the "chief Actors," Peter, belonging to Samuel Thompson of Surry, had escaped, and a reward of £10 alive or £5 dead was offered for his recapture.

The episode had a happier ending for Robert Ruffin's Will. After he had given away the insurrection, it became necessary to move him to the Northern Neck because some of the other Negroes threatened his life. Then at its meeting in the fall of 1710 the Assembly voted him his freedom as a reward for his service to the colony, the occasion being marred only by the complaint of his former master, Ruffin, that the £40 voted by the Assembly was less than he had been offered for the Negro by a prospective buyer.

Another plan for an uprising was headed off in 1722, prompting Governor Drysdale to include in his first message to the Assembly a request for improving the militia and for passing stricter laws as a protection against Negroes. The slave code was, in fact, strengthened that year.

The years of 1729 and 1730 seem to have brought a relatively longer period of unrest among slaves which may have continued through most of the decade of the 30's. The first incident occurred in June of 1729 on a new plantation near the head of the James River. There a group of about fifteen Negroes seized arms, provisions, and tools and made off for the mountains. The search party found them already settled in a secluded area, where they had even begun to clear ground for crops. A brief exchange of gunfire brought about the surrender of the slaves, however, and their small colony was destroyed.

There was more trouble the next year, touched off by a rumor that former Governor Spotswood, just back from England, had brought an order from the Crown to free all Christian slaves. This was more a matter of general unrest than a concerted plot. The governor, at the time Gooch, reported that by "keeping the Militia to their Duty, by Imprisonment and severe whipping of the most Suspected, this Disturbance was very soon Quashed, and until about six weeks afterwards we were easy. . . ." Then there was more trouble. About two hundred slaves in Norfolk and Princess Anne counties gathered on a Sunday at church time and elected officers to lead an intended rebellion. In this instance four of the Negroes involved were executed. A certain amount of continuing uneasiness is reflected in Gooch's address to the Assembly in 1736, in which he recommended strengthening the militia as a means of policing the slaves; in his proclamation of October 29, 1736, on the same subject; and in the 1738 revision of the law requesting the militia to include a system of four-men patrols to police slave quarters and suspected gathering places of Negroes in every county.

Another unsettled period occurred in and near Williamsburg during the 1770's. The number of runaways advertised seemed noticeably large, and accounts of trouble with slaves in York, James City, and Hanover counties circulated in newspapers as far away as New York. This was in part responsible for the establishment of a night watch in Williamsburg in 1772 to consist of four people to patrol the streets, cry the hours, and "use their best Endeavours to preserve Peace and good Order, by apprehending and bringing to Justice all disorderly People, Slaves, as well as others." About the same time there was a strict patrol in Yorktown, and Negroes found on the street were picked up and held overnight.

For suppression of an incipient revolt the colony relied largely on the county militia and, after 1738, the system of Patrols, reinforced by such local activity as the Williamsburg night watch. From what we know about the colonial militia, it is not likely that these men were over-diligent, until there was an indication of trouble. Still, the colony proved able to act swiftly in an emergency. Real emergencies, however, were relatively infrequent; for well-laid plots by slaves were much rarer in eighteenth-century Virginia than what could be more correctly described as periods of unusual restiveness.

The Plantation South

The United States was formed out of highly distinctive regions, so much so, that not until almost a century after the republic was born, did the nation establish, through civil war, its supremacy over its sections. The roots of sectionalism go back into America's colonial period. The New England, middle, and southern colonies each had enough common characteristics to distinguish them from one another. On the other hand, a heightened sense of sectional identity awaited the struggle for independence that propelled Americans into a national political arena where they competed and became more self-conscious of their differences.

Two institutions defined the American South before the Civil War, and both emerged in the colonial period: slavery and the plantation system. Slave labor made plantation agriculture possible. Most colonists were farmers, who relied principally on the labor of large families. Consequently, the amount of land they could cultivate was limited, since agricultural technology was still primitive. Plantations, however, employed capital and labor to produce commercial crops, such as tobacco and rice, on a large scale. Aubrey C. Land shows in the following essay that though there were relatively few plantations — that is, large-scale enterprises — there were many "planters."

The explanation of this paradox is that most southern farmers considered themselves planters even though they operated small family farms, occasionally with a slave or two. Yet almost all aspired to a life of ease and elegance on a large, impressive estate, with a great mansion and thousands of acres, tilled by hundreds of slaves. Few achieved this dream. Land was easy to acquire, but not many accumulated the necessary capital to buy slaves. Some tried by plowing back profits from tobacco or rice into acquiring more slaves. With these they could cultivate more land, raise larger crops, and buy still more slaves. Eventually, they could lift themselves into the ranks of the leading planters. But there were other, even more important, routes to the top. According to Professor Land, enterprising southerners also engaged in trade and manufacturing, practiced law, and speculated in land. Profits from these activities provided capital for the developing plantations. Still another important source came from wealthy English merchants who advanced credit to Americans while helping market southern exports overseas. Those most skillful and aggressive in taking advantage of these opportunities formed the plantation elite, proud of their elegant, gracious life and contemptuous of the commercial spirit that they ascribed to the money-grubbing, boorish Yankee sharpers.

FOR FURTHER READING:

MORTON, LOUIS. *Robert Carter of Nomini Hall: A Virginia Tobacco Planter of the Eighteenth Century.* Charlottesville, Va.: University Press of Virginia, 1964.*

PHILLIPS, ULRICH B. *Life and Labor in the Old South.* Boston: Little, Brown & Company, 1929.*

WOODMAN, HAROLD D. *Slavery and the Southern Economy: Sources and Readings.* New York: Harcourt, Brace & World, 1966.*

Asterisk denotes a paperback edition.

Economic Base and Social Structure: The Northern Chesapeake in the Eighteenth Century   AUBREY C. LAND

The *Maryland Gazette* for 18 October 1749 carried an obituary of more than common interest:

> On the Eleventh Instant Died, at his Seat on Wye River in Queen Anne's County, Richard Bennett, Esq. in the Eighty-third Year of his Age, generally lamented by all that knew him. As his great fortune enabled him to do much good, so (happily for many) his Inclination was equal to his Ability, to relieve the indigent and distressed, which he did very liberally, without regarding of what Party, Religion or Country, they were. As he was the greatest Trader in this Province, so great Numbers fell in his Debt, and a more merciful Creditor could not be, having never deprived the Widows or Orphans of his Debtors of a Support; and when what the Debtors left, was not sufficient for that purpose, frequently supply'd the deficiency. His long Experience and great Knowledge in Business, as well as his known Candor and generosity, occasion'd many to apply to him for Advice and Assistance, and none were ever disappointed of what was in his Power, and several by his means, extricated out of great Difficulties. . . .

A later issue adds some particulars:

> On Wednesday last was solemnized the Funeral of Richard Bennett, Esq. of Wye River, in a very handsome and decent Manner, by the Direction of his sole executor, the Hon. Col. Edward Lloyd. Mr. Bennett, by his Will, has forgiven above one hundred and fifty of his poor Debtors, and has made Provision for the Maintainance of many of his Overseers, and other poor Dependents, and settled a Sum of Money to be paid annually to the Poor of a Parish in Virginia: and done many other Acts of Charity and Munificence. He was supposed to be the Richest Man on the Continent. . . .

Bennett's obvious virtues as a Christian gentleman need no underscoring, but two comments of the eulogist should be noted; his great wealth and his calling as a "trader." Perhaps the enthusiastic editor went beyond the exact truth in estimating Bennett's fortune, though probably not much. The field certainly included a few other candidates for the richest man. A neighbor across the Bay, Charles Carroll, counted his total worth at something like a hundred thousand pounds sterling, including £ 30,000 loaned at 6 per cent interest. Robert Carter, south of the Potomac in Virginia, could reckon himself worth nearly as much. The second William Byrd had left an impressive heritage which his son of the same name had already begun to dissipate. Even by the standards of London these were wealthy men.

All three alternate possibilities for the title of richest man are better known than Bennett, because they have had biographers, or because they played important political roles, or both. They belong to what has been variously called the aristocracy, the ruling oligarchy, or the squirearchy. The pejorative connotations of all three terms incline me toward a label suggested by a profound student of early American social and cultural history, "the southern agrarian leaders." We can understand them in a sense as leaders of an agrarian area. But when we inquire about the eco-

Source: Aubrey C. Land, "Economic Base and Social Structure: The Northern Chesapeake in the Eighteenth Century," *Journal of Economic History,* vol. 25 (1965), pp. 639–654.

nomic milieu in which they flourished or seek the mechanisms by which they acquired their dominant positions, we are faced with some difficulties.

The traditional historiography has leaned heavily on literary evidence, and when
it does not ignore these questions often gives impressions that are positively misleading. As sources, personal letters, travel accounts, and memoirs have the great merit
of being relatively easy to put into context and ideal to paraphrase. A few dozen up
to a few thousand items of this kind can be quilted into interesting and convincing
patterns. The procedure has the limitations of the sources. Even the most acute observer focuses on objects of high visibility. The high tor eclipses the molehill in the
landscape until the king falls to his death because of the "little gentleman in black
velvet."

In the eighteenth-century Chesapeake, the "great planters" were the element of
high visibility. They held slaves, owned vast estates, and built magnificent houses
that have survived as showpieces. Visitors came under the spell of these gracious
livers and left charming accounts of their balls, their tables, and their luxury. Planters themselves contributed to the effect. They wrote letters and a few left diaries
that have survived along with their great houses. Viewed through these sources they
cut large figures and play the star roles in the arrangements that the people of the
Chesapeake made for themselves in that period. These personages are accurately
enough drawn, but they are a detail, though an important one, in the total production. Unfortunately the supporting cast and stage hands that made the production
possible receive next to no attention, sometimes not even the courtesy of a billing.
Just as *Hamlet* cannot be successfully staged without Hamlet, there can hardly be a
play with Hamlet alone.

Not much literary evidence for the minor figures has come down; but another
kind does exist and, even though bristling with difficulties and overawing in bulk, it
can be compelled to yield some data for a fuller view. This body of material has
been brought together in two despositories, the Maryland Hall of Records and the
Virginia State Archives, and properly canvassed will fill in some gaps in our knowledge of Chesapeake affairs. It consists of inventories and accounts of the estates in
personalty of all free men at the time of their death. The argument in this paper
applies only to Maryland, for which a statistical analysis has been completed. The
Virginia counties that have been analyzed give me the clear impression that differences between the areas north and south of the Potomac are not very great in respect
of the basic contention here. Both were a part of a single economic region which
political boundaries could not split asunder and were treated as a unit in contemporary British commercial records.

To obtain from the voluminous Maryland records a sample that faithfully reflects
conditions in the northern Chesapeake, some of the usual economies are not possible. Geographical sampling by selected counties is ruled out. The process of carv-
ing new counties out of large older counties went on continuously from 1690 to the
Revolution. Consequently the county of one decade is not necessarily the same unit
in a later decade. Accordingly, all counties of the province are included. Over the
entire eighty-year period 1690–1770 for which the records are reasonably complete
the alternate decades from 1690–1699 to 1750–1759 have been tabulated. If it can
be assumed that these sizable samples reflect with reasonable accuracy the spectrum
of planters' estates, then we have some basis for understanding an otherwise shad-
owy aspect of the Chesapeake economy.

The profile of estates in the decade January 1, 1690, to December 31, 1699, shows an unexpected imbalance. Three quarters of these estates (74.6 per cent, to be precise) are of the magnitude £ 100 sterling or less. In the next bracket, £ 100 to £ 200, the percentage drops to 12.1, and in succeeding hundred-pound brackets to 5.5 per cent, 2.7 per cent, 1.4 per cent, 1.3 per cent, 0.6 per cent, and 0.3 per cent. After a break in the distribution, a meager 1.5 per cent at the top are valued at £ 1,000 sterling or greater.

Beyond the obvious fact that the less affluent far outnumber the better off, this analysis tells us little. The estates, small or great, are all those of planters — a handful of physicians, mariners, and clergymen specifically excepted. "Planter," then, simply describes an occupation without indicating economic status of the individual. To get at what this distribution means in terms of worldly goods, standard of living, and possibly social status, it is necessary to look at particulars in the inventories themselves. Here impressions become vivid.

The planters at the bottom of the scale, those with estates of £ 100 or less, have at best a "country living": a saddle horse or two, half a dozen or fewer cows, a few swine to furnish fresh or salt meat for the table according to the season, a modest assortment of household utensils — sometimes nothing more than a cooking pot or skillet, a few tools and agricultural implements. Many essentials of a household — for instance, plates and cups — are missing in fully half the inventories, an omission indicating that makeshifts such as wooden bowls and gourds took the place of these articles. The appraisers of estates overlooked no article, not even a cracked cup without a handle or a single glass bottle. In brief the standard of living might be described as rude sufficiency. The self-styled poet laureate of Maryland, Eben Cooke, calls planters at this level "cockerouses."

The inventories also speak to the productivity of these small planters. In those inventories made during the autumn and winter after the tobacco had been cut the appraisers carefully estimated the size of the deceased's crop. Crop entries range from twelve hundred pounds, a trifle over two hogsheads, up to three thousand pounds, or about six hogsheads. This represented the producer's cash crop, almost his entire annual income, excepting possibly the occasional sale of a heifer, a pig, or a few bushels of corn to a neighbor or local trader. Reckoning the price of tobacco at ten shillings a hundred, these small producers could count their disposable incomes at a figure between £ 6 and £ 15 a year.

Even taking into account the small planter's self-sufficiency in fresh vegetables from the kitchen garden, cereals from whatever field crops he grew besides tobacco, and meat from his own farm animals, an income of this size imposed iron limitations on him. Between investment and consumption he had no choice. Such necessities as thread, needles, powder and shot, coarse fabrics for clothing or featherbeds, and an occasional tool or a household utensil strained his credit at the country store until his crop was sold. For the small planter, provincial quitrents, church tithes, and taxes represented a real burden. He cast his ballot for a representative who could resist the blandishments of governors and hold public expenses to the barest minimum. In good part the pressures from men of his kind kept investment in the public sector to lowest dimensions, whether the object was a county courthouse, a lighthouse, or a governor's mansion. As a private person he could not invest from savings because he had none. With tobacco crops barely sufficient to cover his debt to the country merchant, a disastrous year could prostrate him. A lawsuit, the death of cattle in a winter freeze, or a fire in house or barn forced him to contract debts which had often not been paid at the time of his death and which ate up his entire personal estate, leaving his heirs without a penny. Not infrequently his administrator actually overpaid his estate in order to save trifling family heirlooms more precious than their valuation in the inventory. Investment in a slave or indentured servant to increase his productivity, though not completely out of the question, was very difficult.

The small planter clearly was not the beneficiary of the planting society of the Chesapeake. He bred his increase and added to the growing population that filled up vacant land from the shoreline to the mountains before the Revolution. In the language of the courts he qualified as a planter. Considering the circumstances of his life, it would stretch the usual meaning of the term to call him a yeoman, particularly if he fell in the lower half of his group.

In the brackets above £ 100, different characteristics of the estates immediately strike the eye. Sumptuary standards of planters above this line were obviously higher. Kitchens had ampler stocks of utensils; and for dining, earthenware and china replaced the gourds and wooden makeshifts that apparently were the rule on tables of families in the lowest economic bracket. Ticking stuffed with flock gave way to bedsteads and bedding. Even more striking is the prevalence of bond labor, both indentured servants and slaves, in this higher stratum. The transition comes abruptly. In estates below £ 100, servants or slaves rarely appear and then only in those within a few pounds of the line. In the estates at £ 100 to £ 200, the inventories of eight out of ten estates list bond labor — a higher percentage, actually, than in any of the succeeding £ 100 brackets up to £ 500.

In fact, these estates falling between £ 100 and £ 500 form a relatively homogeneous group. Altogether they comprise 21.7 per cent of all estates. Though existence for the planter is less frugal, his worldly goods show few signs of real luxury. Not a single estate was debt free, though fewer than a tenth had debts amounting to more than half the value of the inventory. The number of slaves in single estates does not run high: from one to five in 90 per cent of the estates that had them at all. Yet even this small number represented between half and two thirds of the appraised valuation. Reflecting the additional hands for husbandry, tobacco crops ran higher roughly in proportion to the number of slaves or indentured servants. Crops ranged from twelve hundred pounds (planters with no bond labor) up to nearly twenty thousand pounds, or from a little over two up to forty hogsheads. Again using ten shillings per hundred for transforming tobacco values to sterling, we can put the incomes from tobacco production alone between £ 6 and £ 100 a year. Other sources of income for families with bond labor should not be ruled out. Doubtless off-season occupations such as riving staves or shingles, sawing plank, and making cereal crops occupied some productive time. Unfortunately only occasional data on this type of product appear, enough to call for acknowledgment but insufficient for measurement.

Nevertheless, with annual incomes of these dimensions from their tobacco crops, planters in this group had alternatives not open to the lowest income group. As respectable citizens with community obligations to act as overseers of roads, appraisers of estates and similar duties, they might choose to lay by something to see their sons and daughters decently started in turn as planters or wives of planters. Or they might within the limitations of their estates live the good life, balancing consumption against income. Social pressure must have urged them in this direction, to a round of activities that included local politics and such country entertainments as dances, horseracing, and cockfights, occasionally punctuated with drinking brawls complete with eye-gougings and other practices not usually associated with the genteel life of the planter. Whatever the choice it is difficult to see how the planter in these circumstances could add appreciably to his estate in a short period of years, or even in a lifetime.

Still further up the scale, the estates appraised at sums above £ 500 form an even smaller percentage of the total. The five £ 100 brackets between £ 500 and £ 1,000 include altogether 2.2 per cent of all estates. At first glance this small group appears to be a plusher version of the preceding: somewhat more slaves, larger tobacco crops, more personal goods including some luxury items. These are planters of substance, much closer to the stereotype, as the character and contents of their inventories show. And in their activities they moved on a higher plane. One had represented his county for a term in the General Assembly and another had served on the county court as a justice of the peace. In the matter of indebtedness, however, some interesting differences appear. Just over half the inventories list debts owed to the estate among the major assets. In a few cases the portion of total assets in the form of debts owed the estate runs to half or more.

What I think we see here is an emerging business or entrepreneurial element, a small group of planters with sources of income other than planting alone. All were planters in the sense that they, or their bond labor, produced tobacco crops. But the appreciable number in the creditor category have other concerns. The nature of these concerns appear more clearly in the most affluent element, whose members can be studied individually as cases.

This element includes all persons with estates inventoried at more than £ 1,000 sterling. In the decade 1690–1699, they represent 1.6 per cent of the total. They were the "great planters" of the day.

The smallest estate in personalty, that of Nicholas Gassaway of Anne Arundel County, was inventoried at £ 1,017 14s. 11½d. sterling; the largest, that of Henry Coursey of Talbot County, at £ 1,667 17s. 1¼d. Perhaps estates of this size would have cut a mean figure beside those of the sugar planters of the West Indies. In the northern Chesapeake of the closing years of the seventeenth century, they loom high.

The composition of these largest estates varies a bit from what we might expect of the great planter's holdings. Slaves comprise less than a quarter of the assets and, in several, less than a fifth. It should be remembered that this decade lies in the transition period when slaves were displacing indentured servants as field labor. Even so, the numbers seem unimpressive — often no greater than slave holdings in estates a third as large. By contrast, the number and the amount of assets in the form of debts owed the estate are striking. Altogether they comprised between a quarter and a half of the assets in individual estates. In one of the largest estates, debts owed the deceased came to 78 per cent of the total assets.

The inventories themselves give some clues as to how these large planters had become creditors. Occasionally an industrious appraiser included information on how the debtor had incurred his obligation: for a pipe of wine, for a parcel of steers, for corn, for rent of a certain property, for goods. In short, the great planter had also become a "trader." Frequently a portion of the inventory is simply labeled "in the store" and the contents of that room or building listed under this heading. Then the origin of the debts becomes clear. Sometimes they ran well over a hundred major items and were carefully listed under captions "sperate debts" and "desperate debts."

Putting this cross section or sample against the general outlines of the Chesapeake economy, I suggest the hypothesis that the men of first fortune belonged functionally to a class whose success stemmed from entrepreneurial activities as much as, or even more than, from their direct operations as producers of tobacco. The Chesapeake closely resembles pioneer economies of other times and places. It was a region with a relatively low ratio of population to resources and an equally low ratio of capital to resources. External commerce was characterized by heavy staple exports and high capital imports. Internally this flow created a current of high capital investment, full employment, profit inflation, and rising property values. The tobacco staple did not lend itself to bonanza agriculture, as did sugar in the West India islands where fortunes could be made in a decade. Consequently the Chesapeake planters did not go "back home" to dazzle the populace with their wealth. Their returns derived in the first instance from tobacco production, which afforded a competence, and secondly from enterprise, which gave greater rewards. As entrepreneurs, they gave the Chesapeake economy both organization and direction. They took the risks, made the decisions, and reaped the rewards or paid the penalties. And they worked unremittingly at these tasks, which could not be performed in their absence by the small planter or by overseers.

It is not easy to analyze the activities of this economic elite into neat categories. They were at once planters, political leaders, and businessmen. The first two roles tend to obscure the last. Their role in politics is a textbook commonplace. As planters they lived in the great tradition, some even ostentatiously. On this point testimony is abundant and unambiguous. Had they depended solely on the produce of their tobacco fields, they doubtless would have lived up to or beyond current income. And some did. But in fact many among them increased their fortunes substantially and a few spectacularly, while still maintaining their reputations as good livers. During the early years of the eighteenth century, when the tobacco trade was far from booming, some of the first families of the Chesapeake established themselves as permanent fixtures. Several had come to the first rank, or very near it, both in politics and wealth by 1700: the Taskers, the Catholic Carrolls, the Lloyds, and the Trumans. Others, less well known but eventually architects of equal or greater fortunes, were rising in the scale within another decade: the Bordleys, the Chews, the Garretts, the Dulanys, the Bennetts, and the Protestant Carrolls. The secret of their success was business enterprise, though almost to a man they lived as planters separated from the kind of urban community in which their more conspicuously entrepreneurial counterparts to the north had their residences and places of business. An examination of the chief forms of enterprise discloses the mechanisms by which they came to the top of the heap.

One of the most profitable enterprises and one most commonly associated with the great planters of the Chesapeake, land speculation, appears early in the eighteenth century in both Virginia and Maryland. The Virginia Rent Roll of 1704, admitted as imperfect but the best that could be done at the time, shows half a dozen holdings that suggest speculative intent. After these tentative beginnings, speculators moved quite aggressively during the administration of Spotswood and his successors, when huge grants in the vacant back country became commonplace events for privileged insiders, with the governors themselves sharing the spoils of His Majesty's bounty. In the more carefully regulated land system of Maryland, agents of the Lords Baltimore made a few large grants to favored persons like Charles Carroll the Settler in the first two decades of the century. During these same decades other wary speculators took up occasional large grants. The Maryland system compelled speculators to be cautious, because it exacted some money for the patents and made evasion of quitrents nearly impossible. But by the 1730's, eager speculators had glimpsed a vision of the possible returns and kept the land office busy issuing warrants for unpatented areas. For a relatively modest outlay a small number of Marylanders obtained assets with which they experimented for years before discovering the last trick in turning them to account.

Speculators capitalized their assets in two chief ways, both enormously profitable. First, as landlords of the wild lands, they leased to tenants who paid rents and at the same time improved their leaseholds by clearing, planting orchards, and erecting houses, barns, and fences. Almost exclusively long-term leases, either for years (commonly twenty-one) or for lives, these instruments specified the improvements to be made. Tenants who could not save from current income thus under compulsion contributed their bit to capital formation to the ultimate benefit of the landlord. Literary sources give the impression that tenancy was not very widespread, but the records tell another story. Something over a third of the planters in the lowest £ 100 bracket in Maryland leased their land. Secondly, the large landholder sold off plantation-size parcels as settlement enveloped his holdings and brought values to the desired level. Not content to leave this movement to chance, many speculators hastened the process by encouraging immigration and by directing the movement of settlers toward their own properties. Jonathan Hagar in Maryland and William Byrd in Virginia are two among many who attempted to enhance the value of their properties in this way. It is difficult to determine profits even for single speculators except for short periods. Experience must have varied widely, and undoubtedly some speculators failed. But some of the successful ones made incredible gains in a relatively short span of years.

Even more ubiquitous than the planter-speculator was the planter-merchant. The inventories and accounts contain much evidence on the organization of commerce in the tobacco counties of the Chesapeake. Hardly a parish lacked one or more country stores, often no more than a tiny hut or part of a building on the grounds of a planter who could supply, usually on credit, the basic needs of neighboring small producers — drygoods, hoes and other small implements, salt, sugar, spices, tea, and almost always liquor. Inventories show some small stores with a mere handful of those articles in constant demand. Others had elaborate stocks of women's hats, mirrors, mourning gloves, ribbons, patent medicines, and luxury goods. The names of several great families are associated with country stores, particularly in the earlier generations of the line. Frequently, storekeeping duties fell to a trusted servant or to a younger member of the family as a part of his training. Occasionally, an apprentice from one of the county families came to learn the mysteries of trade by measuring out fabrics or liquors and keeping the accounts.

As with land speculation, determining profits of merchants is next to impossible. Consumers complained bitterly of high markups, and a few storekeepers boasted of them. Even so, the country merchant's profits were not limited to sale of goods alone. He stood to gain on another transaction. He took his payment in tobacco, the crops of the two- to six-hogshead producers. The small planter participated directly in the consignment system of the early eighteenth century only to a limited extent. His petty wants and his small crop hardly justified the London merchant's time and trouble in maintaining him as a separate account. His nexus to the overseas market was the provincial merchant, who took tobacco at prices that allowed at least a small profit to himself on every hogshead.

Closely allied to merchandising, moneylending presents almost as great problems of analysis. The Chesapeake economy operated on an elaborate network of credit arrangements. Jefferson's famous remark that Virginia planters were a species of property attached to certain great British merchant houses may have been true of some planters, as it was of Jefferson himself. But the observation has created a mischievous view of credit relations between England and the tobacco colonies and does not describe the debt pattern within the area at all accurately. A full account awaits the onslaught of an industrious graduate student armed with electronic tapes and computers. Meanwhile the accounts can tell us something. Country merchants had to be prepared to extend credit beyond that for goods purchased by their customers. They paid for some of their customers at least the church tithes, the tax levies, and the freedom dues of indentured servants who had served their terms. These petty book debts could be collected with interest in any county court. Loans to artisans — the shoemakers, tanners, and blacksmiths who multiplied in number toward mid century — were of a different order. For working capital, the artisan in need of £ 5 to £ 20 and upward turned to men of means, the "traders." Far from abating, the demand for capital increased as the century wore on.

Investment opportunities were never lacking for planters with ready money or with credit in England. As lenders, they squarely faced the conflict of the law and the profits. By law they could take interest at 6 per cent for money loans and 8 per cent for tobacco loans. One wonders why the Carrolls chose to loan their £ 30,000 sterling at 6 per cent, even on impeccable securities. Could the answer be in part that returns at this rate equaled those from further investment in planting? At any rate they did choose to lend, following the example of Bennett and a dozen or so others.

Far more profitable as an investment opportunity, manufacturing exercised an enduring fascination on imaginative men of the Chesapeake. During Virginia Company days, before the first settlement of Maryland, glass and iron had figured among the projects launched under Company stimulus. Although these had come to ruin in the massacre of 1622, Virginians never gave up hope of producing iron. Their success was limited; but in the upper reaches of the Bay a combination of easily worked ore, limitless forests for charcoal, oyster shell, and water transportation from the furnace site invited exploitation. British syndicates moved first to establish the Principio Works and later the Nottingham and Lancashire works. These remained in British hands until the Revolutionary confiscations. Last of the big four, the Baltimore Iron Works (1733) became the largest producer and the biggest money-maker. Five Maryland investors subscribed the initial capital of £ 3,500 sterling. The Baltimore enterprise was a triumph for native capital, though technicians and technology were both imported from Britain. After the first three years of operation the partners received handsome dividends but always plowed a substantial part of the profits back into the enterprise. By the early 1760's the share of each partner was valued at £ 6,000 sterling. The five partners were among the first fortunes in Maryland.

Beyond iron making, other forms of enterprise (mostly small-scale manufacturing or processing) attracted investment capital. In nearly all areas of the Chesapeake some shipbuilding, cooperage, and milling establishments provided essential local services or commodities. None of these required either the capital outlay or the organization of an ironworks. Consequently, as enterprises they were attractive to investors with modest capital but large ambitions. In the area of Baltimore, flour milling developed major proportions after mid century, as the upper counties of Maryland found grain more profitable than tobacco as a field crop.

An astonishing percentage of the personal fortunes of the northern Chesapeake had their roots in law practice. While not entrepreneurial in a technical sense, the rewards went to the enterprising. During the seventeenth century lawyers were neither numerous nor always in good odor. Private persons attended to their own legal business in the courts. By 1700, the fashion had changed as the courts insisted on greater formality in pleading and as the cumbersome machinery of the common law compelled the uninstructed to turn to the professional. Pleading "by his attorney" swiftly replaced appearances *in propria persona*. Still the legal profession remained trammeled. Laws strictly regulated fees attorneys could take and kept these at levels low enough that the ablest members of the Maryland bar went on strike in the 1720's. What lawyers lacked in size of fees they made up in number of cases. An attorney might, and frequently did, bring thirty or forty cases to trial in a three- or four-day session of a county court. Had these been litigation over land, an impression widely held by students who use the *Virginia Reports* and the *Maryland Reports,* attorneys might have spent their entire time in title searches, examining witnesses, and preparing their cases. The court proceedings at large, however, show fifty cases of debt collection for every case over land; and sometimes the ratio runs as high as a hundred to one. One traveler to the Chesapeake, remarking on the "litigious spirit," wryly concluded that this spectacle of everybody suing everybody else was a kind of sport peculiar to the area. In fact, the numbers of suits grew out of the very arrangements — a tissue of book debts, bills of exchange, and promissory notes — that kept the mechanism operating.

In this milieu the lawyer had an enviable position. From his practice he derived a steady income freed from direct dependence on returns from the annual tobacco fleet. In a phrase, he had ready money the year 'round. Furthermore, he had an intimate knowledge of the resources and dependability of the planters in the county — and, indeed, throughout the province if he also practiced at the bar of the superior courts. Consequently he could take advantage of opportunities on the spot, whether they were bargains in land, sales of goods or produce, or tenants seeking leases. He could besides avoid the costs of litigation that inevitably arose as he involved himself in land speculation, lending, or merchandising, as many did. As a rule the lawyers did well, and the most enterprising moved into the highest brackets of wealth. Perhaps the most spectacular example, Thomas Bordley, a younger son of a Yorkshire schoolmaster, came from an impecunious immigrant apprentice in a Maryland law office to distinction in the law, in politics, and in Maryland society within the span of a short lifetime. After his premature death in 1726 his executors brought to probate the largest estate in the history of the province to that time.

Quite commonly, lawyers added a minor dimension to their income from office holding. A fair percentage of Maryland offices were sinecures that could be executed by deputies for a fraction of the fees. Most carried modest stipends, but a few eagerly-sought prizes paid handsomely. Baltimore's provincial secretary received £ 1,000 per annum.

This is not the place to argue the returns from planting, pure and simple. Many planters did well without other sources of income. But impressive fortunes went to those who, in addition, put their talents to work in some of the ways described above. A few engaged in all. The list is finite, for we are referring here to a small percentage of planters, those with estates above £ 1,000: in the decade 1690–1699 to 1.6 per cent, in 1710–1719 to 2.2 per cent, in 1730–1739 to 3.6 per cent, and in 1750–1759 to 3.9 per cent. When tabulated and examined for group characteristics, they resemble functionally a type that could easily come under that comprehensive eighteenth-century term, merchant. They look very unlike the planter of the moonlight-and-magnolias variety. It is a commentary on the prosperity of the northern Chesapeake that, as this favored category increased in percentage and in absolute numbers, so did the magnitude of its members' individual fortunes. The sample taken just before the turn of the century shows top fortunes between £ 1,000 and £ 2,000, with none above. The sample decade 1730–1739 includes an appreciable number over £ 2,000. The two largest were those of Samuel Chew (£ 9,937) and Amos Garrett (£ 11,508), both merchants. Even these did not match the fortunes left by Dr. Charles Carroll and Daniel Dulany the Elder in the decade 1750–1759, nor that of Benjamin Tasker in the next.

The poor were not excluded, individually or as a group, from the general prosperity of the Chesapeake. Four individuals — Thomas Macnemara, Thomas Bordley, Daniel Dulany, and Dr. Charles Carroll — moved up the scale from nothing to the top bracket of wealth, two of them from indentured servitude. These were extraordinary men, but their careers indicate the avenues open to their combination of talents for the law, land speculation, moneylending, merchandising, and manufacturing in which they engaged. Of course all were planters as well.

But for the mass, advance was by comparison glacial. The composition of the base on which such performances took place changed more slowly. In the fourth decade of the eighteenth century the percentage of planters in the lowest economic group, those with estates of £ 100 or less, had fallen to 54.7 per cent, in marked contrast to the 74.6 per cent of the decade 1690–1699. Between the same two sample decades the percentage in the next higher category of estates (£ 100 to £ 500) had increased to 35.7 per cent from 21.7 per cent. If this means that the poor were getting richer, it also means for the great majority that they were doing so by short and slow steps. Together, these two lowest categories still made up 90.4 per cent of the planting families in 1730–1739, as compared with 96.3 per cent in the last decade of the seventeenth century. Nonetheless, the shift toward a higher standard of living within this huge mass of lesser planters is quite as important a commentary on the economic well-being of the Chesapeake as is the growth in numbers and magnitude of the great fortunes.

It is never easy to know just how much to claim for statistical evidence. Perhaps there is enough here to raise doubts about the descriptive accuracy of reports from Chesapeake planters themselves. These sound like a protracted wail of hard times, rising occasionally in crescendo to prophesies of impending ruin. Yet even during the early and least prosperous decades, the northern Chesapeake experienced some growth. During the second quarter of the century and on into the following decades the samples made for this study indicate a quickened rate. The results worked no magic change in the way of life or economic station for the small planter, the mass of Maryland. These were always the overwhelming percentage of the producers. As a social group they come in for little notice. Their lives lack the glitter and incident that has made the great planter the focus of all eyes. By the standards of the affluent society theirs was a drab, rather humdrum, existence bound to the annual rhythm of the field crop. The highest rewards were for those who could transcend the routine of producing tobacco and develop the gainful activities that kept the economy functioning.

Religion in the New World

"But it does me no injury for my neighbor to say there are twenty gods, or no God. It neither picks my pocket nor breaks my leg," wrote Thomas Jefferson in the 1780s. Few of those who settled America would have agreed with the Sage of Monticello. Most early European settlers, especially the middle classes and the peasantry, which supplied the bulk of the immigrants, believed that man's relations with God were the central experience of life. Yet by Jefferson's time, and increasingly so since, most Americans have been more preoccupied with life in this world than in the next. The emergence of a secular outlook facilitated the ultimate triumph of religious tolerance and the separation of church and state, since people who are indifferent toward religion are less likely to insist on conformity from dissenters and persecute them for heterodoxy, than those who are preoccupied with salvation and certain that their faith is the only true road to Heaven.

Tolerance and separation of church and state — two foundations of the American religious tradition — did not simply await the corrosive effects of secularism on religious belief, as Perry Miller explains in the following essay. Most colonists brought across the ocean the common assumption of the time that no well-ordered society could exist without an established church to which all people belonged, which all supported financially, and which all accepted as the "true" faith. The Protestant Reformation, however, had divided Christendom into dozens of competing denominations, each claiming to be the only authentic interpretation of Christianity. It also triggered a century of religious wars and persecutions that sent defeated minorities in search of refuge to America. Puritans came to Massachusetts, Catholics to Maryland, Quakers and German Lutherans to Pennsylvania. But the persecuted, with some exceptions, did not seek freedom for all men. Their formula was freedom for themselves, but not for others who were "heretics." Diversity, however, played havoc with efforts to create in the colonies state churches that tolerated no dissent. In some, as in Virginia and Massachusetts, dissenters became so numerous and influential that eventually the established churches grudgingly made concessions and later, during the Revolutionary era, lost their privileged positions. Elsewhere, such as in Pennsylvania, there was never a state church because the Quaker founders believed, as a matter of principle rather than of Jeffersonian expediency, that faith was a private and holy affair between man and God and that state involvement would only corrupt the church and oppress those seeking God.

FOR FURTHER READING:

GREENE, EVARTS B. *Religion and the State: The Making & Testing of an American Tradition.* Ithaca, N.Y.: Cornell University Press, 1959.*
MEAD, SIDNEY E. *The Lively Experiment.* New York: Harper & Row, Publishers, 1963.*
SWEET, WILLIAM W. *Religion in Colonial America.* New York: Cooper Square Publishers, 1942.*

Asterisk denotes paperback edition.

The Contribution of the Protestant Churches to Religious Liberty in Colonial America PERRY MILLER

While endeavouring to formulate these remarks I have come to suspect that there may possibly lurk in the title of my paper a misleading implication. The word "contribution" would seem to connote on the part of the Protestant churches a deliberate and concerted effort toward the triumph of religious liberty. Those of us who prize ecclesiastical freedom would like to feel that our colonial ancestors of their own free will and choice undertook the march to liberty. Liberal-minded historians in particular are prone to sing the praises of this individual or that church for furthering this advance; they are inclined to gloss over or to apologize for the men and the institutions that hindered it.

Such an attitude, though inspired by the most admirable of motives, has been, I am convinced, an encumbrance to the student of history. There is no way to deny — and as far as I can see, no use in denying — that Protestants coming to this country in the seventeenth century were almost unanimous in their conviction that toleration was a dangerous and heathen notion. They came fresh from Europe of the Reformation, where experience had demonstrated that if two divergent churches were permitted to exist within striking distance of each other, it would only be a question of time before throats were cut. And Protestants were far from deploring this belligerency. If you believe, as men believed in that era, that you are altogether on the Lord's side, and that your enemies are and must be entirely on the devil's, you can see no virtue in the idea of tolerating them. Statesmen knew that a policy of toleration would not work; theologians were grimly determined that it never should work. As the Reverend Nathaniel Ward of Ipswich in Massachusetts Bay emphatically declared:

> He that is willing to tolerate any Religion, or descrepant way of Religion besides his own, unless it be in matters merely indifferent, either doubts of his own, or is not sincere in it. He that is willing to tolerate any unsound Opinion, that his own may also be tolerated, though never so sound, will for a need hang God's Bible at the Devil's girdle.

When a Protestant church came into a colony at the beginning of settlement, with no other churches on the ground, with a clear field before it, that church deliberately set up an exclusive régime, it conscientiously strove to establish one official church in absolute uniformity, it frankly employed the civil power to compel all inhabitants to conform and contribute. Both Virginia and Massachusetts furnish examples of this disposition. The Anglicans in the one colony and the Puritans in the other, entertaining utterly different conceptions of polity and theology, were at one in their philosophy of uniformity. Among the early enactments of the House of Burgesses was a statute demanding that there "be a uniformity in our Church as near as may be to the Cannons in England, both in substance and in circumstance, and that all persons yield obedience under pain of censure." Puritan ministers and the Puritan settlement at Nansemond were driven out, and in 1671 that picturesque and outspoken governor, Sir William Berkeley, reported with glowing pride that no free

Source: Perry Miller, "The Contribution of the Protestant Churches to Religious Liberty in Colonial America," *Church History*, vol. 4 (1935), pp. 57-66.

schools disgraced the landscape in Virginia: "I hope we shall not have [them] these hundred years: for learning has brought disobedience and heresy and sects into the world." This, quite clearly, is nipping religious liberty in the bud.

The Puritans were equally clear and decisive. Many writers have already called attention to the fact that though the Puritans came to New England to escape persecution, they did not come to bestow upon those who disagreed with them any such immunity within the confines of their colonies. John Cotton patiently explained their position to Roger Williams thus: anybody in possession of his senses must recognize what is true and what is false when a learned Congregational minister demonstrates truth and falsehood to him. If a man, after such instruction, then maintains certain errors, he deserves punishment, not for being in error, but for persisting in it. In his heart of hearts, his own better judgment must acknowledge as much, even if he won't admit it. Accordingly, the laws of Massachusetts and the explicit pronouncements of her apologists pile up incontrovertible evidence that the leaders of the Bay Colony were intentionally and consistently intolerant; the banishment of Williams and Anne Hutchinson, the fining of Dr. Child, the whipping of Obadiah Holmes, and the dangling bodies of four Quakers hanged on Boston Common attest the fidelity with which the Puritans scouted the idea of toleration.

Speaking still as a historian, I must confess my gratitude to such men as Berkeley and Cotton. We know, at any rate, where we stand with them. With many figures of this stripe for our authorities, we can confidently assert that the Protestant *intention* in America was not towards religious toleration, let alone liberty. Yet it is also true that the colonies of Virginia and Massachusetts were the exceptions; they were the only colonies in which a program of intolerance had any real success, the only colonies in which a religious uniformity was achieved, and even in them for a relatively short time. The colonial period witnessed a fairly steady growth of practical religious freedom. From time to time some men in one or another of the churches might foresee the end and even approve. But by and large, I can find very little evidence that the Protestant churches ever really entertained the conception of complete liberty as their ultimate goal, or that they often moved in that direction unless forced to do so by the pressure of events or by the necessities of the social environment. As I say, there are exceptions, notably of course Williams and Penn, but the contribution of the majority of the Protestant churches must in the final analysis be described as inadvertent.

My time is limited, and it would manifestly be impossible to relate the whole narrative here. I wish therefore only to indicate, however briefly, what seems to my mind to be three important factors determining the development of religious liberty in America. To enumerate them roundly, they seem to me to have been, first the practical situation of the sects in the colonies, second the influence and interference of England, and third the shift in issues and concerns produced by the introduction or development of both the rationalistic and evangelical temper in the eighteenth century.

Most of the colonies were not as fortunate as Virginia or Massachusetts; they did not begin with unsettled expanses, or they could not people them with men of only one persuasion. The proprietors of the Carolinas, for instance, intended some day to establish the Church of England in their domains, but from the beginning had to reckon with a hopeless variety of creeds, Puritans from England and from New England, Huguenots, Dutch Calvinists, Scotch Calvinists, Quakers and several sorts of Baptists. The uniformity for which the noble proprietors hoped was impossible, unless they were prepared to expel nine-tenths of their settlers. So religious principle gave way to economic interest; practical toleration became the rule. The official clique still contemplated a full establishment of the Anglican church and in 1704 felt themselves strong enough in South Carolina to enact legislation excluding dissenters from the assembly and establishing an ecclesiastical court. A revolution was averted only when these acts were annulled by Parliament and toleration was restored.

The story in New York is much the same. The Dutch had been fairly tolerant and hospitable, following the national policy at home. When the English took over the colony, the number of sects already flourishing precluded any effective establishment. As Governor Dongan complained in 1687:

> Here bee not many of the Church of England; few Roman Catholics; abundance of Quaker preachers, men and women especially; Singing Quakers; Ranting Quakers; Sabbatarians; Anti-Sabbatarians; some Anabaptists; some Independents; some Jews; in short, of all sorts of opinions there are some, and the most part of none at all. The most prevailing opinion is that of the Dutch Calvinists. . . . As for the King's natural born subjects that live on Long Island, and other parts of the Government, I find it a hard task to make them pay their Ministers.

The governors did what they could, but the best they could wring from a predominantly Dutch Calvinistic assembly was the peculiar Ministry Act of 1693, which established in four counties six Protestant churches, not necessarily Anglican. Very few denominations were clearly advocating religious liberty on principle in New York; they were all opposing an established church, and the result was that religious liberty in large measure they all had. Circumstances placed insuperable obstacles in the way of intolerance. Where a multiplicity of creeds checkmate each other, they find themselves to their surprise maintaining religious liberty.

Indeed, the reasons that made uniformity difficult or ineffective in the Carolinas or in New York ultimately made it impossible in Virginia and Massachusetts. The established order in Virginia was never a very efficient organization; as early as 1629 the Burgesses were endeavouring to stop the clergy from "drinking or ryott" or "playing at dice." Meantime the dissenters began trickling in, Quakers and Baptists, and then the Scotch-Irish with their militant Presbyterianism streamed down the Shenandoah. Many of these were valuable settlers, particularly on the frontier, and the government had to give them allowance, either by express enactment or by tacit agreement. In Massachusetts also Quakers and Baptists forced an opening, and Anglicans came to stay in the train of the royal governors. By the 1730's the province had to allow some dissenters from the established Congregational order to pay their rates to churches of their own persuasion.

Thus in the colonies a generous amount of liberty or at least of toleration had come to prevail by the time of the Revolution. But this situation was hardly the result of conscious and deliberate theory; it was the result of circumstances. Diversity of belief compelled it. Rhode Island is, of course, an exception to this statement, thanks to the teachings of Roger Williams. Inspiring a figure as Williams may be, he nevertheless devised theories that were not palatable to the majority of Protestant churches in his day. Williams may speak for the essentially individualistic tendency inherent in all Protestantism; in the perspective of time we may see that his was the only solution for the ecclesiastical problem in a Protestant world, but Protestants in the colonies did not want to think so. If we desire to state accurately the "contribution" of the Protestant churches in all colonies beside Rhode Island and Pennsylvania to the development of religious liberty, we are forced to say that they made it inevitable by their dogged persistence in maintaining their own beliefs and practices. They persisted so resolutely that the governments had either to exterminate them or to tolerate them. In this connection it is worth noting that once a sect was tolerated it was generally ready to thrust itself into intolerance if it could get the upper hand. The Anglicans in Maryland, for example, given toleration by the Catholic proprietor in 1649, spent every effort to secure a Protestant establishment and the disfranchisement of their benefactors. Once the Church of England was established in Maryland, we have the old story again; the dissenting sects that had opposed the proprietor's church at once banded together, with the Catholics this time, to antagonize the royal governor's. By 1776 the established church in Maryland had become a shadow. The New Side Presbyterians and the Baptists in eighteenth century Virginia brought down upon their own heads the official persecution to which they were subjected by their own scurrility in assaulting the deplorable established church. "They treat all other modes of worship with the utmost scorn and contempt," complained the broad-minded Governor Gooch in 1745. The Protestant churches in America finally accepted the idea of religious liberty because they had become habituated to it. Most of them had not moved toward it with intelligent foresight; they had been forced to accustom themselves to it, because experience demonstrated the futility of exclusive domination by any one church, because settlers were too valuable to be antagonized over-much by acts of conformity, and because there were simply so many Protestant organizations that no power on earth could whip them into a system of uniformity.

A second source of liberal developments in colonial America is to be found in the example of English opinion and English law. The many sects that sprang up like mushrooms in the frenzied years of the Civil Wars had banded together with the English Independents against the Presbyterians to demand toleration. The dissenters were finally given toleration by the Parliament and the Established Church in the act of 1689. Though this act by no means created religious liberty, it marked the demise in England of that philosophy of absolute uniformity and enforced conformity which had characterized all Protestant churches during the Reformation.

It is with this development of opinion in England that we are to connect the experiment of William Penn. The Quakers were one of the enthusiastic groups that came into being during the wars. They began their existence when the idea of toleration had already been embraced by the Independents. Although in the first flush of their zeal the Quakers had flung themselves against all other churches in a spirit that betrayed little comprehension of toleration, they soon aligned themselves with the Independents. Their peculiar theology made it possible for them to admit, much more easily than other creeds could do, that men might be holy and good even if they belonged to other organizations. In that spirit Penn founded his colony, on an explicit theory of liberty for all churches, though his conceptions were still not as broad as those of Williams and he would not enfranchise Jews or give harbor to atheists. His plan was a little too broad for the home government, so that in 1705 the colony yielded to compulsion from Queen Anne and required the test-oath to be taken by office-holders, thus excluding Catholics from official positions.

Yet if the English government was instrumental in curtailing religious liberty in Pennsylvania, the act of 1689 fashioned a weapon by which minority groups in other colonies could pry loose the laws of conformity. The dissenters of South Carolina successfully appealed to the Whigs in Parliament to block the exorbitant acts of 1704. Francis Makemie, by demanding a license to preach in Virginia under the terms of the act of 1699, compelled the Burgesses to incorporate them into Virginia law. Samuel Davies appealed to the act again in 1753 to procure liberty for itinerant ministers. The Royal charter of Massachusetts, drawn up in 1691, guaranteed that "there shall be liberty of conscience allowed, in the worship of God, to all Christians (except Papists)." When Connecticut in 1708 grudgingly gave toleration to dissenters from the Congregational system, it specifically cited "the act of William and Mary." Thus once more, liberty was forced upon the colonies from without. The Quakers were intentionally libertarian; the other churches used English principles and laws for self-protection. In the end they furthered the growth of religious liberty, but not with malice aforethought; they achieved that end in the course of securing relief and opportunities for themselves.

The eighteenth century saw a steady extension of toleration in the colonies until with the Revolution established churches collapsed, in Massachusetts and Connecticut somewhat belatedly. But again an examination of the activity and statements of the churches before the Revolution does not offer much evidence that they took the lead. In the shift of the general intellectual climate, and the pressure of one or two political factors, religious liberty came to seem attractive. A complete account of this transformation would entail a chapter in intellectual history that has yet to be written; lacking that chapter we can here only enumerate a few of the factors. Before the Revolution the dissenting churches were thrown into co-operation and alliance against the threat of an Anglican bishop; this served to lessen the hostility of one toward another. Furthermore, in this century the question of church-polity ceased to be a serious issue; the young Jonathan Edwards would as soon serve in a Presbyterian as in a Congregational parish. Probably the most irritating of controversies was thus minimized. Then also, the differences between the sects began to seem of minor significance in the face of the towering danger of scientific rationalism and deism, which threatened all traditional creeds alike. Against the spread of "infidelity" all the churches drew closer together. Finally the movement for religious liberty was carried to a speedy triumph in the Revolutionary decades because the leadership was taken by a rational aristocracy, shot through with deistical beliefs, willing to see any number of religions have their freedom because they believed in none of them. As Nathaniel Ward had said, nothing is easier than to tolerate when you do not seriously believe that differences matter. So the Adamses, Masons, Franklins, and Jeffersons could advocate dis-establishment and religious liberty in a spirit which is, from an orthodox Christian point of view, simply cynical. As James Madison cheerfully put it: "In a free government, the security for civil rights must be the same as that for religious rights; it consists in the one case in a multiplicity of interests and in the other in the multiplicity of sects." At the same time the transformation of religious issues wrought by the Great Awakening and the introduction of revivalistic evangelicalism had created a situation in which the new Protestant groups were able to see clearly that a policy of religious liberty offered them definite advantages. Evangelical Baptists and New Side Presbyterians, and eventually the Methodists, came to perceive that they were opposing conceptions of institutionalized civic religion inherited from the previous century; they had to demolish established churches along with intricate theological structures in order to have the track cleared for their own program of spiritual regeneration and impassioned zeal. I do not think it has ever been sufficiently emphasized, or that it can be too much stressed, that there is a subtle and close connection between the shift of vital religious interest from elaborate intellectual systems of theology to the simplified emotional fervor of the new revivalism and the turning of Protestant Americans from a concern with ecclesiastical exclusiveness to the demand for liberty to all churches. It is not only that two or three more militant minorities now existed to contend for privileges against vested institutions, but that the whole bent and temper of this evangelicalism required that organization, external regulation and formal discipline become subordinated to the reawakening of the spirit and the revivifying of morality. It is in Massachusetts where the ruling classes most stoutly resisted what they considered the crude mysticism of the camp meetings that the retention of an established church was the most protracted. Such apparent champions of religious liberty as the Baptists Backus and Manning, or the Presbyterian Davies, have about them an apparent liberalism which is inspiring to behold, which yet can easily be made too much of. The truth of the matter was that they understood the situation, they realized that old institutions had to be replaced by less systematized forms if the sort of religious incitement they prized was to have full opportunity. James Manning — symbolizing the vast difference of evangelical Protestantism in the eighteenth century from Puritanism of the seventeenth, as we have seen that Puritanism incarnated in Nathaniel Ward — said to the Massachusetts delegates to the Continental Congress in October, 1774, "Establishments may be enabled to confer worldly distinctions and secular importance. They may make hypocrites, but cannot create Christians." So for the time being such leaders often made common cause with the rational aristocracy to attack established order and medieval theology. Yet all the time they were perfectly aware that their cause would not be lost, but in reality furthered, if various denominations were allowed to practise it in various ways. In terms of an ideal of ethics rather than of evangelical emotion, the same ultimately became true of the Unitarians. As Professor Hall has remarked, "It was easier for Harvard College to take up Unitarianism than it would have been to introduce at that date sports on Sunday."

It therefore seems to me that it is possible to speak too glibly of the "contributions" of Protestant groups to religious liberty; we can be easily betrayed by our own approbation for the idea into prizing and unduly exalting such instances of advance as we can find in our forebears. It has often seemed to me that the worshippers of Roger Williams have done more harm than good not only to the Puritans of the Bay but to their hero himself by their extravagant laudation of his ideas without at the same time maintaining sufficient historical perspective upon the general intellectual background from which he so dramatically emerged. Exceptionally liberal men in Protestant ranks undoubtedly exist, and they deserve all honor and veneration; but by and large Protestants did not contribute to religious liberty, they stumbled into it, they were compelled into it, they accepted it at last because they had to, or because they saw its strategic value. In their original intention, Protestants were intolerant; because of the sheer impossibility of unifying colonies made up of a hodge-podge diversity, because of the example of toleration set and enforced by England, and because of a complete shift in the intellectual situation in the eighteenth century, whereby religious liberty became a perfect solution for new issues — for these reasons, the Protestant churches did not so much achieve religious liberty as have liberty thrust upon them.

Class and Status in the New World

"In America," reported a South Carolina newspaper toward the end of the colonial period, "every Tradesman is a Merchant, every Merchant is a Gentleman, and every Gentleman one of the Noblesse. . . . We are a Country of Gentry. . . . We have no such Thing as a common People among us. . . ." In reality there was no shortage of "common people" in the American colonies as the following analysis by James Henretta of Boston's changing social structure makes clear. Nonetheless, the American social order differed in significant ways from the European.

In the absence of a hereditary, landed aristocracy, America's elite was perforce self-made, at least at the beginning. Forming the colonial ruling class were merchants, planters, and professionals who acquired substantial wealth; and wealth, rather than birth or blood, was the principal basis of social differentiation. As Henretta notes, this elite differed from its European counterpart in another respect: it did not form a closed caste. For one thing, its eminence was not based on inherited privilege. For another, there was a good deal more access to the leading circles than was the case in Britain. In a new society with seemingly limitless resources and social opportunities, the ambitious had a far better chance of moving up the social ladder. As a result, those on top constantly received infusions of new blood from enterprising newcomers. Moreover, those on top could not sit back and rest on their past achievements. Both trade and planting required constant attention. Those who neglected them for other business, as did Jefferson and Washington, saw their fortunes decline.

Incomplete at top, the social structure was also incomplete at the bottom. Unlike in Europe, in America the masses of country folk were neither landless peasants, nor city proletarians. Most were freehold farmers, or artisans and mechanics, who could vote and participate in government. As a result, the American social order was more open, and social distinctions not quite so clear-cut. Titles, such as mister or madame, which located a person's position in the more precisely graded social structure of England, lost much of their meaning in the colonies. Petty traders insisted on calling themselves merchants, and newly "arrived" merchants considered themselves gentlemen. And no one could stop them or their wives from wearing finery that in the Old World was the mark of a superior social class.

Though American society was more open and fluid than European, James Henretta discovered that it became less so as a city such as Boston matured. In the eighteenth century, a few families accumulated large fortunes and came to engross a disproportionate share of the town's wealth. At the same time, the percentage of the propertyless increased, though they were still substantially in the minority just before the Revolution, and even they could hold town office. A somewhat similar process occurred in the older rural regions. Here, when the best lands were taken up and a farmer's sons preferred to stay and settle on marginal lands rather than migrate to greener pastures far away from relatives, friends, and familiar sights, a landless group began to appear. Yet, to acute European observers the abundance of free land was the most distinctive characteristic of America. It transformed European peasants, they claimed, "from nothing to start into being; from a servant to the rank of a master; from being the slave of some despotic prince to become a freeman, invested with lands to which every municipal blessing is annexed."

FOR FURTHER READING:

BRIDENBAUGH, CARL. *Myths and Realities: Societies of the Colonial South.* New York: Atheneum Publishers, 1963.*

MAIN, JACKSON T. *Social Structure of Revolutionary America.* Princeton: Princeton University Press, 1965.*

TOLLES, FREDERICK B. *Meeting House and Counting House.* New York: W. W. Norton & Company, 1963.*

Asterisk denotes paperback edition.

Economic Development and Social Structure in Colonial Boston

JAMES A. HENRETTA

A distinctly urban social structure developed in Boston in the 150 years between the settlement of the town and the American Revolution. The expansion of trade and industry after 1650 unleashed powerful economic forces which first distorted, then destroyed, the social homogeneity and cohesiveness of the early village community. All aspects of town life were affected by Boston's involvement in the dynamic, competitive world of Atlantic commerce. The disruptive pressure of rapid economic growth, sustained for over a century, made the social appearance of the town more diverse, more complex, more modern — increasingly different from that of the rest of New England. The magnitude of the change in Boston's social composition and structure may be deduced from an analysis and comparison of the tax lists for 1687 and 1771. Containing a wealth of information on property ownership in the community, these lists make it possible to block out, in quantitative terms, variations in the size and influence of economic groups and to trace the change in the distribution of the resources of the community among them.

The transformation of Boston from a land-based society to a maritime center was neither sudden nor uniform. In the last decade of the seventeenth century, a large part of the land of its broad peninsula was still cultivated by small farmers. Only a small fraction was laid out in regular streets and even less was densely settled. The north end alone showed considerable change from the middle of the century when almost every house had a large lot and garden. Here, the later-comers — the mariners, craftsmen, and traders who had raised the population to six thousand by 1690 — were crowded together along the waterfront. Here, too, in the series of docks and shipyards which jutted out from the shore line, were tangible manifestations of the commercial activity which had made the small town the largest owner of shipping

Source: James A. Henretta, "Economic Development and Social Structure in Colonial Boston," *William and Mary Quarterly,* 3d ser., vol. 22 (1965), pp. 75–92.

and the principal port of the English colonies. Over 40 per cent of the carrying capacity of all colonial-owned shipping was in Boston hands.

Dependence on mercantile endeavor rather than agricultural enterprise had by 1690 greatly affected the extent of property ownership. Boston no longer had the universal ownership of real estate characteristic of rural Massachusetts to the end of the colonial period. The tax list for 1687 contained the names of 188 polls, 14 per cent of the adult male population, who were neither owners of taxable property of any kind nor "dependents" in a household assessed for the property tax. Holding no real estate, owning no merchandise or investments which would yield an income, these men constituted the "propertyless" segment of the community and were liable only for the head tax which fell equally upon all men above the age of sixteen. Many in this group were young men, laborers and seamen, attracted by the commercial prosperity of the town and hoping to save enough from their wages to buy or rent a shop, to invest in the tools of an artisan, or to find a start in trade. John Erving, a poor Scotch sailor whose grandson in 1771 was one of the richest men in Boston, was only one propertyless man who rose quickly to a position of wealth and influence.

But many of these 188 men did not acquire either taxable property or an established place in the social order of Boston. Only sixty-four, or 35 per cent, were inhabitants of the town eight years later. By way of contrast, 45 per cent of the polls assessed from two to seven pounds on the tax list, 65 per cent of those with property valued from eight to twenty pounds, and 73 per cent of those with estates in excess of twenty pounds were present in 1695. There was a direct relation between permanence of residence and economic condition. Even in an expanding and diversifying economic environment, the best opportunities for advancement rested with those who could draw upon long-standing connections, upon the credit facilities of friends and neighbors, and upon political influence. It was precisely these personal contacts which were denied to the propertyless.

A second, distinct element in the social order consisted of the dependents of property owners. Though propertyless themselves, these dependents — grown sons living at home, apprentices, and indentured servants — were linked more closely to the town as members of a tax-paying household unit than were the 188 "unattached" men without taxable estates. Two hundred and twelve men, nearly one sixth of the adult male population of Boston, were classified as dependents in 1687. The pervasiveness of the dependency relationship attested not only to the cohesiveness of the family unit but also to the continuing vitality of the apprenticeship and indenture system at the close of the seventeenth century.

Yet even the dependency relationship, traditionally an effective means of alleviating unemployment and preventing the appearance of unattached propertyless laborers, were subjected to severe pressure by the expansion of the economy. An urgent demand for labor, itself the cause of short indentures, prompted servants to strike out on their own as soon as possible. They became the laborers or semiskilled craftsmen of the town, while the sons of the family eventually assumed control of their father's business and a share of the economic resources of the community.

The propertied section of the population in 1687 was composed of 1,036 individuals who were taxed on their real estate or their income from trade. The less-skilled craftsmen, 521 men engaged in the rougher trades of a waterfront society, formed the bottom stratum of the taxable population in this pre-industrial age. These carpenters, shipwrights, blacksmiths, shopkeepers owned only 12 per cent of the taxable wealth of the town. Few of these artisans and laborers had investments in shipping or in merchandise. A small store or house, or a small farm in the south end of Boston, accounted for their assessment of two to seven pounds on the tax list. (Tables 1 and 3.)

Between these craftsmen and shopkeepers and the traders and merchants who constituted the economic elite of the town was a middle group of 275 property owners with taxable assets valued from eight to twenty pounds. Affluent artisans employing two or three workers, ambitious shopkeepers with investments in commerce, and entrepreneurial-minded sea masters with various maritime interests, bulked large in this center portion of the economic order. Of the 275, 180 owned real estate assessed at seven pounds or less and were boosted into the third quarter of the distribution of wealth by their holdings of merchandise and shares in shipping. (Table 3.) The remaining ninety-five possessed real estate rated at eight pounds or more and, in addition, held various investments in trade. Making up about 25 per cent of the propertied population, this middle group controlled 22 per cent of the taxable wealth in Boston in 1687. Half as numerous as the lowest group of property owners, these men possessed almost double the amount of taxable assets. (Table 1.)

Merchants with large investments in English and West Indian trade and individuals engaged in the ancillary industries of shipbuilding and distilling made up the top quarter of the taxable population in 1687. With taxable estates ranging from twenty to 170 pounds, this commercial group controlled 66 per cent of the town's wealth. But economic development had been too rapid, too uneven and incomplete, to allow the emergence of a well-defined merchant class endowed with a common outlook and clearly distinguished from the rest of the society. Only eighty-five of these men, one third of the wealthiest group in the community, owned dwellings valued at as much as twenty pounds. The majority held landed property valued at ten pounds, only a few pounds greater than that of the middle group of property holders. The merchants had not shared equally in the accumulated fund of capital and experience which had accrued after fifty years of maritime activity. Profits had flowed to those whose daring initiative and initial resources had begun the exploitation of the lucrative colonial market. By 1687, the upper 15 per cent of the property owners held 52 per cent of the taxable assets of the town, while the fifty individuals who composed the highest 5 per cent of the taxable population accounted for more than 25 per cent of the wealth. (Table 1.)

By the end of the seventeenth century widespread involvement in commerce had effected a shift in the locus of social and political respectability in Boston and distinguished it from the surrounding communities. Five of the nine selectmen chosen by the town in 1687 were sea captains. This was more than deference to those accustomed to command. With total estates of £83, £29, £33, £33, and £24, Captains Elisha Hutchinson, John Fairweather, Theophilus Frary, Timothy Prout, and Daniel Turell were among the wealthiest 20 per cent of the population. Still, achievement in trade was not the only index of respectability. Henry Eames, George Cable, Isaac Goose, and Elnathan Lyon, the men appointed by the town to inspect the condition of the streets and roads, had the greater part of their wealth, £105 of £130, invested in land and livestock. And the presence of Deacon Henry Allen among the selectmen provided a tangible indication of the continuing influence of the church.

These legacies of an isolated religious society and a stable agricultural economy

TABLE 1   Distribution of Assessed Taxable Wealth in Boston in 1687*

Total Value of Taxable Wealth	Number of Taxpayers in Each Wealth Bracket	Total Wealth in Each Wealth Bracket	Cumulative Total of Wealth	Cumulative Total of Taxpayers	Cumulative Percentage of Taxpayers	Cumulative Percentage of Wealth
£ 1	0	£ 0	£ 0	0	0.0%	0.0%
2	152	304	304	152	14.6	1.8
3	51	153	457	203	19.5	2.7
4	169	676	1,133	372	35.9	6.8
5	33	165	1,298	405	39.0	7.8
6	97	582	1,880	502	48.5	11.3
7	19	133	2,013	521	50.2	12.1
8	43	344	2,357	564	54.4	14.2
9	22	198	2,555	586	56.6	15.4
10	45	450	3,005	631	60.9	18.1
11	17	187	3,192	648	62.5	19.2
12	30	360	3,552	678	65.4	21.4
13	13	169	3,721	691	66.6	22.4
14	12	168	3,889	703	67.9	23.4
15	22	330	4,219	725	69.9	25.4
16	21	336	4,555	746	72.0	27.5
17	1	17	4,572	747	72.0	27.6
18	18	324	4,896	765	73.8	29.5
19	1	19	4,915	766	73.9	29.6
20	30	600	5,515	796	76.8	33.2
21–25	41	972	6,487	837	80.7	39.0
26–30	48	1,367	7,854	885	85.4	47.3
31–35	29	971	8,825	914	88.2	53.1
36–40	21	819	9,644	935	90.2	58.1
41–45	19	828	10,472	954	92.1	63.1
46–50	16	781	11,253	970	93.6	67.8
51–60	16	897	12,150	986	95.1	73.2
61–70	19	1,245	13,395	1,005	97.0	80.7
71–80	7	509	13,904	1,012	97.8	83.8
81–90	3	253	14,157	1,015	97.9	85.3
91–100	7	670	14,827	1,022	98.6	89.3
100–	14	1,764	16,591	1,036	100.0	100.0

* Money values are those of 1687. Many of the assessments fall at regular five pound intervals and must be considered as an estimate of the economic position of the individual. No attempt was made to compensate for systematic overvaluation or undervaluation inasmuch as the analysis measures relative wealth. The utility of a relative presentation of wealth (or income) is that it can be compared to another relative distribution without regard to absolute monetary values. See Mary Jean Bowman, "A Graphical Analysis of Personal Income Distribution in the United States," *American Economic Review, XXXV* (1944–45), 607–628, and Horst Mendershausen, *Changes in Income Distribution during the Great Depression* (New York, 1946).

disappeared in the wake of the rapid growth which continued unabated until the middle of the eighteenth century. In the fifty years after 1690, the population of the town increased from 6,000 to 16,000. The farms of the south end vanished and the central business district became crowded. In the populous north end, buildings which had once housed seven people suddenly began to hold nine or ten. Accompanying this physical expansion of Boston was a diversification of economic endeavor. By 1742, the town led all the colonial cities in the production of export furniture and shoes, although master craftsmen continued to carry on most industry on a small scale geared to local needs. Prosperity and expansion continued to be rooted, not in the productive capacity or geographic position of the town, but in the ability of the Boston merchants to compete successfully in the highly competitive mercantile world.

After 1750, the economic health of the Massachusetts seaport was jeopardized as New York and Philadelphia merchants, exploiting the rich productive lands at their backs and capitalizing upon their prime geographic position in the West Indian and southern coasting trade, diverted a significant portion of European trade from the New England traders. Without increasing returns from the lucrative "carrying" trade, Boston merchants could no longer subsidize the work of the shopkeepers, craftsmen, and laborers who supplied and maintained the commercial fleet. By 1760, the population of Boston had dropped to 15,000 persons, a level it did not exceed until after the Revolution.

The essential continuity of maritime enterprise in Boston from the late seventeenth to the mid-eighteenth century concealed the emergence of a new type of social system. After a certain point increases in the scale and extent of commercial endeavor produced a new, and more fluid, social order. The development of the economic system subjected the family, the basic social unit, to severe pressures. The fundamental link between one generation and another, the ability of the father to train his offspring for their life's work, was endangered by a process of change which rendered obsolete many of the skills and assumptions of the older, land-oriented generation and opened the prospect of success in new fields and new places. The well-known departure of Benjamin Franklin from his indenture to his brother was but one bright piece in the shifting mosaic of colonial life.

The traditional family unit had lost much of its cohesiveness by the third quarter of the eighteenth century. The Boston tax lists for 1771 indicate that dependents of property owners accounted for only 10 per cent of the adult male population as opposed to 16 per cent eighty-five years earlier. Increasingly children left their homes at an early age to seek their own way in the world.

A second factor in the trend away from dependency status was the decline in the availability of indentured servants during the eighteenth century. Fewer than 250 of 2,380 persons entering Boston from 1764 to 1768 were classified as indentured servants. These were scarcely enough to replace those whose indentures expired. More and more, the labor force had to be recruited from the ranks of "unattached" workers who bartered their services for wages in a market economy.

This laboring force consisted of the nondependent, propertyless workers of the community, now twice as numerous relative to the rest of the population as they had been a century before. In 1687, 14 per cent of the total number of adult males were without taxable property; by the eve of the Revolution, the propertyless accounted for 29 per cent. The social consequences of this increase were manifold. For every wage earner who competed in the economy as an autonomous entity at the end of the seventeenth century, there were four in 1771; for every man who slept in the back of a shop, in a tavern, or in a rented room in 1687, there were four in the later period. The population of Boston had doubled, but the number of propertyless men had increased fourfold.

The adult males without property, however, did not form a single unified class, a monolithic body of landless proletarians. Rather, the bottom of society consisted of a congeries of social and occupational groups with a highly transient maritime element at one end of the spectrum and a more stable and respected artisan segment at

TABLE 2   Distribution of Assessed Taxable Wealth in Boston in 1771*

Total Value of Taxable Wealth	Number of Taxpayers in Each Wealth Bracket	Total Wealth in Each Wealth Bracket	Cumulative Total of Wealth	Cumulative Total of Taxpayers	Cumulative Percentage of Taxpayers	Cumulative Percentage of Wealth
£ 3–30	78	£1,562	£1,562	78	5.0%	0.3%
31–40	86	2,996	4,558	164	10.6	0.9
41–50	112	5,378	9,936	276	17.9	2.2
51–60	74	4,398	14,334	350	22.6	3.5
61–70	33	3,122	17,456	383	24.7	3.8
71–80	165	12,864	30,320	548	35.4	6.5
81–90	24	2,048	32,368	572	36.9	7.0
91–100	142	13,684	46,052	714	46.1	10.0
101–110	14	494	46,546	728	47.1	10.1
111–120	149	17,844	64,390	877	56.7	13.9
121–130	20	2,570	66,960	897	58.0	14.5
131–140	26	4,600	71,560	923	59.7	15.5
141–150	20	2,698	74,258	943	60.9	16.1
151–160	88	14,048	88,306	1,031	66.6	19.1
161–170	11	1,846	90,152	1,042	67.4	19.6
171–180	18	3,128	93,280	1,060	68.6	20.3
181–190	10	1,888	95,168	1,070	69.2	20.7
191–200	47	9,368	104,536	1,117	72.2	22.7
201–300	126	31,097	135,633	1,243	80.4	29.4
301–400	60	21,799	157,432	1,303	84.2	34.1
401–500	58	24,947	182,379	1,361	88.0	39.6
501–600	14	7,841	190,220	1,375	88.9	41.3
601–700	24	15,531	205,751	1,399	90.4	44.6
701–800	26	19,518	225,269	1,425	92.2	48.9
801–900	20	17,020	242,289	1,445	93.4	52.6
901–1,000	16	15,328	257,617	1,461	95.4	55.9
1,001–1,500	41	48,364	305,963	1,502	97.1	66.4
1,501–5,000	37	85,326	391,289	1,539	99.5	84.9
5,001–	7	69,204	460,493	1,546	100.0	100.0

* The extant tax list is not complete. In ward 3, there are two pages and 69 polls missing; in ward 7, one page and 24 polls; in ward 12, an unknown number of pages and 225 polls. Only the total number of polls (224) is known for ward 11. The missing entries amount to 558, or 19.3 per cent of the total number of polls on the tax list. Internal evidence (the totals for all wards are known) suggests the absent material is completely random. Nevertheless, it should be remembered that this table represents an 80 per cent sample.

The value of shipping investments and of "servants for life" was not included in the computation of the table as it was impossible to determine the assessor's valuation. For the law regulating the assessment, see *The Arts and Resolves, Public and Private, of the Province of the Massachusetts Bay . . . IV* (Boston, 1881), 985–987. Money values are those of 1771.

the other. Although they held no taxable property, hard-working and reputable craftsmen who had established a permanent residence in Boston participated in the town meeting and were elected to unpaid minor offices. In March 1771, for instance, John Dyer was selected by the people of the town as "Fence Viewer" for the following year. Yet according to the tax and valuation lists compiled less than six months later, Dyer was without taxable property. At the same town meeting, four carpenters, Joseph Ballard, Joseph Edmunds, Benjamin Page, and Joseph Butler, none of whom was listed as an owner of taxable property on the valuation lists, were chosen as "Measurers of Boards." That propertyless men should be selected for public office indicates that the concept of a "stake in society," which provided the theoretical underpinning for membership in the community of colonial Boston, was interpreted in the widest possible sense. Yet it was this very conception of the social order which was becoming anachronistic under the pressure of economic development. For how could the growing number of propertyless men be integrated into a social order based in the first instance on the principle that only those having a tangible interest in the town or a definite family link to the society would be truly interested in the welfare of the community?

Changes no less significant had taken place within the ranks of the propertied groups. By the third quarter of the eighteenth century, lines of economic division and marks of social status were crystalizing as Boston approached economic maturity. Present to some degree in all aspects of town life, these distinctions were very apparent in dwelling arrangements. In 1687, 85 per cent of Boston real estate holdings had been assessed within a narrow range of two to ten pounds; by the seventh decade of the eighteenth century, the same spectrum ran from twelve to two hundred pounds. (Table 3.) Gradations in housing were finer in 1771 and had social connotations which were hardly conceivable in the more primitive and more egalitarian society of the seventeenth century. This sense of distinctiveness was reinforced by geographic distribution. Affluent members of the community who had not transferred their residence to Roxbury, Cambridge, or Milton built in the spacious environs of the south and west ends. A strict segregation of the social groups was lacking; yet the milieu of the previous century, the interaction of merchant, trader, artisan, and laborer in a waterfront community, had all but disappeared.

The increasing differences between the social and economic groups within the New England seaport stemmed in part from the fact that craftsmen, laborers, and small shopkeepers had failed to maintain their relative position in the economic order. In the eighty-five years from 1687 to 1771, the share of the taxable wealth of the community controlled by the lower half of the propertied population declined from 12 to 10 per cent. (Table 2.) If these men lived better at the end of the century than at the beginning, it was not because the economic development of Boston had effected a redistribution of wealth in favor of the laboring classes but because the long period of commercial prosperity had raised the purchasing power of every social group.

The decline in the economic distinctiveness of the middle group of property holders, the third quarter of the taxable population in the distribution of wealth, is even more significant. In 1771, these well-to-do artisans, shopkeepers, and traders (rising land values had eliminated the farmers and economic maturity the versatile merchant-sea captain) owned only $12\frac{1}{2}$ per cent of the taxable wealth, a very substantial decrease from the 21 per cent held in 1687. These men lived considerably better than their counterparts in the seventeenth century; many owned homes and possessed furnishings rarely matched by the most elegant dwellings of the earlier period. But in relation to the other parts of the social order, their economic position had deteriorated drastically. This smaller middle group had been assessed for taxable estates twice as large as the bottom 50 per cent in 1687; by 1771 the assets of the two groups were equal.

On the other hand, the wealthiest 25 per cent of the taxable population by 1771 controlled 78 per cent of the assessed wealth of Boston. This represented a gain of 12 per cent from the end of the seventeenth century. An equally important shift had taken place within this elite portion of the population. In 1687, the richest 15 per cent of the taxpayers held 52 per cent of the taxable property, while the top 5 per cent owned 26.8 per cent. Eighty-five years later, the percentages were 65.9 and 44.1. (Tables 1 and 2 and Chart A.)

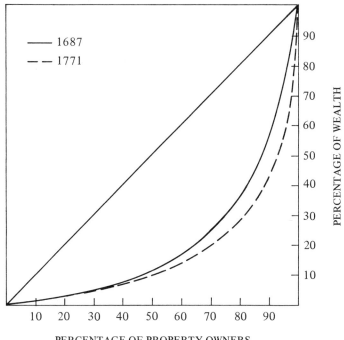

CHART A
*Lorenz Curves Showing the Distribution
of Wealth in Boston in 1687 and 1771
(Drawn from Data in Tables 1 and 2)*

PERCENTAGE OF WEALTH

PERCENTAGE OF PROPERTY OWNERS

Certain long-term economic developments accounted for the disappearance of a distinct middle group of property owners and the accumulation of wealth among a limited portion of the population. The scarcity of capital in a relatively underdeveloped economic system, one in which barter transactions were often necessary because of the lack of currency, required that the savings of all members of the society be tapped in the interest of economic expansion. The prospect of rapid commercial success and the high return on capital invested in mercantile activity attracted the small investor. During the first decade of the eighteenth century, nearly one of every three adult males in Boston was involved directly in trade, owning at least part of a vessel. In 1698 alone, 261 people held shares in a seagoing vessel. Trade had become "not so much a way of life as a way of making money; not a social condition but an economic activity." This widespread ownership of mercantile wealth resulted in the creation of a distinct economic "middle class" by the last decades of the seventeenth century.

A reflection of a discrete stage of economic growth, the involvement of disparate occupational and social groups in commerce was fleeting and transitory. It lasted only as long as the economy of the New England seaport remained underdeveloped, without large amounts of available capital. The increase in the wealth and resources of the town during the first half of the eighteenth century prompted a growing spe-

TABLE 3   Real Estate Ownership in Boston in 1687 and 1771*

| | 1687 | | | 1771 | |
Assessed Total Value of Real Estate	Number of Owners	Cumulative Total of Owners	Assessed Annual Worth of Real Estate	Number of Owners	Cumulative Total of Owners
£ 1	0	0	£ 1	0	0
2	168	168	2	1	1
3	75	243	3	9	10
4	203	446	4	49	59
5	85	531	5	22	81
6	167	698	6	79	160
7	3	701	7	0	160
8	54	755	8	115	275
9	2	757	9	3	278
10	107	864	10	91	369
11	0	864	11	4	373
12	24	888	12	43	416
13	0	888	13	163	579
14	3	891	14	10	589
15	25	916	15	3	592
16	8	924	16	148	740
17	0	924	17	6	746
18	7	930	18	7	753
19	1	931	19	5	758
20	46	932	20	236	994
21–30	25	1,003	21–25	41	1,035
31–40	11	1,014	26–30	163	1,198
41–50	2	1,016	31–35	93	1,291
			36–40	92	1,383
			41–45	5	1,388
			46–50	42	1,430
			51–60	32	1,462
			61–70	10	1,472
			71–80	9	1,481
			81–90	3	1,484
			91–100	3	1,487

* The assessed annual worth of real estate in the 1771 valuation must be multiplied by six to give the total property value.

cialization of economic function; it was no longer necessary to rely on the investments of the less affluent members of the community for an expansion of commerce. This change was slow, almost imperceptible; but by 1771 the result was obvious. In that year, less than 5 per cent of the taxable population of Boston held shares in shipping of ten tons or more, even though the tonnage owned by the town was almost double that of 1698. Few men had investments of less than fifty tons; the average owner held 112 tons. By way of contrast, the average holding at the end of the seventeenth century had been about twenty-five tons. Moreover, on the eve of the Revolution ownership of shipping was concentrated among the wealthiest men of the community. Ninety per cent of the tonnage of Boston in 1771 was in the hands of those whose other assets placed them in the top quarter of the population. With the increase in the wealth of the town had come a great increase in the number of propertyless men and a bifurcation of the property owners into (1) a large amorphous body of shopkeepers, artisans, and laborers with holdings primarily in real estate and (2) a smaller, somewhat more closely defined segment of the population with extensive commercial investments as well as elegant residences and personal possessions.

A similar trend was evident in other phases of town life. In the transitional decades of the late seventeenth and early eighteenth century, the fluidity inherent in the primitive commercial system had produced a certain vagueness in the connotations of social and economic status. Over 10 per cent of the adult males in Boston designated themselves as "merchants" on the shipping registers of the period from 1698 to 1714, indicating not only the decline in the distinctiveness of a title traditionally limited to a carefully defined part of the community but also the feeling that any man could easily ascend the mercantile ladder. Economic opportunity was so evident, so promising, that the social demarcations of the more stable maritime communities of England seemed incongruous. By the sixth decade of the eighteenth century, however, rank and order were supplanting the earlier chaos as successful families tightened their control of trade. The founding in 1763 of a "Merchants Club" with 146 members was a dramatic indication that occupations and titles were regaining some of their traditional distinctiveness and meaning.

An economic profile of the 146 men who composed this self-constituted elite is revealing. Of those whose names appeared on the tax and valuation lists of 1771, only five had estates which placed them in the bottom three quarters of the distribution of wealth. Twenty-one were assessed for taxable property in excess of £1,500 and were thus in the top 1 per cent of the economic scale. The taxable assets of the rest averaged £650, an amount which put them among the wealthiest 15 per cent of the population.

That 146 men, 6½ per cent of the adult male population, were considered eligible for membership in a formal society of merchants indicates, however, that mercantile activity was not dominated by a narrow oligarchy. The range of wealth among the members of the top quarter of the propertied population was so great and the difference of social background so large as to preclude the creation of a monolithic class or guild with shared interests and beliefs.

Yet the influence of this segment of society was pervasive. By the third quarter of the eighteenth century, an integrated economic and political hierarchy based on mercantile wealth had emerged in Boston to replace the lack of social stratification of the early part of the century and the archaic distinctions of power and prestige of the religious community of the seventeenth century. All of the important offices of the town government, those with functions vital to the existence and prosperity of the town, were lodged firmly in the hands of a broad elite, entry into which was conditioned by commercial achievement and family background. The representatives to the General Court and the selectmen were the leaders of the town in economic endeavor as well as in political acumen. John Hancock's taxable wealth totaled £18,000; James Otis was assessed at £2,040, while Colonel Joseph Jackson had property valued at £1,288. Other levels of the administrative system were reserved for those whose business skills or reputation provided the necessary qualifications. Samuel Abbot, John Barrett, Benjamin Dolbeare, John Gore, William Phillips, William White, and William Whitewell, Overseers of the Poor in 1771, had taxable estates of £815, £5,520, £850, £1,747, £5,771, £1,953, and £1,502 respectively. All were among the wealthiest 7 per cent of the property owners; and Barrett and Phillips were two of the most respected merchants of the town. John Scollay, a distiller with an estate of £320, and Captain Benjamin Waldo, a shipmaster assessed at £500, who were among those chosen as "Firewards" in 1771, might in an earlier period have been dominant in town affairs; by the seventh decade of the century, in a mature economic environment, the merchant prince had replaced the man of action at the apex of the social order.

Gradations continued to the bottom of the scale. Different social and occupational levels of the population were tapped as the dignity and responsibility of the position demanded. It was not by accident that the estates of the town assessors, Jonathan Brown, Moses Deshon, and John Kneeland, were £208, £200, and £342. Or that those of the "Cullers of Staves," Henry Lucas, Thomas Knox, and Caleb Hayden, totaled £120, £144, and £156. The assumption of a graded social, economic, and political scale neatly calibrated so as to indicate the relation of each individual to the whole was the basic principle upon which the functioning of town-meeting "democracy" depended. William Crafts, with a taxable estate of £80, was elected "Fence Viewer." Half this amount qualified William Barrett to be "Measurer of Coal Baskets," while Henry Allen and John Bulfinch, "Measurers of Boards," were assessed at £80 and £48. The design was nearly perfect, the correlation between town office and social and economic position almost exact.

As in 1687, the distribution of political power and influence in Boston conformed to the standards and gradations of a wider, more inclusive hierarchy of status, one which purported to include the entire social order within the bounds of its authority. But the lines of force which had emerged on the eve of the American Revolution radiated from different economic and social groups than those of eighty-five years before, and now failed to encompass a significant portion of the population. The weakening of the "extended" family unit and the appearance of a large body of autonomous wage earners, "proletarians" in condition if not in consciousness, had introduced elements of mobility and diversity into the bottom part of society. Equally significant had been the growing inequality of the distribution of wealth among the propertied segment of the community, notably the greater exclusiveness and predominance of a mercantile "elite." Society had become more stratified and unequal. Influential groups, increasingly different from the small property owners who constituted the center portion of the community, had arisen at either end of the spectrum. Creations of the century-long development of a maritime economy in an urban setting, these "merchant princes" and "proletarians" stood out as the salient characteristics of a new social order.

The State of the Union: 1800

By 1815, the United States had successfully passed through the initial stages of national development. It had avoided internal disruption and had successfully defended its interests against other nations. The revolutionary generation, preoccupied with founding a republic on a lasting basis, was passing from the scene. Taking its place after 1815 was a new generation that looked westward and became preoccupied with developing the vast resources of the American continent, now doubled in size as a result of Jefferson's Louisiana Purchase.

In the following selections from his monumental eight-volume history of the United States during the administrations of Jefferson and Madison, Henry Adams (1838–1918), probably the greatest historian America has produced, surveys the state of the union in 1800. Adams plays upon the contrast between the extraordinary creativity of the revolutionary generation in the field of politics and government and the backwardness of the country's material and intellectual life. The American Revolution altered the structure of government and the locus of authority, but it left the economic and social structures largely intact. In vivid strokes of the pen, Adams reminds us how rude a society America was in 1800 — its roads and technology primitive, its intellectual and cultural life thin, its resources enormous but largely unexploited. And he tries to explain why a people, so adventurous politically, was so backward in other respects. Americans, Adams argues, were a conservative people preoccupied with individual enterprise, so much so that they refused to support internal improvements or scientific learning until they glimpsed that these held the keys to far greater wealth. That discovery, made by more and more Americans in the decades after 1815, unleashed new energies that spread settlement to the Pacific in one generation, and touched off a transportation revolution which, in turn, stimulated the growth of manufacturing. At the time Adams wrote, the United States was becoming the world's leading industrial nation. How and why Americans threw off the conservatism that Adams believed held back economic progress for so long, becomes clearer as one studies the history of the American people in the nineteenth century as explored in the next group of selections.

FOR FURTHER READING:

DANGERFIELD, GEORGE. *The Awakening of American Nationalism.* New York: Harper & Row, Publishers, Torchbooks, 1965.*

SMELSER, MARSHALL. *The Democratic Republic, 1801–1815.* New York: Harper & Row, Publishers, Torchbooks, 1968.*

YOUNG, JAMES S. *The Washington Community.* New York: Columbia University Press, 1966.*

Asterisk denotes paperback edition.

From *History of the United States During the Administrations of Jefferson and Madison* HENRY ADAMS

According to the census of 1800, the United States of America contained 5,308,483 persons. In the same year the British Islands contained upwards of fifteen millions; the French Republic, more than twenty-seven millions. Nearly one fifth of the American people were negro slaves; the true political population consisted of four and a half million free whites, or less than one million able-bodied males, on whose shoulders fell the burden of a continent. Even after two centuries of struggle the land was still untamed; forest covered every portion, except here and there a strip of cultivated soil; the minerals lay undisturbed in their rocky beds, and more than two thirds of the people clung to the seaboard within fifty miles of tide-water, where alone the wants of civilized life could be supplied. The centre of population rested within eighteen miles of Baltimore, north and east of Washington. Except in political arrangement, the interior was little more civilized than in 1750, and was not much easier to penetrate than when La Salle and Hennepin found their way to the Mississippi more than a century before.

A great exception broke this rule. Two wagonroads crossed the Alleghany Mountains in Pennsylvania — one leading from Philadelphia to Pittsburg; one from the Potomac to the Monongahela; while a third passed through Virginia southwestward to the Holston River and Knoxville in Tennessee, with a branch through the Cumberland Gap into Kentucky. By these roads and by trails less passable from North and South Carolina, or by water-ways from the lakes, between four and five hundred thousand persons had invaded the country beyond the Alleghanies. At Pittsburg and on the Monongahela existed a society, already old, numbering seventy or eighty thousand persons, while on the Ohio River the settlements had grown to an importance which threatened to force a difficult problem on the union of the older States. One hundred and eighty thousand whites, with forty thousand negro slaves, made Kentucky the largest community west of the mountains; and about ninety thousand whites and fourteen thousand slaves were scattered over Tennessee. In the territory north of the Ohio less progress had been made. A New England colony existed at Marietta; some fifteen thousand people were gathered at Cincinnati; half-way between the two, a small town had grown up at Chillicothe, and other villages or straggling cabins were to be found elsewhere; but the whole Ohio territory contained only forty-five thousand inhabitants. The entire population, both free and slave, west of the mountains, reached not yet half a million; but already they were partly disposed to think themselves, and the old thirteen States were not altogether unwilling to consider them, the germ of an independent empire, which was to find its outlet, not through the Alleghanies to the seaboard, but by the Mississippi River to the Gulf.

Nowhere did eastern settlements touch the western. At least one hundred miles of mountainous country held the two regions everywhere apart. The shore of Lake

Source: Henry Adams, *History of the United States During the Administrations of Jefferson and Madison* (New York: Charles Scribner's Sons, 1891–1896), vol. 1, pp. 1–5, 16–19, 20–23, 27–33, 39–40, 43, 60–63, 65–67, 72–74.

Erie, where alone contact seemed easy, was still unsettled. The Indians had been pushed back to the Cuyahoga River, and a few cabins were built on the site of Cleveland; but in 1800, as in 1700, this intermediate region was only a portage where emigrants and merchandise were transferred from Lake Erie to the Muskingum and Ohio valleys. Even western New York remained a wilderness: Buffalo was not laid out; Indian titles were not extinguished; Rochester did not exist; and the county of Onondaga numbered a population of less than eight thousand. In 1799 Utica contained fifty houses, mostly small and temporary. Albany was still a Dutch city, with some five thousand inhabitants; and the tide of immigration flowed slowly through it into the valley of the Mohawk, while another stream from Pennsylvania, following the Susquehanna, spread toward the Genesee country.

The people of the old thirteen States, along the Atlantic seaboard, thus sent westward a wedge-shaped mass of nearly half a million persons, penetrating by the Tennessee, Cumberland, and Ohio rivers toward the western limit of the Union. The Indians offered sharp resistance to this invasion, exacting life for life, and yielding only as their warriors perished. By the close of the century the wedge of white settlements, with its apex at Nashville and its flanks covered by the Ohio and Tennessee rivers, nearly split the Indian country in halves. The northern half — consisting of the later States of Wisconsin, Michigan, Illinois, Indiana, and one third of Ohio — contained Wyandottes and Shawanese, Miamis, Kickapoos, and other tribes, able to send some five thousand warriors to hunt or fight. In the southern half, powerful confederacies of Creeks, Cherokees, Chickasaws, and Choctaws lived and hunted where the States of Mississippi, Alabama, and the western parts of Georgia, Tennessee, and Kentucky were to extend; and so weak was the State of Georgia, which claimed the southwestern territory for its own, that a well-concerted movement of Indians might without much difficulty have swept back its white population of one hundred thousand toward the ocean or across the Savannah River. The Indian power had been broken in halves, but each half was still terrible to the colonists on the edges of their vast domain, and was used as a political weapon by the Governments whose territory bounded the Union on the north and south. The governors-general of Canada intrigued with the northwestern Indians, that they might hold in check any aggression from Washington; while the Spanish governors of West Florida and Louisiana maintained equally close relations with the Indian confederacies of the Georgia territory.

With the exception that half a million people had crossed the Alleghanies and were struggling with difficulties all their own, in an isolation like that of Jutes or Angles in the fifth century, America, so far as concerned physical problems, had changed little in fifty years. The old landmarks remained nearly where they stood before. The same bad roads and difficult rivers, connecting the same small towns, stretched into the same forests in 1800 as when the armies of Braddock and Amherst pierced the western and northern wilderness, except that these roads extended a few miles farther from the seacoast. Nature was rather man's master than his servant, and the five million Americans struggling with the untamed continent seemed hardly more competent to their task than the beavers and buffalo which had for countless generations made bridges and roads of their own. . . .

If the physical task which lay before the American people had advanced but a short way toward completion, little more change could be seen in the economical conditions of American life. The man who in the year 1800 ventured to hope for a new era in the coming century, could lay his hand on no statistics that silenced doubt. The machinery of production showed no radical difference from that familiar to ages long past. The Saxon farmer of the eighth century enjoyed most of the comforts known to Saxon farmers of the eighteenth. The eorls and ceorls of Offa and Ecgbert could not read or write, and did not receive a weekly newspaper with such information as newspapers in that age could supply; yet neither their houses, their clothing, their food and drink, their agricultural tools and methods, their stock, nor their habits were so greatly altered or improved by time that they would have found much difficulty in accommodating their lives to that of their descendants in the eighteenth century. In this respect America was backward. Fifty or a hundred miles inland more than half the houses were log-cabins, which might or might not enjoy the luxury of a glass window. Throughout the South and West houses showed little attempt at luxury; but even in New England the ordinary farmhouse was hardly so well built, so spacious, or so warm as that of a well-to-do contemporary of Charlemagne. The cloth which the farmer's family wore was still homespun. The hats were manufactured by the village hatter; the clothes were cut and made at home; the shirts, socks, and nearly every other article of dress were also homemade. Hence came a marked air of rusticity which distinguished country from town — awkward shapes of hat, coat, and trousers, which gave to the Yankee caricature those typical traits that soon disappeared almost as completely as coats of mail and steel headpieces. The plough was rude and clumsy; the sickle as old as Tubal Cain, and even the cradle not in general use; the flail was unchanged since the Aryan exodus; in Virginia, grain was still commonly trodden out by horses. Enterprising gentlemen-farmers introduced threshing-machines and invented scientific ploughs; but these were novelties. Stock was as a rule not only unimproved, but ill cared for. The swine ran loose; the cattle were left to feed on what pasture they could find, and even in New England were not housed until the severest frosts, on the excuse that exposure hardened them. Near half a century afterward a competent judge asserted that the general treatment of cows in New England was fair matter of presentment by a grand jury. Except among the best farmers, drainage, manures, and rotation of crops were uncommon. The ordinary cultivator planted his corn as his father had planted it, sowing as much rye to the acre, using the same number of oxen to plough, and getting in his crops on the same day. He was even known to remove his barn on account of the manure accumulated round it, although the New England soil was never so rich as to warrant neglect to enrich it. The money for which he sold his wheat and chickens was of the Old World; he reckoned in shillings or pistareens, and rarely handled an American coin more valuable than a large copper cent.

At a time when the wealth and science of London and Paris could not supply an article so necessary as a common sulphur-match, the backwardness of remote country districts could hardly be exaggerated. Yet remote districts were not the only sufferers. Of the whole United States New England claimed to be the most civilized province, yet New England was a region in which life had yet gained few charms of sense and few advantages over its rivals. Wilson, the ornithologist, a Pennsylvania Scotchman, a confirmed grumbler, but a shrewd judge, and the most thorough of American travellers, said in 1808: "My journey through almost the whole of New England has rather lowered the Yankees in my esteem. Except a few neat academies, I found their schoolhouses equally ruinous and deserted with ours; fields covered with stones; stone fences; scrubby oaks and pine-trees; wretched orchards; scarcely one grain-field in twenty miles; the taverns along the road dirty, and filled with loungers brawling about lawsuits and politics; the people snappish and extortioners, lazy, and two hundred years behind the Pennsylvanians in agricultural improvements." The description was exaggerated, for Wilson forgot to speak of the districts where fields were not covered with stones, and where wheat could be grown to advantage. . . .

A better measure of the difficulties with which New England struggled was given by the progress of Boston, which was supposed to have contained about eighteen thousand inhabitants as early as 1730, and twenty thousand in 1770. For several years after the Revolution it numbered less than twenty thousand, but in 1800 the census showed twenty-five thousand inhabitants. In appearance, Boston resembled an English market-town, of a kind even then old-fashioned. The footways or sidewalks were paved, like the crooked and narrow streets, with round cobblestones, and were divided from the carriage way only by posts and a gutter. The streets were almost unlighted at night, a few oil-lamps rendering the darkness more visible and the rough pavement rougher. Police hardly existed. The system of taxation was defective. The town was managed by selectmen, the elected instruments of town-meetings whose jealousy of granting power was even greater than their objection to spending money, and whose hostility to city government was not to be overcome.

Although on all sides increase of ease and comfort was evident, and roads, canals, and new buildings, public and private, were already in course of construction on a scale before unknown, yet in spite of more than a century and a half of incessant industry, intelligent labor, and pinching economy Boston and New England were still poor. A few merchants enjoyed incomes derived from foreign trade, which allowed them to imitate in a quiet way the style of the English mercantile class; but the clergy and the lawyers, who stood at the head of society, lived with much economy. Many a country clergyman, eminent for piety and even for hospitality, brought up a family and laid aside some savings on a salary of five hundred dollars a year. President Dwight, who knew well the class to which he belonged, eulogizing the life of Abijah Weld, pastor of Attleborough, declared that on a salary of two hundred and twenty dollars a year Mr. Weld brought up eleven children, besides keeping a hospitable house and maintaining charity to the poor.

On the Exchange a few merchants had done most of the business of Boston since the peace of 1783, but a mail thrice a week to New York, and an occasional arrival from Europe or the departure of a ship to China, left ample leisure for correspondence and even for gossip. The habits of the commercial class had not been greatly affected by recent prosperity. Within ten or fifteen years before 1800 three Banks had been created to supply the commercial needs of Boston. One of these was a branch Bank of the United States, which employed there whatever part of its capital it could profitably use; the two others were local Banks, with capital of $1,600,000, toward which the State subscribed $400,000. Altogether the banking capital of Boston might amount to two millions and a half. A number of small Banks, representing in all about two and a half millions more, were scattered through the smaller New England towns. The extraordinary prosperity caused by the French wars opened to Boston a new career. Wealth and population were doubling; the exports and imports of New England were surprisingly large, and the shipping was greater than that of New York and Pennsylvania combined; but Boston had already learned, and was to learn again, how fleeting were the riches that depended on foreign commerce, and conservative habits were not easily changed by a few years of accidental gain.

Of manufactures New England had many, but none on a large scale. The people could feed or clothe themselves only by household industry; their whaleoil, salt fish, lumber, and rum were mostly sent abroad; but they freighted coasters with turners' articles, home-made linens and cloths, cheese, butter, shoes, nails, and what were called Yankee Notions of all sorts, which were sent to Norfolk and the Southern ports, and often peddled from the deck, as goods of every sort were peddled on the flat-boats of the Ohio. Two or three small mills spun cotton with doubtful success; but England supplied ordinary manufactures more cheaply and better than Massachusetts could hope to do. A tri-weekly mail and a few coasting sloops provided for the business of New England with domestic ports. One packet sloop plied regularly to New York.

The State of New York was little in advance of Massachusetts and Maine. In 1800 for the first time New York gained the lead in population by the difference between 589,000 and 573,000. The valuation of New York for the direct tax in 1799 was $100,000,000; that of Massachusetts was $84,000,000. New York was still a frontier State, and although the city was European in its age and habits, travellers needed to go few miles from the Hudson in order to find a wilderness like that of Ohio and Tennessee. . . .

As a rule American capital was absorbed in shipping or agriculture, whence it could not be suddenly withdrawn. No stock-exchange existed, and no broker exclusively engaged in stock-jobbing, for there were few stocks. The national debt, of about eighty millions, was held abroad, or as a permanent investment at home. States and municipalities had not learned to borrow. Except for a few banks and insurance offices, turnpikes, bridges, canals, and land-companies, neither bonds nor stocks were known. The city of New York was so small as to make extravagance difficult; the Battery was a fashionable walk, Broadway a country drive, and Wall Street an uptown residence. Great accumulations of wealth had hardly begun. The Patroon was still the richest man in the State. John Jacob Astor was a fur-merchant living where the Astor House afterward stood, and had not yet begun those purchases of real estate which secured his fortune. Cornelius Vanderbilt was a boy six years old, playing about his father's ferryboat at Staten Island. New York city itself was what it had been for a hundred years past — a local market. . . .

Of all parts of the Union, Pennsylvania seemed to have made most use of her national advantages; but her progress was not more rapid than the natural increase of population and wealth demanded, while to deal with the needs of America, man's resources and his power over Nature must be increased in a ratio far more rapid than that which governed his numbers. Nevertheless, Pennsylvania was the most encouraging spectacle in the field of vision. Baltimore, which had suddenly sprung to a population and commerce greater than those of Boston, also offered strong hope of future improvement; but farther South the people showed fewer signs of change.

The city of Washington, rising in a solitude on the banks of the Potomac, was a symbol of American nationality in the Southern States. The contrast between the immensity of the task and the paucity of means seemed to challenge suspicion that the nation itself was a magnificent scheme like the federal city, which could show only a few log-cabins and negro quarters where the plan provided for the traffic of

London and the elegance of Versailles. When in the summer of 1800 the government was transferred to what was regarded by most persons as a fever-stricken morass, the half-finished White House stood in a naked field overlooking the Potomac, with two awkward Department buildings near it, a single row of brick houses and a few isolated dwellings within sight, and nothing more; until across a swamp, a mile and a half away, the shapeless, unfinished Capitol was seen, two wings without a body, ambitious enough in design to make more grotesque the nature of its surroundings. The conception proved that the United States understood the vastness of their task, and were willing to stake something on their faith in it. Never did hermit or saint condemn himself to solitude more consciously than Congress and the Executive in removing the government from Philadelphia to Washington: the discontented men clustered together in eight or ten boarding-houses as near as possible to the Capitol, and there lived, like a convent of monks, with no other amusement or occupation than that of going from their lodgings to the Chambers and back again. Even private wealth could do little to improve their situation, for there was nothing which wealth could buy; there were in Washington no shops or markets, skilled labor, commerce, or people. Public efforts and lavish use of public money could alone make the place tolerable; but Congress doled out funds for this national and personal object with so sparing a hand, that their Capitol threatened to crumble in pieces and crush Senate and House under the ruins, long before the building was complete.

A government capable of sketching a magnificent plan, and willing to give only a half-hearted pledge for its fulfilment; a people eager to advertise a vast undertaking beyond their present powers, which when completed would become an object of jealousy and fear — this was the impression made upon the traveller who visited Washington in 1800, and mused among the unraised columns of the Capitol upon the destiny of the United States. As he travelled farther south his doubts were strengthened, for across the Potomac he could detect no sign of a new spirit. Manufactures had no existence. Alexandria owned a bank with half a million of capital, but no other was to be found between Washington and Charleston, except the branch Bank of the United States at Norfolk, nor any industry to which loans and discounts could safely be made. Virginia, the most populous and powerful of all the States, had a white population of 514,000, nearly equal to that of Pennsylvania and New York, besides about 350,000 slaves. Her energies had pierced the mountains and settled the western territory before the slow-moving Northern people had torn themselves from the safer and more comfortable life by the seaboard; but the Virginia ideal was patriarchal, and an American continent on the Virginia type might reproduce the virtues of Cato, and perhaps the eloquence of Cicero, but was little likely to produce anything more practical in the way of modern progress. The Shenandoah Valley rivalled Pennsylvania and Connecticut in richness and skill of husbandry; but even agriculture, the favorite industry in Virginia, had suffered from the competition of Kentucky and Tennessee, and from the emigration which had drawn away fully one hundred thousand people. The land was no longer very productive. Even Jefferson, the most active-minded and sanguine of all Virginians — the inventor of the first scientific plough, the importer of the first threshing-machine known in Virginia, the experimenter with a new drilling-machine, the owner of one hundred and fifty slaves and ten thousand acres of land, whose negroes were trained to carpentry, cabinet-making, house-building, weaving, tailoring, shoe-making — claimed to get from his land no more than six or eight bushels of wheat to an acre, and had been forced to abandon the more profitable cultivation of tobacco. Except in a few favored districts like the Shenandoah Valley, land in Virginia did not average eight bushels of wheat to an acre. The cultivation of tobacco had been almost the sole object of land-owners, and even where the lands were not exhausted, a bad system of agriculture and the force of habit prevented improvement.

The great planters lavished money in vain on experiments to improve their crops and their stock. They devoted themselves to the task with energy and knowledge; but they needed a diversity of interests and local markets, and except at Baltimore these were far from making their appearance. Neither the products, the markets, the relative amount of capital, nor the machinery of production had perceptibly changed. "The Virginians are not generally rich," said the Duc de Liancourt, "especially in net revenue. Thus one often finds a well-served table, covered with silver, in a room where for ten years half the window panes have been missing, and where they will be missed for ten years more. There are few houses in a passable state of repair, and of all parts of the establishment those best cared for are the stables." Wealth reckoned in slaves or land was plenty; but the best Virginians, from President Washington downward, were most outspoken in their warnings against the Virginia system both of slavery and agriculture. . . .

If any portion of the United States might hope for a sudden and magnificent bloom, South Carolina seemed entitled to expect it. Rarely had such a situation, combined with such resources, failed to produce some wonderful result. Yet as Washington warned Sinclair, these advantages were counterbalanced by serious evils. The climate in summer was too relaxing. The sun was too hot. The sea-coast was unhealthy, and at certain seasons even deadly to the whites. Finally, if history was a guide, no permanent success could be prophesied for a society like that of the low country in South Carolina, where some thirty thousand whites were surrounded by a dense mass of nearly one hundred thousand negro slaves. Even Georgia, then only partially settled, contained sixty thousand slaves and but one hundred thousand whites. The cotton States might still argue that if slavery, malaria, or summer heat barred civilization, all the civilization that was ever known must have been blighted in its infancy; but although the future of South Carolina might be brilliant, like that of other oligarchies in which only a few thousand freemen took part, such a development seemed to diverge far from the path likely to be followed by Northern society, and bade fair to increase and complicate the social and economical difficulties with which Americans had to deal.

A probable valuation of the whole United States in 1800 was eighteen hundred million dollars, equal to $328 for each human being, including slaves; or $418 to each free white. This property was distributed with an approach to equality, except in a few of the Southern States. In New York and Philadelphia a private fortune of one hundred thousand dollars was considered handsome, and three hundred thousand was great wealth. Inequalities were frequent; but they were chiefly those of a landed aristocracy. Equality was so far the rule that every white family of five persons might be supposed to own land, stock, or utensils, a house and furniture, worth about two thousand dollars; and as the only considerable industry was agriculture, their scale of life was easy to calculate — taxes amounting to little or nothing, and wages averaging about a dollar a day.

Not only were these slender resources, but they were also of a kind not easily converted to the ready uses required for rapid development. Among the numerous difficulties with which the Union was to struggle, and which were to form the interest of American history, the disproportion between the physical obstacles and the material means for overcoming them was one of the most striking.

The growth of character, social and national — the formation of men's minds — more interesting then any territorial or industrial growth, defied the tests of censuses and surveys. No people could be expected, least of all when in infancy, to understand the intricacies of its own character, and rarely has a foreigner been gifted with insight to explain what natives did not comprehend. Only with diffidence could the best-informed Americans venture, in 1800, to generalize on the subject of their own national habits of life and thought. . . .

. . . The path their development might take was one of the many problems with which their future was perplexed. Such few habits as might prove to be fixed, offered little clew to the habits that might be adopted in the process of growth, and speculation was useless where change alone could be considered certain.

If any prediction could be risked, an observer might have been warranted in suspecting that the popular character was likely to be conservative, for as yet this trait was most marked, at least in the older societies of New England, Pennsylvania, and Virginia. Great as were the material obstacles in the path of the United States, the greatest obstacle of all was in the human mind. Down to the close of the eighteenth century no change had occurred in the world which warranted practical men in assuming that great changes were to come. Afterward, as time passed, and as science developed man's capacity to control Nature's forces, old-fashioned conservatism vanished from society, reappearing occasionally, like the stripes on a mule, only to prove its former existence; but during the eighteenth century the progress of America, except in political paths, had been less rapid than ardent reformers wished, and the reaction which followed the French Revolution made it seem even slower than it was. In 1723 Benjamin Franklin landed at Philadelphia, and with his loaf of bread under his arm walked along Market Street toward an immortality such as no American had then conceived. He died in 1790, after witnessing great political revolutions; but the intellectual revolution was hardly as rapid as he must, in his youth, have hoped.

In 1732 Franklin induced some fifty persons to found a subscription library, and his example and energy set a fashion which was generally followed. In 1800 the library he founded was still in existence; numerous small subscription libraries on the same model, containing fifty or a hundred volumes, were scattered in country towns; but all the public libraries in the United States — collegiate, scientific, or popular, endowed or unendowed — could hardly show fifty thousand volumes, including duplicates, fully one third being still theological.

Half a century had passed since Franklin's active mind drew the lightning from heaven, and decided the nature of electricity. No one in America had yet carried further his experiments in the field which he had made American. This inactivity was commonly explained as a result of the long Revolutionary War; yet the war had not prevented population and wealth from increasing, until Philadelphia in 1800 was far in advance of the Philadelphia which had seen Franklin's kite flying among the clouds. . . .

Noah Webster, who before beginning his famous dictionary edited the "New York Commercial Advertiser," and wrote on all subjects with characteristic confidence, complained of the ignorance of his countrymen. He claimed for the New Englanders an acquaintance with theology, law, politics, and light English literature; "but as to classical learning, history (civil and ecclesiastical), mathematics, astronomy, chemistry, botany, and natural history, excepting here and there a rare instance of a man who is eminent in some one of these branches, we may be said to have no learning at all, or a mere smattering." Although defending his countrymen from the criticisms of Dr. Priestley, he admitted that "our learning is superficial in a shameful degree . . . our colleges are disgracefully destitute of books and philosophical apparatus . . . and I am ashamed to own that scarcely a branch of science can be fully investigated in America for want of books, especially original works. This defect of our libraries I have experienced myself in searching for materials for the History of Epidemic Diseases. . . . As to libraries, we have no such things. There are not more than three or four tolerable libraries in America, and these are extremely imperfect. Great numbers of the most valuable authors have not found their way across the Atlantic."

This complaint was made in the year 1800, and was the more significant because it showed that Webster, a man equally at home in Philadelphia, New York, and Boston, thought his country's deficiencies greater than could be excused or explained by its circumstances. George Ticknor felt at least equal difficulty in explaining the reason why, as late as 1814, even good schoolbooks were rare in Boston, and a copy of Euripides in the original could not be bought at any book-seller's shop in New England. For some reason, the American mind, except in politics, seemed to these students of literature in a condition of unnatural sluggishness; and such complaints were not confined to literature or science. If Americans agreed in any opinion, they were united in wishing for roads; but even on that point whole communities showed an indifference, or hostility, that annoyed their contemporaries. . . .

. . . So strong was the popular prejudice against paying for the privilege of travelling on a highway that in certain States, like Rhode Island and Georgia, turnpikes were long unknown, while in Virginia and North Carolina the roads were little better than where the prejudice was universal.

In this instance the economy of a simple and somewhat rude society accounted in part for indifference; in other cases, popular prejudice took a form less easily understood. So general was the hostility to Banks as to offer a serious obstacle to enterprise. The popularity of President Washington and the usefulness of his administration were impaired by his support of a national bank and a funding system. Jefferson's hostility to all the machinery of capital was shared by a great majority of the Southern people and a large minority in the North. For seven years the New York legislature refused to charter the first banking company in the State; and when in 1791 the charter was obtained, and the Bank fell into Federalist hands, Aaron Burr succeeded in obtaining banking privileges for the Manhattan Company only by concealing them under the pretence of furnishing a supply of fresh water to the city of New York.

This conservative habit of mind was more harmful in America than in other communities, because Americans needed more than older societies the activity which could alone partly compensate for the relative feebleness of their means compared with the magnitude of their task. Some instances of sluggishness, common to Europe and America, were hardly credible. For more than ten years in England the steam-engines of Watt had been working, in common and successful use, causing a revolution in industry that threatened to drain the world for England's advantage;

yet Europe during a generation left England undisturbed to enjoy the monopoly of steam. France and Germany were England's rivals in commerce and manufactures, and required steam for self-defence; while the United States were commercial allies of England, and needed steam neither for mines nor manufactures, but their need was still extreme. Every American knew that if steam could be successfully applied to navigation, it must produce an immediate increase of wealth, besides an ultimate settlement of the most serious material and political difficulties of the Union. Had both the national and State Governments devoted millions of money to this object, and had the citizens wasted, if necessary, every dollar in their slowly filling pockets to attain it, they would have done no more than the occasion warranted, even had they failed; but failure was not to be feared, for they had with their own eyes seen the experiment tried, and they did not dispute its success. For America this question had been settled as early as 1789, when John Fitch — a mechanic, without education or wealth, but with the energy of genius — invented engine and paddles of his own, with so much success that during a whole summer Philadelphians watched his ferry-boat plying daily against the river current. No one denied that his boat was rapidly, steadily, and regularly moved against wind and tide, with as much certainty and convenience as could be expected in a first experiment; yet Fitch's company failed. He could raise no more money; the public refused to use his boat or to help him build a better; they did not want it, would not believe in it, and broke his heart by their contempt. Fitch struggled against failure, and invented another boat moved by a screw. The Eastern public still proving indifferent, he wandered to Kentucky, to try his fortune on the Western waters. Disappointed there, as in Philadelphia and New York, he made a deliberate attempt to end his life by drink; but the process proving too slow, he saved twelve opium pills from the physician's prescription, and was found one morning dead.

Fitch's death took place in an obscure Kentucky inn, three years before Jefferson, the philosopher president, entered the White House. Had Fitch been the only inventor thus neglected, his peculiarities and the defects of his steamboat might account for his failure; but he did not stand alone. . . .

Possibly Fulton and Fitch, like other inventors, may have exaggerated the public apathy and contempt; but whatever was the precise force of the innovating spirit, conservatism possessed the world by right. Experience forced on men's minds the conviction that what had ever been must ever be. At the close of the eighteenth century nothing had occurred which warranted the belief that even the material difficulties of America could be removed. Radicals as extreme as Thomas Jefferson and Albert Gallatin were contented with avowing no higher aim than that America should reproduce the simpler forms of European republican society without European vices; and even this their opponents thought visionary. The United States had thus far made a single great step in advance of the Old World — they had agreed to try the experiment of embracing half a continent in one republican system; but so little were they disposed to feel confidence in their success, that Jefferson himself did not look on this American idea as vital; he would not stake the future on so new an invention. "Whether we remain in one confederacy," he wrote in 1804, "or form into Atlantic and Mississippi confederations, I believe not very important to the happiness of either part." Even over his liberal mind history cast a spell so strong, that he thought the solitary American experiment of political confederation "not very important" beyond the Alleghenies.

The task of overcoming popular inertia in a democratic society was new, and seemed to offer peculiar difficulties. Without a scientific class to lead the way, and without a wealthy class to provide the means of experiment, the people of the United States were still required, by the nature of their problems, to become a speculating and scientific nation. They could do little without changing their old habit of mind, and without learning to love novelty for novelty's sake. Hitherto their timidity in using money had been proportioned to the scantiness of their means. Henceforward they were under every inducement to risk great stakes and frequent losses in order to win occasionally a thousand fold. In the colonial state they had naturally accepted old processes as the best, and European experience as final authority. As an independent people, with half a continent to civilize, they could not afford to waste time in following European examples, but must devise new processes of their own. A world which assumed that what had been must be, could not be scientific; yet in order to make the Americans a successful people, they must be roused to feel the necessity of scientific training. Until they were satisfied that knowledge was money, they would not insist upon high education; nor until they saw with their own eyes stones turned into gold, and vapor into cattle and corn, would they learn the meaning of science.

PART 2

The Middle Period
1815-1914

The Urban Wage Earner in the Early Republic

The period between independence and about 1830 was one of considerable progress in the economic institutions of the United States. During the confederation period, the basic outlines of federal land policy were drawn. New trade routes were opened up, following the end of British trade restrictions. Businessmen increasingly adopted the corporate form for private business enterprise. The first true commercial banks were established in major port cities. Following 1787, the new Constitution established a government equipped to protect American economic interests abroad and to encourage economic integration at home. During the administration of Washington, the Hamiltonian program reestablished public credit and created a national bank to stimulate commerce and industry. These and other institutional changes set the stage for rapid economic progress in later years, but the period itself was probably one of slow advance in income and welfare of the average American. Evidently, war, the heavy costs of opening up the West, the slow improvement in technology — all conspired to confine improvement per person in the output of the farms and workshops of the nation to modest dimensions.

In 1830, most Americans were still rural farm folk. Of the four million men, women, and children in the labor force in 1830, almost 3 million were still on farms, with many others employed in other extractive industries. The urban wage-earning class was still relatively small, though growing in size. They were not factory workers, as David Montgomery notes, but craftsmen, seamen, apprentices, and common laborers. They lived in a transitional period in the economy: between the era when many jobs were performed by self-employed craftsmen and the era when many of these working folk would be gathered into large factories.

They were not, it is clear, affluent people, yet they were far better off than their European counterparts, and they found it possible to move up the social ladder. Despite the relatively slow pace of economic growth in this period, it would seem that the lot of the working man was generally better than it had been in eighteenth-century Boston, as described earlier by James Henretta.

FOR FURTHER READING:

Hugins, Walter. *Jacksonian Democracy and the Working Class: A Study of the New York Workingmen's Movement.* Stanford, Cal.: Stanford University Press, 1967.*

Taylor, George R. *The Transportation Revolution.* New York: Harper & Row, Publishers, 1968.*

Ware, Norman. *The Industrial Worker 1840–1860.* Chicago: Quadrangle Books, 1964.*

Asterisk denotes paperback edition.

The Working Classes of the Pre-Industrial American City, 1780–1830

DAVID MONTGOMERY

In the years since Raymond W. Goldsmith submitted to Congress his statistical findings on the rise of per capita income in the United States many economic historians have come to date the beginnings of sustained industrial growth at some time during the 1830s. This chronology has provided historians of the working class with a significant bench-mark to guide their own research and analysis. Among other things it raises questions concerning the sources, size, and character of the labor supply which was at hand before the acceleration of economic growth and the ideological baggage (attitudes, customs, institutions) which the available workers carried with them when they entered the industrial era. The objective of this article is to suggest some parameters for both sets of questions derived from an examination of the working classes in the young nation's four northern cities: Boston, New York, Philadelphia, and Baltimore.

During the five decades before 1830 these cities were essentially depots for transoceanic shipping, and their labor force was largely tied to maritime commerce. Surrounding each of them was "a vast scene of household manufacturing" where, wrote Alexander Hamilton, country folk produced clothing, shoes, and other necessities, "in many instances, to an extent not only sufficient for the supply of the families in which they are made, but for sale, and even, in some cases, for exportation." Such a countryside Albert Gallatin found twenty years later in New Hampshire, where the average farmer's house had at least one spinning wheel, and every second house boasted a loom on which from 100 to 600 yards of saleable cloth were woven annually (at a time when journeymen weavers in their homes averaged only 829 yards per year and factory looms, 1,111 yards). Most manufacturing, in other words, was carried on outside of the major cities. By 1820 some 12 percent of the nation's labor force was engaged in manufacturing and construction, and 28 percent in all non-agricultural occupations, but at that time the residents of these cities and their contiguous suburbs totalled only 356,452, or 3.7 percent of the American people.

The merchant elite of these communities, furthermore, was concerned not so much with hiring labor as with vending the produce of labor, both agricultural and mechanical. Mathew Carey went so far as to accuse the merchants of hostility toward manufacturing interests, of striving "to impress upon the public mind, that the national prosperity depended almost altogether on commerce; that the protection of manufactures by duties on imports was impolitic and unjust." Understandably the broadsides of Carey, Gallatin, Tench Coxe, and other promoters of manufacturing bore the aspect of appeals to the dominant agricultural and commercial interests of the land to pay some heed to the needs of industry and to believe that the growth of domestic manufactures could take place without depriving farmers and merchants of either manpower or customers.

But Carey's conception of the merchant as industry's relentless foe slighted the

Source: David Montgomery, "The Working Classes of the Pre-Industrial American City, 1780–1830," *Labor History,* vol. 9 (1968), pp. 3–22.

encouragement offered manufacturing by the commercial city itself. The concentration of population in seaports required by a growing flow of commerce prevented urban residents from producing their own necessities in the fashion of farm families. It generated a social division of labor within the city itself and hence a need for sedentary artisans. The accumulation of merchant fortunes, furthermore, created a demand for luxury goods and thus for expert craftsmen: for silversmiths, goldbeaters, clockmakers, wig and peruke makers, printers of books and journals, tailors, and cordwainers familiar with European fashions and capable of reproducing them. By the end of the eighteenth century, moreover, seaboard merchants had opened a substantial oceanic trade in shoes, clothing, barrels, and ironwares with the regions of slave plantations. This trade encouraged the development of both the putting-out system and the early efforts toward factory organization of production.

Although most manufacturing was carried on outside the great urban centers, the seaport itself, therefore, generated a demand for labor in production as well as trade. In the eighteenth century most manufacture had been performed in the workshops of mechanics who, with the aid of family, apprentices, and occasional journeymen, made the wares they vended themselves. The printer, for example, was usually a bookseller and a journalist as well, in the manner of Mathew Carey, who in the 1790s composed his own editorials in type and then hawked the paper about Philadelphia. Only after 1810 did urban newspapers gravitate into the hands of publishers who were not printers but, in the language of the journeymen, "speculators on the labor of printers" who installed "hireling editors" to write the columns printers now set in type.

The colonial conception of a journeyman as tomorrow's master mechanic was neither dead nor fully obsolete by 1820, for vertical mobility was still remarkable. Among the early members of the Franklin Typographical Association of New York, a trade society of journeymen founded in 1799, were David Bruce, the future owner of the city's largest printing shop and a pioneer typefounder; Thurlow Weed, a future boss of state politics; Samuel Woodworth, the poet of "Old Oaken Bucket" fame; and Peter Force, America's most eminent historical archivist. Two of the master shoemakers who testified against the cordwainers union in Philadelphia's 1805 conspiracy trial were former journeymen and union members, as were two of the employers at the similar Pittsburgh trial ten years later. But by the first two decades of the nineteenth century the emergence of distinct societies of journeymen and of masters among printers, tailors, shoemakers, carpenters, stone cutters, and other trades in every seaport indicated a new awareness of distinct class interests. The seventeen benevolent societies of Philadelphia carpenters, ship masters, stone cutters, and other trades listed by James Mease in 1811 were clearly organizations of master mechanics. Their initiation fees ranging from $10 up and their annual dues of four or five dollars contrast remarkably with the one dollar initiation and the 25 cents monthly dues (waived after ten years' membership) charged by that city's printers union. Societies of journeymen that sought to combine benevolent functions with the enforcement of union wage scales ultimately found it necessary to either expel members who had risen to the rank of employers, or to succumb to the urgings of "alimoners" in their midst and abandon the effort to regulate trade conditions. Thus the printers' organizations in Philadelphia and Boston during the 1820s converted themselves into friendly societies open to employers and workmen alike, while the New York society, bent on controlling wages and aware that "the interests of the journeymen are separate and in some respects opposite to those of the employers," resolved in 1817 "that when any member of this society shall become an employing printer he shall be considered without the limits of this society."

The myth of harmonious personal relationships among masters, journeymen, and apprentices in a setting of domestic paternalism may be quite anachronistic when applied to post-Revolutionary decades. Ian Quimby's study of apprentice contracts in eighteenth century Philadelphia revealed a persistent erosion of filial duties and loyalties by the emerging ethos of commercialism. The mutual moral obligations of apprentices and masters in such matters as work expected of the boy, and the education and clothing due him were converted over the course of the century into money values and specified in ever-increasing detail in the contracts. The experience of cabinetmakers, furthermore, suggests that journeymen seldom remained long enough with any master to develop a sense of personal attachment. The journeymen of Samuel Ashton's Philadelphia cabinet shop between 1795 and 1803 averaged scarcely six months in his employ. So rapid was the turnover of craftsmen that, though Ashton rarely needed more than five workmen at a time, forty-nine different men worked for him during those eight years. Under such circumstances class antagonisms based on chronic disputes over wages could be quite consistent with a high level of upward social mobility.

By the 1820s, therefore, the urban working classes comprised recognizable and self-conscious elements of urban society. The "classes . . . who are wholly dependent upon wages," wrote Reverend Joseph Tuckerman, "are very numerous" and, he continued:

> would, indeed, be numerous, if we looked for them among only those who have no trade, and who are generally distinguished alone, as labouring men. This large division includes shop, market, and other porters; carmen; those who are employed in lading, and unlading vessels; wood-sawyers; hod carriers; house servants; those employed by mechanics in a single branch of their business; and multitudes, who are men and women of any work, occasionally required in families, as washing, scouring, etc.; or on the wharves, or in the streets of the city. Besides these, the number is great of those, who are journeymen, and many of whom will never be anything but journeymen, in the various mechanic arts; and considerable numbers are also employed in the different departments of large manufactories, who possess no capital; and who know, and will continue to know, little or nothing in any other department of these establishments, except that in which they are themselves employed. All these, in the strictest sense, and in the common acceptation of the term, are dependent on the wages which they obtain for their services.

Tuckerman's definition of the wage earning classes suggests that journeymen, mechanics, casual laborers, and factory operatives must be analyzed separately. Even though many mechanics would "never be anything but journeymen," they enjoyed the highest incomes and status of any wage earners and were psychologically the most firmly wedded to the social values and practices of the traditional artisan. Apprenticeship was the historic route of access to "the art and mysteries" of any trade, and the journeymen of this period strove to bar any other avenue of entry. The Philadelphia Typographical Society, which sought with occasional success to reserve all printing positions in town for its own members, excluded from membership anyone "who shall not have served an apprenticeship satisfactory to the board of directors" of the union, and subsequently tried to keep from the presses anyone who had "broken into the trade" after he was twenty-one years old. Both the income and the honor associated with the printer's art were thus to be reserved to those who elected to ply it when they first attained the age of productive manhood at fifteen or sixteen years old. Altogether Philadelphia's complete records of apprentices bound between October 1771 and October 1773 revealed 1,075 youths apprenticed to sixty-eight trades (including many girls indentured to learn "housewifery"). Ten percent of them were to learn the cordwainer's art, and the trades of tailor, mariner, carpenter, and cooper followed shoemaking in order of preference.

Sons of mechanics apprenticed to trades were supplemented by those of farmers who, for example, constituted the bulk of Massachusetts' supply of shoemakers, and in Baltimore by young slaves. The emancipation of northern slaves meant the eclipse of Negro apprenticeship in most urban trades elsewhere. Because the training of slave craftsmen had rarely been complete, freed Negro artisans, who faced intense animosity from white craftsmen and had lost the protection of their masters, rarely survived in positions where they could train apprentices of their own race, and even fewer whites would engage black youth for training. The influx of white farm boys to urban trades, on the other hand, was inhibited by that "desire of being an independent proprietor of land" which Alexander Hamilton believed would always keep small the numbers of those "who would be diverted from it towards manufacturers." Youths who did elect urban trades, furthermore, often fled their apprenticeships after only a year or two of service and, to the great distress of established journeymen, easily found employment as half-trained workmen at substandard wages. The supply of labor was thus rapidly increased at the expense of its quality. The founding of mechanics' institutes (vocational schools) in every major northern city in the 1820s bears witness to the breakdown of traditional apprenticeship training.

The fact remains that residents of rural areas in the Northeast were being lured toward the city, just as others were migrating westward, and frequently such migrants had been craftsmen, rather than (or as well as) farmers. In every decade between 1790 and 1840, the population of all four cities under review grew at a rate substantially above the 33 percent to 36 percent growth for the nation as a whole, with two exceptions: both Philadelphia and New York grew at less than the national rate between 1810 and 1820, and Baltimore's increase after 1820 was chronically below the national pace. This urbanization of native Americans was supplemented by the arrival of European immigrants, but the extent of the trans-oceanic contribution to the growth of these seaports is difficult to measure. Although newcomers to America totaled 400,000 between 1790 and 1830, with 1801–1807, 1816 and 1828–1830 being the years of greatest influx, the bulk of them came not to the American seaport but through it. It was the demand for farm laborers in the hinterland which produced, for example, the large scale trafficking in redemptioners Frances Wright witnessed in the Philadelphia of 1818.

Among the immigrants who tarried in the city, however, were many skilled mechanics. British emigrants and British trade union practices (complete to the oaths sworn over union scales and the trappings of secrecy necessitated in the old country by the Combination Acts but retained here as a matter of custom) showed up in every conspiracy trial of union journeymen. When the prosecutor charged Philadelphia cordwainers in 1805 with "crimes" committed by union members a decade earlier, the defense replied with only slight exaggeration that none of the journeymen on trial had been in America when those acts were committed. Stocking weavers in Germantown and Kensington outside of Philadelphia had almost all learned their trade in Leicester or Nottingham or the Rhineland. Linen weavers had poured out of northern Ireland in the early 1770s and again at the close of the American Revolution, many of them coming to the new republic. In 1784 alone 11,000 passengers embarked from Dublin, most of them emigrants of this type.

An extreme case of immigrants' providing an industry with its skilled labor was offered by the thousand or so carpet weavers in the country in the early 1830s, at least nine-tenths of whom were Scots, largely from Kilmarnock and Ayr. So well did these mechanics know each other that when sixty-three of them struck the Thompsonville Carpet Manufacturing Company in Connecticut, they quickly assembled, compiled from memory a list of the eleven other principal carpet manufactories in the nation, wrote personal letters to friends in each of them explaining the dispute, notified the Blue Bonnet Tavern in New York City, which served as the country's hiring hall for carpet weavers, to divert men from the struck plant, and dispatched an appeal to the *Old Countryman* in that city to warn off any Scots not reached by the other methods.

Such incidents suggest the hypothesis that America was then a land of opportunity for handicraftsmen whose skills were being undermined by the industrial revolution in England but still in high demand in the more backward American economy. True, the number of handloom weavers and stockingers working in England continued to grow rapidly down to 1820 and perhaps beyond, despite the unmistakeable deterioration of income and status in those trades. Many older craftsmen, Arthur Redford found, moved to manufacturing cities in England, there continuing to ply their obsolete trades while depending increasingly on the earnings of their factory-employed children. The Scottish carpet weavers brought to trial in Connecticut for their strike, however, were remarkably young men, twenty-two years of age or less. The presumption is that the craftsman-immigrant tended to be neither the daring innovator nor the veteran artisan who could not quit his obsolescent trade, but the mobile youth who spurned Briton's factory for the possibility of plying the (to him) preferable family trade in a new location.

This hypothesis is consistent with Hamilton's belief that "the disparity" between the "dearness of labor" in America and that in England was "much less in regard to artificers and manufacturers, than in regard to country labourers," a belief recently concurred in by H. J. Habakkuk and Stuart Bruchey. During the first two decades of the nineteenth century skilled tradesmen in England engaged in "hounourable work" (a high quality work not yet subjected to a division of labor and deterioration of apprenticeship standards) looked upon 30s. weekly ($7.50) as an expected income, while some earned £3 and over. Such a 30s. standard fell below the $8.25 of an American shoemaker or the $9 a more seasonal carpenter might ordinarily have expected when working at union standards by precisely the differential of 12 percent-20 percent in America's favor which J. Leander Bishop found for glass workers. True, American workmen paid considerably fewer taxes than their English counterparts, and as D. B. Warden observed of Philadelphia, "Smiths, shoemakers, weavers, and tailors have generally one or two acres of land, which afford pasture for a cow, fuel, and esculent plants." But such bucolic benefits were by no means unknown to English weavers, croppers, and shoemakers, most of whom still worked in their cottages in rural villages.

Far more extreme was the contrast between the American municipal or canal laborer's expectation of some $4.50 a week (often paid partly in board) and the earnings of the English casual laborer, which then ranged from perhaps 11s. weekly in cotton factories to 1s. a day for wheelbarrow men in Birmingham. Taking 10s. (i.e.,

$2.50) as good weekly pay for such laborers in the second decade of the century, the unskilled American enjoyed a premium of 80 percent over his British counterpart. That the wage differential was less rather than greater for the artisan than for casual labor is thus evident even without investigation of the real values of money wages in the two countries. Yet British craftsmen did migrate, spurred by the deteriorating conditions in their trades at home and lured, as one emigrant manual declared, by the openings in American trades left by "the strong emulation of the *cute* native Yankee to elevate himself above the common labour class."

Whether graduates of American or British apprenticeships, urban tradesmen were both geographically mobile enough and sufficiently well informed about the state of the labor market elsewhere to maintain rather uniform wage standards throughout the northeastern cities. When Philadelphia shoemakers demanded a schedule of prices based on $4 a pair for back strap boots in October 1805, they were aware that the New York union had established precisely that scale in March. Similarly, when Pittsburgh shoemakers unionized at the end of that decade, they quickly drove up their prices from 75 cents below the Philadelphia wage to parity with it — but when they sought a scale higher than Philadelphia's, they were roundly defeated by their masters. Both the New York and Washington societies of printers undertook — by correspondence with their counterparts in Philadelphia, Baltimore, Boston, and Albany — to establish uniform scales, and all these societies exchanged "rat lists" with each other, so that typographers who violated union rules and standards could not find refuge in other communities. At times employers cooperated with these efforts of the journeymen, as did master printers in New York in 1815, or, more dramatically, the master weavers of Baltimore, who in 1829 did everything in their power to ostracize a fellow employer for slashing his journeymen's wages below the city norm.

Although the mechanic was ranked by Tuckerman within the wage-earning classes, there is little evidence that prior to the 1830s he either identified himself with "the poor" or felt in any way alienated from the existing social order. Despite the absence from common American parlance of the rigid British distinction between "honourable" and "dishonourable" work, only the scale of the New York shoemakers out of all the union price lists which have been preserved from that period (mainly those of printers, shoemakers, tailors, and weavers) included a specified wage for coarse work, partially completed work, or the work of helpers. While the Pittsburgh shoemakers union did explicitly deem coarse work "out of society" and posed no objections to non-members performing such tasks, there is no such clear evidence from any of the seaport cities. It is remarkable, however, that the prosecutor in the New York shoemakers' trial, while conceding that many journeymen were not members, insisted that "all the best workmen were of the society." Similarly Philadelphia shoemakers considered themselves fully unionized between 1798 and 1804, when their society had 100 to 150 members, while the city directory for 1798 listed 292 shoemakers and cordwainers. A plausible inference is that cheap shoes for slaves and for auction sale, which did not appear in the union's scale of prices, were deliberately relegated to inferior workmen whom the society made no effort to recruit.

The mechanics proudly preserved an ideological heritage blended of Ben Franklin's maxims and Tom Paine's "rights of man." The best local legal talent defended their societies in the several conspiracy trials to which they were subjected, as witness Philadelphia's shoemakers enlisting Caesar Rodney, whom President Jefferson was soon to appoint Attorney General of the United States. When seventeen years earlier that city's mechanics had paraded with their masters in joyous celebration of the ratification of the federal constitution, they had borne such emblems as "the weavers' flag, a rampant lion in a green field, holding a shuttle in his dexter paw — motto — *'may the government* protect us,'" the boat builders' flag (atop the thirty-three foot schooner *Federal Union* drawn down Market Street for the occasion) bearing "an axe and an adze crossing each other — motto, 'by these we live,'" or the bricklayers' flag, with "the federal city rising out of a forest, workmen building it, and the sun illuminating it," motto, "*'both buildings and rulers are the works of our hands.'*" At the close of the procession, bakers distributed bread to the poor, victuallers slew their "two stately oxen" and gave away the meat, and millers provided the needy with flour. The best the printers could do was to read the destitute a poem, but clearly the citizen craftsmen were dispensers, not recipients, of charity.

Very different was the outlook of the impoverished residents of the Rittenhouse Square vicinity, who petitioned the Philadelphia city council in 1830 to halt the dumping in the square of offal swept from neighboring streets, "which being in heaps, occasions numerous ponds of stagnant and putrescent water in the immediate spots, which in summer send forth pestilential vapours wafted by every breeze to the dwellings of your petitioners, whose only comfort, health, is thus destroyed." These poor argued that "being of the working class, their whole time is indispensably employed in various labour to maintain their families," so that sickness is "a scourge the most severe." Here was a group whose annual incomes ranged far closer to $200 than to $400 or $425 expected by craftsmen, a group who Reverend Tuckerman feared" have lived, and to a great extent are living, as a *caste* — cut off from those in more favoured circumstances; and doomed to find their pleasures, and sympathy in their suffering, alone among themselves."

The seaport poor were by no means a new phenomenon at the end of the 1820s. James Henretta has clearly traced their emergence in eighteenth-century Boston as a function of the growth of overseas commerce. He discovered from the Boston tax rolls of 1687 that only 14 percent of the adult male population of the city, that is, 188 men, were neither "dependent" nor owners of property. In contrast to them stood the 17 percent of the adult males who as servants, apprentices, or participants in family home enterprise were classified as dependent. The propertied classes numbered 1,036 (69 percent of the adult males) and included 521 poor craftsmen, 275 artisans of the "middling sort" with two or three journeymen apiece, and the wealthier tradesmen, professionals, and merchants. By 1771 only 10 percent of the adult males were dependent in the traditional sense, while 29 percent were neither dependent nor propertied. These were wage earners in the full meaning of the term, and while the city's population had doubled between the two counts, their number had increased fourfold. They ranged in occupation from seamen and longshoremen at one end of the scale to journeymen at the other, but, while the latter ranked close to the small property-holding mechanic, the division of wealth between the upper and lower halves of property owners was far sharper than had been the case in the seventeenth century.

Most day laborers participated directly in transportation and commerce. It was the demand for seamen, longshoremen, carters, and domestic servants which absorbed unskilled wage earners already in the eighteenth century. By the early nineteenth century, construction work, wood cutting, and road building employed many, while thousands of Philadelphia's poor, Mathew Carey found, "travel hundreds of miles in quest of employment on canals at 62½, 75 and 87½ cents per day, paying a dollar and a half or two dollars per week for their board, leaving families behind, depending on them for support." By 1830 Carey estimated "labourers, hodmen, seamstresses, families of workmen on canals and rail-roads" at 40 percent of the working classes and 25 percent of the total population of Philadelphia.

Many laborers reached the city from the farm by way of the sea. The merchant fleet of Massachusetts, wrote Samuel Eliot Morison, "was manned by successive waves of adventure-seeking boys, and officered by such of them as determined to make the sea their calling." The great majority on the crew lists professed "to be native-born Yankees, and probably were." Seamen would register with federal revenue agents after 1796 and receive, for a fee of 25 cents, papers certifying their United States citizenship. Between that year and 1812, 106,757 seamen collected their papers, and of them only 1,530, or 1.4 percent were naturalized citizens. The registrations reported for the years after 1808 were certainly still incomplete, for district revenue collectors were very tardy in submitting their reports to Washington. The fact that registration was heaviest in years such as 1797 and 1805, when the danger of British impressment was most severe, indicates that enrollment was never very thorough. These figures, nevertheless, can suggest the large number of native Americans who took to the sea.

So high were the rates of promotion, death, and desertion that the man who spent more than twelve years before the mast was rare indeed. No other occupation offered an unskilled farmboy so great an opportunity to rise quickly in wealth and standing — or to topple from yardarm into the cold Atlantic. Few seamen dwelt long in any port, but while ashore they augmented the local casual labor supply significantly. Illustrative of their role was young Charles Erskine, whose mother moved to Boston in the early 1820s after his father (a currier) had deserted her. Playing about the docks, Erskine heard the tales of sailors and through them was lured to sea. Between voyages he and his mates earned their keep ashore by whatever employment was available wherever they happened to be. He once helped construct an aqueduct in Washington and at another time worked in a Philadelphia hook and eye factory.

In marked contrast to the artisan's tendency to ply for life the trade he had learned in his adolescence, the laborer was the epitome of versatility. To move from the sea to canal digging to hod carrying to factory work was well within the realm of possibility. Many of the half-trained journeymen and "botches" who bedevilled mechanics' efforts to retain high quality and wage standards were of this sort. New England's first factory to use cotton spinning machinery, founded in Beverly, Massachusetts, in 1787, wasted precious quantities of material in training its workmen, then was driven close to ruin when it had to raise wages to prevent its partly-taught employees from deserting to rival firms. Mercifully, perhaps, the factory burned down in 1808. A happier experience with such labor was reported by a cotton mill near Providence, which employed fifty-three workers in the factory and 125 on putting-out by 1810. The owners, reported Albert Gallatin, at first suffered "in being put to much expense by English workmen, who pretended to much more knowledge in the business than they really possessed." But the phony Samuel Slaters were discharged, "and Americans, as apprentices, &c. are getting the art very fast," though the company did not anticipate dividends "for a considerable time."

The fact that machine operatives could be trained made the "factory controversy" of this period focus not on the fate of the workers, as was to be the case in the 1830s and 1840s, but on the potential impact of manufacturing upon the nation's supply of farm labor. Wages of farm hands, Henry Carey reported, were higher in the vicinity of the cities than in more rustic settings. Whether this differential in money wages was a sign of competition from urban employments or simply an indication that the market economy was more mature near the cities (that a smaller portion of the farm laborer's income was paid in kind and more in cash than was the case to the West) is not clear. Whichever it meant, advocates of governmental aid to manufactures from Coxe through Carey felt obliged to echo Hamilton's famous assurance that manufacturing would not attract able-bodied men away from the land, that it would rather "afford occasional and extra employment to industrious individuals and families," through which farmers could profit by the home produce of their wives and daughters, and provide steady employment for "persons who would otherwise be idle, and in many cases a burthen on the community," and render women and children "more useful, and the latter more early useful . . . than they should otherwise be."

At this period, therefore, it was impossible to speak of the factory labor force without directing attention to women, children, and charitable institutions. This was the case long before the mills of Lowell arose. Philadelphia's first large-scale use of spinning jennies was undertaken by the United Company of Philadelphia for Promoting American Manufactures, founded by patriotic subscriptions in 1775. By the late 1780s it employed 400 women, most of them recruited from the city's poor rolls. Despite the pride with which the Society displayed a jenny of eighty spindles in the Federal Procession of 1788, and boasted that the woman operating it was "a native of and instructed in this city," the company's building was destroyed by an arsonist only two years later. Newly-inaugurated President Washington found a similar labor force when he visited a Boston sail duck factory. Here pairs of little girls spun and wove flax from eight in the morning until six at night, but their demeanor favorably impressed the President, who described them as "daughters of decayed families" and "girls of character — none others are admitted."

Two decades later the Secretary of the Treasury reported that eighty-seven cotton mills then in operation or about to commence operations in the United States needed a labor force of about 500 men and 3,500 women and children. Such a work force was for Gallatin proof positive that manufacturing need not lure men from the farm. Tench Coxe agreed:

> Female aid in manufactures, which prevents the diversion of men and boys from agriculture, has greatly increased. Children are employed, as well as the infirm and the crippled. The assylums of the poor and unfortunate, and the penitentiaries of indiscretion and immorality are improved and aided by the employment and profits of manufactures.

The markets of seamstresses were especially crowded with unmarried and widowed women, not to speak of those whose husbands were "travelling" — in the informal divorce procedure of the day. When such women bid on sewing work, they competed with both married women trying to supplement their own families' meager incomes and recipients of work relief. While female operatives in Philadelphia factories earned two or three dollars a week in the 1820s, seamstresses rarely surpassed $1.25, and the city's home relief system helped keep those earnings low. In slack seasons so many women applied to the Provident Society and other charities for work to tide them over that the scale offered by almshouses became, during the 1820s, the standard price offered by private firms. Thus the U.S. War Department offered seamstresses 12½ cents a shirt, the very wage given by the Provident Society. In reply to a plea that such a price reduced the seamstresses "to the degradation of pauperism," the Secretary of War termed the subject "of such delicacy, and so intimately connected with the manufacturing interests, and the general prices of this kind of labour in the city of Philadelphia" that he dared not change his Department's practice.

While the seamstress stood with one foot in the poor house, this was not the case with the weaver, for in the urban areas most cloth was still put out to families with handlooms. The city and county of Philadelphia in 1809 produced 65,326 yards of cloth in its six factories on both hand and power looms, but its home production amounted to 233,232 yards. Furthermore, the spinning mills, while they continued to be staffed primarily by women and children, tended to free themselves by the second decade of the century from dependence on public charities. The reason is that unmarried women, widows, and orphaned families gravitated toward them by free choice.

Especially was this the case in New England, where the textile mill became a means of emancipation for the "maiden aunts" who lived with so many of the region's families. In Massachusetts the 1810 male population under the age of sixteen outnumbered females of the same age in the ratio of 104 to 100. Between the ages of sixteen and forty-five, however, the proportions were reversed. During the marrying season (ages sixteen through twenty-five) there were 103 women for every 100 men, but in the post twenty-six age of the spinster, women outnumbered men by a ratio of 107 to 100. And Massachusetts had 3,335 more women of that age than it had men. Theirs was the choice, at best, of boarding with parents, or a married sister, or entering a mill. Since the loss of males was a result of the westward movement, it would seem that, as far as New England's early textile industry is concerned, the famous "safety-valve" worked in reverse. The migration of men to the West created a surplus of female labor in the East.

Neither New York State nor Pennsylvania exhibited such an imbalance of the sexes, for both were receiving substantial immigration, and considerable westward movement still occurred within their boundaries. But within the cities of New York and Philadelphia free white women between the ages of sixteen and twenty-five sharply outnumbered the men of the same age. The New York ratio in 1820, for example, was 119 women to 100 men in that age bracket, while in Philadelphia women of this marriageable age outnumbered men 122 to 100. Similarly, the Boston ratio was 127 to 100, and that of Baltimore 108 to 100. Although the terrible toll of childbirth, among other hazards, more than corrected the balance of the sexes in all four cities after the age of twenty-six, each of the seaports was naturally provided with a sizeable force of women for whom there was no prospect of marriage and for whom entry into the labor market was a necessity.

Each of these groups of city workers of the pre-industrial epoch (journeymen mechanics, male laborers, and women) merits careful historical study. Little new work has been done in this area since David J. Saposs contributed his chapters to John R. Commons' *History of Labour in the United States* in 1917, and because of this deficiency the labor historian's view of this period has fallen seriously out of phase with that of the economic historian. For example, Saposs' contention that "the wages of the unskilled were going up while those of the skilled were kept down by the merchant-capitalist" in the century's first two decades finds no support in the wage data of this article or in recent economic studies.

The problem assumes considerable significance in the light of George Rogers Taylor's hypothesis that per capita income in America declined rather steadily between 1807 and the early 1830s. The impact of such a trend could logically have been different for mechanics, for factory operatives, for casual laborers, and for women sewing in their rented rooms. Only specific studies of particular groups of workers can yield conclusive data on the standard of living. Jackson Turner Main and James Henretta have shown that enough evidence exists in tax rolls, judicial records, and the press of the eighteenth century to enable the historian to reconstruct patterns of property and income distribution quite clearly. Their work challenges other historians to trace the evolution of these patterns in early nineteenth-century city life and to reduce their reliance on impressionistic evidence.

Still greater is the need for research into the cultural and intellectual life of the working classes of this period. We need to know what the urban poor expected of life, how they reacted to the commercial ethos of their cities, and how they conceived their relationship to the governing merchant elites. Were they, as some historians have recently portrayed the poor of Naples or London, simultaneously devoted to the traditional social order, aware of their power as a mob, confident the city would care for them in times of want, and, profoundly hostile toward the emerging impersonal and amoral market economy? Was it such a mentality which made some 200 assembled New York sailors, idled by the embargo, respond obediently when Mayor Marinus Willet commanded them to disperse, with assurances that the embargo was "the *Captain's Orders,*" and that the city would "do everything possible for your relief"? Such questions cannot yet be answered because a fixation on the clash of "agrarian" and "industrial" values has distracted us from exploring pre-industrial urban values and customs.

Similarly American historians have yet to probe the culture of the American mechanic as, say, E. P. Thompson did for his British counterpart. Our concern has been either with the journeyman's economic circumstances (where there is still much to be learned) or with whether he voted for Andrew Jackson (and may we be spared that debate for a while). Because the mechanics were frequently organized and far more articulate than the urban poor, research into the mind of the journeyman should prove relatively easy. The ideas suggested in this article need careful testing, to begin with, and beyond them lie several major issues for research. How open was economic mobility for the journeymen, and what changes did the post-Revolutionary generation experience in this regard? Why did this class provide most of the country's early nineteenth-century adherents to deism, and just how widespread and significant was infidelity among them? What new circumstances made craftsmen in every major city between 1827 and 1837 expand the horizons of their concern beyond the limits of their own trades, create city Trades' Unions as new institutions to fuse the efforts of the several crafts, undertake unprecedented united action with the unskilled laborers, giving rise to something worthy of the name labor movement?

These problems suggest that we have rushed ahead to evaluate labor's response to industrialism without first ascertaining labor's pre-industrial behavior and attitudes. In exploring the shock of change after the Civil War our attention has been directed half a century too late, and our concern with the fate of agrarian values has led us to ignore the impact of the spreading factory system on the cultural heritage of urban America's lower orders.

The Frontier and American Society

One of the most impressive attempts to explain the special qualities of America and Americans was the frontier thesis of Frederick Jackson Turner. Long before Turner, observers of the United States had assigned a distinctive place to the West in the molding of American thought and institutions. But the brilliant analysis by Turner of that role in his 1893 paper "On the Significance of the Frontier in American History" raised the observations of commentators to the level of a powerful theory and profoundly influenced the way both historians and laymen thought about the American past.

Turner's thesis was that "the existence of an area of free land, its continuous recession, and the advance of American settlement westward, explain American development." This central fact explained American politics, for democracy, in its various manifestations, came from the frontier. It explained American affluence and social stability, for the West was a land of economic opportunity and a "safety valve" for the deprived and the unsuccessful. It explained American individualism, for in the new western communities each man had only himself to rely on for safety and survival. All these traits of character and mind and these institutional distinctions were what made America exceptional and what, Turner might well have said, made America better.

Turner's seminal essay, and its elaboration in a dozen or so articles and a number of books, swept away the earlier emphasis by historians on the continuities between America and the European, particularly the Anglo-Saxon, heritage. Even during his lifetime, Turner was not unchallenged, but at least half of the historians of the country, for the first thirty years of this century, might be labeled "Turner's disciples." During these years the history of the West and the frontier flourished, and analyses of American politics emphasizing East–West conflict became standard elements in textbooks. In the 1930s, Turner went into eclipse. The scholars' disenchantment with capitalism and individualism during the depression made them skeptical of Turner's belief in American uniqueness. They subjected his insights to close scrutiny and often found them seriously wanting. Democracy did not seem to flow from the West; universal manhood suffrage came earlier in the East. The safety valve did not operate; farm-making costs were too high for the unemployed labor of the cities to take advantage of unoccupied land. Individualism was not particularly western; the West often demanded cooperation and conformity for survival.

One of Turner's most persistent and intelligent followers is Ray Allen Billington of the Huntington Library in San Marino, California. Billington is by no means an uncritical disciple. He finds much in Turner's concept of frontier individualism that is exaggerated and simplistic. On the other hand, he sees more merit in the picture of the West as egalitarian and mobile, a region where men did not defer to rank and wealth, and where both were within grasp of the able and the lucky. In the end, he concludes, America has still not entirely lost some of the exceptional qualities it inherited from its frontier past.

FOR FURTHER READING:

BILLINGTON, RAY ALLEN. *America's Frontier Heritage.* New York: Holt, Rinehart & Winston, 1967.*
SMITH, HENRY NASH. *Virgin Land: The American West as Symbol and Myth.* New York: Random House, Vintage Books, 1957.*
TURNER, FREDERICK JACKSON. *On the Significance of the Frontier in American History.* New York: Frederick Ungar Publishing Co., 1963.*

Asterisk denotes paperback edition.

Frontier Democracy: Social Aspects

RAY ALLEN BILLINGTON

To understand the uniqueness of *American* democracy we must consider not only the form of government and the extent of popular participation, but the way in which the people of the United States view government and society as a whole. Do they regard the state as the master or servant of its citizens? Do they consider their fellow men as equals, or as inferiors and superiors? In seeking answers to these questions, our concern is not with what *is,* but with what is *thought* to be. If the image of the social order common among Americans differs from that usual among Europeans, and if the differences can be explained by the pioneering experience, we can conclude that the frontier has altered the national character as well as institutions.

In this quest, two concepts are especially important: that of "individualism" and that of "equality." Visitors from abroad feel that the people of the United States have endowed these words with distinctive meanings. In no other nation is the equality of all men so loudly proclaimed; in no other country is the right of individual self-assertion (within certain areas) so stoutly defended. Travelers have also noted the relationship between the two concepts. Because all men are judged to be equal, all are assured the same freedom of individual expression. "They are apt to imagine," wrote Alexis de Tocqueville in the early nineteenth century, "that their whole destiny is in their own hands." Tocqueville believed that this attitude was dangerous, threatening as it did the atomization of society.

His fears were groundless, for even as he wrote conformity was displacing individualism as a national cult, save in one important aspect. To Ralph Waldo Emerson and Henry David Thoreau society may have been the sum of atomized individuals, but to the generations that followed the emergence of an industrial-urban complex that made social interdependence essential to survival was one of the stark realities of life. In this integrated society, the fact of individualism, if not the *theory* of individualism, was gradually altered. In theory individualism meant the right of every person to make his own decisions and choices without regard to their effect on the

Source: Ray Allen Billington, *America's Frontier Heritage* (New York: Holt, Rinehart & Winston, 1966), chap. 7, "Frontier Democracy: Social Aspects," pp. 139–157.

social group. In practice, this was acceptable only in the sphere of economic activity. In that realm, a sink-or-swim philosophy gained acceptance and still prevails. If a man makes a wrong decision, and a business fails or a job is lost, no one is to blame but the person himself. If his decision is correct and he does well, we believe that he should be rewarded by advancement to positions of ever higher prestige. The direction in which he moves is his responsibility alone; the successful person enjoys a sense of his own greatness quite unrelated to those around him. Individualism in the economic world seems fair to Americans as long as equal and plentiful opportunity exists for all, and who can doubt its existence in a land of abundance? Social-security systems, unemployment benefits, Medicare, and a host of other security measures today challenge the fact of economic individualism, but the theory is still vigorously defended.

Individualism in its distinctly American usage does not apply to the noneconomic world. It grants no license for freedom of personal expression; no respectable citizen would dream of exhibiting a unique personality in the clothes that he wears, the manners he adopts, or the behavior that he exhibits in public. The Frenchman instinctively distrusts the outsider and shuns cooperation; the American instinctively follows the herd. "Americans," observed Peter Ustinov, "are always attempting to run away from conformity, but unfortunately they always start running in the same direction." Twentieth-century travelers have pointed out the monotonous uniformity of the streets, the towns, the cities, of the United States. "Not a single American," wrote one, "can distinguish Main Street in one town from Main Street in one of hundreds of others." Let a Hollywood actress or a spotlighted pop singer adopt a new hair style and women rush to their hairdressers to imitate her. Let a public figure appear in a novel hat, or trousers, or haircut, and men fall into line. Even political behavior is regimented, as Americans dutifully cast their ballots for Democratic or Republican candidates rather than for the dozens of parties that range across the political spectrum in Europe. And woe unto the American who defends a belief that is currently unpopular, either of the extreme left or the extreme right.

The oft-defended individualism of the United States is no guarantee of the individual's freedom of expression, but is manifested in two ways, each related to the other. One is a relative lack of respect for the law; the typical American is more inclined to flaunt regulations, or to whittle a few illegal dollars from his income tax, than his British cousins. The other is a resentment of governmental meddling in private affairs. Some Americans preached individual freedom when the Eighteenth Amendment told them what not to drink, and the bootleggers' paradise of the 1920s was the result. Some raised an umbrella of "rugged American individualism" over their heads when the regulatory measures of Progressivism or the New Deal threatened to interfere with their free use of property. Some, living in the Southern states, hoisted the banner of states' rights when federal agencies told them to integrate their schools, but what they really defended was the right of every individual to like or dislike persons of his own choice, whatever the effect on society. All were proclaiming their defiance of the government, and demanding that it cease telling them how to live or manage their affairs. The American is willing to conform if he personally decides to conform, as he does in adopting the style of his clothes or the brand of popular music that he will enjoy. But the American is not willing to allow his elected representatives to decide that conformity is for him. This is the essential difference between the individualism of the United States and that of Europe.

As long as we dwell in the realm of theory, nothing could be easier than to link this distinctly American faith with the frontier experience. The modern American believes that each person shall be allowed to rise or fall in the workaday world as his own grit and ability decrees; he also clings to the belief that the government should not interfere. Such a system could operate only in a land of equal opportunity, where the dispossessed could begin life anew without too much difficulty, where new jobs were being created to absorb an expanding population, and where resources were so abundant that all could share in their wealth without governmental intervention in the role of umpire. Only in frontier America did this combination of beatitudes exist. Hence American individualism is the product of the frontiering experience. So men reasoned in the nineteenth century, and so many believe today.

This myth has been fastened on the public mind by the plausibility of logic. Nothing is more obvious than that the pioneer would resent social controls, or that he would be able to escape dependence on society. He had, after all, fled his fellows to battle the wilderness alone. In his new home the solitude in which he lived, the vastness of the world about him, and the assurance that he acquired as he combatted nature, contributed to a spirit of self-reliance that was universal among pioneers. This was accentuated by the richness of the land, and the equally shared opportunity to exploit those riches. Where all were potential millionaires, property assumed a new importance, even to the propertyless. Men on the frontier, Americans of the nineteenth century believed, were so confident of affluence that they needed no help from society and wanted no meddling by society. "Here," wrote a visitor to the Colorado mines, "a man looks upon the wealth of others as held in trust for himself, and will suffer no diminution of its sanctity." This attitude fostered rugged American individualism in its truly American sense.

Just as persuasive was the frequent testimony of travelers and Westerners that the West actually was a land of unbridled liberty where men behaved according to the dictates of their consciences, and devil take their neighbors. "Liberty here," wrote an Englishman from the Kentucky backwoods, "means to do each as he pleases, to care for nothing and nobody." This was natural in the borderlands, where men were free to shape the course of their lives without nearby neighbors inflicting their wills or watchful officials meddling in their affairs. There every man was king, and kings could rule themselves. When passengers on a keelboat tried to stop a frontiersman from singing on the Sabbath they were heatedly informed that they were in a "land of liberty" and had no right to interfere. A recruit among the fur trappers of the Rocky Mountain country was told by an old-timer that he had only to mind his own affairs to get along. "If you see a man's mule running off," the newcomer was advised, "don't stop it — let it go to the devil; it isn't yourn. If his possibles sack falls off, don't tell him of it; He'll find it out." A pioneer who told a visitor that he was moving from Arkansas to Texas because he "had heern there was no sich thing as a government there, and not one varmint of a lawyer in the *hull* place" only personified what the United States believed to be the spirit of the whole frontier.

This nineteenth-century image of the West perpetuated the belief that the pioneer was opposed to all governmental regulation of economic activity. If steamboats had accidents that killed hundreds of persons yearly, nothing should be done, for steamboats were the lifeblood of the Mississippi Valley, and a few lives were a cheap price to pay for the economic activity that they fostered. If speculators absorbed the best lands, or miners appropriated mineral wealth, or lumbermen stripped away the forests, or "Sooners" illegally usurped the prime acreage in land openings, the social losses were insignificant compared to the benefits that accrued when the free-enterprise spirit was unleashed amidst the West's resources. These were the tales spread across the nation by the frontiersmen and their visitors, until they became a part of the nation's folklore. The frontier was a land of individualism, and American individualism was its natural offspring. This was a myth accepted throughout the nineteenth century and beyond.

Actually, the legend of frontier individualism rested on what people thought should be true, rather than what was true. The West was in truth an area where cooperation was just as essential as in the more thickly settled East. The danger of Indian attack, the joint efforts needed to clear the forests or break the prairie sod, the community of labor required for the variety of enterprises necessary in establishing a settlement, all decreed that new communities be occupied by groups, and never by solitary individuals. "In a young country," noted a visiting Englishman, "they must assist each other, if they wish to be assisted themselves — and there always will be a mutual dependence." Alexis de Tocqueville expressed nothing less than the truth when he observed that "In no country in the world has the principle of association been more successfully used, or applied to a greater multitude of objects, than in America."

This "principle of association" was more essential on the frontier than in the East. Cooperative enterprise is instinctive among all groups, even of the most primitive tribesmen, for habits of mutual dependence developed by family life during infancy are extended as people realize that the benefits of joint activity compensate for the work involved. Cooperation is normal within every in-group, but accentuates when the in-group is in conflict with an out-group and group solidarity is strengthened. This was the situation in frontier communities, where conflicts with Indians, with raw nature, and with dominating Easterners heightened the spirit of interdependence. In the West social cohesiveness, standardized behavior, and restrictive limitations on individual freedom were more acceptable than in the East.

So closely knit were pioneer groups that privacy of person or mind was virtually unattainable. Where neighbors were relatively few and newcomers a treasured rarity, every stranger was of rapt interest and a heaven sent opportunity to relieve the tedium of existence. "You are in a house of glass," complained one annoyed traveler as he endured the probing of the frontiersmen; another added that "privacy, either in eating, sleeping, conversation, or government, seems quite unknown, and unknowable." So prevailing was the community spirit that no one dared express individuality; people lived and dressed and thought exactly alike. "Whoever ventures to differ essentially from the mass," recorded a newcomer to the Michigan frontier, "is sure to become the object of unkind feeling, even without supposing any bitter personal animosity." And Charles Dickens, vitriolic as usual in his impressions of the Mississippi Valley pioneers, complained of "such a deadly, leaden people; such systematic plodding weary insupportable heaviness." These may have been exaggerations, but they were accurate in the over-all estimate of the spirit of cohesiveness existing in pioneer communities. Amidst the anonymity of a city, a person might dare to be different; amidst the intimacy of the frontier, he did not.

Much of this spirit was rooted in the stark realities of backwoods life, for cooperation was as essential to survival as a "Kentucky" rifle or a Colt revolver. Men went west in groups to minimize the Indian danger and the hardships of travel. When the journey was long and difficult, they organized a walking republic, complete with administrative and judicial officials to whom they delegated needed authority. As soon as they reached their destination they provided for the common defense by building a blockhouse or forming a militia company. These log or adobe forts became the centers of neighborhood life, especially in time of danger when the whole community "forted up" and shared guard duty until the threat passed. "Their common security," a pioneer told a traveler, "locked them in amity." Years after the times of danger a frontiersman remembered the pleasure they had provided because "we were so kind and friendly to one another." Commonly shared perils were a cohesive force among the homesteaders of the Great Plains no less than among earlier pioneers, for there grass fires, grasshopper invasions, and cattle wars banded the people together to combat mutual enemies. Any who refused to share were banished as traitors to society; there was no place for the uncooperative eccentric in a land where joint effort was the key to survival.

Cooperation was just as essential in times of peace as in times of war. Needed goods were imported by mutually owned caravans. Neighbors assisted in the "cabin raisings" and "barn raisings" that provided every newcomer with a home, and in the "logrollings" that helped him clear his fields. They joined in "corn huskings" and "quilting bees" and "fulling parties" where newly woven cloth was prepared for the housewife's needle. Scarce an activity in a frontier community that did not lend itself to neighborhood enterprise; records of pioneer settlements bristle with accounts of spinning parties, goose pickings, apple parings, rag cuttings, carpet tackings, wool pickings, and a dozen more. "A life in the woods," observed a visitor from Britain, "teaches many lessons, and this among the rest, that you must both give assistance to your neighbor, and receive it in return, without either grudging or pouting." Little wonder that students of the frontier refer to the "principle of mutuality" when speaking of life in the West.

The community benefited no less than individuals from mutual enterprise, because the necessity of common labor for society's good was cheerfully accepted as a part of pioneer life. Was a new church required, or a new school to be built, all hands turned out with axes and adzes to buckle to the task. "The neighbors divided themselves into choppers, hewers, carpenters, and masons," recalled an Indiana settler. "Those who found it impossible to report for duty might pay an equivalent in nails, boards, or other materials." When a road was to be constructed, or a bridge thrown across a stream, all were expected to help, since on the frontier division of labor was little known. Communities organized "Claim Clubs" to guard land from or for speculators, and in the Great Plains country recruited members to drive cattle from planted fields. Pioneer farmers, wherever they lived, were not so wedded to individualism that they would scorn help when help was needed.

Even these crown princes of individualism, the ranchers and miners, depended far more on joint effort than on self-prowess. Cattlemen on the Great Plains lost no time in forming associations that not only supervised the semiannual roundups, but that seriously restricted private enterprise by regulating pasturage on the open range. Community activity also quickened in time of emergency, furnishing men and horses to hunt down herds scattered by fire or drought. Cowboys as well as ranchers recognized the value of group activity; in 1883 some 325 in Texas organized to demand a $20 monthly raise, which they won after striking five ranches at roundup time. So did miners. The lone prospector is a figure from fiction rather than reality, for no single man could live long in the rugged mountain country of the early West. Most prospecting was done in groups of five to twenty men, usually well-mounted and provisioned, and led by a miner sufficiently versed in geology that no time was wasted on unlikely spots. Mining was never an individual enterprise, but was conducted by partners or teams who divided the labor and shared the profits. The rugged individualist, defending his claim with a six-shooter, had no place in the real Far West. "The Americans," wrote a Scottish visitor to the California gold fields, "have a very great advantage, for . . . they are certainly of all people in the world the most prompt to organize and combine to carry out a common object."

On all frontiers community effort found particular expression in law enforcement. Renegades from society posed a problem in new settlements, attracted as they were by the hope of quick wealth and the absence of machinery to administer justice, but when they became sufficiently numerous to threaten life and property, the sober citizens banded together to meet the situation head on. Known variously as Regulators or the Regulation in the forested regions, as Anti-Horse-Thief Associations on the Great Plains, and as Vigilantes in the Far West, they served as law officers, courts, and executioners, rounding up the worst offenders, subjecting them to a summary trial, and either hanging them to the nearest tree or banishing them from the community. So effective were they that in one California mining district 500 miles long, occupied by a hundred thousand turbulent men who had riches to tempt the outlaw but neither government nor locks as protection, "there was," noted a visitor in 1850, "as much security of life and property as in any part of the Union." This security was won at a grim price; vigilantes sometimes degenerated into lynching mobs that took the life of many an innocent man. Yet the readiness of frontiersmen to cooperate for protection, and their instinctive skill in organizing, underlines the myth of frontier individualism.

This was made even more obvious by the willingness of pioneers to accept governmental regulations that might have aroused protests in eastern cities. Blue laws were commonplace in many areas, restricting private behavior in a manner reminiscent of seventeenth-century Boston. Ohio in 1816 levied heavy fines for swearing by God, Christ, or the Holy Ghost; shooting bullets across a stream; and running horses in towns. Still heavier penalties awaited anyone guilty of arranging a puppet show, wire dancing, or tumbling. Illinois decreed a fine of $25 for any person selling cards, dice, or billiard balls. Towns studded their statute books with laws forbidding the playing of ninepins, serenading, or making a noise with "drums, fifes, horns, pans, kettles or with anything whatsoever." Frontiersmen accepted infringements on individual freedom needed to protect the community against gambling, time-wasting entertainment, or sleep-disturbing noise, just as had the Puritans.

Less well known was the willingness of the pioneers to adopt laws governing economic behavior, at least in the infant urban communities of the Midwest. Citizens were required to sweep the streets before their doors, and to conform to certain standards in advertising their products. Trade was regulated more exactly than in the East, because firm measures were necessary in near-monopoly situations to protect the uncertain food supply, prevent speculative pricing in times of shortage, and force licensed merchants to compete honestly with each other. Chicago confined the sale of meats and vegetables to certain times and places where they could be inspected to protect the public health. Other pioneer cities fixed the price of bread, regulated fees of hackmen and carters, and regularly checked the accuracy of weights and measures. Not even private property was too sanctified to escape controls designed for the public good.

Regulation by state and national agencies was equally acceptable to the pioneer — when he judged the laws to be in his own interest. Texas in 1883 set up machinery to control railroad rates and force roads to haul cars of their competitors, although such a measure invaded property rights that had been held sacred. Texan cattlemen welcomed laws governing the conduct of drovers on the "long drives" to the Kansas railroads, even though their own liberties were threatened. A few years later the embattled farmers of the Great Plains raised the banner of Populism to demand governmental regulation of the railroads, a "socialistic" parcel post service, and the curbing of monopolies. To the frontier-oriented Westerner, the government could be a valuable ally as readily as a dangerous enemy, and should be viewed in either light as the immediate situation dictated.

On the basis of this analysis of Western opinion, we can now seek answers to two questions: Was frontier individualism a myth, and if not, how did it differ from traditional individualism? One conclusion is obvious: in the social realm the pioneer was a complete traditionalist, leaning on the community no less than his city cousins. Cooperation with his neighbors was commonplace for defense, the accomplishment of essential pioneering tasks, law enforcement, and a host of other necessities. In the economic realm the frontiersman's attitudes were less sharply defined. Consistency was not one of his sins, he favored regulation that seemed beneficial to his interests, and opposed regulation that threatened immediate or potential profits. His views were, in other words, comparable to those of Eastern business leaders who demanded from the government protective tariffs, railroad land grants, and federal subsidies, while mouthing the virtues of "rugged individualism."

Yet in one sense, the frontiersman moved somewhat beyond his counterparts in the East. He was, to a unique degree, living in a land where everyone was a real or potential capitalist. Nowhere could a stake in society be more easily obtained, and nowhere was the belief that this was possible more strongly entrenched. Moreover the frontier was developed largely by capital imported from the seaboard or from Europe. The fur trade, mining, and cattle raising prospered only because a flow of money from the East and abroad made prosperity possible. "The real peculiarity of our present Pacific civilization," wrote the editor of the *Overland Monthly* in 1883, "is that it is, perhaps, the most completely realized embodiment of the purely commercial civilization on the face of the earth." Dependent as they were on this flow of capital, and certain as they were that the humblest tenant farmers would someday enjoy wealth, Westerners were even more acutely conscious of the value of private property than Easterners, and more grimly determined to defend their right to use property as they wished. They would favor regulatory measures needed to attract capital or assure a healthy return on investments, but they would oppose laws that threatened profits even more vigorously than Easterners.

The frontiersmen, then, were opportunists rather than consistent theorists, but to an even greater degree than the capitalists of the seaboard. They had to be. Gambling against an unpredictable nature, they were willing to follow any path that promised success. If their ends could be achieved by individualistic effort, they preached individualism. If, more commonly, cooperative labor was necessary, or the use of governmental controls, they showed no reluctance in approving these devices. Their purpose was to make a profit, not prove a political theory, and their views swung with the circumstances. Yet the widespread property holdings in the West, and the belief that every man would achieve affluence, inclined the Westerner to insist on his right to profits somewhat more stridently than others. His voice spoke for individualism louder than that of his fellows, even though he was equally willing to find haven in cooperation when danger threatened or need decreed.

The rural Westerner's inclination toward individualism was strengthened by the fact that except in periods of danger or disaster he was somewhat less integrated into society than a city dweller, especially after the frontier on which he lived had passed its pioneer stage. The Easterner, living in a land where the economy was based on division of labor, was only a cog in a machine that must keep on operating if he were to survive. The Westerner, even though he leaned on his neighbors for defense and cabin raisings and husking parties, was relatively more self-sufficient. He harbored the belief that his self-sufficiency would increase, knowing that his own abilities would assure him a prosperous future as he exploited the natural resources about him. He might need government help to regulate rates of railroads that carried his grain to market or prices of manufacturers who sold him his implements, but he wanted no government interference with his freedom as he followed the road to riches.

To this extent, the frontiersman was an individualist, and his brand of individualism was remarkably like that which has persisted in the United States as a whole. The American follows the herd in his social habits, and he is eager to accept government aid that promises benefits to his business. But he is loudest in protest when regulatory measures threaten his profits or his economic freedom. Individualism, in the uniquely American sense, does seem to duplicate the individualism of the pioneer.

Basically, frontier individualism stemmed from the belief that all men were equal (excluding Negroes, Indians, Orientals, and other minority groups), and that all should have a chance to prove their personal capabilities without restraint from society. This seemed fair in a land of plenty, where superabundant opportunity allowed each to rise or fall to his proper level as long as governments did not meddle. Faith in the equality of men was the great common creed of the West. Only an understanding of the depth of this belief can reveal the true nature of social democracy on successive frontiers.

To European visitors, this was the most unique feature of Western life and thought: the attitude that set that region apart from Europe or the East. "There is nothing in America," wrote one, "that strikes a foreigner so much as the real republican equality existing in the Western States, which border on the wilderness." The whole attitude of the people was different; calmly confident of their own future, they looked on all men as their peers and acted accordingly. One Westerner who defined the frontier as a region where a poor man could enter a rich man's house without feeling uneasy or unequal was not far astray. Menial subservience was just as unpopular there as haughty superiority. Dame Shirley, writing from the California gold fields, felt the "I'm as good as you are" spirit all about her, and believed that only an American frontiersman could

> Enter a palace with his old felt hat on —
> To address the King with the title of Mister,
> And ask the price of the throne he sat on.

Everywhere men of all ranks exuded that easy air of confidence that went with complete self-assurance, meeting travelers on terms of equality that charmed those democratically inclined and shocked those of opposite prejudice. "The wealthy man assumes nothing to himself on account of his wealth," marveled one, "and the poor man feels no debasement on account of his poverty, and every man stands on his own individual merits." The spirit of Western democracy was captured by a cow-boy addressing a disagreeable scion of British nobility: "You may be a son of a lord back in England, but that ain't what you are out here."

In the give and take of daily life, Western egalitarianism was expressed in the general refusal to recognize the class lines that were forming in every community. Some of the self-proclaimed "better sort" might hold themselves aloof and put on aristo-cratic airs, but they were atypical of the great mass of the people. The majority, in evaluating those about them, applied value judgments that differed from those in communities where tradition played a stronger role. Men were weighed on their present and future contributions to society, with total disregard for their back-ground. Each played a role in the developing social order, and as long as he played it well he was respected. "To be useful is here the ruling principle," wrote a Swedish visitor to the West; "it is immaterial what one does so long as he is respected and does his work efficiently." Drones and aristocratic idlers were not bearing their fair share and were outcasts; men of menial rank were contributing to the community welfare and were respected. "There is in the West," noted an unusually acute ob-server during the 1830s, "a real equality, not merely an equality to talk about, an equality on paper; everybody that has on a decent coat is a gentleman."

Contemporaries speculated often on the reasons for frontier social democracy. Most agreed that the burgeoning Western economy was basically responsible, offer-ing as it did a chance for the lowliest to acquire prestige through accumulated wealth. All had an equal chance to improve themselves, and so all should be treated as equals; conversely, the servant who believed that he would someday be a million-aire saw no reason to be servile to his temporary betters. This was common sense, since every new community boasted dozens of living examples of rags-to-riches suc-cess: the tenant farmer who was now a county judge, the mechanic newly elected to the legislature, the farmer grown rich by the sale of lands. As a British traveler saw, "the means of subsistence being so easy in the country, and their dependence on each other consequently so trifling, that spirit of servility to those about them so prevalent in European manners, is wholly unknown to them." Why be servile when the man above today might be the man below tomorrow? Why cling to traditional views of rank when the heir apparent to a British earldom could be seen mowing hay, assisted by two sons of a viscount, while nearby the brother of an earl was feed-ing grain into a threshing machine? Clearly standards on the frontier were different, and equality more nearly a fact of life.

The common level of wealth encouraged this spirit, for while differences did exist, the gulf between rich and poor was relatively less in frontier regions than in older societies. Poverty was rare in pioneer communities that had graduated from the backwoods stage; one governor complained that the number of dependent paupers in his state was "scarcely sufficient to give exercise to the virtue of charity in individ-uals." Wealth might and did exist on rural frontiers, but its presence was less obvi-ous than in the East, for money would buy little but land and land was available to all. Ostentatious spending existed but was uncommon, partly because luxuries and leisure were largely unavailable, partly because it would breed hostility in neighbors who resented display. "Their wealth," it was observed, "does very little in the way of purchasing even the outward signs of respect; and as to *adulation*, it is not to be purchased with love or money." This leveling process underlined the sense of equality that was so typical of the frontier.

It was further emphasized by the fact that on the newer frontiers rich and poor lived, dressed, and acted much more alike than in the East. Most owned their own houses, though some might be of logs and some of bricks. Most dressed in homespun clothes and shunned the powdered wigs and knee breeches that were the badge of the gentry in the early nineteenth century; travelers frequently complained that it was impossible to distinguish the well-born from the lowly by the garments they wore. Most bore themselves proudly, scorning the humble mien that marked the lower classes in Europe. "The clumsy gait and bent body of our peasant is hardly ever seen here," wrote an Englishman from Kentucky in 1819; "every one walks erect and easy." When people looked and acted alike, as they did along the frontiers, treating them alike came naturally.

No less important in fanning the spirit of egalitarianism was the newness of the West, and the lack of traditional aristocratic standards there. No entrenched gentry governed social intercourse, setting the practices of those below them and closing their ranks against newcomers. Those who rose in station did not have to surmount the barrier of learning new customs as do those achieving higher status today, for conventions, deferences, and distinctions were rare among the "tree-destroying sovereigns" of the West. A man's ancestry and prior history were less important than the contribution that he could make to a new society badly in need of manpower. One Westerner who remarked: "It's what's above ground, not what's under, that we think on," and another who added: "Not 'What has he done in the East?' but 'What does he intend to do in Kansas and for Kansas?' " summed up the reasons for much of the social democracy that thrived along the frontiers.

This combination of causal forces — economic equality, commonly shared living standards, and the absence of traditional aristocratic values — enshrined belief in equality as the common faith of Western society. Class distinctions did exist, of course; innate differences in talent, ambition, and skill divided the various strata at an early stage in the evolution of every Western community. But relatively, these distinctions played a lesser role in the West than in the East. Instead belief in equality compelled frontiersmen to uplift the lowly and degrade the superior as they sought a common democratic level.

Elevation of the lowly was most commonly expressed by refusal to use terms designating class distinctions. Every man on the frontier, whatever his status in life, was a "gentleman," and every woman a "lady." Travelers from older societies were frequently amused to find the ragged wagoner or the ill-kempt seller of old bones addressed in this fashion; one who asked a tavern keeper in an infant settlement in New York to find his coachman was delighted when that worthy called out: "Where is the gentleman that brought this man here?" "Ladies" were as carelessly designated; one traveling in the West might hear, as did Mrs. Trollope, references to "the lady over the way that takes in washing," or "that there lady, out by the Gulley, what is making dip-candles." If titles could serve as social escalators, no one on the frontiers need stay long in menial ranks.

The leveling spirit of Western democracy sought not only to elevate the lowly but also to dethrone the elite. Any attempt at "putting on airs," was certain to be met with rude reminders of the equality of all men. New settlers were warned by guidebooks to mingle freely and familiarly with neighbors, and above all to pretend no superiority, if they wished to be accepted. They were told that nothing ruined a man's chances on the frontier so fatally as a suspicion of pride, which, once established, would ruin his reputation. "The cry of 'Mad Dog,'" wrote a Michigan pioneer, "is not more surely destructive. Travelers were also instructed to dress in simple fashion, and to avoid display in their clothes or their speech; those garbed as mechanics risked insults far less than those dressed as gentlemen. Those who failed to heed these warnings might be greeted with such remarks as: "Hold on, tha'r, stranger! When ye go through this yer town, go slow, so folks kin take you in," or in dry tones: "Mister, how much do you ask for it?" "For what, sir?" "Well, for the town; you look as though you owned it." One English newcomer who asked to be addressed as "Esquire" found that within a few days not only his host but the hired hands were calling him "Charlie"; another had the brass buttons unceremoniously ripped from his coat by a frontiersman who objected to such display. Texas rangers gambled or gave away the fancy uniforms issued to them, and stole the gold-braided suits of officers so that these aristocratic evidences of rank would not be seen. "Superiority," observed an English visitor, "is yielded to men of acknowledged talent alone."

Outward signs of social snobbery might arouse resentment in the West, but so did any conduct that seemed to suggest superiority. Families with sizable incomes found themselves better accepted if they lived and dressed as simply as their poorest neighbors; politicians soon realized that for success they must insist on being addressed as "Mister" or "Governor," and not as "Excellency." Even such a born-to-the-purple native aristocrat as Theodore Roosevelt took pains to understate his wealth and ancestry when on his Dakota ranch. When Colonel Thomas Dabney appeared at a frontier cabin raising in the Southwest with twenty slaves to do his work he was ostracized by the community; when a traveler had the good sense to dispose of expensive luggage, he was at last accepted on friendly terms. Natives and visitors alike learned that in the West refusal to drink with a stranger was interpreted as a sign of social superiority; unless they could convince their would-be hosts that they had "sworn off," even redeye whisky was preferable to the trouble that followed if word spread that they were "too good" for the community.

So strong was the spirit of equality along the frontiers that any deviation was met with resentment that was sometimes carried to ludicrous ends. Frontier housewives found themselves in disfavor if they kept their homes neater or cleaner than those of their neighbors; one who had waited three years for her first caller was told: "I woulda come before but I heard you had Brussels carpet on the floor." Another who offered to lend teaspoons for a party was rudely informed that no such luxuries were wanted, for the guests would not be used to them. Even those with a few choice possessions apologized; carpets were excused as "*one* way to hide the dirt," a mahogany table as "dreadful plaguy to scour," and kitchen conveniences as "lumberin' up the house for nothin'." When an Englishman remonstrated about the lack of ceremony in Western life he was told: "Yes, that may be quite necessary in England, in order to overawe a parcel of ignorant creatures, who have no share in making the laws; but with us a man's a man, whether he have a silk gown on him or not." The spirit of Western social democracy could have found no more eloquent expression than that.

In practice this spirit found its most outspoken expression in the attitude of hired workers. A "servant" in the traditional sense was impossible to find in the West because any form of servility was demeaning and hence intolerable; some of the most wealthy hosts and hostesses interrupted their dinner parties to wait on table or busy themselves in the kitchen. When servants could be drafted from the ranks of newly arrived immigrants or the families of less well-to-do pioneers they refused to accept that designation, but insisted on being called "helps," or "hired hands," or "ladies." The term "waiter" was equally unpopular, and was likely to call forth a spirited rejoinder from the person so addressed. Still more insulting was the word "master." A misguided traveler asking "Is your master at home?" would probably be told "I have no master"; one in the Wyoming cattle country was heatedly informed that "the son of Baliel ain't been born yet." So deep was the resentment against any implication of servility that young men and women preferred to labor at poor pay under bad conditions rather than accept a post as servant.

Those who did so guarded their respectability by abolishing all traditional symbols of servitude. Livery was never used; bells to summon servants in Western inns were unknown because the "helpers" refused to respond. All insisted on being treated as equals, dining with the family, meeting guests, and joining in all social functions under threat of immediate departure. One who had been told she must eat in the kitchen turned up her lip, announced "I guess that's cause you don't think I'm good enough to eat with you," and flounced from the house. Nor was this rebellious spirit peculiar to household help. The oft-heard remark: "If a man is good enough to work for me, he is good enough to eat with me" was literally applied. A family who had hired several carpenters to build a barn made the mistake of an early breakfast without them one day; the next day they left. A honeymooning couple were abandoned by their hired driver when they tried to eat alone just once. In public houses or conveyances the story was the same; travel accounts abound with tales of stewards who joined the card game after serving drinks, of waitresses who leaned over chairs to join in the conversation or borrow a guest's fan, of messengers who seated themselves and demanded a drink while serving their messages, of waiters in inns who joined their patrons when their tasks were done. In the West men felt equal, and acted the part.

Menial tasks were as resented by servants as were menial titles. Travelers were often forced to clean their own boots in frontier inns, or to rub down their own horses while "helpers" looked on disdainfully. One who asked to be awakened in the morning was answered "call yourself and be damned." On another occasion a titled Englishman in the Wyoming wilds was told to take a swim instead of a bath when he asked his hired helper to fill a tub; when he refused the angry helper shot the tub full of holes, shouting: "You ain't quite the top-shelfer you think you is, you ain't even got a shower-bath for cooling your swelled head, but I'll make you a present of one, boss!" Nor did servants alone resent the suggestion of servility. A pioneer Michigan housewife who tired of seeing a guest attack the roast with his own knife and offered to carve was rudely informed: "I'll help myself, I thankye. I never want no waitin' on."

Travelers who were shocked by these evidences of social democracy in the West were equally appalled by the democratic spirit which prevailed in frontier inns. There no "First Class" or "Second Class" accommodations separated patrons; tradesmen, slave dealers, farmers, congressmen, generals, fur trappers, and roustabouts ate side by side at the long tables, and all were treated the same. Sleeping accommodations were allotted on a first-come-first-serve basis, with governors and herdsmen, senators and farmers, rich and poor, clean and unclean, all crowded three or four to a bed. "It has been my lot," recorded an experienced traveler, "to sleep with a diversity of personages; I do believe from the driver of the stage coach, to men of considerable name." Complaints against these arrangements were summarily rejected by pioneer landlords; one visitor from overseas who objected to using a dirt-encrusted washbowl with a dozen other guests was told that "one rain bathes the just and the unjust, why not one wash-bowl"; another's protest that the sheets were dirty was answered with: "since *Gentlemen* are all alike, people do not see why they should not sleep in the same sheets." The frontier inn was, as one traveler put it, "a most almighty beautiful democratic amalgam."

The social democracy and frontier-type individualism that characterized America's growing period have not persisted unchanged into the twentieth century. Individualism has retreated before the advance of social cohesiveness essential in an urban-industrial society. The nation's folk hero may still be the rugged individualist, but the lone wolves of the past have found that they cannot fight the pack and that in cut-throat competition all throats are cut. At least since the 1890s the economic community had grudgingly accepted the regulation that the pioneer resisted save when it was to his advantage, and today cooperation and reliance on government are almost as commonplace in the United States as in the older countries of Europe. Yet American individualism differs from that of France or England in its continued insistence on a degree of economic freedom that has long since vanished in those countries, and in a glorification of the individual's ability to care for himself despite daily proof that joint effort alone will succeed in a society increasingly enmeshed.

Just as vestiges of frontier individualism remain to distinguish the social attitudes of modern America from those of modern Europe, so do remnants of pioneer democracy. The United States is no longer a country free of class distinctions and so wedded to egalitarianism that manifestations of wealth arouse public resentment. But its social democracy does differ from that of older nations, marked by its relative lack of class awareness, and by the brash assurance of the humble that they are as worthy of respect as the elite. The house painter who addresses a client by his first name, the elevator operator who enters into casual conversation with his passengers, the garage mechanic who condescendingly compares his expensive car with your aging model, could exist only in the United States. Their counterparts are unknown in England or on the Continent partly because America's frontiering experience bred into the people attitudes toward democracy that have persisted down to the present.

Women in Ante-Bellum America

American men have always been confused about women, and in the process have often made women confused about themselves. On the one hand women were thought of as vessels of sin, tempting men from the path of purity and continence. On the other hand, they were represented as temples of virtue and the repositories and protectors of all that was holy in the family. They were treated as if they were delicate and fragile, but they were also burdened with nursing, comforting, teaching, and drudging for their families. Men cherished them, but they also mistreated them, and underneath, often despised them.

Without a doubt, the net effect of all this was not happy for women. Much as slavery frustrated the creative potential of blacks, the prevailing attitudes and mores of ante-bellum America severely limited the self-realization of women. The female mind was considered frail, as was the female body, and the education thought proper for a girl excluded the sciences, the learned professions, and the practical world of affairs. Until Oberlin College admitted women in 1833, higher education was closed to them. The first women who attempted to prepare for the medical profession faced enormous difficulties in forcing their way into medical colleges. Women interested in politics or public issues were ridiculed and abused and held to be "unsexed." When the Grimké sisters, Lucretia Mott, Abbey Kelly, and other strong-willed, idealistic women, sought to lecture for the abolitionists, they caused such a furor that otherwise brave antislavery men endeavored to stop them.

More important to most women of the period were the legal disabilities under which they suffered. The common law made women virtually their husbands' or fathers' chattels. Their property and earnings belonged to their men, and they could be physically abused by their men without the law's intervention. The children of a married woman were her husband's, and in a divorce action, even though he might be the guilty party, the father could claim them along with whatever property his wife possessed. In the realm of civil rights, she was virtually nonexistent, forbidden either to vote or hold office.

And yet it might be suggested that her situation was not all bad. If she was restricted, she was also protected. Most women, in those days, were probably happy to be spared the rough-and-tumble of a man's world. If she happened to be middle class and urban, she could count on servants to ease her household burdens, leaving her free to devote herself to self-adornment, the polite arts, and the pleasures of social intercourse. At least for the prosperous then, the "Cult of True Womanhood," as Barbara Welter shows in the following essay, had its advantages. From our perspective it is hard to say whether they offset the drawbacks.

FOR FURTHER READING:

FLEXNER, ELEANOR. *Century of Struggle.* New York: Atheneum Publishers, 1968.*
O'NEILL, WILLIAM. *Everyone Was Brave: The Rise and Fall of Feminism in America.* Chicago: Quadrangle Books, 1969.*

SINCLAIR, ANDREW. *The Emancipation of the American Woman.* New York: Harper & Row, Publishers, Colophon Books, 1966.*
Asterisk denotes paperback edition.

The Cult of True Womanhood
1820–1860 BARBARA WELTER

The nineteenth-century American man was a busy builder of bridges and railroads, at work long hours in a materialistic society. The religious values of his forebears were neglected in practice if not in intent, and he occasionally felt some guilt that he had turned this new land, this temple of the chosen people, into one vast countinghouse. But he could salve his conscience by reflecting that he had left behind a hostage, not only to fortune, but to all the values which he held so dear and treated so lightly. Woman, in the cult of True Womanhood [1] presented by the women's magazines, gift annuals and religious literature of the nineteenth century, was the hostage in the home.[2] In a society where values changed frequently, where fortunes rose and fell with frightening rapidity, where social and economic mobility provided instability as well as hope, one thing at least remained the same — a true woman was a true woman, wherever she was found. If anyone, male or female, dared to tamper with the complex of virtues which made up True Womanhood, he was damned immediately as an enemy of God, of civilization and of the Republic. It was a fearful obligation, a solemn responsibility, which the nineteenth century American woman had — to uphold the pillars of the temple with her frail white hand.

The attributes of True Womanhood, by which a woman judged herself and was judged by her husband, her neighbors and society could be divided into four cardinal virtues — piety, purity, submissiveness and domesticity. Put them all together and they spelled mother, daughter, sister, wife — woman. Without them, no matter whether there was fame, achievement or wealth, all was ashes. With them she was promised happiness and power.

Religion or piety was the core of woman's virtue, the source of her strength. Young men looking for a mate were cautioned to search first for piety, for if that were there, all else would follow.[3] Religion belonged to woman by divine right, a gift of God and nature. This "peculiar susceptibility" to religion was given her for a reason: "the vestal flame of piety, lighted up by Heaven in the breast of woman" would throw its beams into the naughty world of men.[4] So far would its candle power reach that the "Universe might be Enlightened, Improved, and Harmonized by WOMAN!!"[5] She would be another, better Eve, working in cooperation with the Redeemer, bringing the world back "from its revolt and sin."[6] The world would be reclaimed for God through her suffering, for "God increased the cares and sorrows of woman, that she might be sooner constrained to accept the terms of salvation."[7] A popular poem by Mrs. Frances Osgood, "The Triumph of the Spiritual Over the Sensual" expressed just this sentiment, woman's purifying passionless love bringing an erring man back to Christ.[8]

Source: Barbara Welter, "The Cult of True Womanhood, 1820–1860," *American Quarterly,* vol. 18 (1966), pp. 151–174.

Dr. Charles Meigs, explaining to a graduating class of medical students why women were naturally religious, said that "hers is a pious mind. Her confiding nature leads her more readily than men to accept the proffered grace of the Gospel." [9] Caleb Atwater, Esq., writing in *The Ladies' Repository,* saw the hand of the Lord in female piety: "Religion is exactly what a woman needs, for it gives her that dignity that best suits her dependence." [10] And Mrs. John Sandford, who had no very high opinion of her sex, agreed thoroughly: "Religion is just what woman needs. Without it she is ever restless or unhappy. . . ." [11] Mrs. Sandford and the others did not speak only of that restlessness of the human heart, which St. Augustine notes, that can only find its peace in God. They spoke rather of religion as a kind of tranquilizer for the many undefined longings which swept even the most pious young girl, and about which it was better to pray than to think.

One reason religion was valued was that it did not take a woman away from her "proper sphere," her home. Unlike participation in other societies or movements, church work would not make her less domestic or submissive, less a True Woman. In religious vineyards, said the *Young Ladies' Literary and Missionary Report,* "you may labor without the apprehension of detracting from the charms of feminine delicacy." Mrs. S. L. Dagg, writing from her chapter of the Society in Tuscaloosa, Alabama, was equally reassuring: "As no sensible woman will suffer her intellectual pursuits to clash with her domestic duties" she should concentrate on religious work "which promotes these very duties." [12]

The women's seminaries aimed at aiding women to be religious, as well as accomplished. Mt. Holyoke's catalogue promised to make female education "a handmaid to the Gospel and an efficient auxiliary in the great task of renovating the world." [13] The Young Ladies' Seminary at Bordentown, New Jersey, declared its most important function to be "the forming of a sound and virtuous character." [14] In Keene, New Hampshire, the Seminary tried to instill a "consistent and useful character" in its students, to enable them in this life to be "a good friend, wife and mother" but more important, to qualify them for "the enjoyment of Celestial Happiness in the life to come." [15] And Joseph M' D. Mathews, Principal of Oakland Female Seminary in Hillsborough, Ohio, believed that "female education should be preeminently religious." [16]

If religion was so vital to a woman, irreligion was almost too awful to contemplate. Women were warned not to let their literary or intellectual pursuits take them away from God. Sarah Josepha Hale spoke darkly of those who, like Margaret Fuller, threw away the "One True Book" for others, open to error. Mrs. Hale used the unfortunate Miss Fuller as fateful proof that "the greater the intellectual force, the greater and more fatal the errors into which women fall who wander from the Rock of Salvation, Christ the Saviour. . . ." [17]

One gentleman, writing on "Female Irreligion" reminded his readers that "Man may make himself a brute, and does so very often, but can woman brutify herself to his level — the lowest level of human nature — without exerting "special wonder?" Fanny Wright, because she was godless "was no woman, mother though she be." A few years ago, he recalls, such women would have been whipped. In any case, "woman never looks lovelier than in her reverence for religion" and, conversely, "female irreligion is the most revolting feature in human character." [18]

Purity was as essential as piety to a young woman, its absence as unnatural and unfeminine. Without it she was, in fact, no woman at all, but a member of some lower order. A "fallen woman" was a "fallen angel," unworthy of the celestial company of her sex. To contemplate the loss of purity brought tears; to be guilty of such a crime, in the women's magazines at least brought madness or death. Even the language of the flowers had bitter words for it: a dried white rose symbolized "Death Preferable to Loss of Innocence." [19] The marriage night was the single great event of a woman's life, when she bestowed her greatest treasure upon her husband, and from that time on was completely dependent upon him, an empty vessel,[20] without legal or emotional existence of her own.[21]

Therefore all True Women were urged, in the strongest possible terms, to maintain their virtue, although men, being by nature more sensual than they, would try to assault it. Thomas Branagan admitted in *The Excellency of the Female Character Vindicated* that his sex would sin and sin again, they could not help it, but woman, stronger and purer, must not give in and let man "take liberties incompatible with her delicacy." "If you do," Branagan addressed his gentle reader, "you will be left in silent sadness to bewail your credulity, imbecility, duplicity, and premature prostitution." [22]

Mrs. Eliza Farrar, in *The Young Lady's Friend,* gave practical logistics to avoid trouble: "Sit not with another in a place that is too narrow; read not out of the same book; let not your eagerness to see anything induce you to place your head close to another person's." [23]

If such good advice was ignored the consequences were terrible and inexorable. In *Girlhood and Womanhood: Or Sketches of My Schoolmates,* by Mrs. A. J. Graves (a kind of mid-nineteenth-century *The Group*), the bad ends of a boarding school class of girls are scrupulously recorded. The worst end of all is reserved for "Amelia Dorrington: The Lost One." Amelia died in the almshouse "the wretched victim of depravity and intemperance" and all because her mother had let her be "high-spirited not prudent." These girlish high spirits had been misinterpreted by a young man, with disastrous results. Amelia's "thoughtless levity" was "followed by a total loss of virtuous principle" and Mrs. Graves editorializes that "the coldest reserve is more admirable in a woman a man wishes to make his wife, than the least approach to undue familiarity." [24]

A popular and often-reprinted story by Fanny Forester told the sad tale of "Lucy Dutton." Lucy "with the seal of innocence upon her heart, and a rose-leaf on her cheek" came out of her vine-covered cottage and ran into a city slicker. "And Lucy was beautiful and trusting, and thoughtless: and he was gay, selfish and profligate. Needs the story to be told? . . . Nay, censor, Lucy was a child — consider how young, how very untaught — oh! her innocence was no match for the sophistry of a gay, city youth! Spring came and shame was stamped upon the cottage at the foot of the hill." The baby died; Lucy went mad at the funeral and finally died herself. "Poor, poor Lucy Dutton! The grave is a blessed couch and pillow to the wretched. Rest thee there, poor Lucy!" [25] The frequency with which derangement follows loss of virtue suggests the exquisite sensibility of woman, and the possibility that, in the women's magazines at least, her intellect was geared to her hymen, not her brain.

If, however, a woman managed to withstand man's assaults on her virtue, she demonstrated her superiority and her power over him. Eliza Farnham, trying to prove this female superiority, concluded smugly that "the purity of women is the everlasting barrier against which the tides of man's sensual nature surge." [26]

A story in *The Lady's Amaranth* illustrates this dominance. It is set, improbably, in Sicily, where two lovers, Bianca and Tebaldo, have been separated because her family insisted she marry a rich old man. By some strange circumstance the two are in a shipwreck and cast on a desert island, the only survivors. Even here, however, the rigid standards of True Womanhood prevail. Tebaldo unfortunately forgets himself slightly, so that Bianca must warn him: "We may not indeed gratify our fondness by caresses, but it is still something to bestow our kindest language, and looks and prayers, and all lawful and honest attentions on each other." Something, perhaps, but not enough, and Bianca must further remonstrate: "It is true that another man is my husband, but you are my guardian angel." When even that does not work she says in a voice of sweet reason, passive and proper to the end, that she wishes he wouldn't but "still, if you insist, I will become what you wish; but I beseech you to consider, ere that decision, that debasement which I must suffer in your esteem." This appeal to his own double standards holds the beast in him at bay. They are rescued, discover that the old husband is dead, and after "mourning a decent season" Bianca finally gives in, legally.[27]

Men could be counted on to be grateful when women thus saved them from themselves. William Alcott, guiding young men in their relations with the opposite sex, told them that "Nothing is better calculated to preserve a young man from contamination of low pleasures and pursuits than frequent intercourse with the more refined and virtuous of the other sex." And he added, one assumes in equal innocence, that youths should "observe and learn to admire, that purity and ignorance of evil which is the characteristic of well-educated young ladies, and which, when we are near them, raises us above those sordid and sensual considerations which hold such sway over men in their intercourse with each other." [28]

The Rev. Jonathan F. Stearns was also impressed by female chastity in the face of male passion, and warned woman never to compromise the source of her power: "Let her lay aside delicacy, and her influence over our sex is gone." [29]

Women themselves accepted, with pride but suitable modesty, this priceless virtue. *The Ladies' Wreath,* in "Woman the Creature of God and the Manufacturerer of Society" saw purity as her greatest gift and chief means of discharging her duty to save the world: "Purity is the highest beauty — the true pole-star which is to guide humanity aright in its long, varied, and perilous voyage." [30]

Sometimes, however, a woman did not see the dangers to her treasure. In that case, they must be pointed out to her, usually by a male. In the nineteenth century any form of social change was tantamount to an attack on woman's virtue, if only it was correctly understood. For example, dress reform seemed innocuous enough and the bloomers worn by the lady of that name and her followers were certainly modest attire. Such was the reasoning only of the ignorant. In another issue of *The Ladies' Wreath* a young lady is represented in dialogue with her "Professor." The girl expresses admiration for the bloomer costume — it gives freedom of motion, is healthful and attractive. The "Professor" sets her straight. Trousers, he explains, are "only one of the many manifestations of that wild spirit of socialism and agrarian radicalism which is at present so rife in our land." The young lady recants immediately: "If this dress has any connexion with Fourierism or Socialism, or fanaticism in any shape whatever, I have no disposition to wear it at all . . . no true woman would so far compromise her delicacy as to espouse, however unwittingly, such a cause." [31]

America could boast that her daughters were particularly innocent. In a poem on "The American Girl" the author wrote proudly:

> Her eye of light is the diamond bright,
> Her innocence the pearl,

And these are ever the bridal gems
That are worn by the American girl.[32]

Lydia Maria Child, giving advice to mothers, aimed at preserving that spirit of innocence. She regretted that "want of confidence between mothers and daughters on
delicate subjects" and suggested a woman tell her daughter a few facts when she
reached the age of twelve to "set her mind at rest." Then Mrs. Child confidently
hoped that a young lady's "instinctive modesty" would "prevent her from dwelling
on the information until she was called upon to use it." [33] In the same vein, a book
of advice to the newly-married was titled *Whisper to a Bride*.[34] As far as intimate information was concerned, there was no need to whisper, since the book contained
none at all.

A masculine summary of this virtue was expressed in a poem "Female Charms":

> I would have her as pure as the snow on the mount —
>   As true as the smile that to infamy's given —
> As pure as the wave of the crystalline fount,
>   Yet as warm in the heart as the sunlight of heaven.
> With a mind cultivated, not boastingly wise,
>   I could gaze on such beauty, with exquisite bliss;
> With her heart on her lips and her soul in her eyes —
>   What more could I wish in dear woman than this.[35]

Man might, in fact, ask no more than this in woman, but she was beginning to ask
more of herself, and in the asking was threatening the third powerful and necessary
virtue, submission. Purity, considered as a moral imperative, set up a dilemma
which was hard to resolve. Woman must preserve her virtue until marriage and
marriage was necessary for her happiness. Yet marriage was, literally, an end to innocence. She was told not to question this dilemma, but simply to accept it.

Submission was perhaps the most feminine virtue expected of women. Men were
supposed to be religious, although they rarely had time for it, and supposed to be
pure, although it came awfully hard to them, but men were the movers, the doers,
the actors. Women were the passive, submissive responders. The order of dialogue
was, of course, fixed in Heaven. Man was "woman's superior by God's appointment, if not in intellectual dowry, at least by official decree." Therefore, as Charles
Elliott argued in *The Ladies' Repository,* she should submit to him "for the sake of
good order at least." [36] In *The Ladies Companion* a young wife was quoted approv-
ingly as saying that she did not think woman should "feel and act for herself" because "When, next to God, her husband is not the tribunal to which her heart and
intellect appeals — the golden bowl of affection is broken." [37] Women were warned
that if they tampered with this quality they tampered with the order of the Universe.

The Young Lady's Book summarized the necessity of the passive virtues in its readers' lives: "It is, however, certain, that in whatever situation of life a woman is
placed from her cradle to her grave, a spirit of obedience and submission, pliability
of temper, and humility of mind, are required from her." [38]

Woman understood her position if she was the right kind of woman, a true
woman. "She feels herself weak and timid. She needs a protector," declared George
Burnap, in his lectures on *The Sphere and Duties of Woman.* "She is in a measure dependent. She asks for wisdom, constancy, firmness, perseverance, and she is willing
to repay it all by the surrender of the full treasure of her affections. Woman despises

in man every thing like herself except a tender heart. It is enough that she is effeminate and weak; she does not want another like herself." [39] Or put even more strongly by Mrs. Sandford: "A really sensible woman feels her dependence. She does what she can, but she is conscious of inferiority, and therefore grateful for support." [40]

Mrs. Sigourney, however, assured young ladies that although they were separate, they were equal. This difference of the sexes did not imply inferiority, for it was part of that same order of Nature established by Him "who bids the oak brave the fury of the tempest, and the alpine flower lean its cheek on the bosom of eternal snows." [41] Dr. Meigs had a different analogy to make the same point, contrasting the anatomy of the Apollo of the Belvedere (illustrating the male principle) with the Venus de Medici (illustrating the female principle). "Woman," said the physician, with a kind of clinical gallantry, "has a head almost too small for intellect but just big enough for love." [42]

This love itself was to be passive and responsive. "Love, in the heart of a woman," wrote Mrs. Farrar, "should partake largely of the nature of gratitude. She should love, because she is already loved by one deserving her regard." [43]

Woman was to work in silence, unseen, like Wordsworth's Lucy. Yet, "working like nature, in secret" her love goes forth to the world "to regulate its pulsation, and send forth from its heart, in pure and temperate flow, the life-giving current." [44] She was to work only for pure affection, without thought of money or ambition. A poem, "Woman and Fame," by Felicia Hemans, widely quoted in many of the gift books, concludes with a spirited renunciation of the gift of fame:

> Away! to me, a woman, bring
> Sweet flowers from affection's spring.[45]

"True feminine genius," said Grace Greenwood (Sara Jane Clarke) "is ever timid, doubtful, and clingingly dependent; a perpetual childhood." And she advised literary ladies in an essay on "The Intellectual Woman" — "Don't trample on the flowers while longing for the stars." [46] A wife who submerged her own talents to work for her husband was extolled as an example of a true woman. In *Women of Worth: A Book for Girls,* Mrs. Ann Flaxman, an artist of promise herself, was praised because she "devoted herself to sustain her husband's genius and aid him in his arduous career." [47]

Caroline Gilman's advice to the bride aimed at establishing this proper order from the beginning of a marriage: "Oh, young and lovely bride, watch well the first moments when your will conflicts with his to whom God and society have given the control. Reverence his *wishes* even when you do not his *opinions.*" [48]

Mrs. Gilman's perfect wife in *Recollections of a Southern Matron* realizes that "the three golden threads with which domestic happiness is woven" are "to repress a harsh answer, to confess a fault, and to stop (right or wrong) in the midst of self-defense, in gentle submission." Woman could do this, hard though it was, because in her heart she knew she was right and so could afford to be forgiving, even a trifle condescending. "Men are not unreasonable," averred Mrs. Gilman. "Their difficulties lie in not understanding the moral and physical nature of our sex. They often wound through ignorance, and are suprised at having offended." Wives were advised to do their best to reform men, but if they couldn't, to give up gracefully. "If any habit of his annoyed me, I spoke of it once or twice, calmly, then bore it quietly." [49]

A wife should occupy herself "only with domestic affairs — wait till your husband confides to you those of a high importance — and do not give your advice until he asks for it," advised the *Lady's Token*. At all times she should behave in a manner becoming a woman, who had "no arms other than gentleness." Thus "if he is abusive, never retort." [50] *A Young Lady's Guide to the Harmonious Development of a Christian Character* suggested that females should "become as little children" and "avoid a controversial spirit." [51] *The Mother's Assistant and Young Lady's Friend* listed "Always Conciliate" as its first commandment in "Rules for Conjugal and Domestic Happiness." Small wonder that these same rules ended with the succinct maxim: "Do not expect too much." [52]

As mother, as well as wife, woman was required to submit to fortune. In *Letters to Mothers* Mrs. Sigourney sighed: "To bear the evils and sorrows which may be appointed us, with a patient mind, should be the continual effort of our sex. . . . It seems, indeed, to be expected of us; since the passive and enduring virtues are more immediately within our province." Of these trials "the hardest was to bear the loss of children with submission" but the indomitable Mrs. Sigourney found strength to murmur to the bereaved mother: "The Lord loveth a cheerful giver." [53] *The Ladies' Parlor Companion* agreed thoroughly in "A Submissive Mother," in which a mother who had already buried two children and was nursing a dying baby saw her sole remaining child "probably scalded to death. Handing over the infant to die in the arms of a friend, she bowed in sweet submission to the double stroke." But the child "through the goodness of God survived, and the mother learned to say 'Thy will be done.' " [54]

Woman then, in all her roles, accepted submission as her lot. It was a lot she had not chosen or deserved. As *Godey's* said, "the lesson of submission is forced upon woman." Without comment or criticism the writer affirms that "To suffer and to be silent under suffering seems the great command she has to obey." [55] George Burnap referred to a woman's life as "a series of suppressed emotions." [56] She was, as Emerson said, "more vulnerable, more infirm, more mortal than man." [57] The death of a beautiful woman, cherished in fiction, represented woman as the innocent victim, suffering without sin, too pure and good for this world but too weak and passive to resist its evil forces.[58] The best refuge for such a delicate creature was the warmth and safety of her home.

The true woman's place was unquestionably by her own fireside — as daughter, sister, but most of all as wife and mother. Therefore domesticity was among the virtues most prized by the women's magazines. "As society is constituted," wrote Mrs. S. E. Farley, on the "Domestic and Social Claims on Woman," "the true dignity and beauty of the female character seem to consist in a right understanding and faithful and cheerful performance of social and family duties." [59] Sacred Scripture re-enforced social pressure: "St. Paul knew what was best for women when he advised them to be domestic," said Mrs. Sandford. "There is composure at home; there is something sedative in the duties which home involves. It affords security not only from the world, but from delusions and errors of every kind." [60]

From her home woman performed her great task of bringing men back to God. *The Young Ladies' Class Book* was sure that "the domestic fireside is the great guardian of society against the excesses of human passions." [61] *The Lady at Home* expressed its convictions in its very title and concluded that "even if we cannot reform the world in a moment, we can begin the work by reforming ourselves and our households — It is woman's mission. Let her not look away from her own little family circle for the means of producing moral and social reforms, but begin at home." [62]

Home was supposed to be a cheerful place, so that brothers, husbands and sons would not go elsewhere in search of a good time. Woman was expected to dispense comfort and cheer. In writing the biography of Margaret Mercer (every inch a true woman) her biographer (male) notes: "She never forgot that it is the peculiar province of woman to minister to the comfort, and promote the happiness, first, of those most nearly allied to her, and then of those, who by the Providence of God are placed in a state of dependence upon her." [63] Many other essays in the women's journals showed woman as comforter: "Woman, Man's Best Friend," "Woman, the Greatest Social Benefit," "Woman, A Being to Come Home To," "The Wife: Source of Comfort and the Spring of Joy." [64]

One of the most important functions of woman as comforter was her role as nurse. Her own health was probably, although regrettably, delicate.[65] Many homes had "little sufferers," those pale children who wasted away to saintly deaths. And there were enough other illnesses of youth and age, major and minor, to give the nineteenth-century American woman nursing experience. The sickroom called for the exercise of her higher qualities of patience, mercy and gentleness as well as for her housewifely arts. She could thus fulfill her dual feminine function — beauty and usefulness.

The cookbooks of the period offer formulas for gout cordials, ointment for sore nipples, hiccough and cough remedies, opening pills and refreshing drinks for fever, along with recipes for pound cake, jumbles, stewed calves head and currant wine.[66] The Ladies' New Book of Cookery believed that "food prepared by the kind hand of a wife, mother, sister, friend" tasted better and had a "restorative power which money cannot purchase." [67]

A chapter of The Young Lady's Friend was devoted to woman's privilege as "ministering spirit at the couch of the sick." Mrs. Farrar advised a soft voice, gentle and clean hands, and a cheerful smile. She also cautioned against an excess of female delicacy. That was all right for a young lady in the parlor, but not for bedside manners. Leeches, for example, were to be regarded as "a curious piece of mechanism . . . their ornamental stripes should recommend them even to the eye, and their valuable services to our feelings." And she went on calmly to discuss their use. Nor were women to shrink from medical terminology, since "If you cultivate right views of the wonderful structure of the body, you will be as willing to speak to a physician of the bowels as the brains of your patient." [68]

Nursing the sick, particularly sick males, not only made a woman feel useful and accomplished, but increased her influence. In a piece of heavy-handed humor in Godey's a man confessed that some women were only happy when their husbands were ailing that they might have the joy of nursing him to recovery "thus gratifying their medical vanity and their love of power by making him more dependent upon them." [69] In a similar vein a husband sometimes suspected his wife, "almost wishes me dead — for the pleasure of being utterly inconsolable." [70]

In the home women were not only the highest adornment of civilization, but they were supposed to keep busy at morally uplifting tasks. Fortunately most of housework, if looked at in true womanly fashion, could be regarded as uplifting. Mrs. Sigourney extolled its virtues: "The science of housekeeping affords exercise for the judgment and energy, ready recollection, and patient self-possession, that are the characteristics of a superior mind." [71] According to Mrs. Farrar, making beds was good exercise, the repetitiveness of routine tasks inculcated patience and perseverance, and proper management of the home was a surprisingly complex art: "There is more to be learned about pouring out tea and coffee, than most young ladies are willing to believe." [72] *Godey's* went so far as to suggest coyly, in "Learning vs. Housewifery" that the two were complementary, not opposed: chemistry could be utilized in cooking, geometry in dividing cloth, and phrenology in discovering talent in children. [73]

Women were to master every variety of needlework, for, as Mrs. Sigourney pointed out, "Needle-work, in all its forms of use, elegance, and ornament, has ever been the appropriate occupation of woman." [74] Embroidery improved taste; knitting promoted serenity and economy. [75] Other forms of artsy-craftsy activity for her leisure moments included painting on glass or velvet, Poonah work, tussy-mussy frames for her own needlepoint or water colors, stands for hyacinths, hair bracelets or baskets of feathers. [76]

She was expected to have a special affinity for flowers. To the editors of *The Lady's Token* "A Woman never appears more truly in her sphere, than when she divides her time between her domestic avocations and the culture of flowers." [77] She could write letters, an activity particularly feminine since it had to do with the outpourings of the heart, [78] or practice her drawingroom skills of singing and playing an instrument. She might even read.

Here she faced a bewildering array of advice. The female was dangerously addicted to novels, according to the literature of the period. She should avoid them, since they interfered with "serious piety." If she simply couldn't help herself and read them anyway, she should choose edifying ones from lists of morally acceptable authors. She should study history since it "showed the depravity of the human heart and the evil nature of sin." On the whole, "religious biography was best." [79]

The women's magazines themselves could be read without any loss of concern for the home. *Godey's* promised the husband that he would find his wife "no less assiduous for his reception, or less sincere in welcoming his return" as a result of reading their magazine. [80] *The Lily of the Valley* won its right to be admitted to the boudoir by confessing that it was "like its namesake humble and unostentatious, but it is yet pure, and, we trust, free from moral imperfections." [81]

No matter what later authorities claimed, the nineteenth century knew that girls *could* be ruined by a book. The seduction stories regard "exciting and dangerous books" as contributory causes of disaster. The man without honorable intentions always provides the innocent maiden with such books as a prelude to his assault on her virtue. [82] Books which attacked or seemed to attack woman's accepted place in society were regarded as equally dangerous. A reviewer of Harriet Martineau's *Society in America* wanted it kept out of the hands of American women. They were so susceptible to persuasion, with their "gentle yielding natures" that they might listen to "the bold ravings of the hard-featured of their own sex." The frightening result: "such reading will unsettle them for their true station and pursuits, and they will throw the world back again into confusion." [83]

The debate over women's education posed the question of whether a "finished" education detracted from the practice of housewifely arts. Again it proved to be a case of semantics, for a true woman's education was never "finished" until she was instructed in the gentle science of homemaking. [84] Helen Irving, writing on "Literary Women," made it very clear that if women invoked the muse, it was as a genie of the household lamp. "If the necessities of her position require these duties at her hands, she will perform them nonetheless cheerfully, that she knows herself capable of higher things." The literary woman must conform to the same standards as any other woman: "That her home shall be made a loving place of rest and joy and comfort for those who are dear to her, will be the first wish of every true woman's heart." [85] Mrs. Ann Stephens told women who wrote to make sure they did not sacrifice one domestic duty. "As for genius, make it a domestic plant. Let its roots strike deep in your house. . . ." [86]

The fear of "blue stockings" (the eighteenth-century male's term of derision for educated or literary women) need not persist for nineteenth-century American men. The magazines presented spurious dialogues in which bachelors were convinced of their fallacy in fearing educated wives. One such dialogue took place between a young man and his female cousin. Ernest deprecates learned ladies ("A *Woman* is far more lovable than a *philosopher*") but Alice refutes him with the beautiful example of their Aunt Barbara who "although she *has* perpetrated the heinous crime of writing some half dozen folios" is still a model of "the spirit of feminine gentleness." His memory prodded, Ernest concedes that, by George, there was a woman: "When I last had a cold she not only made me a bottle of cough syrup, but when I complained of nothing new to read, set to work and wrote some twenty stanzas on consumption." [87]

The magazines were filled with domestic tragedies in which spoiled young girls learned that when there was a hungry man to feed French and china painting were not helpful. According to these stories many a marriage is jeopardized because the wife has not learned to keep house. Harriet Beecher Stowe wrote a sprightly piece of personal experience for *Godey's*, ridiculing her own bad housekeeping as a bride. She used the same theme in a story "The Only Daughter," in which the pampered beauty learns the facts of domestic life from a rather difficult source, her mother-in-law. Mrs. Hamilton tells Caroline in the sweetest way possible to shape up in the kitchen, reserving her rebuke for her son: "You are her husband — her guide — her protector — now see what you can do," she admonishes him. "Give her credit for every effort: treat her faults with tenderness; encourage and praise whenever you can, and depend upon it, you will see another woman in her." He is properly masterful, she properly domestic and in a few months Caroline is making lumpless gravy and keeping up with the darning. Domestic tranquillity has been restored and the young wife moralizes: "Bring up a girl to feel that she has a responsible part to bear in promoting the happiness of the family, and you make a reflecting being of her at once, and remove that lightness and frivolity of character which makes her shrink from graver studies." [88] These stories end with the heroine drying her hands on her apron and vowing that *her* daughter will be properly educated, in piecrust as well as Poonah work.

The female seminaries were quick to defend themselves against any suspicion of interfering with the role which nature's God had assigned to women. They hoped to enlarge and deepen that role, but not to change its setting. At the Young Ladies' Seminary and Collegiate Institute in Monroe City, Michigan, the catalogue admitted few of its graduates would be likely "to fill the learned professions." Still, they were called to "other scenes of usefulness and honor." The average woman is to be "the presiding genius of love" in the home, where she is to "give a correct and elevated literary taste to her children, and to assume that influential station that she ought to possess as the companion of an educated man." [89]

At Miss Pierce's famous school in Litchfield, the students were taught that they had "attained the perfection of their characters when they could combine their elegant accomplishments with a turn for solid domestic virtues."[90] Mt. Holyoke paid pious tribute to domestic skills: "Let a young lady despise this branch of the duties of woman, and she despises the appointments of her existence." God, nature and the Bible "enjoin these duties on the sex, and she cannot violate them with impunity." Thus warned, the young lady would have to seek knowledge of these duties elsewhere, since it was not in the curriculum at Mt. Holyoke. "We would not take this privilege from the mother."[91]

One reason for knowing her way around a kitchen was that America was "a land of precarious fortunes," as Lydia Maria Child pointed out in her book *The Frugal Housewife: Dedicated to Those Who Are Not Ashamed of Economy*. Mrs. Child's chapter "How To Endure Poverty" prescribed a combination of piety and knowledge — the kind of knowledge found in a true woman's education, "a thorough religious *useful* education."[92] The woman who had servants today, might tomorrow, because of a depression or panic, be forced to do her own work. If that happened she knew how to act, for she was to be the same cheerful consoler of her husband in their cottage as in their mansion.

An essay by Washington Irving, much quoted in the gift annuals, discussed the value of a wife in case of business reverses: "I have observed that a married man falling into misfortune is more apt to achieve his situation in the world than a single one . . . it is beautifully ordained by Providence that woman, who is the ornament of man in his happier hours, should be his stay and solace when smitten with sudden calamity."[93]

A story titled simply but eloquently "The Wife" dealt with the quiet heroism of Ellen Graham during her husband's plunge from fortune to poverty. Ned Graham said of her: "Words are too poor to tell you what I owe to that noble woman. In our darkest seasons of adversity, she has been an angel of consolation — utterly forgetful of self and anxious only to comfort and sustain me." Of course she had a little help from "faithful Dinah who absolutely refused to leave her beloved mistress," but even so Ellen did no more than would be expected of any true woman.[94]

Most of this advice was directed to woman as wife. Marriage was the proper state for the exercise of the domestic virtues. "True Love and a Happy Home," an essay in *The Young Ladies' Oasis*, might have been carved on every girl's hope chest.[95] But although marriage was best, it was not absolutely necessary. The women's magazines tried to remove the stigma from being an "Old Maid." They advised no marriage at all rather than an unhappy one contracted out of selfish motives.[96] Their stories showed maiden ladies as unselfish ministers to the sick, teachers of the young, or moral preceptors with their pens, beloved of the entire village. Usually the life of single blessedness resulted from the premature death of a fiancé, or was chosen through fidelity to some high mission. For example, in "Two Sisters," Mary devotes herself to Ellen and her abandoned children, giving up her own chance for marriage. "Her devotion to her sister's happiness has met its reward in the consciousness of having fulfilled a sacred duty."[97] Very rarely, a "woman of genius" was absolved from the necessity of marriage, being so extraordinary that she did not need the security or status of being a wife.[98] Most often, however, if girls proved "difficult," marriage and a family were regarded as a cure.[99] The "sedative quality" of a home could be counted on to subdue even the most restless spirits.

George Burnap saw marriage as "that sphere for which woman was originally intended, and to which she is so exactly fitted to adorn and bless, as the wife, the mistress of a home, the solace, the aid, and the counsellor of that ONE, for whose sake alone the world is of any consequence to her." [100] Samuel Miller preached a sermon on women: "How interesting and important are the duties devolved on females as WIVES . . . the counsellor and friend of the husband; who makes it her daily study to lighten his cares, to soothe his sorrows, and to augment his joys; who, like a guardian angel, watches over his interests, warns him against dangers, comforts him under trials; and by her pious, assiduous, and attractive deportment, constantly endeavors to render him more virtuous, more useful, more honourable, and more happy." [101] A woman's whole interest should be focused on her husband, paying him "those numberless attentions to which the French give the title of *petits soins* and which the woman who loves knows so well how to pay . . . she should consider nothing as trivial which could win a smile of approbation from him." [102]

Marriage was seen not only in terms of service but as an increase in authority for women. Burnap concluded that marriage improves the female character "not only because it puts her under the best possible tuition, that of the affections, and affords scope to her active energies, but because it gives her higher aims, and a more dignified position." [103] *The Lady's Amaranth* saw it as a balance of power: "The man bears rule over his wife's person and conduct. She bears rule over his inclinations: he governs by law; she by persuasion. . . . The empire of the woman is an empire of softness . . . her commands are caresses, her menaces are tears." [104]

Woman should marry, but not for money. She should choose only the high road of true love and not truckle to the values of a materialistic society. A story "Marrying for Money" (subtlety was not the strong point of the ladies' magazines) depicts Gertrude, the heroine, rueing the day she made her crass choice: "It is a terrible thing to live without love. . . . A woman who dares marry for aught but the purest affection, calls down the just judgments of heaven upon her head." [105]

The corollary to marriage, with or without true love, was motherhood, which added another dimension to her usefulness and her prestige. It also anchored her even more firmly to the home. "My Friend," wrote Mrs. Sigourney, "If in becoming a mother, you have reached the climax of your happiness, you have also taken a higher place in the scale of being . . . you have gained an increase of power." [106] The Rev. J. N. Danforth pleaded in *The Ladies' Casket,* "Oh, mother, acquit thyself well in thy humble sphere, for thou mayest affect the world." [107] A true woman naturally loved her children; to suggest otherwise was monstrous. [108]

America depended upon her mothers to raise up a whole generation of Christian statesmen who could say "all that I am I owe to my angel mother." [109] The mothers must do the inculcating of virtue since the fathers, alas, were too busy chasing the dollar. Or as *The Ladies' Companion* put it more effusively, the father "weary with the heat and burden of life's summer day, or trampling with unwilling foot the decaying leaves of life's autumn, has forgotten the sympathies of life's joyous springtime. . . . The acquisition of wealth, the advancement of his children in worldly honor — these are his self-imposed tasks." It was his wife who formed "the infant mind as yet untainted by contact with evil . . . like wax beneath the plastic hand of the mother." [110]

The Ladies' Wreath offered a fifty-dollar prize to the woman who submitted the most convincing essay on "How May An American Woman Best Show Her Patriotism." The winner was Miss Elizabeth Wetherell who provided herself with a husband in her answer. The wife in the essay of course asked her husband's opinion. He tried a few jokes first — "Call her eldest son George Washington," "Don't speak

French, speak American" — but then got down to telling her in sober prize-winning truth what women could do for their country. Voting was no asset, since that would result only in "a vast increase of confusion and expense without in the smallest degree affecting the result." Besides, continued this oracle, "looking down at their child," if "we were to go a step further and let the children vote, their first act would be to vote their mothers at home." There is no comment on this devastating male logic and he continues: "Most women would follow the lead of their fathers and husbands," and the few who would "fly off on a tangent from the circle of home influence would cancel each other out."

The wife responds dutifully: "I see all that. I never understood so well before." Encouraged by her quick womanly perception, the master of the house resolves the question — an American woman best shows her patriotism by staying at home, where she brings her influence to bear "upon the right side for the country's weal." That woman will instinctively choose the side of right he has no doubt. Besides her "natural refinement and closeness to God" she has the "blessed advantage of a quiet life" while man is exposed to conflict and evil. She stays home with "her Bible and a well-balanced mind" and raises her sons to be good Americans. The judges rejoiced in this conclusion and paid the prize money cheerfully, remarking "they deemed it cheap at the price." [111]

If any woman asked for greater scope for her gifts the magazines were sharply critical. Such women were tampering with society, undermining civilization. Mary Wollstonecraft, Frances Wright and Harriet Martineau were condemned in the strongest possible language — they were read out of the sex. "They are only semi-women, mental hermaphrodites." The Rev. Harrington knew the women of America could not possibly approve of such perversions and went to some wives and mothers to ask if they did want a "wider sphere of interest" as these nonwomen claimed. The answer was reassuring. " 'NO!' they cried simultaneously, 'Let the men take care of politics, *we will take care of the children!*' " Again female discontent resulted only from a lack of understanding: women were not subservient, they were rather "chosen vessels." Looked at in this light the conclusion was inescapable: "Noble, sublime is the task of the American mother." [112] "Women's Rights" meant one thing to reformers, but quite another to the True Woman. She knew her rights,

> The right to love whom others scorn,
> The right to comfort and to mourn,
> The right to shed new joy on earth,
> The right to feel the soul's high worth . . .
> Such women's rights, and God will bless
> And crown their champions with success.[113]

The American woman had her choice — she could define her rights in the way of the women's magazines and insure them by the practice of the requisite virtues, or she could go outside the home, seeking other rewards than love. It was a decision on which, she was told, everything in her world depended. "Yours it is to determine," the Rev. Mr. Stearns solemnly warned from the pulpit, "whether the beautiful order of society . . . shall continue as it has been" or whether "society shall break up and become a chaos of disjointed and unsightly elements." [114] If she chose to listen to other voices than those of her proper mentors, sought other rooms than those of her home, she lost both her happiness and her power — "that almost magic power, which, in her proper sphere, she now wields over the destinies of the world." [115]

But even while the women's magazines and related literature encouraged this ideal of the perfect woman, forces were at work in the nineteenth century which impelled woman herself to change, to play a more creative role in society. The movements for social reform, westward migration, missionary activity, utopian communities, industrialism, the Civil War — all called forth responses from woman which differed from those she was trained to believe were hers by nature and divine decree. The very perfection of True Womanhood, moreover, carried within itself the seeds of its own destruction. For if woman was so very little less than the angels, she should surely take a more active part in running the world, especially since men were making such a hash of things.

Real women often felt they did not live up to the ideal of True Womanhood: some of them blamed themselves, some challenged the standard, some tried to keep the virtues and enlarge the scope of womanhood.[116] Somehow through this mixture of challenge and acceptance, of change and continuity, the True Woman evolved into the New Woman — a transformation as startling in its way as the abolition of slavery or the coming of the machine age. And yet the stereotype, the "mystique" if you will, of what woman was and ought to be persisted, bringing guilt and confusion in the midst of opportunity.[117]

The women's magazines and related literature had feared this very dislocation of values and blurring of roles. By careful manipulation and interpretation they sought to convince woman that she had the best of both worlds — power and virtue — and that a stable order of society depended upon her maintaining her traditional place in it. To that end she was identified with everything that was beautiful and holy.

"Who Can Find a Valiant Woman?" was asked frequently from the pulpit and the editorial pages. There was only one place to look for her — at home. Clearly and confidently these authorities proclaimed the True Woman of the nineteenth century to be the Valiant Woman of the Bible, in whom the heart of her husband rejoiced and whose price was above rubies.

NOTES

1. Authors who addressed themselves to the subject of women in the mid-nineteenth century used this phrase as frequently as writers on religion mentioned God. Neither group felt it necessary to define their favorite terms, they simply assumed — with some justification — that leaders would intuitively understand exactly what they meant. Frequently what people of one era take for granted is most striking and revealing to the student from another. In a sense this analysis of the ideal woman of the mid-nineteenth century is an examination of what writers of that period actually meant when they used so confidently the vague phrase True Womanhood.
2. The conclusions reached in this article are based on a survey of almost all of the women's magazines published for more than three years during the period 1820–60 and a sampling of those published for less than three years; all the gift books cited in Ralph Thompson, *American Literary Annuals and Gift Books, 1825–1865* (New York, 1936) deposited in the Library of Congress, the New York Public Library, the New York Historical Society, Columbia University Special Collections, Library of the City College of the University of New York, Pennsylvania Historical Society, Massachusetts Historical Society, Boston Public Library, Fruitlands Museum Library, the Smithsonian Institution and the Wisconsin Historical Society; hundreds of religious tracts and sermons in the American Unitarian Society and the Galatea Collection of the Boston Public Library: and the large collection of nineteenth century cookbooks in the New York Public Library and the Academy of Medicine of New York. Corroborative evidence not cited in this article was found in women's diaries, memoirs, autobiographies and personal papers, as well as in all the novels by women which sold over 75,000 copies during this period, as cited in Frank Luther Mott, *Golden Multitudes: The Story of Best Sellers in the United States* (New York, 1947) and H. R. Brown, *The Sentimental Novel in America, 1789–1860* (Durham, N. C., 1940). This latter information also indicated the effect of the cult of True Womanhood on those most directly concerned.

3. As in "The Bachelor's Dream," in *The Lady's Gift: Souvenir for All Seasons* (Nashua, N. H., 1849), p. 37.
4. *The Young Ladies' Class Book: A Selection of Lessons for Reading in Prose and Verse*, ed. Ebenezer Bailey, Principal of Young Ladies' High School, Boston (Boston, 1831). p. 168.
5. A Lady of Philadelphia, *The World Enlightened, Improved, and Harmonized by WOMAN!!!* A lecture, delivered in the City of New York, before the Young Ladies' Society for Mutual Improvement, on the following question proposed by the society, with the offer of $100 for the best lecture that should be read before them on the subject proposed: What is the power and influence of woman in moulding the manners, morals and habits of civil society? (Philadelphia, 1840), p. 1.
6. *The Young Lady's Book: A Manual of Elegant Recreations, Exercises, and Pursuits* (Boston, 1830), p. 29.
7. *Woman As She Was, Is, and Should be* (New York, 1849), p. 206.
8. "The Triumph of the Spiritual Over the Sensual: An Allegory," in *Ladies' Companion: A Monthly Magazine Embracing Every Department of Literature, Embellished With Original Engravings and Music, XVII* (New York) (1842), 67.
9. *Lecture on Some of the Distinctive Characteristics of the Female,* delivered before the class of the Jefferson Medical College, Jan. 1847 (Philadelphia, 1847), p. 13.
10. "Female Education," *Ladies' Repository and Gatherings of the West: A Monthly Periodical Devoted to Literature and Religion, I* (Cincinnati), 12.
11. *Woman, in Her Social and Domestic Character* (Boston, 1842), pp. 41–42.
12. *Second Annual Report of the Young Ladies' Literary and Missionary Association of the Philadelphia Collegiate Institution* (Philadelphia, 1840), pp. 20, 26.
13. *Mt. Holyoke Female Seminary: Female Education. Tendencies of the Principles Embraced, and the System Adopted in the Mt. Holyoke Female Seminary* (Boston, 1839), p. 3.
14. *Prospectus of the Young Ladies' Seminary at Bordentown, New Jersey* (Bordentown, 1836), p. 7.
15. *Catalogue of the Young Ladies' Seminary in Keene, New Hampshire* (n.p., 1832), p. 20.
16. "Report to the College of Teachers, Cincinnati, October, 1840" in *Ladies' Repository, I* (1841), 50.
17. *Woman's Record: or Sketches of All Distinguished Women from 'The Beginning' Till A.D. 1850* (New York, 1853), pp. 665, 669.
18. "Female Irreligion," *Ladies' Companion, XIII* (May–Oct. 1840), 111.
19. *The Lady's Book of Flowers and Poetry,* ed. Lucy Hooper (New York, 1842), has a "Floral Dictionary" giving the symbolic meaning of floral tributes.
20. See, for example, Nathaniel Hawthorne, *The Blithedale Romance* (Boston, 1852), p. 71, in which Zenobia says: "How can she be happy, after discovering that fate has assigned her but one single event, which she must contrive to make the substance of her whole life? A man has his choice of innumerable events."
21. Mary R. Beard, *Woman As Force in History* (New York, 1946) makes this point at some length. According to common law, a woman had no legal existence once she was married and therefore could not manage property, sue in court, etc. In the 1840s and 1850s laws were passed in several states to remedy this condition.
22. *Excellency of the Female Character Vindicated: Being an Investigation Relative to the Cause and Effects on the Encroachments of Men Upon the Rights of Women, and the Too Frequent Degradation and Consequent Misfortunes of The Fair Sex* (New York, 1807), pp. 277, 278.
23. By a Lady (Eliza Ware Rotch Farrar), *The Young Lady's Friend* (Boston, 1837), p. 293.
24. *Girlhood and Womanhood: or, Sketches of My Schoolmates* (Boston, 1844), p. 140.
25. Emily Chubbuck, *Alderbrook* (Boston, 1847), 2nd. ed., *II*, 121, 127.
26. *Woman and Her Era* (New York, 1864), p. 95.
27. "The Two Lovers of Sicily," *The Lady's Amaranth: A Journal of Tales, Essays, Excerpts — Historical and Biographical Sketches, Poetry and Literature in General* (Philadelphia), *II* (Jan. 1839), 17.
28. *The Young Man's Guide* (Boston, 1833), pp. 229, 231.
29. *Female Influence: and the True Christian Mode of Its Exercise; a Discourse Delivered in the First Presbyterian Church in Newburyport, July 30, 1837* (Newburyport, 1837), p. 18.
30. W. Tolles, "Woman The Creature of God and the Manufacturer of Society," *Ladies' Wreath* (New York), *III* (1852), 205.
31. Prof. William M. Heim, "The Bloomer Dress," *Ladies' Wreath, III* (1852), 247.
32. *The Young Lady's Offering: or Gems of Prose and Poetry* (Boston, 1853), p. 283. The American girl, whose innocence was often connected with ignorance, was the spiritual ancestress of the Henry James heroine. Daisy Miller, like Lucy Dutton, saw innocence lead to tragedy.
33. *The Mother's Book* (Boston, 1831), pp. 151, 152.
34. Mrs. L. M. Sigourney, *Whisper to a Bride* (Hartford, 1851), in which Mrs. Sigourney's approach is summed up in this quotation: "Home! Blessed bride, thou art about to enter this sanctuary, and to become a priestess at its altar!," p. 44.
35. S. R. R., "Female Charms," *Godey's Magazine and Lady's Book* (Philadelphia), *XXXIII* (1846), 52.
36. Charles Elliott, "Arguing With Females," *Ladies' Repository, I* (1841), 25.
37. *Ladies' Companion, VIII* (Jan. 1838), 147.
38. *The Young Lady's Book* (New York, 1830), American edition, p. 28. (This is a different book than the one of the same title and date of publication cited in note 6.)

39. *Sphere and Duties of Woman* (5th ed., Baltimore, 1854), p. 47.

40. *Woman*, p. 15.

41. *Letters to Young Ladies* (Hartford, 1835), p. 179.

42. *Lecture*, p. 17.

43. *The Young Lady's Friend*, p. 313.

44. Maria J. McIntosh, *Woman in America: Her Work and Her Reward* (New York, 1850), p. 25.

45. *Poems and a Memoir of the Life of Mrs. Felicia Hemans* (London, 1860), p. 16.

46. Letter "To an Unrecognized Poetess, June, 1846" (Sara Jane Clarke), *Greenwood Leaves* (2nd ed.; Boston, 1850), p. 311.

47. "The Sculptor's Assistant: Ann Flaxman," in *Women of Worth: A Book for Girls* (New York, 1860), p. 263.

48. Mrs. Clarissa Packard (Mrs. Caroline Howard Gilman), *Recollections of a Housekeeper* (New York, 1834), p. 122.

49. *Recollections of a Southern Matron* (New York, 1838), pp. 256, 257.

50. *The Lady's Token: or Gift of Friendship*, ed. Colesworth Pinckney (Nashua, N. H., 1848), p. 119.

51. Harvey Newcomb, *Young Lady's Guide to the Harmonious Development of Christian Character* (Boston, 1846), p. 10.

52. Rules for Conjugal and Domestic Happiness," *Mother's Assistant and Young Lady's Friend*, III (Boston), (April 1843), 115.

53. *Letters to Mothers* (Hartford, 1838), p. 199. In the diaries and letters of women who lived during this period the death of a child seemed consistently to be the hardest thing for them to bear and to occasion more anguish and rebellion, as well as eventual submission, than any other event in their lives.

54. "A Submissive Mother," *The Ladies' Parlor Companion: A Collection of Scattered Fragments and Literary Gems* (New York, 1852), p. 358.

55. "Woman," *Godey's Lady's Book*, II (Aug. 1831), 110.

56. *Sphere and Duties of Woman*, p. 172.

57. Ralph Waldo Emerson, "Woman," *Complete Writings of Ralph Waldo Emerson* (New York, 1875), p. 1180.

58. As in Donald Fraser, *The Mental Flower Garden* (New York, 1857). Perhaps the most famous exponent of this theory is Edgar Allan Poe who affirms in "The Philosophy of Composition" that "the death of a beautiful woman is unquestionably the most poetical topic in the world. . . ."

59. "Domestic and Social Claims on Woman," *Mother's Magazine*, VI (1846), 21.

60. *Woman*, p. 173.

61. *The Young Ladies' Class Book*, p. 166.

62. T. S. Arthur, *The Lady at Home: or, Leaves from the Every-Day Book of an American Woman* (Philadelphia, 1847), pp. 177, 178.

63. Caspar Morris, *Margaret Mercer* (Boston, 1840), quoted in *Woman's Record*, p. 425.

64. These particular titles come from: *The Young Ladies' Oasis: or Gems of Prose and Poetry*, ed. N. L. Ferguson (Lowell, 1851), pp. 14, 16; *The Genteel School Reader* (Philadelphia, 1849), p. 271; and *Magnolia*, I (1842), 4. A popular poem in book form, published in England, expressed very fully this concept of woman as comforter: Coventry Patmore, *The Angel in the Home* (Boston, 1856 and 1857). Patmore expressed his devotion to True Womanhood in such lines as:

> The gentle wife, who decks his board
> And makes his day to have no night,
> Whose wishes wait upon her Lord,
> Who finds her own in his delight. (p. 94)

65. The women's magazines carried on a crusade against tight lacing and regretted, rather than encouraged, the prevalent ill health of the American woman. See, for example, *An American Mother, Hints and Sketches* (New York, 1839), pp. 28 ff. for an essay on the need for a healthy mind in a healthy body in order to better be a good example for children.

66. The best single collection of nineteenth-century cookbooks is in the Academy of Medicine of New York Library, although some of the most interesting cures were in hand-written cookbooks found among the papers of women who lived during the period.

67. Sarah Josepha Hale, *The Ladies' New Book of Cookery: A Practical System for Private Families in Town and Country* (5th ed.; New York, 1852), p. 409. Similar evidence on the importance of nursing skills to every female is found in such books of advice as William A. Alcott, *The Young Housekeeper* (Boston, 1838), in which, along with a plea for apples and cold baths, Alcott says "Every female should be trained to the angelic art of managing properly the sick," p. 47.

68. *The Young Lady's Friend*, pp. 75–77, 79.

69. "A Tender Wife," *Godey's*. II (July 1831), 28.

70. "MY WIFE! A Whisper," *Godey's*, II (Oct. 1831), 231.

71. *Letters to Young Ladies*, p. 27. The greatest exponent of the mental and moral joys of housekeeping was the *Lady's Annual Register and Housewife's Memorandum Book* (Boston, 1838), which gave practical advice on ironing, hair curling, budgeting and marketing, and turning cuffs — all activities which contributed to the "beauty of usefulness" and "joy of accomplishment" which a woman desired (*I*, 23).

72. *The Young Lady's Friend*, p. 230.
73. "Learning vs. Housewifery," *Godey's*, X (Aug. 1839), 95.
74. *Letters to Young Ladies*, p. 25. W. Thayer, *Life at the Fireside* (Boston, 1857), has an idyllic picture of the woman of the house mending her children's garments, the grandmother knitting and the little girl taking her first stitches, all in the light of the domestic hearth.
75. "The Mirror's Advice," *Young Maiden's Mirror* (Boston, 1858), p. 263.
76. Mrs. L. Maria Child, *The Girl's Own Book* (New York, 1833).
77. P. 44.
78. T. S. Arthur, *Advice to Young Ladies* (Boston, 1850), p. 45.
79. R. C. Waterston, *Thoughts on Moral and Spiritual Culture* (Boston, 1842), p. 101. Newcomb's *Young Lady's Guide* also advised religious biography as the best reading for women (p. 111).
80. *Godey's*, I (1828), 1. (Repeated often in *Godey's* editorials.)
81. *The Lily of the Valley*, n. v. (1851), p. 2.
82. For example, "The Fatalist," *Godey's*, IV (Jan. 1834), 10, in which Somers Dudley has Catherine reading these dangerous books until life becomes "a bewildered dream. — O passion, what a shocking perverter of reason thou art!"
83. Review of *Society in America* (New York, 1837) in *American Quarterly Review* (Philadelphia), *XXII* (Sept. 1837), 38.
84. "A Finished Education," *Ladies' Museum* (Providence), I (1825), 42.
85. Helen Irving, "Literary Women," *Ladies' Wreath*, III (1850), 93.
86. "Women of Genius," *Ladies' Companion*, XI (1839), 89.
87. "Intellect vs. Affection in Woman," *Godey's*, XVI (1846), 86.
88. "The Only Daughter," *Godey's*, X (Mar. 1839), 122.
89. *The Annual Catalogue of the Officers and Pupils of the Young Ladies' Seminary and Collegiate Institute* (Monroe City, 1855), pp. 18, 19.
90. *Chronicles of a Pioneer School* from 1792 to 1833: Being the History of Miss Sarah Pierce and Her Litchfield School, Compiled by Emily Noyes Vanderpoel; ed. Elizabeth C. Barney Buel (Cambridge, 1903), p. 74.
91. *Mt. Holyoke Female Seminary*, p. 13.
92. *The American Frugal Housewife* (New York, 1838), p. 111.
93. "Female Influence," in *The Ladies' Pearl and Literary Gleaner: A Collection of Tales, Sketches, Essays, Anecdotes, and Historical Incidents* (Lowell), I (1841), 10.
94. Mrs. S. T. Martyn, "The Wife," *Ladies' Wreath*, II (1848–49), 171.
95. *The Young Ladies' Oasis*, p. 26.
96. "On Marriage," *Ladies' Repository*, I (1841), 133; "Old Maids," *Ladies' Literary Cabinet* (Newburyport), II (1822) (Microfilm), 141; "Matrimony," *Godey's*, II (Sept. 1831), 174; and "Married or Single," *Peterson's Magazine* (Philadelphia) IX (1859), 36, all express the belief that while marriage is desirable for a woman it is not essential. This attempt to reclaim the status of the unmarried woman is an example of the kind of mild crusade which the women's magazines sometimes carried on. Other examples were their strictures against an overly-genteel education and against the affectation and aggravation of ill health. In this sense the magazines were truly conservative, for they did not oppose all change but only that which did violence to some cherished tradition. The reforms they advocated would, if put into effect, make woman even more the perfect female, and enhance the ideal of True Womanhood.
97. *Girlhood and Womanhood*, p. 100. Mrs. Graves tells the stories in the book in the person of an "Old Maid" and her conclusions are that "single life has its happiness too" for the single woman "can enjoy all the pleasures of maternity without its pains and trials" (p. 140). In another one of her books, *Woman in America* (New York, 1843), Mrs. Graves speaks out even more strongly in favor of "single blessedness" rather than "a loveless or unhappy marriage" (p. 130).
98. A very unusual story is Lela Linwood, "A Chapter in the History of a Free Heart," *Ladies' Wreath*, *III* (1853), 349. The heroine, Grace Arland, is "sublime" and dwells "in perfect light while we others struggled yet with the shadows." She refuses marriage and her friends regret this but are told her heart "is rejoicing in its *freedom.*" The story ends with the plaintive refrain:

> But is it not a happy thing,
>   All fetterless and free,
> Like any wild bird, on the wing,
>   To carol merrily?

But even in this tale the unusual, almost unearthly rarity of Grace's genius is stressed; she is not offered as an example to more mortal beings.
99. Horace Greeley even went so far as to apply this remedy to the "dissatisfactions" of Margaret Fuller. In his autobiography, *Recollections of a Busy Life* (New York, 1868) he says that "noble and great as she was, a good husband and two or three bouncing babies would have emancipated her from a deal of cant and nonsense" (p. 178).
100. *Sphere and Duties of Woman*, p. 64.
101. *A Sermon: Preached March 13, 1808, for the Benefit of the Society Instituted in the City of New-York, For the Relief of Poor Widows with Small Children* (New York, 1808), pp. 13, 14.

102. *Lady's Magazine and Museum: A Family Journal* (London) *IV* (Jan. 1831), 6. This magazine is included partly because its editorials proclaimed it "of interest to the English speaking lady at home and abroad" and partly because it shows that the preoccupation with True Womanhood was by no means confined to the United States.

103. *Sphere and Duties of Woman*, p. 102.

104. "Matrimony," *Lady's Amaranth, II* (Dec. 1839), 271.

105. Elizabeth Doten, "Marrying for Money," *The Lily of the Valley*, n. v. (1857), p. 112.

106. *Letters to Mothers*, p. 9.

107. "Maternal Relation," *Ladies' Casket* (New York, 1850?), p. 85. The importance of the mother's role was emphasized abroad as well as in America. *Godey's* recommended the book by the French author Aimeé-Martin on the education of mothers to "be read five times," in the original if possible (*XIII*, Dec. 1842, 201). In this book the highest ideals of True Womanhood are upheld. For example: "Jeunes filles, jeunes épouses, tendres mères, c'est dans votre âme bien plus que dans les lois du législateur que reposent aujourd'hui l'avenir de l'Europe et les destinées du genre humain," L. Aimeé-Martin, *De l'Education des Mères de famille ou De la civilisation du genre humain par les femmes* (Bruxelles, 1857), *II*, 527.

108. *Maternal Association of the Amity Baptist Church: Annual Report* (New York, 1847), p. 2: "Suffer the little children to come unto me and forbid them not, is and must ever be a sacred commandment to the Christian woman."

109. For example, Daniel Webster, "The Influence of Woman," in *The Young Ladies' Reader* (Philadelphia, 1851), p. 310.

110. Mrs. Emma C. Embury, "Female Education," *Ladies' Companion, VIII* (Jan. 1838), 18. Mrs. Embury stressed the fact that the American woman was not the "mere plaything of passion" but was in strict training to be "the mother of statesmen."

111. "How May An American Woman Best Show Her Patriotism?" *Ladies' Wreath, III* (1851), 313. Elizabeth Wetherell was the pen name of Susan Warner, author of *The Wide Wide World* and *Queechy*.

112. Henry F. Harrington, "Female Education," *Ladies' Companion, IX* (1838), 293, and "Influence of Woman — Past and Present," *Ladies' Companion, XIII* (1840), 245.

113. Mrs. E. Little, "What Are the Rights of Women?" *Ladies' Wreath, II* (1848–49), 133.

114. *Female Influence*, p. 18.

115. *Ibid.*, p. 23.

116. Even the women reformers were prone to use domestic images, i.e. "sweep Uncle Sam's kitchen clean," and "tidy up our country's house."

117. The "Animus and Anima" of Jung amounts almost to a catalogue of the nineteenth-century masculine and female traits, and the female hysterics whom Freud saw had much of the same training as the nineteenth-century American woman. Betty Friedan, *The Feminine Mystique* (New York, 1963), challenges the whole concept of True Womanhood as it hampers the "fulfillment" of the twentieth-century woman.

The Black Slave

If America was exceptional, it was so not only in positive but also in negative ways. By 1860, the "land of the free" was also the home of four million black slaves, who constituted 13 percent of the whole population. Some of these bondsmen were African by birth; many more were descended from the wretched victims stolen from Africa by slavers in the colonial period. By the eve of the Civil War, blacks had been in North America for as long as Europeans, yet the overwhelming majority were chattel slaves, a "peculiar species of property," whose status would become more controversial with each passing year.

Slavery in the ante-bellum South was not a benign institution. Most masters sought to avoid using the lash and the branding iron to enforce their will, but everywhere in the South some slaves were punished brutally and peremptorily. More important, slavery denied its subjects' fundamental human needs by weakening the ties between husband and wife, children and parents. It also wasted tremendous human potential. A few slaves were able to develop and exercise their minds and their skills, but most were locked permanently into a life of mindless, backbreaking, common toil.

Yet human beings can adjust to many frustrating and coercive experiences. Most bondsmen learned to survive within the system by virtue of avoiding its penalties as much as they were able. Slaves shirked their duties, or did them in the easiest, and often the most inefficient, way possible. They expressed their resistance to the regime by feigning clumsiness or stupidity, by breaking tools and equipment, by mistreating farm stock. They often ran away. Sometimes they struck back physically at the master, though the penalty for such behavior was savage and summary punishment. A number of times during the slave era, bloody slave uprisings took place, upheavals that sent tremendous shocks through all of southern society.

Though slavery was founded on coercion, it would be a mistake to assume that the average bondsmen encountered nothing but beatings and brandings in his day-to-day existence. Work, rather than force, was the most common experience of the slave. They were employed in almost every conceivable occupation and in almost every conceivable setting in the Old South. Bondsmen were used as house servants in every capacity, from butler and cook to laundress, housemaid, and stable boy. A few worked at the skilled trades — carpentry, masonry, blacksmithing, and numerous others — both on the plantation and in the towns. They were common laborers on canals and railroads and were even employed as operatives in the South's cotton mills and iron works.

But above all they were agricultural laborers. The South was overwhelmingly agrarian. By 1860, the North, particularly the Northeast, was beginning to industrialize. The South had some industry too, but was well behind New England and the Middle Atlantic states in the size, number, and output of its factories and workshops. In colonial times, southern slaves had grown tobacco, rice, and indigo along the Chesapeake and the Carolina and Georgia coasts. Tobacco and rice continued to be cultivated in these older regions by slave labor, but by the 1790s these were no longer expanding crops, and it looked to many men as if slavery were doomed. The slave population continued to expand by natural increase, but it became more and more difficult to find profitable labor for it. Then came cotton and the rapid spread of slavery through the entire lower South. Thousands of slaves were drawn off to the burgeoning cotton kingdom to grow the white fiber. Men got rich, slave prices rose, and slavery once more became a viable and profitable labor system. By 1830, the South was a prosperous part of the American and the world economy, fiercely committed to the perpetuation of the plantation system and the labor regime that sustained it.

In the selection that follows, Kenneth M. Stampp, of the University of California at Berkeley, describes the work of the slave on the plantations and in the homes and workshops of the South. Stampp does not sentimentalize slavery. His book *The Peculiar Institution* is deeply colored by his repugnance for chattel slavery. Although he seeks to evaluate the institution objectively, he refuses to believe that, at heart, it was more than a way of squeezing profits from the lives and toil of black men.

FOR FURTHER READING:

ELKINS, STANLEY. *Slavery: A Problem in American Institutional and Intellectual Life.* Chicago: University of Chicago Press, 1968.*

JORDAN, WINTHROP. *White Over Black.* Baltimore: Penguin Books, Pelican, 1969.*

PHILLIPS, ULRICH B. *American Negro Slavery.* Magnolia, Mass.: Peter Smith, 1966.*

Asterisk denotes paperback edition.

From Day Clean to First Dark

KENNETH M. STAMPP

The day's toil began just before sunrise. A visitor on a Mississippi plantation was regularly awakened by a bell which was rung to call the slaves up. "I soon hear the tramp of the laborers passing along the avenue. . . . All is soon again still as midnight. . . . I believe that I am the only one in the house that the bell disturbs; yet I do not begrudge it a few minutes' loss of sleep it causes me, it sounds so pleasantly in the half dreamy morning." [1] On James H. Hammond's South Carolina plantation a horn was blown an hour before daylight. "All work-hands are [then] required to rise and prepare their cooking, etc. for the day. The second horn is blown just at good day-light, when it is the duty of the driver to visit every house and see that all have left for the field." [2] At dusk the slaves put away their tools and returned to their quarters.

The working day was shorter in winter than in summer, but chiefly because there was less daylight, not because there was much less to do. Seldom at any time of the year was the master at a loss to find essential work to keep his hands busy. Those

Source: Kenneth M. Stampp, *The Peculiar Institution: Slavery in the Ante-Bellum South* (New York: Alfred A. Knopf, 1956), chap. 2, "From Day Clean to First Dark," pp. 44–85.

who planned the routine carefully saved indoor tasks for rainy days. An Alabama planter told his father in Connecticut that cotton picking continued until January, "and after that [we] gathered our corn which ripened last August. We then went to work with the waggons ha[u]ling rails and repairing and rebuilding fences, say two weeks, we then knocked down cotton stalks and pulled up corn stalks and commenced plowing. There is no lying by, no leisure, no long sleeping season such as you have in New England."[3] The terse plantation records of the year-round routine of slaves whose principal work was growing cotton usually ran something like this:

January–February: Finished picking, ginning, and pressing cotton and hauling it in wagons to the point of shipment; killed hogs and cut and salted the meat; cut and hauled wood; cut and mauled fence rails; repaired buildings and tools; spread manure; cleaned and repaired ditches; cleared new ground by rolling and burning logs and grubbing stumps; knocked down corn and cotton stalks and burned trash; plowed and "bedded up" corn and cotton fields; planted vegetables.

March–April: Opened "drills," or light furrows, in the corn and cotton beds; sowed corn and cotton seeds in the drills and covered them by hand or with a harrow; replanted where necessary; cultivated the vegetable garden; plowed and hoed in the corn fields.

May–August: "Barred" cotton by scraping dirt away from it with plows; "chopped" cotton with hoes to kill weeds and grass and to thin it to a "stand"; "molded" cotton by "throwing dirt" to it with plows; cultivated corn and cotton until it was large enough to be "laid by"; made repairs; cleared new ground; "pulled fodder," i.e., stripped the blades from corn stalks; cleaned the gin house.

September–December: Picked, ginned, pressed, and shipped cotton; gathered peas; hauled corn and fodder; dug potatoes; shucked corn; cleaned and repaired ditches; repaired fences; cut and hauled wood; cleared new ground.[4]

Thus the operations of one growing cycle overlapped those of the next. There were, of course, variations from planter to planter and differences in the time of planting crops in the upper and lower parts of the cotton belt. Slaves who grew long-staple, or sea-island, cotton in the coastal areas of South Carolina and Georgia had to exercise greater care in picking, ginning, and packing this finer and more expensive variety. But these were differences only in detail. The routine work of cotton growers was essentially the same everywhere, and their basic tools were always the hoe and the plow.

Slaves who cultivated sugar, rice, tobacco, or hemp were involved in a similar year-round routine. They used the same basic tools and much of the time performed the same kinds of supplementary tasks. But each of the staples required special techniques in planting, cultivating, harvesting, and preparing for market.

Some slaves in Texas, Florida, Georgia, and other scattered places in the Deep South produced a little sugar, but those who worked on plantations lining the rivers and bayous of southern Louisiana produced ninety-five per cent of this crop. Most of them were attached to large estates whose owners had heavy investments in land, labor, and machinery. On sugar plantations in the late fall and winter the slaves prepared the land with plows and harrows; before the end of February they planted the seed cane in deep furrows. The shoots grew from eyes at the joints of the seed cane, or ratooned from the stubble of the previous crop. Then came months of cultivation with hoes and plows until the crop was laid by in July. Meanwhile, other slaves cut huge quantities of wood and hauled it to the sugar house, and coopers made sugar hogsheads and molasses barrels. Much heavy labor also went into ditching to provide drainage for these lands which sloped gently from the rivers toward the swamps.

The first cane cut in October was "matalayed" (laid on the ground and covered with a little dirt) to be used as the next year's seed cane. During the frantic weeks from then until December most of the slaves worked at cutting the cane and stripping the leaves from the stalks, loading it into carts, and hauling it to the sugar house. At the mill other slaves fed the cane through the rollers, tended the open kettles or vacuum pans, kept the fires burning, hauled wood, and packed the unrefined sugar into hogsheads. When the last juice was boiled, usually around Christmas, it was almost time to begin planting the next crop.[5]

Soon after the Revolution South Carolina planters abandoned the cultivation of one of their staples — indigo.[6] But to the end of the ante-bellum period rice continued to be the favorite crop of the great planters along the rivers of the South Carolina and Georgia Low Country. Slaves had turned the tidal swamps into fertile rice fields by constructing an intricate system of banks, "trunks" (sluices), and ditches which made possible periodic flooding and draining with the rising and falling tides. Throughout the year slaves on rice plantations devoted much of their time to cleaning the ditches, repairing the banks and trunks, and keeping the tide-flow irrigation system in efficient operation.

In winter the slaves raked the rice fields and burned the stubble. After the ground was broken and "trenched" into drills, the seeds were planted in March and early April. During the first flooding (the "sprout flow") other crops on higher ground were cultivated. When the rice fields were drained and dried they were hoed to loosen the ground and to kill grass and weeds. The next flooding (the "stretch flow") was followed by a long period of "dry growth" during which hoeing went on constantly. Then came the final flooding (the "harvest flow") which lasted until September when the rice was ready to be cut. The slaves cut the rice with sickles, tied it into sheaves, and stacked it to dry. After it had dried they carried the rice to the plantation mill to be threshed, "pounded" to remove the husks from the kernels, winnowed, screened, and packed in barrels.[7] The other crops grown on lands above the swamps were gathered in time to begin preparations for the next year's planting.

The Tobacco Kingdom stretched into the border states of Maryland, Kentucky, and Missouri, but in the ante-bellum period its heart was still the "Virginia District." This district embraced the piedmont south of Fredericksburg, including the northern tier of counties in North Carolina. Here the plantations were smaller than in the Lower South, because each hand could cultivate fewer acres and because the crop had to be handled with great care. The unique aspects of tobacco culture included the preparing of beds in which the tiny seeds were sown during the winter, the transplanting of the shoots in May, and the worming, topping, and suckering of the plants during the summer months. In the late summer the tobacco stalks were split, cut, and left in the fields to wilt. Then they were carried to the tobacco houses to be hung and cured during the fall and winter. The following year, when work had already begun on the next crop, the leaves were stripped from the stalks, sorted, tied into bundles, and "prized" into hogsheads.[8]

The Bluegrass counties of Kentucky and the Missouri River Valley were the chief hemp producing regions of the Old South. Slaves were almost always the working force on hemp farms, because free labor avoided the strenuous, disagreeable labor required to prepare a crop for market. After the ground was prepared, the seeds were sown broadcast in April and May and covered lightly with a harrow or shovel plow. Unlike the other staples, hemp required no cultivation during the growing season, and slaves were free to tend other crops. In late summer the hemp was cut, laid on the ground to dry, and then tied in sheaves and stacked. In November or December it was again spread out in the fields for "dew rotting" to loosen the fiber. A month or so later the hemp was stacked once more, and the lint was laboriously separated from the wood with a hand "brake." The fiber was taken to the hemp house where it was hackled or sold immediately to manufacturers.[9]

In 1850, the Superintendent of the Census estimated that 2,500,000 slaves of all ages were directly employed in agriculture. Of these, he guessed that 60,000 were engaged in the production of hemp, 125,000 in the production of rice, 150,000 in the production of sugar, 350,000 in the production of tobacco, and 1,815,000 in the production of cotton. Somewhat casually he observed that these slaves also produced "large quantities of breadstuffs." [10] This was scarcely adequate recognition of the amount of time they devoted to such crops, even on many of the plantations which gave chief attention to one of the five staples.

To be sure, some planters in the Lower South were so preoccupied with staple production that they grew almost nothing else — not even enough corn and pork to feed their slaves. This pattern was common in the Louisiana sugar district. One planter explained that when sugar sold for fifty dollars a hogshead, "it is cheaper to buy pork[,] for it is utterly impossible to raise hogs here without green pastures and plenty of corn[,] and all lands here fit for pasturage will make a hogshead [of] sugar pr acre — The great curse of this country is that we are all planters and no farmers." [11] An Alabama cotton planter was alarmed when pork failed to arrive from Tennessee: "All of our towns and most of our large Planters are dependent on Drovers for their meat." Even some of the cotton and tobacco planters in North Carolina bought food supplies for their slaves.[12] Such planters were convinced that it was most profitable to concentrate on the production of a single cash crop.

Most planters, however, did not share this point of view. Almost all of the hemp and tobacco growers of the Upper South planted many acres of food crops to supply their own needs — and frequently additional acres to produce surpluses for sale. A major feature of the agricultural revival in ante-bellum Virginia was an improved system of crop rotation with increased emphasis upon corn, wheat, and clover.[13] Many of the tobacco planters gave enough attention to these and other crops to approximate a system of diversified farming. Their field-hands often devoted less than half of their time to tobacco.

Few planters in the Deep South approached such levels of diversification, but most of them produced sizeable food crops for their families and slaves. In southern agricultural periodicals they constantly admonished each other to strive for self-sufficiency. They instructed their overseers to produce adequate supplies of corn, sweet potatoes, peas, and beans, and to give proper attention to the poultry, hogs, and cattle. A Mississippi planter warned his overseer "that failure to make a bountiful supply of corn and meat for the use of the plantation, will be considered as notice that his services will not be required for the succeeding year." [14] The average planter, however, was tempted to forgive a great deal if his overseer managed to make enough cotton. Interest in other crops tended to vary with fluctuations in cotton prices. Even so, most of the field-hands on cotton plantations were at least familiar with the routine of corn cultivation.

Though southern planters showed that slaves could grow other crops besides the five great staples, there was a widespread belief that it was impractical to devote plantations to them exclusively. But here and there in the Lower South a planter disproved this assumption. In Richmond County, Georgia, an owner of more than a hundred slaves successfully used his labor force to raise grain and meat for sale in Augusta.[15]

In the Upper South many large slaveholders grew neither tobacco nor hemp but engaged in diversified farming. In Talbot County, Maryland, Colonel Edward Lloyd worked his two hundred and seventy-five slaves on profitable farms which produced wheat, corn, hams, wool, and hides.[16] On Shirley Plantation on the James River, Hill Carter, like many of his Virginia neighbors, made wheat his major cash crop. An incomplete list of the products of a plantation in King and Queen County included wheat, corn, oats, rye, vegetables, Irish potatoes, sweet potatoes, wool, hogs, apples, and strawberries.[17]

In North Carolina, corn was the chief crop on a number of Roanoke River plantations. In Tyrrell County, Ebenezer Pettigrew annually shipped thousands of bushels of wheat and corn to Norfolk and Charleston.[18] Clearly, the slave-plantation system had greater flexibility and was less dependent upon the production of a few staples than some have thought.

There is a different tradition about the agricultural operations of farmers who owned less than ten slaves. Here a high degree of diversification is assumed — presumably the smaller farms were better adapted to this type of farming than to the cultivation of the staples. Thousands of slaveholders in this group did engage in what was almost subsistence farming with cash incomes well below five hundred dollars a year. Others, especially in the Upper South, marketed large surpluses of pork, corn, and wheat. The amount of commercialization in the operations of non-staple producing small slaveholders depended upon the quality of their lands, their proximity to markets and transportation, and their managerial skill.

But a large proportion of these slaveholding farmers depended upon one of the five southern staples for a cash crop. In Kentucky and Missouri many of them produced a few tons of hemp; there and in Virginia and North Carolina they often gave tobacco their chief attention. A few small slaveholders in the Deep South even planted rice and sugar — sometimes surprisingly large amounts — in spite of the handicaps they faced in trying to compete with the planters. In St. Mary Parish, Louisiana, for example, an owner of seven slaves in 1859 produced forty hogsheads of sugar. These small operators depended upon their neighbors' sugar making facilities or ran their own crude horse-driven mills.[19]

In cotton production those with modest slaveholdings faced no overwhelming competitive disadvantage. Some of the smaller cotton growers were as preoccupied with this staple as were their neighbors on the large plantations. Some even depended upon outside supplies of food. Many of them reported astonishing cotton-production records to the census takers, the number of bales per hand easily matching the records of the planters.[20]

Nevertheless, the majority of small slaveholders did engage in a more diversified type of agriculture than most of the large planters. Slavery could be, and was, adapted to diversified agriculture and to the labor needs of small farms. It did not necessarily depend upon large plantations or staple crops for its survival.

For the owner of a few slaves, labor management was a problem of direct personal relationships between individuals. For the owner of many, the problem was more difficult and required greater ingenuity. Both classes of masters desired a steady and efficient performance of the work assigned each day. They could not expect much cooperation from their slaves, who had little reason to care how much was produced. Masters measured the success of their methods by the extent to which their interest in a maximum of work of good quality prevailed over the slaves' predilection for a minimum of work of indifferent quality. Often neither side won a clear victory.

Slaveowners developed numerous variations of two basic methods of managing their laborers: the "gang system" and the "task system." Under the first of these systems, which was the one most commonly used, the field-hands were divided into gangs commanded by drivers who were to work them at a brisk pace. Competent masters gave some thought to the capacities of individual slaves and to the amount of labor that a gang could reasonably be expected to perform in one day. But the purpose of the gang system was to force every hand to continue his labor until all were discharged from the field in the evening.

Under the task system, each hand was given a specific daily work assignment. He could then set his own pace and quit when his task was completed. The driver's job was to inspect the work and to see that it was performed satisfactorily before the slave left the field. "The advantages of this system," according to a Georgia rice planter, "are encouragement to the laborers, by equalizing the work of each agreeable to strength, and the avoidance of watchful superintendence and incessant driving. As . . . the task of each [slave] is separate, imperfect work can readily be traced to the neglectful worker." [21]

The task system was best adapted to the rice plantation, with its fields divided into small segments by the network of drainage ditches. Outside the Low Country of South Carolina and Georgia planters occasionally used this system or at least experimented with it, but many of them found it to be unsatisfactory. For one thing, they could get no more work out of their stronger slaves than out of their weaker ones, since the tasks were usually standardized. The planters also found that the eagerness of slaves to finish their tasks as early as possible led to careless work. After using the task system for twenty years, an Alabama planter abandoned it because of evils "too numerous to mention." A South Carolina cotton planter, who also gave it up, noted with satisfaction that under the gang system his slaves did "much more" and were "not so apt to strain themselves." [22]

Actually, most planters used a combination of the two systems. Cotton planters often worked plow-hands in gangs but gave hoe-hands specific tasks of a certain number of cotton rows to hoe each day. Each hand was expected to pick as much cotton as he could, but he might be given a minimum quota that had to be met. Sugar, rice, and tobacco planters applied the task system to their coopers, and hemp growers used it with hands engaged in breaking or hackling hemp. Masters generally tasked their hands for digging ditches, cutting wood, or mauling rails.

Thus most slaves probably had some experience with both systems. From their point of view each system doubtless had its advantages and drawbacks. A strong hand might have preferred to be tasked if he was given an opportunity to finish early. But many slaves must have been appalled at the ease with which they could be held responsible for the quality of their work. The gang system had the disadvantages of severe regimentation and of hard driving which was especially onerous for the weaker hands. But there was less chance that a slave would be detected and held individually responsible for indifferent work. In the long run, however, the rigors of either system were determined by the demands of masters and overseers.

The number of acres a slaveholder expected each of his field-hands to cultivate depended in part upon how hard he wished to work them. It also depended upon the nature of the soil, the quality of the tools, and the general efficiency of the agricultural enterprise. Finally, it depended upon the crop. Cotton growers on flat prairies and river bottoms planted as many as ten acres per hand but rarely more than that. Those on hilly or rolling lands planted from three to eight acres per hand. Since a slave could ordinarily cultivate more cotton than he could pick, acreage was limited by the size of the available picking force. By the 1850's each hand was expected to work from nine to ten acres of sugar but seldom more than five acres of rice or three of tobacco, plus six or more of corn and other food crops.[23] The yield per acre and per hand varied with the fertility of the soil, the care in cultivation, the damage of insects, and the whims of the weather.

When calculating his yield per field-hand a slaveholder was not calculating his yield per slave, for he almost always owned fewer field-hands than slaves. Some of his slaves performed other types of work, and the very young and the very old could not be used in the fields. The master's diseased, convalescing, and partially disabled slaves, his "breeding women" and "sucklers," his children just beginning to work in the fields, and his slaves of advanced years were incapable of laboring as long and as hard as full-time hands.

Most masters had systems of rating such slaves as fractional hands. Children often began as "quarter hands" and advanced to "half hands," "three-quarter hands," and then "full hands." As mature slaves grew older they started down this scale. "Breeding women" and "sucklers" were rated as "half hands." Some planters organized these slaves into separate gangs, for example, into a "sucklers gang." Children sometimes received their training in a "trash gang," or "children's squad," which pulled weeds, cleaned the yard, hoed, wormed tobacco, or picked cotton. Seldom were many more than half of a master's slaves listed in his records as field-hands, and always some of the hands were classified as fractional. Olmsted described a typical situation on a Mississippi cotton plantation: "There were 135 slaves, big and little, of which 67 went to the field regularly — equal, the overseer thought, to 60 able-bodied hands." [24]

The master, not the parents, decided at what age slave children should be put to work in the fields. Until they were five or six years old children were "useless articles on a plantation." Then many received "their first lessons in the elementary part of their education" through serving as "water-toters" or going into the fields alongside their mothers.[25] Between the ages of ten and twelve the children became fractional hands, with a regular routine of field labor. By the time they were eighteen they had reached the age when they could be classified as "prime field-hands."

Mature slaves who did not work in the fields (unless they were totally disabled or extremely old) performed other kinds of valuable and productive labor. Old women cooked for the rest of the slaves, cared for small children, fed the poultry, mended and washed clothes, and nursed the sick. Old men gardened, minded stock, and cleaned the stable and the yard.

Old or partially disabled slaves might also be put to spinning and weaving in the loom houses of the more efficient planters. The printed instructions in a popular plantation record book advised overseers to adopt this policy: "Few instances of good management will better please an employer, than that of having all the winter clothing spun and woven on the place. By having a room devoted to that purpose . . . where those who may be complaining a little, or convalescent after sickness, may be employed in some light work, and where all of the women may be sent in wet weather, more than enough of both cotton and woolen yarn can be spun for the supply of the place." [26] One planter reported that he had his spinning jenny "going at a round rate[.] Old Charles [is] Spinning and Esther reeling the thread. . . . Charles will in this way be one of my most productive laborers and so will several of the women[.]" [27] Thus a master's productive slaves were by no means limited to those listed as field-hands.

The bondsmen who were valued most highly were those who had acquired special skills which usually exempted them from field work entirely. This select group of slave craftsmen included engineers, coopers, carpenters, blacksmiths, brickmakers, stone masons, mechanics, shoemakers, weavers, millers, and landscapers. The excellence of the work performed by some of them caused slaveowners to make invidious comparisons between them and the free artisans they sometimes employed. An Englishman recalled an interview with the overseer on a Louisiana sugar plantation: "It would have been amusing, had not the subject been so grave, to hear the overseer's praises of the intelligence and skill of these workmen, and his boast that they did all the work of skilled laborers on the estate, and then to listen to him, in a few minutes, expatiating on the utter helplessness and ignorance of the black race, their incapacity to do any good, or even to take care of themselves." [28]

Domestic servants were prized almost as much as craftsmen. The number and variety of domestics in a household depended upon the size of the establishment and the wealth of the master. They served as hostlers, coachmen, laundresses, seamstresses, cooks, footmen, butlers, housemaids, chambermaids, children's nurses, and personal servants. On a large plantation specialization was complete: "The cook never enters the house, and the nurse is never seen in the kitchen; the wash-woman is never put to ironing, nor the woman who has charge of the ironing-room ever put to washing. Each one rules supreme in her wash-house, her ironing-room, her kitchen, her nursery, her house-keeper's room; and thus . . . a complete system of domesticdom is established to the amazing comfort and luxury of all who enjoy its advantages." [29]

But the field-hands remained fundamental in the slave economy. Though their work was classified as unskilled labor, this of course was a relative term. Some visitors described the "rude" or "slovenly" manner in which slaves cultivated the crops, how "awkwardly, slowly, and undecidedly" they moved through the fields.[30] But other observers were impressed with the success of many masters in training field-hands to be efficient workers, impressed also by the skill these workers showed in certain crucial operations in the production of staple crops. Inexperienced hands had their troubles in sugar houses and rice fields, in breaking and hackling hemp, and in topping, suckering, sorting, and prizing tobacco. Even the neophyte cotton picker soon wondered whether this was unskilled labor, as one former slave testified: "While others used both hands, snatching the cotton and depositing it in the mouth of the sack, with a precision and dexterity that was incomprehensible to me, I had to seize the boll with one hand, and deliberately draw out the white, gushing blossom with the other." On his first day he managed to gather "not half the quantity required of the poorest picker." [31]

Field workers kept up a ceaseless struggle to make the lands fruitful, against the contrary efforts of the insects and the elements. The battle seemed at times to be of absorbing interest to some of the slaves, conscripts though they were. In a strange and uneasy kind of alliance, they and their masters combatted the foes that could have destroyed them both.

In 1860, probably a half million bondsmen lived in southern cities and towns, or were engaged in work not directly or indirectly connected with agriculture. Some farmers and planters found it profitable, either temporarily or permanently, to employ part of their hands in non-agricultural occupations. Along the rivers slaves cut wood to provide fuel for steamboats and for sale in neighboring towns. In swamplands filled with juniper, oak, and cypress trees they produced shingles, barrel and hogshead staves, pickets, posts, and rails. In North Carolina's Dismal Swamp slave gangs labored as lumberjacks.[32] In the eastern Carolina pine belt several thousand slaves worked in the turpentine industry. An owner of one hundred and fifty slaves in Brunswick County, North Carolina, raised just enough food to supply his force; he made his profits from the annual sale of thousands of barrels of turpentine. Many smaller operators also combined turpentine production with subsistence farming.[33]

Elsewhere in the South bondsmen worked in sawmills, gristmills, quarries, and fisheries. They mined gold in North Carolina, coal and salt in Virginia, iron in Kentucky and Tennessee, and lead in Missouri. On river boats they were used as deck hands and firemen. Slave stokers on a Mississippi River steamer bound for New Orleans, who sang as they fed wood to the boiler fires, intrigued a European traveler: "It was a fantastic and grand sight to see these energetic black athletes lit up by the wildly flashing flames . . . while they, amid their equally fantastic song, keeping time most exquisitely, hurled one piece of firewood after another into the yawning fiery gulf." [34]

Other slaves were employed in the construction and maintenance of internal improvements. They worked on the public roads several days each year in states which required owners to put them to such use. For many years slaves owned by the state of Louisiana built roads and cleared obstructions from the bayous. Slaves also worked for private internal improvements companies, such as the builders of the Brunswick and Altamaha Canal in Georgia and the Cape Fear and Deep River Navigation Company in North Carolina. In Mississippi a hundred were owned by a firm of bridge contractors, the Weldon brothers.[35]

Railroad companies employed bondsmen in both construction and maintenance work. As early as 1836 the Richmond, Fredericksburg, and Potomac Railroad Company advertised for "a large number" of slave laborers. In the same year the Alabama, Florida, and Georgia Railroad Company announced a need for five hundred "able-bodied negro men . . . to be employed in felling, cutting, and hewing timber, and in forming the excavations and embankments upon the route of said Rail Road." During the 1850's southern newspapers carried the constant pleas of railroad builders for slaves. Almost every railroad in the ante-bellum South was built at least in part by bondsmen; in Georgia they constructed more than a thousand miles of roadbed. In 1858, a Louisiana newspaper concluded: "Negro labor is fast taking the place of white labor in the construction of southern railroads." [36]

Bondsmen in southern cities and towns, in spite of the protests of free laborers, worked in virtually every skilled and unskilled occupation. They nearly monopolized the domestic services, for most free whites shunned them to avoid being degraded to the level of slaves. Many of the Southerners who owned just one or two slaves were urban dwellers who used them as cooks, housekeepers, and gardeners. The wealthier townspeople often had staffs of domestic servants as large as those of rural planters. Other domestics found employment in hotels and at watering places.

Town slaves worked in cotton presses, tanneries, shipyards, bakehouses, and laundries, as dock laborers and stevedores, and as clerks in stores. Masters who owned skilled artisans such as barbers, blacksmiths, cabinet makers, and shoemakers often provided them with shops to make their services available to all who might wish to employ them. Many white mechanics used slave assistants. In short, as a visitor to Natchez observed, town slaves included "mechanics, draymen, hostlers, labourers, hucksters, and washwomen, and the heterogeneous multitude of every other occupation, who fill the streets of a busy city — for slaves are trained to every kind of manual labour. The blacksmith, cabinet-maker, carpenter, builder, wheelwright — all have one or more slaves labouring at their trades. The negro is a third arm to every working man, who can possibly save money enough to purchase one. He is emphatically the 'right-hand man' of every man." [37] The quality of the work of slave artisans had won favorable comment as early as the eighteenth century. Among them were "many ingenious Mechanicks," wrote a colonial Georgian, "and as far as they have had opportunity of being instructed, have discovered as good abilities, as are usually found among people of our Colony." [38]

Some Southerners were enthusiastic crusaders for the development of factories which would employ slaves. They were convinced that bondsmen could be trained in all the necessary skills and would provide a cheaper and more manageable form of labor than free whites. "When the channels of agriculture are choked," predicted an industrial promoter, "the manufacturing of our own productions will open new channels of profitable employment for our slaves." Others thought that slavery was one of the South's "natural advantages" in its effort to build industries to free it from "the incessant and vexatious attacks of the North." [39] They believed that industrialization and slavery could proceed hand in hand.

Southern factory owners gave evidence that this was more than idle speculation. Every slave state had industrial establishments which made some use of slave labor. In Kentucky, the "ropewalks" which manufactured cordage and the hemp factories which produced cotton bagging and "Kentucky jeans" employed slaves extensively.[40] Almost all of the thirteen thousand workers in the tobacco factories of the Virginia District were bondsmen. The majority of them were employed in the three leading tobacco manufacturing cities — Richmond, Petersburg, and Lynchburg. These slave workers were not only a vital part of this industry but also a curiously paradoxical element in the society of the tobacco towns.[41]

From its earliest beginnings the southern iron industry depended upon skilled and unskilled slaves. Negro iron workers were employed in Bath County, Kentucky, and along the Cumberland River in Tennessee. In the Cumberland country the majority of laborers at the iron furnaces were slaves. Montgomery Bell, owner of the Cumberland Iron Works, engaged his own three hundred slaves and many others in every task connected with the operation of forge and furnace.[42] In the Great Valley of Virginia, where the southern industry was centered during the early nineteenth century, slaves constituted the chief labor supply.

Until the 1840's, the famed Tredegar Iron Company in Richmond used free labor almost exclusively. But in 1842, Joseph R. Anderson, then commercial agent of the company, proposed to employ slaves as a means of cutting labor costs. The board of directors approved of his plan, and within two years Anderson was satisfied with "the practicability of the scheme." In 1847, the increasing use of slaves caused the remaining free laborers to go out on strike, until they were threatened with prosecution for forming an illegal combination. After this protest failed, Anderson vowed that he would show his workers that they could not dictate his labor policies: he refused to re-employ any of the strikers. Thereafter, as Anderson noted, Tredegar used "almost exclusively slave labor except as the Boss men. This enables me, of course, to compete with other manufacturers." [43]

But it was upon the idea of bringing textile mills to the cotton fields that southern advocates of industrialization with slave labor pinned most of their hopes. In cotton factories women and children were needed most, and hence it was often argued that they would provide profitable employment for the least productive workers in agriculture. Though the majority of southern textile workers were free whites, and though some believed that this work ought to be reserved for them, a small number of slaves were nevertheless employed in southern mills.

Occasionally mill owners managed to work slaves and free whites together with a minimum of friction. A visitor found equal numbers of the two groups employed in a cotton factory near Athens, Georgia: "There is no difficulty among them on account of colour, the white girls working in the same room and at the same loom with the black girls; and boys of each colour, as well as men and women, working together without apparent repugnance or objection." [44] But even if some white workers would tolerate this, slaveowners ordinarily looked upon it as a dangerous practice.

The southern press gave full reports of cotton mills which used slave labor and ecstatic accounts of their success. A Pensacola newspaper cited the local Arcadia Cotton Factory, which employed only slaves, to prove that "with the native skill and ingenuity of mere labor — the labor of the hands — the negro is just as richly endowed as the white." The Saluda mill, near Columbia, South Carolina, operated on the "slave-labor, or anti free-soil system." The white managers testified to the "equal efficiency, and great superiority in many respects" of slaves over free workers.[45] During the 1830's and 1840's, a half dozen other cotton mills in South Carolina's Middle and Low Country employed bondsmen. Most other southern states could point to one or more mills which used this type of labor. To many observers the enterprises of Daniel Pratt at Prattsville, near Montgomery, Alabama, provided models for other Southerners to copy. Pratt worked slaves not only in his cotton mill but also in his cotton gin factory, iron foundry, sash and door factory, machine shop, and carriage and wagon shop.[46]

Actually, the ante-bellum South had relatively few cotton mills, and most of them were small enterprises manufacturing only the coarser grades of cloth. In 1860, the fifteen slave states together had only 198 mills each employing an average of 71 workers, whereas Massachusetts alone had 217 mills each employing an average of 177 workers. Many of the southern factories resembled the one owned by a small manufacturer in East Tennessee which contained only three hundred spindles operated by fourteen slave hands.[47]

Still, in these textile mills and in what little other industry existed in the Old South there was abundant evidence that slaves could be trained to be competent factory workers. The evidence was sufficient to raise serious doubts that slavery was tied to agriculture, as some defenders and some critics of the institution believed.

Each year, around the first of January, at southern crossroad stores, on the steps of county courthouses, and in every village and city, large crowds of participants and spectators gathered for "hiring day." At this time masters with bondsmen to spare and employers in search of labor bargained for the rental of slave property. Thus thousands of nonslaveholders managed temporarily to obtain the services of slaves and to enjoy the prestige of tenuous membership in the master class. Thus, too, many bondsmen found it their lot to labor for persons other than their owners. Hired slaves were most numerous in the Upper South; during the 1850's perhaps as many as fifteen thousand were hired out annually in Virginia alone. But slave-hiring was a common practice everywhere.[48]

In December and January southern newspapers were filled with the advertisements of those offering or seeking slaves to hire. Some of the transactions were negotiated privately, some by auctioneers who bid slaves off at public outcry, and some by "general agents" who handled this business for a commission. In Richmond, P. M. Tabb & Son, among many others, advertised that they attended "to the hiring out of negroes and collecting the hires" and promised to give "particular attention . . . through the year to negroes placed under their charge." [49]

Though slaves were occasionally hired for short terms, it was customary to hire them from January until the following Christmas. Written contracts specified the period of the hire, the kind of work in which the slaves were to be engaged, and the hirer's obligation to keep them well clothed. Usually an owner could spare only a few, but occasionally a single master offered as many as fifty and, rarely, as many as a hundred. Though most slaves were hired in the vicinity of their masters' residences, many were sent long distances from home. Hamilton Brown, of Wilkes County, North Carolina, hired out slaves in Virginia, Tennessee, and Georgia; and Jeremiah Morton, of Orange County, Virginia, hired out fifty-two of his Negroes through an agent in Mobile.[50]

A variety of circumstances contributed to this practice. If for some reason the owner was unable to use his slaves profitably, if he was in debt, or if he had a surplus of laborers, he might prefer hiring to selling them. Executors hired out slave property while estates were being settled. Sometimes lands and slaves together were rented to tenants. Heirs who inherited bondsmen for whom they had no employment put them up for hire. Many spinsters, widows, and orphans lived off the income of hired slaves who were handled for them by administrators. Masters often directed in their wills that slaves be hired out for the benefit of their heirs, or that cash be invested in slave property for this purpose. A widow in Missouri hired out most of her slaves, because she found it to be "a better business" than working them on her farm.[51] Occasionally a slaveowner endowed a church or a benevolent institution with slaves whose hire was to aid in its support.

In addition, urban masters often hired out the husbands or children of their female domestics. Both they and planters who had more domestics than they could use or afford disposed of them in this manner. It was also very common for urban and rural owners of skilled slaves to hire them to others at least part of the time. Planters hired their carpenters and blacksmiths to neighbors when they had no work for them and thus substantially augmented their incomes. A master sometimes hired a slave to a white artisan with the understanding that the slave was to be taught his skill. For example, a contract between a North Carolina master and a white blacksmith provided that the hirer was to work a slave "at the Forge during the whole time and learn him or cause him to be learned the arts and mysteries of the Black Smith's trade." [52]

A few Southerners bought slaves as business ventures with the intention of realizing profits solely through hiring them to others. Between 1846 and 1852, Bickerton Lyle Winston, of Hanover County, Virginia, purchased at least fifteen slaves for this purpose. Winston kept careful records of these investments, noting the purchase prices, the annual income from and expenses of each slave, and the net profit. The slaves Randal and Garland were his first speculations. Randal's record ended abruptly in 1853 with the terse notation: "Deduct medical and funeral expenses: $20." Four years later Winston recorded the fact that "Garland came to his end . . . by an explosion in the Black Heath Pits." [53] Some overseers pursued a similar course by investing in slaves whom they hired to their employers. A resident in Mississippi knew families "who possess not an acre of land, but own many slaves, [and] hire them out to different individuals; the wages constituting their only income, which is often very large." [54]

Farmers and planters frequently hired field-hands to neighbors for short periods of time. Cotton growers who finished their picking early contracted to help others pick their cotton for a fee. When a planter's crop was "in the grass" he tried to borrow hands from neighbors with the understanding that the labor would be repaid in the future. Small slaveholders sometimes made less formal agreements to help each other. A Virginia farmer lent his neighbor two mules and received in return "the labor of one man for the same time." [55] Many masters were generous in lending the labor of their slaves to friends.

The demand for hired slaves came from numerous groups. The shortage of free agricultural labor caused planters to look to this practice as a means of meeting their seasonal needs for additional workers. During the grinding season sugar growers hired hands from Creole farmers or from cotton planters after their crops were picked.[56] Small farmers who could not afford to buy slaves were well represented in the "hiring-day" crowds. Some landowners employed free Negroes, Indians, or poor whites, but they generally preferred to hire slaves when they were available.

The great majority of hired slaves, however, were employed by those who sought a supply of nonagricultural labor. Many urban families hired rather than owned their domestic servants. Advertisements such as these appeared in every southern newspaper: "Wanted immediately, a boy, from 14 to 19 years of age, to do house work. One that can be well recommended from his owner." "Wanted a Black or Colored Servant, to attend on a Gentleman and take care of a Horse." [57] Hotels and watering places hired most of their domestics; laundries, warehouses, shipyards, steamships, cotton presses, turpentine producers, mine operators, lumberers, and drayage companies all made considerable use of hired slaves. Free artisans seldom could afford to own bondsmen and therefore hired them instead. Even a free Negro cooper in Richmond for many years hired a slave assistant.[58]

In most cases southern railroad companies did not own the slaves they employed; rather, they recruited them by promising their owners generous compensation. Railroad builders obtained most of their hands in the neighborhood of their construction work, but they often bid for them in distant places. In 1836, the Alabama, Florida, and Georgia Railroad Company advertised for a hundred slaves in Maryland, Virginia, and North Carolina. The Florida Railroad Company, in 1857, announced that for the past two years it had been employing slaves from Virginia and the Carolinas and offered to give masters evidence "of the health, climate, and other points of interest connected with the country and work." [59]

An advertisement in a Kentucky newspaper for "twenty-five Negro Boys, from thirteen to fifteen years old, to work in a woolen factory" pointed to another source of the demand for hired slaves. Gristmills, sawmills, cotton factories, hemp factories, iron foundries, and tobacco factories used them extensively, especially the smaller enterprises with limited capital. In 1860, about half of the slave laborers in Virginia tobacco factories were hired.[60]

A small group of slaves obtained from their masters the privilege of "hiring their own time." These bondsmen enjoyed considerable freedom of movement and were permitted to find work for themselves. They were required to pay their masters a stipulated sum of money each year, but whatever they could earn above that amount was theirs to do with as they wished. Almost all of the slaves who hired their own time were skilled artisans; most of them were concentrated in the cities of the Upper South. Though this practice was illegal nearly everywhere and often denounced as dangerous, there were always a few slaves who somehow managed to work in this manner under the most nominal control of their owners.

By permitting a trusted slave artisan to hire his own time the master escaped the burden of feeding and clothing him and of finding employment for him. Then, as long as his slave kept out of trouble, the master's sole concern was getting his payments (which were almost the equivalent of a quitrent) at regular intervals. Frederick Douglass described the terms by which he hired his own time to work as a calker in the Baltimore shipyards: "I was to be allowed all my time; to make all bargains for work; to find my own employment, and to collect my own wages; and, in return for this liberty, I was required, or obliged, to pay . . . three dollars at the end of each week, and to board and clothe myself, and buy my own calking tools. A failure in any of these particulars would put an end to my privilege. This was a hard bargain." [61]

But whatever the terms, most slave artisans eagerly accepted this arrangement when it was offered to them. A Negro blacksmith in Virginia pleaded with his master for the privilege of hiring his own time: "I would . . . be much obliged to you if you would authorize me to open a shop in this county and carry it on. . . . I am satisfied that I can do well and that my profits will amount to a great deal more than any one would be willing to pay for my hire." [62]

This slave had his wish granted, but few others shared his good fortune. It was the lot of the ordinary bondsman to work under the close supervision of his master or of some employer who hired his services. For him bondage was not nominal. It was what it was intended to be: a systematic method of controlling and exploiting labor.

Mammy Harriet had nostalgic memories of slavery days: "Oh, no, we was nebber hurried. Marster nebber once said, 'Get up an' go to work,' an' no oberseer ebber said it, neither. Ef some on 'em did not git up when de odders went out to work, marster nebber said a word. Oh, no, we was nebber hurried." [63] Mammy Harriet had been a domestic at "Burleigh," the Hinds County, Mississippi, estate of Thomas S. Dabney. She related her story of slave life there to one of Dabney's daughters who wrote a loving volume about her father and his cotton plantation.

Another slave found life less leisurely on a plantation on the Red River in Louisiana: "The hands are required to be in the cotton field as soon as it is light in the morning, and, with the exception of ten or fifteen minutes, which is given them at noon to swallow their allowance of cold bacon, they are not permitted to be a moment idle until it is too dark to see, and when the moon is full, they often times labor till the middle of the night." Work did not end when the slaves left the fields. "Each one must attend to his respective chores. One feeds the mules, another the swine — another cuts the wood, and so forth; besides the packing [of cotton] is all done by candle light. Finally, at a late hour, they reach the quarters, sleepy and overcome with the long day's toil." [64] These were the bitter memories of Solomon Northup, a free Negro who had been kidnapped and held in bondage for twelve years. Northup described his experiences to a Northerner who helped him prepare his autobiography for publication.

Mammy Harriet's and Solomon Northup's disparate accounts of the work regimen imposed upon slaves suggest the difficulty of determining the truth from witnesses, Negro and white, whose candor was rarely uncompromised by internal emotions or external pressures. Did Dabney's allegedly unhurried field-hands (who somehow produced much cotton and one of whom once tried to kill the overseer) feel the same nostalgia for slavery days? How much was Northup's book influenced by his amanuensis and by the preconceptions of his potential northern readers?

And yet there is nothing in the narratives of either of these ex-slaves that renders them entirely implausible. The question of their complete accuracy is perhaps less important than the fact that both conditions actually did exist in the South. Distortion results from exaggerating the frequency of either condition or from dwelling upon one and ignoring the other.

No sweeping generalization about the amount of labor extracted from bondsmen could possibly be valid, even when they are classified by regions, or by occupations, or by the size of the holdings upon which they lived. For the personal factor transcended everything else. How hard the slaves were worked depended upon the demands of individual masters and their ability to enforce them. These demands were always more or less tempered by the inclination of most slaves to minimize their unpaid toil. Here was a clash of interests in which the master usually, but not always, enjoyed the advantage of superior weapons.

Not only must glib generalizations be avoided but a standard must be fixed by which the slave's burden of labor can be judged. Surely a slave was overworked when his toil impaired his health or endangered his life. Short of this extreme there are several useful standards upon which judgments can be based. If, for example, the quantity of labor were compared with the compensation the inevitable conclusion would be that most slaves were overworked. Also by present-day labor standards the demands generally made upon them were excessive. These, of course, were not the standards of the nineteenth century.

Another standard of comparison — though not an altogether satisfactory one — is the amount of work performed by contemporary free laborers in similar occupations. Independent farmers and artisans set their own pace and planned their work to fit their own convenience and interests, but they nevertheless often worked from dawn to dusk. Northern factory workers commonly labored twelve hours a day. This was arduous toil even for free laborers who enjoyed the advantages of greater incentives and compensation. Yet contemporaries did not think that slaves were overworked when their masters respected the normal standards of their day. Some slaveowners did respect them, and some did not.

Unquestionably there were slaves who escaped doing what was then regarded as a "good day's work," and there were masters who never demanded it of them. The aphorism that it took two slaves to help one to do nothing was not without its illustrations. After lands and slaves had remained in the hands of a single family for several generations, planters sometimes developed a patriarchal attitude toward their "people" and took pride in treating them indulgently. Such masters had lost the competitive spirit and the urge to increase their worldly possessions which had characterized their ancestors. To live gracefully on their declining estates, to smile tolerantly at the listless labor of their field-hands, and to be surrounded by a horde of pampered domestics were all parts of their code.

In Virginia, the easygoing manner of the patricians was proverbial. But Virginia had no monopoly of them; they were scattered throughout the South. Olmsted visited a South Carolina rice plantation where the tasks were light enough to enable reasonably industrious hands to leave the fields early in the afternoon. Slaves on several sea-island cotton plantations much of the time did not labor more than five or six hours a day.[65]

The production records of some of the small slaveholding farmers indicated that neither they nor their slaves exerted themselves unduly. These masters, especially when they lived in isolated areas, seemed content to produce little more than a bare subsistence. In addition, part of the town slaves who hired their own time took advantage of the opportunity to enjoy a maximum of leisure. The domestics of some wealthy urban families willingly helped to maintain the tradition that masters with social standing did not examine too closely into the quantity or efficiency of their work.

From these models proslavery writers drew their sentimental pictures of slave life. The specific cases they cited were often valid ones; their profound error was in generalizing from them. For this leisurely life was the experience of only a small fraction of the bondsmen. Whether they lived in the Upper South or Deep South, in rural or urban communities, on plantations or farms, the labor of the vast majority of slaves ranged from what was normally expected of free labor in that period to levels that were clearly excessive.

It would not be too much to say that masters usually demanded from their slaves a long day of hard work and managed by some means or other to get it. The evidence does not sustain the belief that free laborers generally worked longer hours and at a brisker pace than the unfree. During the months when crops were being cultivated or harvested the slaves commonly were in the fields fifteen or sixteen hours a day, including time allowed for meals and rest.[66] By ante-bellum standards this may not have been excessive, but it was not a light work routine by the standards of that or any other day.

In instructions to overseers, planters almost always cautioned against overwork, yet insisted that the hands be made to labor vigorously as many hours as there was daylight. Overseers who could not accomplish this were discharged. An Arkansas master described a work day that was in no sense unusual on the plantations of the Deep South: "We get up before day every morning and eat breakfast before day and have everybody at work before day dawns. I am never caught in bed after day light nor is any body else on the place, and we continue in the cotton fields when we can have fair weather till it is so dark we cant see to work, and this history of one day is the history of every day."[67]

Planters who contributed articles on the management of slaves to southern periodicals took this routine for granted. "It is expected," one of them wrote, "that servants should rise early enough to be at work by the time it is light. . . . While at work, they should be brisk. . . . I have no objection to their whistling or singing some lively tune, but no *drawling* tunes are allowed in the field, for their motions are almost certain to keep time with the music." [68] These planters had the businessman's interest in maximum production without injury to their capital.

The work schedule was not strikingly different on the plantations of the Upper South. Here too it was a common practice to regulate the hours of labor in accordance with the amount of daylight. A former slave on a Missouri tobacco and hemp plantation recalled that the field-hands began their work at half past four in the morning. Such rules were far more common on Virginia plantations than were the customs of languid patricians. An ex-slave in Hanover County, Virginia, remembered seeing slave women hurrying to their work in the early morning "with their shoes and stockings in their hands, and a petticoat wrapped over their shoulders, to dress in the field the best way they could." [69] The bulk of the Virginia planters were businessmen too.

Planters who were concerned about the physical condition of their slaves permitted them to rest at noon after eating their dinners in the fields. "In the Winter," advised one expert on slave management, "a hand may be pressed all day, but not so in Summer. . . . In May, from one and a half to two hours; in June, two and a half; in July and August, three hours rest [should be given] at noon." [70] Except for certain essential chores, Sunday work was uncommon but not unheard of if the crops required it. On Saturdays slaves were often permitted to quit the fields at noon. They were also given holidays, most commonly at Christmas and after the crops were laid by.

But a holiday was not always a time for rest and relaxation. Many planters encouraged their bondsmen to cultivate small crops during their "leisure" to provide some of their own food. Thus a North Carolina planter instructed his overseer: "As soon as you have laid by the crop give the people 2 days but . . . they must work their own crops." Another planter gave his slaves a "holiday to plant their potatoes," and another "holiday to get in their potatoes." James H. Hammond once wrote in disgust: "Holiday for the negroes who fenced in their gardens. Lazy devils they did nothing after 12 o'clock." In addition, slave women had to devote part of their time when they were not in the fields to washing clothes, cooking, and cleaning their cabins. An Alabama planter wrote: "I always give them half of each Saturday, and often the whole day, at which time . . . the women do their household work; therefore they are never idle." [71]

Planters avoided night work as much as they felt they could, but slaves rarely escaped it entirely. Night work was almost universal on sugar plantations during the grinding season, and on cotton plantations when the crop was being picked, ginned, and packed. A Mississippi planter did not hesitate to keep his hands hauling fodder until ten o'clock at night when the hours of daylight were not sufficient for his work schedule.[72]

Occasionally a planter hired free laborers for such heavy work as ditching in order to protect his slave property. But, contrary to the legend, this was not a common practice. Most planters used their own field-hands for ditching and for clearing new ground. Moreover, they often assigned slave women to this type of labor as well as to plowing. On one plantation Olmsted saw twenty women operating heavy plows with double teams: "They were superintended by a male negro driver, who carried a whip, which he frequently cracked at them, permitting no dawdling or delay at the turning." [73]

Among the smaller planters and slaveholding farmers there was generally no appreciable relaxation of this normal labor routine. Their production records, their diaries and farm journals, and the testimony of their slaves all suggest the same dawn-to-dusk regimen that prevailed on the large plantations.[74] This was also the experience of most slaves engaged in nonagricultural occupations. Everywhere, then, masters normally expected from their slaves, in accordance with the standards of their time, a full stint of labor from "day clean" to "first dark."

Some, however, demanded more than this. Continuously, or at least for long intervals, they drove their slaves at a pace that was bound, sooner or later, to injure their health. Such hard driving seldom occurred on the smaller plantations and farms or in urban centers; it was decidedly a phenomenon of the large plantations. Though the majority of planters did not sanction it, more of them tolerated excessively heavy labor routines than is generally realized. The records of the plantation regime clearly indicate that slaves were more frequently overworked by calloused tyrants than overindulged by mellowed patriarchs.

That a large number of southern bondsmen were worked severely during the colonial period is beyond dispute. The South Carolina code of 1740 charged that "many owners . . . do confine them so closely to hard labor, that they have not sufficient time for natural rest." [75] In the nineteenth century conditions seemed to have improved, especially in the older regions of the South. Unquestionably the ante-bellum planter who coveted a high rank in society responded to subtle pressures that others did not feel. The closing of the African slave trade and the steady rise of slave prices were additional restraining influences. "The time has been," wrote a planter in 1849, "that the farmer could kill up and wear out one Negro to buy another; but it is not so now. Negroes are too high in proportion to the price of cotton, and it behooves those who own them to make them last as long as possible." [76]

But neither public opinion nor high prices prevented some of the bondsmen from suffering physical breakdowns and early deaths because of overwork. The abolitionists never proved their claim that many sugar and cotton growers deliberately worked their slaves to death every seven years with the intention of replacing them from profits. Yet some of the great planters came close to accomplishing that result without designing it. In the "race for wealth" in which, according to one Louisiana planter, all were enlisted, few proprietors managed their estates according to the code of the patricians.[77] They were sometimes remarkably shortsighted in the use of their investments.

Irresponsible overseers, who had no permanent interest in slave property, were frequently blamed for the overworking of slaves. Since this was a common complaint, it is important to remember that nearly half of the slaves lived on plantations of the size that ordinarily employed overseers. But planters could not escape responsibility for these conditions simply because their written instructions usually prohibited excessive driving. For they often demanded crop yields that could be achieved by no other method.

Most overseers believed (with good reason) that their success was measured by how much they produced, and that merely having the slave force in good condition at the end of the year would not guarantee re-employment. A Mississippi overseer with sixteen years of experience confirmed this belief in defending his profession:

"When I came to Mississippi, I found that the overseer who could have the most cotton bales ready for market by Christmas, was considered best qualified for the business — consequently, every overseer gave his whole attention to cotton bales, to the exclusion of everything else." [78]

More than a few planters agreed that this was true. A committee of an Alabama agricultural society reported: "It is too commonly the case that masters look only to the yearly products of their farms, and praise or condemn their overseers by this standard alone, without ever once troubling themselves to inquire into the manner in which things are managed on their plantations, and whether he may have lost more in the diminished value of his slaves by over-work than he has gained by his large crop." This being the case, it was understandably of no consequence to the overseer that the old hands were "worked down" and the young ones "over-strained," that the "breeding women" miscarried, and that the "sucklers" lost their children. "So that he has the requisite number of cotton bags, all is overlooked; he is re-employed at an advanced salary, and his reputation increased." [79]

Some planters, unintentionally perhaps, gave overseers a special incentive for overworking slaves by making their compensation depend in part upon the amount they produced. Though this practice was repeatedly denounced in the ante-bellum period, many masters continued to follow it nevertheless. Cotton growers offered overseers bonuses of from one to five dollars for each bale above a specified minimum, or a higher salary if they produced a fixed quota. A Louisiana planter hired an overseer on a straight commission basis of $2.75 per bale of cotton and four cents per bushel of corn. A South Carolina rice planter gave his overseer ten per cent of the net proceeds. And a Virginian offered his overseer "the seventh part of the good grain, tobacco, cotton, and flax" that was harvested on his estate. "Soon as I hear [of] such a bargain," wrote a southern critic, "I fancy that the overseer, determined to save his salary, adopts the song of 'drive, drive, drive.'" [80]

Masters who hired their slaves to others also helped to create conditions favoring ruthless exploitation. The overworking of hired slaves by employers with only a temporary interest in their welfare was as notorious as the harsh practices of overseers. Slaves hired to mine owners or railroad contractors were fortunate if they were not driven to the point where their health was impaired. The same danger confronted slaves hired to sugar planters during the grinding season or to cotton planters at picking time. Few Southerners familiar with these conditions would have challenged the assertion made before a South Carolina court that hired slaves were "commonly treated more harshly . . . than those in possession of their owner[s]." [81]

But the master was as responsible for the conduct of those who hired his slaves as he was for the conduct of the overseers he employed. Overworked slaves were not always the innocent victims of forces beyond his control; there were remedies which he sometimes failed to apply. A stanch defender of slavery described a set of avaricious planters whom he labeled "Cotton Snobs," or "Southern Yankees." In their frantic quest for wealth, he wrote indignantly, the crack of the whip was heard early and late, until their bondsmen were "bowed to the ground with over-tasking and over-toil." [82] A southern physician who practiced on many cotton plantations complained, in 1847, that some masters still regarded "their sole interest to consist in large crops, leaving out of view altogether the value of negro property and its possible deterioration." During the economic depression of the 1840's, a planter accused certain cotton growers of trying to save themselves by increasing their cotton acreage and by driving their slaves harder, with the result that slaves broke down from overwork. An Alabama newspaper attributed conditions such as these to "avarice, the desire of growing rich." [83]

On the sugar plantations, during the months of the harvest, slaves were driven to the point of complete exhaustion. They were, in the normal routine, worked from sixteen to eighteen hours a day, seven days a week.[84] Cotton planters who boasted about making ten bales per hand were unconsciously testifying that their slaves were overworked. An overseer on an Arkansas plantation set his goal at twelve bales to the hand and indicated that this was what his employer desired. On a North Carolina plantation a temporary overseer assured the owner that he was a "hole hog man rain or shine" and boasted that the slaves had not been working like men but "like horses." "I'd ruther be dead than be a nigger on one of these big plantations," a white Mississippian told Olmsted.[85]

Sooner or later excessive labor was bound to take its toll. In the heat of mid-summer, slaves who could not bear hard driving without sufficient rest at noon simply collapsed in the fields. In Mississippi a planter reported "numerous cases" of sunstroke in his neighborhood during a spell of extreme heat. His own slaves "gave out." On a Florida plantation a number of hands "fainted in the field" one hot August day. Even in Virginia hot weather and heavy labor caused "the death of many negroes in the harvest field." [86]

NOTES

1. Joseph H. Ingraham (ed.), *The Sunny South; or, The Southerner at Home* (Philadelphia, 1860), pp. 51–52.
2. Plantation Manual in James H. Hammond Papers.
3. Henry Watson, Jr., to his father, February 24, 1843 (copy), Henry Watson, Jr., Papers.
4. This is a generalized description obtained from the records of many slaveholders who grew cotton in widely scattered parts of the cotton belt.
5. J. Carlyle Sitterson, *Sugar Country: The Cane Sugar Industry in the South, 1753–1950* (Lexington, Kentucky, 1953), pp. 112–56.
6. Michael Gramling, a small planter in the Orangeburg District, who was still producing indigo as late as 1845 was a rare exception. Michael Gramling Ms. Record Book.
7. Duncan Clinch Heyward, *Seed from Madagascar* (Chapel Hill, 1937), pp. 27–44; J. H. Easterby (ed.), *The South Carolina Rice Plantation as Revealed in the Papers of Robert F. W. Allston* (Chicago, 1945), pp. 31–32; Phillips, *Life and Labor in the Old South*, pp. 115–18.
8. Joseph Clarke Robert, *The Tobacco Kingdom* (Durham, 1938), pp. 32–50.
9. James F. Hopkins, *A History of the Hemp Industry in Kentucky* (Lexington, Kentucky, 1951), pp. 24–30, 39–64; Harrison A. Trexler, *Slavery in Missouri, 1804–1865* (Baltimore, 1914), pp. 23–25.
10. *Compendium of the Seventh Census* (Washington, 1854), p. 94.
11. Kenneth M. Clark to Lewis Thompson, June 20, 1853, Lewis Thompson Papers.
12. Columbus Morrison Ms. Diary, entry for November 27, 1845; Rosser H. Taylor, *Slaveholding in North Carolina: An Economic View* (Chapel Hill, 1926), pp. 36–37.
13. Avery O. Craven, *Soil Exhaustion as a Factor in the Agricultural History of Virginia and Maryland* (Urbana, Illinois, 1926), pp. 122–61; Robert, *Tobacco Kingdom*, pp. 18–19.
14. *De Bow's Review, X* (1851), pp. 625–27.
15. Ralph B. Flanders, *Plantation Slavery in Georgia* (Chapel Hill, 1933), p. 158.
16. Records of sales in Lloyd Family Papers. See also Frederick Law Olmsted, *A Journey in the Seaboard Slave States* (New York, 1856), p. 10.
17. Shirley Plantation Ms. Farm Journal; John Walker Ms. Diary.
18. Pettigrew Family Papers; Bennett H. Wall. "Ebenezer Pettigrew. An Economic Study of an Ante-Bellum Planter" (unpublished doctoral dissertation, University of North Carolina, 1946), *passim; Farmer's Journal, I* (1852), p. 147.
19. Sitterson, *Sugar Country*, pp. 50–51.
20. This information about small slaveholders was derived from a study of their production records in representative counties throughout the South as reported in the manuscript census returns for 1860.
21. *Southern Agriculturist, VI* (1833), p. 576.

22. Sellers, *Slavery in Alabama*, p. 67; Hammond Diary, entry for May 16, 1838.
23. These are generalized figures from a survey of many plantation records. See also *De Bow's Review, II* (1846), pp. 134, 138; *X* (1851), p. 625; Sydnor, *Slavery in Mississippi*, pp. 13–14; Gray, *History of Agriculture, II*, pp. 707–708; Sitterson, *Sugar Country*, pp. 127–28; Robert, *Tobacco Kingdom*, p. 18.
24. Olmsted, *Back Country*, p. 47; *id., Seaboard*, p. 433; *Southern Agriculturist, VI* (1833), pp. 571–73; Sydnor, *Slavery in Mississippi*, pp. 18–20; Sellers, *Slavery in Alabama*, p. 66.
25. [Joseph H. Ingraham], *The South-West. By a Yankee* (New York, 1835), *II*, p. 126; Charles S. Davis, *The Cotton Kingdom in Alabama* (Montgomery, 1939), p. 58.
26. Thomas Affleck, *The Cotton Plantation Record and Account Book* (Louisville and New Orleans, 1847–).
27. Gustavus A. Henry to his wife, December 3, 1846, Gustavus A. Henry Papers; Herbert A. Kellar (ed.), *Solon Robinson, Pioneer and Agriculturist* (Indianapolis, 1936), *II*, p. 203.
28. William H. Russell, *My Diary North and South* (Boston, 1863), p. 273.
29. Ingraham (ed.), *Sunny South*, pp. 179–81.
30. Henry Watson, Jr., to Theodore Watson, March 3, 1831, Watson Papers; Olmsted, *Seaboard*, pp. 18–19.
31. Solomon Northup, *Twelve Years a Slave* (Buffalo, 1853), pp. 178–79.
32. Gustavus A. Henry to his wife, December 12, 1848, Henry Papers; John Nevitt Ms. Plantation Journal; William S. Pettigrew to James C. Johnston, January 24, 1856, Pettigrew Family Papers; Olmsted, *Seaboard*, pp. 153–55.
33. Olmsted, *Seaboard*, pp. 339–42; Guion G. Johnson, *Ante-Bellum North Carolina* (Chapel Hill, 1937), pp. 487–88.
34. Fredrika Bremer, *The Homes of the New World* (New York, 1853), *II*, p. 174.
35. Joe Gray Taylor, "Negro Slavery in Louisiana" (unpublished doctoral dissertation, Louisiana State University, 1951), pp. 43–44, 115–17; Raleigh *North Carolina Standard*, June 6, 1855; August 13, 1859; Horace S. Fulkerson, *Random Recollections of Early Days in Mississippi*, (Vicksburg, 1885), pp. 130–31.
36. Richmond *Enquirer*, August 2, 1836; Sellers, *Slavery in Alabama*, pp. 200–220; Flanders, *Plantation Slavery in Georgia*, pp. 197–98; Taylor, "Negro Slavery in Louisiana," pp. 112–13.
37. [Ingraham], *South-West, II*, p. 249.
38. Quoted in Flanders, *Plantation Slavery in Georgia*, p. 47. See also Leonard P. Stavisky, "Negro Craftsmanship in Early America," *American Historical Review, IV* (1949), pp. 315–25.
39. *De Bow's Review, VIII* (1850), p. 76; *IX* (1850), pp. 432–33.
40. Hopkins, *Hemp Industry*, pp. 135–37; J. Winston Coleman, Jr., *Slavery Times in Kentucky* (Chapel Hill, 1940), pp. 81–82.
41. Robert, *Tobacco Kingdom*, pp. 197–203; Alexander MacKay, *The Western World; or Travels in the United States in 1846–47* (London, 1849), *II*, p. 74.
42. Coleman, *Slavery Times in Kentucky*, p. 64; Robert E. Corlew, "Some Aspects of Slavery in Dickson County," *Tennessee Historical Quarterly, X* (1951), pp. 226–29.
43. Kathleen Bruce, *Virginia Iron Manufacture in the Slave Era* (New York, 1931), pp. 231–38.
44. James S. Buckingham, *The Slave States of America* (London, [1842]), *II*, p. 112.
45. Pensacola *Gazette*, April 8, 1848; *De Bow's Review, IX* (1850), pp. 432–33.
46. E. M. Lander, Jr., "Slave Labor in South Carolina Cotton Mills," *Journal of Negro History, XXXVIII* (1953), pp. 161–73; Charles H. Wesley, *Negro Labor in the United States, 1850–1925* (New York, 1927), pp. 15–20; *American Cotton Planter and Soil of the South, I* (1857), pp. 156–57.
47. William B. Lenoir to William Lenoir, May 18, 1833, Lenoir Family Papers.
48. Frederic Bancroft, *Slave-Trading in the Old South* (Baltimore, 1931), pp. 404–405.
49. Richmond *Enquirer*, January 1, 1850; Bancroft, *Slave-Trading*, p. 149.
50. Hamilton Brown Papers; Memorandum dated December 15, 1860, in Morton-Halsey Papers.
51. S. F. Lenoir to her sisters, November 18, 1851, Lenoir Family Papers; Bancroft, *Slave-Trading*, pp. 145–47.
52. Contract between William Frew and R. S. Young, dated December 30, 1853, in Burton-Young Papers.
53. Rickerton Lyle Winston Ms. Slave Account Book.
54. [Ingraham], *South-West, II*, pp. 251–52.
55. Edmund Ruffin, Jr., Farm Journal, entry for September 7, 1843.
56. Sitterson, *Sugar Country*, pp. 61–62; Taylor, "Negro Slavery in Louisiana," p. 94.
57. Charleston *Courier*, August 16, 1852.
58. Copies of letters to "James Sims a Colored man," in Walker Diary.
59. Richmond *Enquirer*, August 8, 1836; Wilmington (N.C.) *Journal*, December 28, 1857.
60. Lexington *Kentucky Statesman*, December 26, 1854; Robert, *Tobacco Kingdom*, p. 198.
61. Frederick Douglass, *My Bondage and My Freedom* (New York, 1855), p. 328.
62. Charles White to Hamilton Brown, December 20, 1832, Hamilton Brown Papers.
63. Susan Dabney Smedes, *Memorials of a Southern Planter* (Baltimore, 1887), p. 57.
64. Northup, *Twelve Years a Slave*, pp. 166–68.
65. Olmsted, *Seaboard*, pp. 431–36; Guion G. Johnson, *A Social History of the Sea Islands* (Chapel Hill, 1930), pp. 124–25; E. Merton Coulter, *Thomas Spalding of Sapelo* (Baton Rouge, 1940), p. 85.

66. Gray, *History of Agriculture, I,* pp. 556–57.
67. Gustavus A. Henry to his wife, November 27, 1860, Henry Papers.
68. *Southern Cultivator, VIII* (1850), p. 163.
69. William W. Brown, *Narrative of William W. Brown, a Fugitive Slave* (Boston, 1847), p. 14; Olmsted, *Seaboard,* p. 109; *De Bow's Review, XIV* (1853), pp. 176–78; Benjamin Drew, *The Refugee: or the Narratives of Fugitive Slaves in Canada* (Boston, 1856), p. 162.
70. *Southern Cultivator, VIII* (1850), p. 163.
71. Henry K. Burgwyn to Arthur Souter, August 6, 1843, Henry King Burgwyn Papers; John C. Jenkins Diary, entries for November 15, 1845; April 22, 1854; Hammond Diary, entry for May 12, 1832; *De Bow's Review, XIII* (1852), pp. 193–94.
72. Jenkins Diary, entry for August 7, 1843.
73. Olmsted, *Back Country,* p. 81; Sydnor, *Slavery in Mississippi,* p. 12.
74. See, for example, Marston Papers; Torbert Plantation Diary; *De Bow's Review, XI* (1851), pp. 369–72; Drew, *Refugee;* Douglass, *My Bondage,* p. 215; Trexler, *Slavery in Missouri,* pp. 97–98.
75. Hurd, *Law of Freedom and Bondage, I,* p. 307; Flanders, *Plantation Slavery in Georgia,* p. 42.
76. *Southern Cultivator, VII* (1849), p. 69.
77. Kenneth M. Clark to Lewis Thompson, December 29, 1859, Thompson Papers.
78. *American Cotton Planter and Soil of the South, II* (1858), pp. 112–13.
79. *American Farmer, II* (1846), p. 78; *Southern Cultivator, II* (1844), pp. 97, 107.
80. *North Carolina Farmer, I* (1845), pp. 122–23. Agreements of this kind with overseers are in the records of numerous planters.
81. Catterall, *Judicial Cases, II,* p. 374.
82. Hundley, *Social Relations,* pp. 132, 187–88.
83. *De Bow's Review, I* (1846), pp. 434–36; *III* (1847), p. 419; Selma *Free Press,* quoted in Tuscaloosa *Independent Monitor,* July 14, 1846.
84. This is apparent from the records of sugar planters. See also Sitterson, *Sugar Country,* pp. 133–36; Olmsted, *Seaboard,* pp. 650, 667–68.
85. P. Weeks to James Sheppard, September 20, 1854, James Sheppard Papers; Doctrine Davenport to Ebenezer Pettigrew, April 24, 1836, Pettigrew Family Papers; Olmsted, *Back Country,* pp. 55–57, 202.
86. Jenkins Diary, entries for August 9, 1844; July 7, 1846; June 30, 1854; Ulrich B. Phillips and James D. Glunt (eds.), *Florida Plantation Records from the Papers of George Noble Jones* (St. Louis, 1927), p. 90; John B. Garrett Ms. Farm Journal, entry for July 19, 1830.

Ante-Bellum Reform

In the history of all nations, periods of change alternate with periods of relative stability. This generalization seems to hold true particularly in the realm of ideas and values. The years between 1815 and 1860 were just such an era of intellectual and ideological ferment in the United States, a period marked by a willingness to think everything, propose everything, try everything.

Though related to the momentous romantic revolution of sensibility that influenced every aspect of art, thought, politics, and perception in the Western world, it developed distinctive qualities in the United States. American society as a whole was more fluid and open, of course, than European. Political democracy was matched by a kind of intellectual democracy that made the ordinary American extraordinarily receptive to new ideas and new social nostrums. New thoughts, new proposals, new speculations were not confined to a small elite, but were shared by a large middle element of the population. The profoundly religious bent of the American people also gave the romantic revolution its unique cast in the United States. In pious Protestant America, the romantic sensibility was to take the form of an intense zeal for improving men and institutions. At times, it appeared to contemporaries that every man wanted to remake religion, society, the economy, the government, or the world as a whole.

Humanitarian reform was not uniformly diffused throughout the country. It was centered in the North, and within that section it flourished most exuberantly in New England and in areas where Yankees resided in large numbers, such as western New York and the Western Reserve of Ohio. It scarcely penetrated the South. That section, by the early years of the nineteenth century, had begun to diverge culturally and intellectually from the rest of the country. At the heart of this growing gap was slavery, an institution that not only affronted the earlier values of the Enlightenment, but even more, was incompatible with the romantic spirit. The reformers singled out slavery as one of their chief targets. This in itself was enough to convince southerners that reform and speculative social thought were dangerous to the whole fragile structure of slave society and to make them declared enemies of northern "isms." By 1860, romantic reform had helped to create two fairly distinct and antagonistic societies within the political limits of the United States.

FOR FURTHER READING:

FILLER, LOUIS. *The Crusade Against Slavery.* New York: Harper & Row, Publishers, Torchbooks, 1963.*
SMITH, TIMOTHY L. *Revivalism and Social Reform: American Protestantism on the Eve of the Civil War.* New York: Harper & Row, Publishers, Torchbooks, 1965.*
TYLER, ALICE FELT. *Freedom's Ferment: Phases of American Social History from the Colonial Period to the Outbreak of the Civil War.* New York: Harper & Row, Publishers, Torchbooks, 1962.*

Asterisk denotes paperback edition.

Romantic Reform in America, 1815–1865   JOHN L. THOMAS

Confronted by the bewildering variety of projects for regenerating American society, Emerson concluded his survey of humanitarian reform in 1844 with the observation that "the Church, or religious party, is falling away from the Church nominal, and . . . appearing in temperance and nonresistance societies; in movements of abolitionists and of socialists . . . of seekers, of all the soul of the soldiery of dissent." Common to all these planners and prophets, he noted, was the conviction of an "infinite worthiness" in man and the belief that reform simply meant removing "impediments" to natural perfection.[1]

Emerson was defining, both as participant and observer, a romantic revolution which T. E. Hulme once described as "spilt religion."[2] A romantic faith in perfectibility, originally confined by religious institutions, overflows these barriers and spreads across the surface of society, seeping into politics and culture. Perfectibility — the essentially religious notion of the individual as a "reservoir" of possibilities — fosters a revolutionary assurance "that if you can so rearrange society by the destruction of oppressive order then these possibilities will have a chance and you will get Progress." Hulme had in mind the destructive forces of the French Revolution, but his phrase is also a particularly accurate description of the surge of social reform which swept across Emerson's America in the three decades before the Civil War. Out of a seemingly conservative religious revival there flowed a spate of perfectionist ideas for the improvement and rearrangement of American society. Rising rapidly in the years after 1830, the flood of social reform reached its crest at midcentury only to be checked by political crisis and the counterforces of the Civil War. Reform after the Civil War, though still concerned with individual perfectibility, proceeded from new and different assumptions as to the nature of individualism and its preservation in an urban industrial society. Romantic reform ended with the Civil War and an intellectual counterrevolution which discredited the concept of the irreducible self and eventually redirected reform energies.

Romantic reform in America traced its origins to a religious impulse which was both politically and socially conservative. With the consolidation of independence and the arrival of democratic politics the new nineteenth-century generation of American churchmen faced a seeming crisis. Egalitarianism and rising demands for church disestablishment suddenly appeared to threaten an inherited Christian order and along with it the preferred status of the clergy. Lyman Beecher spoke the fears of more than one of the clerical party when he warned that Americans were fast becoming "another people." When the attempted alliance between sound religion and correct politics failed to prevent disestablishment or improve waning Federalist fortunes at the polls, the evangelicals, assuming a defensive posture, organized voluntary benevolent associations to strengthen the Christian character of Americans and save the country from infidelity and ruin. Between 1815 and 1830 nearly a dozen moral reform societies were established to counter the threats to social equilibrium posed by irreligious democrats. Their intense religious concern could be read in the

Source: John L. Thomas, "Romantic Reform in America, 1815–1865," *American Quarterly*, vol. 17 (1965), pp. 658–681.

titles of the benevolent societies which the evangelicals founded: the American Bible Society, the American Sunday School Union, the American Home Missionary Society, the American Tract Society. By the time of the election of Andrew Jackson the benevolent associations formed a vast if loosely coordinated network of conservative reform enterprises staffed with clergy and wealthy laymen who served as self-appointed guardians of American morals.[3]

The clerical diagnosticians had little difficulty in identifying the symptoms of democratic disease. Infidelity flourished on the frontier and licentiousness bred openly in seaboard cities; intemperance sapped the strength of American working-men and the saving word was denied their children. Soon atheism would destroy the vital organs of the republic unless drastic moral therapy prevented. The evangelicals' prescription followed logically from their diagnosis: large doses of morality injected into the body politic under the supervision of Christian stewards. No more Sunday mails or pleasure excursions, no more grog-shops or profane pleasures, no family without a Bible and no community without a minister of the gospel. Accepting for the moment their political liabilities, the moral reformers relied on the homeopathic strategy of fighting democratic excess with democratic remedies. The Tract Society set up three separate printing presses which cranked out hundreds of thousands of pamphlets for mass distribution. The Home Missionary Society subsidized seminarians in carrying religion into the backcountry. The Temperance Union staged popular conventions; the Peace Society sponsored public debates; the Bible Society hired hundreds of agents to spread its propaganda.

The initial thrust of religious reform, then, was moral rather than social, preventive rather than curative. Nominally rejecting politics and parties, the evangelicals looked to a general reformation of the American character achieved through a revival of piety and morals in the individual. By probing his conscience, by convincing him of his sinful ways and converting him to right conduct they hoped to engineer a Christian revolution which would leave the foundations of the social order undisturbed. The realization of their dream of a nonpolitical "Christian party" in America would ensure a one-party system open to moral talent and the natural superiority of Christian leadership. Until their work was completed, the evangelicals stood ready as servants of the Lord to manage their huge reformational apparatus in behalf of order and sobriety.

But the moral reformers inherited a theological revolution which in undermining their conservative defenses completely reversed their expectations for a Christian America. The transformation of American theology in the first quarter of the nineteenth century released the very forces of romantic perfectionism that conservatives most feared. This religious revolution advanced along three major fronts: first, the concentrated anti-theocratic assault of Robert Owen and his secular utopian followers, attacks purportedly atheistic and environmentalist but in reality Christian in spirit and perfectionist in method; second, the revolt of liberal theology beginning with Unitarianism and culminating in transcendentalism; third, the containment operation of the "new divinity" in adapting orthodoxy to the criticism of liberal dissent. The central fact in the romantic reorientation of American theology was the rejection of determinism. Salvation, however, variously defined, lay open to everyone. Sin was voluntary; men were not helpless and depraved by nature but free agents and potential powers for good. Sin could be reduced to the selfish preferences of individuals, and social evils, in turn, to collective sins which, once acknowl-edged, could be rooted out. Perfectionism spread rapidly across the whole spectrum of American Protestantism as different denominations and sects elaborated their own versions of salvation. If man was a truly free agent, then his improvement be-came a matter of immediate consequence. The progress of the country suddenly seemed to depend upon the regeneration of the individual and the contagion of example.

As it spread, perfectionism swept across denominational barriers and penetrated even secular thought. Perfection was presented as Christian striving for holiness in the "new heart" sermons of Charles Grandison Finney and as an immediately at-tainable goal in the come-outer prophecies of John Humphrey Noyes. It was de-scribed as an escape from outworn dogma by Robert Owen and as the final union of the soul with nature by Emerson. The important fact for most Americans in the first half of the nineteenth century was that it was readily available. A romantic religious faith had changed an Enlightenment doctrine of progress into a dynamic principle of reform.

For the Founding Fathers' belief in perfectibility had been wholly compatible with a pessimistic appraisal of the present state of mankind. Progress, in the view of John Adams or James Madison, resulted from the planned operation of mechanical checks within the framework of government which balanced conflicting selfish inter-ests and neutralized private passions. Thus a properly constructed governmental machine might achieve by artifact what men, left to their own devices, could not — gradual improvement of social institutions and a measure of progress. Perfection-ism, on the contrary, as an optative mood demanded total commitment and imme-diate action. A latent revolutionary force lay in its demand for immediate reform and its promise to release the new American from the restraints of institutions and precedent. In appealing to the liberated individual, perfectionism reinforced the Jacksonian attack on institutions, whether a "Monster Bank" or a secret Masonic order, entrenched monopolies or the Catholic Church. But in emphasizing the un-fettered will as the proper vehicle for reform it provided a millenarian alternative to Jacksonian politics. Since social evils were simply individual acts of selfishness compounded, and since Americans could attempt the perfect society any time they were so inclined, it followed that the duty of the true reformer consisted in educat-ing them and making them models of good behavior. As the sum of individual sins social wrong would disappear when enough people had been converted and rededi-cated to right conduct. Deep and lasting reform, therefore, meant an educational crusade based on the assumption that when a sufficient number of individual Amer-icans had seen the light, they would automatically solve the country's social prob-lems. Thus formulated, perfectionist reform offered a program of mass conversion achieved through educational rather than political means. In the opinion of the ro-mantic reformers the regeneration of American society began, not in legislative en-actments or political maniuplation, but in a calculated appeal to the American urge for individual self-improvement.

Perfectionism radically altered the moral reform movement by shattering the be-nevolent societies themselves. Typical of these organizations was the American Peace Society founded in 1828 as a forum for clerical discussions of the gospel of peace. Its founders, hoping to turn American attention from the pursuit of wealth to the prevention of war, debated the question of defensive war, constructed hypo-thetical leagues of amity, and in a general way sought to direct American foreign policy into pacific channels. Perfectionism, however, soon split the Peace Society into warring factions as radical nonresistants, led by the Christian perfectionist Henry C. Wright, denounced all use of force and demanded the instant creation of an American society modeled on the precepts of Jesus. Not only war but all governmental coercion fell under the ban of the nonresistants who refused military service and political office along with the right to vote. After a series of skirmishes the nonresistants seceded in 1838 to form their own New England Non-Resistant Society; and by 1840 the institutional strength of the peace movement had been completely broken.

The same power of perfectionism disrupted the temperance movement. The founders of the temperance crusade had considered their reform an integral part of the program of moral stewardship and had directed their campaign against "ardent spirits" which could be banished "by a correct and efficient public sentiment." Until 1833 there was no general agreement on a pledge of total abstinence: some local societies required it, others did not. At the first national convention held in that year, however, the radical advocates of temperance, following their perfectionist proclivities, demanded a pledge of total abstinence and hurried on to denounce the liquor traffic as "morally wrong." Soon both the national society and local and state auxiliaries were split between moderates content to preach to the consumer and radicals bent on extending moral suasion to public pressure on the seller. After 1836 the national movement disintegrated into scattered local societies which attempted with no uniform program and no permanent success to establish a cold-water America.

By far the most profound change wrought by perfectionism was the sudden emergence of abolition. The American Colonization Society, founded in 1817 as another key agency in the moral reform complex, aimed at strengthening republican institutions by deporting an inferior and therefore undesirable Negro population. The cooperation of Southerners hoping to strengthen the institution of slavery gave Northern colonizationists pause, but they succeeded in repressing their doubts until a perfectionist ethic totally discredited their program. The abolitionist pioneers were former colonizationists who took sin and redemption seriously and insisted that slavery constituted a flat denial of perfectibility to both Negroes and whites. They found in immediate emancipation a perfectionist formula for casting off the guilt of slavery and bringing the Negro to Christian freedom. Destroying slavery, the abolitionists argued, depended first of all on recognizing it as sin; and to this recognition they bent their efforts. Their method was direct and intensely personal. Slaveholding they considered a deliberate flouting of the divine will for which there was no remedy but repentance. Since slavery was sustained by a system of interlocking personal sins, their task was to teach Americans to stop sinning. "We shall send forth agents to lift up the voice of remonstrance, of warning, of entreaty, and of rebuke," the Declaration of Sentiments of the American Anti-Slavery Society announced. Agents, tracts, petitions and conventions — all the techniques of the moral reformers — were brought to bear on the consciences of Americans to convince them of their sin.

From the beginning, then, the abolitionists mounted a moral crusade rather than an engine of limited reform. For seven years, from 1833 to 1840, their society functioned as a loosely coordinated enterprise — a national directory of antislavery opinion. Perfectionist individualism made effective organization difficult and often impossible. Antislavery delegates from state and local societies gathered at annual conventions to frame denunciatory resolutions, listen to endless rounds of speeches and go through the motions of electing officers. Nominal leadership but very little power was vested in a self-perpetuating executive committee. Until its disruption in 1840 the national society was riddled with controversy as moderates, disillusioned by the failure of moral suasion, gradually turned to politics, and ultras, equally disenchanted by public hostility, abandoned American institutions altogether. Faced with the resistance of Northern churches and state legislatures, the perfectionists, led by William Lloyd Garrison, deserted politics for the principle of secession. The come-outer abolitionists, who eventually took for their motto "No Union with Slaveholders," sought an alternative to politics in the command to cast off church and state for a holy fraternity which would convert the nation by the power of example. The American Anti-Slavery Society quickly succumbed to the strain of conflicting philosophies and warring personalities. In 1840 the Garrisonians seized control of the society and drove their moderate opponents out. Thereafter neither ultras nor moderates were able to maintain an effective national organization.

Thus romantic perfectionism altered the course of the reform enterprise by appealing directly to the individual conscience. Its power stemmed from a millennial expectation which proved too powerful a moral explosive for the reform agencies. In one way or another almost all of the benevolent societies felt the force of perfectionism. Moderates, attempting political solutions, scored temporary gains only to receive sharp setbacks. Local option laws passed one year were repealed the next. Despite repeated attempts the Sunday School Union failed to secure permanent adoption of its texts in the public schools. The Liberty Party succeeded only in electing a Democratic president in 1844. Generally, direct political action failed to furnish reformers with the moral leverage they believed necessary to perfect American society. The conviction spread accordingly that politicians and legislators, as Albert Brisbane put it, were engaged in "superficial controversies and quarrels, which lead to no practical results." [4] Political results, a growing number of social reformers were convinced, would be forthcoming only when the reformation of society at large had been accomplished through education and example.

The immediate effects of perfectionism, therefore, were felt outside politics in humanitarian reforms. With its confidence in the liberated individual perfectionism tended to be anti-institutional and exclusivist; but at the same time it posited an ideal society in which this same individual could discover his power for good and exploit it. Such a society would tolerate neither poverty nor suffering; it would contain no condemned classes or deprived citizens, no criminals or forgotten men. Impressed with the necessity for saving these neglected elements of American society, the humanitarian reformers in the years after 1830 undertook a huge rescue operation.

Almost to a man the humanitarians came from moral reform backgrounds. Samuel Gridley Howe was a product of Old Colony religious zeal and a Baptist education at Brown; Thomas Gallaudet, a graduate of Andover and an ordained minister; Dorothea Dix, a daughter of an itinerant Methodist minister, school mistress and Sunday school teacher-turned-reformer, E. M. P. Wells, founder of the reform school, a pastor of a Congregational church in Boston. Louis Dwight, the prison reformer, had been trained for the ministry at Yale and began his reform career as a traveling agent for the American Tract Society. Robert Hartley, for thirty years the secretary of the New York Association for Improving the Condition of the Poor, started as a tract distributor and temperance lecturer. Charles Loring Brace served as a missionary on Blackwell's Island before founding the Children's Aid Society.

In each of these cases of conversion to humanitarian reform there was a dramatic disclosure of deprivation and suffering which did not tally with preconceived notions of perfectibility — Dorothea Dix's discovery of the conditions in the Charlestown reformatory, Robert Hartley's inspection of contaminated milk in New York slums, Samuel Gridley Howe's chance conversation with Dr. Fisher in Boston. Something very much like a conversion experience seems to have forged the decisions of the humanitarians to take up their causes, a kind of revelation which furnished them with a ready-made role outside politics and opened a new career with which they could become completely identified. With the sudden transference of a vague perfectionist faith in self-improvement to urgent social problems there emerged a new type of professional reformer whose whole life became identified with the reform process.

Such, for example, was the conversion of Dorothea Dix from a lonely and afflicted schoolteacher who composed meditational studies of the life of Jesus into "D. L. Dix," the militant advocate of the helpless and forgotten. In a very real sense Miss Dix's crusade for better treatment of the insane and the criminal was one long self-imposed subjection to suffering. Her reports, which recorded cases of unbelievable mistreatment, completed a kind of purgative rite in which she assumed the burden of innocent suffering and passed it on as guilt to the American people. The source of her extraordinary energy lay in just this repeated submission of herself to human misery until she felt qualified to speak out against it. Both an exhausting schedule and the almost daily renewal of scenes of suffering seemed to give her new energies for playing her romantic reform role in an effective and intensely personal way. Intense but not flexible: there was little room for exchange and growth in the mood of atonement with which she approached her work. Nor was her peculiarly personal identification with the victims of American indifference easily matched in reform circles. Where other reformers like the abolitionists often made abstract pleas for "bleeding humanity" and "suffering millions," hers was the real thing — a perfectionist fervor which strengthened her will at the cost of psychological isolation. Throughout her career she preferred to work alone, deploring the tendency to multiply reform agencies and ignoring those that existed either because she disagreed with their principles, as in the case of Louis Dwight's Boston Prison Discipline Society, or because she chose the more direct method of personal appeal. In all her work, even the unhappy and frustrating last years as superintendent of nurses in the Union Army, she saw herself as a solitary spokesman for the deprived and personal healer of the suffering.

Another reform role supplied by perfectionism was Bronson Alcott's educator-prophet, the "true reformer" who "studied man as he is from the hand of the Creator, and not as he is made by the errors of the world." Convinced that the self sprang from divine origins in nature, Alcott naturally concluded that children were more susceptible to good than people imagined and set out to develop a method for uncovering that goodness. With the power to shape personality the teacher, Alcott was sure, held the key to illimitable progress and the eventual regeneration of the world. The teacher might literally make society over by teaching men as children to discover their own divine natures. Thus true education for Alcott consisted of the process of self-discovery guided by the educator-prophet. He sharply criticized his contemporaries for their fatal mistake of imposing partial and therefore false standards on their charges. Shades of the prison house obscured the child's search for perfection, and character was lost forever. "Instead of following it in the path pointed out by its Maker, instead of learning by observation, and guiding it in that path; we unthinkingly attempt to shape its course to our particular wishes. . . ." [5]

To help children avoid the traps set by their elders Alcott based his whole system on the cultivation of self-awareness through self-examination. His pupils kept journals in which they scrutinized their behavior and analyzed their motives. Ethical problems were the subject of frequent and earnest debate at the Temple School as the children were urged to discover the hidden springs of perfectibility in themselves. No mechanical methods of rote learning could bring on the moment of revelation; each child was unique and would find himself in his own way. The real meaning of education as reform, Alcott realized, came with an increased social sense that resulted from individual self-discovery. As the creator of social personality Alcott's teacher was bound by no external rules of pedagogy: as the primary social reformer he had to cast off "the shackles of form, of mode, and ceremony" in order to play the required roles in the educational process.

Alcott's modernity lay principally in his concept of the interchangeability of roles — both teacher and pupils acquired self-knowledge in an exciting give-and-take. Thus defined, education became a way of life, a continuing process through which individuals learned to obey the laws of their own natures and in so doing to discover the laws of the good society. This identification of individual development with true social unity was crucial for Alcott, as for the other perfectionist communitarians, because it provided the bridge over which they passed from self to society. The keystone in Alcott's construction was supplied by the individual conscience which connected with the "common conscience" of mankind. This fundamental identity, he was convinced, could be demonstrated by the learning process itself which he defined as "sympathy and imitation, the moral action of the teacher upon the children, of the children upon him, and each other." He saw in the school, therefore, a model of the good community where self-discovery led to a social exchange culminating in the recognition of universal dependency and brotherhood. The ideal society — the society he hoped to create — was one in which individuals could be totally free to follow their own natures because such pursuit would inevitably end in social harmony. For Alcott the community was the product rather than the creator of the good life.

Fruitlands, Alcott's attempt to apply the lessons of the Temple School on a larger scale, was designed to prove that perfectionist educational reform affected the "economies of life." In this realization lay the real import of Alcott's reform ideas; for education, seen as a way of life, meant the communitarian experiment as an educative model. Pushed to its limits, the perfectionist assault on institutions logically ended in the attempt to make new and better societies as examples for Americans to follow. Communitarianism, as Alcott envisioned it, was the social extension of his perfectionist belief in education as an alternative to politics.

In the case of other humanitarian reformers like Samuel Gridley Howe, perfectionism determined even more precisely both the role and intellectual content of their proposals. Howe's ideal of the good society seems to have derived from his experiences in Greece where, during his last year, he promoted a communitarian plan for resettling exiles on the Gulf of Corinth. With government support he established his colony, "Washingtonia," on two thousand acres of arable land, selected the colonists himself, brought cattle and tools, managed its business affairs, and supervised a Lancastrian school. By his own admission these were the happiest days of his life:

"I laboured here day & night in season & out; & was governor, legislator, clerk, constable, & everything but patriarch."[6] When the government withdrew its support and brigands overran the colony, Howe was forced to abandon the project and return home. Still, the idea of an entire community under the care of a "patriarch" shouldering its collective burden and absorbing all its dependents in a cooperative life continued to dominate the "Doctor's" reform thinking and to determine his methods.

The ethical imperatives in Howe's philosophy of reform remained constant. "Humanity demands that every creature in human shape should command our respect; we should recognise as a brother every being upon whom God has stamped the human impress." Progress he likened to the American road. Christian individualism required that each man walk separately and at his own pace, but "the rear should not be left too far behind . . . none should be allowed to perish in their helplessness . . . the strong should help the weak, so that the whole should advance as a band of brethren." It was the duty of society itself to care for its disabled or mentally deficient members rather than to shut them up in asylums which were "offsprings of a low order of feeling." "The more I reflect upon the subject the more I see objections in principle and practice to asylums," he once wrote to a fellow-reformer. "What right have we to pack off the poor, the old, the blind into asylums? They are of us, our brothers, our sisters — they belong in families. . . ."[7]

In Howe's ideal society, then, the handicapped, criminals and defectives would not be walled off but accepted as part of the community and perfected by constant contact with it. Two years of experimenting with education for the feeble-minded convinced him that even "idiots" could be redeemed from what he called spiritual death. "How far they can be elevated, and to what extent they may be educated, can only be shown by the experience of the future," he admitted in his report to the Massachusetts legislature but predicted confidently that "each succeeding year will show even more progress than any preceding one."[8] He always acted on his conviction that "we shall avail ourselves of special institutions less and the common schools more" and never stopped hoping that eventually all blind children after proper training might be returned to families and public schools for their real education. He also opposed the establishment of reformatories with the argument that they only collected the refractory and vicious and made them worse. Nature mingled the defective in common families, he insisted, and any departure from her standards stunted moral growth. He took as his model for reform the Belgian town of Geel where mentally ill patients were boarded at public expense with private families and allowed maximum freedom. As soon as the building funds were available he introduced the cottage system at Perkins, a plan he also wanted to apply to reformatories. No artificial and unnatural institution could replace the family which Howe considered the primary agency in the perfection of the individual.

Howe shared his bias against institutions and a preference for the family unit with other humanitarian reformers like Robert Hartley and Charles Loring Brace. Hartley's "friendly visitors" were dispatched to New York's poor with instructions to bring the gospel of self-help home to every member of the family. Agents of the AICP dispensed advice and improving literature along with the coal and groceries. Only gradually did the organization incorporate "incidental labors" — legislative programs for housing reform, health regulations and child labor — into its system of reform. Hartley's real hope for the new urban poor lay in their removal to the country where a bootstrap operation might lift them to sufficiency and selfhood. "Escape then from the city," he told them, " — for escape is your only recourse against the terrible ills of beggary; and the further you go, the better." [9] In Hartley's formula the perfectionist doctrine of the salvation of the individual combined with the conservative appeal of the safety-valve.

A pronounced hostility to cities also marked the program of Charles Loring Brace's Children's Aid Society, the central feature of which was the plan for relocating children of the "squalid poor" on upstate New York farms for "moral disinfection." The Society's placement service resettled thousands of slum children in the years before the Civil War in the belief that a proper family environment and a rural setting would release the naturally good tendencies in young people so that under the supervision of independent and hard-working farmers they would save themselves. [10]

There was thus a high nostalgic content in the plans of humanitarians who emphasized pastoral virtues and the perfectionist values inherent in country living. Their celebration of the restorative powers of nature followed logically from their assumption that the perfected individual — the truly free American — could be created only by the reunification of mental and physical labor. The rural life, it was assumed, could revive and sustain the unified sensibility threatened by the city. A second assumption concerned the importance of the family as the primary unit in the reconstruction of society. As the great debate among social reformers proceeded it centered on the question of the limits to which the natural family could be extended. Could an entire society, as the more radical communitarians argued, be reorganized as one huge family? Or were there natural boundaries necessary for preserving order and morality? On the whole, the more conservative humanitarians agreed with Howe in rejecting those communal plans which, like Fourier's, stemmed from too high an estimate of "the capacity of mankind for family affections." [11]

That intensive education held the key to illimitable progress, however, few humanitarian reformers denied. They were strengthened in their certainty by the absolutes inherited from moral reform. Thus Howe, for example, considered his work a "new field" of "practical religion." The mental defective, he was convinced, was the product of sin — both the sin of the parents and the sin of society in allowing the offspring to languish in mental and moral darkness. Yet the social evils incident to sin were not inevitable; they were not "inherent in the very constitution of man" but the "chastisements sent by a loving Father to bring his children to obedience to his beneficent laws." [12] These laws — infinite perfectibility and social responsibility — reinforced each other in the truly progressive society. The present condition of the dependent classes in America was proof of "the immense space through which society has yet to advance before it even approaches the perfection of civilization which is attainable." [13] Education, both the thorough training of the deprived and the larger education of American society to its obligations, would meet the moral challenge.

The perfectionist uses of education as an alternative to political reform were most thoroughly explored by Horace Mann. Mann's initial investment in public school education was dictated by his fear that American democracy, lacking institutional checks and restraints, was fast degenerating into "the spectacle of gladiatorial contests" conducted at the expense of the people. Could laws save American society? Mann thought not.

> With us, the very idea of legislation is reversed. Once, the law prescribed the actions and shaped the wills of the multitude; here the wills of the multitude prescribe and shape the

law . . . now when the law is weak, the passions of the multitude have gathered irresistible strength, it is fallacious and insane to look for security in the moral force of law. Government and law . . . will here be moulded into the similitude of the public mind. . . . [14]

In offering public school education as the only effective countervailing force in a democracy Mann seemingly was giving vent to a conservative dread of unregulated change in a society where, as he admitted, the momentum of hereditary opinion was spent. Where there was no "surgical code of laws" reason, conscience and benevolence would have to be provided by education. "The whole mass of mind must be instructed in regard to its comprehensive and enduring interests." In a republican government, however, compulsion was theoretically undesirable and practically unavailable. People could not be driven up a "dark avenue" even though it were the right one. Mann, like his evangelical predecessors, found his solution in an educational crusade.

> Let the intelligent visit the ignorant, day by day, as the oculist visits the blind mind, and detaches the scales from his eyes, until the living sense leaps to light. . . . Let the love of beautiful reason, the admonitions of conscience, the sense of religious responsibility, be plied, in mingled tenderness and earnestness, until the obdurate and dark mass of avarice and ignorance and prejudice shall be dissipated by their blended light and heat. [15]

Here in Mann's rhetorical recasting was what appeared to be the old evangelical prescription for tempering democratic excess. The chief problem admittedly was avoiding the "disturbing forces of party and sect and faction and clan." To make sure that education remained nonpartisan the common schools should teach on the *"exhibitory"* method, "by an actual exhibition of the principle we would inculcate."

Insofar as the exhibitory method operated to regulate or direct public opinion, it was conservative. But implicit in Mann's theory was a commitment to perfectionism which gradually altered his aims until in the twelfth and final report education emerges as a near-utopian device for making American politics simple, clean and, eventually, superfluous. In the Twelfth Report Mann noted that although a public school system might someday guarantee "sufficiency, comfort, competence" to every American, as yet "imperfect practice" had not matched "perfect theory." Then in an extended analysis of social trends which foreshadowed Henry George's classification he singled out "poverty" and "profusion" as the two most disturbing facts in American development. "With every generation, fortunes increase on the one hand, and some new privation is added to poverty on the other. We are verging toward those extremes of opulence and penury, each of which unhumanizes the mind." [16] A new feudalism threatened; and unless a drastic remedy was discovered, the "hideous evils" of unequal distribution of wealth would cause class war.

Mann's alternative to class conflict proved to be nothing less than universal education based on the exhibitory model of the common school. Diffusion of education, he pointed out, meant wiping out class lines and with them the possibility of conflict. As the great equalizer of condition it would supply the balance-wheel in the society of the future. Lest his readers confuse his suggestions with the fantasies of communitarians Mann hastened to point out that education would perfect society through the individual by creating new private resources. Given full play in a democracy, education gave each man the "independence and the means by which he can resist the selfishness of other men."

Once Mann had established education as an alternative to political action, it remained to uncover its utopian possibilities. By enlarging the "cultivated class" it would widen the area of social feelings — "if this education should be universal and complete, it would do more than all things else to obliterate factitious distinctions in society." Political reformers and revolutionaries based their schemes on the false assumption that the amount of wealth in America was fixed by fraud and force, and that the few were rich because the many were poor. By demanding a redistribution of wealth by legislative fiat they overlooked the power of education to obviate political action through the creation of new and immense sources of wealth.

Thus in Mann's theory as in the programs of the other humanitarians the perfection of the individual through education guaranteed illimitable progress. The constantly expanding powers of the free individual ensured the steady improvement of society until the educative process finally achieved a harmonious, self-regulating community. "And will not the community that gains its wealth in this way . . . be a model and a pattern for nations, a type of excellence to be admired and followed by the world?" The fate of free society, Mann concluded, depended upon the conversion of individuals from puppets and automatons to thinking men who were aware of the strength of the irreducible self and determined to foster it in others.

As romantic perfectionism spread across Jacksonian society it acquired an unofficial and only partly acceptable philosophy in the "systematic subjectivism" of transcendental theory. [17] Transcendentalism, as its official historian noted, claimed for all men what a more restrictive Christian perfectionism extended only to the redeemed. Seen in this light, self-culture — Emerson's "perfect unfolding of our individual nature" — appeared as a secular amplification of the doctrine of personal holiness. In the transcendentalist definition, true reform proceeded from the individual and worked outward through the family, the neighborhood and ultimately into the social and political life of the community. The transcendentalist, Frothingham noted in retrospect, "was less a reformer of human circumstances than a regenerator of the human spirit. . . . With movements that did not start from this primary assumption of individual dignity, and come back to that as their goal, he had nothing to do." [18] Emerson's followers, like the moral reformers and the humanitarians, looked to individuals rather than to institutions, to "high heroic example" rather than to political programs. The Brook-Farmer John Sullivan Dwight summed up their position when he protested that "men are anterior to systems. Great doctrines are not the origins, but the product of great lives." [19]

Accordingly the transcendentalists considered institutions — parties, churches, organizations — so many arbitrarily constructed barriers on the road to self-culture. They were lonely men, Emerson admitted, who repelled influences. "They are not good citizens; not good members of society. . . ." [20] A longing for solitude led them out of society, Emerson to the woods where he found no Jacksonian placards on the trees, Thoreau to his reclusive leadership of a majority of one. Accepting for the most part Emerson's dictum that one man was a counterpoise to a city, the transcendentalists turned inward to examine the divine self and find there the material with which to rebuild society. They wanted to avoid at all costs the mistake of their Jacksonian contemporaries who in order to be useful accommodated themselves to institutions without realizing the resultant loss of power and integrity.

The most immediate effect of perfectionism on the transcendentalists, as on the humanitarians, was the development of a set of concepts which, in stressing reform by example, opened up new roles for the alienated intellectual. In the first place, self-culture accounted for their ambivalence toward reform politics. It was not simply Emerson's reluctance to raise the siege on his hencoop that kept him apart, but a genuine confusion as to the proper role for the reformer. If government was simply a "job" and American society the senseless competition of the marketplace, how could the transcendentalist accept either as working premises? The transcendentalist difficulty in coming to terms with democratic politics could be read in Emerson's confused remark that of the two parties contending for the presidency in 1840 one had the better principles, the other the better men. Driven by their profound distaste for manipulation and chicanery, many of Emerson's followers took on the role of a prophet standing aloof from elections, campaigns and party caucuses and dispensing wisdom (often in oblique Emersonian terminology) out of the vast private resources of the self. In this sense transcendentalism, like Christian perfectionism, represented a distinct break with the prevailing Jacksonian views of democratic leadership and the politics of compromise and adjustment.

One of the more appealing versions of the transcendental role was the hero or genius to whom everything was permitted, as Emerson said, because "genius is the character of illimitable freedom." The heroes of the world, Margaret Fuller announced, were the true theocratic kings: "The hearts of men make music at their approach; the mind of the age is like the historian of their passing; and only men of destiny like themselves shall be permitted to write their eulogies, or fill their vacancies." [21] Margaret Fuller herself spent her transcendentalist years stalking the American hero, which she somehow confused with Emerson, before she joined the Roman Revolution in 1849 and discovered the authentic article in the mystic nationalist Mazzini.

Carlyle complained to Emerson of the "perilous altitudes" to which the transcendentalists' search for the hero led them. Despite his own penchant for hero-worship he came away from reading the *Dial* "with a kind of shudder." In their pursuit of the self-contained hero they seemed to separate themselves from "this same cotton-spinning, dollar-hunting, canting and shrieking, very wretched generation of ours." [22] The transcendentalists, however, were not trying to escape the Jacksonian world of fact, only to find a foothold for their perfectionist individualism in it. They sought a way of implementing their ideas of self-culture without corrupting them with the false values of materialism. They saw a day coming when parties and politicians would be obsolescent. By the 1850s Walt Whitman thought that day had already arrived and that America had outgrown parties.

> What right has any one political party, no matter which, to wield the American government? No right at all . . . and every American young man must have sense enough to comprehend this. I have said the old parties are defunct; but there remains of them empty flesh, putrid mouths, mumbling and speaking the tones of these conventions, the politicians standing back in shadow, telling lies, trying to delude and frighten the people. . . .[23]

Whitman's romantic alternative was a "love of comrades" cementing an American brotherhood and upholding a redeemer president.

A somewhat similar faith in the mystical fraternity informed Theodore Parker's plan for spiritual revolution. Like the other perfectionists, Parker began by reducing society to its basic components — individuals, the "monads" or "primitive atoms" of the social order — and judged it by its tendency to promote or inhibit individualism. "Destroy the individuality of those atoms . . . all is gone. To mar the atoms is to mar the mass. To preserve itself, therefore, society is to preserve the individuality of the individual." [24] In Parker's theology perfectionist Christianity and transcendental method merged to form a loving brotherhood united by the capacity to apprehend primary truths directly. A shared sense of the divinity of individual man held society together; without it no true community was possible. Looking around him at ante-bellum America, Parker found only the wrong kind of individualism, the kind that said, "I am as good as you, so get out of my way." The right kind, the individualism whose motto was "You are as good as I, and let us help one another," [25] was to be the work of Parker's spiritual revolution. He explained the method of revolution as one of *"intellectual, moral* and *religious* education — everywhere and for all men." Until universal education had done its work Parker had little hope for political stability in the United States. He called instead for a new "party" to be formed in society at large, a party built on the idea that "God still inspires men as much as ever; that he is immanent in spirit as in space." Such a party required no church, tradition or scripture. "It believes God is near the soul as matter to the sense. . . . It calls God father and mother, not king; Jesus, brother, not redeemer, heaven home, religion nature." [26]

Parker believed that this "philosophical party in politics," as he called it, was already at work in the 1850s on a code of universal laws from which to deduce specific legislation "so that each statute in the code shall represent a fact in the universe, a point of thought in God; so . . . that legislation shall be divine in the same sense that a true system of astronomy be divine." Parker's holy band represented the full fruition of the perfectionist idea of a "Christian party" in America, a party of no strict political or sectarian definition, but a true reform movement, apostolic in its beginnings but growing with the truths it preached until it encompassed all Americans in a huge brotherhood of divine average men. Party members, unlike time-serving Whigs and Democrats, followed ideas and intuitions rather than prejudice and precedent, and these ideas led them to question authority, oppose legal injustice and tear down rotten institutions. The philosophical party was not to be bound by accepted notions of political conduct or traditional attitudes toward law. When unjust laws interpose barriers to progress, reformers must demolish them.

So Parker himself reasoned when he organized the Vigilance Committee in Boston to defeat the Fugitive Slave Law. His reasoning epitomized perfectionist logic: every man may safely trust his conscience, properly informed, because it is the repository for divine truth. When men learn to trust their consciences and act on them, they naturally encourage others to do the same with the certainty that they will reach the same conclusions. Individual conscience thus creates a social conscience and a collective will to right action. Concerted right action means moral revolution. The fact that moral revolution, in its turn, might mean political revolt was a risk Parker and his perfectionist followers were willing to take.

Both transcendentalism and perfectionist moral reform, then, were marked by an individualist fervor that was disruptive of American institutions. Both made heavy moral demands on church and state; and when neither proved equal to the task of supporting their intensely personal demands, the transcendentalists and the moral reformers became increasingly alienated. The perfectionist temperament bred a come-outer spirit. An insistence on individual moral accountability and direct appeal to the irreducible self, the faith in self-reliance and distrust of compromise, and a substitution of universal education for partial reform measures, all meant that normal political and institutional reform channels were closed to the perfectionists. Alternate routes to the millennium had to be found. One of these was discovered by a new leadership which made reform a branch of prophecy. Another was opened by the idea of a universal reawakening of the great god self. But there was a third possibility, also deeply involved with the educational process, an attempt to build the experimental community as a reform model. With an increasing number of reformers after 1840 perfectionist anti-institutionalism led to heavy investments in the communitarian movement.

The attraction that drew the perfectionists to communitarianism came from their conviction that the good society should be simple. Since American society was both complicated and corrupt, it was necessary to come out from it; but at the same time the challenge of the simple life had to be met. Once the true principles of social life had been discovered they had to be applied, some way found to harness individual perfectibility to a social engine. This urge to form the good community, as John Humphrey Noyes experienced it himself and perceived it in other reformers, provided the connection between perfectionism and communitarianism, or, as Noyes put it, between "Revivalism" and "Socialism." Perfectionist energies directed initially against institutions were diverted to the creation of small self-contained communities as educational models. In New England two come-outer abolitionists, Adin Ballou and George Benson, founded cooperative societies at Hopedale and Northampton, while a third Garrisonian lieutenant, John Collins, settled his followers on a farm in Skaneateles, New York. Brook Farm, Fruitlands and the North American Phalanx at Redbank acquired notoriety in their own day; but equally significant, both in terms of origins and personnel, were the experiments at Raritan Bay under the guidance of Marcus Spring, the Marlboro Association in Ohio, the Prairie Home Community of former Hicksite Quakers, and the Swedenborgian Brocton Community. In these and other experimental communities could be seen the various guises of perfectionism.

Communitarianism promised drastic social reform without violence. Artificiality and corruption could not be wiped out by partial improvements and piecemeal measures but demanded a total change which, as Robert Owen once explained, "could make an immediate, and almost instantaneous, revolution in the minds and manners of society in which it shall be introduced." Communitarians agreed in rejecting class struggle which set interest against interest instead of uniting them through association. "Whoever will examine the question of social ameliorations," Albert Brisbane argued in support of Fourier, "must be convinced that *the gradual perfecting of Civilization* is useless as a remedy for present social evils, and that the only effectual means of doing away with indigence, idleness and the dislike for labor is to do away with civilization itself, and organize Association . . . in its place." [27] Like the redemptive moment in conversion or the experience of self-discovery in transcendentalist thought, the communitarian ideal pointed to a sharp break with existing society and a commitment to root-and-branch reform. On the other hand, the community was seen as a controlled experiment in which profound but peaceful change might be effected without disturbing the larger social order. Massive change, according to communitarian theory, could also be gradual and harmonious if determined by the model.

Perfectionist religious and moral reform shaded into communitarianism, in the case of a number of social reformers, with the recognition that the conversion of the individual was a necessary preparation for and logically required communal experimentation. Such was John Humphrey Noyes' observation that in the years after

1815 "the line of socialistic excitement lies parallel with the line of religious Revivals. . . . The Revivalists had for their one great idea the regeneration of the soul. The great idea of the Socialists was the regeneration of society, which is the soul's environment. These ideas belong together and are the complements of each other." [28] So it seemed to Noyes' colleagues in the communitarian movement. The course from extreme individualism to communitarianism can be traced in George Ripley's decision to found Brook Farm. Trying to win Emerson to his new cause, he explained that his own personal tastes and habits would have led him away from plans and projects. "I have a passion for being independent of the world, and of every man in it. This I could do easily on the estate which is now offered. . . . I should have a city of God, on a small scale of my own. . . . But I feel bound to sacrifice this private feeling, in the hope of the great social good." That good Ripley had no difficulty in defining in perfectionist terms:

> . . . to insure a more natural union between intellectual and manual labor than now exists; to combine the thinker and the worker, as far as possible, in the same individual; to guarantee the highest mental freedom, by providing all with labor, adapted to their tastes and talents, and securing to them the fruits of their industry; to do away with the necessity of menial services, by opening the benefits of education and the profits of labor to all; and thus to prepare a society of liberal, intelligent, and cultivated persons, whose relations with each other would permit a more simple and wholesome life, than can be led amidst the pressure of our competitive institutions. [29]

However varied their actual experiences with social planning, all the communitarians echoed Ripley's call for translating perfectionism into concerted action and adapting the ethics of individualism to larger social units. Just as the moral reformers appealed to right conduct and conscience in individuals the communitarians sought to erect models of a collective conscience to educate Americans. Seen in this light, the communitarian faith in the model was simply an extension of the belief in individual perfectibility. Even the sense of urgency characterizing moral reform was carried over into the communities where a millennial expectation flourished. The time to launch their projects, the social planners believed, was the immediate present when habits and attitudes were still fluid, before entrenched institutions had hardened the American heart and closed the American mind. To wait for a full quota of useful members or an adequate supply of funds might be to miss the single chance to make the country perfect. The whole future of America seemed to them to hinge on the fate of their enterprises.

Some of the projects were joint-stock corporations betraying a middle-class origin; others were strictly communistic. Some, like the Shaker communities, were pietistic and rigid; others, like Oneida and Hopedale, open and frankly experimental. Communitarians took a lively interest in each others' projects and often joined one or another of them for a season before moving on to try utopia on their own. The division between religious and secular attempts was by no means absolute: both types of communities advertised an essentially religious brand of perfectionism. Nor was economic organization always an accurate means of distinguishing the various experiments, most of which were subjected to periodic constitutional overhauling and frequent readjustment, now in the direction of social controls and now toward relaxation of those controls in favor of individual initiative.

The most striking characteristic of the communitarian movement was not its apparent diversity but the fundamental similarity of educational purpose. The common denominator, or "main idea" Noyes correctly identified as *the enlargement of home — the extension of family union beyond the little man-and-wife circle to large corporations.*[30] Communities as different as Fruitlands and Hopedale, Brook Farm and Northampton, Owenite villages and Fournier phalanstaeries were all, in one way or another, attempting to expand and apply self-culture to groups. Thus the problem for radical communitarians was to solve the conflict between the family and society. In commenting on the failure of the Brook Farmers to achieve a real community, Charles Lane, Alcott's associate at Fruitlands, identified what he considered the basic social question of the day — "whether the existence of the marital family is compatible with that of the universal family, which the term 'Community' signifies."[31] A few of the communitarians, recognizing this conflict, attempted to solve it by changing or destroying the institution of marriage. For the most part, the perfectionist communitarians shied away from any such radical alteration of the family structure and instead sought a law of association by which the apparently antagonistic claims of private and universal love could be harmonized. Once this law was known and explained, they believed, then the perfect society was possible — a self-adjusting mechanism constructed in accordance with their recently discovered law of human nature.

Inevitably communitarianism developed a "science of society," either the elaborate social mathematics of Fourier or the constitutional mechanics of native American perfectionists. The appeal of the blueprint grew overwhelming: in one way or another almost all the communitarians succumbed to the myth of the mathematically precise arrangement, searching for the perfect number or the exact size, plotting the precise disposition of working forces and living space, and combining these estimates in a formula which would ensure perfect concord. The appeal of Fourierism stemmed from its promise to reconcile productive industry with "passional attractions." "Could this be done," John Sullivan Dwight announced, "the word 'necessity' would acquire an altogether new and pleasanter meaning; the outward necessity and the inward prompting for every human being would be one and identical, and his life a living harmony."[32] Association fostered true individuality which, in turn, guaranteed collective accord. In an intricate calculation involving ascending and descending wings and a central point of social balance where attractions equalled destinies the converts to Fourierism contrived a utopian alternative to politics. The phalanx represented a self-perpetuating system for neutralizing conflict and ensuring perfection. The power factor — politics — had been dropped out; attraction alone provided the stimulants necessary to production and progress. Here in the mathematical model was the culmination of the "peaceful revolution" which was to transform America.

The communitarian experiments in effect were anti-institutional institutions. In abandoning political and religious institutions the communitarians were driven to create perfect societies of their own which conformed to their perfectionist definition of the free individual. Their communities veered erratically between the poles of anarchism and collectivism as they hunted feverishly for a way of eliminating friction without employing coercion, sure that once they had found it, they could apply it in a federation of model societies throughout the country. In a limited sense, perhaps, their plans constituted an escape from urban complexity and the loneliness of alienation. But beneath the nostalgia there lay a vital reform impulse and a driving determination to make American society over through the power of education.

The immediate causes of the collapse of the communities ranged from loss of funds and mismanagement to declining interest and disillusionment with imperfect human material. Behind these apparent reasons, however, stood the real cause in the person of the perfectionist self, Margaret Fuller's "mountainous me," that proved too powerful a disruptive force for even the anti-institutional institutions it had created. It was the perfectionist ego which allowed the communitarian reformers to be almost wholly nonselective in recruiting their membership and to put their trust in the operation of an atomistic general will. Constitution-making and paper bonds, as it turned out, were not enough to unite divine egoists in a satisfactory system for the free expression of the personality. Perfectionist individualism did not make the consociate family. The result by the 1850s was a profound disillusionment with the principle of association which, significantly, coincided with the political crisis over slavery. Adin Ballou, his experiment at Hopedale in shambles, summarized the perfectionist mood of despair when he added that "few people are near enough right in heart, head and habits to live in close social intimacy." [33] Another way would have to be found to carry divine principles into social arrangements, one that took proper account of the individual.

The collapse of the communitarian movement in the 1850s left a vacuum in social reform which was filled by the slavery crisis. At first their failure to consolidate alternative social and educational institutions threw the reformers back on their old perfectionist individualism for support. It was hardly fortuitous that Garrison, Mann, Thoreau, Howe, Parker, Channing, Ripley and Emerson himself responded to John Brown's raid with a defense of the liberated conscience. But slavery, as a denial of freedom and individual responsibility, had to be destroyed by institutional forces which could be made to sustain these values. The antislavery cause during the secession crisis and throughout the Civil War offered reformers an escape from alienation by providing a new identity with the very political institutions which they had so vigorously assailed.

The effects of the Civil War as an intellectual counterrevolution were felt both in a revival of institutions and a renewal of an organic theory of society. The war brought with it a widespread reaction against the seeming sentimentality and illusions of perfectionism. It saw the establishment of new organizations like the Sanitary and the Christian Commissions run on principles of efficiency and professionalism totally alien to perfectionist methods. Accompanying the wartime revival of institutions was a theological reorientation directed by Horace Bushnell and other conservative churchmen whose longstanding opposition to perfectionism seemed justified by the war. The extreme individualism of the ante-bellum reformers was swallowed up in a Northern war effort that made private conscience less important than saving the Union. Some of the abolitionists actually substituted national unity for freedom for the slave as the primary war aim. Those reformers who contributed to the war effort through the Sanitary Commission or the Christian Commission found a new sense of order and efficiency indispensable. Older perfectionists, like Dorothea Dix, unable to adjust to new demands, found their usefulness drastically confined. Young Emersonians returned from combat convinced that professionalism, discipline and subordination, dubious virtues by perfectionist standards, were essential in a healthy society. A new emphasis on leadership and performance was replacing the benevolent amateurism of the perfectionists.

Popular education and ethical agitation continued to hold the post-war stage, but the setting for them had changed. The three principal theorists of social reform in post-war industrial America — Henry George, Henry Demarest Lloyd and Edward Bellamy — denounced class conflict, minimized the importance of purely political reform, and, like their perfectionist precursors, called for moral revolution. The moral revolution which they demanded, however, was not the work of individuals in whom social responsibility developed as a by-product of self-discovery but the ethical revival of an entire society made possible by the natural development of social forces. Their organic view of society required new theories of personality and new concepts of role-playing, definitions which appeared variously in George's law of integration, Lloyd's religion of love, and Bellamy's economy of happiness. And whereas Nemesis in the perfectionist imagination had assumed the shape of personal guilt and estrangement from a pre-established divine order, for the post-war reformers it took on the social dimensions of a terrifying relapse into barbarism. Finally, the attitudes of the reformers toward individualism itself began to change as Darwinism with the aid of a false analogy twisted the pre-war doctrine of self-reliance into a weapon against reform. It was to protest against a Darwinian psychology of individual isolation that Lloyd wrote his final chapter of *Wealth Against Commonwealth*, declaring that the regeneration of the individual was only a half-truth and that "the reorganization of the society which he makes and which makes him is the other half."

> We can become individual only by submitting to be bound to others. We extend our freedom only by finding new laws to obey. . . . The isolated man is a mere rudiment of an individual. But he who has become citizen, neighbor, friend, brother, son, husband, father, fellow-member, in one is just so many times individualized.[34]

Lloyd's plea for a new individualism could also be read as an obituary for perfectionist romantic reform.

NOTES

1. Ralph Waldo Emerson, "The New England Reformers," *Works* (Centenary ed.), *III*, 251; "Man the Reformer," Works, *I*, 248–49.
2. T. E. Hulme, "Romanticism and Classicism," *Speculations: Essays on Humanism and the Philosophy of Art*, ed. Herbert Read (London, 1924), reprinted in *Critiques and Essays in Criticism, 1920–1948*, ed. Robert Wooster Stallman (New York, 1949), pp. 3–16.
3. For discussions of evangelical reform see John R. Bodo, *The Protestant Clergy and Public Issues, 1812–1848* (Princeton, 1954) and Clifford S. Griffin, *Their Brothers' Keepers* (New Brunswick, N. J., 1960).
4. Albert Brisbane, *Social Destiny of Man: or, Association and Reorganization of Industry* (Philadelphia, 1840), introduction, p. vi.
5. For a careful analysis of Alcott's educational theories see Dorothy McCuskey, *Bronson Alcott, Teacher* (New York, 1940), particularly pp. 25–40 from which these quotations are taken.
6. Letter from Howe to Horace Mann, 1857, quoted in Harold Schwartz, *Samuel Gridley Howe* (Cambridge, 1956), p. 37.
7. Letter from Howe to William Chapin, 1857, quoted in Laura E. Richards, *Letters and Journals of Samuel Gridley Howe* (2 vols.; New York, 1909), *II*, 48.
8. Second Report of the Commissioners on Idiocy to the Massachusetts Legislature (1849), quoted in Richards, *Howe, II*, 214.
9. New York A.I.C.P., *The Mistake* (New York, 1850), p. 4, quoted in Robert H. Bremner, *From the Depths: the Discovery of Poverty in the United States* (New York, 1956), p. 38.
10. Brace's views are set forth in his *The Dangerous Classes of New York and Twenty Years Among Them* (New York, 1872). For a brief treatment of his relation to the moral reform movement see Bremner, *From the Depths*, chap. iii.
11. Letter from Howe to Charles Sumner, Apr. 8, 1847, quoted in Richards, *Howe, II*, 255–56.
12. First Report of the Commissioners on Idiocy (1848), quoted in Richards, *Howe, II*, 210–11.
13. *Ibid.*, pp. 210–11.
14. Horace Mann, "The Necessity of Education in a Republican Government," *Lectures on Education* (Boston, 1845), pp. 152, 158.
15. "An Historical View of Education; Showing Its Dignity and Its Degradation," *Lectures on Education*, pp. 260, 262.

16. This quotation and the ones from Mann that follow are taken from the central section of the *Twelfth Report* entitled "Intellectual Education as a Means of Removing Poverty, and Securing Abundance," Mary Peabody Mann, *Life of Horace Mann* (4 vols.; Boston, 1891), *IV*, 245–68. See also the perceptive comments on Mann in Rush Welter, *Popular Education and Democratic Thought in America* (New York, 1962), pp. 97–102, from which I have drawn.

17. The phrase is Santayana's in "The Genteel Tradition in American Philosophy." For an analysis of the anti-institutional aspects of transcendentalism and reform see Stanley Elkins, *Slavery* (Chicago, 1959), chap. iii.

18. Octavius Brooks Frothingham, *Transcendentalism in New England* (Harper Torchbooks ed.: New York, 1959), p. 155.

19. John Sullivan Dwight as quoted in Frothingham, *Transcendentalism*, p. 147.

20. "The Transcendentalist," *Works, I,* 347–48.

21. Such was her description of Lamennais and Beranger as quoted in Mason Wade, *Margaret Fuller* (New York, 1940), 195.

22. Quoted in Wade, *Margaret Fuller,* pp. 88–89.

23. Walt Whitman, "The Eighteenth Presidency," an essay unpublished in Whitman's lifetime, in *Walt Whitman's Workshop*, ed. Clifton Joseph Furness (Cambridge, 1928), pp. 104–5.

24. Quoted in Daniel Aaron, *Men of Good Hope* (Oxford paperback ed.: New York, 1961), p. 35.

25. Theodore Parker, "The Political Destination of America and the Signs of the Times" (1848) excerpted in *The Transcendentalists,* ed. Perry Miller (Anchor ed.: Garden City, N. Y., 1957), p. 357.

26. Quoted in R. W. B. Lewis, *The American Adam* (Chicago, 1955), p. 182.

27. Albert Brisbane, *Social Destiny of Man,* p. 286, quoted in Arthur Eugene Bestor, *Backwoods Utopias: The Sectarian and Owenite Phases of Communitarian Socialism in America: 1663–1829* (Philadelphia, 1950), p. 9.

28. John Humphrey Noyes, *History of American Socialism* (Philadelphia, 1870), p. 26.

29. Letter from Ripley to Ralph Waldo Emerson, Nov. 9, 1840, in *Autobiography of Brook Farm,* ed. Henry W. Sams (Englewood Cliffs, N. J., 1958), pp. 5–8.

30. Noyes, *American Socialisms,* p. 23.

31. Charles Lane, "Brook Farm," *Dial, IV* (Jan. 1844), 351–57, reprinted in Sams, *Brook Farm,* pp. 87–92.

32. John Sullivan Dwight, "Association in its Connection with Education," a lecture delivered before the New England Fourier Society, in Boston, Feb. 29, 1844. Excerpted in Sams, *Brook Farm,* pp. 104–5.

33. Letter from Ballou to Theodore Weld, Dec. 23, 1856, quoted in Benjamin P. Thomas, *Theodore Weld: Crusader for Freedom* (New Brunswick, N. J., 1950), p. 229.

34. Henry Demarest Lloyd, *Wealth Against Commonwealth* (Spectrum paperback ed.: Englewood Cliffs, N. J., 1963), pp. 174, 178.

Black Reconstruction in the South

Resuming full partnership within the Union was one half of the reconstruction process after 1865. The other half was reconstructing southern society to accommodate the changes the war had produced. Part of this was purely physical. Much of the upper South had been a battleground for the contending armies and had been devastated. Where Sherman's army had swung through Georgia and the Carolinas, it had created a blackened swath of destruction. Substantial towns like Columbia and Atlanta had been almost totally burned out. The South's railroads and factories had either been destroyed or had worn out from excessive use and poor maintenance. Financial loss was added to physical damage. Millions of dollars of paper assets were swept away with the bankruptcy of the Confederate government and the collapse of the banks.

More serious was the social disruption produced by emancipation and the end of slavery. As has often been noted, Lincoln's Emancipation Proclamation of 1863, applying as it did only to regions of the South out of reach of federal power, did not itself free a single slave. But Union armies did, in vast numbers, and by the time of Confederate surrender in April 1865, slavery was dead. This event profoundly disturbed the South's social and economic arrangements. Four million former slaves, without previous experience as citizens or as breadwinners, were suddenly told that they were on their own. The Freedmen's Bureau, it is true, attempted to provide some economic help and guidance for ex-slaves, but it was spasmodic, inconsistent, short-lived, and, as we would say today, underfunded. Political help came from so-called scalawags, southerners who embraced the new order, and carpetbaggers, northerners who came south to take advantage of it. Moved by both civic spirit and avarice, these white men helped organize the freedmen politically within the ranks of the Republican party. Joining with talented black leaders, these white radicals succeeded in modernizing and liberalizing the constitutions of the former Confederate states and in providing expanded social services and educational opportunities for all southerners, white and black.

But though the ex-slave was now a citizen, he was also still part of the labor force, and a part that was largely unskilled and illiterate. Could the blacks be reintegrated into the southern economy as free men without massive economic disruption? Slavery had done little to prepare them for the market economy the nation endorsed, and many white men were fearful that, under the new regime, ex-slaves would not be willing to work, and the southern economy would stagnate.

Interwoven with this was the social issue: Would the blacks become a wage-earning proletariat, or would they be encouraged to become owners of property? Prevailing Jeffersonian values hallowed the yeoman and the family farm, and held that both the political and economic health of society demanded that there be a large class of small landholders. The recent Homestead Act had embodied this Jeffer-

sonian ideal, but the lands to which it applied were largely in the Northwest, far removed from the South and from the cotton culture that the ex-slaves knew best.

Given these circumstances, it would have surely been wise for the federal government to have provided land for the freedmen. A number of prominent Radicals saw
this clearly and sought to redistribute the land of prominent Confederates among
them. Some land actually passed to ex-slaves through the efforts of the Freedmen's
Bureau. But on the whole, little was done by Congress to create a black yeomanry.
In the following essay, Joel Williamson discusses the actual economic readjustments
that occurred in one southern state, South Carolina, in the absence of federal guidance.

FOR FURTHER READING:

DuBois, William E. B. *Black Reconstruction in America, 1860–1880.* New York: Atheneum Publishers,
1969.*

Stampp, Kenneth M. *The Era of Reconstruction, 1865–1867.* New York: Random House, Vintage
Books, 1965.*

Wharton, Vernon Lane. *The Negro in Mississippi, 1865–1890.* Harper & Row, Publishers, Torchbooks,
1965.*

Asterisk denotes paperback edition.

New Patterns in Economics

JOEL WILLIAMSON

Before the end of Reconstruction, the Negro in South Carolina found that the
pattern of his employment was already well defined. In agriculture, he belonged to
one or more of four distinct groups. Either he rented the land upon which he
worked, labored for wages, sold his supervisory skills as a foreman or a manager, or
owned his own land.

In the first days of freedom, the Negro agrarian usually found himself in one of
the first two categories. His desire to rent land was strong and persistent. He was
also averse to working for wages and, especially, to working in gangs under direct
supervision. David Golightly Harris, visiting Spartanburg village on January 4,
1866, observed: "The negroes all seem disposed to rent land, & but few are willing
to hire by the day, month or year." Occasionally, the desire to rent became a mania.
"I am about renting some land on the aint (Aunt) Juriy Hemphill place to Bek,
Smith Sam & Peggy," wrote a Chester County planter in November, 1869. "They
have hardly corn for Bread & will make nothing but are rent Crazy & must be
gratified."

In the first years after manumission, renting was poor economics for most freedmen. Few had the managerial experience, and fewer still had the capital necessary
to succeed as independent renters. Moreover, the late 1860's was a period of agricultural depression. Landowners were aware of these problems and, in addition to
their aversion to renting land to Negroes for social and political reasons, they op-

---

Source: Joel Williamson, *After Slavery: The Negro in South Carolina During Reconstruction, 1861–1877* (Chapel Hill:
University of North Carolina Press, 1965), chap. 5, "New Patterns in Economics," pp. 126–163.

---

posed the practice as economically unsound. "Negroes will not do to rely upon as croppers," journalized David Harris in the spring of 1869. "They will not [look] far enough ahead to do any good." As buildings, fences, ditches, and lands deteriorated under the neglect of successive tenants, resistance to renting to either blacks or whites became stronger among landowners. In the spring of 1868, Harris recorded a complaint frequently heard: "I have no little trouble to get my renters to do such work [maintenance], & have almost determined never to rent again. I sometimes think that if I can [not] hire hands to work my land as I want it done, it shall not be worked at all."

Possibly, the Negro renter made his choice against the clear dictates of agrarian economy because he wanted to free himself from the pattern of life he had known as a slave. As a wage laborer, he would have continued to live in the plantation village and to work in gangs under the eye of the white man. As a renter, he labored independently and lived with his family upon his own farm, having either moved a cabin from the plantation village or, as frequently happened, having built a new one upon his plot of earth.

Statistically, the "rent crazy" Negroes often had their way. A generation after emancipation, 37 per cent of the Negro farmers in the state were renters, a large majority occupying plots of less than fifty acres. Indeed, renting became the usual form of land tenure in the upcountry. For instance, of thirty-four Negro farmers who testified on the subject before a Congressional committee in the spring of 1871, twenty-one were renters, eight were wage laborers, and five owned their own land. Further, renting existed in considerable degree in every part of the state. "The negroes who cultivated cotton, as a general rule, rented land from their former masters," reported one native several decades later.

Negro renters paid their landlords in a variety of ways, but, generally, the method of payment belonged to one of two broad categories. In South Carolina in 1880, about one-quarter of the farm operators of both races compensated landlords with a share of the crop. Renting land for a share of the proceeds tended particularly to pervade those areas where cotton was grown; and, even after the return of prosperity, many planters (or landowners) continued to adhere to the system, deeming it more profitable than slavery. This was especially true in the upcountry. "In the upper counties the negroes work better and the masters treat them fairly, so that in some cases farms are still worked on shares with a profit to both parties," reported a Northern correspondent in 1874.

The proportion of the crop paid for the use of land normally varied from one-half to three-quarters, depending largely on the goods and animals that the landlord supplied in addition to the land. The share arrangement was thus capable of endless variety and complexity. For instance, in Edgefield District in 1866, Alfred rented a certain acreage from his late master for one-third the expected crop. However, for the cultivation of another plot, Alfred was to get a tenth of the gross yield in payment for his services as stockminder, then the owner was to have a third of the remainder as rent, and the last two-thirds was to go to Alfred as wages.

In 1880, slightly less than a quarter of the farm operators in South Carolina were renters who paid their landlords a fixed-cash rental. Like share-renting, the term fixed-cash renting covered a wide variety of methods of payment. A common device was the payment of the rent by a specific quantity of a given crop. Thus, in St. Paul's Parish, Colleton District, in December, 1865, "Miles (a Freedman of Colour) and Alfred E. Stokes of the same place" agreed to rent sixteen acres of land from

Charles H. Rice for the coming season. The rental was to be paid in November, 1866, and consisted of sixty-four bushels of corn and a third of the "peace and fodder that may be made." Frequently, Negro renters paid a money rental for their land. For instance, a planter near Adams Run filled his plantation with renters at five dollars per acre, whereas another planter in St. Andrews Parish, in 1872, had difficulty finding renters at three dollars an acre. Occasionally, labor was given in total or partial payment of rent. In Spartanburg County, David G. Harris recorded the terms of a contract with a Negro renter for 1869: "Prince morris has built a house[,] garden[,] cut a ditch & cleared an small field. He gives me Sim's [his son's] labour this year for this land."

To meet the needs of the renter, the landlord, the crop, and of the land itself, rental arrangements often assumed a bewildering complexity as various methods of sharing and paying produce, cash, and labor were combined to provide a satisfactory rental. In 1871 in Colleton County, seven renters (two of whom may have been white) agreed to six different arrangements with the same landowner. Benjamin Kelley agreed to pay the owner a fourth share which was to be used by Kelley himself to improve the house on his rented plot. A pair of renters agreed to work a mule for the owner on a given field and to pay the owner a half of the yield from this field in addition to the fourth due from their main plot. Didemus Allen agreed to farm four acres and to pay the owner two bushels of corn per acre and a fourth of all else he grew. Jerry Smith, a Negro, agreed to pay on Christmas Day, 1871, $12.00 plus a fourth of the produce from a twenty-acre plot that he was allowed to use. In the following year, Jerry contracted with the owner to set up ten thousand turpentine boxes on his land and to divide the profits of the enterprise evenly.

Contrary to the general impression, the plantations of South Carolina did not at the end of the war immediately crumble into many small parts. Indeed, probably most plantations continued to be worked, on a reduced scale, as integral units using wage labor. In the rice districts, fragmentation was impossible since the production of that crop required dikes, ditches, and flood gates which could only be constructed and maintained by a number of laborers organized under a well-financed management. Although few rice plantations were restored to full productivity during Reconstruction, many of these were operated as units. On the other hand, many cotton plantations were indeed divided into small farms and operated under the rental system. Even in the cotton areas, however, some plantations continued to be operated as units for some time after the war, and many planters who rented portions of their lands to others frequently retained large "home places" which they managed themselves.

Employers placed restrictions upon Negro wage laborers that were much more onerous than those imposed upon renters by landlords. The amount, the time, and, frequently, the quality of the wage hand's labor were closely prescribed in his contract, and any delinquency in his performance was severely penalized by fines. In the early years of Reconstruction, the task — the unit of labor used in the slave period — was widely utilized. Ideally, a task was an amount of work which an adult Negro of average abilities could do well in a day's time. The contract signed by thirty-six wage laborers on the Peter B. Bacot plantation in Darlington District in 1867 was typical: "The said servants agreed to perform the daily tasks hitherto usually allotted on said plantation, to wit: 125 to 150 rails; cutting grain 3 to 6 acres; ditching & banking 300 to 600 feet; hoeing cotton 70 to 300 rows an acre long; corn 4000 to 6000 hills. In all cases where tasks cannot be assessed, they agree to labor diligently ten hours a day." While the task system of measuring labor tended to persist in the rice areas, elsewhere there was a general trend toward substituting a given number of hours of labor per day. Ten hours daily was the usual requirement, beginning at or shortly after sunrise and ending at sunset, with greater and lesser periods of freedom allowed for the noon meal as the days lengthened and shortened. Often, attempts were made to control the quality of labor by including in contracts provisions binding Negroes to work "as heretofore," or to "the faithful discharge of his duties as an industrious farm labourer doing whatever he is directed to do . . ." The fine for "absence, refusal or neglect" was everywhere fifty cents for each day lost, and illness gave no exemption from the penalty. Absence from the plantation without leave was subject to fine at the rate of two dollars a day. Persistent absence or misbehavior was punishable by expulsion from the plantation and forfeiture of any claim to wages at the end of the year.

Contracts also included a host of minor regulations designed to enhance the efficiency of the laborer. Typically, the laborer was "not to leave the premises during work hours without the consent of the Proprietor or his Agent," and "not to bring visitors without permission." On some plantations, laborers were committed to observe silence in their cabins after nine o'clock in the evening, "to bring no ardent spirits at any time upon the plantation," and not to have private livestock or pets or to converse with one another in the fields. Often, the laborers as a group were required to supply from their numbers a foreman, a nurse when sickness occurred, a stockminder, and a watchman for the harvested crop. Employers also sought to use the contract to enforce a proper demeanor upon their Negro employees. Thus, laborers were often bound to "perfect obedience," promptness, diligence and respectful conduct," or "to conduct themselves faithfully, honestly & civilly," or to be "peaceable, orderly and pleasant," or "reliable and respectful and to mind all directions," or "to be kind and respectful to Employer and Agent," or to "treat the Employer with due respect." Disrespectful behavior, evidenced by "impudence, swearing; or indecent and unseemly language," was often punishable by fines. Finally, the laborer was invariably bound to pay for the loss or injury of tools and animals either through neglect or by his willful act.

In return for his toil, the agricultural laborer was paid by combinations of goods, services, and cash. In the early postwar years, most received at the end of the season a share of the crop, commonly a third of the gross yield. As with share-renting, the proportion taken by the employer depended largely on the degree to which he maintained his employees. In 1869, an upcountry editor averred that contracts usually granted the laborer a third of the crop in lieu of wages. However, he added, if the employer fed the laborer a weekly ration of four pounds of meat and one peck of meal with small allowances of coffee, salt, sugar, and lesser items, the share granted was a fourth. Share-wage arrangements were often very complicated. For example, on the MacFarland plantation in Chesterfield District, in 1866, twenty-five Negro workers agreed to share evenly with the landowner the net profit of the year after a fourth of the cotton crop or seven bales, whichever was less, was deducted for rent and the overseer's wages and other expenses had been paid.

Neither the share nor the specific amount of money the laborers received for their share was the ultimate measure of the individual's wages. On virtually every plantation, wage laborers contracted as a group, and the share which they earned collectively was divided among them in proportion to the working capacity of each as agreed upon in the contract itself. Thus, a full hand was paid a certain amount, while three-quarter, half, and quarter hands received proportionately less. In addition, employers promised "to furnish each family with quarters on his plantation & a garden plot and the privilege of getting firewood from some portion of the premises indicated by the Employer . . ." Also, laborers were sometimes allowed an "outside crop." A. H. Boykin, in Kershaw County, in 1875, permitted his dozen workers to cultivate as much land as "each thinks he can work every other saturday . . ." Further, he promised to let each employee keep "one cow & one hog," not unusual concessions ten years after emancipation. Occasionally, special allowances were made for family chores. On Dean Hall plantation on the lower Cooper River, in 1866, the contract provided that "only half a day's work on Saturdays will be required of female employees who are heads of families." Employers usually agreed to advance goods and services to their employees, the costs of which were deducted from their share at the end of the season. Whether a part of the contract or not, most employers were forced to supply rations to their employees to enable them to finish the season. In addition, they often advanced other items: tobacco, salt, molasses, blankets, overcoats, shoes, taxes, medical care, and even, with striking frequency, preachers' salaries, coffins, and grave sites. Sometimes, too, the laboring force was required to pay a fraction of the cost of fertilizer, insurance, bagging, and rope — all of which were advanced in the same manner by the employer.

Although it was true that many impoverished planters had no other resort in the early postwar years when cash was scarce, there are indications that many planters and laborers deliberately elected, at first, to use the share system. "I found very few [planters] — not more than one or two, who were offering monthly wages," wrote the owner of extensive lands on the Cooper River in February, 1866. "All on the Cooper River as far as I could learn were offering a share in the crops whether from a want of ability to pay wages &c or because they believed an interest in the crop would secure a more steady course of labor and prevent stealage, I know not, perhaps both." Many Negro workers, themselves, preferred shares to cash wages. "The negroes will not contract for wages," reported a lowcountry planter in the winter of 1866. In the fall of the same year, the majority of a large meeting of Negro laborers gathered in Sumter rejected a suggestion to change to cash wages, clinging "to their preference for a moiety of the crops." One planter thought the Negroes preferred goods to money because they feared: "Maybe it git lak Confeddick money."

Nevertheless, the great majority of planters shifted to money wages within the first few years after the war. Even in 1867, the number of planters paying cash wages, either entirely or partly, greatly increased. A cotton planter on Cooper River who ran "ten steady plows & more as the necesity [sic] calls for them and 30 hoe hands" wrote to a friend in the spring of 1867 that "We pay money for our labour half cash at the End of Each month." A Northern correspondent reported in that year that the few Sea Island planters who could afford it had shifted to monthly wages; and another, writing in 1874, asserted that the share system had been "entirely abandoned" in the lowcountry a year or two after the war and that most planters "now pay their hands monthly wages."

A preference for cash wages also spread among Negro laborers. In June, 1874, a planter on the Combahee River reported that "The negroes now work for money & I have to send out & pick them up where I can get them, & am obliged to take what I can get in order to get along." Such was still the case in the following winter:

"Uncle Hawk is here with some hands that know how to work & will work here all the week, they work for money, exclusively, & don't draw from the Commissary." As described earlier, the Combahee Riots in 1876 were partly caused by the desire of Negro laborers for payment of their wages in cash.

Definitions of the amount of labor demanded of an employee who worked for cash and the manner in which his wages were paid varied widely. On the whole, however, both were much less complicated than share agreements, and the parties concerned often dispensed entirely with formal, written contracts. A Combahee planter described one of his arrangements in 1875: "I have hired John Barnwell to Plow & attend to the mules at $5.00 per month, & give him 2 lbs meat & a package of flour per week . . ." In the early postwar years, planters, suspicious of the constancy of Negro labor, were prone to withhold a portion of their employees' wages until the crop was harvested. In Newberry District, in 1866, for instance, an employer contracted to retain half the wages due his employees until "after summer work begins," and the other half until the end of the year to insure "faithful performance." By the end of Reconstruction, however, most wage laborers were paid daily, weekly, or monthly, had contracted with their employers individually rather than collectively, and had taken a giant step away from the organizational forms of slavery.

Cash wages were also paid for part-time labor. Employees working on shares were paid cash for extra work. For instance, in 1867, the owner of Dirleton plantation on the Pee Dee contracted to pay fifty cents per day in wages to those share-laborers who would do "plantation work," particularly "carpenter work," beyond the terms of their contract. Extra labor, on and off the plantation, was hired "to get the crop out of the grass," or to assist in its harvesting. Gathering in the cotton crop was a usual occasion for hiring additional laborers, and the standard rate of fifty cents per hundred pounds of cotton picked soon became the fixed wage. In the lowcountry, many Negroes owning or renting small plots worked as day laborers whenever they could. In 1868, the Reverend John Cornish was breakfasting with John Jenkins at Gardenia Hall near Adams Run when "quite a gang of negroes came up the avenue with their hoes in hand, looking for work — John sent them into his cotton field — gives them 20cts a task — if very hard 25cts. In this way John is cultivating 30 odd acres of cotton this year — has but one hand constantly employed, & that is his plough man — "

In the Sea Islands generally, and on some rice plantations on the Cooper River, the payment of wages by a combination of land allotments and cash called the "two-day system" came to be widely practiced. As applied to cotton on the Sea Islands, the system involved the laborer's giving two days of work a week (usually Monday and Tuesday) during the ten-month working season in return for quarters, fuel, and five to seven acres of land to work as he wished. Additional labor performed for the planter was paid for in cash at the rate of fifty cents a day or task. "Laborers prefer this system," asserted an agricultural expert in 1882. The system was also applied to rice culture. Gabriel Manigault, having just completed the 1876 season on Rice Hope on the Cooper River, urged his brother Louis, who had had an unsuccessful year in rice on a Georgia Sea Island, to exchange land for two days' labor a week and to hire workers for two more, thereby cutting his cash expenses from $5,000 to $3,000 a year and avoiding "the paying of wages at every step." The "two-day system," too, was capable of infinite variation. In 1868, for instance, rice planters near Adams Run were said to give two and a half acres of rice land, two pounds of bacon, and four quarts of corn in exchange for three days of labor each week. Here again, possibly, the preference of the Negro worker for the "two-day system" marked his desire for greater independence in economic pursuits.

A third class of Negro agricultural worker emerged under the title of "foreman," or, less frequently, "agent" or "manager." Functionally, the foreman was the all too familiar "driver" of the slave period trading under a new label. Francis Pickens inadvertently recognized this fact when he drafted his first contract to employ his exslaves as free laborers. In that document he, at first, bound his workers "to obey faithfully the Overseer or Driver." Having second thoughts, he crossed out the word "Driver" and substituted "Agent." The primary function of the foreman (as that of the driver had been) was the day-to-day assignment of tasks to individual laborers and seeing that they were properly done. Unlike the driver, however, the foreman did not carry a whip as his badge of office, and his demeanor was often in sharp contrast with that of the driver. In 1868, the mistress of El Dorado, a lowcountry plantation, noted this development with disgust. "The work here consists in going out at 9 & hoeing in a very leisurely manner till 12 — when they disappear for the day," she reported. "The 'foreman' escorts the women with an air of gallantry — & Mary P. one day heard him saying in the most courteous manner — 'Hide your grass, ladies, hide your grass.'" Further, the foreman frequently assumed the obligations of a full field hand, laboring alongside his charges and, thus, becoming more of a leader among equals than a superior. Contracts typically bound all hands to obey the foreman equally with the owner, and occasionally, foremen possessed the power to discharge "disrespectful and idle or unfaithful" employees. Foremen were doubtless numerous because plantations which continued to be farmed as a unit invariably relied upon the services of at least one member of this class.

The foreman sometimes earned only as much as a full hand, sometimes more. In 1866, H. L. Pinckney made James, an ex-slave who had not been a driver, foreman over some thirty-three field hands on his Sumter District plantation. For his trouble, James seems to have received only a full hand's share of the crop. Two years later, Pinckney broke his force into three groups of which James, Mitchell (another Negro), and the owner himself were the leaders. James and Mitchell, apparently, received only the shares due full hands. Francis Pickens, in contrast, was very liberal in compensating his foremen. In 1866, he agreed to pay Jacob, who had been one of his drivers in the slave period, $100 at the end of the year and to keep him and his five dependents "in the old fashion." Comparatively, two years later, Pickens employed a "field labourer" for the year at $60 and maintenance.

Largely out of the ranks of the foremen, there arose a higher level of agricultural supervisors who might be described collectively as the "managerial class." Managers differed from foremen in that their primary concern was with yearly, rather than daily, operations, though they usually performed both functions. In essence, the manager substituted for the absentee owner. He planned the crops, scheduled the various phases of cultivation and harvesting, executed the schedules, kept the records, attended to the health, welfare, and efficiency of the laboring force, and prepared, shipped, and frequently marketed the finished product. The manager might also do field work, but he was clearly more than a field hand. He was the fully authorized agent of the owner, filling an office which before the war was dominated by whites. Frequently, the manager received a special share of the profits from the owner. Occasionally, he became the lessee of the plantation and operated it for his own profit and, thus, passed into the entrepreneurial class where he competed directly with white men.

The Negro manager in action was personified by Adam R. Deas. He had been born a slave, the son of Robert, a driver on The Grove, a rice plantation near Adams Run belonging to John Berkeley Grimball. In July, 1863, during an inland raid conducted by Union gunboats and a portion of the First South Carolina Volunteers, he fled to the Union lines along with the entire Negro population of The Grove, including his father, his mother Amy, and his grandmother Sally. Like so many refugee families, they pre-emptied a plot on Edisto Island in the spring of 1865 and remained there through 1866. In the spring of 1866, however, Robert contracted with Grimball to serve as caretaker of The Grove and an adjacent rice plantation, Pinebury, which was also owned by Grimball. In return, Robert was allowed to farm whatever portion of land he chose with a mule provided by Grimball. Adam's mother and grandmother, however, elected to remain on Edisto, partly because they had already begun a crop.

Through 1868, Grimball attempted unsuccessfully to resume profitable operations on his two rice plantations. In 1865 and 1866, he and his son, Arthur, were unable to induce their ex-slaves to return from their Edisto homes. In 1867, Robert persuaded a few Negroes to plant rice on The Grove, paying a third of the produce as a rental. Since Grimball did not provide seed rice and advances, some of these laborers had to earn expenses by working on neighboring plantations and the yield was both late and scanty. In 1868, Pinebury, the buildings of which had been razed and the fields neglected since 1863, was taken up by a Negro manager named Henry Jenkins with the same unsatisfactory results.

In November, 1868, Grimball sent for Adam Deas. Deas, in a letter written in his clear, squarish script, promised to come to Grimball in Charleston within a week. "I was at the Grove on Thursday afternoon," he wrote, catching a scene. "The people are all busy thrashing & I met my father cleaning out the house, expecting you up. I hope the family are all well." In Charleston, early in December, he called on Grimball and agreed to act as the owner's agent in restoring Pinebury to productivity. What happened to Pinebury during the next eleven years was adequate testimony to Deas's worth as a manager. On December 5, Adam returned to the country and on December 9 he wrote: "The time being so Short I was out from 6 oclock this morning up [to] 10½ oclock to night, the Place being in Such bad order & no Building. It is a hard Task for me to gat any one, but up to this date the 9th, I have the Promise of 15 hands who Expect to move Right on the Plantation." On December 21, while laborers were searching for places for the coming year, he again reported to Grimball: "Everybody & my Self are Standing quite Still at present Waiting for Jan . . . So you must allow me a little Chance, I cant go to Work With a Rush, because I have no money." In concluding, he advised Grimball to take any offer for the lease of The Grove which he might receive.

In January, 1869, Deas mustered a score of rice hands on Pinebury and by early February was hard at work. Apparently, however, he had located his family on the Gibbes' plantation, near Willtown, perhaps because there were no buildings remaining on Pinebury. ". . . I was down to the Plantation Purty Much all this Week, and We are trying to do the Best We Can," he informed Grimball. "Just now the men are Buisy Building & preparing Some Where to Put their Provision & Seed Rice." He rejected Grimball's idea of transferring some Pinebury acreage to the Grove. "I don't think Sir that you aught to take a way any of the Pinebury land to Put with the Grove because If We Should not be able to Plant all of It this Season We will Want It to put in order this Summer for the next Season and I am trying to get the Place full up." Several days later, Deas wrote that nothing had been done on the Grove for the coming season. On April 1, while some planters were still seeking laborers, he reported: "We are trying to Push things through in the Best Way We Can We have one Square under water & in a day or 2 We Will have 2 more." By the end of June, the crop was planted. "We have Planted 74 acres of Rice & 50 acres of Corn. We are Now trying to Keep the Grass out of What is Planted." During 1869, Deas acted as Grimball's "agent and nominal leasee" for Pinebury. The payment for his services was a fifth of Berkeley's rental fee of five bushels of rice for each acre of rice land planted and one bushel of rice for each acre of high ground cultivated. On October 26, Deas's commission produced $142.92 in cash.

In 1870, Deas worked on Pinebury under the same terms, but a better yield on increased acreage raised his income to $233.74. In 1871, he received $243.84 for his portion of the crop. In July, 1871, Deas journeyed to Charleston where he signed a three-year contract with Grimball to "cash" rent Pinebury himself for 1000 bushels of rice a year. Hardly had Deas returned to Pinebury when the area was lashed by a hurricane. Nevertheless, by September 3, he reported that the laboring force was hard at work and would soon repair the damage to flood gates, dikes, ditches, and the crop. In 1872, Deas actually leased Pinebury for himself, generously agreeing to pay Grimball the rental which the owner would have received under the previous system only if the plantation were under maximum cultivation. Deas, apparently, intended to profit by using the two-day system to pay his laborers, a system which Grimball had steadfastly refused to utilize. Deas's income from Pinebury in 1872 was about $800, roughly half the salary of a South Carolina circuit judge. By some means Grimball broke the three-year lease, and, in 1873, Deas agreed to manage Pinebury for two-thirds of the yield of 105 acres of rice to be planted. Grimball's share of the crop sold for $946 and Deas's for twice that amount. Deducting $600 in expenses, Deas's income for the year was approximately $1300. Thus, Deas, for the first time, derived a higher income from managing Pinebury than its owner received as a rental.

Grimball was unhappy with the contract for 1873. Even in April, 1873, he had pressed Deas to plant more than the 105 acres stipulated in the agreement. However, a scarcity of laborers prevented further expansion. On June 30, Grimball met Deas in the Charleston office of their marketing agent, Ingraham, and told him he would only agree to share equally both expenses and profits in 1874. In August, Grimball thought that Deas was unwilling to agree to these terms, "says he has made nothing by planting," and complained that even the present terms were too high. Deas was to write his decision. Ultimately, Deas offered Grimball a cash rental of $1200, due on December 1, 1874, and Grimball accepted. The rent was no longer fixed by the acreage planted, and Deas expanded to the fullest the area under cultivation. Perhaps with the benefit of information from the marketing agent, Grimball estimated that Deas's sales grossed $4975 in the year 1874. If this were true, after deducting the expense of planting the increased acreage, Deas's income for the year was about $3,000, a handsome figure in view of the fact that the governor of South Carolina earned only $3,500 during the same period. Grimball agreed to a cash rental in 1875 also, and Deas's profits were probably similar to those of 1874.

Again unhappy with the terms of the contract, Grimball offered, in the summer of 1875, to rent Pinebury to Deas in 1876 for either $1625 in cash or one-third of the net profits. Finally, they agreed to plant at least 150 acres in rice, and the owner was to get a third of the net profits. However, a poor crop and poorer prices produced only about $900 for Grimball and twice as much for Deas. In 1877, they agreed to share both expenses and profits equally. At the end of the year, Grimball resolved to offer Deas a straight 10 per cent commission on profits to act as his manager. It is not clear whether Deas accepted or not, but he did remain in control of Pinebury in 1878 and 1879.

Finally, on December 20, 1879, in a letter addressed to John Berkeley Grimball at 19 Lynch Street, Charleston, Deas severed his connection with Pinebury and gave the owner some parting advice: "It is true I don't expect to plant pinebury next year but things there are moving too slowly. Other planters are moving and you should too, otherwise you allow the hands to Scatter off And it is so much trouble to Get them together again. I know that you dont like to Commence your work until January, but you throw things to far back why Sir you ought [to] be Ploughing now, Giving the Lands to the Rain and Frost." Unfortunately for Pinebury, Grimball did not take Deas's advice. At the end of the year, he gave management of the plantation to his son Lewis, a physician and druggist who had been singularly and repeatedly unsuccessful in his profession. Grimball, himself, remained in Charleston, visiting old friends and being visited, presiding over sessions of the Charleston Library Society, ordering books for the Library, and writing over and over again ever-diminishing lists of the ill-paying stocks and bonds of his and his wife's estates.

A similar story could be told of Bacchus Bryan, a Negro who managed five other hands in planting rice, cotton, and provision crops on a plantation in the vicinity of Adams Run. From 1866 through 1876, Bacchus agreed with the owner, Reverend John Cornish, each year to pay half the yield in return for the use of the land and the advance of supplies. Bacchus's profits were much less spectacular than those of Adam Deas but were probably nearer those of the average manager. For instance, in 1869, Bacchus's share of the cotton crop sold for about $160, and this probably constituted nearly the whole of his cash income for the year.

The Negro manager was a persistent figure in post-Reconstruction South Carolina. In 1888, a Northerner returning to the Sea Islands twenty-five years after he had first come there as a teacher, found that Cuffee, who had been a foreman on one of the plantations, was managing a stock farm for a Northern firm. In 1900, however, there were only 180 farm managers among the 85,000 Negro farm operators in South Carolina, and probably most of these were less like the entrepreneurs Adam Deas and Bacchus Bryan than the salaried Cuffee.

"We all know that the colored people want land," cried the carpetbag delegate from Barnwell District to the members of the Constitutional Convention which assembled in Charleston in January, 1868. "Night and day they think and dream of it. It is their all in all." The speaker hardly exaggerated; yet, at that time, relatively few Negroes had entered the class of agricultural landholders. Some free Negroes had owned land (and, indeed, slaves) before the war, a negligible number had been given lands by their late masters after emancipation, and some two thousand had secured titles to lands on the Sea Islands. But, in view of the desires of Negro agrarians, these were, after all, mere tokens. Under the circumstances, it is hardly surprising that Negro agriculturalists simply shifted the focus of their expectations from the federal to the state government, and that local Republican leaders, mindful of where their strength lay, were anxious to accommodate them.

Doubtless, many Negro voters would have favored confiscation. "I know how hard it was to beat down that idea," declared a Massachusetts man on the floor of the Constitutional Convention. "It has been in their minds that government would some day present them with their old homes and old farms. There is no gentleman on this floor from the country who does not know how much he has had to contend with when he has had to oppose that desire which has been uppermost in the hearts of the people." A few of the most radical of Republican leaders endorsed confiscation. A scalawag delegate to the organizing convention of the Republican party, held in May, 1867, was "perfectly disgusted with the negroes, that they advocate confiscation of lands . . ."; and as late as the campaign of 1870, the scalawag boss of Laurens County was vigorously preaching confiscation with the result, one resident observed, that "none of the men want to work, all looking forward to next month when they expect to get land & houses." White anxiety concerning confiscation was partially justified, but much of the furor was generated by an overly timorous white community. In Spartanburg, in November, 1867, a prospective purchaser of a plot of land was too cautious when he reneged because he was "afraid of confiscation." Furthermore, there were Conservative politicians who were not above promoting and playing upon the anxieties of their friends. "Knowing that the Radicals had scared the Southern people with *Confiscation* by Congress, from the path of honor and patriotism, I thought I would scare them back again with *Confiscation* by the negroes," B. F. Perry wrote to one of his supporters in the spring of 1867. "You have lived long enough in the world . . . to know that most persons are influenced more by their *fears* than by their honor," concluded that gentleman of highly vaunted democratic reputation.

Confiscation met with the early, persistent, and successful opposition of the main body of Republican leadership. In the convention of the party in July, 1867, the idea was not even formally introduced; in the field, campaigners subsequently adopted the same attitude; and the Constitutional Convention of 1868 with the full assent of its Negro delegates pointedly asserted that "The only manner by which any land can be obtained by the landless will be to purchase it." Two years later, in a political meeting at Christ Church, native Negro A. J. Ransier was still answering the charge that Republicans had offered Negroes forty acres and a mule. "We had never," he declared, "promised any such thing, but on the contrary advised the people to buy lands by saving their money, and not to expect confiscation or the possession of lands that were not theirs, nor ours to give them . . ."

To some extent, Republicans rejected confiscation as inexpedient — that is, that titles conferred might be impermanent, that Congress might disallow such a measure, or that whites might be driven to violence. Primarily, however, they refused confiscation because they felt it was contrary to the natural laws of economic morality; it would be useless, they argued, even pernicious, to legislate against the fiats of classical economics. "The sooner the public mind is disabused of that impression, the sooner every man knows that to acquire land he must earn it," declared W. J. Whipper, a Northern-born Negro delegate, to the convention, "the sooner he feels the Government has no lands to dispose of or to give him the better. Do what is necessary to protect the laborer in his labor and you will effect the greatest possible good."

Republican leaders were strong in their rejection of confiscation, but by no means did they abandon the use of political power to achieve the popular goal of a division of large landed estates among their supporters. Ultimately, they settled upon two complementary but separate programs. One of these involved the purchase of lands by the state for division and resale to actual settlers. By the spring of 1869, acting upon an ordinance of the Constitutional Convention, the Republican legislature had created a Land Commission which was to purchase, by the issue of bonds guaranteed by the state, lands at public sales and "otherwise." Under a land commissioner these acquisitions were to be surveyed, divided into smaller tracts, and sold to settlers at the purchase price. The settler would pay taxes on the land and 7 per cent interest yearly on the principal of the loan. One half the plot was to be under cultivation within three years, at which time payments on the purchase price would begin and would extend over such period as the legislature directed.

Almost from its inception the land program was hamstrung by political involvement. At least some Radical politicians thought that the partisan purposes of the relocation scheme were as important as the economic goals. In October, 1869, for instance, a leading Republican concurred in a statement by the land commissioner that party interest dictated "That in the upper counties it is necessary to purchase large tracts, so that colonies may be planted of sufficient strength to help, & protect each other, and to be the nucleas [*sic*] of education &c &c &c. . . . We must draw the union people to points where they will be a power & mutual supporters." In addition, the office of land commissioner, itself, soon became a political pawn. The first incumbent was Charles P. Leslie, an aging, erratic, unscrupulous New Yorker who was given the office, it was said, to compensate him for losing the United States marshalship which he really wanted. Whatever talents Leslie may have possessed were turned immediately to filling his own pockets, an occupation at which he was very adept. Using $200,000 in bonds authorized by the legislature, Leslie began to buy land at a rapid rate.

A very few purchases were well made at sheriff's sales, from the executors of estates, and by conscientious agents with an eye for a bargain. For instance, Henry E. Hayne, an ex-sergeant of the First South Carolina, acting as Leslie's agent in Marion County, arranged to buy 1734 acres of land for $1,500. The tract contained, by Hayne's report, 200 acres of "good swamp land, a splendid range for cattle &c and good corn and grain land. The balance is good upland, a large portion of woodland. There is good water on the place, several good buildings." The tract was then rented for $100 yearly, suggesting that the offered price was reasonable. But more to the point: "A number of citizens are prepared to purchase small tracts of this property from the State."

Unfortunately, most purchases were made by men less reliable than Hayne. In Darlington County, Leslie's agent bought lands at a sheriff's sale supposedly for the land agency. He later changed the titles to indicate that he had bought them on his own account and then re-sold the land to the state at twice the price he had paid. Throughout the life of the commission, a suspiciously large number of purchases were made from men directly involved in Republican politics — including Governor Scott, himself.

The secretary of state, Francis L. Cardozo, a Negro, had never approved of the choice of Leslie as land commissioner and soon refused to participate as a member of the advisory board. As rumors of fraud and mismanagement in the Land Commission began to circulate, Cardozo and other Negro leaders — including Rainey, Whipper, Elliott, Ransier, and Nash — moved to force Leslie out of his post. Dominant in the legislature in the winter of 1870, these men refused to pass a proposed bill authorizing the issuance of an additional $500,000 in bonds for the use of the commission. Leslie and others were very anxious to win the new issue because they had already overspent the amount initially authorized. It was arranged, finally, that Leslie would resign and the legislature would sanction the new issue. According to the subsequent testimony of N. G. Parker, treasurer of the state until 1872, Leslie demanded and got $25,000 in return for his resignation and the surrender of his one-twelfth share in the Greenville and Columbia Railroad. To raise this money, Parker arranged the fraudulent purchase by the commission of some 27,000 acres (one portion of which was appropriately known as "Hell Hole Swamp") for about $119,000 nominally, but actually for much less. D. H. Chamberlain, then attorney-general, discovered that the title to one of these tracts was faulty and that Parker and his associates were aware of the fault. However, he did not expose his findings.

One of the demands of the Negro legislators was the appointment of a Negro as land commissioner. The stipulation was met, but the choice was unfortunate, falling upon R. C. De Large, a native Charlestonian, still young in 1870 and very ambitious politically. Parker later asserted that De Large was Scott's choice and that the latter arranged his appointment so that De Large could steal enough money to unseat scalawag Congressman C. C. Bowen of Charleston, Scott's most bitter personal and political enemy. True or not, De Large was in fact immediately caught up in a year-long, vitriolic campaign against Bowen from which he emerged victorious. During De Large's absence, the scalawag comptroller-general, apparently, took the lead in administering the land program. Again, most purchases were made at exorbitant prices through the agency of or directly from officers of the state, and by 1871 the funds of the commission were exhausted. They were never renewed, but the quality of lands purchased during De Large's tenure did improve somewhat. The improvement may have resulted from the closer scrutiny to which Cardozo and Chamberlain subjected prospective transactions. Since Cardozo, as secretary of state, had to record purchases and Chamberlain, as attorney-general, was responsible for the legitimacy of titles, each man was in a position to block suspicious transactions. During the De Large period, interested parties were, apparently, willing to solicit their approval for purchases and the degree of control which they exercised was considerable.

Criticism within the Republican party during the spring and summer of 1870 forced many officials to defend their connections with purchases made by the commission. Chafing under charges that professional politicians were obstructing the efficient administration of the land program, an aroused legislature ordered the land commissioner to report immediately, formed a joint committee to investigate the program, and passed legislation clarifying the conditions of settlement on state lands. Ultimately, the legislature assigned the duties of the land commissioner to the secretary of state, and, thus, Cardozo, himself, assumed responsibility for the program. A very able administrator, Cardozo quickly systematized the haphazardly kept records of the office, ascertained the location of the one hundred thousand acres in twenty-three counties which belonged to the state, investigated the degree to which these lands were settled, and arranged to receive regular payments from the settlers. In April, 1872, the advisory board permitted the commissioner to base the price of lots (those already sold, as well as those remaining unsold) upon their actual value rather than the price which the state had paid for them. Immediately, a wave of additional settlers moved onto state lands. On one state-owned plantation on St.

John's Island, for instance, fifteen lots which had lain barren for two years were promptly settled by Negro families.

Henry E. Hayne, who succeeded Cardozo as secretary of state in 1872, continued the good work. He improved the administration of the program still more by appointing a single agent, J. E. Green, to replace the many county agents. Green familiarized himself with each tract, encouraged settlement, and made collections. In 1874, Hayne reported that the administration of the program under the new system cost only 8 per cent of collections, whereas before expenses had often exceeded revenues. On one occasion, when settlers were about to be evicted from their Darlington County plots because of a fault in the title purchased by the state, Hayne used the resources of the commission to correct the deficiency. The humane policy of the state was further revealed in February, 1874, when the legislature, following a poor farming season in some areas and a money scarcity which generally prevailed after the panic of 1873, authorized the commissioner to postpone payments in cases where subsistence was endangered.

Strangely enough, although they did not buy new lands to perpetuate the program, the Redeemers continued and improved still further the administration of the Land Commission. Through litigation they added about 1300 acres to the program, the only addition made after 1870. Further, they refunded taxes paid by settlers before titles were granted, it being customary for titleholders to pay tax claims against real estate, in this case the state itself. In November, 1877, about 47,000 acres or one-half of the state's lands remained unsettled. The Redeemers reduced prices on unsold plots, surveyed tracts more suitably, allowed occupants to reduce the size of their farms to adjust to their ability to pay, and passed on the lands of those unable to pay to other settlers.

The end result was that by the late 1880's nearly all the state's lands had been disposed of to actual settlers; and by the early 1890's approximately 2,000 families had obtained titles to farms through the agency of the Land Commission.

Perhaps the most effective scheme of land redistribution implemented by Republicans in South Carolina was also the most subtle. In its earliest form, it was conceived as a heavy tax on unused land. This tax was expected to force owners of such lands either to bear the burden of the tax from their other resources, to put the land under cultivation and thus employ laborers or renters, or to allow the land to be sold either to the state for resale or directly to private parties. As it matured, the basic concept expanded. Not only would unused lands be heavily taxed, but all property, real and personal, used and unused, would be so burdened. Thus, all capital would be forced into full productivity, or, in essence, would be confiscated and sold. One anticipated result of the program was that a large quantity of land would be offered for sale at prices that the landless could afford to pay. Also, heavy taxation would support a prospective expansion of public services rendered by the state: internal improvements; care for the insane, orphans, and indigents; a modern penitentiary; a streamlined and efficient judiciary; and, most important, a system of public education from primary to university levels. Heavy taxation, then, was the core of the Republican program in Reconstruction South Carolina. It was a program designed to give its supporters land, educational opportunity, and other benefits that would imbue them with a spirit of loyalty to the party and insure its continuance in power.

From its birth, the Republican party in South Carolina consciously and deliberately advocated land division through taxation. "We must drive them to the wall by taxation," cried one carpetbagger to a Republican convention in the summer of 1867. While the convention was more circumspect in its choice of words, its resolution on the subject was commonly interpreted as an endorsement of a tax program which, as one Negro delegate observed, "would force owners of large tracts of waste lands to sell and give us a chance." As the campaign for the Constitutional Convention of 1868 proceeded, the tax program supplanted confiscation in popularity. Such a program, one observer noted, would be as effective as confiscation, "and yet avoid the strenuous opposition that any scheme of general land pillaging would infallibly meet with in the North." Perhaps, with this criticism in mind, the Convention itself decided to tax all real and personal property at a single, uniform rate based upon actual values. This amendment did not mean that the party had deserted the tax program. The carpetbag delegate who was soon to become the treasurer of South Carolina put the case succinctly:

> Taxes are always (at least in hard times) a burden, will be assessed yearly upon all lands, and they must be paid. The expenses of the State (constantly increasing, will be a continual drag upon those who attempt to carry on large landed estates with a small amount of money,) will alone force sufficient lands upon the market at all times to meet the wants of all the landless. This Convention will cost the State quite a large sum of money. A legislature will soon assemble, and that will cost money. Education, once limited, is to be general, and that will be expensive; and, to keep up with the age, it is fair to presume that the State tax will be greater next year than this, and increase yearly; this will be felt, and will be the stimulus to many for owning less land, and cause them to see the necessity for disposing of their surplus.

The Convention adopted other measures which were to supplement the tax program. It requested and obtained from the military authorities a stay law — or rather order — designed to delay forced sales of lands to allow the landless an opportunity to accumulate capital and the tax program time to depress land prices. Once the agriculturalist had acquired a small holding, the Convention sought to protect him against the direct effects of forced sales in civil actions by a constitutional provision that exempted from such sales a homestead worth $1000 and personal property worth $500. A suggested corollary to the tax program would have required state officers to subdivide all tracts sold for taxes into plots of 160 acres or less. This proposal met with the sympathy of the Convention, but the majority ultimately decided that no satisfactory defense could be made against monied men buying as many plots as they chose.

Once in power on the state level, Republicans hastened to carry out the tax program. The burden of taxation was shifted from mercantile interests to landed property, and the total tax bill increased rapidly to astounding heights. During Reconstruction, the amount of taxes levied and collected every year was well over a million dollars; before 1860 it had always been considerably less, and, during the Orr regime, had been only about $600,000 — less than one dollar each for every man, woman, and child in the state.

Some Republican politicians contended that the state tax rate in South Carolina was no more than in some Northern states. Such, indeed, was the case, but the whole story of taxation in South Carolina was not told by the *state tax rate*. Actually, the rate was kept deliberately low, but other variables in the tax equation were manipulated to raise the tax bill ever higher. In addition to the state levy, each county taxed its property owners for the administration of regular county affairs and for special purposes such as new buildings and roads. Furthermore, the school tax was often quoted separately. Thus, E. Gelzer, in Abbeville County in 1871, paid a state tax of only $59.64; but, at the same time, he paid a $25.56 county tax and an $8.52 school tax. Property owners residing in towns and cities paid municipal taxes as well. Census returns indicate that Carolinians paid $2,800,000 in state and local taxes in 1870, an enormous sum by prewar standards. Of this amount, $1,600,000, including the school tax, went to Columbia, while almost half was consumed locally.

A second variable in the tax equation was the value placed on property for tax purposes. Before the advent of the Republican regime, the tendency was to under-value property in assessing it for tax purposes; after, the tendency was drastically reversed. This weapon for increasing taxes was sharpened by the authority given to the governor to appoint and remove assessors within each county and by the creation of a State Board of Equalization with power to decrease or increase (two- or threefold if it wished) the assessment of a given county. There was abundant evidence that this power was abused during the first six years of Republican rule. A meeting of Conservative white leaders in Columbia in 1871 admitted that the state tax rate (about 1 per cent at that time) was not excessive but complained that assessments were unduly high. Wide fluctuations in the total of assessments between 1869 and 1873 show clearly that this power was freely used. For instance, in 1870, the figure was placed at $184,000,000. In the hard election year of 1872, it was reduced to $146,000,000, only to be raised again after the election. Even some Republicans deprecated such blatant unfairness. Martin R. Delany, the former major, stated in 1871 that lands were often sold at one-half to one-fourth of the assessed value. "Land in South Carolina is greatly depreciated," he declared, "while taxes have become proportionately higher." "Taxes are enormous," exclaimed a Northern businessman residing in Charleston, voicing a fact all too well known among his land-owning Carolina contemporaries.

Astonishing as the tax bill was in the aggregate, it was even more astounding to the individual taxpayer. In May, 1871, a Chester County planter lamented: "I have paid $400.00 Dollars of Tax this year & expect to pay about $300.00 in the fall making $700 in all. before the war my Tax was from 30 to 50 Dollars. Where does the money go?" By January 6, 1873, he had paid $365 in taxes for that year and would have to pay another large tax bill before the year ended. "I can go to some other place (say Augusta) & live comfortably on my Tax," he asserted.

Republican reform Governor Daniel H. Chamberlain, who held office from November, 1874, until he was ousted by Hampton in April, 1877, made a determined and partly successful attempt to reduce the tax burden. In this he was ably assisted by Secretary of the Treasury Francis L. Cardozo. In 1874, Chamberlain recommended to the legislature an across-the-board reduction in expenditures and, soon thereafter, executed a re-assessment of taxable property throughout the state which very nearly equalized assessed and market values. When the legislature passed a tax bill in the spring that exceeded his recommendations, Chamberlain courageously vetoed it, and in the legislative session of 1875–1876 he succeeded in reducing the rate of taxation from 13 to 11 mils.

Chamberlain won much praise and considerable support from the native white community for his efforts, but other circumstances were operating in the fall of 1875 to turn the tide of taxpayer sentiment against him. In the counties and cities where corruptionists remained entrenched, local tax rates were largely beyond the control of the governor. In spite of Chamberlain's reforms, these drove the total tax bill for their areas to great heights. In heavily agricultural Kershaw County, yearly taxes (county and education, as well as state) amounted to about 2 per cent of the total value of taxable property. Taxpayers, under such circumstances, were hardly impressed with the fact that Chamberlain had saved them from a 2.2 per cent levy. One upcountry editor queried, "Does this mean reform or confiscation?" Even in counties under native white control, where local levies had been kept at a consistent minimum, Chamberlain's moderate gains were more than offset by the decline in cotton profits and the increase in food costs which began in the fall of 1875. "Our crops are poorer, the prices range much lower than for years past, while flour and bacon are higher," complained an Anderson County editor early in December. When he learned that the tax rate for his county was to be about 1.5 per cent he cried, "Thus our worst fears are realized."

The results of the Republican tax program were everything that its authors anticipated — and more. Vast quantities of land were forfeited to the state every year, and others passed under the hammer to satisfy judgments rendered in civil suits. When the Republicans took office, the state held only about 23,000 acres of land forfeited for taxes. This figure dwindled into insignificance as tax foreclosures by the Radical government proceeded. In the early 1870's, the local press, particularly in the middle and lower counties, abounded in advertisements of tax sales. During the state fiscal year which ended October 31, 1873, officials reported 270,000 acres of land as forfeited for about $21,000 in taxes; and in the following year the figure rose to more than 500,000 acres. Interestingly, the twelve counties in which the most land was forfeited were precisely those dozen counties in which the proportion of Negro to white voters was highest.

White landowners in the lower counties were convinced that Republican tax collectors were, indeed, conspiring to "drive them to the wall." One Georgetown plantation owner complained in the spring of 1869 that the county tax collector had told him he did not know how much his tax would be or when it would be determined. "The scallawags and capt Baggers would no doubt like right well to see my place advertised and sold for taxes," he surmised. "I trust they will not be gratified." John Berkeley Grimball could have added that confiscation by hook was fully as possible as by crook. In the spring of 1873, he was surprised to see that Pinebury, which Adam Deas was operating, was up for sale within two weeks for delinquent taxes. Hasty inquiry revealed that his tax payment had gone astray and much ado at the county seat eventually brought rectification. In January of the following year, when the tax collector visited Charleston for the convenience of residents owning land in Colleton County, Grimball proceeded to the appointed place prepared to pay his dues, only to find that the collector had fled to avoid meeting a rival claimant to his office. For some days, he tried to locate the elusive collector, always arriving just after the tax agent had departed, pursued by his rival. Finally, he succeeded in passing the duty to the post office by resorting to the use of registered mail.

In the fall of 1875, as agricultural profits declined and the price of foods increased, economic distress began to spread into the white counties. In 1873, no land had been forfeited for taxes in Anderson County, and, in 1874, only two acres were lost to the state. In December, 1875, however, the editor of the local newspaper noted that "a very large amount of property was sold" at the monthly sheriff's sales for the execution of tax and civil judgments against property.

The losses of property owners were not entirely reckoned in the number of acres forfeited. Obviously, all labored under the burden of paying unusually high taxes on lands which had never yielded so little income. J. B. Grimball paid state and local taxes on Pinebury amounting to $119.36 in 1873 and $136.08 in 1874. During the same period, he received about $1200 yearly by leasing the plantation to Adam Deas. Thus, the tax on the property amounted to about 10 and 11 per cent of the gross income in 1873 and 1874 respectively, and, in terms of productivity, these were banner years for Pinebury. Taxpayers were also distressed by the extremes to which they were forced to save their lands from the sheriff. The widow of the most prominent Know-Nothing leader in ante-bellum South Carolina complained to a friend in 1874: "Having six pieces of property not yielding me one dollar, and those demons after taking my Plantation from me, have this year levied 50 per cent Taxes which I have had to sell Silver to pay." Similarly, in 1872, a Charlestonian, noting that the ownership of a plantation "will *cost* me a good deal" during the year, complained: "I don't think you cd get any attempt at resistance in any part of the Old State to an immediate Confiscation of all the property of the whites if the so called Legislature ordered it."

The price of land in South Carolina was depressed after the war and continued to decline until 1868. Even after prosperity returned, prices remained relatively low. In some measure, this was a result of the uncertain political situation; but, more particularly, it was the fruit of the Republican tax program. In 1870, one upcountry farmer painted the picture rather deftly:

> Our country is in a bad condition. Negroes have every thing in their own hands, and do as they please. The Legislature is radical out and out. All or nearly all of our County officers are negroes. The consequence is that lands and every other kind of property is taxed so high that they have decline twenty five percent in value since last fall. Every little negro in the county is now going to school and the public pays for it. There is a negro school near Billy Turners, with over fifty schollars and lands principally are taxed to pay for them. This is a hell of a fix but we cant help it, and the best policy is to conform as far as possible to circumstance . . .

It is evident that many Negroes took advantage of these conditions to acquire lands by purchase. Unfortunately, no census of Negro farm owners was taken in South Carolina before 1890, but in that year 13,075 Negro farmers owned farms of some size. Since only about 4,000 Negroes obtained lands through government agencies, roughly 9,000 Negro farmers must have bought farms through their own efforts during the generation that followed emancipation. A large portion of these realized their desire for land during the eight years of Republican rule. In 1870, Reuben Tomlinson, a Northern missionary who came to the Sea Islands during the war and remained to become a Bureau educator and a state legislator, declared on the floor of the House of Representatives that "If we could get together the statistics of the laboring men who have during the past year become land owners through their own exertions and industry, we would be perfectly astounded." Random evidence seems to bear out this assumption, for one cannot travel far into contemporary writings without encountering numerous incidental references to the sale of land to Negroes.

It is improbable that many Negroes acquired land through cooperative purchases, but on at least two occasions, Negroes formed associations for the purchase of lands. In January, 1868, in the low country, F. L. Cardozo described one such operation to his colleagues in the Constitutional Convention: "About one hundred poor colored men of Charleston met together and formed themselves into a Charleston Land Company. They subscribed for a number of shares at $10 per share, one dollar payable monthly. They have been meeting for a year. Yesterday they purchased 600 acres of land for $6,600 that would have sold for $25,000 or $50,000 in better times. They would not have been able to buy it had not the owner through necessity been compelled to sell." In 1872, a similar group acquired a 750-acre estate on Edisto Island.

The Negro generally paid his poll tax and his one- or two-dollar levy on personal property cheerfully, but once he had acquired lands, he was subject to the same adverse effects of the Republican tax program as his white neighbors. Contrary to the design of the politicians, small holders suffered equally with large. In 1874, a Northern traveler visited the home of a Negro farmer who had bought his land two years previously with two hundred hard-saved dollars. "Now the cabin has fallen into decay, the rain and wind come through great cracks in the walls of the one cheerless room, the man and his wife are in rags, and the children run wild about the parched and stony fields, clothed very much as they were when they first saw the light. Negro voters are not exempt from the visits of the tax gatherer, and it is almost certain that the poor fellow's place will, with many others, be forfeited to the State at the next sale for delinquent taxes." It is hardly surprising that Negro property owners were observed in one lowcountry community in January, 1877, paying taxes for the support of the Hampton government while a Republican still sat in the governor's office.

Native white resistance to the aggressive tax program of the Republicans was at first tentative and cautious. There was, after all, no assurance that Republican rule through Negro voters would ever end and an imprudent resistance might close doors which could never be re-opened. Nevertheless, almost as soon as the first Republican tax bills reached the taxpayers a quiet desperation crept into Conservative politics. "Negro laws will ruin any people," an upcountry farmer advised his brother during the summer of 1869, "those that was not broke by the old debts will be by tax my tax was 57 dollars & 30 cents. I have paid but how long I can do so I dont no but we still hope for better times we think in the year 1870 we will be able to change the law making power . . ." In 1870, native whites looked anxiously to the polls and placed their trust in a "Reform" Republican candidate for governor. "If the Radicals gain the day what is to become of us, I don't see how we can stay in the country," a Laurens resident wrote to her son on the eve of the elections "for our taxes will be increased, and we will be under the very heels of the Radicals." The election was lost and taxes rose as expected. Among John Berkeley Grimball's papers there is an artifact, a clipping from a March, 1871, issue of a Charleston paper. What Grimball saved was an article which concluded with the sentence: "This is a TAXATION which is tantamount to CONFISCATION." Several weeks later, an upcountry woman wrote to her cousin: "I have nothing of a political nature to communicate that would interest you, — nothing much talked of these days except Taxation & the Ku Klux."

It was characteristic of the native white community that their anxiety should lead to meetings and that meetings should soon assume some state-wide organization. The state-wide conference took place in May, 1871, under the name of the Taxpayers' Convention. Even though the convention included Negroes, carpetbaggers, and scalawags, as well as rising young professional politicians within the ranks of the Conservatives, it was dominated by the prewar aristocracy — men such as Chesnut, Kershaw, Aldrich, Trenholm, Porter, Trescot, Bonham, and Hagood. Indeed, it was generally conceded that no comparably distinguished body of men had met in the state since the Secession Convention. Nevertheless, the leadership remained cautious. The debates were temperate, no Republican officeholder was personally impugned, and the resolutions were innocuous: it was in essence a whitewash of the Republican regime.

The Moses administration (1872–1874) brought still higher taxes and consequent agitation among the whites. ". . . our tax this year is full one third higher than last year and it looks to me like that it will finally result in confiscation of the land by Taxation," wrote a Laurens planter in February, 1873. The whites called another Taxpayers' Convention for February, 1874. "Things are blue enough here & the taxation is practically confiscation," wrote a resident of Georgetown in January, "I trust there may be some good in the Taxpayer's [sic] Convention *this time*." The desperation of the whites rapidly became less quiet, particularly as they began to read signs outside the state which suggested that Negro rule might not be perpetual. The tone of the convention of 1874 was radically different from that of 1871. An impressive delegation of gentlemen from the convention journeyed to Washington where they formally presented to both Grant and the House of Representatives a vigorous indictment of the Republican regime in South Carolina. "It has been openly avowed by prominent members of the Legislature," the memorial of the convention declared, "that taxes should be increased to a point which will compel the sale of the great body of the land, and take it away from the former owners." Perhaps the most important result of the convention was the legacy of organization which it left to the white community. Largely under the leadership of the "Bourbons," local Tax Unions were formed which were to function as the watchdogs of persons in office. These organizations were very active in the 1874 campaign and in supporting the reform programs of the Chamberlain administration. In the fall of 1875, however, the Tax Union rapidly lost ground to more radical elements among the native whites and, by 1876, had virtually ceased to exist.

During 1876, native whites stymied the Republican tax program by extra-legal means. In the fall of 1876, they refused to pay taxes to the Chamberlain government which claimed victory in the November elections while they voluntarily paid 10 per cent of the previous year's levy to the Hampton government. By general concert, native whites also refused to buy lands being sold for taxes. In December, 1876, in Charleston County numerous parcels of land had been forfeited for some $200,000 in taxes and costs, but not one single purchaser could be found for any of these. Once firmly in power, the Redeemers hastened to restore forfeited lands to the tax books and allow delinquents generous limits within which to repair their deficiencies.

Although the great mass of Negroes in Reconstruction South Carolina earned their living through agricultural pursuits, others worked as domestics, as skilled or unskilled laborers, and as business and professional men.

With the exception of agriculture, the domestic class was by far the most numerous economic group. These found employment in various capacities in the homes of the whites. Negro men became butlers, valets, coachmen, gardeners, and handy men. Negro women became housemaids, personal maids, cooks, laundresses, nurses, and serving girls. As described earlier, a general reduction in household staffs occurred immediately after the war. As Reconstruction progressed, further reductions ensued. Typical was the H. L. Pinckney plantation near Statesburg, in Sumter District, in June, 1866, where a unique arrangement prevailed in which ten domestics — two cooks, two houseboys, a house servant, a gardener, a nurse, a housemaid, a washer, and "Louisia — (little)" — were included with thirty-nine agricultural workers in a contract by which all would receive a third of the crop. By 1868, the total work force had been reduced to sixteen, only three of whom were domestics.

In relations with his employer, the Negro domestic experienced grievances similar to those felt by his agrarian contemporaries. His responses, too, were much the same. In a sense, however, he was freer to express his dissatisfaction since desertion — the ultimate reply to unsatisfactory conditions — could follow the daily or weekly payday and he need not forfeit or await the division of a crop. Occasionally, individual domestics revealed a persistent reluctance to remain with any single employer very long. In 1872, in Charleston a Negro cook told her employer that she was leaving the household, not because she was dissatisfied with her position but "because, ma'am, it look like old time to stay too long in one place." However, like their brothers in agriculture, most Negro servants adjusted to the new order during the first years of Reconstruction and established rather permanent relations with a single employer. For instance, in 1870, a lady residing in a large household in the village of Chicora wrote: "We have only made one change in our domestic arrangements since you left [a year previously] & that is in the outdoor department, the indoor servants are all with us still & we go on so smoothly & comfortably that I hope it will be long before we have to make any change."

A glimpse into the life of a servant girl working in one of the Campbell households in Charleston in 1868 is preserved in a letter from her to her aunt in Camden. The girl, Celia Johnson, was a member of a "free" Negro family living in Camden and had come to Charleston as a servant. To her aunt's invitation to visit Camden, she replied that she would like to, but it was too "hard to get away from Mrs. Campbell, and hard to get money." Not all of Celia's life was drudgery. "I spent last Sunday night with sister Mary Stewart, and went to a meetin to the African church. We heard a blind man preacher and had good times." But, there was work to be done. "Excuse this short letter as I am very busy ironing," she concluded. "All the way I will get to go home is to promise to come back in October. If I don't I will make hard feelings . . . I have been sleeping upstairs so long that you will have [to] get me an upstairs room when I get there. I don't know how to sleep down stairs."

In slavery, large numbers of Negroes had performed relatively unskilled labor in the lumbering and turpentine industries and in construction, particularly railroad construction. In freedom, many laborers continued the occupations which they had learned as slaves and these were joined by freedmen who had never before had an opportunity to leave the fields. Frequently, the choice was made even more attractive by the prospect of higher and certain wages in industry. In 1873, a resident of the once rice-rich county of Georgetown noted the growing profitability of the production of naval stores and commented: "The turpentine interest being very lucrative, controls a great deal of labor & the Rice fields suffer thereby." The war, itself, promoted the growth of the laboring population outside of agriculture. During and after the war, hundreds of Negro laborers found employment in the Quartermaster and Engineering departments of the army and in the Freedmen's Bureau. The dislocations of the war and of the months immediately following left large numbers of

Negroes in Charleston and in the towns and villages of the interior. These often earned a subsistence by working as stevedores, street cleaners, yardkeepers, porters, draymen, messengers, and at other unskilled jobs. The repair of war-worn and torn rail lines and a boom in the construction of new lines gave at least temporary employment to several thousand Negro laborers. Many others found jobs in a new and fantastically profitable industry — the mining of phosphates for processing into fertilizers. Some of the rock was dug from tidewater river beds by giant dredges, but large deposits lay on or near the surface of the land. These "land deposits" were mined with pick and shovel, wielded by Negroes under the supervision of white foremen. "A common laborer will raise a ton a day, for which he is paid $1.76," wrote an agricultural expert in 1882. "The product of the land rock is about 100,000 tons a year." Negroes struggling to retain their small farms in the Sea Islands during the hard years following emancipation must have viewed the rise of the phosphate industry as providential.

Many of the free Negroes of Charleston had long earned their living as artisans. A month after their liberation, the Negro tradesmen of the city participated in a parade, described earlier, which indicated the diversity of their occupations and the solidity of their organization. Free Negroes in other centers of population followed much the same pattern on minor scales. Further, emancipation freed numerous slaves who had been trained in the trades, particularly in those connected with plantation maintenance. Thus, literally thousands of more or less proficient blacksmiths, carpenters, wheelrights, masons, plasterers, millers, mechanics, and engineers (who had operated steam engines supplying power to rice threshers, cotton gins, sawmills, and flour mills) became "free" economic agents.

Many of these, of course, were only partially trained for their occupations, and many combined the practice of their trade with other pursuits (e.g., farming) in order to support themselves. Still, a few Negro tradesmen attained eminence as artists in their work. The Noisette family in Charleston, for instance, was nationally praised for the products of their nursery and the elder Noisette gained a creditable reputation as botanist. Ben Williams, a Negro shoemaker in Columbia, was awarded a premium in November, 1869, "for the second best lot of shoes" exhibited at the annual fair of the State Agricultural and Mechanical Society.

In Reconstruction South Carolina, Negroes tended to withdraw or abstain from entering certain trades, leaving them entirely to whites. "The well wishers of the negro race see with regret that they seem to have little inclination to take to mechanical pursuits," reported a Northern journalist from Charleston in 1870. ". . . it is a rare thing to find a negro adopting the trade of blacksmith, or carpenter, or any other requiring skilled labor." This particular gentleman was apparently suffering from myopia induced by the fact that he did not, in truth, wish very well for the Negro race, but he did glimpse a part of a large trend among tradesmen. The results of this retirement of the Negro tradesman is evident in the business directory of the state published in 1880. In the entire state, it listed no Negroes among the cigarmakers, coopers, or coppersmiths, and only one Negro dyer and cleaner was polled. Furthermore, outside of Charleston there were no Negroes listed as tailors, dressmakers, tinners, upholsterers, wheelwrights, or builders and repairmen; in Charleston about half of the tradesmen engaged in each specialty were Negroes. Although the evidence is by no means conclusive, for obviously many Negro tradesmen continued to serve white customers, there was also a trend toward Negro tradesmen serving Negro customers exclusively. In Spartanburg District, in the winter of 1867,

David Golightly Harris probably touched a deep reason for this tendency. Vexed at the inefficiency of the white man he had chosen to run his flour mill, he had reached the point of exasperation. "I have an idea of puting Paschal to the mill," he wrote. "But some say a negro will drive all the customers away. . . . Everything is a botheration." Charleston, again, was perhaps exceptional in this respect.

Probably most Negro tradesmen worked independently and a few worked for established white employers, but many were also businessmen in that they kept shops in which their goods or services were sold. In addition to those in the trades, a large number of Negroes engaged in small enterprises, such as the flourishing trade in supplying firewood to Charleston from the neighboring islands. More typical of small Negro-owned businesses, perhaps, were those of Beverly Nash who operated a produce stand in Columbia in 1867 and later opened a coal and wood yard, and of Samuel Nuckles, a political refugee from Union County, who, in 1871, operated a drayage wagon in the same city. Occasionally, Negroes embarked upon large-scale undertakings in business. For instance, in the spring of 1866, "The Star Spangled Banner Association" led by Tom Long, a veteran of the First South, raised $20,000 by $15 to $100 subscriptions with which they opened a store at Beaufort and acquired a steamer to operate along the coast under the captaincy of Robert Smalls. During the Republican ascendency, Negro politicians participated in ventures darkened in greater or lesser degree by partisan shadows. Thus, F. L. Cardozo and J. H. Rainey were two of the twelve stockholders in the Greenville and Columbia Railroad Company and, with several other Negro leaders, charter members of the Columbia Street-Railway Company. However, the most striking successes in business were made by individuals in private life who gradually accumulated capital and expanded the scope of their operations. John Thorne, who had apparently led in a cooperative land purchase on Edisto Island in 1872, ten years later owned 250 acres of land on the island, "an extensive store and storehouse," and a comfortable residence. "He also runs a gin-house with six gins, and last year ginned out upwards of 400 bags of cotton of 300 pounds each, for which work he received four cents per pound. He advanced largely to several colored planters, and is worth from $15,000 to $20,000."

Although not numerous, the Negro professional class was very influential during and after Reconstruction. Ministers, politicians, and lawyers led the professions, while teachers and medical doctors formed a rather weak second rank, both in popular influence and economic importance.

Social Mobility in Urban America

One of the most important components of social health in any nation is the degree of social mobility that exists. It has always been traditional to assert the extraordinary social fluidity of the United States in the era of the family farm. The most convincing statement of this fact is the Turnerian Safety Valve Thesis which we have noted previously. But even Turner was concerned when he observed the apparent disappearance of the frontier at the end of the nineteenth century. With the end of free land for would-be farmers, what could the nation expect but growing class rigidities and growing class strife?

What Turner and his followers failed to observe was the immense social impact of the cities in the late nineteenth century. This was the period of the most rapid urban growth in our history. Between 1860 and 1910, the cities of the country increased their population by 35 million, while during the same years the nation as a whole grew by some 61 million. Between 1880 and 1910, urban population trebled; rural population increased only one-third. Many of these new urban folk derived from the natural increase of the cities themselves. Many were European immigrants. The largest contingent was composed of native-born rural Americans who found the farms straitened and sterile places to live. Increasingly then, the cities were serving as the safety valve for excess rural population, rather than the other way around.

Obviously America permitted a good deal of geographical movement. But did it also allow much mobility in wealth, occupation, and status? We must, surely, assume that geographical mobility must also have encouraged social mobility. Men would not have continued to come to the cities from the farms unless they had been able rather consistently to improve their economic lot. No doubt, a good deal of the moving about from city to city that afflicted American families represented the ebb and flow of restless failures. This is one of the points that Thernstrom emphasizes in the following essay. But could the steady movement from country to town have persisted over generations without a fair degree of success for the movers? That the migrants to cities knew what to expect when they arrived is attested to by the acceleration of urban growth during prosperous periods and its deceleration during hard times.

This conclusion is deductive. Is there also direct evidence of social mobility? Thernstrom's essay, though based on incomplete and tentative evidence, concludes that there was a considerable amount of such social movement, though it was far less than unbiased boosters of America, both contemporary and modern, would have us believe. In the end, he thinks, it was this fluidity that made the American social order a stable entity in a time of rapid industrialization and urbanization.

FOR FURTHER READING:

McKelvey, Blake. *The Urbanization of America, 1860–1915.* New Brunswick, N. J.: Rutgers University Press, 1967.

Schlesinger, Arthur M. *The Rise of the City, 1878–1898.* New York: The Macmillan Company, 1957.

Thernstrom, Stephan. *Poverty and Progress: Social Mobility in a Nineteenth-Century City.* New York: Atheneum Publishers, 1969.*

Asterisk denotes paperback edition.

Urbanization, Migration, and Social Mobility in Late Nineteenth-Century America STEPHAN THERNSTROM

The United States, it has been said, was born in the country and has moved to the city. It was during the half-century between the Civil War and World War I that the move was made. In 1860, less than a quarter of the American population lived in a city or town; by 1890, the figure had reached a third; by 1910, nearly half. By more sophisticated measures than the mere count of heads, the center of gravity of the society had obviously tilted cityward well before the last date.

If to speak of "the rise of the city" in those years is a textbook cliché, the impact of this great social transformation upon the common people of America has never been sufficiently explored. This essay is intended as a small contribution toward that task. It sketches the process by which ordinary men and women were drawn to the burgeoning cities of post-Civil War America, assesses what little we know about how they were integrated into the urban class structure, and suggests how these matters affected the viability of the political system.

The urbanization of late nineteenth-century America took place at a dizzying pace. Chicago, for instance, doubled its population every decade but one between 1850 and 1890, growing from 30,000 to over a million in little more than a generation. And it was not merely the conspicuous metropolitan giants but the Akrons, the Duluths, the Tacomas that were bursting at the seams; no less than 101 American communities grew by 100 percent or more in the 1880s.[1]

Why did Americans flock into these all too often unlovely places? There were some who were not pulled to the city but rather pushed out of their previous habitats and dropped there, more or less by accident. But the overriding fact is that the cities could draw on an enormous reservoir of people who were dissatisfied with their present lot and eager to seize the new opportunities offered by the metropolis.

Who were these people? It is conventional to distinguish two broad types of migrants to the American city: the immigrant from another culture, and the farm lad who moved from a rural to an urban setting within the culture. It is also conventional in historical accounts to overlook the latter type and to focus on the more exotic of the migrants, those who had to undergo the arduous process of becoming Americanized.

This is regrettable. To be sure, immigration from abroad was extremely important in the building of America's cities down to World War I. But the most important source of population for the burgeoning cities was not the fields of Ireland and Austria, but those of Vermont and Iowa. The prime cause of population growth in nineteenth-century America, and the main source of urban growth, was simply the high fertility of natives living outside the city.

We tend to neglect internal migration from country to city, partly because the im-

Source: Stephan Thernstrom, "Urbanization, Migration, and Social Mobility in Late Nineteenth-Century America," in *Towards a New Past: Dissenting Essays in American History,* ed. Barton J. Bernstein (New York: Pantheon Books, 1968), pp. 158–175.

migrants from abroad seem exotic and thus conspicuous, partly because of the unfortunate legacy left by Frederick Jackson Turner's frontier theory, one element of which was the notion that the open frontier served as a safety valve for urban discontent. When there were hard times in the city, according to Turner, the American worker didn't join a union or vote Socialist; he moved West and grabbed some of that free land. This theory has been subjected to the rather devastating criticism that by 1860 it took something like $1,000 capital to purchase sufficient transportation, seed equipment, livestock, and food (to live on until the first crop) to make a go of it; that it took even more than $1,000 later in the century; and that it was precisely the unemployed workmen who were least likely to have that kind of money at their command. It is estimated that for every industrial worker who became a farmer, twenty farm boys became urban dwellers.[2] There was an urban safety valve for rural discontent, and an extremely important one. The dominant form of population movement was precisely the opposite of that described by Turner.

Since scholarly attention has been focused upon immigrants from abroad, upon Oscar Handlin's "Uprooted," it will be useful to review what is known about their movement to the American city and then to ask how much the same generalizations might hold for native Americans uprooted from the countryside and plunged into the city.

Immigration is as old as America, but a seismic shift in the character of European immigration to these shores occurred in the nineteenth century, as a consequence of the commercial transformation of traditional European agriculture and the consequent displacement of millions of peasants.[3] Compared to earlier newcomers, these were people who were closer to the land and more tradition-bound, and they generally had fewer resources to bring with them than their predecessors. One shouldn't overwork this; a substantial fraction of the German and Scandinavian immigrants had enough capital to get to the West to pick up land. But some of the Germans and Scandinavians, and most men of other nationalities, had just enough cash to make it to the New World and were stuck for a time at least where they landed — New York, Boston, or wherever. They swelled the population appreciably and the relief rolls dramatically, particularly in the pre-Civil War years, when they entered cities which were basically commercial and had little use for men whose only skill in many cases was that they knew how to dig. Eventually, however, the stimulus of this vast pool of cheap labor and the demands of the growing city itself opened up a good many unskilled jobs — in the construction of roads, houses, and commercial buildings, and in the manufacturing that began to spring up in the cities.

That they were driven off the land in the Old World, that they arrived without resources, immobilized by their poverty, and that they often suffered a great deal before they secured stable employment is true enough. But these harsh facts may lead us to overlook other aspects which were extremely significant.

One is that immigration was a *selective* process. However powerful the pressures to leave, in no case did everyone in a community pull up stakes. This observation may be uncomfortably reminiscent of the popular opinion on this point: that it was the best of the Old World stock that came to the New — the most intelligent, enterprising, courageous. But this should not lead us to neglect the point altogether. The traits that led some men to leave and allowed them to survive the harrowing journey to the port, the trip itself, and the perils of the New World, could be described in somewhat different terms: substitute cunning for intelligence, for example, or ruthlessness for courage. Still, whatever the emphasis, the fact remains: as weighed in the scales of the marketplace, those who came — however driven by cruel circumstance — were better adapted to American life than those who remained in the village or died on the way.

The other main point about the immigrants, and especially those who suffered the most extreme hardships — the Irish in the 1840s and 1850s, the French Canadians in the 1870s, the Italians and various East Europeans after 1880 — is that they appraised their new situations with standards developed in peasant society. Lowell was terrible, with its cramped stinking tenements, and factory workers labored from dawn till dark for what seems a mere pittance. Children were forced to work at a brutally early age; the factories and dwellings were deathtraps. But Lowell was a damn sight better than County Cork, and men who knew from bitter experience what County Cork was like could not view their life in Lowell with quite the same simple revulsion as the middle-class reformers who judged Lowell by altogether different standards. It is not so much the objectively horrible character of a situation that goads men to action as it is a nagging discrepancy between what *is* and what is *expected*. And what one expects is determined by one's reference group — which can be a class, an ethnic or religious subculture, or some other entity which defines people's horizon of expectation.[4] Immigration provided an ever renewed stream of men who entered the American economy to fill its least attractive and least well rewarded positions, men who happen to have brought with them very low horizons of expectation fixed in peasant Europe.

That those Americans with greatest reason to feel outrageously exploited judged their situation against the dismally low standards of the decaying European village is an important clue to the stunted growth of the labor movement and the failure of American Socialism. Working in the same direction was what might be called the Tower of Babel factor. A firm sense of class solidarity was extremely difficult to develop in communities where people literally didn't speak each other's language. Even in cases where groups of immigrant workers had unusually high expectations and previous familiarity with advanced forms of collective action — such as the English artisans who led the Massachusetts textile strikes in the 1870s — they found it hard to keep the other troops in line; a clever Italian-speaking or Polish-speaking foreman could easily exploit national differences for his own ends, and if necessary there were always the most recent immigrants of all (and the Negroes) to serve as scabs to replace the dissenters en masse.

A somewhat similar analysis applies to the migrants who left the Kansas farms for Chicago. They were linguistically and culturally set apart from many of their fellow workers; they too had low horizons of expectation fixed in the countryside and brought to the city. The latter point is often missed because of the peculiar American reverence for an idealized agrarian way of life. As we have become a nation of city dwellers, we have come more and more to believe that it is virtuous and beautiful to slave for fourteen hours a day with manure on your boots. Recently that sturdy small farmer from Johnson City, Texas, remarked that "it does not make sense on this great continent which God has blessed to have more than 70 percent of our people crammed into one percent of the land." A national "keep them down on the farm" campaign is therefore in the offing.[5] But it is damnably hard to keep them down on the farm after they've seen New York (or even Indianapolis), and it was just as hard a century ago, for the very good reason that the work is brutal, the profits are often miserably low, and the isolation is psychologically murderous. Virtuous this life may be, especially to people who don't have to live it, but enjoyable it is not — not, at least, to a very substantial fraction of our ever shrinking farm population.

This applies particularly to young men and women growing up on a farm. Their parents had a certain stake in staying where they were, even if it was a rut. And the eldest son, who would inherit the place eventually, was sometimes tempted by that. But the others left in droves, to tend machines, to dig and haul and hammer — or in the case of the girls, to sell underwear in Marshall Field's, to mind someone else's kitchen, or in some instances to follow in the footsteps of Sister Carrie.

There were some large differences between native-born migrants to the cities and immigrants from another land, to be sure. But the familiar argument that native workmen "stood on the shoulders" of the immigrant and was subjected to less severe exploitation is somewhat misleading. The advantages enjoyed by many America-born laborers stemmed more from their urban experience than their birth, and they did not generally accrue to freshly arrived native migrants to the city. The latter were little better off than their immigrant counterparts, but then they too were spiritually prepared to endure a great deal of privation and discomfort because even the bottom of the urban heap was a step up from the farms they had left behind. The two groups were one in this respect, and perceptive employers recognized the fact. In 1875, the Superintendent of one of Andrew Carnegie's steel mills summed up his experience this way: "We must steer clear as far as we can of Englishmen, who are great sticklers for high wages, small production and strikes. My experience has shown that Germans and Irish, Swedes and what I denominate 'Buckwheats' — young American country boys, judiciously mixed, make the most honest and tractable force you can find." [6]

The move to the city, therefore, was an advance of a kind for the typical migrant. Were there further opportunities for advancement there, or did he then find himself crushed by circumstance and reduced to the ranks of the permanent proletariat? Did his children, whose expectations were presumably higher, discover correspondingly greater opportunities open to them? Remarkably little serious research has been devoted to these issues. Historians who see American history as a success story have been content to assume, without benefit of data, that the American dream of mobility was true, apparently on the principle that popular ideology is a sure guide to social reality. Dissenting scholars have been more inclined to the view that class barriers were relatively impassable, an assumption based upon generalized skepticism about American mythology rather than upon careful empirical study. Some recent work, however, provides the basis for a tentative reappraisal of the problem.

We know most about mobility into the most rarified reaches of the social order regarding such elite groups as millionaires, railroad presidents, directors of large corporations, or persons listed in the *Dictionary of American Biography*. What is most impressive about the literature on the American elite is that, in spite of many variations in the way in which the elite is defined, the results of these studies are much the same. It is clear that growing up in rags is not in the least conducive to the attainment of later riches, and that it was no more so a century ago than it is today.[7] There have been spectacular instances of mobility from low down on the social scale to the very top — Andrew Carnegie for instance. But colorful examples cannot sustain broad generalizations about social phenomena, however often they are impressed into service toward that end. Systematic investigation reveals that even in the days of Andrew Carnegie, there was little room at the top, except for those who started very close to it.

Furthermore, this seems to have been the case throughout most of American history, despite many dramatic alterations in the character of the economy. It seems perfectly plausible to assume, as many historians have on the basis of impressionistic evidence, that the precipitous growth of heavy industry in the latter half of the nineteenth century opened the doors to men with very different talents from the educated merchants who constituted the elite of the preindustrial age, that unlettered, horny-handed types like Thomas Alva Edison and Henry Ford, crude inventors and tinkerers, then came into their own; that the connection between parental wealth and status and the son's career was loosened, so that members of the business elite typically had lower social origins and less education, and were often of immigrant stock. Plausible, yes, but true, no. It helped to go to Harvard in Thomas Jefferson's America, and it seems to have helped just about as much in William McKinley's America. There were the Edisons and Fords, who rose spectacularly from low origins, but there were always a few such. Cases like these were about as exceptional in the late nineteenth century as they were earlier. The image of the great inventor springing from common soil, unspoiled by book-larnin', is a red herring. It is doubtful, to say the least, that the less you know, the more likely you are to build a better mousetrap. And in any event it was not the great inventor who raked in the money, in most cases — Henry Ford never invented anything — but rather the organizer and manipulator, whose talents seem to have been highly valued through all periods of American history.

These conclusions are interesting, but an important caution is in order. It by no means follows that if there was very little room at the top, there was little room anywhere else. It is absurd to judge the openness or lack of openness of an entire social system solely by the extent of recruitment from below into the highest positions of all. One can imagine a society in which all members of the tiny elite are democratically recruited from below, and yet where the social structure as a whole is extremely rigid with that small exception. Conversely, one can imagine a society with a hereditary ruling group at the very top, a group completely closed to aspiring men of talent but lowly birth, and yet with an enormous amount of movement back and forth below that pinnacle. Late nineteenth-century America could have approximated this latter model, with lineage, parental wealth, and education as decisive assets in the race for the very peak, as the business elite studies suggest, and yet with great fluidity at the lower and middle levels of the class structure.

Was this in fact the case? The evidence available today is regrettably scanty, but here are the broad outlines of an answer, insofar as we can generalize from a handful of studies.[8] At the lower and middle ranges of the class structure there was impressive mobility, though often of an unexpected and rather ambiguous kind. I will distinguish three types of mobility: geographical, occupational, and property, and say a little about the extent and significance of each.

First is geographical mobility, physical movement from place to place, which is tied up in an interesting way with movement through the social scale. Americans have long been thought a restless, footloose people, and it has been assumed that the man on the move has been the man on the make; he knows that this little town doesn't provide a grand enough stage for him to display his talents, and so he goes off to the big city to win fame and fortune, *or* to the open frontier to do likewise. When you examine actual behavior instead of popular beliefs, however, you discover that things are more complicated than that.

It proves to be true that Americans are indeed a footloose people. In my work on Newburyport, a small industrial city, I attempted to find out what fraction of the families present in the community in the initial year of my study — 1850 — were still living there in the closing year, 1880, one short generation. Less than a fifth of them, it turned out — and this not in a community on the moving frontier, like Merle Curti's Trempealeau County, where you would expect a very high turnover. There the true pioneer types, who liked to clear the land, became nervous when there was another family within a half day's ride of them and sold out to the second wave of settlers (often immigrants who knew better than to try to tame the wilderness without previous experience at it). But to find roughly the same volatility in a city forty miles north of Boston suggests that the whole society was in motion.

The statistics bear out the legend that Americans are a restless people. What of the assertion that movement and success go hand in hand, that physical mobility and upward social mobility are positively correlated? Here the legend seems more questionable. It seems likely that some who pulled up stakes and went elsewhere for a new start did improve their positions; they found better land, or discovered that they possessed talents which were much more highly valued in the big city than in the place they came from. What ever would have happened to Theodore Dreiser in small-town Indiana had there been no Chicago for him to flee to?

But the point to underline, for it is less commonly understood, is that much of this remarkable population turnover was of quite a different kind. As you trace the flow of immigrants into and then out of the cities, you begin to see that a great many of those who departed did so in circumstances which make it exceedingly hard to believe that they were moving on to bigger and better things elsewhere. There is no way to be certain about this, no feasible method of tracing individuals once they disappear from the universe of the community under consideration. These questions can be explored for contemporary America by administering questionnaires to people and collecting life histories which display migration patterns, but dead men tell no tales and fill out no questionnaires, so that part of the past is irrevocably lost. But some plausible inferences can be drawn about the nature of this turnover from the fact that so many ordinary working people on the move owned no property, had no savings accounts, had acquired no special skills, and were most likely to leave when they were unemployed. They were, in short, people who had made the least successful economic adjustment to the community and who were no longer able to hang on there. At the lower reaches of the social order, getting out of town did not ordinarily mean a step up the ladder somewhere else; there is no reason to assume that in their new destinations migrant laborers found anything but more of the same. When middle-class families, who already had a niche in the world, moved on, it was often in response to greater opportunities elsewhere; for ordinary working people physical movement meant something very different.

That is a less rosy picture than the one usually painted, but I think it is more accurate. And we should notice one very important implication of this argument: namely, that the people who were least successful and who had the greatest grievances are precisely those who never stayed put very long in any one place. Students of labor economics and trade union history have long been aware of the fact that there are certain occupations which are inordinately difficult to organize simply because they have incessant job turnover. When only 5 percent or 1 percent of the men working at a particular job in a given city at the start of the year are still employed twelve months later, as is the case with some occupations in the economic underworld today (short-order cooks or menial hospital workers, for instance), how do you build a stable organization and conduct a successful strike?

An analogous consideration applies not merely to certain selected occupations but to a large fraction of the late nineteenth-century urban working class as a whole. The Marxist model of the conditions which promote proletarian consciousness presumes not only permanency of membership in this class — the absence of upward mobility — but also, I suggest, some continuity of class membership *in one setting* so that workers come to know each other and to develop bonds of solidarity and common opposition to the ruling group above them. This would seem to entail a stable labor force in a single factory; at a minimum it assumes considerable stability in a community. One reason that a permanent proletariat along the lines envisaged by Marx did not develop in the course of American industrialization is perhaps that few Americans have *stayed* in one place, one workplace, or even one city long enough to discover a sense of common identity and common grievance. This may be a vital clue to the divergent political development of America and Western Europe in the industrial age, to the striking weakness of socialism here, as compared to Europe — though we can't be sure because we don't definitely know that the European working-class population was less volatile. I suspect that it was, to some degree, and that America was distinctive in this respect, but this is a question of glaring importance which no one has yet taken the trouble to investigate.

When I first stumbled upon this phenomenon in sifting through manuscript census schedules for nineteenth-century Newburyport, I was very doubtful that the findings could be generalized to apply to the big cities of the period. It seemed reasonable to assume that the laborers who drifted out of Newburyport so quickly after their arrival must have settled down somewhere else, and to think that a great metropolis would have offered a more inviting haven than a small city, where anonymity was impossible and where middle-class institutions of social control intruded into one's daily life with some frequency, as compared to a classic big-city lower-class ghetto, where the down-and-out could perhaps huddle together for protective warmth and be left to their own devices — for instance, those Irish wards of New York where the police made no attempt to enforce law and order until late in the century. Here if anywhere one should be able to find a continuous lower-class population, a permanent proletariat, and I began my Boston research with great curiosity about this point.

If Boston is any example, in no American city was there a sizable lower class with great continuity of membership. You can identify some more or less continuously lower-class areas, but the crucial point is that *the same people do not stay in them.* If you take a sample of unskilled and semi-skilled laborers in Boston in 1880 and look for them in 1890, you are not much more likely to find them still in the city than was the case in Newburyport.[9]

The bottom layer of the social order in the nineteenth-century American city was thus a group of families who appear to have been permanent transients, buffeted about from place to place, never quite able to sink roots. We know very little about these people, and it is difficult to know how we can learn much about them. You get only occasional glimpses into the part of this iceberg that appears above the surface, in the person of the tramp, who first is perceived as a problem for America in the 1870s and reappears in hard times after that — in the 1890s and in the great depression most notably. But what has been said here at least suggests the significance of the phenomenon.

So much for geographical mobility. What can be said about the people who come to the city and remain there under our microscope so that we can discern what happened to them? I have already anticipated my general line of argument here in my discussion of migration out of the city — which amounted to the claim that the city was a kind of Darwinian jungle in which the fittest survived and the others drifted on to try another place. Those who did stay in the city and make their way there did, in general, succeed in advancing themselves economically and socially. There was very impressive mobility, though not always of the kind we might expect.

In approaching this matter, we must make a distinction which is obscured by applying labels like "open" or "fluid" to entire whole social structures. There are, after all, two sets of escalators in any community; one set goes down. To describe a society as enormously fluid implies that there are lots of people moving down while lots of others are moving up to take their place. This would obviously be a socially explosive situation, for all those men descending against their will would arrive at the bottom, not with low horizons of expectation set in some peasant village, but with expectations established when they were at one of the comfortable top floors of the structure.

Downward mobility is by no means an unknown phenomenon in American history. There have been socially displaced groups, especially if you take into account rather subtle shifts in the relative status of such groups as professionals.[10] But the chief generalization to make is that Americans who started their working life in a middle-class job strongly tended to end up in the middle class; sons reared in middle-class families also attained middle-class occupations in the great majority of cases. Relatively few men born into the middle class fell from there; a good many born into the working class either escaped from it altogether or advanced themselves significantly within the class. There is a well-established tradition of writing about the skilled workman, associated with such names as the Hammonds, the Lynds, Lloyd Warner, and Norman Ware, which holds the contrary, to be sure.[11] This tradition still has its defenders, who argue that with industrialization "class lines assumed a new and forbidding rigidity" and that "machines made obsolete many of the skilled trades of the antebellum years, drawing the once self-respecting handicraftsmen into the drudgery and monotony of factory life, where they were called upon to perform only one step in the minutely divided and automatic processes of mass production." [12] Rapid technological change doubtless did displace some skilled artisans, doubtless produced some downward mobility into semiskilled positions. But defenders of this view have built their case upon little more than scattered complaints by labor leaders, and have not conducted systematic research to verify these complaints.

Careful statistical analysis provides a very different perspective on the matter. Two points stand out. One is that as certain traditional skilled callings became obsolete, there was an enormous expansion of *other* skilled trades, and, since many of the craftsmen under pressure from technological change had rather generalized skills, they moved rapidly into these new positions and thus retained their place in the labor aristocracy.[13] Second, it is quite mistaken to assume that the sons of the threatened artisan were commonly driven down into the ranks of the factory operatives; they typically found a place either in the expanding skilled trades or in the even more rapidly expanding white-collar occupations.[14]

As for workers on the lower rungs of the occupational ladder, the unskilled and semiskilled, they had rarely drifted down from a higher beginning point. Characteristically, they were newcomers to the urban world. A substantial minority of them appear to have been able to advance themselves a notch or two occupationally, especially among the second generation; a good many of their sons became clerks, salesmen, and other petty white-collar functionaries. And the first generation, which had less success occupationally, was commonly experiencing mobility of another kind — property mobility. Despite a pathetically low (but generally rising) wage level, despite heavy unemployment rates, many were able to accumulate significant property holdings and to establish themselves as members of the stable working class, as opposed to the drifting lower class.[15]

It may seem paradoxical to suggest that so many Americans were rising in the world and so few falling; where did the room at the top come from? The paradox is readily resolved. For one thing, our attention has been fastened upon individuals who remained physically situated in one place in which their careers could be traced; an indeterminate but substantial fraction of the population was floating and presumably unsuccessful. By no means everyone at the bottom was upwardly mobile; the point is rather that those who were not were largely invisible. Furthermore, the occupational structure itself was changing in a manner that created disproportionately more positions in the middle and upper ranges, despite the common nineteenth-century belief that industrialization was homogenizing the work force and reducing all manual employees to identical robots. The homogenizing and degrading tendencies that caught the eye of Marx and others were more than offset, it appears, by developments which made for both a more differentiated and a more top-heavy occupational structure. Third, there were important sources of social mobility that could be attained without changing one's occupation, most notably the property mobility that was stimulated by the increases in real wages that occurred in this period. Finally, there was the so-called "demographic vacuum" created by the differential fertility of the social classes, best illustrated in the gloomy late nineteenth-century estimate that in two hundred years 1,000 Harvard graduates would have only 50 living descendants while 1,000 Italians would have 100,000. The calculation is dubious, but the example nicely clarifies the point that high-status groups failed to reproduce themselves, thus opening up vacancies which had necessarily to be filled by new men from below.

For all the brutality and rapacity which marked the American scene in the years in which the new urban industrial order came into being, what stands out most is the relative absence of colective working-class protest aimed at reshaping capitalist society. The foregoing, while hardly a full explanation, should help to make this more comprehensible. The American working class was drawn into the new society by a process that encouraged accommodation and rendered disciplined protest difficult. Within the urban industrial orbit, most of its members found modest but significant opportunities to feel that they and their children were edging their way upwards. Those who did not find such opportunities were tossed helplessly about from city to city, from state to state, alienated but invisible and impotent.

NOTES

1. C. N. Glaab and A. T. Brown, *A History of Urban America* (New York, 1967), pp. 107–11.
2. Fred Shannon, "A Post Mortem on the Labor-Safety-Valve Theory," *Agricultural History, XIX* (1954), 31–37.
3. For general accounts, see Marcus L. Hansen, *The Atlantic Migration, 1607–1860* (paperback ed.; New York, 1961); Oscar Handlin, *The Uprooted* (Boston, 1951).
4. For discussion of the sociological concepts of reference groups and the theory of relative deprivation, see Robert K. Merton, *Social Theory and Social Structure*, rev. ed. (Glencoe, Ill., 1957) and the literature cited there. The problem of assessing the level of expectations of any particular migratory group in the past is extremely complicated, and it is obvious that there have been important differences between and within groups. But the generalizations offered here seem to me the best starting point for thinking about this issue.
5. *Boston Globe*, February 5, 1967.
6. Quoted in Oscar Handlin, *Immigration as a Factor in American History* (Englewood Cliffs, N.J., 1959), pp. 66–67.
7. For a convenient review of this literature, see Seymour M. Lipset and Reinhard Bendix, *Social Mobility in Industrial Society* (Berkeley, Cal., 1959), Ch. 4.
8. The main sources for the generalizations which follow, unless otherwise indicated, are: Stephen Thernstrom, *Poverty and Progress: Social Mobility in a Nineteenth Century City* (Cambridge, Mass., 1964); Merle E. Curti, *The Making of an American Frontier Community* (Stanford, Cal., 1959); Donald B. Cole, *Immigrant City: Lawrence, Massachusetts, 1845–1921* (Chapel Hill, N.C., 1963)–for my reservations about this work, however, see my review in the *Journal of Economic History*, XXIV (1964), 259–61; Herbert G. Gutman, "Social Status and Social Mobility in 19th Century America: Paterson, N.J., A Case Study," unpublished paper for the 1964 meetings of the American Historical Association; Howard Gitelman, "The Labor Force at Waltham Watch During the Civil War Era," *Journal of Economic History, XXV* (1965), 214–43; David Brody, *Steelworkers in America: The Nonunion Era* (Cambridge, Mass., 1960); Pauline Gordon, "The Chance to Rise Within Industry" (unpublished M.A. thesis, Columbia University); Robert Wheeler, "The Fifth-Ward Irish: Mobility at Mid-Century" (unpublished seminar paper, Brown University, 1967); and the author's research in progress on social mobility in Boston over the past century, in which the career patterns of some 8,000 ordinary residents of the community are traced.
9. Recent work suggesting that even the most recent U.S. Census seriously undernumerated the Negro male population may make the critical reader wonder about the accuracy of the census and city directory canvases upon which I base my analysis. Some elaborate checking has persuaded me that these nineteenth-century sources erred primarily in their coverage–their lack of coverage, rather–of the floating working-class population. For a variety of reasons it seems clear that families which had been in the community long enough to be included in one of these canvases–and hence to be included in a sample drawn from them–were rarely left out of later canvases if they were indeed still resident in the same city. A perfect census of every soul in the community on a given day would therefore yield an even higher, not a lower, estimate of population turnover for men at the bottom, which strengthens rather than weakens the argument advanced here.
10. The assumption that discontent stemming from social displacement has been the motive force behind American reform movements has exerted great influence upon American historical writing in recent years. See for instance David Donald, "Toward a Reconsideration of Abolitionists," *Lincoln Reconsidered* (New York, 1956), pp. 19–36; Richard Hofstadter, *The Age of Reform: From Bryan to F.D.R.* (New York, 1955). Donald's essay is easily demolished by anyone with the slightest acquaintance with sociological method. Hofstadter's work, while open to a very serious objection, is at least sufficiently suggestive to indicate the potential utility of the idea.
11. J. L. and Barbara Hammond, *The Town Labourer (1760 – 1832)* (London, 1917); Robert S. and Helen M. Lynd, *Middletown* (New York, 1929), and *Middletown in Transition* (New York, 1937); W. Lloyd Warner and J. O. Low, *The Social System of the Modern Factory* (New Haven, Conn., 1947); Norman J. Ware, *The Industrial Worker, 1840 – 1860* (Boston, 1924).
12. Leon Litwak, ed., *The American Labor Movement* (Englewood Cliffs, N.J., 1962), p. 3.
13. This is evident from aggregated census data and from my Boston investigation, but we badly need an American counterpart to Eric Hobsbawm's splendid essay on "The Labour Aristocracy in Nineteenth Century Britain," in *Labouring Men: Studies in the History of Labour* (London, 1964), pp. 272–315.
14. So, at least, the evidence from Boston and Indianapolis indicates; for the latter, see Natlic Rogoff, *Recent Trends in Occupational Mobility* (Glencoe, Ill., 1953).

15. The clearest demonstration of this is in Thernstrom, *Poverty and Progress,* Ch. 5. It might be thought, however, that the remarkable property mobility disclosed there depended upon the existence of an abundant stock of cheap single-family housing available for purchase. It could be that where real estate was less readily obtainable, laborers would squander the funds that were accumulated with such sacrifice in places where home ownership was an immediate possibility. It appears from Wheeler's unpublished study of nineteenth-century Providence, however, that the working-class passion for property did not require an immediate, concrete source of satisfaction like a home and a plot of land. The Irish workmen of Providence were just as successful at accumulating property holdings as their Newburyport counterparts; the difference was only that they held personal rather than real property.

Advent of Urban Slums

Thernstrom's urbanites were the relatively successful ones, the ones who left records behind, and records, generally, of some occupational or income mobility. Obviously there were others who were not so lucky. Doubtless some of these fall into Thernstrom's category of the "perpetual failures" whose way of dealing with disaster was to move periodically from place to place, always seeking to escape misfortune. Many of these people drifted into the big city. There they were joined by masses of European immigrants who were attempting to find an economic niche in American life. Neither group found urban life ideal. The cities were simply growing too fast to maintain the amenities. But, in addition, imaginative social planning was an alien concept in laissezfaire America. As they grew, the cities were virtually at the mercy of private developers, building contractors, traction magnates, and all those who wanted to make money out of their growing housing, transit, sanitation, and health needs. In the end, the cities were left with a legacy of physical disorder and aesthetic blight.

The "problems of the inner city," then, are not unique to our own day. They first appeared in serious form in the years after the Civil War in our largest cities, and with particular virulence in New York where overcrowding took an extreme form. Then, as now, there were problems of crime, poverty, poor sanitation, inadequate transportation, and social disorder. Today we connect many of these social ills with racial bigotry. But the late nineteenth century often assigned responsibility to physical congestion and bad housing, and frequently devoted a disproportionate amount of reformist zeal to improving the physical environment of the poor. In the essay that follows, Roy Lubove describes the growth of the New York slums and the efforts made by reformers to solve the difficult and still intractable problem of adequately housing the inhabitants of our largest cities.

FOR FURTHER READING:

ADDAMS, JANE. *Twenty Years at Hull House*. New York: New American Library, Signet, 1965.*
RIIS, JACOB. *How the Other Half Lives*. Magnolia, Mass.: Peter Smith, 1959.*
SINCLAIR, UPTON. *The Jungle*. New York: New American Library, Signet, 1960.*

Asterisk denotes paperback edition.

The Tenement Comes of Age, 1866–1890   ROY LUBOVE

The jurisdiction of the newly established Metropolitan Board of Health extended over New York, Kings, Westchester, and Richmond counties and a few towns in the present Borough of Queens. The Board consisted of nine commissioners — four appointed by the governor, three of whom had to be physicians; the health officer of the Port of New York; and four police commissioners. A sanitary superintendent, appointed by the Board, supervised the work of fifteen sanitary inspectors.

The Board's authority to regulate tenement conditions was embodied in the Tenement House Law of 1867. This law was enacted upon the recommendation of a state legislative committee which had investigated the New York and Brooklyn tenements shortly after the establishment of the Metropolitan Board of Health. The committee discovered that the 15,511 tenements reported by the Council of Hygiene had increased to over 18,000. More than half were in "bad sanitary condition." The squalor of basement and cellar habitations defied imagination. In the lower streets of the city they were "subject to regular periodical flooding by tide water, to the depth of from six inches to a foot; frequently so much as to keep the children of the occupants in bed until ebb-tide." The committee's findings generally confirmed the low estimate placed upon New York's sanitary condition by the Council of Hygiene.

The housing act of 1867 defined a tenement as follows:

> A tenement house within the meaning of this act shall be taken to mean and include every house, building, or portion thereof which is rented, leased, let or hired out to be occupied, or is occupied as the home or residence of more than three families living independently of another, and doing their cooking upon the premises, or by more than two families on a floor, so living and cooking, but have a common right in the halls, stairways, water closets or privies, or some of them.

The "more than three families" provision was a serious error. Some of the city's worst tenements were occupied by only three families. Twenty years passed before this fault was corrected. Otherwise, the legal definition of a tenement remained the same into the twentieth century.

On the whole, the standards established by the Tenement House Law of 1867 were low. Many of its provisions were vague, leaving too much discretionary authority with the Board of Health. In relation to fire protection, for example, the law required all tenements to have a fire escape *or some other means of egress* approved by the inspector of public buildings in Manhattan and in Brooklyn by the assistant sanitary superintendent. An inconveniently located wooden ladder thus satisfied the legal requirements, if approved by these officials. To ventilate dark interior bedrooms, the law compelled only the construction of a window connecting with a room which did communicate with the outer air. The law set no limit to the percentage of the lot which a tenement might cover. Although ten feet had to separate the rear of any building from another, a tenement might extend to the lot line if no other building existed. The Board of Health was authorized to modify even this modest ten foot requirement.

Source: Roy Lubove, *The Progressives and the Slums: Tenement House Reform in New York City, 1890–1917* (Pittsburgh: University of Pittsburgh Press, 1962), chap. 2, "The Tenement Comes of Age, 1866–1890," pp. 25–48.

The reports of the inspectors for the Council of Hygiene were glutted with uncomplimentary references to the poor sanitary and drainage systems in tenement districts. Privies, often unconnected to sewers and located in rear yards, overflowed. In some places, the contents seeped through rotten foundations into cellars. The sanitary requirements set by the act of 1867 represented little progress. Cesspools were forbidden — except where unavoidable. Water closets and privies had to connect with sewers — where such existed. A landlord was obligated to provide only one water closet or privy for every twenty inhabitants, and it could be located in the yard. The manner and material of water closet construction was left again to the discretion of the Board of Health. Finally the tenement landlord satisfied the law if he furnished a water tap somewhere in the house or yard.

The Tenement House Law of 1867 at least had symbolic value. It represented the acceptance in principle of the community's right to limit the freedom of the tenement landlord and builder. However, the low standards of the law and its successors through 1901 involved a very shaky compromise between entrepreneurial rights and the rights of the community to protect its citizens. Housing legislation before 1901 was also characterized by inadequate provision for enforcement. An understaffed Board of Health, often subject to political pressures from landlords or builders influential with Tammany, found it difficult to ensure compliance with the law. Burdened with many other duties, the Board of Health had not the time or resources to inspect periodically thousands of tenements or to prod indefinitely uncooperative landlords. It was difficult to force elusive "estates, receivers, agents and non-residents" to obey the legislation, and the "poverty of small owners, struggling to retain property heavily mortgaged" intensified the problems of enforcement. Legal compulsion was at best a slow and often futile procedure. Two major problems inherited by Progressive housing reformers were an ineffective tenement code and the creaky machinery of enforcement.

Housing reformers of the post-Civil War decades experimented further with the model tenement program which had its small beginnings in the AICP's [Association for Improving the Condition of The Poor] "Workmen's Home" and in the program of sanitary legislation urged by the Council of Hygiene. A key development of the period was the emergence of Alfred T. White of Brooklyn as the chief spokesman for the model tenement ideal. The example of White's three groups of model tenements, built between 1877 and 1890, greatly influenced a generation of reformers seeking a solution to the problem of the ever-expanding tenement slums.

The discrepancy in standards between the model tenements erected by White and other "investment philanthropists" and the ordinary commercial tenement built under the housing laws, was very apparent; but the few built housed only a small fraction of New York's tenement population and the vast majority had to depend for their protection upon legislative restrictions over builders and landlords. Conceivably, had the housing reformer not overestimated the potentialities of the model tenement, he might have pressed harder for legislation which would make all tenements model, at least in relation to such basic necessities as light, air, ventilation, fire protection, and sanitary facilities. One consequence of the minimal legislative controls over building development was the birth and proliferation after 1879 of the notorious dumb-bell tenement. The dumb-bell, indeed, did not even originate in the minds of building speculators, but was the contribution of reformers willing to accept the terms imposed by the commercial builder.

The history of the dumb-bell begins in 1877 when Henry C. Meyer established a trade journal, the *Plumber and Sanitary Engineer*. Shortly after the Cvil War, Meyer had founded a company which manufactured water, gas, and steam installation supplies. Anxious to boost sales, he hoped that his journal would convince architects, plumbers, and engineers of the safety of his type of equipment. Meyer chose Charles F. Wingate, a civil engineer, as his editor. A relative of the secretary of the AICP, Wingate had assisted in the preparation of the Association's annual reports and in the process had become an authority on the housing problem. Wingate interested Meyer in housing reform, and the latter decided that a competition for an improved tenement sponsored by his journal would increase circulation. Accordingly, the *Plumber and Sanitary Engineer* in December 1878, announced a prize competition for a tenement on a 25 x 100 foot lot. The design which best combined maximum safety and convenience for the tenant, and maximum profitability for the investor, would win.

In the next few months approximately two hundred plans were submitted by architects. Exhibited at the Leavitt Art Gallery on Clinton Place, they aroused considerable public interest. The plans were judged by a committee of five: R. G. Hatfield, a consulting architect, Charles F. Chandler, president of the Board of Health; Robert Hoe, a printing press manufacturer; and two clergymen, Dr. Potter of Grace Church and Dr. John Hall, Meyer's own clergyman. The gentlemen of this committee, despite their explicit denial that the "requirements of physical and moral health" could be satisfied by a tenement on a 25 x 100 foot lot, awarded first prize to the dumb-bell design of James E. Ware.

The widespread adoption of the dumb-bell by builders was assured by a provision of the Tenement House Law of 1879. Partly as a result of the interest in tenement reform stimulated by the *Plumber and Sanitary Engineer* competition, a group of clergymen and laymen held a conference early in February 1879. This conference, which included Dr. Stephen Smith, Alfred T. White, and Charles Loring Brace of the Children's Aid Society, resolved that the clergy of the city would preach on the tenement problem on Sunday, February 23. After the ministers had spoken, two public meetings were held in the evening and various speakers explained the pressing urgency of tenement reform. The following week Mayor Cooper presided over an important public meeting at Cooper Union, which resulted in the formation of a Committee of Nine to plot a reform strategy. Upon the recommendation of this committee, an Improved Dwellings Association was formed to provide housing for "persons unable to pay more than eight to ten dollars per month." The "New York Sanitary Reform Society," a voluntary private association designed to work for the improvement of tenement conditions, also originated in the Committee's recommendations. Finally, the Committee of Nine prepared and introduced into the state legislature a bill amending the Tenement House Law of 1867. After considerable delay "owing to the vigorous opposition of many landlords through the agency of their representatives at Albany," the legislation passed. It required, significantly, that every tenement bedroom have a window opening directly to the street or yard unless sufficient light and ventilation could be provided "in a manner and upon a plan approved by the board of health." This provision of the law requiring a window in all tenement bedrooms, combined with the discretionary authority granted to the Board of Health, paved the way for the dumb-bell tenement.

Ware's prize tenement, with various modifications, was the characteristic type of multiple dwelling erected for the working class in New York between 1879 and 1901. The dumb-bell was essentially a front and rear tenement connected by a hall.

Situated on a pinched 25 x 100 foot lot, the dumb-bell was usually five or six stories high and contained fourteen rooms to a floor, seven on either side running in a straight line. One family occupied the first four of these seven rooms, a second family the remaining three rooms to the rear. The dumb-bell thus harbored four families to a floor. The hallways and stairwell were dimly lit by windows fronting upon the air shaft. Water closets, two to a floor or one to every two families, were located opposite the stairs.

Of the fourteen rooms on each floor, ten depended for light upon the narrow air shaft. This was an indentation at the side of the building about twenty-eight inches wide and enclosed on all sides. It proved to be not only inadequate for the purpose of providing light and air, but a positive hindrance to the health and comfort of tenants. The shaft was a fire hazard, acting as a duct to convey flames from one story to the next. It became a receptacle for garbage and filth of all kinds. It was noisy with the quarrels and shouts of twenty or more families. Its stale air reeked with the cooking odors from twenty or more kitchens.

Meyer and his associates had attempted the impossible; the architect could not reconcile the tenant's welfare and the investor's profit. Two dozen families could not be housed comfortably in a six-story building compressed into a lot 25 x 100 feet in dimension. The building occupied 75 per cent to 90 per cent of the lot. The front parlor, the most spacious room, measured only $10\frac{1}{2}$ x 11 feet. Bedrooms were about 7 x $8\frac{1}{2}$ feet in size. Amenities such as landscaping or children's play areas were out of the question.

Meyer explained his acquiescence in the 25 x 100 foot lot on the grounds that "the problem in New York then was the single lot, and that any architect could make a design for a large block; but that it was an attempt to emphasize and solve the New York problem that the competition was instituted." Far more useful, however, would have been an attempt by Meyer or the Committee of Nine to condemn the single lot as unfit for tenement construction. The 25 x 100 foot lot mostly benefited land owners, speculators, realtors, builders, and landlords who found it a convenient parcel to buy, build upon, and sell. This narrow subdivision may have made sense in 1800, when most dwellings were built for single-family occupancy. By 1879 it had outlived its usefulness.

The prize awards of the *Plumber and Sanitary Engineer* were criticized by contemporaries who realized that the dumb-bell was a negative contribution to the solution of the housing problem. The New York *Times* observed that if the prize plans were the best possible, then the housing problem was virtually insolvable. Perhaps, the *Times* sardonically reflected, "the gentlemen who offered the prizes really desired to demonstrate this to the public before proposing any other scheme." Dr. A. N. Bell, editor of the *Sanitarian,* complained that "the prizes were won by the most ingenious designs for dungeons." If the dumb-bell is the best, then "how much is the best worth?" wondered the *American Architect and Building News.*

The housing legislation between 1879 and 1890 contained some useful provisions, but did nothing to alter the dumb-bell pattern. The 1879 law limited, for the first time, the amount of lot space a tenement could occupy. The 65 per cent limitation, however, was nullified by the discretionary authority granted the Board of Health. A provision requiring a window of at least twelve square feet in any room used for sleeping was also diluted by discretionary power given the Board of Health, which could approve a substitute. Finally, the law provided for thirty sanitary police, under the Board's supervision, to enforce the housing code.

The widespread interest in housing conditions stimulated by the *Plumber and Sanitary Engineer* competition subsided until 1884, when a series of lectures by Felix Adler, founder of the Ethical Culture Society, again aroused and coalesced the energies of reformers. Growing out of Adler's denunciation of the tenement blight in 1884 was the first of a series of official state tenement house commissions. The investigations and report of the Tenement House Commission of 1884, which included Adler and Charles F. Wingate among its membership, resulted in further amendments to the tenement code in 1887, mostly of a superficial character. The number of sanitary police was increased from thirty to forty-five. The law established a standing (and quite ineffectual) tenement house commission composed of New York's mayor and several department heads. Tenement landlords now had to provide one water closet for every fifteen instead of every twenty inhabitants, as well as running water on every floor. For administrative purposes, the law required owners of tenements to file their names and addresses annually with the Board of Health. Moreover, the Board was required to make semiannual inspections of every tenement. Neither of these latter provisions was successfully enforced.

We have suggested, although it would be difficult to prove, that reformers might have labored for higher standards of restrictive legislation had they not been so dazzled by the potentialities of the model tenement. The intense interest in model tenements throughout the period was always disproportionate to the actual accomplishments of "investment philanthrophy." The model tenement, in theory, had many advantages over restrictive legislation. It circumvented the troublesome task of enacting and enforcing housing codes, a process which often involved the compromise of standards and principles. Second, even if restrictive legislation prevented the worst tenements from being built, it did not guarantee a sufficient supply of good ones at moderate rentals. The model tenement, a strictly private venture accompanied by voluntary limitations upon profit, promised a safe, sane solution to the housing problem in a capitalist society.

One of the first notable model tenement projects after the Civil War emerged not in New York but in Boston, where Dr. H. P. Bowditch helped organize the Boston Cooperative Building Company in 1871. Limiting dividends to 7 percent, the Company opened its first buildings in 1872 and ultimately constructed five tenement estates. The tenements were small, with one family to a floor, and each apartment contained running water. This latter convenience, however, was canceled out by cellar toilets. A few years after the Company began operations, Robert Treat Paine decided to offer workers the benefits of model homes rather than tenements. He financed the construction of four- to six-room single-family homes, with bath, and arranged for long-term mortgage payments. Paine organized a limited-dividend Workingmen's Building Association in 1880 to expand his operations.

Despite the work of Paine and the Boston Cooperative Building Company, the undisputed evangelist of model-tenement gospel in the postwar period was Alfred T. White of Brooklyn. Born in 1846, White was educated at Rensselaer Polytechnical Institute. After the Civil War he joined his father as a partner in the importing firm of W. A. and A. M. White. A wealthy man in search of a philanthropy, White discovered in housing reform an outlet for his benevolent impulse: "It is time to recognize that if the intelligent and wealthy portion of the community do not provide homes for the working classes, the want will be continually supplied by the less intelligent class and after the old fashion." In White's estimation, the need for improved low-income housing had become imperative, for "the badly constructed, unventilated, dark and foul tenement houses of New York . . . are the nurseries of the epidemics which spread with certain destructiveness into the fairest homes; they are the hiding-places of the local banditti; they are the cradles of the insane who fill the asylums and of the paupers who throng the almshouses; in fact, they produce these noxious and unhappy elements of society as surely as the harvest follows the sowing. . . ."

In 1872 White began preparing plans for a model tenement when he learned of Sir Sydney Waterlow's philanthropic work in London. Waterlow in 1863 had erected a tenement whose distinctive features were an exterior stairwell and two-room-deep apartments. White patterned his own buildings after the Langbourn Estate of Waterlow's Improved Industrial Dwellings Company, including the outside stairwell which dispensed with the "foulness of interior dark unventilated halls and stairways," and served as a sturdy, accessible fire escape. Located in Brooklyn and completed in 1877, White's initial tribute to "philanthropy and 5 per cent" was an immediate, influential success. He demonstrated, presumably, that a capitalist could provide "well-ventilated, convenient, and agreeable" housing for workers. According to White, his "Home Buildings" on Hicks and Baltic Streets near the Brooklyn waterfront swiftly captured the attention of the Children's Aid Society, the AICP, and the State Charities Aid Association. Among the visitors, "keen in their interest," were Theodore Roosevelt, Sr., and Louisa Lee Schuyler, both of the State Charities Aid Association, D. Willis James, at whose home the first conference leading to the formation of the Committee of Nine had been held, and Josephine Shaw Lowell, founder of the New York Charity Organization Society, who referred to the new tenements as a "realization of an Arabian Night's Dream."

The "Home Buildings" accommodated forty families; and each apartment, only two rooms deep to ensure sufficient light and ventilation, included a sink and water closet. White completed a second adjoining unit the same year and then purchased a 200 x 250 foot tract on the next block. The "Tower Buildings" arose on this site (Hicks, Warren, and Baltic Streets) in 1878–79. Finally White compressed thirty-four cottages into a narrow alley or passageway running from Warren to Baltic Street. These were attached six- to nine-room houses, arranged in two parallel rows. Altogether White was landlord to 267 families. He prohibited boarders or lodgers, set high standards of maintenance and upkeep for his tenants, and demanded prompt weekly payments of rent in advance.

Following White's lead, others promoted model tenement companies in the next decade. The Improved Dwellings Association, organized in 1879 as a consequence of the Committee of Nine's recommendations, opened its Manhattan tenements for occupancy in 1882. The Tenement House Building Company, organized in 1885, was ready for business two years later. Its property was located on squalid Cherry Street in the fourth ward. Pratt Institute inaugurated another philanthropic venture in 1887, when it opened its Astral Apartments in Greenpoint, Brooklyn, and White rounded out the decade's good works with his "Riverside Buildings" in 1890.

White's objectives were representative of most other model tenement enthusiasts of the period. He insisted, above all, that such tenements must be profitable. Otherwise, they would not inspire imitators. And if model tenements failed financially, opponents of restrictive legislation would use this as an argument "*against* efforts to secure legislative action seeking to impose healthful restrictions on existing or future buildings." Furthermore, the reformer must never view housing as a charity in which the poor got something for nothing, thus weakening their character and self-reliance. It was a business venture; the purpose of the model tenement was to prove that good housing paid.

White advised prospective investors to build in districts already invaded by speculators. "You can afford to pay as much for land as they can; and high cost is no detriment, *provided* the value is made by the pressure of people seeking residence there." White's insistence upon profitability and his advice to philanthropists to emulate the example of the speculative builder indicate his essentially conservative outlook. Neither White nor his contemporary housing reformers were radicals, toying with imaginative reconstructions of the social and economic order. Their aim was more modest — to provide safe, comfortable, and even pleasant housing for low-income groups within the framework of the capitalist-profit system. Apart from the genuine structural merits of the model tenement, it is not surprising that the businessmen, clergymen, and social workers who participated in the housing movement were so united in its endorsement. The model tenement represented no challenge whatever to economic orthodoxy. It was a painless and ostensibly effective solution to the housing problem.

White recommended that model tenement investors determine the prevailing rents in the neighborhood selected for construction. The buildings should then be planned to return the same average rentals and simultaneously assure tenants "as many conveniences as this average rental will allow." White's last unit, the "Riverside Buildings," are a good example of his objectives in practice and they indicate, generally, the kind of accommodations which the model tenement companies hoped to provide. The Riverside Buildings were six stories high. They contained 3 one-room, 91 two-room, 161 three-room and 23 four-room apartments. Rents ranged from $1.40 a week for a single room with scullery on the ground floor to $3.60 a week for a four-room apartment. These rents, which the unskilled worker could afford to pay, were unusually low even by the standards of the model tenement. White, of course, built in Brooklyn, where land prices were much cheaper than in Manhattan. The Riverside Buildings provided a separate water closet for each family and such outdoor amenities as children's sandboxes, grass-lined courts and summer band concerts. Most important of all, White broke from the confines of the 25 x 100 foot lot and grouped his buildings around a large central court. They covered only half the land and since no apartment was more than two rooms deep, every room was assured plentiful light and ventilation.

Model tenement zealots like White were certain that the policy of investment philanthropy would inspire widespread emulation. After all, the model tenement idea courted two of the strongest instincts in human nature — self-interest and altruism. By helping the poor at a profit, one served both humanity and one's pocket. Unfortunately, capitalists in the 1880's were no more prepared to minister to humanity in this fashion that had been their counterparts in the 1850's, when the AICP had sponsored its model tenement. Why should wealthy businessmen with loose capital accept dividends of only 4 or 5 per cent in an age of great material expansion when more profitable investments beckoned elsewhere?

Housing, as a rule, did not attract the large aggregations of capital necessary to build model tenements in contrast to the cheaper dumb-bells with their smaller lot dimensions and lower structural standards. Concentrated ownership of tenement land or property, such as that of the Astor family or Trinity Church, was not typical. Low-income housing appealed mostly to the capitalist (builder or landlord) of relatively small means. It required a comparatively modest equity, which was all he could afford. Yet the tenement landlord might anticipate average profits of 6 or 7 per cent on his investment. Tenement property in the 1880's sometimes paid much more — even 15 or 18 per cent. In effect, those who could afford the large capital investment required to build model tenements were not particularly interested; they had better uses for their capital which did not involve the annoyance of dealing with ignorant or careless tenants. On the other hand the small entrepreneurs, sometimes immigrants themselves, who owned the lion's share of New York tenements, were not prepared to sacrifice their profits for the sake of humanity. The altruism and self-restraint upon which model-tenement enthusiasts depended were remote from the realities of the market place. Until reformers could incorporate the standards of the model tenement in restrictive legislation, housing conditions would not improve for the majority of workers.

Why was it that an affluent and comfortably situated gentleman like Alfred T. White devoted so much time, energy, and money to improving the housing of the poor? Why, in the words of the AICP, was there "no social question, except that of labor itself, of deeper interest to the community at large?" We cannot wholly appreciate the attitudes and goals of housing reformers until we grasp the full social implications of the tenement problem. The tenement slum was the product of mighty social and economic upheavals in American society. For most reformers it was also a cause.

The quality of a city's housing is inextricably linked to broader social and economic trends. It is related, for example, to the generally accepted standard of living, the pace of urban and industrial expansion, the level of technology, the accepted role of government in the urban economy, and social and moral ideals. The decade or two after the Civil War has been described as the age of the robber barons, the gilded age, the age of enterprise, the great barbecue. Its dominant features —industrialization, urbanization, immigration, westward expansion — were not new phenomena in American life, but their magnitude was unprecedented. In 1860 there were only nine cities with over 100,000 population. By 1880 there were twenty. The nine cities in 1860 contained a little over 2,500,000 inhabitants. The corresponding figure for the twenty cities in 1880 was 6,000,000. In 1854, some 400,000 immigrants from Europe landed in the United States, the record number before the Civil War. After 1880, yearly immigration rarely fell below 400,000. In 1859, approximately 1,300,000 wage earners toiled in 140,000 industrial establishments. By 1889, over 4,000,000 labored in 355,000 factories. The value of manufactured products in the same thirty-year period rose from less than two billion dollars to more than nine billion.

However one might characterize the two decades after the Civil War, one thing is certain. The machine and the city had shattered the Jeffersonian–Jacksonian vision of the yeoman, agrarian republic. The economic vitality of the new era centered in the factory, not the farm. The city, rather than the small town, became the undisputed symbol of America's productive energies, cultural and intellectual attainments, economic and social opportunities. New men of wealth in the great cities superseded the older planter and merchant aristocracy and, as Veblen explained, created new canons of consumption. The stone and marble palaces of the rich lined Fifth Avenue in New York. The lavish excesses of the wealthy excited the imagination of *hoi polloi.* It became the custom on New Year's day, for example, to leave window curtains partly undrawn on Fifth Avenue, permitting strollers to view "the richly furnished, brightly lighted drawing rooms, with their elegantly dressed occupants." The excitement and diversity of city life, its economic possibilities most vividly manifested by the *nouveau riche,* attracted those persons dissatisfied with the stale routine of the farm or village.

But the color of the city, the avenues it opened to material success and cultural stimulation, were balanced by less glamorous features. The city reflected as well the acute social tensions and maladjustments of an expanding and fluid industrial society.

The Jeffersonian–Jacksonian ideal had been that of a roughly equalitarian society. A nation composed of small property owners, mostly farmers and artisans, would insure political democracy, widely diffused intelligence, virtue, and patriotism. Although extreme Jacksonians had certain qualms about the unsettling effects on the economy of business enterprise, most Americans could easily reconcile enterprise with stability and virtue. Men would be rewarded for their toil in proportion to their thrift, initiative, ability, and sobriety. Work and business were thus tests of character, and the entrepreneur the instrument of the community's moral and economic progress. Even the most doctrinaire Jacksonian agreed that the threat to social stability came not from business enterprise as such, but from monopoly and special privilege.

What happened to the certainties of the equalitarian society in an industrial-urban age? They lingered on in men's minds, but they obviously had less applicability in the urban metropolis, with its striking contrasts between wealth and poverty. The artisan became a wage earner in a factory. No longer the master of his economic destiny, he found that his standard of living and his range of opportunities were increasingly controlled by remote and impersonal forces — the absentee capitalist, the laws of the market place, technological innovations. A permanent laboring class had formed that owned neither its homes nor the tools of its trade. But the equalitarian dream was based upon a nation of men who owned their homes, worked for themselves, and lived close to the soil. Could the new proletariat be relied upon to exercise sound political judgment when it had no material interest in honest government? No wonder corruption and bossism pervaded urban politics. Could such a class appreciate the rights of property and not look with envy upon the acquisitions of the more prosperous and successful? No wonder the middle class reacted furiously to such assertions of working-class discontent as the railroad strikes of 1877 and the Haymarket explosion of 1886. Were these a portent of the future — a nation of cities filled with a rootless, ignorant proletariat ogling the wealth of their betters and prepared to expropriate it by violent means? "The city's beautiful homes, splendid with costly furniture; the prancing horses and sparkling carriages; the silks and seal-skins and the bright and dainty dresses of rich children," seemed to the worker "to have been filched from his own poor fireside and from his shabby little ones." What did one have in common with a man who believed that "you and your class have wronged him?"

At the same time that the city exposed the breakdown of America's ideal of the classless society, it revealed a corresponding division by race and nationality. Large cities like New York, Chicago, and Boston developed foreign quarters whose life and culture seemed to diverge at every point from that of native, middle-class Americans. Here was another serious menace to America's social homogeneity and the stability of her institutions.

Could these foreigners, most of them belonging to the wage-earning proletariat and many of them Catholics, be depended upon to preserve the "pure high faith of our fathers," the faith that had "promoted at once free-thinking and right-thinking, power and purity, personal liberty and personal responsibility?" How many of these same foreigners — whose ranks after 1880 increasingly included the hot-tempered, unpredictable Italian and the querulous, clannish Jew plucked from the Pale and ghettos of eastern Europe — would "join the ranks of the misguided and incorrigible men who openly or secretly long for the coming of anarchy and chaos?" The presence of the foreigner not only intensified the "great and growing gulf . . . between the working class and those above them," but created an even worse class problem than existed in Europe. In America disparities in wealth were intensified by "still greater differences in race, language, and religion."

Within the urban community, the most vivid expression of the class and ethnic tensions troubling American society was the slum. Here the working-class and immigrant population concentrated. Measured by American standards of physical health, moral deportment, language, customs, traditions, and religion, the tenement population almost seemed to belong to a different species of humanity. The housing reformer believed that if he could improve the housing of the poor, this would reduce the class and ethnic conflict splitting the urban community into enemy camps. Better housing was needed not only to protect the health of the entire community, but to Americanize the immigrant working-class population, to impose upon it the middle-class code of manners and morals.

Charles F. Wingate, former editor of the *Plumber and Sanitary Engineer,* included among the moral disadvantages of tenement life "the growth of intemperance and immorality," "the disruption of families, the turning of children into the street, the creation and fostering of crime." If such charges were true, then New York had indeed allowed a civic Frankenstein to gestate within its womb. By 1890, the city's 81,000 dwellings included 35,000 tenements. These tenements, however, contained an overwhelming percentage of the city's total population of approximately 1,500,000. Those tenements alone which housed twenty-one persons or more contained a total population in excess of 1,000,000.

In the American hierarchy of values, stable and harmonious family life loomed high. Whatever else failed, the moral influence of the family unit over the individual would maintain the integrity of the community. But New York was a city of the homeless. Many of its people grew up "without the education, discipline, and moral influence of a separate family life and the interest in the community which the owning of a bit of land gives." These were the "natural tool of demagogues." A generation of tenement life had already "destroyed in a great measure the safeguards which a genuine home erects around a people." This left "vice and ignorance as the foundation stones of the municipality."

As in the past, the feature of tenement life which critics singled out most frequently was the enforced overcrowding. The tenement heaped people and families together; by force of example, the impure infected the virtuous. As Wingate explained: "Every tenement-house is a community in itself, and the malign example of vice cannot fail to exert its full influence. The drunkard, the wife or child beater, the immoral woman, and the depraved child infect scores of their neighbors by their vicious acts. How is it possible to preserve purity amid such homes, or to bring up children to be moral and decent?"

There in the tenements "young girls are found sleeping on the floor in rooms where are crowded men, women, youths and children. Delicacy is never known; purity is lost before its meaning is understood. . . ." Boys growing up in the company of thieves and vagabonds formed into gangs of "toughs" who roamed the city in search of thrills. These, the children of immigrants, were described by Charles Loring Brace as "the dangerous classes of New York." Ignorant and insensitive, they were "far more brutal than the peasantry from whom they descend." When the parent could no longer control his child, the tenement indeed had sapped the roots of the family.

The tenement environment responsible for crime, hoodlumism, and sexual impurity also fostered alcoholism. Poor food, filthy surroundings, and "the constant inhalation of vitiated air" poisoned the organism and predisposed "these unfortunates to a continual desire for stimulation." The environment was more responsible for intemperance than any inherent addiction of the tenement poor to liquor. If "Mr. Millions" had to suffer through life in a cramped tenement apartment, one sympathetic observer noted, he would very likely be inclined to send for his bottle of rum and "solace himself with the great East Side comforter."

How could the immigrant and his children develop into desirable citizens, how could they be assimilated into the American community if the tenement warped their personalities? It even warped their bodies. The poor fell prey to "the slow process of decay . . . called 'tenement-house rot'." Infantile life was "nipped in the bud." Deformed youth gave way at the age of thirty to "loathsome" decrepitude. The typical immigrant was "a European peasant, whose horizon has been narrow, whose moral and religious training has been meager or false, and whose ideas of life are low." How could he possibly be rescued if, segregated in his tenement ghetto, he remained impervious to the elevating influence of American moral and cultural doctrine? Perhaps it was necessary to restrict immigration, the source of so much turmoil. The foreigners who came here to "herd together like sheep in East Side tenement-houses" were more an incubus than a boon to the nation.

Although the American middle-class community and the immigrant worker were conscious of each other's existence, there was little personal association between them. The city became a world marked by physical proximity and social distance. The American reacted with hostile contempt to the foreigner's unwillingness or inability to shed his old world customs, language, and companions. He blamed the foreigner for having caused the tenement blight. He resented the fact that "all forms of misgovernment and political corruption in the City feed on this un-Americanized mass, which has now grown so great that the native element is merely tolerated." The foreigner, for his part, could either ignore or rankle under the whiplash of such criticism. Whatever his reaction, he could not suddenly shed his foreignness and merge silently into the American community. The city was divided into two worlds.

If the homogeneity of urban society had disintegrated under the strains caused by industrialism and immigration, the tenement system in the eyes of reformers thwarted any possibilities of reintegration. Since "the bad almost inevitably drag down the good; and the good have not the chance to lift up the bad," it was impossible for the foreigner to adopt the standards of personal cleanliness and behavior essential to his Americanization.

The tenement reformer had great faith in the reformatory powers of an improved housing environment. It was true, as some complained, that many "perfectly honest and virtuous" persons conscientiously abstained from soap and water, twisted out balusters for kindling wood, and unhesitatingly emptied garbage from the nearest window. Reformers replied to such pessimism that the poor could not always help themselves, that they "never knew cleanliness or comfort or anything but squalor." It was their normal condition. On the other hand, such squalor not only served to "prevent the adoption of better habits," but threatened to "produce a race adapted to the surroundings." Thus John Cotton Smith, rector of Ascension Church, admitted that it was useless to carry on mission work among the poor until their physical conditions had been improved. They would only remain impervious to elevating moral influences. In words reminiscent of the AICP, the New York *Times* argued that it was futile to expect "decency, purity of life, and obedience to moral and political law" to arise out of wretched physical squalor.

Conceivably, housing reformers placed excessive faith in the potency of a changed physical environment. The latter cannot necessarily transcend the limitations imposed by historical and cultural conditioning. The slum, after all, was a way of life, not simply houses. Habits and attitudes of the tenement population were affected by such fundamental influences as ethnic background, level of education, employment opportunities, and personal ambitions. The immigrant's adaptation to American life was influenced also by what he expected from this country. The immigrant who viewed his residence here as only temporary did not always care how he lived, so long as he found work, and this transient immigrant would remain especially resistant to efforts to transform his life. Because the quality and tone of tenement life were moulded by factors other than overcrowding, poor sanitary facilities, a paucity of light or ventilation, and similar inconveniences, housing reform had limited applicability as an instrument of social control. As Thomas and Znaniecki have explained in their analysis of the Polish peasant, changes of material environment will not necessarily affect "mentality and character of individuals and groups." A change of material conditions might "help or hinder . . . the development of corresponding lines of behavior, but only if the tendency is already there, for the way in which they will be used depends on the people who use them."

Tenement reformers, however, did not usually ponder such subtleties. They exposed the moral and physical condition of the tenement population and arraigned the tenement itself as the nursery of the squalor and degradation spreading incessantly before their eyes. They transmitted their faith in the beneficent powers of better housing conditions to most reformers of the Progressive generation.

The Decline of Intellectual Orthodoxy

The period from 1885 to 1910 was one of great intellectual unrest and creativity. Previously, for almost a generation, Americans had been content to acquiesce in traditional wisdom and to build on the intellectual certainties of the past. In large measure this conservatism was the legacy of the Civil War. Before 1860, the intellectual mood of the nation was bold, dissenting, and innovative. This was the period of skepticism about institutions and received values. It had produced an intense wave of reform and an impressive literary renaissance.

The war taught the nation's creative thinkers the importance of institutions and of the conventional ways of looking at society and values. Indeed it burned the lesson in too deeply, for during the following decades the intellectual life of the country was relatively sterile and conformist. It was dominated by mechanical views of the way social institutions operated. The social mechanism was very much like the Newtonian solar system — fixed, changeless, and logically predictable.

The system, as Morton White notes in the following selection, was peculiarly abstract. It did not need to make much contact with the hurly-burly of the actual world. Instead of the realities of American business with its tendency toward monopoly, the prevailing orthodoxy taught the free market economics of Adam Smith and John Stuart Mill. History was dominated by the idea that the doings of princes and parliaments alone mattered. Law meant the immutable principles of the British Common Law or of the federal Constitution. These were like the Ten Commandments, and all that judges needed do was to refer to the principles contained in these fundamental sources.

By the 1880s, these orthodoxies began to come under attack. A major element in the change was the gradual penetration of evolutionary notions into the field of social thought. To evolutionists the social mechanism was growing, evolving, everchanging. Its proper analogue was not the inert machine but the live organism. Institutions and values, accordingly, were not fixed for all time. They changed with time, and we had to recognize that change and accommodate ourselves to it.

FOR FURTHER READING:

AARON, DANIEL. *Men of Good Hope: A Story of American Progressives.* New York: Oxford University Press, 1961.*

MAY, HENRY. *The End of American Innocence: A Study of the First Years of Our Own Time.* Chicago: Quadrangle Books, 1964.*

NOBLE, DAVID. *The Progressive Mind, 1890–1917.* New York: Rand McNally & Company, 1969.*

Asterisk denotes paperback edition.

The Revolt Against Formalism

MORTON G. WHITE

The movements of thought with which we shall be most concerned cannot be fully understood without some sense of their relation to the ideas which dominated the nineteenth century. That century transcended the eighteenth through its concern with change, process, history, and culture. It was the century of history, evolutionary biology, psychology and sociology, historical jurisprudence and economics; the century of Comte, Darwin, Hegel, Marx, and Spencer. It is not surprising, therefore, to find American intellectuals ranging themselves, in the eighteen-nineties, against formalism, since they had been convinced that logic, abstraction, deduction, mathematics, and mechanics were inadequate to social research and incapable of containing the rich, moving living current of social life. So convinced had some American intellectuals become that their earliest work touched off a large-scale revolt against formalism in philosophy and the social sciences. The battle for history and culture may have been won on the Continent, but here in America it was only beginning, and the last bastions of formalist philosophy, economics, law, and political science were being besieged. Dewey, Holmes, and Veblen were the leaders of a campaign to mop up the remnants of formal logic, classical economics and jurisprudence in America, and to emphasize that the life of science, economics, and law was not logic but experience in some streaming social sense.

It is very hard to give an exact definition of the word "formalism," but I think its meaning will become clearer as we consider examples. It may be that the term as applied to movements in different fields — in law, philosophy, and economics — does not retain precisely the same meaning, but there is a strong family resemblance, strong enough to produce a feeling of sympathy in all who opposed what they called formalism in their respective fields. Anti-formalists like Holmes, Dewey, Veblen, and Beard called upon social scientists in all domains, asked them to unite, and urged that they had nothing to lose but their deductive chains.

This attack on formalism or abstractionism leads to two important positive elements in the thought of these men — "historicism" and what I shall call "cultural organicism." These are frequently identified in discussions of nineteenth-century thought, but it seems to me that they can be distinguished in a rather simple way. By "historicism" I shall mean the attempt to explain facts by reference to earlier facts; by "cultural organicism" I mean the attempt to find explanations and relevant material in social sciences other than the one which is primarily under investigation. The historicist reaches back in time in order to account for certain phenomena; the cultural organicist reaches into the entire social space around him. In many cases these two tendencies exist side by side in the thought of a single man, and in fact this is precisely what happens with most of the figures we shall treat. They are all under the spell of history and culture. Holmes is the learned historian of the law and one of the heroes of sociological jurisprudence; Veblen is the evolutionary and sociological student of economic institutions; Beard urges us to view political instruments as

Source: Morton G. White, *Social Thought in America: The Revolt Against Formalism* (Boston: Beacon Press, 1957), chap. 2, "The Revolt Against Formalism," pp. 11–31.

more than documents; Robinson construes history as the ally of all the social disciplines and the study of how things have come to be as they are; Dewey describes his philosophy alternately as "evolutionary" and "cultural" naturalism. All of them insist upon coming to grips with life, experience, process, growth, context, function. They are all products of the historical and cultural emphases of the nineteenth century, following, being influenced by, reacting from its great philosophers of change and process. The present chapter is an attempt to delineate somewhat specifically the early roots of this outlook. It lays great stress upon the fact that Dewey violently attacked formal logic in his earliest writings, that Veblen devoted great energy to deprecating the abstract-deductive method of classical political economy, that Beard fought against the formal-juridical approach to the Constitution, that Holmes proclaimed in 1881 what later became the slogan of generations of legal realists: "The life of the law has not been logic: it has been experience."

In the case of Dewey the roots are very clear. His early thought began under the domination of neo-Hegelianism with its unqualified condemnation of the formal and the mechanical. It was supported (in his own mind) by the results of Darwinian biology. Dewey was first a disciple of G. S. Morris, the obscure American idealist. His first philosophical work was also under the influence of Thomas H. Green and Edward Caird. Not only his views of logic and metaphysics but also the earliest expression of his political philosophy found their roots here. Veblen, by an interesting coincidence, was also a graduate student at Johns Hopkins, and he too listened to Morris. Although Veblen did not go through a serious early Hegelian stage with Dewey, he shared Dewey's tremendous admiration for Darwin. It is interesting to observe that Veblen constantly compared the Hegelian and Darwinian conceptions of change, always to the detriment of the former, whereas there was a period in Dewey's development when he tried to defend his Hegelianism with arguments from Darwinism. In spite of their early differences on Hegel, Dewey and Veblen were part of a reaction against English and Scottish empiricism, and their early thought expressed this quite vividly. One berated the philosophical wing of the tradition, the other attacked the economists. And sometimes, of course, they converged on the same figures — Hume, Adam Smith, Bentham, or John Stuart Mill.

It is extremely important to take into account this aversion to British empiricism — a phenomenon which can surprise only those who casually link Dewey and Veblen with all "empiricists." The paradox, if any, was almost solved by Leslie Stephen when he remarked in his study of the utilitarians that, although the latter were frequently appealing to experience, they had a very low opinion of the value of historical study. Now Holmes was certainly less opposed to the British tradition. Nevertheless Holmes selected for his special attack the prime exponent of utilitarian jurisprudence — John Austin. Holmes was disputing as early as 1874 Austin's view of the law as the command of the sovereign. For if the law is the command of the sovereign, then the judge is to find it rather than make it, and this conflicted with Holmes' main positive view. I emphasize the fact that Austin was a Benthamite in order to indicate the centrality of Bentham in the camp of the enemy. When Dewey first published books on ethics, it was hedonism, and utilitarianism, which he most severely attacked; when Veblen criticized the foundations of classical economics, it was Bentham's calculus of pains and pleasures that he was undermining; when Holmes was advancing his own view of the law, it was the tradition of Bentham he was fighting against; when Beard came to treat the Constitution as a social document and not simply as an abstract system to be logically analyzed, he found Bentham's shadow, made longer by Austin on Bentham's shoulders. That Robinson, the historian, should not have found a comparable sparring partner among the utilitarians does not destroy the generality of my thesis; on the contrary, it confirms it, for there were no utilitarian historians of comparable stature. And it was precisely utilitarianism's alleged failure to deal with social phenomena in a historical-cultural manner that led to the attack on the tradition of Bentham. Dewey attacked utilitarian ethics, psychology, and logic for failing to study the actual workings of the human mind; Veblen attacked the hedonic calculus as well as the failure to study economic institutions in their wider cultural setting; Beard opposed the analytical school for treating the Constitution as if it were axiomatized geometry rather than a human, social document; and Holmes regarded Austin's theory as an inaccurate account of law as it was practiced.

These general reflections give a fair idea of what I mean when I connect all of these men as anti-formalist revolutionaries; I turn now to some concrete expressions of this attitude in their early writings.

Oliver Wendell Holmes, Jr.

Because Holmes was the oldest of these men, and because he was the first of them to present a mature and clear statement of his position, I want to treat him first. I want particularly to consider some of the more general aspects of his work *The Common Law* (1881) in order to focus upon its important role in the revolt against formalism.

His purpose, Holmes tells us on the first page, is to present a general view of the subject. And then, as if to dissociate himself from a view which he might have expected his readers to assign to him, he announces that "other tools are needed besides logic" in order to accomplish this task. May we infer that there were some expositors of the common law who believed that *only* logic was necessary as a tool? I doubt it; but certainly there were some who conceived of logic as the fundamental tool. Of what logic is Holmes speaking? If it were not for the fact that he published his book in 1881, when the world was being swamped with two-volume studies in idealistic logic, such a question might not be raised. But I raise it only to make explicit the fact that he was not referring to these works or to the discipline which they claimed to expound, but rather that he had in mind traditional Aristotelian logic. It was syllogistic logic that did not suffice for presenting a general view of the common law. Moreover, we can be sure that Holmes was not rejecting Aristotelian logic because of any failure which might be remedied by modern, mathematical logic. Of the latter he knew almost nothing, and in it he had little interest. No enrichment of syllogistic logic in the modern manner would have changed the situation for Holmes' purposes. It was simply his conviction that deductive logic did not suffice, no matter how enriched. Holmes was not about to give a list of legal axioms in the manner of Euclid and promptly to deduce theorems with the help of logic. If this had been his sole purpose, logic would have been the sole tool necessary in addition to the legal principles expressed in his axioms. But on this he says: "The law embodies the story of a nation's development through many centuries, and it cannot be dealt with as if it contained only the axioms and corollaries of a book of mathematics."

We see at once the historical emphasis in Holmes. It is because the law embodies the *history* of a nation that it cannot be treated deductively. Although Holmes does not explicitly formulate them, we may indicate at least two questions which are introduced by his statement, in order to be clearer about what he is saying. 1. Can we formulate the law accepted at a given time in a deductive fashion, beginning with legal axioms or fundamental principles? 2. Has the law in its actual historical course developed in a logico-deductive manner? In other words, did the axioms, for example, reveal themselves to man before the theorems? Now we must not forget that in this place Holmes is concerned with the latter question, and his answer is that we cannot explain legal history in terms of logical processes alone. Legal history does not unfold as if it were created by a logician. The life of the law has not been logic in this sense. He follows this statement with a statement of other factors to which we must refer if we are to understand why and how certain legal rules were developed: "The felt necessities of the time, the prevalent moral and political theories, intuitions of public policy, avowed or unconscious, even the prejudices which judges share with their fellow men, have a good deal more to do than the syllogism in determining the rules by which men should be governed." The theory, we see, is predominantly a theory of historical development of law, and it is anti-formalistic in so far as it rejects the view that the law evolves in accordance with a formal-logical pattern.

The positive implications of this attack on formalism are fairly obvious. Holmes is led to an intensive study of the history and theories of legislation in order to explain the meanings of certain legal terms and rules and why they emerged when they did. The first chapter of *The Common Law,* for example, is an exercise in historical explanation; it is a study of early forms of liability in order to show that they are rooted in passion and vengeance. The entire study, the details of which we need not consider, is permeated with a historical outlook, specifically with the spirit of an epoch-making work in anthropology. *The Common Law* followed the publication of E. B. Tylor's *Primitive Culture* by ten years, and the impact of the latter was still considerable. Not only is Tylor cited by Holmes on certain factual questions, but some of his general ideas are also absorbed. For example, Holmes remarks on what he calls a "very common phenomenon," and one which is "very familiar to the student of history": "The customs, beliefs, or needs of a primitive time establish a rule or a formula. In the course of centuries the custom, belief, or necessity disappears, but the rule remains. The reason which gave rise to the rule has been forgotten, and ingenious minds set themselves to inquire how it is to be accounted for. Some ground of policy is thought of, which seems to explain it and to reconcile it with the present state of things; and then the rule adapts itself to the new reasons which have been found for it, and enters on a new career. The old form receives a new content, and in time even the form modifies itself to fit the meaning which it has received."

The point of view expressed here is closely related to Tylor's conception of survival, treated at length in the third and fourth chapters of *Primitive Culture.* In the case of Tylor, the study of primitive culture is motivated, in part, by a desire to ferret out just those elements of his own culture which are mere survivals of a more backward and less civilized age. The study of the past is not exclusively archaeological or antiquarian for Tylor. He urges that we try to get rid of those practices which have nothing to commend them but the fact that they are survivals of the past. It is for this reason that he concludes his great work with the following statement: "It is a harsher, and at times even painful, office of ethnography to expose the remains of prude old culture which have passed into harmful superstition, and to mark these out for destruction. Yet this work, if less genial, is not less urgently needful for the good of mankind. Thus, active at once in aiding progress and in removing hindrance, the science of culture is essentially a reformer's science."

Tylor's conception of the science of culture as a reformer's science must be underscored if we are to appreciate the link between the historicism and the liberalism of our American thinkers. Tylor's view shows conclusively that historicism is not necessarily associated with a veneration of the past. Here the study of the past is construed as instrumental to the solution of present problems — to the elimination of contemporary irrationality. The student of the past need not have a stake in the past. If the example of Marx is not sufficient to show this, certainly that of Tylor is worth mentioning. The statement of this idea is of great value in helping us to understand the evolutionary and historical orientation of Holmes, Veblen, Dewey, Beard, and Robinson. It helps us to distinguish the motivation of their historicism and organicism from that which inspired European reactionaries in the nineteenth century.

John Dewey

In 1882, one year after the publication of *The Common Law*, Dewey's first published contribution to philosophy appeared. With it he began a series of investigations into philosophy and psychology, under the influence of British neo-idealism. This influence was to continue until the emergence of his distinctly instrumentalist, pragmatist, or experimentalist outlook. Dewey was even more anti-formalist than Holmes. Under the more direct influence of Morris he came to scorn the epistemology of the British empiricists, and to single out for criticism their dualistic separation of mind from the object of knowledge. This separation was construed by Dewey as "formal" and "mechanical" and hence attacked in the manner of Hegel. The "new psychology" was a movement, according to Dewey, which was to free psychology from the analytical dissections of associationism. Hegel provided him with the concept of a universal consciousness which embraced everything and which provided the link between individual consciousness and the objects of knowledge, the link which supposedly showed them to be more than formally related. The *objective mind* of idealism was made central, and, as Dewey tells us later, it was the ancestor of his insistence upon the influence of the cultural environment in shaping ideas, beliefs, and intellectual attitudes. It was this which united him with the spirit of *The Common Law* — this emphasis on the need for regarding human action (in Holmes the special case of legal action) as part of what Dewey later called a "cultural matrix." Although Holmes was not a Hegelian, I think there is no doubt that he and Dewey were motivated by similar considerations in their attack on formalism. In the light of this great similarity in their early years, and their mutual respect in later years, the convergence of pragmatism and legal realism should occasion little surprise. It was in the eighties that Dewey was also attacking formal logic. Now Holmes was no admirer of Hegel's *Logic;* certainly he would not have agreed that it represented "the quintessence of the scientific spirit," as Dewey maintained in 1891. But the classic excerpt from *The Common Law* about the life of the law not being logic can be matched with several from Dewey, the most striking being Dewey's claim in 1891 that formal logic was *"fons et origo malorum* in philosophy."

In addition to sharing Holmes' attitude toward the role of formal logic, and toward what I have called cultural organicism, Dewey shared his respect for the historical or genetic method. We have seen how this functioned in Holmes' early work. In Dewey's thought the use of genetic method is positively motivated, whereas his opposition to formalism is the product of a polemic on Hegelian grounds against British empiricism. This is not to say that his historicism had no connections with his Hegelianism. What must be emphasized is the fact that Dewey's Hegelianism directed him against formalism, and that this was fortified by his study of Darwin. It is not surprising, therefore, to find his use of genetic method taking on an evolutionary cast. This links him not only to Holmes but also to Veblen, as we shall see when we examine the latter's regretful complaint in 1898 that economics was not then an evolutionary science.

Dewey's application of evolutionary method to morality not only is useful for establishing his connection with Holmes and Veblen; it also helps to illuminate some of the ties between his historicism and his experimentalism, between his early Hegelian emphasis on change and history and his later pragmatic emphasis on experiment and control. In expounding the nature of evolutionary method he tries to formulate the sense in which experimental method is itself genetic. His answer is rather simple. In conducting experiments on the nature of water, to use his own example, we perform certain acts of combination and we see that water is formed as a consequence. The entire process is one in which water is "called into being." The experimental process, therefore, is viewed as genetic in character, precisely because it "calls into being" certain phenomena as a result of experimental manipulation. Now there are some domains, Dewey thought at the time, in which experimental control is impossible. We are able to use experiment in chemistry, he argues but we cannot apply it to "those facts with which ethical science is concerned. We cannot," he says, "take a present case of parental care, or of a child's untruthfulness, and cut it into sections, or tear it into physical pieces, or subject it to chemical analysis." What we can do, however, is study "how it came to be what it is," that is, study it historically. History, therefore, is construed, according to Dewey, as "the only available substitute for the isolation and for the cumulative recombination of experiment. The early periods present us in their relative crudeness and simplicity with a substitute for the artificial operation of an experiment: following the phenomenon into the more complicated and refined form which it assumes later, is a substitute for the synthesis of experiment."

We see then that for Dewey at this time history was the only available substitute for experiment and, moreover, that he viewed experiment itself as a kind of historical enterprise. The notion of history as a possible alternative for experiment was not original with Dewey; in fact his whole argument is reminiscent of the kind of discussion one finds in *A System of Logic,* especially where Mill considers the various methods and their applicability in the social sciences. Mill also concluded that experiment was not possible in at least one of the "moral sciences," namely, economics, but he argued that the best substitute was the deductive method, and not history. That Mill and Dewey should have divided in this way is quite understandable in the light of Dewey's avowed opposition to formalism. It is important to see, moreover, how this permits Veblen to enter the picture. For it was precisely this aspect of Mill's methodology which Veblen attacked in his own critique of classical economics. And Veblen, like Dewey, appealed to history, to the need for an "evolutionary science."

Thorstein Veblen

Like Holmes and Dewey, Veblen was strongly influenced by new developments in anthropology. If anything, he was more interested and more learned in that field than they were. So strong was this influence that he began his famous attack on all previous schools of economics by approving the following statement: "Anthropology is destined to revolutionize the political and the social sciences as radically as bacteriology has revolutionized the science of medicine." But economics, he complained, was not then in tune with this new note. In short, it was not an evolutionary science.

But why wasn't it an evolutionary science? To understand this we might best turn to John Stuart Mill for the light he sheds on Veblen's lament, and in this way observe concretely how Mill represents, with Bentham and Austin, the ideology against which so many of the pioneers of American social science revolted. The doctrine of economic method associated with Mill is well expressed in *A System of Logic,* but it is even more sharply defined in a brilliant essay which he wrote in 1830 when he was twenty-four years old, "On the Definition of Political Economy; and the Method of Investigation Proper to It." For Mill, political economy is to be distinguished from what he calls social economy or speculative politics — the latter treating "the whole of man's nature as modified by the social state." Political economy is rather a branch of social economy, because it does not deal with the whole of man's nature. It is concerned with man "solely as a being who desires to possess wealth, and who is capable of judging of the comparative efficacy of means for attaining that end. It predicts only such of the phenomena of the social state as take place in consequence of the pursuit of wealth. It makes entire abstraction of every other human passion or motive; except those which may be regarded as perpetually antagonizing principles to the desire of wealth, namely, aversion to labour, and desire of the present enjoyment of costly indulgences." The important point in Mill's statement of the nature of political economy is his use of the subjunctive conditional mode of assertion in the following passage (the italics are mine): "Political economy considers mankind as occupied solely in acquiring and consuming wealth, and aims at showing what is the course of action into which mankind, living in a state of society, *would* be impelled, *if* that motive, except in the degree in which it is checked by the two perpetual counter-motives above adverted to, *were* absolute ruler of all their actions." I emphasize the subjunctive mood of the statement, for it is clear that Mill is not saying that in fact the pursuit of wealth is the sole motive of man. Indeed he goes on to say that the economist does *not* put this forth as a description of man's actual behavior. He denies that any "political economist was ever so absurd as to suppose that mankind are really thus constituted." But later critics of Mill, pre-eminently Veblen and his followers, have treated this view of the economic man as though it were an unconditional assertion in the indicative mood about man's actual psychology. We can see, therefore, why Veblen rejected the view and why he should have found himself in agreement with Dewey on this point. For Veblen this is the acme of "faulty psychology," and what is worse than faulty psychology for an institutionalist? It is simply not true to say that man is governed by this single motive (even where the qualifications about counter-motives are made). And since this is an "assumption" of classical economics which is false, everything which is "deduced" from it is suspect in the eyes of a Veblenian.

There are other aspects of Mill's methodology of economics which contribute to an understanding of what was troubling Veblen. Mill suggests that the economist ought to treat man much as the astronomer treats planets. The astronomer frequently talks about what *would* happen to a planet if it were not subject to the sun's attraction. (This, of course, occurs when he considers it as a particle subject only to Newton's first law of motion.) In such a case, Mill says, he *abstracts* and considers the planet *as if* it were a body outside the sun's gravitational field (although he knows it is not). Just as astronomers pursue this method successfully, so, it is urged, may economists. By considering first how men *would* behave if they were simply dominated by a single motive, Mill believes that economists will come to a good approximation of how they do in fact behave. "This approximation," he points out, "is then to be corrected by making proper allowance for the effects of any impulses of a different description, which can be shown to interfere with the result in any particular case.

There can be no doubt that this was the tradition against which Veblen was rebelling when he rejected the method of classical economics. I don't think he ever clearly formulated for himself the methodological tenets of Mill in a way that left them defensible, but it was a doctrine of this kind that he rejected. I say "of this kind," not to exclude the possibility that there were classical economists who were less able than Mill in methodology, and less cautious in what they asserted about the actual psychology of man. In any case, it should be evident that classical economics was formalistic for Veblen in a sense related to that in which formal logic was formalistic for Dewey, and Austin's jurisprudence was formalistic for Holmes. Dewey in his earliest attack on it construed formal logic as a description of how we think, and contemptuously dismissed it. Holmes insisted that when we study law "we are not studying a mystery but a well-known profession," and what could be more mysterious than the abstract dicta of Austin, formally conceived and having nothing to do with the "bad man" — the man who pays the lawyer to advise him how to keep out of jail? It is for this reason that Holmes, Dewey, and Veblen found themselves arrayed against three apostles of empiricism — Bentham, Mill, and Austin: they weren't empirical enough.

When Veblen complained that economics was not an evolutionary science he was voicing precisely this attitude. Now what was evolutionary science as Veblen understood it? In his essay on it he is, unfortunately, too occupied with asserting that all the traditional schools were not evolutionary, and little concerned with saying what an evolutionary science is. He insists that some things which might be expected to make a science evolutionary really don't. Hence the historical school — Schmoller, Hildebrand, Ashley, Cliffe-Leslie — was "realistic" in so far as it dealt with "facts," but this is not enough, according to Veblen. It failed, in his opinion, to formulate a theory concerning those facts. For him an evolutionary science must present a "theory of a process, of an unfolding sequence." When he comes to the classical economists he finds that even where they do refer to empirical data, and even where they try to present a theory of process, they still fall short of the evolutionary ideal. What, then, is the difference? As we press on we find a statement to the effect that the difference is one of "spiritual attitude" — a rather tender expression for one so tough-minded as Veblen. We press further and find that what he is disturbed about in the classical economists is their addiction to natural law. He is opposed to their formulating an ideal situation and generalizing about that situation without attending to actual economic facts. In some of Veblen's writings this amounts to an objection to the use of a subjunctive conditional like that used by Mill. We cannot,

Veblen seems to urge, use hypotheses like "If man were subject to only one motive," "If perfect competition prevailed," because they are false. At other times Veblen seems to be objecting not so much to the use of such hypotheses in science but rather to the fact that certain classical economists also had a moral attitude toward them. They thought either that these hypotheses formulated socially and morally desirable states, or that society was tending toward those states. In both cases Veblen held that some kind of belief in natural law was present. The first alternative involved a moral judgment on society; the second a faith in progress.

We may become a little clearer about Veblen's objection if we compare the situation of the student of mechanics with that of the classical political economist. The former tells us how the distance fallen by a freely falling body depends on the time it takes to fall. He points out, of course, that this law holds only in a vacuum. Thus far his procedure is analogous to that of the economist who insists that his laws hold only for economic vacuums, so to speak — cases where only one motive is in operation. But the physicist does not add, "And indeed the vacuum is a highly prized state," or, "The atmosphere tends more and more toward a vacuum." But the analogous economist, according to Veblen, not only uses ideal concepts like "economic man" and "perfect competition," but also admires these kinds of men and states of society, and looks upon them as ends toward which man and society are moving.

Thus far we have considered Veblen's attack on the use of abstraction in classical economics, but we have not considered his attitude toward the use of a priori method in economics. To understand this we must return to Mill's view.

Mill distinguished between two types of minds — the "practicals" and the "theorists," as he called them. The difference between them may be exhibited by his own illustration. Suppose we were faced with the following question: Are absolute kings likely to employ the powers of government for the welfare or for the oppression of their subjects? How would the practicals go about settling it? They would try, Mill says, to examine the conduct of particular despotic monarchs in history and to find out how they behaved. But the theorists, he says, "would contend that an observation of the tendencies which human nature has manifested in the variety of situations in which human beings have been placed, and especially observation of what passes in our own minds, warrants us in inferring that a human being in the situation of a despotic king will make a bad use of power; and that this conclusion would lose nothing of certainty even if absolute kings had never existed, or if history furnished us with no information of the manner in which they had conducted themselves. The practical uses the a posteriori method, the theorist the a priori method.

We see how Mill regarded economics as both abstract and a priori in method — abstract because it abstracted one aspect of man's behavior and tried to discover how he would behave if he had only one motive; a priori because it avoided the laborious and painstaking methods of statistical research. To verify hypotheses by reference to history was for Mill "not the business of science at all, but the application of science." It should be evident why Mill's doctrine was opposed by historicism and institutionalism. It is plain how Dewey's early views also ran counter to Mill's. Dewey's suggestion that we use history as a substitute for experiment where the latter is not possible was clearly the method of the "practical" for Mill — a label which the later Dewey would have accepted gladly.

It is evident how much the historical, evolutionary, cultural attitude united Dewey and Veblen against the abstract and a priori method of Mill. It is also clear why American thinkers rejected so much of the "empiricism" of Bentham and Mill: they were revolting against the least empirical elements of the tradition — apriorism, abstractionism, the hedonic calculus, formal jurisprudence. The grounds of Veblen's rejection of the method of classical economics are very similar to those which led Dewey to reject what he called scholastic formalism in psychology and logic. They also resemble the considerations which led Holmes to reject the so-called mechanical theory of the law as existing in advance and awaiting the judge's discovery of it. Furthermore, to complete the pattern, Veblen also turned to history and culture, to a cross-sectional study of the institutional context of economic behavior as well as to a study of the temporal development of society. Like Dewey and Holmes, he looked to temporal antecedents and cultural concomitants. For this reason we may say that Dewey, Holmes, and Veblen were united in an attempt to destroy what they conceived of as three fictions — the logical, legal, and economic man. In this way they began a tradition in recent American thought which Beard and Robinson continued in political science and history.

James Harvey Robinson and Charles A. Beard

The connections between Robinson, Beard, and the revolt against formalism are evident as early as 1908 — the year in which they delivered lectures on history and politics respectively at Columbia University, in a series devoted to science, philosophy, and art. Considered in terms of the revolt, Robinson's work is an expression of historicism, the evolutionary movement in social science, and genetic method. Robinson was anxious to establish the scientific character of history, but at the same time to distinguish his own from Ranke's version of scientific method in history. According to Robinson, historians from Thucydides to Macaulay and Ranke had examined the past "with a view of amusing, edifying, or comforting the reader." None of these motives, however, can be described as scientific, according to Robinson. He says: "To scan the past with the hope of discovering recipes for the making of statesmen and warriors, of discrediting the pagan gods, of showing that Catholic or Protestant is right, of exhibiting the stages of self-realization of the *Weltgeist,* of demonstrating that Liberty emerged from the forests of Germany never to return thither — none of these motives are scientific although they may go hand in hand with much sound scholarship. But by the middle of the nineteenth century the muse of history, *semper mutabile,* began to fall under the potent spell of natural science. She was no longer satisfied to celebrate the deeds of heroes and nations with the lyre and shrill flute on the breeze-swept slopes of Helicon; she no longer durst attempt to vindicate the ways of God to man. She had already come to recognize that she was ill-prepared for her undertakings and had begun to spend her mornings in the library, collating manuscripts and making out lists of variant readings. She aspired to do even more and began to talk of raising her chaotic mass of information to the rank of a science."

It is evident from this passage that Robinson was anxious to free historical research from moralism and estheticism, a concern which linked him with Holmes and Veblen in their attempt to distinguish their disciplines from morals; it is also connected with the early (though not the later) views of Beard, who held in 1908 that "it is not the function of the student of politics to praise or condemn institutions or theories, but to understand and expound them; and thus for scientific purposes it is separated from theology, ethics, and patriotism." We must remember that this amoralism occurred at a time when the confusion of factual and ethical questions was usually viewed as an instrument of conservatism and reaction. Objectivity was eagerly sought. Social theorists wanted to expose, to rake the facts, and to achieve scientific status. Indeed, on this point they were not seriously opposed to the tradition of Bentham and Mill. Like the utilitarians, they were part of a reforming movement, and they too sought to distinguish between what was and what ought to have been. Nevertheless it should be remembered that the desire to make this distinction was not regarded as incompatible with the view that moral judgments are theoretically capable of empirical verification. Certainly this was Dewey's view at the time.

Although Robinson was anxious to exclude moral considerations from the writing of history, he was also anxious to go beyond a mere report of what actually happened. Past historians, he said, "did take some pains to find out how things really were — *wie es eigentlich gewesen,* to use Ranke's famous dictum." Moreover, "to this extent they were scientific, although their motives were mainly literary, moral or religious." What they failed to do, however, was to "try to determine how things had come about — *wie es eigentlich geworden.*" And so Robinson concluded that history had remained for two or three thousand years a record of past events — a definition, he said, which still satisfied "the thoughtless." "It is one thing to describe what once was; it is quite another to attempt to determine how it came about." The old history, he thought, functioned as a dead formula rather than as a living picture of the past.

His view of history as itself a genetic account of how things come to be emphasized the concept of development, and was therefore part of the movement I have called historicism. It was quite like Holmes' conception of history as something which furnished explanations of the emergence and meaning of legal rules; it was wholly sympathetic with Veblen's critique of the historical school; it was like Dewey's view of history as a statement of "how the thing came to be as it is." How did it compare with Beard's view? Let us turn to the latter's lecture on "Politics," delivered in the same year, in the same place, and before much the same audience.

Beard's major complaint about his predecessors revolved about their error in studying juridical-formal relations in the abstract without attention to their roots in the social process. He warned his audience that "official performances are not really separable from other actions of the governmental agents themselves or from many of the actions of the citizens at large." Political facts are organically related to the social process as a whole. "The jural test of what constitutes a political action draws a dividing line where none exists in fact, and consequently any study of government that neglects the disciplines of history, economics, and sociology will lack in reality what it gains in precision. Man as a political animal acting upon political, as distinguished from more vital and powerful motives, is the most unsubstantial of all abstractions. The recognition of this truth has induced students of politics to search in many fields for a surer foothold than law alone can afford." And now just one more quotation to give the flavor of Beard's early conception of political science: "We are coming to realize that a science dealing with man has no special field of data all to itself, but is rather merely a way of looking at the same thing — a view of a certain aspect of human action. The human being is not essentially different when he is depositing his ballot from what he is in the counting house or at the work bench. In the place of a 'natural' man, an 'economic' man, a 'religious' man, or a 'political' man, we now observe the whole man participating in the work of government."

Robinson and Beard taken together present us with a historicist view of history and an organic view of political science. The connection with Dewey, Holmes, and Veblen is only too obvious. In the case of Beard, moreover, even the influence of some of the other historicists is evident. He was younger than they, and his work appeared later. One need only point to the fact that he cites Holmes, Pound, Good-now, and Bentley in the *Economic Interpretation of the Constitution* (1913) in order to show the intimate ties between his own cultural organicism and that of the key figures in some of the most important intellectual trends of the century — legal real-ism, sociological jurisprudence, pragmatism. Many of them, of course, did not ac-cept the main thesis of his book on the Constitution, but this must not obscure the broad ground on which Beard was united with the rest in a struggle against what I have called formalism and in an attempt to break down artificial barriers between the social disciplines. Like them, he embarked on a historical and cultural study of man.

Changing Morals in the Progressive Era

The tight nuclear family was largely a product of the nineteenth century. In earlier years, whatever we may conventionally assume, the family had not been as cohesive. In medieval and early modern times, social historians now believe, the family had a much looser structure. It often included servants, kinsmen, various sorts of retainers, and generally more than just the two generations of parents and children. Within this "extended family," relations were rather casual. High infant mortality rates made a large emotional investment in children hazardous, and they were not generally deferred to or taken very seriously. Individuals passed into and out of family units casually and without trauma. Moral authority was no doubt exercised by the family patriarch, but his control was rather diffuse and brief in duration for any given member.

By the nineteenth century, this porous social entity had been compacted into the nuclear family. Better suited to the highly competitive and mobile life of an industrial society, it was also much more repressive than its precursor. The family head, the father, was now a despot whose dominance over the lives of his spouse and his children was almost absolute. We have already seen to what extent this authoritarian regime reduced and confined the potential of women. Still more did the family patriarch command the lives of his children. It is suggestive that the title "governor" was often given to the father in a Victorian household of the mid-nineteenth century.

This environment was frequently stifling to its members. It was probably an important element in the repressiveness of instinctual outlets that Sigmund Freud observed among his patients in the years he was formulating his theories of neurosis and personality development. But neurosis was scarcely a healthy accommodation to the new family structure. A better one was divorce. When the marriage relationship became intolerable one could always escape by terminating it legally. Moralists might denounce the growing incidence of divorce in the Progressive Era, as William O'Neill shows in the following selection, but as he demonstrated elsewhere, it made the survival of the tight nuclear family possible. Divorce did not threaten the family; it actually strengthened it in many ways by providing an escape hatch for the truly bad mismatches that often occurred. Without it, conceivably, the hazards of mismating would have deterred many people from entering into the "blissful state of matrimony."

FOR FURTHER READING:

LASCH, CHRISTOPHER. *The New Radicalism in America.* New York: Random House, Vintage Books, 1965.*
O'NEILL, WILLIAM L. *Divorce in the Progressive Era.* New Haven: Yale University Press, 1967.

Asterisk denotes paperback edition.

Divorce in the Progressive Era

WILLIAM L. O'NEILL

During the Progressive years the divorce rate, which had been rising steadily since the Civil War, attained critical dimensions. Consequently, Americans of this period took a graver view of the problem than any subsequent generation. Their varied responses proved to be decisive as far as the future of divorce itself was concerned, and they illuminate aspects of the Progressive Era which have received little attention from historians.

The precipitate growth of the divorce rate can be easily demonstrated. In 1880 there was one divorce for every twenty-one marriages; in 1900 there was one divorce for every twelve marriages; in 1909 the ratio dropped to one in ten, and by 1916 it stood at one in nine.[1] Naturally this dramatic increase in the divorce rate stimulated public alarm.

In 1881 the New England Divorce Reform League was established to conduct research on family problems, educate the public and lobby for more effective legislative curbs on divorce.[2] Under the leadership of Samuel Dike, a Congregational minister, the league enjoyed a long and useful life, but Dike's reluctance to advance legislative solutions to the divorce problem failed to deter others from resorting to politics.

Efforts to arrest the spread of divorce by legal means took two forms. State campaigns were waged to amend local divorce laws, and repeated attempts were made to achieve uniform marriage and divorce laws either through a constitutional amendment or through the voluntary enactment of uniform codes by the several states.[3] Typical of the many local fights to alter state divorce laws was the successful battle in 1893 to end South Dakota's status as a divorce colony. After their admission to the Union in 1889 North and South Dakota retained Dakota Territory's generous ninety-day residence requirement. Sioux City, largest and most accessible town in the two states, soon developed a substantial divorce trade and gained national fame as a divorce colony. The resulting notoriety provoked local resentment which was mobilized by the return from Japan of the popular Episcopal Bishop William Hobart Hare, who in 1893 led Protestants, Catholics and Populists in an attack on the ninety-day residence requirement. The state legislature was successfully petitioned to extend the residence requirement to six months and the migratory divorce trade was diverted to North Dakota.[4]

The South Dakota campaign conformed to what was already an established pattern. It was led by conservative clergymen, supported by women's groups, and met little apparent opposition. Although these local campaigns did not succeed anywhere in abolishing divorce, they were part of a widespread tendency toward stricter divorce legislation.[5] When such local crusades failed, it was usually because of public apathy, sometimes coupled with undercover resistance from commercial and legal interests which profited from the divorce trade.

Serious attempts to secure uniform marriage and divorce legislation through a constitutional amendment began in 1892 when James Kyle, the Populist Senator

Source: William L. O'Neill, "Divorce in the Progressive Era," *American Quarterly,* vol. 17 (1965), no. 2, pt. 1, pp. 203–217.

from South Dakota, introduced a joint resolution which read in full: "The Congress shall have the exclusive power to regulate marriage and divorce in the several states, Territories, and the District of Columbia." [6] Senator Kyle's resolution died in committee as did all later resolutions, presumably because of a disinclination on the part of Congress to increase the power of the Federal government at the expense of the states.[7]

More popular, if equally unsuccessful, was the movement to secure voluntary uniformity through the drafting of model statutes which were to be enacted by the states. The most persistent of the organizations dedicated to this goal was the National Conference of Commissioners on Uniform State Laws, which met annually in connection with the American Bar Association. It was established by the Bar Association in 1889 to frame model codes on a wide range of subjects. The Commissioners were usually appointed by their state governors, and over the years drafted seven model statutes concerning marriage and divorce.[8] However, few of the states demonstrated an interest in these models, and by 1916 the Commissioners were forced to admit that their approach had been a failure.

If the experience of the National Conference of Commissioners on Uniform State Laws to 1906 had not been conclusive, the fate of the National Divorce Congress in that year was. A national meeting to draft uniform legislation had been talked about for years on the grounds that it would attract sufficient attention to succeed where the more diffident Commissioners had failed. In 1906 President Roosevelt was persuaded to request a new census study of marriage and divorce, and the interest aroused by this led Governor Pennypacker of Pennsylvania to call a national conference to draft model uniform legislation on these subjects. The Congress met twice, once in Washington to appoint committees, and again in Philadelphia to ratify the proposed statutes. The first meeting was attended by delegates from 42 of the 45 states and consisted largely of clergymen and lawyers, many of the latter having also been members of the NCCUSL. Despite the widespread approval which met their efforts, few states adopted their model statutes.[9]

The antidivorce forces were also active within the established Protestant churches. During the Progressive Era repeated efforts were made in almost all the great Protestant denominations to stiffen their positions on divorce. The Episcopal Church, traditionally more hostile to divorce than most Protestant bodies, was in the van of this movement, thanks principally to William Croswell Doane, Bishop of Albany, New York. Doane was perhaps the most vocal and consistent enemy of divorce in the whole country. He favored prohibiting divorce altogether, and his activities within the Episocpal Church were directed at the canon which allowed the innocent party in an adultery suit to remarry. This canon was only slightly less severe than the refusal of the Roman Catholic Church to allow any divorced person to remarry, but it seemed dangerously lax to Doane and he regularly introduced an amendment which would have denied the sacraments to all divorced persons without exception.

In 1898 the House of Bishops, usually more conservative than the lower House, which included laymen, at the policy-making Triennial Convention, rejected Doane's amendment 31 to 24.[10] In 1901 his amendment was defeated by a narrower margin, but in 1904 it passed the House of Bishops only to fail in the House of Deputies, whose members felt that it was too far removed from the spirit of the country.[11] Thereafter enthusiasm within the Episcopal Church for the Doane amendment declined, and while it was re-introduced at later conventions, it failed to pass even in the House of Bishops. Similar efforts were made in the other Protestant denominations with what proved to be an equal lack of success.[12]

American attitudes toward marriage and divorce during the Progressive years must be seen in terms of the widespread fear of divorce demonstrated by these examples. It is not too much to say that there was a national crisis generated by divorce. It was a crisis to begin with because people believed it was. As Daniel Bell has demonstrated in his *The End of Ideology,* it is not necessary for activities seen to be antisocial actually to increase in order to create a crisis atmosphere — it is enough if people simply believe that such activities are increasing.[13]

An even better example perhaps was the white slave panic of 1912–13. If anything, prostitution was declining, but irrespective of the facts, widespread public alarm over this presumed social evil was triggered by local investigations and newspaper publicity.[14]

However, divorce actually was increasing by leaps and bounds. When one marriage in twelve ended in divorce, there were legitimate grounds for concern. These were crucial years for divorce, finally, because the Progressive period was the last time when public opinion could reasonably have been expected to support genuinely repressive action. With the 1920s and the advent of the revolution in morals the opportunity to abolish or seriously restrict divorce was lost forever. Some of the anti-divorce leaders sensed that time was running out for them, and this awareness gave their strictures an urgent tone which became more shrill with the years.

Although divorce had political, psychological and other dimensions, the increase of divorce was usually seen as a moral and social problem.[15] It is difficult, if indeed not actually pointless, to try to determine which of these two aspects alarmed critics of divorce the most. The enemies of divorce invariably regarded it as both immoral and antisocial. Since most opponents of divorce were either clergymen or strongly religious people, it seems fair to assume that the moral side of the divorce question was what first engaged their attention, but having once declared divorce to be immoral, there is little more one can say in that direction, and most of the serious attacks on divorce emphasized its antisocial character.[16]

The attack on divorce hinged on the common belief that divorce destroyed the family, which was the foundation of society and civilization. Theodore Schmauk, editor of the *Lutheran Church Review,* President of the Lutheran General Council and a leading theologian, characterized the family as "the great and fundamental institution in social life." [17] *The Catholic World* in an attack on H. G. Wells' view of divorce felt that it had demolished his position when it observed that Wells failed to see that the family "was the cradle of civil society." [18] Lyman Abbott, an influential Progressive editor and associate of Theodore Roosevelt, once charged a prominent divorcee with being "the worst type of anarchist" because divorce, like anarchy, threatened to destroy society altogether.[19] President Roosevelt, in addressing Congress on the need for uniform legislation, described marriage as being "at the very foundation of our social organization. . . ." [20] Marriage and the family are, of course, quite different institutions, but the critics of divorce did not usually distinguish between them.

Felix Adler took this contention a step further when he insisted that divorce menaced "the physical and spiritual existence of the human race. . . ." [21] Adler was in some ways a surprising figure to find on this side of the divorce question. The founder of Ethical Culture and a leading advocate of liberal religion, he consistently attacked dogma and orthodoxy and supported a wide variety of social reforms.[22] He had earlier supported divorce, but by 1915 had changed his mind and accepted the point, usually advanced by the theologically orthodox, that divorce had to be suppressed as a matter of social survival. His conversion showed how this argument operated independently of its conservative religious base, and helps to explain why some enemies of divorce attached such importance to their campaign. One could hardly play for higher stakes.

A related theme which engaged the attention of divorce critics was the role of woman. It was generally believed that the family was woman's special responsibility and its protection her primary concern. Moreover women were thought to be more active than men in securing divorces (and they probably were since about two-thirds of all divorces were awarded to women). *The North American Review* reflected this point of view when it entitled one of its divorce symposiums, "Are Women to Blame?"[23] The *Review*'s female panelists charged women with responsibility for the divorce rate, and accused them of being spoiled, romantic, impatient, jealous of men and usurpers of the male's time-honored functions. Many of these women were successful writers, as was Anna B. Rogers, a popular essayist, who repeated the same charges in her book, *Why American Marriages Fail*, nineteen years later.[24]

While the critics of divorce, especially the men, were inclined to argue that women were really happier when they stayed at home and held the family together, the more tough-minded accepted the fact that the woman's traditional role was often painful and difficult.[25] Few had a clearer picture of what was involved than the respected novelist Margaret Deland. Mrs. Deland was a warm supporter of many Progressive causes and a woman with courage enough to defend the rights of unwed mothers in Victorian Boston. But she believed that civilization "rests on the permanence of marriage."[26] For this reason women dared not turn to divorce, for it would mean the end of everything. "If we let the flame of idealism be quenched in the darkness of the senses," she cried, "our civilization must go upon the rocks."[27] Even adultery was no excuse for giving up the fight, she continued, because men were instinctively promiscuous and their lapses from grace had to be tolerated for the sake of the greater good.

Implicit in these arguments was the belief that the individual was less important than the group. Most opponents of divorce agreed that divorce was part of an unwholesome tendency toward a "dangerous individualism." Margaret Deland bewailed the absence of team-play among women and Professor Lawton called frankly for the "suppression of the individual in favor of the community."[28] Samuel Dike in his Cook Lecture attributed divorce to the rising tide of individualism menacing all progressive societies, while Felix Adler as early as 1890 was tracing the whole ugly business back to Rousseau's "false democratic ideals."[29] Although, as we shall see, most leading sociologists believed in divorce, Charles A. Ellwood did not. This future president of the American Sociological Society, despite his Progressive sympathies, also attributed divorce to excessive individualism.[30] Francis Peabody, an eminent theologian and student of the Higher Criticism, believed that the family's major enemies were scientific socialism and "the reactionary force of self-interested individualism. . . ."[31]

The opponents of divorce were more varied and had much more to say than I have been able to indicate, but the foregoing gives at least some idea of who they were and what they thought. The defenders of divorce, by way of contrast, were fewer in number and easier to locate. Opinion against divorce was so widespread and diffuse that it cannot be attributed to a handful of groups, but the sentiment favoring divorce was largely confined to sociologists, liberal clergymen and feminists. The defenders of divorce, like its enemies, viewed the problem primarily in moral and social terms. But unlike the critics of divorce, its supporters, who were with few exceptions liberals, were much more interested in the morality of divorce and more inclined to see its moral and social dimensions as too interrelated for separate discussion and analysis.

The case for divorce gained initial momentum in the 1880s and 1890s when a trickle of protest against Victorian marriage began to make itself heard. The plays of Henrik Ibsen, especially *A Doll's House* (1879) and *Ghosts* (1881), were affecting English audiences in the late 1880s and American opinion somewhat later. By the 1890s a number of Englishmen were attacking marriage and the views of Mona Caird and Grant Allen became well known in the United States through their own writings, and through the publicity given their ideas by the American press. Mona Caird was a feminist whose essays appeared for the most part in high-quality limited circulation periodicals. Her most controversial proposal was an attempt to substitute for divorce short-term marriage contracts whose expiration would leave both parties free to separate or to negotiate a new contract.[32]

Grant Allen's best-known statement on the question was a sensational novel boosting feminism and free love entitled *The Woman Who Did.*[33] Allen was really calling for an end to marriage altogether, but his polemics against the institution supported divorce as much as free love. Within a few years the radical attack on marriage enlisted such big guns as H. G. Wells, who in a characteristically exuberant preview of the future in 1901 announced that monogamy was dissolving and sexual standards relaxing to the point where in a hundred years the present moral code "would remain nominally operative in sentiment and practice, while being practically disregarded. . . ."[34] Marriage was also under fire from the new moralists like the mystical Edward Carpenter, Havelock Ellis and his wife Edith, and the South African feminist Olive Schreiner, among others.[35]

The effect of this stream of marriage propaganda was to invigorate and inspire those Americans who believed in the right to divorce. Few respectable Americans were prepared to go as far as new moralists like Wells and Carpenter, but a substantial number of liberals were beginning to feel that traditional marriage was needlessly tyrannical and repressive, that it discriminated against women, and that divorce was not only an escape hatch for abused women, but offered real opportunities for a reform of the whole marriage system. At the bottom of most, if not all, of this sentiment was the feminist impulse, for most divorce liberals were acutely conscious of the usefulness of divorce as an instrument for the emancipation of women.

Unlike the new moralists whose feminism was concerned with freeing women for a fuller sex life, the American feminist was inclined to defend divorce because it freed women from sex. Benjamin O. Flower, who edited the populistic *Arena,* called for easier divorce laws as a way of protecting women from the excessive sexual appetites of their husbands. He argued that the common prostitute was "far freer than the wife who is nightly the victim of the unholy passion of her master. . . ."[36] By 1914 this argument had become so familiar that it was thought fit for the respectable readers of the cautious *Good Housekeeping* magazine. In that year Jesse Lynch Williams, feminist and playwright, asked rhetorically, "is allowing herself to be owned body and soul by a man she loathes doing right?" before going on to delicately suggest "that seems rather like a dishonorable institution more ancient than marriage." [37]

Many feminists contended that not only did traditional marriage make women the sexual victims of their husbands, but it also exaggerated the importance of sex by denying women the chance to develop their other traits of character through work and education, and by forcing them to compete in the marriage market largely on the basis of their sexual attractions. The most desirable women had the best marital opportunities and so, through a kind of natural selection, sexuality prospered at the expense of other attributes. Divorce, along with expanded opportunities for education and employment, was a way of combatting this pernicious tendency.[38]

If the impulse to defend divorce came first from feminists who agreed with Elizabeth Cady Stanton on the need for a "larger freedom in the marriage relation," social scientists performed a crucial service in coping with the public's fear of the social consequences of divorce.[39] The first man of stature to defend divorce was Carrol Wright, U.S. Commissioner of Labor Statistics and a self-trained social scientist, who at the national Unitarian convention in 1891 boldly declared himself for liberal divorce laws. A few years later he wrote:

> The pressure for divorce finds its impetus outside of laws, outside of our institutions, outside of our theology; it springs from the rebellion of the human heart against that slavery which binds in the cruelest bonds human beings who have by their haste, their want of wisdom, or the intervention of friends, missed the divine purpose as well as the civil purpose of marriage.[40]

But it was not until 1904 that a leading professionally trained social scientist joined the fight. In his massive *A History of Matrimonial Institutions* and subsequent writings George E. Howard, an eminent historian and sociologist, tried to show how the divorce rate was the product of forces which were dramatically improving American society.[41] He argued that industrialization, urbanization and the other pressures which were breaking up the old patriarchal family produced not only more divorces, but a new kind of marriage marked by higher spiritual standards and greater freedom. Closing with the problem of individualism which so alarmed the enemies of divorce, he declared that the growing power of the state was tending to make the individual and not the family the functional unit of society and that this process not only freed the individual from familial authoritarianism but elevated the family by abolishing its coercive power and transforming it into a "spiritual and psychic association of parent and child based on persuasion." [42]

Within a few years Wright and Howard were joined by a host of social scientists including most of the leading men in the field.[43] The weight of sociological opinion was solidly on the side of divorce by 1908 when the American Sociological Society devoted its third annual meeting to the family.[44] President William G. Sumner, the crusty, aging president of the society who had done so much to establish sociology as an academic discipline, opened the proceedings by observing gloomily that "the family has to a great extent lost its position as a conservative institution and has become a field for social change." [45] The program of the convention confirmed Sumner's fears for virtually every paper described the changes affecting the family, called for more changes, or did both. Charlotte P. Gilman read a paper summarizing her *Women and Economics,* and a group of papers dealt with the damage inflicted on the family by urban, industrial life.[46]

The high point of the meeting was George Howard's "Is the Freer Granting of Divorce an Evil?" Howard repeated his now familiar views and touched off a controversy which showed the drift of professional opinion.[47] He was attacked by Samuel Dike, who insisted that divorce was produced by a dangerous individualism and the decline of ideals, and by Walter George Smith. Smith was a prominent Catholic lawyer who had advocated stricter divorce laws for many years and was a leader in the campaign for uniform divorce legislation. His criticisms stressed divorce's incompatibility with orthodox religion and he accused Howard of condoning a social revolution that destroyed the divinely constituted order of things. Nothing, he declared, could alter the fact of feminine inferiority. Howard replied that marriage was a purely social institution "to be freely dealt with by men according to human needs." [48]

Despite this unusually spirited clash, Smith and his friends were making an illusory show of strength. The moralistic flavor of their language, so different in tone from Howard's, revealed their professional isolation. Theirs was the faintly anachronistic rhetoric of a discredited tradition of social criticism. The opponents of Howard's position were, moreover, all laymen with the exception of President Sumner and Albion Small, while on his side were ranged most of the speakers, including E. A. Ross, James Lichtenberger and other leading scientists. As a profession then, sociology was committed to a positive view of divorce at a time when virtually every other organized group in the country was opposed to it. But although heavily outnumbered, the sociologists were the only people who could claim to speak on the problem with expert authority, and in the Progressive Era expertise was coming to be highly valued. As experts, the social scientists conferred respectability on the cause of free divorce at the same time as they did much to allay public anxiety over its effects.

A final problem that remained for the divorce liberals was finding some way to weaken the general conviction that divorce was forbidden by the Bible, and to diminish the impact of the clergy's opposition to divorce. It was here that the handful of liberal ministers who supported divorce performed a signal, and indeed indispensable, service. Simply by saying that divorce was a morally acceptable device, the liberal ministers endowed it with a certain degree of legitimacy. If supporting divorce with their moral prestige was the more important function performed by the liberal ministers, some went beyond this and effectively disputed the traditional charge that the Bible specifically prohibited divorce.

One of the most impressive statements of the liberal position was delivered by William G. Ballentine, classicist, Bible scholar, onetime president of Oberlin College and for twenty years editor of the *Bibliotheca Sacra*. Ballentine argued that "even if all thoughtful Christian men were today united in a resolute purpose of conformity to the letter of Scripture the path of duty would be far from plain." [49] He pointed out that a Biblical injunction against divorce cited by Bishop Doane in a recent magazine article appeared in the same passage as the admonition to resist evil. How, he asked, were Christians to know which commandment to obey and which to ignore? Ballentine described the life of Jesus as a struggle against Talmudic literalism:

> During His whole life, He fought against the tyranny of mere words, and for the lordship of the present living spiritual man. In his discourse He suggested great truths by parables, by questions, by metaphors, by paradoxes, by hyperboles, by every device that could elude the semblance of fixed judicial formulas. It is the irony of history that such language should be seized upon for statute law.[50]

Other scholars, theologians and Higher Critics attacked the presumed Biblical sanctions against divorce in different ways, but the effect of their work was to undercut the general belief that the Bible clearly forbade divorce.[51]

On a more popular level the Rev. Minot J. Savage declared that as love was the essence of marriage two people who no longer loved each other had every reason to get divorced.[52] This same conviction informed the writings of John H. Holmes, a great civil libertarian and advocate of liberal Christianity, who believed that the passing of love destroyed marriage in fact if not in name.[53]

Gradually the climate of opinion began to change. As noted earlier there was a substantial organized opposition to divorce during the Progressive period, but despite local victories, the movement to retard divorce by legal and political means was resoundingly unsuccessful. There were other signs which demonstrated that attitudes were being modified. Samuel Dike died in 1913 and his League expired shortly thereafter. It was essentially a one-man operation, but it was supported by the enemies of divorce, whose financial contributions had declined sharply even before his death, to the point where receipts after 1910 were about half of what they had been in the 1890s.[54] The Committee on the Family which was routinely formed by the Federal Council of Churches in 1911 was singularly inactive, and in 1919 it was dropped altogether.[55]

At the same time the solid wall of opposition to divorce maintained by the nation's press was repeatedly breached. Before 1900 no important American magazine defended the right to divorce except the radical *Arena*. Articles favorable to divorce were very rare in the general press. After about 1900, however, a few bold magazines like the *Independent* endorsed the right of divorce editorially, and many more began to print occasional articles defending divorce. The *North American Review*, which was more interested in the problem than any other major periodical, began the new century with a rousing attack on the opponents of divorce by the aging but still magnificent Elizabeth Cady Stanton.[56] Other magazines, too numerous to mention, also began to print articles favoring divorce. Even the uncompromisingly hostile *Outlook* unbent to this extent, and in 1910 it conceded editorially that there were times when divorce was permissible.[57] This shift influenced popular as well as serious magazines. In 1910 the slick monthly *World's Work* announced that "The True View of Increasing Divorce" was that the divorce rate was not alarming, and that divorces should not be subject to excessive restrictions.[58]

Obviously the changes in public opinion which these articles represented did not constitute a general recognition of the desirability of divorce. Although a few journals accepted the liberal argument that divorce was a therapeutic social mechanism, most did not. In many cases nothing more was involved than the admission that there were probably two sides to the question. This of itself, however, was a form of moral relativism on the issue which would have been unthinkable in the 1890s. This new tolerance of divorce coincided with the eruption of a number of curious phenomena like the dance craze and the white slave panic which marked the onset of the revolution in morals.[59]

Divorce was a part of the complex transformation of moral values and sexual customs which was to help give the 1920s their bizarre flavor. It was not only the most visible result of this vast social upheaval, but in many ways it was the most compatible with traditional modes of thought. It was, on the whole, an orderly, public and institutionalized process which took due account of the formal difference between right and wrong, guilt and innocence. It had the blessings of the highest sociological authorities, and it was recommended by many feminists as a cure for the brutalizing sexual indignities known to occur in some marriages. Conservatives could, therefore, more easily resign themselves to divorce than to other, more extravagant, demonstrations of the changing moral order.

Although divorce has today assumed proportions undreamed of in the Progressive Era, the nature of the American response to mass divorce was determined at that time. Between 1905, when the magnitude of divorce as a social problem had become fully apparent, and 1917, when the movement to limit or direct the spread of divorce had clearly failed, something of importance for American social history had occurred. This was the recognition by moral conservatives that they could not prevent the revolution in morals represented by mass divorce. Their failure of morale in the immediate prewar period paved the way for the spectacular changes which took place after the war.

NOTES

1. The definitive statistical study is Paul H. Jacobson, *American Marriage and Divorce* (New York, 1959). Two great government reports contain the raw materials — they are U. S. Bureau of Labor, *Marriage and Divorce 1867–1887* (1889), and the later more comprehensive U. S. Bureau of the Census, *Marriage and Divorce 1867–1906* (1909). Interesting contemporary analyses are contained in E. A. Ross, *Changing America* (New York, 1912) and William B. Bailey, *Modern Social Conditions* (New York, 1906).
2. Its origins are described in an untitled autobiographical manuscript by Samuel Warren Dike in the Dike Papers, Library of Congress.
3. The legal and political history of divorce is described very fully in Nelson Manfred Blake, *The Road to Reno* (New York, 1962).
4. See M. A. DeWolfe Howe, *The Life and Labors of Bishop Hare* (New York, 1912), *passim;* Blake, "Divorce in South Dakota," *Nation, IX* (January 26, 1893), 61.
5. National League for the Preservation of the Family, *Some Fundamentals of the Divorce Question* (Boston, 1909). A pamphlet written by Samuel Dike and published by his organization, which had undergone two changes of name since its founding, deals with these changes at some length. They involved extending the time required to obtain divorces, and limiting the causes for which they could be granted.
6. U. S. Congressional Record, 52 Cong., 1st Sess. (February 3, 1892), p. 791.
7. See Senator Shortridge's candid remarks to this effect during hearings on a similar resolution years later. *Senate Judiciary Committee,* "Hearings on S. J. Res. 31" (November 1, 1921), *passim.*
8. "Secretary's Memorandum," *Proceedings of the 26th Annual Meeting of the NCCUSL* (1916).
9. See Blake, 140–45, and *Proceedings of the Adjourned Meeting of the National Congress on Uniform Divorce Laws* (Harrisburg, Pa., 1907).
10. "The Canon on Marriage and Divorce," *Public Opinion,* October 27, 1898.
11. "Remarriage After Divorce," *Outlook,* October 22, 1904.
12. The positions of the principal denominations on divorce and the efforts to change them are summarized in James P. Lichtenberger, *Divorce: A Study in Social Causation* (New York, 1909), chap. vii.
13. Daniel Bell, "The Myth of Crime Waves" (New York, 1961), pp. 151–74.
14. Roy Lubove, "The Progressives and the Prostitute," *The Historian, XXIV* (May 1962), 308–29.
15. Generalizations of this sort which depend upon a close acquaintance with the popular literature are notoriously hard to document. My own conclusions are derived from an examination of almost everything dealing with marriage and divorce published either in book form or in more than thirty leading periodicals from 1889 through 1919. For details see my unpublished, "The Divorce Crisis of the Progressive Era" (Doctor's dissertation, Berkeley, Calif., 1963).
16. By dismissing the moral side of the opposition to divorce so casually I do not mean to imply that it was not important, but only that it was unremarkable and required no detailed analysis. Divorce was considered immoral because it was forbidden by the New Testament, and because it encouraged lust. Naturally the clergymen who opposed divorce supported themselves with Scriptural citations. One of the most elaborate efforts to relate divorce to licentiousness was Samuel Dike's first major address on the subject, reprinted in *Christ and Modern Thought: The Boston Monday Lectures 1880–81,* ed. Joseph Cook (Boston, 1882).
17. "The Right to Be Divorced," *Lutheran Church Review, XXVIII* (October 1909), 661.
18. W. E. Campbell, "Wells, the Family, and the Church," *Catholic World, XCI* (July 1910), 483.

19. "The Worst Anarchism," *Outlook,* August 11, 1906, p. 826.
20. Bureau of the Census, *Marriage and Divorce 1867–1906,* p. 4.
21. *Marriage and Divorce* (New York, 1915), p. 15.
22. Henry Neumann, *Spokesmen for Ethical Religion* (Boston, 1951), deals with Adler's career at some length.
23. Rebecca Harding Davis, Rose Terry Cooke, Marion Harland, Catherine Owen, Amelia E. Barr, *North American Review, CXLVIII* (May 1889).
24. Boston, 1909.
25. Among the frequent male efforts to sentimentalize over the role and nature of woman were Lyman Abbott, *Christianity and Social Problems* (Boston, 1896), and Robert Lawton, *The Making of a Home* (Boston, 1914).
26. "The Change in the Feminine Ideal," *Atlantic Monthly, CV* (March 1910), 295; see also her interesting autobiography *Golden Yesterdays* (New York, 1940).
27. *Ibid.,* p. 297.
28. *The Making of a Home,* p. 594.
29. "The Ethics of Divorce," *Ethical Record, II* (April 1890), 207.
30. *Sociology and Modern Social Problems* (New York, 1913).
31. *Jesus Christ and the Social Question* (New York, 1903), p. 145.
32. *The Morality of Marriage and Other Essays on the Status and Destiny of Women,* London, 1897. A collection of articles which had previously appeared in the *North American Review,* the *Fortnightly Review,* the *Westminster Review* and the *Nineteenth Century.* Typical of the American press's treatment of her ideas are "The Millennium of Marriage — Mona Caird's Views," *Current Literature, XVI* (July 1894), reprinted from the *Boston Herald.* "The Practice of Marriage," *Current Literature, XVIII* (October 1895), reprinted from the *Saturday Review.*
33. Boston, 1895.
34. "Anticipations; An Experiment in Prophecy — II," *North American Review, CLXXIII* (July 1901), 73–74.
35. Carpenter, *Love's Coming of Age* (New York, 1911). *Little Essays of Love and Virtue* (New York, 1921), summarized the ideas Havelock Ellis had been advocating for years and the *New Horizon in Love and Life* (London, 1921), contains the thoughts of his wife, who died in 1916. Schreiner, *Women and Labor* (New York, 1911).
36. "Prostitution Within the Marriage Bond," *Arena, XIII* (June 1895), 68.
37. "The New Marriage," *Good Housekeeping, LII* (February 1914), 184.
38. Charlotte Perkins Gilman, *Women and Economics* (Boston, 1898), was an especially influential exposition of this point of view. For other information on this remarkable woman's life and work see Carl N. Degler's appreciative article, "Charlotte Perkins Gilman on the Theory and Practice of Feminism," *American Quarterly, VIII* (Spring 1956). See also Rheta Childe Dorr, *What Eight Million Women Want* (Boston, 1910), and C. Gasquoine Hartley, *The Truth About Women* (London, 1914).
39. "Divorce vs. Domestic Warfare," *Arena, I* (April 1890), 568. Alone of the great feminist leaders, Mrs. Stanton was a lifelong supporter of divorce, and in her later years it became one of her major interests. In this respect she was hardly a typical feminist, for while most divorce liberals were also feminists, they remained very much a minority within the women's movement.
40. *Outline of Practical Sociology* (New York, 1900), p. 176.
41. Chicago, 1904.
42. "Social Control and the Function of the Family," Congress of Arts and Sciences, *Proceedings, VII* (St. Louis, 1904), 701. This abbreviated summary may not bring out the markedly utopian flavor which permeated discussions on the family by liberal sociologists and feminists during the Progressive period. Indeed, they entertained hopes for the future of the family which seem fantastically imaginative by the standards of our own more somberly clinical age. This visionary strain in Progressive social thought has been underestimated by historians in recent years, especially by Richard Hofstadter, whose influential *The Age of Reform* (New York, 1955), ignores the role played by feminism and the new morality in shaping the Progressive mood.
43. So many statements were made on marriage and divorce by sociologists during these years that I can list only a few of them here. Walter F. Willcox, *The Divorce Problem* (New York, 1891), was a seminal monograph that laid the statistical base for most later studies of divorce, but which was not well known outside of the profession and did not have the impact of other works which were more widely publicized. Elsie Clews Parsons, *The Family* (New York, 1906), caused a minor sensation by calling for trial marriages. Mrs. Parsons was a student of Franz Boas and the most radical of the academicians who dealt with the problem. Arthur W. Calhoun, *A Social History of the American Family, From the Civil War* (Cleveland, 1919), Vol. III, was written from an avowedly socialist point of view and is still the only comprehensive work on the history of the American family.
44. *Papers and Proceedings of the American Sociological Society, III* (Chicago, 1909).
45. *Ibid.,* p. 15.
46. "How Home Conditions React Upon the Family," *Papers . . . of American Sociological Society,* pp. 16–29. Margaret F. Byington, "The Family in a Typical Mill Town," pp. 73–84. Edward T. Devine, "Results of the Pittsburgh Survey," pp. 85–92; Charles R. Henderson, "Are Modern Industry and City Life Unfavorable to the Family?" pp. 93–105, among others.

47. *Papers . . . of American Sociological Society,* pp. 150–60.
48. *Ibid.,* p. 180.
49. "The Hyperbolic Teachings of Jesus," *North American Review, CLXXIX* (September 1904), 403.
50. *Ibid.,* p. 447.
51. E.g., Ernest D. Burton, "The Biblical Teaching Concerning Divorce," *Biblical World, XXIX* (February and March 1907). Norman Jones, "Marriage and Divorce: The Letter of the Law," *North American Review, CLXXXI* (October 1905). Thomas S. Potwin, "Should Marriage Be Indissoluble?" *New Englander and Yale Review, LVI* (January 1892).
52. *Men and Women* (Boston, 1902).
53. *Marriage and Divorce* (New York, 1913).
54. *Annual Reports* of the National League for the Protection of the Family.
55. *Annual Reports* of the Executive Committee of the Federal Council of Churches of Christ in America.
56. "Are Homogenous Divorce Laws in All the States Desirable?" *North American Review, CLXX* (March 1900).
57. E. R. Stevens, "Divorce in America: The Problem," *Outlook,* June 1, 1907; "Just Grounds for Divorce," November 23, 1910.
58. *World's Work, XIX* (January 1910).
59. Henry F. May, *The End of American Innocence* (New York, 1959), *II,* Part IV, 333, 343–44.

Immigration after the Civil War

In the century between 1815 and the outbreak of World War I, some 30 million Europeans crossed the Atlantic to the United States. They came from every part of the old continent and represented every stratum of European population. Preponderantly, however, they were the little men, the peasants and the common laborers, leavened a bit by businessmen, professionals, and middle-class political refugees. Their goal was a better life for themselves and their families, and the magnets that drew the great majority of them was cheap land and high wages.

They did not come in a homogeneous, steady stream. Between 1815 and 1830 their numbers were small. During the 1830s, the number swelled to 600,000, followed by the deluge of 1.7 million in the 1840s, and 2.3 million in the following decade. The Civil War discouraged immigrants from coming, but the later 1860s and early 1870s, until the hard times following the 1873 panic, saw a tremendous additional burst. Another revival in the 1880s was followed by another decline during the lean years of the following decade. From 1900 through 1915, all-time yearly peaks were reached with the total number of arrivals soaring to over one million in each of six years during the fifteen-year period.

The reception these immigrants received on our shores was not uniform. While Americans often took pride in their open door, they were also frequently appalled at the foreign "hordes" that arrived. The immigrants not only peopled this empty land and did the hard work of building the nation physically, they also brought crime, and poverty, and alien ways. Protestant North Europeans — Germans, Scandinavians, and above all the English — groups whose cultural patterns most closely approximated those of the United States were most welcome. The Britons, particularly, who spoke English were scarcely noticed and quickly merged with the native-born population. Other groups did not receive as friendly a greeting. Before 1860, the Irish-Catholics were regarded as "a noisy, drinking and brawling rabble," whose Catholic faith was a danger to free institutions. Though nothing was done to restrict their coming, they found themselves treated as outcasts, their position in society and economy fixed, not only by their relative lack of skill, but also by bigotry and intolerance.

The Civil War period was a time of healing in the relations between natives and foreign-born. Though the Irish, particularly, were often skeptical of Republican policies, the immigrants' performance in the war, and the patriotism they exhibited in defense of the Union, resulted in ethnic reconciliation. Then, in the 1880s, a new wave of foreign arrivals from southern and eastern Europe upset the equilibrium. Except for the Jews these were largely Slavs, Hungarians, Greeks, and Italians who, like the Irish, were mostly peasants and Catholics. Once more native Americans became alarmed, and nativism began to flourish as an intellectual and social force.

As in the past, much of this nativism was fed by religious and especially anti-

Catholic prejudice. In the 1890s, the American Protective Association encouraged anti-Catholic feelings by playing on the economic fears of Protestant workingmen during the economically bad years after 1893. At one point, the organization disseminated a bogus Papal encyclical purporting to absolve Catholics from any oath of loyalty to the United States and encouraging them "to exterminate all heretics."

This crude religious bigotry was only effective among the ignorant and the simpleminded. Unfortunately, a more subtle and sophisticated force, racism, soon began to feed the fires of intolerance. Racism was not new to America. In the form of Negrophobia it had thrived in the pre–Civil War period when it had been used to justify slavery. The post–Civil War version of racism, however, was broader in its rejections and was buttressed by science, or rather pseudo-science, derived from "biology" and anthropology. Included now among the proscribed groups were southern and eastern Europeans who were held to be inferior intellectually and morally to the Nordic stock of northern Europe. The Nordic races had been the truly creative peoples of the world, declared men like Madison Grant, and America was allowing itself to be debased by permitting the mobs of inferior whites, "Alpines" and "Mediterraneans," to invade its shores.

The way in which racist thinking was applied to American immigration policy by the Immigration Commission in the early years of the twentieth century is the subject of Oscar Handlin's essay. A key assumption of immigration restrictionists, he notes, was the concept that the "old immigration" of the years before 1880 was Nordic and superior, that of the post–1880 period, the "new immigration," non-Nordic and inferior in talent, health, character, and the inherent ability to assimilate American democratic values.

FOR FURTHER READING:

ERICKSON, CHARLOTTE. *American Industry and the European Immigrant, 1860–1885.* New York: Russell & Russell, Publishers, 1967.
HIGHAM, JOHN. *Strangers in the Land.* New York: Atheneum Publishers, 1963.*
RISCHIN, MOSES. *The Promised City, New York's Jews, 1870–1914.* New York: Corinth Books, 1964.*

Asterisk denotes paperback edition.

Old Immigrants and New   OSCAR HANDLIN

Between 1917 and 1924 American immigration policy took a sharp and decisive turn. From the earliest days of the republic until the First World War the United States had deliberately permitted newcomers of whatever origin to enter freely through its gates. Unrestricted immigration had significantly furthered national development. Yet suddenly this long-standing tradition yielded to a new attitude which thereafter was so firmly fixed in the American consciousness that it has not yet been shaken off.

A combination of circumstances was responsible for the abrupt shift. The fears and distrust bred by the war and the unsuccessful peace nurtured suspicion of all

Source: Oscar Handlin, *Race and Nationality in American Life* (New York: Doubleday & Company, 1957), chap. 5, "Old Immigrants and New," pp. 73–110.

that was foreign, of immigration as well as of the League of Nations. In addition some groups within the United States had come to consider their interests imperiled by the newcomers. The old Yankee families of New England, for instance, viewed with misgivings the rising percentage of foreign born about them. The organized labor movement, made up predominantly of skilled workers, had become convinced that only a sharp limitation of the labor supply could protect its interests. In the first decade of the twentieth century substantial blocs of Southerners, former Populists and Progressives, each for its own reasons, came to regard the continuation of immigration as undesirable. The gradual accretion of strength in these groups contributed to the ultimate shift in policy.

Prior to 1910 there was no indication that all these dissatisfied groups would see the solution to their own problems in the restriction of immigration in the actual form restriction took. For the new policy aimed not simply to limit the total numbers of entrants; it intended also to select among them. The new policy drew a sharp distinction between the immigrants of northern and western Europe and those from southern and eastern Europe. In the minds of those who framed the laws of 1917–1924 that distinction was more important than restriction itself.

Basic to that distinction was a "scientific" assumption, one that subsequently proved false, but that was sincerely and conscientiously held in the early decades of this century. That assumption seemed for a time to have been validated and confirmed by the report of a governmental commission which devoted a great deal of time and energy to its investigation. Since vestiges of that assumption still influence our laws, it is imperative that we look closely at the commission which gave it authoritative expression. To do so will also clarify some of the problems of science as an instrument for directing government policy.

One fundamental premise lay behind the immigration legislation of 1917–1924 and animated also the McCarran-Walter Act of 1952. Embodied in the quota system, this premise held that the national origin of an immigrant was a reliable indication of his capacity for Americanization. It was averred, and science seemed to show, that some people, because of their racial or national constitution, were more capable of becoming Americans than others. Furthermore, it was argued that the "old immigrants," who came to the United States before 1880, were drawn from the superior stocks of northern and western Europe, while those who came after that date were drawn from the inferior breeds of southern and eastern Europe.

There was a demonstrable connection between the diffusion of this assumption and the course of immigration legislation in the first quarter of the century. Those who argued in favor of a restrictionist policy did so not merely, perhaps not primarily, because they wished to reduce the total volume of immigration, but, more important, because they wished to eliminate the "new" while perpetuating the "old" immigration. This was the logic of the literacy test. Writing in the midst of the battle for its enactment, one of its leading proponents, Prescott F. Hall, pointed out that the test furnished "an indirect method of excluding those who are undesirable, not merely because of their illiteracy, but for other reasons." After all, Hall noted, "the hereditary tendencies of the peoples illiterate abroad . . . cannot be overcome in a generation or two." And, looking back at the accomplished fact, the Commissioner General of Immigration pointed out in 1923 that the widespread popularity of the literacy test was "based quite largely upon a belief . . . that it would reduce the stream of new immigration . . . without seriously interfering with the coming of the older type."

The literacy law, passed over President Wilson's veto in 1917, did not, however, accomplish what had been expected of it. The end of the war brought a resumption of immigration and, with it, a renewed demand that the objective of keeping out the "new" while admitting the "old" immigrants be attained through the national-origin device. The result was passage of the Johnson Act of 1921. The intent of the act was clear. On the question of whether the base year should be 1910 or 1920, for instance, Representative Box pointed out that "the number of the older and better immigrants coming has been relatively much smaller during the last 10 years, and the number from southern Europe, Italy, and Russia much greater, which will be reflected in the 1920 census. The making of the 1910 census the basis will give us more of the better and less of the less desirable immigration than if it were based on the census of 1920." The act of 1924, which pushed the base quota year back to 1890 and consolidated the theory of national origins, was motivated by similar convictions as to the inferiority of the "new" immigrants. Congressman Vestal, arguing in favor of the measure, put the idea clearly: the southern and eastern immigrants of Europe, he said, "have not been of the kind that are readily assimilated or absorbed by our American life."

It thus becomes a matter of considerable importance to ascertain how the conception originated and gained currency that the peoples of southern and eastern Europe were inferior to those of northern and western Europe. At root this concept could be traced to the racist beliefs, freely expressed in the 1890's, that the peoples of the Mediterranean region were biologically different from those of northern and western Europe and that the difference sprang from an inferiority of blood and could be observed in certain social characteristics.

The argument was given forceful expression by the distinguished anthropologist of the American Museum of Natural History in an enormously popular book, one adjudged by *Science* a "work of solid merit." In *The Passing of the Great Race* (1916), Madison Grant adopted the line of Gobineau and insisted that the new immigrants were not "members of the Nordic race as were the earlier ones. . . . The new immigration contained a large and increasing number of the weak, the broken, and the mentally crippled of all races drawn from the lowest stratum of the Mediterranean basin and the Balkans, together with hordes of the wretched, submerged populations of the Polish ghettos. Our jails, insane asylums, and almshouses are filled with this human flotsam and the whole tone of American life, social, moral, and political, has been lowered and vulgarized by them."

These theories were bitterly and inconclusively debated through the early years of the twentieth century. The decisive turn in the argument came when they seemed to receive validation from the reports of two governmental investigations. The first was the detailed study by the Immigration Commission under the chairmanship of Senator Dillingham. The second was a report by Dr. Harry H. Laughlin of the Carnegie Institution, "the expert eugenics agent" of the House Committee on Immigration and Naturalization.

These reports had a direct impact upon subsequent legislation, for they supported theoretical opinions privately held with what appeared to be official and presumably scientific proof. The Immigration Commission, appointed in 1907, presented its conclusions in 1910 in an impressive forty-two-volume report. Widely quoted, the report figured prominently in the deliberations which produced the Johnson Act of 1921. Congressman Box thus took for granted that "the great immigration commission, which some years ago spent hundreds of thousands of dollars in investigation and study of this great question," had produced "conclusive reasons why we should encourage the coming in of the class which has been extolled so highly as an element which has contributed so much to our life and why it should discourage that which comes from Russia and southern Europe." In the same way the Laughlin report, presented in 1922 and printed in 1923, laid the groundwork for the legislation of 1924. This latter report was widely quoted in quasi-scientific articles and entered prominently into the debate as a result of which the act of 1924 was enacted. It therefore becomes a matter of prime importance to investigate the preparation of these reports and the soundness of their conclusions.

The Dillingham Commission was the outgrowth of a renewed attempt to enact a literacy test in 1906. The opponents of that measure hoped to block it, or at least to postpone immediate action, by calling for a commission to study the whole problem. Congressman Bartholdt, who proposed the creation of such a body, undoubtedly had in mind a congressional committee such as those which had already conducted similar investigations in 1891 and 1892. This was also the expectation of Speaker Cannon, who opposed any airing of the immigration question on the ground that it was an issue likely to divide the Republican party politically.

Although the question was one primarily for congressional action, it also deeply concerned President Theodore Roosevelt. In part he was moved by such considerations as influenced Speaker Cannon. In part he was also concerned because he was even then engaged in delicate diplomatic discussions with the Japanese. Ultimately these negotiations would lead to the controversial Gentlemen's Agreement to limit Japanese immigration by the voluntary action of the Tokyo government. At the moment Roosevelt feared that agitation of the general question of immigration might upset these negotiations. Finally, the President had great faith in the efficiency of fact-finding agencies as devices to evade the necessity for clear-cut political decisions.

Although Theodore Roosevelt accepted and supported the idea of such a commission, he subtly modified the conception of what it should be and do. He proposed to the Congress that the study be entrusted not to the usual congressional investigating committee, but rather to a number of experts, whom he would himself appoint. While the question was still being debated in Congress, he confidentially requested Commissioner of Labor Neill to proceed at once to "as full an investigation of the whole subject of immigration as the facilities at hand will permit."

As enacted on February 20, 1907, the law was a compromise between presidential and congressional wishes. It provided for an investigating commission of nine, three to be chosen by the President of the Senate, three by the Speaker of the House, and three experts by the President. In this form the proposal secured the acquiescence of all parties to the debate and also drew the support of a great number of social workers and social theorists attracted by the idea of an impartial, scientific investigation as an instrument of the social engineering of which there was then much talk.

At this stage, therefore, there was a widespread expectation that out of the deliberations of the commission would come a body of verified and indisputable facts which would supply the groundwork for future action. President Roosevelt summed up these expectations in a private message to Speaker Cannon when he expressed the hope that from the work of the commission would come the information that he could then use "to put before the Congress a plan which would amount to a definite solution of this immigration business."

The circumstances of its establishment account for the great hopes that were held out for the report of the commission and the prestige that was ultimately attached to its findings. That prestige was certainly added to when the commission took more than three years to investigate, spent a million dollars, employed a staff of about three hundred, and published its results in forty-two impressive volumes.

A view of the actual circumstances of the compilation and of the methods used shows, however, that the commission's report was neither impartial nor scientific, and that confidence in it was not altogether justified. No public hearings were held, no witnesses cross-examined by the members of the commission. Largely the study was conducted by experts who each compiled voluminous reports which were not printed until *after* the commission had reached its conclusions. It is doubtful whether the senators and congressmen on the commission ever had the time to examine the bulky reports in manuscript. It is most likely they were compelled rather to rest their judgment upon a two-volume summary prepared for them by a group of experts on the staff. The final report was "adopted within a half hour of the time when, under the law, it must be filed." The identity of the experts must therefore be of some significance.

The key individual was the economist Jeremiah W. Jenks. Jenks was chosen because he had served for a decade in a similar capacity on other fact-finding investigations set up to deal with trusts and other questions. He had already expressed himself on the subject of immigration; and, as a teacher, had long argued the necessity of restricting the number of newcomers along the lines the commission would later recommend. The other public members were Commissioner of Labor Neill and William R. Wheeler, active in Republican politics in San Francisco, which was then being shaken by the Japanese question. The crucial post of secretary was given, on the recommendation of Senator Henry Cabot Lodge, an outspoken restrictionist, to Morton E. Crane, described by the senator as "absolutely safe and loyal" on the immigration question. Roosevelt was perhaps less concerned with impartiality than with the likelihood of producing a tactically safe report. In any case, he warned Jenks, "Don't put in too many professors."

Despite its scientific pretensions, therefore, the report began by taking for granted the conclusions it aimed to prove — that the new immigration was essentially different from the old and less capable of being Americanized. This assumption is clearly stated at the very beginning of the report:

> The old and the new immigration differ in many essentials. The former was . . . largely a movement of settlers . . . from the most progressive sections of Europe. . . . They entered practically every line of activity. . . . Many of them . . . became landowners. . . . They mingled freely with the native Americans and were quickly assimilated. On the other hand, the new immigration has been largely a movement of unskilled laboring men who have come . . . from the less progressive countries of Europe. . . . They have . . . congregated together in sections apart from native Americans and the older immigrants to such an extent that assimilation has been slow.

The assumption with which the commission started conditioned the preparation of the whole report and made it certain that the conclusions would confirm the prejudgment. To quote the commission's own words:

> Consequently the Commission paid but little attention to the foreign-born element of the old immigrant class and directed its efforts almost entirely to . . . the newer immigrants.

The notion that the old immigration stood clearly apart from the new was directly reflected in the techniques through which the commission operated. There was no effort to give a time dimension to its data; there was some talk of including a history of immigration, but such a study was never prepared. There was therefore no opportunity to trace the development of various problems or to make comparisons between earlier and later conditions. For the same reason the commission made no use of any information except that gathered by its own staff at the moment. The enormous store of data in the successive state and federal censuses was hardly touched. For fifty years state bureaus of labor statistics had been gathering materials on the conditions of industrial labor; the commission disregarded those entirely. Instead it planned, but never finished, a mammoth census of all industrial workers. It overlooked similarly the wealth of information contained in almost a century of investigations by other governmental and private bodies.

Finally, the commission consistently omitted from its calculations and judgments the whole question of duration of settlement. Time and again it assumed that a group which had lived in the United States for five years could be treated on the same footing as one that had lived here for thirty-five. In a few cases there was enough information to make out the distortions that followed upon that premise. In most cases, however, the commission did not even possess the data on which a reasoned judgment could be based.

Taking for granted the difference between old and new immigrants, the commission found it unnecessary to prove that the difference existed. In most cases the individual reports — on industry, crime, nationality, and the like — did not contain the materials for a proper comparison of old and new. *But in the summary the commission followed the procedure of presenting the introduction and conclusion of each individual report, together with its own interpretive comments, which supplied the judgment on the inferiority of the new immigrants.* Those comments sprang from its own a priori assumption, not from any evidence — whatever that was worth; sometimes, indeed, they ran altogether against such evidence.

The substance of the report fell into a number of general categories. Volumes I and II were summary volumes. Volume III, a statistical survey of immigration, 1819–1910, and Volume XXXIX, an analysis of legal provisions, were noncontroversial. Volume XL was a study of immigration in other countries, with no bearing upon the general conclusions.

The critical material in the other volumes fell into nine general categories:

1. A Dictionary of Races. Volume V, summarized in Volume I, 209 ff.
2. Emigration Conditions in Europe. Volume IV, summarized in Volume I, 165 ff.
3. Economic Effects of Immigration. Volumes VI–XXVIII, summarized in Volume I, 285 ff.
4. Education and Literacy. Volumes XXIX–XXXIII, summmarized in Volume II, 1 ff.
5. Charity and Immigration. Volumes XXXIV–XXXV, summarized in Volume II, 87 ff.
6. Immigration and Crime. Volume XXXVI, summarized in Volume II, 159 ff.
7. Immigration and Vice. Volume XXXVII, summarized in Volume II, 323 ff.
8. Immigration and Insanity. Volume II, 223 ff. Complete report.
9. Immigration and Bodily Form. Volume XXXVIII, summarized in Volume II, 501 ff.

It will be profitable to scrutinize each of these categories individually.

The Dictionary of Races

In considering the monumental *Dictionary of Races* compiled by the commission it is necessary to take account of the views of race held by its expert, Dr. J. W. Jenks, and by the anthropologist, Daniel Folkmar, who was charged with the responsibility for preparing that section of the report. Neither man consciously accepted the notion that such people as Italians or Armenians were set apart by purely biological distinctions; such a notion could not have been applied to differentiate among the masses of immigrants. But both agreed that there were innate, ineradicable race distinctions that separated groups of men from one another, and they agreed also as to the general necessity of classifying these races to know which were fittest, most worthy of survival. The immediate problem was to ascertain "whether there may not be certain races that are inferior to other races . . . to discover some test to show whether some may be better fitted for American citizenship than others."

The introduction to the *Dictionary of Races* explained that while mankind may be divided into five divisions "upon physical or somatological grounds," the subdivision of these into particular races is made "largely upon a linguistic basis." According to the dictionary, this linguistic basis of classification was not only practical, in the sense that immigrant inspectors could readily determine the language spoken, but it also had "the sanction of law in immigration statistics and in the census of foreign countries."

Yet, in practice, the dictionary concerned itself with much more than a classification by language. Through it ran a persistent, though not a consistent, tendency to determine race by physical types, to differentiate the old from the new immigrants racially, and to indicate the superiority of the former to the latter.

■ **The Biological Sources of Race.** Although the dictionary presumably rested upon a linguistic basis, it often considered biological inheritance the critical element in determining racial affiliation. The following examples will illustrate:

The Finns, it stated, linguistically belonged to the Finno-Tartaric race, along with the Hungarians, Turks, and Japanese. But the western Finns, who actually came to the United States, though they spoke the same language, were descended from "the blondest of Teutons, Swedes."

The Armenians linguistically "are more nearly related to the Aryans of Europe than to their Asiatic neighbors," but "are related physically to the Turks, although they exceed these . . . in the remarkable shortness and height of their heads. The flattening of the back of the head . . . can only be compared to the flattened occiput of the Malay."

Although "English has been the medium of intercourse for generations," the dictionary defined as Irish those descended from people whose "ancestral language was Irish."

Among the Japanese, who all spoke the same language, "the 'fine' type of the aristocracy, the Japanese ideal, as distinct from the 'coarse' type recognized by students of the Japanese to-day," was due to "an undoubted white strain." The "fine" type were the descendants of "the Ainos, the earliest inhabitants of Japan . . . one of the most truly Caucasian-like people in appearance."

■ **The Differentiation of Old and New Immigrants.** All these racial identifications were confused by the evident desire of the commission to demonstrate that the old immigration was different in racial type from the new. Thus Jewish immigrants, though in language and physical characteristics akin to the Germans, were reckoned among the Slavs or eastern Europeans. In the same way it was suggested that a large part of the Irish were "English or Scotch in blood, Teutonic ('Nordic') in type rather than 'Celtic.'" The Dutch were the "Englishmen of the mainland."

■ **The Inferiority of the New Immigrants.** Throughout the dictionary and its summary were sprinkled reflections in scattered phrases and sentences upon the lesser capacity of the new immigrants to be Americanized. The English and the Irish came to the United States "imbued with sympathy for our ideals and our democratic institutions." The "Norse" make "ideal farmers and are often said to Americanize more rapidly than do the other peoples who have a new language to learn. . . . There is no need to speak of peculiarities in customs and the many important elements which determine the place of the German race in modern civilization." For "the German is too well known in America to necessitate further discussion." By contrast, the Serbo-Croatians had "savage manners," the South Italians "have not attained distinguished success as farmers" and are given to brigandry and poverty; and although "the Poles verge toward the 'northern' race of Europe," being lighter in color than the Russians, "they are more high-strung," in this respect resembling the Hungarians. "All these peoples of eastern and southern Europe, including the Greeks and the Italians . . . give character to the immigration of today, as contrasted with the northern Teutonic and Celtic stocks that characterized it up to the eighties. All are different in temperament and civilization from ourselves."

It need hardly be said there was no evidence in the report to support these characterizations. If the material in the dictionary proved anything, it proved that the people of Europe were so thoroughly intermixed, both physically and linguistically, that they could not be separated into distinct races. Nevertheless, the dictionary significantly established a pseudoscientific basis for the designation of various races. In the balance of the report the reservations and conditional statements in the dictionary dropped away, and the various immigrant groups were treated as fixed races, with well-defined characteristics. Furthermore, throughout, the commission proceeded on the assumption that these races could be combined into the two clear-cut categories, the old and new.

Emigration Conditions in Europe

The commission studied the background of immigration by an extensive tour of Europe and through the examination of some of the relevant documents. It was interested in the causes of emigration, the surrounding conditions, the selective factors that operated in it, and the means by which the movement was effected.

In this section of its work, too, the commission deprived itself of the means of making appropriate comparisons between the old and the new immigrants, and then proceeded to make such comparisons to the disadvantage of the new immigrants, without the necessary evidence.

In approaching the subject the commission "was not unmindful of the fact that the widespread apprehension in the United States relative to immigration is chiefly due" to the shift in the source of immigration from the northwestern regions to the southeastern regions of Europe. It therefore "paid particular attention" to the latter group. Almost three hundred pages of the report dealt with the situation in Italy,

Russia, Austria-Hungary, and Greece. These discussions were, on the whole, fair and factual. But they were preceded by a general survey of some hundred and thirty pages which drew less fair inferential comparisons between the emigration from these places and that from western Europe. The extensive account of the difficulties of life in the countries of the new emigration and the omission of any such account for the countries of the old emigration left the impression that the circumstances which caused the one differed from those which caused the other.

In the general survey the old and the new immigrations were said to differ on four main points—permanence of settlement, sex distribution, occupation, and the causes of emigration. In the summary (Volume I) these differences were stated even more strongly than in the more extended report in Volume IV. It will be worth examining each of these differences in turn.

■ **Permanent or Transient Emigration.** The matter of permanent or transient emigration was important because the commission presumed that those immigrants who came with the intention of staying made better citizens and residents than the "birds of passage" who came merely with the intention of working for a few years, then to depart. The commission stated flatly, "In the matter of stability or permanence of residence in the United States there is a very wide difference between European immigrants of the old and new classes." This conclusion it proved by comparing the number of arrivals in 1907 with the number of departures in 1908 as follows:

	Immigrants Admitted 1907	Aliens Departing 1908
Per cent of old immigration	22.7	8.9
Per cent of new immigration	77.3	91.1
Total	100.	100.

If, however, the same data is taken for particular groups and presented in terms of the relationship of the number of departures to the number of arrivals, the case is by no means so clear. Such peoples as the south Italians and the Croatians would still show a high rate of departures; but, on the other hand, such "old" groups as the English, the Germans, and the Scandinavians would show higher rates of departure than such "new" groups as the Armenians, the Dalmatians, the Hebrews, and the Portuguese.

Taken even at its face value, this data would not justify a correlation between old immigration and permanence of settlement and between new immigration and transience of settlement. Indeed, the commission had available other kinds of data which pointed to the completely contrary conclusion. Most important of all, the discussion did not take account here of various conditioning factors, such as recency of migration. As an agent of the committee pointed out in another place:

> It is true, no doubt, that most of the recent immigrants hope at first to return some day to their native land, but . . . with the passing years and the growth of inevitable ties, whether domestic, financial, or political, binding the immigrant to his new abode, these hopes decline and finally disappear.

■ **Sex Distribution of Immigrants.** The identical criticism applies to the commission's opinion that the new immigration contained a higher proportion of single men than did the old. Again, that judgment was superficially supported by throwing all the old and all the new immigrants together into two distinct groups; that is the basis of the commission's table:

Per Cent of Males Among Immigrants, 1899–1909	
Old immigration	58.5
New immigration	73.0

But the specific groups of immigrants, taken individually, show no such clear-cut demarcation:

Per Cent of Males Among Immigrants, 1899–1909	
Irish	47.2
Hebrew	56.7
Bohemian	56.9
French	58.6
Portuguese	59.0
German	59.4
Scandinavian	61.3
English	61.7
Scotch	63.6
Welsh	64.8
Dutch	65.5
Finnish	65.8
Syrian	68.2
Polish	69.2
Slovak	70.0

Here, too, the factor of recency of immigration affected the validity of the generalizations. But even taking the data as presented it is significant that such new groups as the Hebrews, the Bohemians, and the Portuguese stand better than such old ones as the Germans, Scandinavians, and English.

■ Occupations. The commission attempted to prove that the new immigration brought to the United States a significantly larger percentage of unskilled laborers than did the old. Its data did not show this. For the purposes of this discussion only, therefore, the Hebrews were defined as not part of the new immigration. That still, however, did not account for the large proportion of servants among the old immigrants. Furthermore, an examination of the specific immigrant groups once more reveals that the Germans and Scandinavians among the old immigrants boasted fewer skilled laborers than such new groups as the Armenians, Bohemians, Hebrews, and Spanish; and the Irish were lower in the list than the south Italians. There was certainly no basis here for the commission's distinction between old and new.

■ The Causes of Emigration. By confining the discussion of economic pressures on emigration to the countries of southern and eastern Europe the commission left the inference that the new immigration was more conditioned by such factors than the old. Thus the report stated, "a large proportion of the emigration from southern and eastern Europe may be traced directly to the inability of the peasantry to gain an adequate livelihood in agricultural pursuits." The statement could just as well have been applied to the peasantry of northern and western Europe.

Similarly the summary in the report asserted, "the fragmentary nature of available data relative to wages in many European countries makes a satisfactory comparison with wages in the United States impossible. It is well known, however, that even in England, Germany, France, and other countries of western Europe wages are below the United States standard, while in southern and eastern Europe the difference is very great." Actually the report itself made it clear in another place that the only evidence the commission had was on the disparity between wages in the United States and those in France, Germany, and Great Britain. It admitted that there was no data on southern and eastern Europe. Yet by assuming that wages in the latter places were necessarily lower than in the former, the data on the old immigration was made to prove the inferiority of the new.

Economic Effects of Immigration

This section of the subject absorbed the major portion of the commission's attention. Fully twenty (*VI–XXV*) of the forty-two volumes were devoted to it. The commission's agents accumulated an enormous store of data in all parts of the country; they examined twenty-one industries intensively, and sixteen others only slightly less so. Much of the material so gathered was, and remains, useful. But the conclusions drawn from it by the commission were often unsound and misleading, almost invariably so when it came to comparisons between the old and the new immigrants.

The commission began with the dubious assertion that:

> the older immigrant labor supply was composed principally of persons who had had training and experience abroad in the industries which they entered after their arrival in the United States. . . . In the case of the more recent immigrations from southern and eastern Europe this condition of affairs has been reversed. Before coming to the United States the greater proportion were engaged in farming or unskilled labor and had no experience or training in manufacturing or mining.

By the commission's own figures this statement was untrue; less than twenty per cent of the old immigrants (1899–1909) were skilled laborers, and the percentage in earlier periods was probably smaller still. Starting with the misapprehension that there was a correlation between the old immigration and skilled labor and between the new and unskilled, the committee proceeded to draw from its material far-reaching conclusions as to the effects of the new immigration upon native and old-immigrant labor, unionization, industrial methods, new industries, unemployment and depressions, and agriculture.

■ **Effects of the New Immigration upon Native and Old-Immigrant Labor.** The commission wished to demonstrate the adverse effects of the new immigration upon the existing labor supply. At one point it actually suggested that the new immigration diminished the volume of the old and reduced the native birth rate. But it did not push that suggestion far.

Instead it argued that in many industries the "new" immigrants *pushed out* the old labor force. It could not, however, explain this "racial displacement" by the mere willingness of newcomers to work at lower wages, for the commission discovered that in the case of the industries covered by its investigation it was not usual "for employers to engage recent immigrants at wages actually lower than those prevailing at the time of their employment." The line of argument took another course, therefore. The presence of the newcomers, it was said, produced unsafe working conditions and lowered the standards of labor to a degree that "the Americans and older immigrants have considered unsatisfactory." To have proved that would have called for a historical investigation of the industries concerned from which evidence might be drawn for the presumed deterioration of conditions. There was no such study and no such evidence. Indeed, this section seems to have been inserted into the summary arbitrarily, for it did not correspond with any section of the extended report itself.

On the other hand, the report did contain material, not used by the commission, that threw a different light upon the process of displacement. The investigators discovered that "the chief reason for the employment of immigrants" was "the impossibility of securing other labor to supply the demand caused by the expansion of the industry. Without the immigrant labor supply, the development of the cotton-goods industry to its present status in New England and other North Atlantic States could not have taken place." All these changes were part of the complex development of the American economy. The rapid industrial expansion of the half century before the investigation had been accompanied by a swift technological transformation which mechanized many aspects of production and thereby eliminated the skill of the old craftsmen. That accounted for the displacement. But the commission also found that those displaced, in large measure, moved upward to better-paying jobs made available by the rapid expansion of the economy. To the extent that immigrants contributed to that expansion they actually helped to lift the condition of the laborers they found already there.

In any case, no connection was established between the specific qualities of the new immigrants and the whole process of displacement. Indeed, the report itself pointed out that the shifts in the labor force went back to early in the nineteenth century and had once involved such old groups as the Irish. That might have suggested to the commission, but unfortunately did not, that what was involved was not some peculiarity of the immigrants from southern and eastern Europe, but rather a general factor characteristic of all immigrants, and varying with the recency of the group.

■ **Unionization.** The commission made the blanket accusation that "the extensive employment of southern and eastern European immigrants in manufacturing and mining has in many places resulted in the weakening of labor organizations or in their complete disruption." This statement was made without a shred of evidence. The commission did not include in its report any data on union membership, either for the country as a whole or for specific industries or specific unions. It had no way of knowing what the trend of union membership was, or what the relationship of immigration was to that trend.

The accusation quoted above derived not from evidence, but from the commission's assumption as to the nature of the new immigration:

> The members of the larger number of races of recent entrance to the mines, mills, and factories as a rule have been tractable and easily managed. This quality seems to be a

temperamental one acquired through present or past conditions of life in their native land.

The lengths to which the commission was willing to go to maintain views of the effects of immigration on unions in accord with its prejudices emerge from a comparison of the account of the labor organizations in the cotton industry as it appeared in the extended report of the investigators with the same account "summarized" in the summary by the commission.

Speaking of the cotton-goods industry, the original report pointed out that unions were confined to the skilled branches of the trade while the immigrants were largely unskilled. The latter occupations "are not organized, and the coming of the foreigner there does not concern the textile unions." Since the organized branches of the trade were "protected, by the long time required to attain proficiency, from any sudden or immediate competition of unorganized foreigners, these unions are not strongly opposed to the immigrants gradually working into their trades." But "they manifest little interest in the immigrant employees until they have advanced to the occupations controlled by the labor organizations." Though the mass of laborers thus remained outside the union, the report continued, "all the operatives are strongly union in their sympathies and in the case of labor troubles have stood with the union people."

How was this summarized? Only an extended quotation will show the extent of the distortion:

> The more recent immigrant employees from southern and eastern Europe and Asia, however, have been a constant menace to the labor organizations and have been directly and indirectly instrumental in weakening the unions and threatening their disruption. . . . The recent immigrants have also been reluctant to identify themselves with the unions.

This dictum inserted into the summary, in direct contradiction to the evidence, while the conclusions of the original report were omitted, demonstrated the total unreliability of the commission's observations on the question of unionization and immigration.

■ Industrial Methods.   The commission's finding that an increase in the number of accidents was one of the effects of employing the new immigrants in industry has already been mentioned above. In addition reference should be made to the careful examination of the commission's conclusions on the subject by Dr. I. A. Hourwich (*Immigration and Labor* [2d. ed., N.Y., 1922], 458 ff.). Dr. Hourwich showed that the commission merely accepted the mine operators' point of view, which was to ascribe all accidents to employee negligence rather than to deficiencies in equipment. Reconstructing the history of mine accidents, Dr. Hourwich showed that their incidence varied with the output of industry rather than with the character of the labor force; and a comparison of mines in Oklahoma, Tennessee, and Alabama, which employed very few immigrants, with those of Pennsylvania, where the bulk of the miners were immigrants, exposed clearly the falsity of the commission's views. The commission, eager to reach its own final judgments, considered none of these types of evidence.

The conclusions of the commission also contained numerous miscellaneous statements as to the deterioration of the conditions of labor and of wages as the results of immigration. In this connection it is necessary only to emphasize again the fact that the commission had no evidence whatsoever to support these contentions. Such evidence could have come only by a comparative historical study which would actually trace the development of labor conditions over a substantial period. The commission made no such study. The hypothetical and speculative nature of its conclusions is evident in the following example:

Acknowledging that there was no evidence that immigrants actually worked at lower wages, the commission went on to say, "It is hardly open to doubt, however, that the availability of the large supply of recent immigrant labor prevented the increase in wages which otherwise would have resulted during recent years from the increased demand for labor."

■ **New Industries.** The commission drew another unfavorable comparison between the old and the new immigration with regard to the capacity of the latter for stimulating economic innovation. The arrival of the newest comers, it argued, did not result "in the establishment of new industries of any importance." But, "by way of contrast, it will be recalled that a large proportion of the earlier immigrant laborers were originally induced to come to this country to contribute their skill and experience toward the establishment of new industries, such as mining and textile, glass, and iron and steel manufacturing." This assertion sprang from the unreal fantasy to which the commission clung, that the old immigration was largely made up of skilled artisans. It disregarded also the obvious difference between industrial conditions in the United States in 1840 and 1900. It was, indeed, easier to create new industries at the earlier date; but that reflected the undeveloped economy of the country rather than the quality of the immigration.

■ **Unemployment and Depressions.** The conclusions of the report also contain a number of statements implying a relationship between the new immigration and unemployment and depressions. These are nowhere proved. In any case, as elsewhere, the commission found it unnecessary to show that the old immigration had stood in a different relationship; it took that for granted.

■ **Agriculture.** Here the discussion centered on a fairly sympathetic survey of many communities of recent immigrants. But the summary was preceded by an introduction, not particularly related to the report itself, which drew an invidious distinction between the old and the new immigrants with regard to the likelihood of their entry into agriculture. The comments disregarded two critical factors: first, that the number of farmers increased with the prolongation of a group's experience in the United States (this was revealed quite clearly in the commission's data, which showed that for all groups there was a greater percentage of farmers among the second than among the first generation); and second, that the American economy had changed after 1890. With industrialization there came a general growth of urban at the expense of rural population; even the sons of native farmers were being drawn to the city. Whatever difference existed between the old and the new immigrants was not the product of their inherent characteristics but of the conditions they had found and the length of time they had lived in the United States.

Education and Literacy

The agitation for the literacy test that occupied popular attention while the commission worked gave particular importance to its discussion of literacy and education, and to its attempt to establish a difference, in this regard, between the old and the new immigration.

The background was established in the account of emigration conditions in Europe, which clearly indicated a substantial difference in the rate of illiteracy. The original report examined the various reasons for the high rate of illiteracy in southern and eastern Europe and concluded, "But probably the most apparent cause of illiteracy in Europe, as elsewhere, is poverty. The economic status of a people has a very decided effect upon the literacy rate." It then went on to predict a steady improvement in the future. The commission's own investigators abroad thus recognized that the inability to read was a product of environmental rather than of racial deficiencies. The summary, however, omitted this optimistic discussion and instead made the sweeping suggestion that the high rate of illiteracy among the new immigrants was due to "inherent racial tendencies."

The commission also labored the point that the new immigrants in the United States were less literate than the old. The supporting documentation was nowhere brought systematically together; it was instead scattered through the reports on industries and agriculture. Criticism in detail is therefore difficult. But the general fallacy of the argument is evident enough.

The commission almost everywhere failed to take account of duration of settlement in arriving at the conclusion that "a much higher degree of illiteracy prevails among the immigrants of recent years from southern and eastern Europe than among those of old immigration from Great Britain and northern Europe." That is, in comparing the natives of Italy in the United States with the natives of Scotland, it calmly disregarded the fact that the former had lived in the country for a far shorter period than the latter. Yet that circumstance was of critical importance, as may be gathered from the data on the ability of employees in clothing manufacture to learn English, which does take account of it:

Percentage of Foreign-Born Employees Who
Speak English by Years in the United States

Years in the United States	Per Cent
Under 5	38.8
5 to 9	66.5
10 or over	83.0

The failure of the commission to reckon with the duration of settlement invalidated its whole comparison of old and new immigrants.

Its difficulties with the more general problems of education were even more obvious. The commission had apparently thought it would be possible to measure the capacity of the old and new immigrants to be schooled. Discussing the question, Jenks had pointed out, "Anyone who has observed, even in a small way, the different classes of people that come into this country knows that some are very much inclined toward making the best possible use of our schools, while others make no attempt whatever to get in touch with our educational system." The commission planned to make such measurements through an elaborate investigation of more than two million school children in order to discover which races were most likely to be retarded.

Although four volumes of tables came forth from this investigation, they proved nothing. To begin with, the data was defective since it was based upon questionnaires sent to teachers who did not understand them. "In a considerable proportion of cases," the commission acknowledged, "the teachers have assigned a 'cause of retardation' for pupils who are the normal age or even younger than the normal age for the grade." The commission nevertheless used the bulk of material gathered in its elaborate tables on "retardation," the very meaning of which many teachers did not understand.

The volumes of statistics that the commission reprinted thus reflect not the care and accuracy of the survey, but, rather, the fact that it was not able to shape its material to the conclusions at which it wished to arrive.

There was no basis in the data for dividing the old from the new immigrants on the performance of their children in schools. But the information in the tables did show a wide variation from place to place in the achievements of children within any given group. Thus 55 per cent of the German children in St. Louis were retarded, but only 21.2 per cent in Scranton; similarly the English showed 56.2 per cent in St. Louis, 19.1 per cent in Scranton, and 13.9 per cent in Worcester.

That might have suggested that the quality of schools and the social environment were more significant variables than parentage. But not to the commission.

Too, through the tables there ran a good deal of material that emphasized the importance of recency of settlement, so much so that the original report pointed out:

Length of residence in the United States has an important bearing on progress of pupils. It can hardly be expected that children of immigrants who have been in the United States only a few months or even years can make the same progress as children of those who have been here long enough to become more or less adjusted to their new surroundings.

But this reasonable comment did not seem worthy of inclusion in the summary.

Charity and Immigration

The data on pauperism, dependence, and admissions to institutions did not provide the basis for any general comparisons between the old and new immigration, except insofar as the old were more subject to alcoholism than the new.

Immigration and Crime

"Statistics show," said the commission, "that the proportion of convictions for crimes according to the population is greater among the foreign-born than among the native-born." Furthermore, it concluded that "the proportion of the more serious crimes of homicide, blackmail, and robbery, as well as the least serious offences, is greater among the foreign-born." These statements followed smoothly from the conception of racial propensities defined in the *Dictionary of Races.* But to support them with statistical evidence was more difficult.

When the commission turned to the only existing body of information, the *United States Census Report on Prisoners,* it discovered a disconcerting situation. This data, gathered by a body which did not have to prove any conclusions, showed that "immigration has not increased the volume of crime to a distinguishable extent, if at all"; indeed, that the percentage of immigrants among prisoners had actually fallen between 1890 and 1904, and that native Americans "exhibited in general a tendency to commit more serious crimes than did the immigrant."

Obviously such statistics would not do. The commission proceeded to gather its own. For its study the commission accumulated a very large number of cases, fully 1,179,677, extracted from court records over a period of seven years. These were, however, derived from relatively few sources. Of them some 1,130,000 were drawn from New York and Chicago, the two cities with the largest number of foreign-born in the United States, and 30,000 more came from Massachusetts, also a state of high immigrant density. (The remainder were the 12,000 aliens in federal institutions.) Apparently it was unnecessary to sample the experience of such places as New Orleans, Memphis, San Francisco, or Atlanta.

No inferences drawn from this partial data could possibly support the sweeping generalizations of the conclusions. Such a sampling would hardly be illuminating for the country as a whole, nor could it measure the pressure of the immigrant in the national crime problem. At most it might throw light on the peculiar problems of the two cities from which the bulk of the cases were taken.

The commission did not, however, use the source material as if it applied only to the communities from which it was drawn; if it had, its conclusions could not stand. Nor did it examine the frequency of crime relative to the number of the foreign-born and the natives. To attempt such a correlation, it felt, would not be feasible. Instead the commission organized the data to show how immigration had changed the character of crime in the United States. Its evidence, the commission imagined, proved that immigration had increased:

> the commission of offenses of personal violence (such as abduction and kidnaping, assault, homicide, and rape) and of that large class of violations of the law known as offenses against public policy (which include disorderly conduct, drunkenness, vagrancy, the violation of corporate ordinances, and many offenses incident to city life) . . . [as well as] offenses against chastity, especially those connected with prostitution.

It must be emphasized again that at no point did the commission have the evidence to support its general conclusions that the immigrants committed a higher proportion of crimes than did the natives. Furthermore, it *did not* show that such a result had followed upon immigration. It had, indeed, no basis at all for comparison with earlier periods.

What it did was quite different. It traced the distribution of various types of crimes attributable to each group of immigrants and to the much larger group of native Americans. Within each group it compared the incidence of each specific type of crime with the total number of crimes in that group. That is, it reckoned up all the crimes charged to Italians and then computed what percentage of that number were homicides, larcenies, and the like. It did the same for every other group by nativity and then compared the resultant percentages for larceny or homicide. When, therefore, it said that the foreign-born were more prone than the natives to crimes of personal violence, it did not mean that the foreign-born committed *more such crimes* than the natives either absolutely or relative to their percentage in the total population. It meant only that such crimes accounted for a larger part of the total criminality of the group.

One illustration will suffice to show the meaning of this difference. The New York county and Supreme courts, in 1907 and 1908, showed the following cases of assault, by nativity:

Country of Birth	Number
United States	630
Italy	342
Russia	73
Austria-Hungary	62
Germany	47
Ireland	38
Canada	15
Poland	14
England	8

This data was presented by the commission in a table headed "Relative Frequency" of such offenses, as follows:

Country of Birth	Per Cent of Total
Italy	28.9
Austria-Hungary	15.0
Poland	14.6
Ireland	13.7
Canada	12.1
Russia	11.3
Germany	9.1
United States	8.7
England	5.0

Only the wariest reader could avoid concluding from this tricky presentation that Italians committed more such crimes than the natives, whereas the exact opposite was true.

The table last cited could be accurately understood only if one remembered that "per cent of total" meant per cent of crimes of this category of the total number of crimes committed by the nativity group concerned. The high position of the Italians, for example, was not due to the fact that they perpetrated more assaults than the natives, but to the fact that they were responsible for fewer crimes of other types. In almost every instance the low rating of natives of the United States seemed due to the fact that the total number of crimes they committed was much larger than that of other groups. As the commission presented this data, it was never very meaningful, often misleading, and in no case supported the commission's general contentions.

Immigration and Vice

The commission's finding on the "white slave traffic" was moderate in tone and factual in content. It was on the whole free of the conjectural elements that marred so much of the rest of the report. Perhaps the only objection to it was the failure adequately to place the problem in its context. Dealing exclusively with the immigrants, it gave the impression, unintentionally, that prostitution was largely a responsibility of the foreign-born, although fragmentary data in the report indicated that the immigrants were only a minor element in a more general American problem.

Immigration and Insanity

The commission did not make a firsthand investigation of this subject. Its data was drawn from the census and other sources. While the available information seemed to indicate that the foreign-born supplied more than their share of the insane, it also indicated that it was the old, rather than the new, immigration that was chiefly responsible. The Irish, the Germans, and the Scandinavians showed the greatest relative responsibility, or, as the report put it:

> It appears that insanity is relatively more prevalent among the foreign-born than among the native-born, and relatively more prevalent among certain immigrant races and nationalities than among others. In general the nationalities furthest advanced in civilization show, in the United States, a higher proportion of insane than do the more backward races.

Changes in Bodily Form among the Descendants of Immigrants

The commission considered within the scope of its inquiry the whole problem of the physical characteristics of the immigrants. To the *Dictionary of Races,* which rested upon information gathered from other sources, it wished to join its own findings on the physical characteristics of immigrants and their descendants. This was an important question because it was theretofore assumed that such characteristics of a race as bodily form were fixed and permanent. It was not imagined that they would change in the course of immigration; and if they did not, that might conspicuously affect the assimilation of the immigrants.

Professor Franz Boas of Columbia University, the distinguished anthropologist charged with responsibility for the study, discovered surprising results, however. It appeared that:

> the head form, which has always been considered one of the most stable and permanent characteristics of human races, undergoes far-reaching changes due to the transfer of the people from European to American soil. . . . This fact shows . . . that not even those characteristics of a race which have proved to be most permanent in their old home remain the same under the new surroundings; and we are compelled to conclude that when these features of the body change, the whole bodily and mental make-up of the immigrants may change. . . . All the evidence is now in favor of a great plasticity of human types.

The commission was certainly surprised with these results. It perforce quoted them—but cautiously, and with the reservation that a good deal more study was needed before they could be accepted. The commission, however, did not allow these findings to influence the materials in the *Dictionary of Races* or to stand in the way of its allusion to the fixed nature of the temperaments of the races it discussed through the body of the report.

Summary Evaluation of the Commission's Findings

In summary it may be said the commission did not use the opportunity afforded it to make the open, objective study of the problem it might have. It began with preconceived ideas as to the difference between the old and the new immigration. It did not find the evidence to substantiate that assumption. But it devoted much of its effort to bending what evidence it could find to that end. Its conclusions were largely invalidated by those distortions and offered an unsound basis for the legislation that followed.

Less than a decade after the submittal of the Dillingham Commission's report the proponents of more restrictive legislation sought further scientific support for their theories. They found it in the "Analysis of America's Modern Melting Pot," by Dr. Harry Laughlin, a highly qualified geneticist associated with the Eugenics Records Office. This inquiry, commissioned by the government, was designed to correct the inability of the earlier investigation to demonstrate conclusively the social inferiority of the new immigrants. Laughlin's report originated in a hearing of the House Immigration Committee (April 16, 17, 1920), which asked him to study the relationship of biology to immigration, particularly as that bore on the problems of social degeneracy.

Laughlin's analysis was presented to the committee in November 1922. Congressman Albert Johnson, chairman of the committee, examined the report and certified that "Dr. Laughlin's data and charts . . . are both biologically and statistically thorough, and apparently sound." Whatever the chairman's competence to pass upon these matters, he was satisfied that the investigation had proved the inferiority of the new immigrants.

The opinions that were before long to be reflected in legislation were summarized by Dr. Laughlin:

> The outstanding conclusion is that, making all logical allowances for environmental conditions, which may be unfavorable to the immigrant, the recent immigrants as a whole, present a higher percentage of inborn socially inadequate qualities than do the older stocks.

This conclusion was accompanied by the assurance that it was based upon "data and conditions," and not on "sentiment or previous attitudes."

Before advancing to an examination of that data it will, however, be worth making note of Dr. Laughlin's own sentiments as he explicitly stated them to the committee:

> We in this country have been so imbued with the idea of democracy, or the equality of all men, that we have left out of consideration the matter of blood or natural inborn hereditary mental and moral differences. No man who breeds pedigreed plants and animals can afford to neglect this thing.

Dr. Laughlin thus purported to be studying the "natural inborn hereditary" tendencies of the new immigrants to the significant social disorders. His method was to examine the distribution of various national stocks in 445 state and federal institutions in 1921.

This procedure was inherently defective, for commitments to public institutions did not actually measure the hereditary tendencies Dr. Laughlin presumed he was measuring. In the case of insanity, for instance, the standard of commitment was most inadequate, since the availability of facilities in various sections varied greatly, as did the willingness of certain social, economic, and ethnic groups to make use of those facilities in preference to private institutions or to home care. All the generalization based on such data must be dubious.

Furthermore, Laughlin's sample was faulty and he treated his material crudely, failing to make corrections for occupational, age, or sex distribution. His critical statistical device, "the quota fulfillment plan of analysis," was based upon a comparison of committal records of 1921 with the distribution of population in 1910, *al-*

though the census data of 1920 was available to him. By this means he certainly magnified the relative number of the immigrants among the socially inadequate.

But all these methodological faults, grave as they are, shrink in importance when compared with a more basic criticism. *The data, faulty as it is, simply does not say what Laughlin says it says.* His conclusions can find support, of a sort, only by throwing together all forms of inadequacy in a few gross, and arbitrary, divisions, as follows:

	Per Cent of Quota Fulfillment
Native white, native parentage	84.33
Native white, foreign parentage	109.40
Native white, mixed parentage	116.65
Northwestern Europe immigrants	130.42
Southeastern Europe immigrants	143.24

Laughlin's own materials do not support his conclusions if the various national groups are treated separately, whether for inadequacy as a whole or for particular types of inadequacy. In the chart which follows, the various nationalities are ranked according to their order in Laughlin's rating of quota fulfillment for each category and for the total. The ranking is in the order of descending desirability, that is, those at the top are most desirable, those at the bottom, least.[1]

Feeblemindedness

1. Ireland
2. Switzerland
3. All Asia
4. Greece
5. France
6. Germany
7. Scandinavia
8. Austria-Hungary
9. Canada
10. Rumania
11. Italy
12. Great Britain
13. Turkey
14. Russia and Poland
15. Bulgaria
16. U.S., native parents
17. U.S., foreign parents
18. U.S., mixed parents
19. Australia
20. Serbia

Insanity

1. Japan
2. Switzerland
3. U.S., native parents
4. Rumania
5. U.S., mixed parents
6. U.S., foreign parents
7. Canada
8. All Asia
9. Austria-Hungary
10. Great Britain
11. Italy
12. France
13. Greece
14. Germany
15. Scandinavia
16. Turkey
17. Russia and Poland
18. Bulgaria
19. Ireland
20. Serbia

Crime

1. Switzerland
2. Ireland
3. Germany
4. Scandinavia

Epilepsy

1. Scandinavia
2. France
3. Switzerland
4. All Asia

Crime

5. Great Britain
6. Canada
7. Austria-Hungary
8. U.S., native parents
9. U.S., foreign parents
10. U.S., mixed parents
11. France
12. Russia-Poland
13. Rumania
14. Japan
15. Italy
16. Turkey
17. All Asia
18. Greece
19. Bulgaria
20. Serbia

Epilepsy

5. Greece
6. Austria-Hungary
7. Germany
8. Canada
9. Italy
10. U.S., native parents
11. Turkey (European)
12. Ireland
13. Russia-Poland
14. Rumania
15. Great Britain
16. U.S., foreign parents
17. U.S., mixed parents

Tuberculosis

1. Switzerland
2. Germany
3. Austria-Hungary
4. Great Britain
5. U.S., native parents
6. Canada
7. U.S., mixed parents
8. U.S., foreign parents
9. Italy
10. Ireland
11. All Asia
12. Russia-Poland
13. Scandinavia
14. Greece

Dependency

1. Austria-Hungary
2. Italy
3. All Asia
4. Russia-Poland
5. Scandinavia
6. U.S., mixed parents
7. U.S., foreign parents
8. U.S., native parents
9. Switzerland
10. Germany
11. Greece
12. Canada
13. Great Britain
14. France
15. Turkey
16. Ireland

All Types of Social Inadequacy

1. Switzerland
2. Japan
3. U.S., native parents
4. Austria-Hungary
5. Canada
6. Rumania
7. Germany
8. U.S., foreign parents
9. Great Britain
10. U.S., mixed parents
11. Scandinavia
12. France
13. All Asia
14. Italy
15. Russia-Poland
16. Greece
17. Turkey
18. Ireland
19. Bulgaria
20. Serbia

A candid examination of these rankings will reveal that, whatever their intrinsic value, they did not show any consistent order of superiority or inferiority among the various nationality groups concerned. Furthermore, they certainly did not show that the new nationalities could, in any sense, conceivably have been said to rank below the old nationalities. All the inferences of the Laughlin report should therefore have been categorically rejected.

They were not. Instead they were widely accepted and significantly influenced American policy. The newspaper reader, like the member of Congress, took their results uncritically and without question. The one jarring note, struck by the Boas investigation into bodily forms, was quietly disregarded and not, for several decades, further pursued. Unfortunately the means of critical appraisal of these biased reports had long since been dulled by science itself, which had already led men to expect the results Dillingham and Laughlin found.

The studies that have here been examined have a historical interest insofar as they have contributed to the adoption of the national-origins quota system, which is still a part of American immigration legislation. By giving governmental and scientific validation to existing prejudices against the new immigrants, they helped to justify the discriminations against them in the laws of 1921 and 1924.

But these studies have also a larger significance: they show how vulnerable science was, at the beginning of the twentieth century, to penetration by images and conceptions charged with popular emotions. Those emotions sprang from a deep uneasiness in the hearts of disturbed men. To understand the hatreds and the fears that spilled over into the laboratories and that biased the computing machines, it will be necessary to look beyond the world of science at the human condition from which they sprang.

NOTES

1. Not all Laughlin's entries are included, and Negroes are excluded, so that "native" refers to native white.

PART 3

Recent America
1914-Present

Intolerance in the 1920s

In the aftermath of World War I, the Ku Klux Klan experienced a phenomenal revival. Nearly moribund for the first five years after its resurrection in 1915, the KKK suddenly exploded into life in 1920. By 1925, it had recruited perhaps five million men into its hooded ranks. Identical to the Klan of Reconstruction days in regalia and ritual, the KKK of the 1920s actually drew on a much broader base of support. The object of its hatred now included many others than the black man, and its strength extended far outside the South. During the first half of the decade, the Klan exerted immense power, dominating the politics of some states and imposing its standards of "Americanism" far more widely. The downward slide was no less swift, however. By the end of the 1920s, the Klan had become a negligible force and would remain so until the civil-rights revolution called it forth for a second resurrection in the modern era.

The Klan of the 1920s, Robert Moats Miller argues in the following essay, must be treated not as an aberration, but as part of the American mainstream. On the one hand, it drew on dark strains of intolerance, authoritarianism, and violence deep-rooted in the nation's history. The Klan attracted its clientele not primarily from America's blackguards and dispossessed, but from its decent, God-fearing citizenry. On the other hand, the Klan expressed the deep anxieties about the social revolution taking place in the country. For the American drawn to the Klan—Anglo-Saxon, fundamentalist, rural at least by birth—the 1920s seemed a time of profound and threatening change. A massive stream of immigrants, supposedly unassimilable and inferior, had poured into the country; the dreaded Roman Catholics constituted a third of the population; city dwellers were about to become a national majority; manners and morals had grown loose and impure. All of these threats to the older America, no less than the continuing determination to preserve white supremacy, had stimulated the growth of the KKK. Its equally fast decline was a sign of easing tensions, either through adjustment to the new world or, as in the case of the political radical and the black man, through suppression of the danger. By his analysis, Robert Miller rescues the KKK from the realm of historical curiosity. The hooded organization becomes rather a key for understanding the American experience in the 1920s.

FOR FURTHER READING:

CHALMERS, DAVID M. *Hooded Americanism.* New York: Doubleday & Company, 1965.*
HIGHAM, JOHN. *Strangers in the Land.* New York: Atheneum Publishers, 1963.*
MURRAY, ROBERT K. *Red Scare: A Study in National Hysteria.* New York: McGraw-Hill Book Company, 1964.*

Asterisk denotes paperback edition.

The Ku Klux Klan ROBERT MOATS MILLER

The Ku Klux Klan of the 1920's is a study in anxiety rather than in abnormality. The citizens of the Invisible Empire were deeply anxious men, but they were not, save for the psychotic few, moral monsters; and to dismiss these five million hooded Americans as peculiarly depraved is to blink away the banality of evil. The Klan illuminates the need of mediocre men to flee to the mysticism of the primitive collectivity, and serves, therefore, to remind us that Americans are implicated in the totalitarian temper of the modern world. To discern more than a casual relationship between the Klan and twentieth-century collectivism, however, is not to say that the Klan is a study in un-Americanism. These True Believers of the twenties were not converts to an alien ideology; rather, they confessed to a creed shared, in whole or in part, by many Americans in every generation. The Klan illuminates the persistency of dark strains in American history, strains that have been eased but never entirely erased by faithfulness to the countervailing ideals of decency and fair play. Why, however, should these strains become acutely manifest in a decade fondly deemed the apogee of "normalcy"? Admitting that all men in the modern world bear the burden of anxiety, acknowledging the racism, nativism, and irrationalism flawing the American past, it remains our task to comprehend what there was in the social and psychic air of the early 1920's making many Americans so terribly anxious as to compel them to seek release in a secret, hooded order which, if spawned in Europe, would have carried the designation "fascist."

Any attempt to resolve this paradox must begin with the understanding that the Klan was a many-splintered thing or, less invidiously, a many-splendored thing. The Knights were troubled souls, but that which tried their souls varied from region to region and, indeed, from Knight to Knight. It was as though an outraged citizenry participated in a gigantic police line-up to identify the enemies of society, with each "good" American fingering a different suspect: uppity Negro, conspiratorial Catholic, avaricious Jew, dirty Mexican, wily Oriental, bloody-handed Bolshevik, scabrous bootlegger, fancy "lady," oily gambler, fuzzy internationalist, grafting politico, Sabbath desecrator, wife-beater, home-breaker, atheistic evolutionist, feckless-faithed Modernist, scoffing professor, arrogant intellectual, subversive socialist, slick urbanite, simpering pacifist, corrupt labor organizer. Of necessity, the line of suspects was endless because the evils threatening America appeared legion: miscegenation, mongrelization, Romanism, socialism, urbanism, skepticism, secularism, paganism, modernism, radicalism, internationalism, materialism, Freudianism, relativism, surrealism, alcoholism, sexualism.

These myriad dangers appeared more clear and present in some regions and to some citizens than others; consequently, it is imprecise to speak of the Klan of the 1920's. Rather, there existed many local Klans operating as virtually autonomous units, and each unit ranked the dangers in some order of priority, just as each Knight was motivated (whether consciously or not) by his life experiences.

Fragmented and amorphous, the Klan was yet a fellowship of belief, knitted together by a shared anxiety about tomorrow and a shared longing for the return of yesterday. Perhaps, after all, there was only one great enemy: *change!* Made bewil-

Source: Robert Moats Miller, "The Ku Klux Klan," in *Change and Continuity in Twentieth-Century America: The 1920's,* eds. John Braeman et al. (Columbus, Ohio: Ohio State University Press, 1968), pp. 215–238, 246–253.

dered and fearful by the swift and surging forces reshaping "their" country, unwilling or unable to understand this strange, new century, men banded together to offer resistance. Essentially, then, the Klan was a counter-revolutionary movement. Its core appeal was to those Americans who, through consideration of rational self-interes or unconscious emotional needs, dreamed that the clock might be stopped; and who, as they donned their white dream robes, knew a momentary identification with a fanciful older and purer community.

The older and purer community of the Klansman's dream was, of course, a white man's community. "I believe in the Klan. I don't believe the thing to do at this moment is to go out and shoot a nigger in the street. But when the time comes — when it comes — we'll take them down by the busload, by the trainload, that's what we'll do. By the busload. By the carload! . . . We don't hate Negroes. We love 'em, in their place — like shinin' shoes, bell-hoppin', street-sweepin', pickin' cotton, diggin' ditches, eatin' possum, servin' time, totin' buckshot, river-floatin', etc." Thus spoke the voice of the Klan in 1965, as articulated by a Jacksonville, Florida, barber. "Our main and fundamental objective is the MAINTENANCE OF THE SUPREMACY OF THE WHITE RACE in this Republic." Thus spoke the voice of the Klan in 1867, as articulated by the delegates to the organizational meeting of the Reconstruction Klan in Nashville.

Because the Negro was the central target of both the Reconstruction and mid-twentieth-century Klans, because both saw the untrammeled Negro as the nation's greatest menace, the temptation is to interpolate and conclude that the same Negrophobia dominated the Klan of the twenties. Perceptive historians have not succumbed to this temptation, realizing that the Klan that flowered after World War I reflected the coalescence of many different fears and loyalties. Indeed, students of the Klan in the Southwest, Far West, and Midwest deem the black man an inconsequential factor in the growth of the white-robed order. We may concur that the movements of the 1860's, 1920's, and 1960's, although sharing a common name and ritual, were substantively different. We may even concur that in great areas of the country where the Klan was powerful the Negro population was insignificant, and that, in fact, it is probable that had not a single Negro lived in the United States, a Klan-type order would have emerged, such was the pervasive anxiety of the post-Versailles years.

Yet having escaped the errors of simplism and "presentism," perhaps in this very sophistication the principle of Ockham's Razor has been forgotten: complex and refined explanations of observed phenomena must not obscure the simple and evident. Just as there is no more demonic theme in American history, so there is none more persistent than that America was a white man's country. White supremacy was an article of faith with almost all modern Europeans and their descendants in the northern New World. Until almost today it was a faith seemingly supported by much scientific and scholarly evidence. Kluxers of every generation have feared the Negro — and consequently have hated him. And Kluxers in every generation have enjoyed the covert endorsement of large numbers of citizens too timid or too hypocritical to enlist under the banner of the fiery cross. The Klan of the 1920's was first, if not foremost, a movement to keep the black man in his place — if necessary, by digging his grave. Its founder, Colonel William Joseph Simmons, was an Alabaman who with a band of Georgians on Thanksgiving night, 1915, ascended Stone Mountain near Atlanta to call "from its slumber of half a century" that Invisible Empire that once had saved the prostrate South from mongrelization. "The present

Klan," testified Simmons, "is a memorial to the original organization. In a sense it is the reincarnation among the sons of the spirit of the fathers." As gallant southerners had galloped with torch and mask to the defense of their society imperiled by conquering Yankee and former bondsmen, so their sons would band to resist with equal success the present pretensions of "darkies" who, said Simmons, were "getting pretty uppity." Childhood cloudy fantasies of redeeming Klansmen were given sharper focus on the screen of the darkened Atlanta theater as the good Colonel saw repeated performances (on scrounged passes) of that tarnished epic, *The Birth of a Nation*, a film that wrote "history with lightning," to use Woodrow Wilson's words of mindless approbation; and in both fantasy and film Simmons identified the redemption of his beloved South with the preservation of the existing caste system. It is, therefore, not surprising that all prospective Knights vowed to "faithfully strive for the eternal maintenance of white supremacy." Nor is it a matter of astonishment that when Simmons was maneuvered from control, his successor, Hiram Wesley Evans, reaffirmed the ancient dogma that "God Almighty never intended social equality for Negro and white man," and who, with a coterie of Dallas disciples, implemented the Almighty's wishes by branding with acid the initials KKK across the forehead of a Negro bellhop. As the Klan was reborn in Georgia by southerners determined to rekindle with fiery cross the resistance spirit of their fathers, so it was in Dixie in 1920, 1921, and 1922 that the movement first gained strength. To be sure, presently the Klan penetrated other sections and exploited other anxieties, but its southern "style" and essential Negrophobia was never totally lost. And the 1960's have reminded us of the historic fact that white men in the North when put to the test are scarcely color-blind.

The period immediately following World War I was a time of testing for the white man and a time of terror for the Negro. Even as the guns on the Western Front quieted, racial violence in America exploded. Service overseas gave Negro soldiers a taste of equality and a sense of pride. The migration of thousands to northern cities engendered a feeling of independence. And the millions who remained in the South hoped that President Wilson intended to include American Negroes among the beneficiaries of his new world of democracy. By 1920 their hopes had been shattered and their pretensions corrected. America was to remain, as it always had been, a white man's country. This was the hard lesson learned of a thousand floggings, a hundred lynchings, and a score of race riots in the months following the Armistice — a lesson administered over the land from Washington to Omaha and from Chicago to Longview, Texas. Further, it was an instruction to be repeated throughout the 1920's for the benefit of forgetful Negroes by the revived Ku Klux Klan.

If many Americans were made fearful by the rising tide of color, it is possible that an even greater number trembled over the menace of Rome. In truth, the shadow of the Pope seemed darker than that of the Negro, and anti-Catholicism was the key to the Klan's growth in the Far West and Midwest and, though not initially, perhaps in the South as well. Although Colonel Simmons dreamed of resurrecting the Reconstruction Klan, he in fact reawakened two other resistance movements, the Know-Nothings of the 1840's and 1850's and the American Protective Association of the 1880's and 1890's. In these movements there raged the fever of anti-Catholicism, the oldest and stubbornest variety of the disease called "nativism," a disease far too common in the United States to be diagnosed a foreign or un-American strain. If the conquest of America by Rome seemed a freightening possibility to nineteenth-century Protestants, to their twentieth-century sons it was an imminent probability and, in the great northern cities, an actuality. In the twenty-five-year period preceding the incident atop Stone Mountain, the Catholic church gained in membership 114.1 per cent, and in 1920, the year of the Klan's great surge, Catholics comprised 36 per cent of the American religious population. The power, the prestige, the "arrogance" of Catholicism was everywhere evident in American life; and when Alfred Emanuel Smith made his first bid for the presidency in 1924, the last, worst fear of Protestants was at hand: the "Dago of the Tiber" (to borrow a Klansman's characterization of the pope) would now take up residence on the Potomac.

It is impossible to understand the enormity of the peril and consequently the enormous appeal of the Klan unless we comprehend the historic identification between Protestantism and Americanism. Since the first settlements, Protestants had prided themselves on being the senior partners in the American enterprise, and in the nineteenth century the American nation and the Protestant denominations had marched to greatness together. This was entirely appropriate, for there was no discernible tension between the evangelical churches and society, between piety and patriotism. The Protestant way of faith and the American way of life were one. What was good for the churches was good for the country. To be sure, this resulted in a "culture-Protestantism" wherein the churches paid a tragic price for their comfortable relationship with American culture; rarely was it found necessary to cry, "Let the Church be the Church!" The churches were not merely domesticated, they were virtually emasculated, and like the eunuchs of old, served as ornaments without seriously disturbing their master's establishment.

Thus, the prideful cry of the Ohio Klan leader was repeatedly uttered: "We want the country ruled by the sort of people who settled it. This is *our* country and we alone are responsible for its future." Protestants viewed the growing power of Catholicism as not only a threat to their religion but also to their beloved nation. Indeed, since Protestantism and Americanism were inseparable, it was impossible to assault the one without wounding the other. Therefore, the Klan attracted patriots as well as bigots, appealing to nationalist loyalties as well as to religious prejudices. Even irenic-spirited Protestants saw (or thought they saw) in the authoritarian structure of the Catholic church objective reasons for opposing its spread in a democratic society. As in wartime true citizens willingly lay down their lives in defense of their free institutions, so patriots in peacetime should freely spend of themselves in the fight against internal subversion. It is instructive that the "Klan verse" of the New Testament is Romans 12:1: "I beseech you therefore, brethren, by the mercies of God, that ye present your bodies a living sacrifice, holy, acceptable unto God, which is your reasonable service." Perhaps we can now understand why the Klan tapped anti-Catholic hostilities even in areas, such as rural Indiana, where the Catholic population numbered less than 2 per cent. Social conflict between Protestants and Catholics over such matters as schools, local politics, prohibition, and censorship heightened tension in many communities; but even where abrasive contact was absent, patriotic Protestants yet feared for the future of "their" nation.

The very name *Roman* Catholic church was suggestive of sinister foreign influence, underscoring the essential Americanism of the Protestant denominations. The very militancy of Catholicism transmuted Protestant tolerance from a virtue to a weakness. And the very authoritarianism of the Church of Rome sharpened the revelation of Protestantism's fragmentation, rendering efforts to quench the conflagration of Catholicism sweeping the land as feeble and ill-directed as the spray from a leaky hose. The Klan carried the hope of Protestant unity and the promise of Protestant militancy. At long last God-fearing men could know, as they assembled around the blazing hillside cross, identification with a mighty supradenominational movement. Like all crusaders, these Klansmen without conscious hypocrisy could cry, "For God and country," and in their righteousness have no sense of shame as they battled the enemies of their faith and nation. "I've attended a lot of church gatherings and conventions," remarked an Exalted Cyclops after the Klan's 1924 national convention, "but I never attended one where the revival spirit was as pronounced as it was at the Klan Klonvocation."

The operative words are "revival spirit," for though anxiety over Catholicism's growth and ambitions was widespread, few liberal Protestants could bring themselves to join the Klan. Thus, far from being a unifying force, the Klan further sharpened the cleavage between Modernists and Fundamentalists. Though not all Fundamentalists were Klansmen, virtually all Klansmen — aside from the obvious charlatans — were Fundamentalists. Fundamentalism and the Klan were perfectly mated in their anti-intellectualism, their morbid compulsion to destroy that which they did not understand, their passion for emotional release, and their frustration, as well as in their blind faith and total commitment. At the same time we should note the national leadership of American Protestantism, including almost every minister of reputation and every theologian of significance, denounced the hooded order, as did almost every national governing body of the larger denominations. Thus the Klan was not an instrument of American Protestantism in the sense, say, that the Inquisition was of the medieval church. It is crucial to understand that the Protestant denominations did not call forth the Klan; rather, the Klan sought desperately to become identified by Protestants as an ally, and it did so by tapping the historic anti-Catholic bias learned by Protestant children in cradle and conventicle and by exploiting the prideful Protestant assumption that they were the darlings of American history.

The Klan made the identification in many ways. Its symbol was a cross, and "The Old Rugged Cross" became almost the official hymn, sometimes with the alteration, "I will cherish the bright Fiery Cross. . . ." Its Kreed "reverentially" acknowledged the majesty of God. Its code of conduct was drawn from the Ten Commandments. The *Kloran* declared that "the living Christ is a Klansman's criterion of character," and Klan pamphlets bore such titles as "Christ and Other Klansmen." Every Klavern had a chaplain called a Kludd, who opened each meeting with a prayer and closed with a benediction. The fervent religiosity of the meeting reached a crescendo as the Knights gathered before the altar to sing the "Kloxology." And perhaps as they marched from the Klavern to burn a warning cross atop a nearby hill, their voices broke forth in the militant "Onward, Christian Solders." Perhaps, too, a few thoughtful members quieted their troubled consciences with the words from another much loved hymn, "God moves in mysterious ways, His wonders to behold."

Little wonder, then, that the Klan succeeded in attracting thousands of evangelical ministers, men already disturbed by the passing of "Old-Time Religion" and made uneasy by their own declining community status. When a Kleagle entered an area, almost invariably he made his first overtures to the local preachers, offering them membership free of the usual ten-dollar fee. Often a co-operating clergyman was thanked or a stiff-kneed one threatened by a sudden Sunday visitation of white-robed and masked Klansmen who silently entered the sanctuary, marched down the aisles, congregated in front of the pulpit to present a purse of perhaps forty dollars. Additional hundreds of ministers were on the Klan payrolls as organizers, lecturers, and officers; and without their active labors and without the tacit endorsement of a numerically impressive element of the ministry, the Klan could not have flourished. The obscene spectacle of men of God gathered about a cross ignited by their hands is perhaps tempered only by a sense of pity for Christians possessed by such anxiety.

"My country in 1900 is something totally different from my own country of 1860. I am wholly a stranger in it." The writer continued: "The child born in 1900 would . . . be born into a new world which would not be a unity but a multiple." This lament and this prediction were made by that purest of patricians, Henry Adams, grandson and great-grandson of presidents; but the words might have been uttered by the most banal of Klansmen, for the opening years of the twentieth century saw the older Americans overwhelmed by a sense of estrangement as "their" land was flooded by a sea of new immigrants. Historians of immigration make much of the shock of alienation experienced by the "uprooted" as they migrated from the psychological security of their familiar European villages to the unknown New World. These insights are altogether valid, for the immigrant's ordeal was seldom physically easy and never emotionally painless. The obverse side of the coin, however, has been examined by fewer students. How does a man accustomed to power and prestige respond when strangers enter the land to dethrone him — and if perchance the dethronement is only in the man's imagination, it does not lessen the fear.

Between the year William McKinley enlisted as a private in the 23rd Ohio Volunteer Infantry in the Civil War and his assassination at the hands of a twenty-eight-year-old Polish-American with the "sinister" name of Czolgosz, fourteen million people came to the United States, "new" immigrants from southern and eastern Europe accounting for over 50 per cent of the total by the 1890's. In the opening fifteen years of the new century the torrent accelerated rather than slackened, an average of 1,000,000 entering annually, and now the "new" immigrants accounted for 72 per cent. The impulse was temporarily stemmed by the war, but with the coming of peace, it renewed. From June, 1920, to June, 1921, more than 800,000 individuals entered, and consuls in Europe reported that additional millions were planning to leave. Then, in one of the most momentous enactments in American history, Congress virtually closed the gates, and the Statue of Liberty lost all relevance save for returning tourists — and a handful of immigrants. (Probably the whole twenty-five-year period after 1925 saw fewer immigrants to the United States than the single year 1907.)

There was more than a casual relationship between this surge of immigration and the resurgence of the Ku Klux Klan. These "new" immigrants, these "beaten men of beaten races," these mongrel worshipers of Bacchus or Baal or Marx, seemed no less threatening to the cherished America of yesteryear than insolent blacks and arrogant Romans. Inquired Colonel Simmons in explaining the growth of the Klan: "What were the dangers which the white men saw threatening to crush and overwhelm Anglo-Saxon civilization? The dangers were in the tremendous influx of foreign immigration, tutored in alien dogmas and alien creeds, flowing in from all climes and slowly pushing the native-born white American population into the center of the country, there to be ultimately overwhelmed and smothered." The Colonel's successor, Evans, elaborated: "When the Klan first appeared the nation was in the confusion of sudden awakening from the lovely dream of the melting pot, disorganized and helpless before the invasion of aliens and alien ideas. After ten years of the Klan it arms for defense." Nordic Americans, he continued, finally

> decided that even the crossing of salt water did not dim a single spot on a leopard; that an alien usually remains an alien no matter what is done to him, what veneer of education he gets, what oath he takes, nor what public attitudes he adopts. They decided that the melting pot was a ghastly failure, and remembered that the very name was coined by a member of one of the races — the Jews — which most determinedly refuses to melt. They decided that in every way, as well as in politics, the alien in the vast majority of cases is unalterably fixed in his instincts, character, thought and interests by centuries of racial selection and development, that he thinks first for his own people, works only with and for them, and never an American. They decided that in character, instincts, thought, and purposes — in his whole soul — an alien remains fixedly alien to America and all it means.

It is again necessary to insist on a hard point. As the Klan tapped rather than created Negrophobia and anti-Catholicism, so it did not so much inspire as reflect a pervasive Anglo-Saxon racism. The Klan can be understood only in the context of the tribalism of the times: the lynching of Leo Frank and the judicial execution of Sacco and Vanzetti; the subtle anti-Semitic discrimination instituted by eastern clubs, resorts, and universities and the crude slanders leveled at Jews by Henry Ford; the superman notions of Jack London and the elitist concepts of Irving Babbitt; the "Yellow Peril" warnings of Homer Lea and the anti-Oriental practices of native Californians; the findings prideful to Anglo-Saxons and diminishing to other "races" of the Army intelligence tests administered during the war and the conclusions implicit in "objective" sociological studies; and the consensus seemingly reached by geneticists such as Henry Fairfield Osborn, geographers such as Ellsworth Huntington, psychologists such as William McDougall, and a host of pseudo scholars such as Madison Grant, that the American grain was being choked by alien chaff.

It is disconcerting to note the similarities between this xenophobia and European fascism. Both stressed racial purity, a return to a primitive community of one blood, and the purging of alien minority groups. And if the Klan preached 100 per cent Americanism, was this not the national goal during World War I? If the Klan sought to save the country from mongrelization, was this not the intent of the Congressional restriction laws of 1921 and 1924, laws as ardently supported by many patricians, populists, and progressives as by hooded Knights?

John Higham has given a very serviceable definition of nativism: an intense opposition to an internal minority on the ground of its foreign (i.e., "un-American") connections; and he has discerned three major themes each with a separate history reaching back before the Civil War: anti-Catholicism, Anglo-Saxon racism, and antiforeign radicalism. We have seen how the Ku Klux Klan reflected and exploited two of these manifestations. Almost equally central to the Klan's purposes was the stamping out of radicalism in all its variants. Throughout American history, patriots have feared their nation endangered by imported radical ideologies. The Birchites and McCarthyites of the mid-twentieth century experience an apprehension as old as that which impelled the Alien and Sedition acts during the anti-Jacobin hysteria of the 1790's. And when in the 1960's Klansmen proclaim "FIGHT COMMUNISM," the injunction is no more imperative than that given by their fathers to "FIGHT BOLSHEVISM." Today the enemy within is deemed less the alien immigrant than the native-born "fellow traveler" seduced by alien ideas. Following World War I, however, the stereotype of the immigrant radical knew its most tarnished hour.

During the war all Americans, irrespective of race or religion or ethnic background, had rallied 'round the flag, save only for some Socialists, Industrial Workers of the World, and other elements of the left wing. Thus radicalism was equated with wartime treason, the dissenter identified with the Hun. Scarcely had the United States been saved, despite the radicals' activities, than there loomed the menace of Bolshevism. And in America the advance agents of the Comintern were quite obviously aliens who somehow owed a double allegiance to Germany and Russia. Surely alien agitators were responsible for the massive labor unrest, the Seattle general strike, the Boston police strike, the "Great Steel Strike," and the thousands of additional strikes involving millions of workers in 1919 and 1920. Surely no true American laborer, unless deranged by Bolshevik propaganda, would march in May Day parades or shout, "To hell with the United States!" or join the new Communist and Communist-Labor parties. And certainly only foreigners were capable of the bombings and attempted assassinations of public officials that seemed proof positive of a vast revolutionary conspiracy.

Such was the peril, it was not enough to bar future immigration or patiently instruct foreigners in the meaning of Americanism. Heroic surgery was immediately required to cut out the cancerous growth. The "Great Red Scare" was a time of unparalleled intimidation, suppression, imprisonment, deportation — at the local, state, and federal level — because at no time in American history, either before or since, had the American people been seized by such a collective failure of nerve. It is, therefore, altogether fitting that the most feared nativist movement in American history, the revived Ku Klux Klan, should date its take-off point from the "Great Red Scare." The Klan never articulated an economic program, and capitalism was not mentioned in its constitution; but it is evident that the Klan saw Americanism and radicalism in irreconcilable tension and that at least some elements in the business community supported the order as an ally in the war against all forms of radicalism, including as it happened, labor unions.

Hopefully, the anatomy of the revived Ku Klux Klan is becoming discernible. Far from being a uniquely reprehensible episode in an otherwise sunny American pageant, it was the archetype of nativist movements, the receptacle for nativist themes flowing from the distant American past. Far from being an isolated, ugly phenomenon in an age of wonderful nonsense, it reflected the tensions of an age of revolution and embodied the anxieties of a people convulsed by change. Far from being a membership entirely of society's failures, it embraces many citizens who historically had enjoyed power and prestige, the prerogatives of the nation's senior partners. To repeat a point made earlier, the Klan may best be understood as a counterrevolutionary movement called into being by sober individuals to resist a world they neither made nor admired — nor understood. The Klan adopted as one of its mottos the command attributed to George Washington: "Put none but Americans on guard tonight!" Alas, Klansmen would not acknowledge — indeed, could not bear to acknowledge — that Negroes, Catholics, immigrants, or "radicals" had any rightful claim to the coveted title "American."

In 1927 in the southern Alabama farm country of Crenshaw, a group of Klansmen led by a Baptist minister, L. A. Nalls, flogged a divorcée, the mother of two children, who had married a divorced man. After the whipping the Reverend Nalls offered the consoling sermon: "Sister, you were not punished in anger this evening; you were punished in a spirit of kindness and correction, to set your feet aright and to show your children how a good mother should go." A collection for the woman was taken up among her assailants and the resulting three dollars and fifty cents were given her along with a jar of Vaseline for her wounds. This incident and these words reveal still another color of the chameleon-like Klan: its moral authoritarianism, its vigilantism, and its sadism.

Recent scholarship has demonstrated what must have been self-evident to the victims of the Klan's wrath at the time: the hooded Knights, who took as their motto, "Not for self, but for others," regarded themselves as perfect knights, *sans peur et sans reproche,* and therefore the proper guardians of public virtue and private morality. And in the postwar years, public corruption and private depravity seemed endemic. Is it necessary to explicate this point? Is it mandatory to refer once again to Hemingway's heroes and Fitzgerald's heroines and all the beautiful and the damned of the Lost Generation of the Roaring Twenties? The quips about rising skirts and falling morals and the times being out of joint when the word "neck" abruptly became a verb are not merely surface manifestations of a society that remained at its core stable. Bootleggers, speak-easies, rumrunners, syphilitic gangsters, organized gambling, open prostitution, lurid movies, salacious literature, Sabbath sports, easy divorce, family disintegration, sexy dances, purchased politicians, bought policemen — these things, of course, were not unique to the twenties. Yet a social and moral revolution, already apparent before the war, was in fact dislocating the old nineteenth-century Victorian structure. The acids of modernity were in truth dissolving the old verities of piety, patriotism, and moral purity, reverence for church, country, and home. To older Americans this revolution was as menacing as the rising tide of Negroes, Catholics, aliens, and radicals. Indeed, the strangers in the land (together with the proverbially sexually depraved blacks) had introduced these evils into a formerly chaste society, and now, obviously, even the sons and daughters of the American Revolution were being infected.

Read a Klan handbill: "Every criminal, every gambler, every thug, every libertine, every girl runner, every home wrecker, every wife beater, every dope peddler, every moonshiner, every crooked politician, every pagan Papist priest, every shyster lawyer, every K. of C., every white slaver, every black spider — is fighting the Klan. Think it over. Which side are you on?" In torchlight parades white-robed men (and it probably is not happenstance that white, the emblem of purity, was chosen for the robes) carried signs: LAW AND ORDER MUST PREVAIL. COHABITATION BETWEEN WHITES AND BLACKS MUST STOP. BOOT-LEGGERS, PIMPS, HANGERS-ON, GET RIGHT OR GET OUT. WIFE-BEATERS, FAMILY-DESERTERS, HOME-WRECKERS, WE HAVE NO ROOM FOR YOU. LAW VIOLATORS, WE ARE WATCHING YOU. BEWARE. GO JOY RIDING WITH YOUR OWN WIFE. THE SHERIFFS OF BOWIE AND MILLER COUNTIES HAVE MORE DEPUTIES THAN CARRY COMMISSIONS. PURE WOMENHOOD. CRAP SHOOTERS BEWARE. LOVE THY NEIGHBOR AS THYSELF, BUT LEAVE HIS WIFE ALONE. Although the evidence is fragmentary, it is quite possible that the majority of individuals flogged, tarred and feathered, branded, emasculated, and otherwise tortured and intimidated by the Klan were those who had in some way transgressed morally.

When the Klan proclaimed its opposition to "Jew, Jug, and Jesuit," its intimate relationship to Prohibition was merely underscored. There were millions of prohibitionists, of course, who never became Klansmen, but almost all Klansmen *claimed* to be as dry as a powder flask. The harsh, repressive spirit of Prohibition represented a souring of the original humanitarian passion of the early temperance reformers. Just so, the moral passion of the Kluxers was a perversion rather than a denial of progressivism's vision of a redeemed society.

And so it came to pass that thousands of good, decent citizens, genuinely alarmed by civic corruption and moral decay, failed initially to discern the Klan's own corrupt nature and welcomed it as an agency of reform. And seemingly many a community *was* rid of gamblers, bootleggers, and prostitutes because of the Klan's presence. Exulted the editor of a Texas newspaper: "It cost Goose Creek just $1200 to clean up. It cost the boys down there $1200 in fines assessed for flogging to transform a rough and tumble oil camp into a progressive and God-fearing community of industrious toilers. . . . The Ku Klux Klan has made a new and different town of Goose Creek." After one visit from Klan regulators, it was said, a tough town became "almost a Sunday School class." Vigilantism is, after all, as much a sign of a desire for law and order as it is a manifestation of lawlessness. In America vigilantism was an old and not always dishonorable tradition. In fact, in 1920 and 1921 masked farmers roamed the countryside with lighted torch in order to check the sale of cotton, and their acts of intimidation, however justified, provided an example for the Klan to follow.

The dangers of men taking the law into their own hands, the arrogance of men appointing themselves as civic censors, the voyeurism and prurience implicit in Comstockery, the sadism in the act of stripping and whipping "fallen" women, the temptation to exact personal vengeance in the name of "morality" — these things are no less true because obvious. As Sartre observed, "It is *fun* to be an anti-Semite." Undoubtedly, the Klan attracted cranky professional moralists, village vigilantes, local busybodies, prudish Pecksniffs, old ladies of both sexes haunted (as Mencken sneered) by the fear that someone, somewhere, might be happy. But even Klansmen of the purest conscious motives and highest community status failed to heed the words of George Santayana: "Neither prosperity nor empire nor heaven can be worth the winning at the price of a virulent temper, bloody hands, an anguished spirit, and a vain hatred of the rest of the world." In our effort to understand the Klan we might heed the words of John Higham: "Perhaps, in the pageant of American history, the white-robed Klansmen should stand in the place of Santayana's genteel New Englander as the Last Puritan."

When a Klansman addressed a Catholic priest, "You, who wears his collar backwards like a mule," his audience caught the allusion, for they were steeped in agrarian life and lore, and when they dreamed of the past it was of a pastoral community, a virgin land, inhibited by sturdy yeomen, unspotted by the urban world. But urbanization had come to the United States. In fact, the revived Klan emerged at the precise moment when the tides of population, power, and prestige were running heavily to the city, and at the end of the twenties only 40 per cent of the population still lived in rural areas. There is more than a casual correlation between this demographic change and the Klan's rise. Yet it is not a simple relationship.

Most students interpret the Klan as a rural, village, and small-town phenomenon. This is true less in a statistical than in a psychological sense. The Klan was reborn in Atlanta. It enjoyed great strength in the booming cities of the Southwest: Shreveport, Dallas, Tulsa, Little Rock (but not cosmopolitan New Orleans). The Milwaukee unit was the first and largest in the state of Wisconsin, and Detroit was the center of the Klan's power in Michigan. It was strong in Indianapolis, Chicago,

Dayton, and Pittsburgh in the heartland of America, and on the eastern shore in Norfolk and on the West Coast in Portland. Cities as diverse as Denver, Tampa, and Philadelphia were spawning beds. It is therefore misleading to presume that city dwellers were protected by some invisible *cordon sanitaire* from the virus of the Invisible Empire. Yet it remains essentially correct to identify the Klan with the older agrarian angle of vision.

For one thing, the Klan *was* in fact a force in the villages and small towns dotting the land. For another, there had migrated to the cities farmers and villagers who, regardless of how they might be located for census purposes, retained their rural mentality. They were America's own uprooted, as lost and dislocated as the European immigrant. Stripped of their identity by the externalization, impersonalization, and depersonalization of urban industrial life, they sought desperately to define themselves by clinging to the values of their fathers and perhaps of their own childhood. The Klan had held the hope that men might preserve their ancient, agrarian values even as they now lived in an urban environment. Indeed, it was imperative that these values be imposed on the cities. Thus when Klansmen spoke of redeeming the country, in reality they meant saving the great cities of the nation, for rural and village America had not yet been lost. It was in the cities, dominated by alien hordes and ruled by politicians subservient to their wishes, that there flourished gangsterism, alcoholism, skepticism, radicalism, sexualism — in brief, the paganism that threatened to break forth from the metropolitan centers and engulf the entire land. The very enormity of the challenge heightened the Klansman's anxiety and dictated the extremism of his response.

Just as Klansmen were in the twentieth century but dreamed they were not of it, so they hoped their country somehow could be in the world but not of it. The Klan clearly drew from the wellsprings of nineteenth-century American exceptionalism and isolationism. Equally discernible is its marriage with the mood of disenchantment and bitterness that followed the Great Crusade. It is unnecessary to explicate this point at length. The Klan opposed American membership in the World Court and, at least after 1920, in the League of Nations. It did not favor the reduction of war debts or disarmament, and it loathed pacifism. (However, the Klan did not agitate for intervention in Mexico, a foreign adventure associated with the Catholic hierarchy.) It was the old story of American innocence and European wickedness. Klansmen would have concurred in Ben Hecht's sentiment, if not in his imagery, in comparing Wilson at Versailles among the crafty Old World diplomats to "a long-faced virgin trapped in a bawdy house and calling in violent tones for a glass of lemonade." Once again it must be remarked that the spirit of the Klan fused intimately with the general temper of the 1920's. In its ethnocentrism, provincialism, and inability to accept the facts of twentieth-century life, the Klan mirrored perfectly the notion of Fortress America, a nation whose strength was the strength of ten because its heart was pure. And America's purity could be preserved only in isolation. Alas, the Klan's Manichaean view of the international scene was as murky as its vision of an America divided between the children of light and the children of darkness.

Men who see things in this fashion, who make simplistic judgments and draw sharp distinctions between right and wrong, good and evil, who think in terms of stereotypes and moralisms, tend to be prejudiced. They also tend to be anti-intellectual. Ambiguity, irony, paradox, relativism, contingency, skepticism, suspended judgment, speculation, open-mindedness — these are the attributes of the intellectual's glory (and perhaps the source of his misery). The average Klansman was neither blessed nor cursed by them; the intellectual as Klansman was atypical. Indeed, we are of the conviction that while the Klan appealed to an entire host of Americans, poor and prosperous, disinherited and establishment-secure, southerner and Yankee, farmer, villager, and urbanite, scarcely a single intellectual claimed citizenship in the Invisible Empire. Thus the Klan both perpetuated the pervasive anti-intellectualism in American history and illuminated the growing estrangement in the 1920's between artists and scholars and the commonalty. Hiram Wesley Evans put it pointedly and poignantly:

> We are a movement of the plain people, very weak in the matter of culture, intellectual support, and trained leadership. We are demanding, and we expect to win, a return of power into the hands of the everday, not highly cultured, not overly intellectualized, but unspoiled and not de-Americanized, average citizen of the old stock. Our members and leaders are all of this class — the opposition of the intellectuals and liberals who hold the leadership and from whom we expect to wrest control, is almost automatic.
>
> This is undoubtedly a weakness. It lays us open to the charge of being "hicks" and "rubes" and "drivers of second-hand Fords." We admit it. Far worse, it makes it hard for us to state our case and advocate our crusade in the most effective way, for most of us lack skill in language. . . .
>
> Every popular movement has suffered from just this handicap. . . .
>
> The Klan does not believe that the fact that it is emotional and instinctive, rather than coldly intellectual, is a weakness. All action comes from emotion, rather than from ratiocination. Our emotions and the instincts on which they are based have been bred into us for thousands of years; far longer than reason has had a place in the human brain. . . . They are the foundations of our American civilization, even more than our great historic documents; they can be trusted where the fine-haired reasoning of the denatured intellectuals cannot.

Thus spoke the spirit of fundamentalism with its repression through anti-evolution laws and heresy trials and textbook censorship of all in modern science and scholarship threatening to a faith made truly blind by ignorance. Thus spoke the spirit of fascism with its appeal to primitive instincts and tribal symbols. Thus spoke mediocre men maddened by the epithet's "yahoo," "boob," and "Babbitt" flung at them by all the sneering Menckens of the "Smart Set." Thus spoke Klansmen in an age when not only were ancient truths questioned, the very existence of Truth itself was coming to be doubted. . . .

Inevitably the Klan entered politics, and invariably it became a divisive and sinister force. At no time did it sponsor or support a third-party movement, but this fact heightened rather than diminished its malevolent influence. A Klan leader justified this political concern: "Everybody knows that politicians nowadays cater to all kinds of 'elements' mostly selfish, some corrupt, and some definitely anti-American. They cater to the German vote, the Catholic vote, the Jewish vote, the Italian vote, the boot-leg vote, the vice vote, and sometimes even to the violently criminal vote. What the Klan intends to do is to make them pay some attention to the American vote, the Protestant Christian vote, and the decent, God-fearing, law-abiding vote." Candidates were expected to certify their adherence to the Klan's definition of "Americanism" and their sympathy for the Invisible Order — or suffer the consequences. Neither unadvisedly nor lightly could politicians afford (as one of them lamented) to "withstand an incalculable impact, of indefinite forces, from an invisible source, and at an unexpected time."

The Klan became a terrible element in state and local politics from North Carolina to California and from Indiana to Texas. It elected governors in Georgia and

Oregon; a United States senator in Texas; congressmen in several states. In Arkansas it was so politically powerful that it held its own primaries. In Oklahoma it impeaced the hostile governor after a struggle reflecting little credit on either side. In Indiana under Stephenson the Klan was the state. In communities throughout the South, Southwest, Midwest, and Pacific Coast whole municipal establishments, literally from mayor to dogcatcher, were Klansmen or subservient to the order. And the Klan's role in the presidential nominations and elections of 1924 and 1928 suggest that the Invisible Empire came perilously close to achieving the status coveted for it by Imperial Wizard Evans, that of a "great militant political organization."

The cast of Klan leaders seems incredible; that is, until we remember that the scenario was shot in the 1920's. The star of the production, albeit a dim and flickering one, was Colonel William Joseph Simmons, whose fevered imagination called the Klan "from its slumber of half a century to take up a new task." Big and hollow, pious and prissy yet profane, genteely attired in rump-sprung britches and diamond stick pin, laden with lodge badges and heavy gold watch chain, breathing a hopefully deceptive mixture of cloves and bourbon, fond of poker and the ladies (his wife was an invalid), this amiable fraud, this "engaging old reprobate," was as "full of sentiment as a plum is full of juice." What made "Doc" Simmons run? He pursued the same light as Jay Gatsby and Sammy Glick (though he would not have approved of the company) as preacher, drummer of ladies' garters, and professional lodge man (he claimed membership in twelve or fifteen fraternal orders). With his Klan, "The World's Greatest Secret, Social, Patriotic, Fraternal, Beneficiary Order," with its membership, raiment, and life-insurance fees, he whiffed at last the sweet smell of success. Oleaginous, mellifluous, lazy yet lovable, vacuous yet sly, he disarmed the American people as he did investigating congressmen with platitude, piety, and pomposity. "Are we the only people that use a mask?" he asked of his inquisitors. "If so, what about Mardi Gras celebrations in this country, and what about Hallowe'en celebrations? . . . Our mask and robe, I say before God, are as innocent as the breath of an angel." Not even Warren G. Harding could have improved on that. And is it unsporting to inquire what sort of man the sovereign citizens of the United States elected to their highest office in 1920, the precise year of Simmons' ascending star?

Simmons' star ascended in 1920 (until that year his Invisible Empire after a struggling half-decade remained almost literally invisible) because he had the wit to tap the wits of two professional promoters, Edward Young Clarke and Mrs. Elizabeth Tyler. Eyeing the main chance, these inelegant hucksters transformed Simmons' easygoing southern fraternity of patriotic whites into a violently aggressive national organization of chauvinistic native-born white Protestants. It is a compliment to their promotional abilities to say Klan membership skyrocketed under their shrewd guidance. It is a commentary on the Klan to say that in 1919 the dubious duo had been arrested, while drunk and undraped, and fined for disorderly conduct; that Clarke deserted his wife before being deserted by the divorced Mrs. Tyler; that in 1923 Clarke was arrested for transporting whisky, and in 1924 he pleaded guilty to violating the White Slave Act. Perhaps in their way Ed Clarke and Mrs. Tyler were as at home in the Jazz Age as the organization they promoted.

In November, 1922, Simmons (and soon Clarke) was pressured out of power in a palace revolution led by a Dallas dentist, Hiram Wesley Evans. Plumpish, moonfaced, spectacled, benign, platitudinous, Evans called himself the "most average man in America." Evans testifies to the banality of evil, to the sinister consequences of a blind sincerity, to the unhappy fact that sobriety and chastity are not incompatible with bigotry and fanaticism. Like another American in the 1920's, Calvin Coolidge, Evans was a "Puritan in Babylon." The country would not have missed the leadership of either "average" man. As for the gross, tough, amoral David C. Stephenson, it is sufficient to observe that had he exchanged roles with Al Capone, neither Chicago nor Indiana would have been the loser — or the winner.

By late 1924 the KKK claimed a membership of four million, perhaps even five million, though most certainly not eight million as one authority estimates. "They just threw the doors open," complained a once dedicated Knight, "and every man that had the money, they took him in just to get his vote. . . . " It was really not a very exclusive fraternity. One needed only to be white, Protestant, and native-born — and willing to part with $10.

The Klan attracted good men, sincerely anxious about the future of "their" country, seemingly imperiled by Negroes, Catholics, aliens, and radicals. It was a godsend to the frustrated and insecure, unconsciously seeking scapegoats for their sense of failure. Weak men joined because their wills were unequal to the community pressures to conform. The Klan carried enormous appeal to lonely men who would join any fraternal order to erase the monotony of daily existence. Political opportunists saw the Klan as the highroad to power. To hucksters, the society spelled "Ku Klux Kash."

For it's order and trumpet and anger and drum
And power and glory command you to come;
The graves shall fly open and let you all in,
And the earth shall be emptied of mortal sin.

(W. H. Auden, "Danse Macabre")

Yet the membership melted away like chilled aspic on a warm summer afternoon. Immigration no longer seemed a threat after the restriction act of 1924. The task was now one of Americanization through education rather than the immediate intimidation and repression of a once ceaseless flow of new aliens. A Negro rebellion had not materialized, and by the late 1920's the black man was again his docile self. Although the U.S.S.R. failed to wither away, the feeble and feckless condition of both labor unions and socialist parties by the middle of the decade suggested that the fires of radicalism in the United States had now been banked. The general prosperity and the coolness (not to say placidity) of the Coolidge era drained reform ardor. Many Klansmen, like many prohibitionists and, for that matter, progressives, said farewell to reform. Ardor gave way to apathy. Or, perhaps, to a feeling of resignation.

Decent citizens drew back in horror as the evidence of the order's indecency mounted. How could the good people of Indiana, for instance, continue to believe in the moral authority of the Klan after Grand Dragon Stephenson's imprisonment? In fact, everywhere Klan leadership proved either weak or obscene. Internal wrangling was endemic. Unlike fascist movements in Europe, the KKK threw up no charismatic Mussolini or Hitler.

Official American Protestantism with increasing firmness rejected the Klan's representation of itself as a great, militant supradenominational agency. The world of journalism was almost uniformly hostile. Anti-Klan riots, anti-mask bills, and counterboycotts intimidated the timid membership. And prudent politicians increasingly learned that the Klan's blessing was a kiss of death. (After all, native-born white Protestants were themselves in many communities a minority group, as the politician recognized when he arranged to have a cross burned in front of *his* home.) Moreover, when the Klan proved unable to dominate either major party, its failure to found a third party became fatal. But, then, how could the order survive politically when it championed not a single *concrete* economic or social reform. Its appeal was essentially negative, and if it played a part (minor, we think) in the defeat of Smith in 1928, more crucial is its failure to prevent his easy nomination in the first instance. The fact of religious pluralism in America, confirmed in the life of John F. Kennedy, was foreshadowed in the career of Al Smith.

To be sure, most Klansmen remained loyal to their exclusive and prideful definition of Americanism, and they continued to cherish their dreams of an older and purer America. But they lost hope in the Klan as the agency of redemption. They were largely unmoved by rational persuasion or moralistic preaching that they had been wrong, and their drift from the Klan represented a rejection of the order itself, but not necessarily of its ideals.

Ultimately, however, the Knights unmasked and dismounted because an even larger number of Americans recalled and honored Abraham Lincoln's indictment of the Know-Nothing party:

> How could I be [a member]? How can any one who abhors the oppression of Negroes, be in favor of degrading classes of white people? Our progress in degeneracy appears to me to be pretty rapid. As a nation we began by declaring that *'all men are created equal.'* We now practically read it 'all men are created equal, *except Negroes.'* When the Know Nothings get control, it will read, 'all men are created equal except Negroes, *and foreigners, and Catholics.'* When it comes to this I should prefer emigrating to some country where they make no pretence of loving liberty — to Russia, for instance. . . .

The Popular Mind in the New Era

The 1920s ushered in the age of modern America. The impact of industrialism had, to be sure, been powerfully felt in the preceding decades, but only now was there a general acceptance of the new economic order, and only now did Americans fully perceive the way of life that accompanied mature industrialism. The 1920s saw an end to the Progressive resistance to giant economic organization, and the beginning of a mass-consumption society. In the world of the automobile, of the radio and the movie, of the home appliance, installment buying and suburbia, there was no room for the kind of overt fears manifested in populism and progressivism. But if the American had, on the surface, come to terms with modernism, he had not really made peace with himself.

How is the cultural historian to probe the popular mind? Normally, the task is strewn with difficulties. Sometimes, not very often, a single event throws a shaft of light. This, in essence, is what John W. Ward discovers in his penetrating analysis of Charles Lindbergh's solo flight from New York to Paris in 1927. Dramatic as was Lindbergh's exploit, in itself the flight could not account for the massive response it evoked in the American people. What Lindbergh had done, Ward suggests, was to touch basic chords in the popular imagination. The aviator symbolized, at once, the rugged individualism of the frontier past, and the triumph of the machine in America's present and future. By celebrating Lindbergh, the country celebrated the values of yesterday and tomorrow and, at least for the fleeting moment, persuaded itself that it could sustain both.

FOR FURTHER READING:

ALLEN, FREDERICK LEWIS. *Only Yesterday.* New York: Harper & Row, Publishers, 1931.
CARTER, PAUL. *The Twenties in America.* New York: Thomas Y. Crowell Company, 1968.*
LYND, ROBERT and HELEN. *Middletown.* New York: Harcourt, Brace & World, 1929.

Asterisk denotes paperback edition.

The Meaning of Lindbergh's Flight

JOHN W. WARD

On Friday, May 20, 1927, at 7:52 A.M., Charles A. Lindbergh took off in a silver-winged monoplane and flew from the United States to France. With this flight Lindbergh became the first man to fly alone across the Atlantic Ocean. The log of flight 33 of "The Spirit of St. Louis" reads: "Roosevelt Field, Long Island, New York, to Le Bourget Aerodrome, Paris, France. 33 hrs. 30 min." Thus was the fact

---

Source: John W. Ward, "The Meaning of Lindbergh's Flight," *American Quarterly,* vol. 10 (1958), pp. 3–16.

of Lindbergh's achievement easily put down. But the meaning of Lindbergh's flight lay hidden in the next sentence of the log: "(Fuselage fabric badly torn by souvenir hunters.)"

When Lindbergh landed at Le Bourget he is supposed to have said, "Well, we've done it." A contemporary writer asked "Did what?" Lindbergh "had no idea of what he had done. He thought he had simply flown from New York to Paris. What he had really done was something far greater. He had fired the imagination of mankind." From the moment of Lindbergh's flight people recognized that something more was involved than the mere fact of the physical leap from New York to Paris. "Lindbergh," wrote John Erskine, "served as a metaphor." But what the metaphor stood for was not easy to say. The *New York Times* remarked then that "there has been no complete and satisfactory explanation of the enthusiasm and acclaim for Captain Lindbergh." Looking back on the celebration of Lindbergh, one can see now that the American people were trying to understand Lindbergh's flight, to grasp its meaning, and through it, perhaps, to grasp the meaning of their own experience. Was the flight the achievement of a heroic, solitary, unaided individual? Or did the flight represent the triumph of the machine, the success of an industrially organized society? These questions were central to the meaning of Lindbergh's flight. They were also central to the lives of the people who made Lindbergh their hero.

The flight demanded attention in its own right, of course, quite apart from whatever significance it might have. Lindbergh's story had all the makings of a great drama. Since 1919 there had been a standing prize of $25,000 to be awarded to the first aviator who could cross the Atlantic in either direction between the United States and France in a heavier-than-air craft. In the spring of 1927 there promised to be what the *New York Times* called "the most spectacular race ever held — 3,600 miles over the open sea to Paris." The scene was dominated by veteran pilots. On the European side were the French aces, Nungesser and Coli; on the American side, Commander Richard E. Byrd, in a big tri-motored Fokker monoplane, led a group of contestants. Besides Byrd, who had already flown over the North Pole, there were Commander Davis, flying a ship named in honor of the American Legion which had put up $100,000 to finance his attempt, Clarence Chamberlin, who had already set a world's endurance record of more than fifty-one hours in the air in a Bellanca tri-motored plane, and Captain René Fonck, the French war ace, who had come to America to fly a Sikorsky aircraft. The hero was unheard of and unknown. He was on the West Coast supervising the construction of a single-engine plane to cost only ten thousand dollars.

Then fate played its part. It seemed impossible that Lindbergh could get his plane built and east to New York in time to challenge his better equipped and more famous rivals. But in quick succession a series of disasters cleared his path. On April 16, Commander Byrd's "America" crashed on its test flight, crushing the leg of Floyd Bennett who was one of the crew and injuring Byrd's hand and wrist. On April 24, Clarence Chamberlin cracked up in his Bellanca, not seriously, but enough to delay his plans. Then on April 26, Commander Davis and his co-pilot lost their lives as the "American Legion" crashed on its final test flight. In ten days, accidents had stopped all of Lindbergh's American rivals. Nungesser and Coli, however, took off in their romantically named ship, the "White Bird," from Le Bourget on May 8. The world waited and Lindbergh, still on the West Coast, decided to try to fly the Pacific. But Nungesser and Coli were never seen again. As rumors filled the newspapers, as reports came in that the "White Bird" was seen over Newfoundland, over Boston, over the Atlantic, it soon became apparent that Nungesser and Coli had failed, dropping to their deaths in some unknown grave. Disaster had touched every ship entered in the trans-Atlantic race.

Now, with the stage cleared, Lindbergh entered. He swooped across the continent in two great strides, landing only at St. Louis. The first leg of his flight established a new distance record but all eyes were on the Atlantic and the feat received little notice. Curiously, the first time Lindbergh appeared in the headlines of the New York papers was Friday, the thirteenth. By this time Byrd and Chamberlin were ready once again but the weather had closed in and kept all planes on the ground. Then, after a week of fretful waiting, on the night of May 19, on the way into New York to see "Rio Rita," Lindbergh received a report that the weather was breaking over the ocean. He hurried back to Roosevelt Field to haul his plane out onto a wet, dripping runway. After mechanics painfully loaded the plane's gas by hand, the wind shifted, as fate played its last trick. A muddy runway and an adverse wind. Whatever the elements, whatever the fates, the decisive act is the hero's, and Lindbergh made his choice. Providing a chorus to the action, the *Herald Tribune* reported that Lindbergh lifted the overloaded plane into the sky "by his indomitable will alone."

The parabola of the action was as clean as the arc of Lindbergh's flight. The drama should have ended with the landing of "The Spirit of St. Louis" at Le Bourget. That is where Lindbergh wanted it to end. In *"WE,"* written immediately after the flight, and in *The Spirit of St. Louis,* written twenty-six years later, Lindbergh chose to end his accounts there. But the flight turned out to be only the first act in the part Lindbergh was to play.

Lindbergh was so innocent of his future that on his flight he carried letters of introduction. The hysterical response, first of the French and then of his own countrymen, had been no part of his careful plans. In *"WE,"* after Lindbergh's narrative of the flight, the publisher wrote: "When Lindbergh came to tell the story of his welcome at Paris, London, Brussels, Washington, New York, and St. Louis he found himself up against a tougher problem than flying the Atlantic." So another writer completed the account in the third person. He suggested that "the reason Lindbergh's story is different is that when his plane came to a halt on Le Bourget field that black night in Paris, Lindbergh the man kept on going. The phenomenon of Lindbergh took its start with his flight across the ocean; but in its entirety it was almost as distinct from that flight as though he had never flown at all."

Lindbergh's private life ended with his flight to Paris. The drama was no longer his, it was the public's. "The outburst of unanimous acclaim was at once personal and symbolic," said the *American Review of Reviews.* From the moment of success there were two Lindberghs, the private Lindbergh and the public Lindbergh. The latter was the construction of the imagination of Lindbergh's time, fastened on to an unwilling person. The tragedy of Lindbergh's career is that he could never accept the role assigned him. He always believed he might keep his two lives separate. But from the moment he landed at Le Bourget, Lindbergh became, as the *New Republic* noted, *"ours. . . .* He is no longer permitted to be himself. He is US personified. He is the United States." Ambassador Herrick introduced Lindbergh to the French, saying, "This young man from out of the West brings you better than anything else the spirit of America," and wired to President Coolidge, "Had we searched all America we could not have found a better type than young Lindbergh to represent the spirit and high purpose of our people." This was Lindbergh's fate, to be a type. A writer in the *North American Review* felt that Lindbergh represented "the dominant American character," he "images the best" about the United States. And an ecstatic female in the *American Magazine,* who began by saying that Lindbergh "is a sort of symbol. . . . He is the dream that is in our hearts," concluded that the American public responded so wildly to Lindbergh because of "the thrill of possessing, in him, our dream of what *we* really and truly want to be." The act of possession was so complete that articles since have attempted to discover the "real" Lindbergh, that enigmatic and taciturn figure behind the public mask. But it is no less difficult to discern the features of the public Lindbergh, that symbolic figure who presented to the imagination of his time all the yearnings and buried desires of its dream for itself.

Lindbergh's flight came at the end of a decade marked by social and political corruption and by a sense of moral loss. The heady idealism of the First World War had been succeeded by a deep cynicism as to the war's real purpose. The naïve belief that virtue could be legislated was violated by the vast discrepancy between the law and the social habits of prohibition. A philosophy of relativism had become the uneasy rationale of a nation which had formerly believed in moral absolutes. The newspapers agreed that Lindbergh's chief worth was his spiritual and moral value. His story was held to be "in striking contrast with the sordid unhallowed themes that have for months steeped the imaginations and thinking of the people." Or, as another had it, "there is good reason why people should hail Lindbergh and give him honor. He stands out in a grubby world as an inspiration."

Lindbergh gave the American people a glimpse of what they liked to think themselves to be at a time when they feared they had deserted their own vision of themselves. The grubbiness of the twenties had a good deal to do with the shining quality of Lindbergh's success, especially when one remembers that Lindbergh's flight was not as unexampled as our national memory would have it. The Atlantic was not unconquered when Lindbergh flew. A British dirigible had twice crossed the Atlantic before 1919 and on May 8 of that year three naval seaplanes left Rockaway, New York, and one, the NC-4 manned by a crew of five, got through to Plymouth, England. A month later, Captain John Alcock, an Englishman, with Arthur W. Browne, an American, flew the first heavier-than-air land plane across the Atlantic nonstop, from Newfoundland to Ireland, to win twice the money Lindbergh did, a prize of $50,000 offered by the London *Daily Mail.* Alcock's and Browne's misfortune was to land in a soft and somnolent Irish peat bog instead of before the cheering thousands of London or Paris. Or perhaps they should have flown in 1927.

The wild medley of public acclaim and the homeric strivings of editors make one realize that the response to Lindbergh involved a mass ritual in which America celebrated itself more than it celebrated Lindbergh. Lindbergh's flight was the occasion of a public act of regeneration in which the nation momentarily rededicated itself to something, the loss of which was keenly felt. It was said again and again that "Lindy" taught America "to lift its eyes up to Heaven." Heywood Broun, in his column in the *New York World,* wrote that this "tall young man raised up and let us see the potentialities of the human spirit." Broun felt that the flight proved that, though "we are small and fragile," it "isn't true that there is no health in us." Lindbergh's flight provided the moment, but the meaning of the flight is to be found in the deep and pervasive need for renewal which the flight brought to the surface of public feeling. When Lindbergh appeared at the nation's capital, the *Washington Post* observed, "He was given that frenzied acclaim which comes from the depths of the people." In New York, where 4,000,000 people saw him, a reporter wrote that the dense and vociferous crowds were swept, as Lindbergh passed, "with an emotion tense and inflammable." The *Literary Digest* suggested that the answer to the hero-worship of Lindbergh would "throw an interesting light on the psychology of our times and of the American people."

The *Nation* noted about Lindbergh that "there was something lyric as well as heroic about the apparition of this young Lochinvar who suddenly came out of the West and who flew all unarmed and all alone. It is the kind of stuff which the ancient Greeks would have worked into a myth and the medieval Scots into a border ballad. . . . But what we have in the case of Lindbergh is an actual, an heroic and an exhaustively exposed experience which exists by suggestion in the form of poetry." The *Nation* quickly qualified its statement by observing that reporters were as far as possible from being poets and concluded that the discrepancy between the fact and the celebration of it was not poetry, perhaps, but "magic on a vast scale." Yet the *Nation* might have clung to its insight that the public meaning of Lindbergh's flight was somehow poetic. The vast publicity about Lindbergh corresponds in one vital particular with the poetic vision. Poetry, said William Butler Yeats, contains opposites; so did Lindbergh. Lindbergh did not mean one thing, he meant many things. The image of itself which America contemplated in the public person of Lindbergh was full of conflict; it was, in a word, dramatic.

To heighten the drama, Lindbergh did it alone. He was the "lone eagle" and a full exploration of that fact takes one deep into the emotional meaning of his success. Not only the *Nation* found Sir Walter Scott's lines on Lochinvar appropriate: "he rode all unarmed and he rode all alone." Newspapers and magazines were deluged with amateur poems that vindicated one rhymester's wry comment, "Go conquer the perils / That lurk in the skies — / And you'll get bum poems / Right up to your eyes." The *New York Times*, that alone received more than two hundred poems, observed in trying to summarize the poetic deluge that "the fact that he flew alone made the strongest impression." Another favorite tribute was Kipling's "The Winners," with its refrain, "He travels the fastest who travels alone." The others who had conquered the Atlantic and those like Byrd and Chamberlin who were trying at the same time were not traveling alone and they hardly rode unarmed. Other than Lindbergh, all the contestants in the trans-Atlantic race had unlimited backing, access to the best planes, and all were working in teams, carrying at least one co-pilot to share the long burden of flying the plane. So a writer in the New York *Sun*, in a poem called "The Flying Fool," a nickname that Lindbergh despised, celebrated Lindbergh's flight: ". . . no kingly plane for him; / No endless data, comrades, moneyed chums; / No boards, no councils, no directors grim — / He plans ALONE . . . and takes luck as it comes."

Upon second thought, it must seem strange that the long-distance flight of an airplane, the achievement of a highly advanced and organized technology, should be the occasion for hymns of praise to the solitary unaided man. Yet the National Geographic Society, when it presented a medal to Lindbergh, wrote on the presentation scroll, "Courage, when it goes alone, has ever caught men's imaginations," and compared Lindbergh to Robinson Crusoe and the trailmakers in our own West. But Lindbergh and Robinson Crusoe, the one in his helmet and fur-lined flying coat and the other in his wild goatskins, do not easily co-exist. Even if Robinson Crusoe did have a tidy capital investment in the form of a well-stocked shipwreck, he still did not have a ten thousand dollar machine under him.

Lindbergh, in nearly every remark about his flight and in his own writings about it, resisted the tendency to exploit the flight as the achievement of an individual. He never said "I," he always said "We." The plane was not to go unrecognized. Nevertheless, there persisted a tendency to seize upon the flight as a way of celebrating the self-sufficient individual, so that among many others an Ohio newspaper could describe Lindbergh as this "self-contained, self-reliant, courageous young man [who] ranks among the great pioneers of history." The strategy here was a common one, to make Lindbergh a "pioneer" and thus to link him with a long and vital tradition of individualism in the American experience. Colonel Theodore Roosevelt, himself the son of a famous exponent of self-reliance, said to reporters at his home in Oyster Bay that "Captain Lindbergh personifies the daring of youth. Daniel Boone, David Crocket [sic], and men of that type played a lone hand and made America. Lindbergh is their lineal descendant." In *Outlook* magazine, immediately below an enthusiastic endorsement of Lindbergh's own remarks on the importance of his machine and his scientific instruments, there was the statement, "Charles Lindbergh is the heir of all that we like to think is best in America. He is of the stuff out of which have been made the pioneers that opened up the wilderness, first on the Atlantic coast, and then in our great West. His are the qualities which we, as a people, must nourish." It is in this mood that one suspects it was important that Lindbergh came out of the West and rode all alone.

Another common metaphor in the attempt to place Lindbergh's exploit was to say that he had opened a new "frontier." To speak of the air as a "frontier" was to invoke an interpretation of the meaning of American history which had sources deep in American experience, but the frontier of the airplane is hardly the frontier of the trailmakers of the old West. Rather than an escape into the self-sufficient simplicity of the American past, the machine which made Lindbergh's flight possible represented an advance into a complex industrial present. The difficulty lay in using an instance of modern life to celebrate the virtues of the past, to use an extreme development of an urban industrial society to insist upon the significance of the frontier in American life.

A little more than a month after Lindbergh's flight, Joseph K. Hart in *Survey* magazine reached back to Walt Whitman's poem for the title of an article on Lindbergh: "O Pioneer." A school had made Lindbergh an honorary alumnus but Hart protested there was little available evidence "that he was educated in *schools.*" "We must look elsewhere for our explanation," Hart wrote and he looked to the experience of Lindbergh's youth when "everything that he ever did . . . he did by himself. He lived more to himself than most boys." And, of course, Lindbergh lived to himself in the only place conceivably possible, in the world of nature, on a Minnesota farm. "There he developed in the companionship of woods and fields, animals and machines, his audaciously natural and simple personality." The word, "machines," jars as it intrudes into Hart's idyllic pastoral landscape and betrays Hart's difficulty in relating the setting of nature upon which he wishes to insist with the fact that its product spent his whole life tinkering with machines, from motorcycles to airplanes. But except for that one word, Hart proceeds in uncritical nostalgia to show that "a lone trip across the Atlantic was not impossible for a boy who had grown up in the solitude of the woods and waters." If Lindbergh was "clear-headed, naif, untrained in the ways of cities," it was because he had "that 'natural simplicity' which Fenimore Cooper used to attribute to the pioneer hero of his Leatherstocking Tales." Hart rejected the notion that any student "bent to all the conformities" of formal training could have done what Lindbergh did. "Must we not admit," he asked, "that this pioneering urge remained to this audacious youth because he had never submitted completely to the repressions of the world and its jealous institutions?"

Only those who insist on reason will find it strange that Hart should use the industrial achievement of the airplane to reject the urban, institutionalized world of industrialism. Hart was dealing with something other than reason; he was dealing with the emotion evoked by Lindbergh's solitude. He recognized that people wished to call Lindbergh a "genius" because that "would release him from the ordinary rules of existence." That way, "we could rejoice with him in his triumph, and then go back to the contracted routines of our institutional ways [because] ninety-nine percent of us must be content to be shaped and moulded by the routine ways and forms of the world to the routine tasks of life." It is in the word, "must," that the pathos of this interpretation of the phenomenon of Lindbergh lies. The world had changed from the open society of the pioneer to the close-knit, interdependent world of a modern machine-oriented civilization. The institutions of a highly corporate industrial society existed as a constant reproach to a people who liked to believe that the meaning of its experience was embodied in the formless, independent life of the frontier. Like Thomas Jefferson, who identified American virtue with nature and saw the city as a "great sore" on the public body, Hart concluded that "certainly, in the response that the world — especially the world of great cities — has made to the performance of this Midwestern boy, we can read of the homesickness of the human soul, immured in city canyons and routine tasks, for the freer world of youth, for the open spaces of the pioneer, for the joy of battling with nature and clean storms once more on the frontiers of the earth."

The social actuality which made the adulation of Lindbergh possible had its own irony for the notion that America's strength lay in its simple uncomplicated beginnings. For the public response to Lindbergh to have reached the proportions it did, the world had by necessity to be the intricately developed world of modern mass communications. But more than irony was involved. Ultimately, the emotion attached to Lindbergh's flight involved no less than a whole theory about American history. By singling out the fact that Lindbergh rode alone, and by naming him a pioneer of the frontier, the public projected its sense that the source of America's strength lay somewhere in the past and that Lindbergh somehow meant that America must look backward in time to rediscover some lost virtue. The mood was nostalgic and American history was read as a decline, a decline measured in terms of America's advance into an urban, institutionalized way of life which made solitary achievement increasingly beyond the reach of ninety-nine percent of the people. Because Lindbergh's ancestors were Norse, it was easy to call him a "Viking" and extend the emotion far into the past when all frontiers were open. He became the "Columbus" of another new world to conquer as well as the "Lochinvar" who all rode alone. But there was always the brute, irreducible fact that Lindbergh's exploit was a victory of the machine over the barriers of nature. If the only response to Lindbergh had been a retreat to the past, we would be involved with a mass cultural neurosis, the inability of America to accept reality, the reality of the world in which it lived. But there was another aspect, one in which the public celebrated the machine and the highly organized society of which it was a product. The response to

Lindbergh reveals that the American people were deeply torn between conflicting interpretations of their own experience. By calling Lindbergh a pioneer, the people could read into American history the necessity of turning back to the frontier past. Yet the people could also read American history in terms of progress into the industrial future. They could do this by emphasizing the machine which was involved in Lindbergh's flight.

Lindbergh came back from Europe in an American man-of-war, the cruiser *Memphis*. It seems he had contemplated flying on, around the whole world perhaps, but less adventurous heads prevailed and dictated a surer mode of travel for so valuable a piece of public property. The *New Republic* protested against bringing America's hero of romance home in a warship. If he had returned on a great liner, that would have been one thing. "One's first trip on an oceanliner is a great adventure — the novelty of it, the many people of all kinds and conditions, floating for a week in a tiny compact world of their own." But to return on the *Memphis*, "to be put on a gray battleship with a collection of people all of the same stripe, in a kind of ship that has as much relation to the life of the sea as a Ford factory has! We might as well have put him in a pneumatic tube and shot him across the Atlantic." The interesting thing about the *New Republic*'s protest against the unromantic, regimented life of a battleship is that the image it found appropriate was the Ford assembly line. It was this reaction against the discipline of a mechanized society that probably led to the nostalgic image of Lindbergh as a remnant of a past when romance was possible for the individual, when life held novelty and society was variegated rather than uniform. But what the Ford Assembly Line represents, a society committed to the path of full mechanization, was what lay behind Lindbergh's romantic success. A long piece in the Sunday *New York Times,* "Lindbergh Symbolizes the Genius of America," reminded its readers of the too obvious fact that "without an airplane he could not have flown at all." Lindbergh "is, indeed, the Icarus of the twentieth century; not himself an inventor of his own wings, but a son of that omnipotent Daedalus whose ingenuity has created the modern world." The point was that modern America was the creation of modern industry. Lindbergh "reveres his 'ship' as a noble expression of mechanical wisdom. . . . Yet in this reverence . . . Lindbergh is not an exception. What he means by the Spirit of St. Louis is really the spirit of America. The mechanical genius, which is discerned in Henry Ford as well as in Charles A. Lindbergh, is in the very atmosphere of [the] country." In contrast to a sentiment that feared the enforced discipline of the machine there existed an attitude of reverence for its power.

Lindbergh led the way in the celebration of the machine, not only implicitly by including his plane when he said "we," but by direct statement. In Paris he told newspapermen, "You fellows have not said enough about that wonderful motor." Rarely have two more taciturn figures confronted one another than when Lindbergh returned to Washington and Calvin Coolidge pinned the Distinguished Flying Cross on him, but in his brief remarks Coolidge found room to express his particular delight that Lindbergh should have given equal credit to the airplane. "For we are proud," said the President, "that in every particular this silent partner represented American genius and industry. I am told that more than 100 separate companies furnished materials, parts or service in its construction."

The flight was not the heroic lone success of a single daring individual, but the climax of the co-operative effort of an elaborately interlocked technology. The day after Coolidge's speech, Lindbergh said at another ceremony in Washington that the honor should "not go to the pilot alone but to American science and genius which had given years of study to the advancement of aeronautics." "Some things," he said, "should be taken into due consideration in connection with our flight that have not heretofore been given due weight. That is just what made this flight possible. It was not the act of a single pilot. It was the culmination of twenty years of aeronautical research and the assembling together of all that was practicable and best in American aviation." The flight, concluded Lindbergh, "represented American industry."

The worship of the machine which was embodied in the public's response to Lindbergh exalted those very aspects which were denigrated in the celebration of the flight as the work of a heroic individual. Organization and careful method were what lay behind the flight, not individual self-sufficiency and daring romance. One magazine hailed the flight as a "triumph of mechanical engineering." "It is not to be forgotten that this era is the work not so much of brave aviators as of engineers, who have through patient and protracted effort been steadily improving the construction of airplanes." The lesson to be learned from Lindbergh's flight, thought a writer in the *Independent*, "is that the splendid human and material aspects of America need to be organized for the ordinary, matter of fact service of society." The machine meant organization, the careful rationalization of activity of a Ford assembly line, it meant planning, and, if it meant the loss of spontaneous individual action, it meant the material betterment of society. Lindbergh meant not a retreat to the free life of the frontier past but an emergence into the time when "the machine began to take first place in the public mind — the machine and the organization that made its operation possible on a large scale." A poet on this side of the matter wrote, "All day I felt the pull / Of the steel miracle." The machine was not a devilish engine which would enthrall mankind, it was the instrument which would lead to a new paradise. But the direction of history implicit in the machine was toward the future, not the past; the meaning of history was progress, not decline, and America should not lose faith in the future betterment of society. An address by a Harvard professor, picked up by the *Magazine of Business,* made all this explicit. "We commonly take Social Progress for granted," said Edwin F. Gay, "but the doctrine of Social Progress is one of the great revolutionary ideas which have powerfully affected our modern world." There was a danger, however, that the idea "may be in danger of becoming a commonplace or a butt of criticism." The speaker recognized why this might be. America was "worn and disillusioned after the Great War." Logically, contentment should have gone with so optimistic a creed, yet the American people were losing faith. So Lindbergh filled an emotional need even where a need should have been lacking. "He has come like a shining vision to revive the hope of mankind." The high ideals of faith in progress "had almost come to seem like hollow words to us — but now here he is, emblematic of heroes yet to inhabit this world. Our belief in Social Progress is justified symbolically in him."

It is a long flight from New York to Paris; it is a still longer flight from the fact of Lindbergh's achievement to the burden imposed upon it by the imagination of his time. But it is in that further flight that lies the full meaning of Lindbergh. His role was finally a double one. His flight provided an opportunity for the people to project their own emotions into his act and their emotions involved finally two attitudes toward the meaning of their own experience. One view had it that America represented a brief escape from the course of history, an emergence into a new and open world with the self-sufficient individual at its center. The other said that America represented a stage in historical evolution and that its fulfillment lay in the development of society. For one, the meaning of America lay in the past; for the other in the future. For one, the American ideal was an escape from institutions, from the forms of society, and from limitations put upon the free individual; for the other, the American ideal was the elaboration of the complex institutions which made modern society possible, an acceptance of the discipline of the machine, and the achievement of the individual within a context of which he was only a part. The two views were contradictory but both were possible and both were present in the public's reaction to Lindbergh's flight.

The Sunday newspapers announced that Lindbergh had reached Paris, and in the very issue whose front pages were covered with Lindbergh's story the magazine section of the *New York Times* featured an article by the British philosopher, Bertrand Russell. The magazine had, of course, been made up too far in advance to take advantage of the news about Lindbergh. Yet, in a prophetic way, Russell's article was about Lindbergh. Russell hailed the rise to power of the United States because he felt that in the "new life that is America's" in the twentieth century "the new outlook appropriate to machinery [would] become more completely dominant than in the old world." Russell sensed that some might be unwilling to accept the machine, but "whether we like this new outlook or not," he wrote, "is of little importance." Why one might not was obvious. A society built on the machine, said Russell, meant "the diminution in the value and independence of the individual. Great enterprises tend more and more to be collective, and in an industrialized world the interference of the community with the individual must be more intense." Russell realized that while the co-operative effort involved in machine technology makes man collectively more lordly, it makes the individual more submissive. "I do not see how it is to be avoided," he concluded.

People are not philosophers. They did not see how the conflict between a machine society and the free individual was to be avoided either. But neither were they ready to accept the philosopher's statement of the problem. In Lindbergh, the people celebrated both the self-sufficient individual and the machine. Americans still celebrate both. We cherish the individualism of the American creed at the same time that we worship the machine which increasingly enforces collectivized behavior. Whether we can have both, the freedom of the individual and the power of an organized society, is a question that still haunts our minds. To resolve the conflict that is present in America's celebration of Lindbergh in 1927 is still the task of America.

Political Revolution, 1920–1936

Between 1920, when Warren G. Harding carried all but ten southern states, and 1936, when Franklin D. Roosevelt lost only Maine and Vermont, American politics underwent a revolution. The long-term dominance of the Republican party gave way to a Democratic majority. At first, political analysts attributed the Democratic successes to Roosevelt's skill and to the popularity of the New Deal. They did not perceive that a permanent shift had taken place in voting patterns. This was the thesis that Samuel Lubell, an astute political writer specializing in survey analysis, advanced in his seminal work *The Future of American Politics*. Lubell reversed the normal sequence of political analysis: not political personality or platform, but demographic change was the decisive factor. A major population change, Lubell argued, had preceded each shift in party dominance in the nation's history.

In the case of the Democratic resurgence, the key demographic fact was that, by 1930, the cities contained a majority of the nation's population. Two migrations had fueled the urban explosion: the 13 million European immigrants arriving between 1900 and 1914, whose children would become urban voters after 1920, and the rural whites and blacks who moved cityward in massive numbers during and after World War I. That the Democrats should have captured this new vote was by no means foreordained, since neither party had any special claim as an urban party, and it is still not entirely clear why the new voters did not divide rather evenly between them. All we can safely say is that the Democrats proved more responsive to the opportunity.

Actually the Democratic success with the new urban voters *preceded* the New Deal. Hidden by the overall Republican ascendancy during the 1920s, this shift took place during that decade, as Lubell demonstrates by comparing the urban vote of 1920 and 1928. The New Deal consolidated this transfer and brought in the other elements of the urban vote — the native American workingman and the Negro — which had not been attracted by the Democratic cultural politics of the 1920s and, indeed, had been hostile to the immigrants to whom those politics appealed.

Since Lubell published *The Future of American Politics* almost twenty years ago, his thesis has been closely scrutinized and tested by other scholars. On the whole, his pioneering findings have stood the test of time. Equally important, his emphasis on demographic factors has helped liberate American political history from the narrow focus on personalities, campaigns, and platforms.

FOR FURTHER READING:

BURNER, DAVID. *The Politics of Provincialism.* New York: Alfred A. Knopf, 1968.*
HANDLIN, OSCAR. *Al Smith and His America.* Boston: Little, Brown & Company, Atlantic Monthly Press, 1958.*
HUTHMACHER, JOSEPH. *Massachusetts People and Politics.* New York: Atheneum Publishers, 1969.*

Asterisk denotes paperback edition.

From *The Future of American Politics*

SAMUEL LUBELL

A Little Matter of Birth Rates

In the winter of 1910 Congress received the longest report ever submitted by a government investigating body up to that time. From early 1907 a special commission had been studying almost every imaginable aspect of immigration, filling forty-two fat volumes with its findings. Buried in that statistical mountain was at least one table of figures which was to prove peculiarly prophetic for our own times.

This table showed that a majority of the children in the schools of thirty-seven of our leading cities had foreign-born fathers. In cities like Chelsea, Fall River, New Bedford, Duluth, New York and Chicago more than *two out of every three* school children were the sons and daughters of immigrants.

Viewed in today's perspective, it is clear that those figures forecast a major political upheaval some time between 1930 and 1940. By then all of these children, plus baby brothers and sisters not enrolled in school, would have grown to voting age. Massed as they were in the states commanding the largest electoral vote, their sheer numbers would topple any prevailing political balance.

No matter what else had happened, the growing up of these children of the 13,000,000 immigrants who poured into the country between 1900 and 1914 was bound to exert a leveling pull on American society. As it was, the depression — striking when most of them had barely entered the adult world — sharpened all their memories of childhood handicaps. When Roosevelt first took office, no segment of the population was more ready for "a new deal" than the submerged, inarticulate urban masses. They became the chief carriers of the Roosevelt Revolution.

The really revolutionary surge behind the New Deal lay in this coupling of the depression with the rise of a new generation, which had been malnourished on the congestion of our cities and the abuses of industrialism. Roosevelt did not start this revolt of the city. What he did do was to awaken the climbing urban masses to a consciousness of the power in their numbers. He extended to them the warming hand of recognition, through patronage and protective legislation. In the New Deal he supplied the leveling philosophy required by their sheer numbers and by the hungers stimulated by advertising. In turn, the big-city masses furnished the votes which re-elected Roosevelt again and again — and, in the process, ended the traditional Republican majority in this country.

Today this same big-city generation still stands like a human wall between the Republicans and their past dominance. It is this generation — now grown to parenthood and in many cases to home-owning, but still bound by common underdog attitudes — which the Republicans must crack to win the Presidency.

Twice before in American history a majority party has been transformed into a minority party. Each time the change was prefaced by a dramatic reshuffling of population. Jacksonian democracy tramped in to the echoes of the oxcarts which had rolled westward in the twenty years before. In 1800 only one of twenty Ameri-

Source: Samuel Lubell, *The Future of American Politics* (New York: Harper & Row, Publishers, 1952), chap. 3, "Revolt of the City," pp. 28–50.

cans lived west of the Appalachians; when Jackson was inaugurated the transmountain country claimed one of every three Americans.

Similarly, the formation of the Republican party was preceded by a tremendous westward expansion into the Great Lakes and Midwest regions. Between 1840 and 1860 the nation's population almost doubled, swelling another 60 per cent by 1880. If it is true that the pre-Civil War parties were overwhelmed by their inability to dam back the passions stirred by the slavery controversy, it is also true that they were unable to channel the flood of new voters.

There were two population currents which cleared the way for the New Deal:

Between 1910 and 1930 for the first time a majority of the American people came to live in cities. The second population shift might be described as the triumph of the birth rates of the poor and underprivileged over those of the rich and well born.

Searching for families of five or more, the U.S. Immigration Commission's investigators found two-and-a-half times as many among unskilled laborers as among businessmen. In Minneapolis, for example, the second generation of English stock — the backbone of Republican strength — celebrated a blessed event on the average of one every five years. Among the foreign born a new baby arrived every three years.

As late as 1925 wives of miners and laborers were still having twice as many children as the wives of bankers.

Nor was it the birth rates of the immigrants alone which were threatening the Republican majority. The other prolific baby patches were in the farming areas, particularly in the Appalachian hills and in the South. When World War One shut off the flow of European immigrants, it was into these areas of high human fertility and low living standards that industry sent its recruiting agents searching for cheap labor. Whites and Negroes were sucked north into the cities, especially after 1920 when immigration was curtailed sharply.

Between 1920 and 1930 more than 6,500,000 persons were drawn off the farms and hills; 4,500,000 came into New York, Chicago, Detroit and Los Angeles alone. They hit the cities at roughly the same time that the children of the immigrants were growing up and bestirring themselves. The human potential for a revolutionary political change had thus been brought together in our larger cities when the economic skies caved in.

Through the entire Roosevelt era the Republicans labored on the wrong side of the birth rate. Nor was there anything they could do about it, since the birth rates frustrating them were those of 1910 to 1920. During the last years of Republican victory, from 1920 through 1928, roughly 17,000,000 potential new voters passed the age of twenty-one. From 1936 through 1944, the number ran over 21,000,000, most of them coming from poorer, Democratically inclined families.

Whatever inroads into Roosevelt's popularity the Republicans made was offset largely by these new voters. In 1936, for example, nearly 6,000,000 more ballots were cast than in 1932. While the Republicans gained just under 1,000,000, Roosevelt's vote swelled by almost 5,000,000.

Except for the Polish-Americans and Italo-Americans, the wave of new voters among the immigrant groups passed its crest by 1945. Not until the 1970s will the record number of births of recent years register politically. Until then the nation's basal political metabolism is likely to remain more sluggish than during the Roosevelt years. The issues of realignment will have to be fought out primarily among existing population elements, whose instinctive voting attitudes are already largely formed.

This prospect, of no abrupt change in the make-up of the electorate, re-emphasizes the decisive importance of the big-city generation, which came of age through the Roosevelt years. Without their overwhelming urban pluralities the Democrats would not have won in either 1940, 1944 or 1948. The 1948 election was so close because Truman's vote in the twelve largest cities fell more than 1,000,000 below Roosevelt's.

Not only does this generation hold the balance of political power in the nation. It also constitutes a radically new political force in American history. The old Republican dominance was rooted in the Civil War and the transcontinental expansion which followed. Most of the immigrants who peopled our larger cities came to these shores long after the Civil War, even after the exhaustion of free lands in the West. To their children and grandchildren the loyalties of Appomattox and the Homestead Act were details in history books rather than a family experience passed down from grandfather to grandson.

Never having known anything but city life, this new generation was bound to develop a different attitude toward the role of government from that of Americans born on farms or in small towns. To Herbert Hoover the phrase "rugged individualism" evoked nostalgic memories of a rural self-sufficiency in which a thrifty, toiling farmer had to look to the marketplace for only the last fifth of his needs. The Iowa homestead on which Hoover grew up produced all of its own vegetables, its own soap, its own bread. Fuel was cut and hauled from the woods ten miles away, where one could also gather walnuts free. "Sweetness" was obtained from sorghums. Every fall the cellar was filled with jars and barrels which, as Hoover observes in his memoirs, "was social security in itself."

To men and women who regulated their labors by the sun and rain, there was recognizable logic in talking of natural economic laws — although even among farmers the murmur for government intervention grew louder, as their operations became more commercialized and less self-sufficient.

In the city, though, the issue has always been man against man. What bowed the backs of the factory worker prematurely were not hardships inflicted by Mother Nature but by human nature. He was completely dependent on a money wage. Without a job, there were no vegetables for his family, no bread, no rent, no fuel, no soap, no "sweetness." Crop failures, plagues of grasshoppers or searing drought could be put down as acts of God. Getting fired or having one's wages cut were only too plainly acts of the Boss.

A philosophy that called for "leaving things alone" to work themselves out seemed either unreal or hypocritical in the cities, where nearly every condition of living groaned for reform. The wage earner had to look to the government to make sure that the milk bought for his baby was not watered or tubercular; he had to look to government to regulate the construction of tenements so all sunlight was not blocked out. If only God could make a tree, only the government could make a park.

Neither the Republicans nor the New Dealers seem to have appreciated how sharp a wrench from the continuity of the past was involved in the rise of this big-city generation. G.O.P. leaders persisted in regarding Roosevelt's popularity as a form of hero worship, abetted by the radio. Only Roosevelt's personal magnetism and political skill were holding together the varied Democratic elements, reasoned the Republicans. With "that voice" quieted, the coalition would fall apart. The nation would then return to safe and sane Republicanism. What this reasoning overlooked was that the Roosevelt generation had no tradition of Republicanism to go back to. For them the weight of tradition was such that if they were undecided about rival Presidential candidates, they instinctively would give the Democrats preference.

The basic weakness of the Republican party stems from this fact, that it remains rooted in an earlier historical era in which it was dominant. The resilient Democratic strength springs from being so alive — clumsily perhaps, but definitely alive — to the problems with which the newer generation has grown up.

Between the Republican and Democratic appeals, as we shall see, the issue is less one of conservatism versus liberalism than one of timeliness.

The Forgotten Warrior

At the height of Roosevelt's popularity, Republicans used to lament over the youthfulness of so many of the nation's voters. Since they had come of age since 1928, the complaint ran, the only Presidents they knew were Roosevelt and Hoover, who was hopelessly linked with the depression. Still, it would be a mistake to regard the Roosevelt coalition as strictly a product of the depression.

The startling fact — generally overlooked — is that through the booming twenties Republican pluralities in the large industrial centers were dropping steadily. Even when the stock market tickers were clicking most gratifyingly the forces of urban revolt were gathering momentum.

Consider the waning Republican strength revealed in the table below which totals the vote in our twelve largest cities (New York, Chicago, Philadelphia, Pittsburgh, Detroit, Cleveland, Baltimore, St. Louis, Boston, Milwaukee, San Francisco and Los Angeles). In 1920 the Republicans had 1,638,000 more votes than the Democrats in these twelve cities. This net Republican plurality dropped in 1924 and was turned into a Democratic plurality by 1928.

Year	Net Party Plurality
1920	1,638,000 Republican
1924	1,252,000 Republican
1928	38,000 Democratic
1932	1,910,000 Democratic
1936	3,608,000 Democratic
1940	2,210,000 Democratic
1944	2,296,000 Democratic
1948	1,443,000 Democratic

Two things stand out from those figures. First, it was not the depression which made Roosevelt the champion of the urban masses but what he did after he came to the Presidency. Between 1932 and 1936 the Democratic plurality in these cities leaped 80 per cent, the biggest change in any single election. Second, the Republican hold on the cities was broken not by Roosevelt but by Alfred E. Smith. Before the Roosevelt Revolution there was an Al Smith Revolution.

In many ways, Smith's defeat in 1928, rather than Roosevelt's 1932 victory, marked off the arena in which today's politics are being fought. The Happy Warrior and four-time governor of New York first hacked out the rural-city cleavage which generates so much of the force behind the present struggle between Congress and the President. It was Smith who first slashed through the traditional alignments that had held so firmly since the Civil War, clearing the way for the more comprehensive realignment which came later.

Smith split not only the Solid South but the Republican North as well. While Hoover was carrying more than 200 Southern counties which had never gone Republican before, Smith was swinging 122 Northern counties out of the G.O.P. column.

Seventy-seven of these counties are predominantly Catholic. But more than religious sympathy inspired their support of Smith. This is shown clearly by the way these counties have voted since. Fifty-seven have remained staunchly Democratic in every Presidential election from 1928 through 1948. Included are some of our heaviest voting areas — New York, Boston, Providence, St. Louis, San Francisco, Cleveland, Milwaukee and St. Paul, also Butte, Montana, and Burlington, Vermont.

Of the sixty-two Smith counties whose allegiance has wavered, most are German-American in background and therefore broke against Roosevelt in 1940 because of the war. In 1948 Truman gained over Roosevelt in fifty of these counties, with eighteen returning to the Democratic party.

Smith may be today's "Forgotten Warrior" but the line he drew across the map of American politics has never been erased.

How profound a social upheaval stirred beneath the Smith vote can be seen most clearly in the industrial East, where one finds the heaviest concentration of counties which have been Democratic since 1928. Before Smith, no other part of the country was more religiously Republican. None had a heavier proportion of foreign born. Nor were these two factors unrelated.

During the twenty years of heaviest immigration, from 1890 to 1910, coal production tripled and steel output multiplied seven times. It was in the cities with the most immigrants that Bryan's free silver crusade was beaten. To a considerable extent, in short, both the expansion of industry and Republican political dominance rested on the immigrant.

The conditions under which these immigrants worked and lived hardly requires description here. Coming to this country after the free lands were gone, they were thrust into the sectors of the economy with the sorest tensions, into the sweatiest jobs, where wages were not much above subsistence level and where labor unions were feeble. The foreign born made up 60 per cent of the workers in the packing-house plants described by Upton Sinclair's *The Jungle;* 57 per cent of those in iron and steel, 61 per cent of our miners, nearly 70 per cent of those toiling in textiles or clothing.

Probably of greater long-run political significance than their low wages was the segregation in which they lived. In one-industry coal and steel towns the separation of laborers and managers was as complete as that between serfs and lord on a feudal manor. In the larger cities, even where Gold Coast and slum were hardly a block apart, they still constituted two separate worlds. Roosevelt has often been accused of ranging class against class, as if class antagonism did not exist before the New Deal. Yet, certainly since the turn of the century our urban social structure had been a class structure.

For a long time, though, the resentment of the "other half" against those on top merely smoldered submissively. Even had the immigrants been inclined to political activity, they would have found it difficult. In 1910 one of every five among the foreign born spoke no English. Until 1920 the twelve-hour working day, still the rule in iron and steel, left little leisure time. As late as 1933, when the N.R.A. codes were being considered, Secretary of Labor Frances Perkins had to go out into the mill towns to drum up interest among the steelworkers. At Homestead a Catholic priest arranged a meeting with some Polish-American workers, all of whom came scrupulously scrubbed. They spoke no English and the meeting had to be conducted through an interpreter. Mrs. Perkins was visibly touched when several workers rose and spoke and it developed they were asking God to bless the President, much as peasants in Russia might have blessed the czar.

The rise in the educational level is a revealing index to the quickening political pulse of the urban masses. At the turn of the century only one of every fifteen youngsters was going beyond the elementary school. By 1930 every second child of high school age was in high school.

At first, this rising generation found little real identification with either of the major parties. In exchange for a favor or a two-dollar bill the newly naturalized voter would vote the way the political machine instructed. But he was as likely to follow the dictates of a Republican boss in Philadelphia as of Tammany Hall in New York. None of the Republican Presidents stirred that most vital of all political assets: vicarious identification. It was not a matter of postwar disillusionment. Far from feeling like a lost generation, the children of the immigrants were intensely idealistic. But with whom could they identify this idealism? Harding was a dirty story. Calvin Coolidge might be untouched by scandal, but the same Puritanical, small-town qualities which endeared him to Main Street made "Silent Cal" a chilling, pedagogic figure to city kids.

On the Democratic side, Woodrow Wilson had captured the imagination of some of these underdog elements through favorable labor legislation, through his dream of peace and by championing the cause of Europe's minorities. Even today, in appealing to Czechs and Poles, Democratic politicians find it effective to invoke Wilson's memory. But this enthusiasm did not carry over to either James M. Cox, an Ohio publisher, or John W. Davis, a Wall Street lawyer. As for William Jennings Bryan, his revivalist oratory might inflame the Bible belt — but in the city he was a repellent, even comic figure. When the "Great Commoner" rose before the 1924 Democratic Convention in New York to oppose denouncing the Ku Klux Klan by name, contending "We can exterminate Ku Kluxism better by recognizing their honesty and teaching them that they are wrong," he was hissed and booed by the galleries.

By 1924, "the enemy's country," as Bryan called the East, had flung up its own Great Commoner in Al Smith. Prohibition and the Klan were the immediate weapons in the duel Smith and Bryan fought; but behind each antagonist were ranged the habits and prejudices, hopes and frustrations, prides and hatreds of two different cultures and two historical eras.

The very eccentricities and mannerisms of the two men were symbolic. The brown derby and rasping East Side accent, which stamped Smith as "one of our boys" to the sidewalk masses, sent shivers down the spine of Protestant respectability. In turn, the traits which made Bryan seem like the voice of pious morality to his Prohibitionist, rural, Protestant following — the liberal use of Biblical phrases, the resonant Chautauqua tones, the heaven-stomping energy — made him sound like the voice of bigotry to the urban masses.

Both men were mouthpieces of protest — Bryan of the overmortgaged Bible belt, Smith of the underpaid melting pot. Whether either was understood in the other's country is doubtful. Could the factory worker really share the despair of the farmer watching a sheriff tack a foreclosure notice on the barn door? Could the farmer feel the vicarious terror of the factory masses reading of a shirtwaist fire in which 145 women were trapped and burned alive?

The year of this Triangle fire, 1911, was the year Smith first went to Albany. It marked the beginning of his fight to improve factory conditions, reduce the hours of labor for women and for other social legislation. After his relations with Roosevelt had curdled, Smith came to denounce the New Deal's "socialism." But during the 1920's he was the means by which the Democratic party absorbed the agitations — and votes — of the Socialists and their sympathizers.

What Smith really embodied was the revolt of the underdog, urban immigrant against the top dog of "old American" stock. His Catholicism was an essential element in that revolt. The so-called "old" immigration which settled the farms was drawn largely from Protestant countries, England, Norway, Sweden and Germany. The "new" immigration after 1885 which crowded the teeming cities, came mainly from Italy, Poland, Russia, Greece and the disintegrating Hapsburg Empire. The larger part of these new immigrants were Catholic. They also included perhaps 1,500,000 Jews.

Because they came to this country late, these immigrants and their children were concentrated in the lower economic rungs. Moreover, they resented what seemed to them efforts to force conformity to an Anglo-Saxon, Protestant culture, through Sunday Blue Laws, prohibition and the Klan.

Throughout the industrialized East, the make-up of society was such that Protestantism coincided largely with the Republican party, with millowners and financiers, with the snobbish members of exclusive clubs — in short, with the upper class. Catholicism, in turn, coincided largely with discrimination and sweated labor, with immigrant minorities who were looked down upon as inferior beings — in short, the lower class.

In his campaign Smith did not draw the line of class conflict. His campaign manager, John S. Raskob, was a millionaire. So were other ardent supporters like Pierre Du Pont, Herbert Lehman and William F. Kenny, who was reputed to have made $30,000,000 as a contractor. Still, the class and cultural cleavage was there, like a deep fault, in the granite of our national life. Smith's candidacy unavoidably split the rock along that fault.

The viciousness of the 1928 campaign is usually laid to religious prejudice. In view of developments since, one wonders whether it did not also reflect the violence of the realignment which Smith was precipitating. Generally, American elections blur social divisions. But in 1928, economic, racial, religious and cultural differences all sharpened the cleavage.

Before Smith the Democrats were little more of an urban party than were the Republicans. In Pennsylvania, for example, the three counties the Democrats won in

1920 and 1924 were largely rural and native born. These counties swung for Hoover in 1928. In their place, the Democrats captured three mining and industrial counties — Elk, Luzerne and Lackawanna — which had not gone Democratic since at least 1896. In Pennsylvania, Smith pushed the Democratic vote above the million mark for the first time. Throughout New England, whole voting elements such as the French-Canadians and Italo-Americans were swung out of the Republican party never to return.

Smith also made women's suffrage a reality for the urban poor. In better income families, women started voting in 1920 as soon as they were granted the privilege; but among the urban masses the tradition that a woman's place was in the home still held strong until 1928. That year in Massachusetts (which Smith carried along with Rhode Island) the outpouring of women lifted the number of voters by 40 per cent over 1924. The turnout in Boston was 44 per cent heavier.

Although the issues of 1928 have long passed off, the cleavage which Smith's candidacy laid bare still persists. If New England remains the most Republican of the major regions, it is also where the line between unwaveringly Republican and unwaveringly Democratic voters is most rigidly drawn. Between 1932 and 1944, New England's Democratic vote did not shift by more than 2 per cent in any election, while other parts of the country were fluctuating by 5 and 10 percent.

There are Catholic Republicans, of course, as there are Yankee Democrats, but, in the main, the bedrock cleavage in the East remains a Catholic-Protestant one. The divergence in cultures shows up in all sorts of ways. One county carried by Smith in 1928 and which has remained Democratic since is Hillsborough in New Hampshire, which was the site of the "mercy killing" trial of Dr. Herman Sanders. When Sanders went on trial, prayers for his acquittal were voiced in the Congregational Church. When he was freed, the Catholic hospitals barred him from practicing there.

But if Smith lifted the Democratic vote to new heights in some cities, he lost such Democratic strongholds as Oklahoma City, Atlanta, Birmingham, Dallas, Houston. In virtually all the Southern cities, Smith's vote fell off, as well as in cities with heavy Scandinavian populations, reflecting Lutheran distrust of Catholicism; he also lost ground wherever the population was mainly native born or Ku Klux in sympathy.

To sum up, by 1928 the masses in the cities with the most foreign born were already in political revolt. But that part of the urban population which was drawn from native American stock had still to be roused.

The Year of Decision

Bowls of red roses graced the speakers' table while American flags and tricolored bunting draped the walls of the banquet hall. The occasion was the first annual dinner of the Muncie, Indiana, Chamber of Commerce since the depression. Its immediate inspiration had been the news that General Motors, which had stripped its local plant three years before, was moving back. Mindful that the company was returning to escape a strike in Toledo, the Mayor assured the banqueters that "the citizens of Muncie are in no mood for outsiders to come in and agitate."

Returning to the city that June week in 1935 to begin their study of "Middletown in Transition," Robert and Helen Lynd were struck by the eagerness with which Muncie's community leaders were hailing the return of the "good old days."

But if Muncie's businessmen were ready to forget the depression as "just a bad bump in the road," that was not the feeling across the railroad tracks "in the other world of wage earners." Predominantly native born, drawn mainly from near-by farms, Muncie's "cornfeds," as the local workers were called, had seen no point in labor unions before the depression. Out of a working force of 13,000, hardly 700 had carried union cards, fewer than joined the Klan. Al Smith won a lone precinct in the city, losing one of the two precincts which went Democratic in 1924. With every fourth Muncie worker jobless in 1932, Roosevelt carried thirteen precincts, but still lost the city.

As in so many other communities, the N.R.A. brought a rush among Muncie's workers to join labor unions. At the Ball glass factory and the automotive plants — Muncie's two strongest antiunion citadels — the American Federation of Labor was petitioned to send in organizers. But the A.F. of L. was fumbling and inept, while the business community was militantly efficient. The local police force was secretly increased. Persons distributing handbills advertising a union meeting were picked up. One local newspaper front-paged a photograph of a picket in Oregon being dragged through the streets under the caption, THIS PICKET HAD REAL "DRAG" WITH COPS.

By the time the 1936 Presidential campaign opened, the drive to unionize Muncie had been broken. But the workers still had the ballot. To the Lynds the 1936 campaign "witnessed perhaps the strongest effort in the city's history by the local big businessmen (industrialists and bankers) to stampede local opinion in behalf of a single Presidential candidate." When the ballots were in, Muncie had gone for a Democratic President for the first time since the Civil War. Exulted one worker to the Lynds, "We certainly licked the big bosses."

Muncie was not the only Republican citadel which resisted Roosevelt in 1932 but fell in 1936. Twenty-three other countries, which the Republicans held in 1932, swung four years later and — like Muncie — have stayed Democratic. Among these was "Bloody" Harlan in southeast Kentucky, where efforts to organize the miners in the 1930's exploded in assassinations and pitched battles; also the cities of Philadelphia and Wilmington, the home of the Du Ponts. To defeat Roosevelt, various members of the Du Pont clan contributed more than $500,000 to the Republicans, in addition to their donations to the American Liberty League. The net effect seems only to have advertised more sharply who was on whose side.

So overwhelming was Roosevelt's 1936 victory, that its political decisiveness is often overlooked. With only Maine and Vermont remaining Republican, Roosevelt's re-election seemed primarily a vote of gratitude for lifting the country out of a desperate economic crisis. Certainly many people favored him for that reason. But 1936 was also the year of realignment in which the Democrats became the nation's normal majority party. The traditional dominance which the Republicans had enjoyed since the Civil War was washed away and a new era in American politics began.

The depression vote of 1932 still mirrored the orbit of conflict of the old Republican order. The G.O.P. cleavage had been mainly a struggle between the "progressives" of the Midwest and Far West against the industrial East. Roosevelt's first campaign was directed primarily toward splitting off this "progressive" vote. His best showing came in the Western and Mountain states. All six states he lost — Pennsylvania, Delaware, Connecticut, Vermont, New Hampshire and Maine — were in the East.

The shift in the basis of Roosevelt's appeal "from acreage to population," to use

Raymond Moley's phrase, occurred in 1935. Moley credits the change to Huey Long's "Share Our Wealth" agitation and to Roosevelt's ire over the Supreme Court's declaring the N.R.A. unconstitutional. To steal Long's thunder, Roosevelt proposed a "soak the rich" tax bill, which, Moley feels, marked the beginning of the conservative-liberal split inside the Democratic party. Whatever the exact turning point, 1935 saw more social legislation enacted than in any other year in the nation's history — the "wealth tax," the Wagner Labor Relations Act, the Social Security Law, the creation of WPA, the Public Utilities Holding law, the start of the Rural Electrification Administration.

Not only in Washington but throughout the country 1935 was the year of decision. To go back to the old order or to move forward to something different? That was the question posed for decision in 1935, in countless different ways, in every phase of life.

In the early New Deal days how things were done had been less important than getting the stalled economy going again. By 1935 recovery had progressed to the point where there no longer was any question that the country would be saved. The new issue was: Would the "good old days" of unchallenged business dominance be restored? Or was America to be reshaped?

The more articulate business groups had one answer. As in Muncie, they were ready to resume their annual Chamber of Commerce dinners as if there never had been a depression. But the same processes of recovery which restored the courage of businessmen also enabled the leaders of organized labor to recover their nerve. Early in 1933 John L. Lewis, Phil Murray and Tom Kennedy lamented to Roosevelt that the United Mine Workers had barely enough members to pay the union's expenses. "Go home and have a good night's sleep," Roosevelt consoled them. "If I don't do anything else in my administration I am going to give the miners an opportunity to organize in the United Mine Workers of America."

Taking Roosevelt at his word, Lewis nearly emptied the UMW treasury to hire organizers, sending them out to tell the miners, "The President wants you to join a union." By 1934 Lewis could stand before the A.F. of L. convention and boast that the UMW was again a fighting force of 400,000 miners. By 1935 he was ready to demand that the A.F. of L. embrace the principle of industrial unionism or let a new labor movement organize the mass production industries.

The hard right to the jaw which Lewis swung at Bill Hutcheson in Atlantic City that October was symbolic of the fact that at least one group of labor leaders were determined not to go back to the old order.

When the first sit-down strike broke in November 1935, it came — significantly — not among workers of immigrant origin, but among the rubber workers of Akron. That city had drawn so many hillbillies from near-by states that it was often jokingly called "the capital of West Virginia." Before taking their place in the picket line, some rubber workers knelt in prayer. After the last "Amen," they picked up their baseball bats and lead pipes and moved into formation around the factories.

This fervor for unions which swept the native American workers — some observers likened it to a religious revival — was of crucial political importance. Al Smith, as we have seen, stirred a new sense of political consciousness among workers of immigrant and Catholic origin. But the native workers off the farms and hills had always held suspiciously aloof from those of immigrant stock.

The hillbillies had their own sense of group solidarity. Flint, Michigan, had its "Little Missouri" and "Little Arkansas" residential settlements. In Akron, the West

Virginia State Society had 25,000 members and put on an annual West Virginia day picnic. Marked off from the older inhabitants by their accents, manners and dress, the "snake-eaters" were the butt of ridicule and jokes, which were fiercely resented. A judge in Akron suspended sentence on one man on condition that he return to West Virginia. A newspaper reporter wrote up the incident, "Judge Sentences Man to West Virginia for Life." At the next election the hapless judge was badly beaten by the votes of outraged mountaineers.

The formation of the CIO marked the fusing of the interests of the immigrant and native-stock workers. That, I believe, is perhaps the most telling accomplishment of the CIO. Its political importance can hardly be exaggerated. The mass production industries had been the ones in which racial and religious antagonisms among the workers were most divisive. Carnegie-Illinois, for example, had sprinkled clusters of different nationalities in each of its mines, reasoning correctly that a Balkanized working force would be more difficult to unionize. In some industries immigrants and Negroes had first been introduced as strikebreakers or because they would work for lower wages than native-born workers. The failure of the Knights of Labor in the 1880's was largely a failure to unite the immigrant working groups. Much of the A.F. of L.'s reluctance to embark on a real organizing drive in the mass production industries reflected the dislike of the "aristocrats of labor" in the skilled crafts for the immigrant "rubbish."

By 1935, of course, the immigrants had made considerable progress toward Americanization. But the key to the change was the rise of a common class consciousness among all workers. The depression, in making all workers more aware of their economic interests, suppressed their racial and religious antagonisms. Put crudely, the hatred of bankers among the native American workers had become greater than their hatred of the Pope or even of the Negro.

This struggle between the old nativist prejudices and the newer class consciousness still remains one of the crucial behind the scenes battles in the mass production unions. Class feeling or racial-religious feeling? The future of American labor rests largely on which holds the ascendancy.

This rise in class consciousness among native-American workers was a nationwide development. In Muncie the Lynds reported the first evidences of class feeling among the workers, stirred by the sense that the government could do something for them. In "Yankee City" (Newburyport, Mass.) W. Lloyd Warner tells of a similar change among the so-called "Riverbrookers," the proud, clannish, Yankee-stock workers who had always refused to join unions with immigrant workers. When the new shoe union staged the first successful strike in Yankee City's history, the Riverbrookers supplied the leadership.

Negroes were another voting element which was determined to go forward rather than back. In some cities as many as four out of five Negro families were on relief. "Don't Buy Where You Can't work" campaigns were being pressed to force white storeowners to hire Negroes. In Harlem the accumulated tensions of the depression years were exploded suddenly by a trivial incident.

On March 19, 1935, a sixteen-year-old boy snatched a ten-cent bread knife from a five-and-ten cent counter — "just for fun" he later told the police. Two white clerks and the white manager chased the boy to the rear of the store. When they grabbed him, he bit their hands and broke away.

The boy was a Puerto Rican, yet the rumor spread that a Negro had been lynched in the store. Pickets appeared. A soapbox orator on one street corner attracted a growing crowd. When a funeral hearse happened to drive by a woman shrieked, "They've come to take the boy's body!" The Negro mob went on a rampage. When the riot was over, one man was dead — three others died later of injuries — and a hundred or more whites and Negroes had been shot, stabbed or stoned.

The grisly tragedy was lightened only by the action of a Chinese laundryman. When he saw the mob surging through the streets, heaving stones into store windows, he hastily thrust a sign into his window, "Me colored too."

New York City had had four previous race riots, without anything much happening afterward. The 1935 riot, however, set off a series of far-reaching changes. Harlem's shopowners hastily put on Negro employees. Before the year was out Tammany Hall had named its first Negro district leader. Mayor Fiorello La Guardia had appointed the first Negro magistrate. In 1932 most Negro voters in the country were still Republican. In 1936, in many cities two of every three Negro voters were for Roosevelt.

And so it went all through the country. It would be impossible to trace in full all the different ways in which the question — whether to go back or forward — was being asked of the American people. Sometimes the query was put bluntly in so many words. More often it was implicit in the logic of events or in reminders of the depression. At the end of 1935, more than $780,000,000 was still tied up in closed banks, 3,000,000 persons were still on relief; one survey of a group of garment workers showed that half of them had not bought a new coat for four years.

Lifelong Socialists had to ask themselves — did they return to the ivory tower of a futile third party or did they defend their immediate interests by rallying behind Roosevelt? Sidney Hillman and David Dubinsky, whose unions had been saved by the N.R.A., formed a new American Labor party to enable New Yorkers to vote for Roosevelt and still remain independent of the Democrats. Norman Thomas polled 884,000 Socialist votes nationally in 1932 and only 187,000 votes four years later.

On the other side of the political barricades the realignment was equally sharp. In 1932 one fourth of the Democratic campaign funds was contributed by bankers. In 1936 bankers accounted for a mere 3 per cent of the Democratic party's war chest. (Their total contributions to the Democrats were only about a third of the $750,000 spent by organized labor.)

Particularly in rural areas, the 1936 vote showed that sizable numbers of voters were ready to return to the Republicanism of their ancestors. Winston County, which had seceded from Alabama during the Civil War to remain loyal to the union, swung back to the Republican party in 1936; so did thirty-two counties in Missouri, all but eight bone-dry by tradition. Less than a dozen wheat counties in the whole country had stayed Republican in 1932. Four years later, most of the wheat counties were on their way back to the Republican party.

In the industrial centers, however, the political allegiances that had grown out of the Civil War were uprooted for good. In New York, New Jersey and Pennsylvania, alone, the Democratic vote leaped by roughly 1,800,000. Despite the Depression, in 1932, Roosevelt failed to carry a dozen cities with 100,000 or more population — Philadelphia, Scranton and Reading in Pennsylvania; Canton, Youngstown and Columbus in Ohio; Gary, Duluth, Des Moines, Grand Rapids and Springfield, Massachusetts. Everyone swung for Roosevelt in 1936 and except for Grand Rapids have remained Democratic since.

A dramatic glimpse into the nature of this hidden political revolution will be found by comparing the 1928 and 1936 vote in our major cities. While Smith won six of every ten voters in some cities, in others he drew only three out of ten. This disparity had narrowed by 1932, but wide divergencies in voting still prevailed in different parts of the country. With the 1936 election, as the table below shows, the voting of nearly all our major cities hit a common level.

Whether the cities are heavily foreign born or native American in make-up, Catholic or Protestant, with large numbers of Negroes or of whites up from the South, did not make too much difference in their 1936 vote. Nor whether the city had a strong labor tradition like San Francisco or an open shop tradition like Los Angeles, nor whether it was located on the East or West coast or in the Midwest.

CITIES HIGH SMITH			CITIES LOW SMITH		
City	Dem. Percent 1928	Dem. Percent 1936	City	Dem. Percent 1928	Dem. Percent 1936
Lawrence	71	73	Flint	19	72
Boston	67	63	Wichita, Kan.	24	64
Lowell	64	61	Los Angeles	28	67
Fall River	64	67	Akron	31	71
New York	60	75	Des Moines	31	55
New Haven	57	65	San Diego	32	65
Milwaukee	53	76	Seattle	32	64
New Bedford	52	65	Duluth	32	71
Cleveland	52	76	Canton	34	66
St. Louis	51	66	Spokane	35	71
San Francisco	49	72	Detroit	37	65
Chicago	48	65	Indianapolis	39	57
Pittsburgh	47	67	Philadelphia	39	60
Baltimore	47	67	Youngstown	39	74

A new nationalizing force had clearly been injected into American politics. In the past American political realignments have always followed sectional lines. The Revolt of the City, however, had drawn the same class-conscious line of economic interest across the entire country, overriding not only regional distinctions but equally strong cultural differences.

This development was not without its irony. In drawing the line of cleavage between worker and "economic royalist," Roosevelt unquestionably sharpened the sense of class division in American society. Yet, in doing so, he subordinated the old nativistic prejudices of race and religion, which had divided the lower half of American society for so long, bringing these lower income elements a greater degree of social unity than they had ever shared before. Was Roosevelt dividing or unifying the country? That question is worth coming back to later after we have delved more deeply into the implications of the rise of the urban masses.

Labor's Struggle for Power

Of all the changes wrought by the Great Depression, none held greater importance for the future than the emergence of a strong labor movement. For that event spelled a major restructuring of the power relationships within the economy and, beyond that, within the larger society. By the end of the depression era, the American industrial worker, until then a helpless figure in a system of large-scale business organization, would be able, through collective action, to deal with his employer on relatively equal terms.

Three major developments conspired to bring about this labor revolution. For one thing, there was a profound change within American workers: the embittering experience of joblessness created a militancy that had been wholly absent during the prosperous 1920s. For another, the labor movement revamped itself to act more effectively in the mass-production sector: in 1935, John L. Lewis led a group of unions out of the craft-oriented American Federation of Labor and formed a rival federation — the Committee for Industrial Organization — that did a brilliant job of organizing the industrial workers. Finally, the federal government, hitherto committed to a hands-off policy, intervened decisively to regulate labor-management relations: ineffectively at first through Section 7a of the National Industrial Recovery Act (1933) and then successfully in the Wagner National Labor Relations Act (1935), the government protected labor's right to organize and engage in collective bargaining.

American employers did not let the union offensive go uncontested. With all the mighty resources at their command, General Motors, United States Steel, and the other industrial giants fought this unprecedented threat to their managerial prerogatives. From 1933 onward, industrial war raged in the country. The following article, published in *Fortune* in November 1937, assesses that war at the point when it had just about ended in labor's victory. Earlier in the year, General Motors had lost the historic Flint sit-down strike, and U.S. Steel had, to the nation's astonishment, surrendered without a fight. The war was not yet over. During mid-1937, Little Steel (the lesser companies whose antiunion animus exceeded that of the industry's giant, U.S. Steel) defeated the CIO in a bitter and prolonged strike which included the terrible Memorial Day Massacre in South Chicago. Still, if warfare persisted, the tide had turned clearly in labor's favor. That is, indeed, the perspective of the following essay. By the shrewd analysis of five key episodes, beginning with the disastrous textile strike of 1934 and ending with the bloody Little Steel strike of 1937, *Fortune* revealed to its business readers in a concrete way how rank-and-file militancy, effective union organization, and public support were carrying the day for labor in its struggle for power.

FOR FURTHER READING:

BERNSTEIN, IRVING. *Turbulent Years: A History of the American Worker.* Boston: Houghton Mifflin Company, 1969.
DULLES, FOSTER R. *Labor in America.* New York: Thomas Y. Crowell Company, 1960.*
SWARD, KEITH. *The Legend of Henry Ford.* New York: Atheneum Publishers, 1968.*

Asterisk denotes paperback edition.

The Industrial War   FORTUNE

To progressive sociologists it is axiomatic that the U.S., most advanced of the industrial nations, has had the least developed philosophy of labor. These people contend that until the present Administration took office, labor legislation in the U.S., despite innumerable laws and commissions, had resulted in little essential change in organized labor's standing. They especially emphasize such significant facts as that before the current U.S. union drive, no more than 18 per cent of U.S. nonagricultural labor was organized into trade unions, compared with over 35 per cent in Britain and more than 70 per cent in Sweden. And on the basis of these figures and various supplementary observations that we need not develop here, they hold that U.S. labor has lagged behind U.S. industry in the matter of self-fulfillment.

The U.S. businessman does not admit that his labor philosophy is backward. It is of course impossible to speak for *all* businessmen, and in attempting to speak for even a few one runs into insuperable difficulties in social terminology. . . . Here we can only say that in general, as the businessman sees it, this is a free country, with jobs open to all who can get them and the rights of private property inherent in every economic and political fiber. He has on the whole no "objection" to the organization of labor provided that this will not impede his free action as an owner (or representative of owners) of private property; provided he can hire and fire as he sees fit; provided his individual employees can work when they want to; provided, that is to say, that traditional labor relations are not materially changed. If an "advanced" labor philosophy presumes the existence of national labor unions that curtail this familiar freedom of action, then the average American businessman does not want an advanced philosophy. Confronted with the possibility, or the threat, he takes his position upon the sturdy democratic tradition bequeathed to him by his forefathers, thus placing all those who are opposed to him in the awkward predicament of seeming to oppose that tradition. So that they become what Al Smith calls Communists.

Now whether you believe that this philosophy is backward, or whether you believe that it is the best that any democracy has so far devised, depends roughly upon which side of the private-property line your lot is cast. And as between those two irreconcilable extremes it is not the province of this article to choose. We are not here concerned with theory but with fact: the fact, namely, that for the past four and a half years the U.S. has been in the throes of a major labor upheaval, which can fairly be described as one of the greatest mass movements in our history. If one bars the irrepressible conflict of the sixties, the only historical phenomenon comparable to the labor movement is the great trek westward, beginning in the Mississippi Valley and ending on the Pacific Coast. And if that classic American migration looms up to our generation as something far more permanent and vast it is well to remind ourselves that the labor movement likewise has a history. There has been labor unrest ever since there was a factory system, but the movement referred to here can properly be traced back to 1886–87, a period of open warfare characterized for the first time by a series of important strikes on the issue of the right to organize and bargain

---

Source: "The Industrial War," *Fortune*, November 1937, pp. 105–110, 156, 158, 160, 166, 168, 171, 172, 174, 176, 179.

collectively through nationwide unions. The claim to that right, now widely conceded in Britain and the European democracies but still resisted in the U.S., is the keystone of the American labor movement — is indeed what dignifies it as a movement rather than an intermittent and aimless war. Not that employers by and large are opposed to collective bargaining in principle. If they are involved in conflict, even as deeply involved as Mr. Girdler, it is with national unions as instruments for achieving it. The various local unions and independent unions that many employers prefer are in themselves — since the passage of the Wagner Act — an important aspect of the industrial war; but we are here concerned with labor's longer attempt to achieve collective bargaining through nationwide unions such as are organized into the A.F. of L. and the C.I.O.

The history of that struggle can be had from any textbook and need not detain us here. At present we are considering its most modern phase — a phase that, corresponding roughly with the Roosevelt Administration, is in itself a compound affair illustrating an exceedingly rapid change. In the early days of the NRA there was no C.I.O., there was no Wagner Act, there was no La Follette Committee, and no Mohawk Valley Formula, Big Steel had not yet "sold out" to labor, a sitdown strike had never been heard of in lay circles, and the American automobile was still for the most part innocent of unionized hands. Those things and those events were part of an evolution that was in its turn a part of the long labor movement above referred to. Not to understand this is to miss the point of every major event, every tactical decision, every judgment or error in judgment in the current labor world.

As a medical diagnosis can be reached only by a study of the symptoms, so it is necessary in an analysis of industrial warfare to reach into the heart of the problem by way of the strikes. For the strike is the external manifestation of labor's unrest, the thing that happens when an irresistible force meets an immovable body. The modern evolution we are speaking of has made itself manifest by a series of strikes, reaching a tremendous crescendo in the spring of 1937; and for the purpose of obtaining a better perspective on that evolution FORTUNE has isolated five of them, to be examined in some detail presently. As this article will show, strikes resemble wars in this at least — that they seldom break when or where they are expected. But, as of October 1, when this article went to press, there had been a three-month lull in the storm of big strikes. Whether or not this lull is to continue, it seems a likely moment to take stock of the complex modern phase — to recapitulate, to acquire a broader understanding of forces more subject to misapprehension and misinterpretation than any others to which society is heir.

From May, 1933, to July, 1937, a period of a little more than four years, there were some 10,000 strikes drawing out no less than 5,600,000 workers. This was aside from all the thousands of quickies, sitdowns, and other protests that tied up industry during that period — a "strike," as defined by the Department of Labor and used in this article, being an affair involving at least six workers for at least one day. But that was not all. Although a wave of strikes after any economic dislocation such as a war or a depression is supposed to be a normal phenomenon, the present strike wave did not entirely adhere to this pattern. It began conventionally enough with 1,695 strikes in 1933 (as against only 841 in 1932), and it rose on schedule to 1,856 in 1934, 2,014 in 1935, and 2,172 in 1936. In the latter year it gave signs of relaxing, the number of workers involved having dropped from 1,117,000 in 1935 to 789,000. But instead of following these indications the wave took life again in 1937, such that there were some 2,500 strikes in the first six months of this year, or more than in 1936 all together. And these strikes involved some 1,200,000 workers as against 789,000 workers for the full year 1936. During the spring labor observers began to predict an all-time high for 1937, with a total of at least 5,000 strikes, the previous high having been made in 1917 with 4,450.[1]

As already stated, there is now little reason to suppose that the 1917 strike high will be surpassed in 1937. Many an employer feels more secure, and many have fallen back upon the comfortable theory that the 1937 wave, while slightly off pattern, is after all part and parcel of a normal post-depression disturbance. For all anyone knows, these comfortable theorists may be right; but before jumping to that conclusion the wary observer ought to examine the field for himself.

To begin with numbers, the labor movement has been growing prodigiously, displaying an inherent power in the face of numerous emergencies and setbacks. While labor's membership claims are to be taken with some reserve, recent performances make it unwise to discount them too freely. Thus the C.I.O., which had 1,000,000 members in September, 1936, now claims 3,700,000; and the A.F. of L., which then had some 2,600,000 now claims 3,600,000. From these figures, adding in the railway brotherhoods and other independents, one may conservatively estimate the strength of organized labor at over 4,000,000 as of September, 1936, and over 7,500,000 as of September, 1937 — a gain of around 90 per cent in twelve months.

The more spectacular record is of course provided by the C.I.O. Today every passenger automobile manufacturer except Ford, Hupp, and Nash has a signed C.I.O. contract. The big committee claims some 400 contracts in the textile industry, covering 275,000 workers. It has signed up many companies, including such giants as U.S. Steel and American Viscose, without going so far as to call a strike. And while considering this angle of the situation it is well to remember that despite the strike in Little Steel, the Steel Workers' Organizing Committee has continued to grow, and now claims 400 contracts and a membership of 510,000. To visualize the progress that the committee has made in steel the reader might profitably turn to FORTUNE for October, 1936, where the membership of the Amalgamated Association of Iron, Steel & Tin Workers was somewhat cautiously guessed to be 50,000.

Next, it is important to note the very marked increase in the number of strikes that labor has won during the past decade. Labor won about 26 per cent of its 707 strikes in 1927 and made partial gains in 25 per cent more; and things remained at about this level through 1932. But in 1933, bolstered by NRA, 37 per cent of labor's strikes resulted in victories, and in 1936 the victories reached what is probably an all-time high of 46 per cent, another 24 per cent of the strikes involving partial gains. If these mounting percentages are applied to the rising number of strikes, the effect is startling. In 1927 labor won or compromised about 360 strikes; in 1936 about 1,500.

Some of the reasons for this will become apparent as we proceed. Here they may be summarized as: (1) new legislation making illegal a number of practices traditionally used by employers (such as subsidizing company unions); (2) new techniques, especially that of the sitdown; and (3) a more highly developed strategy, for which the C.I.O. has been largely responsible and which has changed the nature of labor warfare. The C.I.O. approaches an industry with elaborate and forethoughtful plans; organizes on the basis of peace just as long as possible; acquaints itself with sales problems and seasonal swings; and ferrets out weaknesses in the balance sheet.

Third, during the same decade there has apparently been a marked trend (in this case downward) in the number of days lost per worker as the result of strikes. The 1927 strikes, while few in number, were painfully prolonged, with the result that each striker lost an average of 108 days of work. This was largely the result of the soft-coal miners' strike, which frittered along into the next year. By 1928 the average was down to only eighty-eight days. During the depression it dropped substantially; and then fell further in 1933 to an average of only eighteen days, and in 1934 to fourteen, and in 1935 to thirteen. A slight rise in 1936 does not materially affect this general trend, which is strongly illustrated by the fact that for the six pre-NRA years the average time out was fifty-one days per worker, while for the four succeeding years it was eighteen.

Various factors have been responsible for this, among them the sitdown and the techniques and strategy already referred to. But for the quicker settlement of their strikes the laborites have above all to thank the U.S. Government. Congress has boosted collective bargaining by a series of recent enactments, beginning in 1926 with the Railway Labor Act. In 1932 came the Norris–La Guardia Anti-Injunction Act; in 1933 the Bankruptcy Act amendment and NRA (including labor's famed Magna Charta); in 1934 an amended Railway Labor Act; and in 1935 the stormy Wagner Act, which was upheld by the Supreme Court shortly before the Little Steel strike in 1937. As between industrial warfare . . . and the orderly process of collective bargaining, Congress has repeatedly condemned the former and embraced the latter, even at the risk of violating what many industrialists are prone to call the American tradition. The Wagner Act was the most radical step in this direction that Congress has ever made, and whatever problems it involves, the Board that this act set up is perhaps the most effective instrument for the settlement of industrial disputes that the country has ever had. The NLRB is cocky, and . . . many employers accuse it of prejudice and unfair procedures. But between August, 1935, when it was established, and October, 1937, over 7,600 labor disputes involving 2,225,000 workers have been dumped on its doorstep, and it has acted on over 4,500 cases. It claims to have averted 392 strikes involving 95,000 workers and it has adjusted 2,679 cases informally in addition to its highly publicized elections, hearings, and decisions.

Fourth, and perhaps most significant of all, there has been a marked trend in the causes of labor disputes, with the emphasis increasingly on the issue of union recognition. A labor movement fighting merely for better wages might or might not be a "movement" in the profound sense: it might be a kind of guerrilla warfare, indicating unrest but without historical direction. On the other hand, when men strike for union recognition they are striking for collective bargaining, which we have already described as the keystone of the American labor movement. This collective bargaining theme has not always been to the fore by any means. Of the great 1919 strikes, only about 24 per cent were fought chiefly on this issue, while 55 per cent were fought chiefly for wages and hours. (The balance were "miscellaneous.") Up through 1926, indeed, the organization issue never represented 25 per cent of the total. Thereafter there was an abrupt rise, stimulated partly by the general prosperity, and by 1929 about 40 per cent of the strikes were fought for collective bargaining. Then, after declining during the depression, the curve proceeded upward, breaking through 40 per cent in 1934, and reaching 50 per cent in 1936 and 53 per cent for the first half of this year — which so far as the record goes is an all-time high. This can be expressed in another way. In the fourteen-year period beginning with 1919 there were in round numbers 20,000 strikes. Of these 5,000 were primarily for union recognition. But in four years beginning with 1933 there were some 7,000 strikes. Of these, 3,000 were primarily for union recognition.

The fact that half of the 1936 strikes were fought for a principle, with the trend continuing into the stormy spring and summer of 1937, is of such significance that those who follow labor closely are inclined to doubt the comfortable theory already mentioned, to the effect that the current wave of strikes is just a normal post-depression phenomenon. Coupled with the prodigious growth of union membership, the increased percentage of strikes won and compromised, and the apparent trend toward quicker settlements, it would seem to indicate the recrudescence of a major mass movement with its roots far in the American past. One must, to be sure, make allowances for Roosevelt "prosperity," which has made it possible for the worker to afford to fight for principles. And one must make a big allowance for assistance rendered by the government. This latter element, however, is itself symptomatic of a real pressure, for the machinery of Washington, unpredictable as its motion may be, does not operate in a vacuum of pure idealism. Washington has strengthened labor's position, not just for the hell of it, but in response to forces that the depression stimulated and revitalized.

So much, at any rate, the realist must admit. It is useless in a situation such as this to hide one's head in the sand — to suppose, as some employers do, that labor's recent drive has been stopped. It may be that the lull in big strikes will continue for some time. But it is possible that even if it does — and even if the violent manifestations of labor's unrest are somehow avoided — labor is in a position to consolidate and even increase its new gains. It has the machinery, whether for peace or for war. And it is rapidly acquiring the men.

The examples of U.S. Steel and American Viscose, which signed with the C.I.O. without waiting for strikes, enable one to speak of peace in connection with a modern labor drive. But certainly peace has not characterized past drives, and it is with these that we are of necessity concerned. As already stated, the modern phase of the labor movement, the post-NRA phase, represents a distinct evolution, and the progress of the evolution has been fraught with warfare of the most harrowing character. It is of course impossible to choose from the 10,000 strikes included in this phase any several that would give a complete evolutionary picture; but it is possible to choose a few strikes to illustrate the more important points. Eliminating the San Francisco General Strike of 1934 as a special affair and the Minneapolis truck drivers' strike of that year on somewhat the same ground, FORTUNE has arbitrarily compiled a list of five samples, which, presented as case histories from an impartial point of view, may at least open the door to an elementary understanding of what has been going on. They are presented herewith.

Textiles, 1934: Mushroom Unions

If you were a union worker in the southern cotton-textile industry on September 1, 1934, your earnings were around $11 a week — and in general you could expect a wage of little more than half the national average for workers in manufacturing. You probably lived in a town of less than 10,000 people. Unlike the 100,000 weavers, spinners, loom fixers, card grinders, smash hands, slubber tenders, and other cotton-textile workers of the North, you lived in a region where the traditions of organized labor were not strong. You were new to industry, and there was much you disliked about it. Your great complaint was what you called the stretch-out, for if, under the NRA cotton-textile code, you worked a basic forty-hour week, you insisted that you produced more than formerly in fifty hours. For instance, you used to make 144 dozen bloomers in ten hours, but now in eight hours you turned out 200 dozen bloomers. You might complain of "docks," of fines, of cases where a week's work brought in $5.88. You were one unit in a vast, disorderly, depressed industry, made up of some 1,200 mills operated by some 850 companies. And, you were probably in a union for the first time in your life.

More immediately, since June your position had grown worse. In that month the cotton-textile code authority had reduced production 25 per cent, which meant a sharp cut in your wages. There was a statewide textile strike in Alabama. The delegates of your local, meeting at the national convention of the United Textile Workers in August, had voted for an industry-wide strike, demanding a thirty-hour week with no wage reduction, more uniform wages in the North and South, establishment of maximum work loads, reinstatement of workers fired for union membership, and — which has most bearing on this article — recognition of the union. Francis Gorman, Fifth Vice President of the Union, had sent the demands to George Arthur Sloan, President of the Cotton-Textile Institute and Chairman of the Cotton Textile Code Authority. He replied that no one could bargain for the entire industry and that the strike was a strike against the code. And the cotton-textile code was no ordinary code. The first of all NRA codes, under which average hourly wages increased 65 per cent in a year, it outlawed child labor, established a labor board to handle disputes, and was generally regarded as one of the most liberal, as Sloan himself was judged a liberal trade-association head. But the union charged that 2,000 cases brought before the board brought no appreciable results. And after six weeks, on September 1, 1934, at 11:30 P.M., you, as a good union man, went on strike.

You were caught up, in fact, in the first surge of the strike wave already described in statistics—and your strike accounted for almost 400,000 of the 1,467,000 workers who were involved that year. Above all, it was a strike of a union that had increased its members enormously under the impetus of the NRA drive, the United Textile Workers having grown from some 15,000 before the NRA to claim 300,000 in cotton textiles alone.

The textile strike was a strike involving primarily workers new to organized labor, pitted against a bitterly depressed industry, which meant that it was violent and brief. Twelve strikers and one deputy were killed in the three weeks that it raged. It was also emotional. "God is with us," cried a southern organizer as the strike began, "He will not desert us in this just struggle for ourselves and our families." It was characterized by what liberal economists politely call "employer resistance to collective bargaining." "Mobs of hoodlums and thugs!" thundered the President of the Alabama Manufacturers' Association, after a clash in the mill town of Boaz, "producing something like civil war in the South!" And the New England trade journal *Fibre and Fabric* asserted: "A few hundred funerals will have a quieting influence." The strike was followed by a period of disillusionment with section 7A and the elaborate mediation apparatus of the New Deal. With consequences that will presently be examined.

Largely because of its mushroom growth, the union could not support a long-drawn-out struggle. Facing enormous expenses, it had less than $1,000,000 in the treasury, and the strike might involve 500,000 cotton-textile workers — to say nothing of about 700,000 other workers in silk, wool, rayon, and other branches of the industry. It had four regional offices covering thirteen states and seventy organizers. When Gorman handed out his orders for simultaneous transmission to 500 locals of the union, he knew that the strike could not last longer than three weeks — or, as time is measured during strikes, he had 500 hours in which to win or lose.

The picket lines of fresh recruits tightened around hundreds of the industry's mills, and they stopped production so effectively that textile trade papers reported, along with indignant accounts of violence, that the employers felt they had been outgeneraled by an "audacious and intelligent minority." In the South, during the first week of the strike, fifty flying squadrons of pickets, with from 200 to 650 men in each column of cars, were operating along a 110-mile front from Gastonia to Greenville in the Carolinas. At Trion, Georgia, a deputy sheriff, a picket, and a strike sympathizer were killed and fifteen strikers were wounded in a two-hour pitched battle; at Greenville another strike sympathizer was killed, and during the strike's course there were clashes between pickets, deputies, non-strikers, and Guardsmen as far afield as Woonsocket, Rhode Island, Lancaster, Pennsylvania, and Augusta, Georgia, where three more strikers were shot, one fatally. At the gate of the Chiquola Manufacturing Co.'s plant at Honea Path, South Carolina, a group of armed men opposing the strike charged the picket line, firing, killing six pickets and wounding fifteen. The union said that the armed group were deputies; the employers said they were nonstriking workers. By the second week of the strike more than 15,000 National Guardsmen had been mobilized in seven states, and a concentration camp for pickets had been set up in Georgia.

The strike's violence created so much bitter controversy that its fundamental issues were obscured. The union's introduction of flying squadrons of pickets, a then relatively unfamiliar weapon that it took over from the coal miners, caused a furor in the press. The employers claimed that the use of these groups of strikers in automobiles, descending on towns suddenly and unexpectedly, was proof that the union had the support of only a minority of the employees in each plant.

For this charge the union's rejoinder ran roughly as follows: the employees in company towns, especially in the South, could not form picket lines because of armed guards employed by the companies. Nor could ordinary organizing procedure be followed. At Rockmart, Georgia, the president of the local was kidnaped and driven from town; at Winfield, Alabama, two union officials were caught by thirty-three armed guards of the Alabama Mills Co. and ordered to leave the county. And so forth. Against such odds, the union said, the only way a picket line could be established was by means of a flying squadron. At Fitchburg, Massachusetts, for instance, Organizer Powers Hapgood led fifty pickets to the edge of town, but was turned back by police. Later he returned with a flying squadron of 500 recruits drawn from a number of striking mills and succeeded in establishing a picket line. Whereupon the plant in Fitchburg also came out.

But underlying this was the matter of a union with limited resources and a vastly increased membership, waging a strike over an enormous area and around hundreds of mills, unevenly organized within the industry, with unexperienced strikers to man its picket lines — picket lines, the union asserts, that were attacked with forces strong enough to demoralize the most seasoned of hard-bitten unionists. And when the Winant Board issued a report that was a moral victory for the textile workers (since it recognized their basic grievances as real) but was a practical defeat (since it made no provisions for immediate or specific relief), the union called the strike off. "The union has won an overwhelming victory," said Gorman, the union complaining three weeks later that 25,000 strikers had been blacklisted. By the next year the membership claim of the United Textile Workers declined by about two-thirds.

Thus, if you were an average textile worker who went on strike on September 1, 1934, you probably came out of it three weeks later burdened with considerable doubt as to the effectiveness of section 7A. You had been a part of a mushroom growth of unionism that came into being with the signing of the NRA and fell away soon after.

Remington Rand: 1936. The Back-to-Work Movement Develops

If you were an aligner, say, in Remington Rand's ancient red brick Ilion plant your union experiences were of a far more complex character. As an aligner you were one of the most skilled workers in the complicated field of typewriter and business-machine manufacture, but during the depression you may have earned as little as $350 a year, and girls in the factory got as little as sixteen cents an hour. You probably owned your own home in Ilion, but it was mortgaged. In 1933, soon after the NRA was signed and while the textile workers were being organized, a federal union was chartered in the factory, the old craft unions expanded, and by intricate steps too numerous to be traced here, you presently found yourself in John Frey's Metal Trades Department of the A.F. of L., organized, along with the employees of the four — later six — Remington Rand plants, into a Joint Protective Board of Office Equipment Workers.

Your union went through some of the typical troubles of the new unions of that period. Mr. Rand would not recognize it as exclusive bargaining agent, and on May 9, 1934, you went on strike. After five weeks, the union was recognized as a bargaining agency for its members (it claimed 90 per cent of the production and maintenance workers).

But the troubles of your union were only beginning. Through the winter of 1936, as a good union man, you were worried at rumors that Remington Rand had bought a huge abandoned automobile factory at Elmira, New York, and planned to move operations there, developing a new typewriter known as the Madame X. The union was worried because of the contract with Rand, covering the employees of six Rand factories. Would the contract apply in the new Elmira plant? And was the plant at Ilion to close? With these questions agitating them, union officials tried to see Rand. They charged, and the Labor Board later upheld them, that Rand's refusal to see them was a violation of their right of collective bargaining. To the company their questions were an unwarranted intrusion into management and an attempt to find out plans that could not be announced without disclosures to competitors. Plant managers conferred with union people discussing other matters of the contract, but could give no satisfactory answer to the crucial question of what was going to happen at Elmira with Madame X. For these and other reasons a strike vote was taken on April 28, and by a vote of 3,200 to 568, union officers were empowered to

call a strike if, in their opinion, "all other means have failed to bring about a satisfactory conclusion."

The union contract contained a confidential clause. It read: "It is understood and
agreed that any discrimination or intimidation on the part of any employee toward
any other employee shall be just cause for discharge." As the union understood it,
this only confirmed the public clause of the contract, which pledged both parties to
the maintenance of peace and harmony — "We were not to bother or harm the few
scabs, and they were to keep their shirts clean," was the union's interpretation. But
on May 21, three weeks after the union authorized the strike, this confidential agreement became the mainspring of action. All employees of Remington Rand had received ballots distributed by the management, reading: *Are you dissatisfied with present working conditions? Are you in favor of a strike?* In the Syracuse plant the union
leaders stopped work until the balloting was called off. Whereupon the company
closed the plant for two weeks. Rand informed the mayor that he would reopen
after the sixteen union leaders had been discharged — the point being, he insisted,
that they had violated the confidential agreement in preventing the balloting. In
Ilion, Syracuse, Tonawanda, Middletown, and Norwood, the union prepared for a
strike, sending a last wire asking Rand if he was not letting "anger instead of reason
rule." There was no reply. The second Remington Rand strike began.

If you were a good union man in Ilion you probably went to the strike meeting at
the Temple Theatre on the night of May 25, listened to the speeches and turned out
on the picket line the next morning. You may have eaten a sandwich at strike headquarters nearby. You may have watched the thirty-odd newly hired guards of Foster's Detective Bureau arriving to patrol the plant interior. And then things began
to happen — not only to you, but to the mayor, the chief of police, a number of
small city businessmen, the employees of Remington Rand in other cities, and a
number of professional guards. In Ilion a Citizen's Committee was started by Barney Allen, Ilion's retail dealer in General Electric supplies. He was afraid Remington Rand would move out of Ilion, taking the $12,000-a-day payroll that was the
town's main income. An organization called the Ilion Typewriter Employees' Protective Association was started by Reginald Boote, a young aligner who opposed the
strike. It opened an office and began signing up employees who wanted to go back
to work. A "For Sale" sign appeared on the factory. There was one tense moment
the second day, with a threatened riot arising out of a brief encounter between strikers and guards. The Citizens' Committee appealed to Governor Lehman to send
state troopers to supplement Ilion's six regular officers. He refused, since there had
been no violence. Failing, the Citizens' Committee demanded that the mayor appoint 300 special deputies. In an atmosphere of growing hysteria, the Citizens'
Committee held a mass meeting, Barney Allen called upon the mayor to coöperate
(but he refused to ring the fire bell to summon the volunteer firemen to be deputized), and 300 deputies were signed up.

On the morning of June 10 the streets near the plant were roped off. Tear-gas
guns were mounted in the factory windows. Across the street members of Reginald
Boote's Ilion Typewriter Employees' Association gathered for an open meeting.
There were a few skirmishes between strikers and nonstrikers, ending when tear-gas
bombs were fired. Then the members and sympathizers of the Ilion Typewriter
Employees' Protective Association (500 says the union, 800 says Reginald Boote)
entered the factory, the flag rose on the factory flagpole, the "For Sale" sign was

taken down, and Rand arrived to address the returning employees. That night a state of emergency was declared in Ilion on the strength of rumors that a flying squadron of strikers from Syracuse was rushing to town to help the Ilion pickets. All roads were blocked. The union headquarters were padlocked. During the "siege of Ilion," as the strikers called it, Union Leader Harold Beer (who had worked for Remington Rand for twenty-five years) entered Ilion by going on foot through the woods that lie behind the town. And the siege ended when the strikers broke, more than 1,200 returning to work two days after the strike began.

If you were a union man in Remington Rand's Ilion plant in 1936 you were one atom in the working out of a new force, which, amid charges and countercharges, accusations of prejudice, partisanship, plotting, and worse, was to be analyzed and defined by the National Labor Relations Board as the Mohawk Valley Formula. The nine steps of the Mohawk Valley Formula it found to include: (1) conducting a forced balloting under the direction of foremen to misrepresent the strength of the union, calling strike leaders "agitators," forming a Citizens' Committee under threat to move the plant; (2) arousing the community by calling for "law and order" because of "wholly imagined violence"; (3) calling mass meetings of citizens; (4) calling for armed deputies; (5) starting a back-to-work movement; (6) setting a date for opening the plant; (7) staging the opening theatrically; (8) turning "the locality into a warlike camp"; (9) keeping up a campaign of publicity to convince the remaining strikers that the plant is in full operation.

Thus the Labor Board pictured Rand as a superstrategist of strikebreaking and the originator of a foolproof strikebreaking technique. It revealed that during the Remington Rand strike the company paid, in all, $25,800 to Pearl L. Bergoff for his services and the services of 200 guards and "missionaries," whose function it was to discourage the strikers, $30,000 more to Captain Foster of Foster's Industrial and Detective Bureau, and an additional $25,000 to Raymond J. Burns of the William J. Burns International Detective Agency, Inc. The latter two, according to the company, for protection because of the recurring violence of the strike, which in some of its six towns lasted longer and was more bitterly fought than at Ilion. The Labor Board found Rand guilty of unfair labor practices and ordered him to offer reinstatement to all strikers unemployed, the case going to the courts, where it still remains. The joint Committee of Remington Rand Employees' Associations (the Board called the one at Ilion "a puppet association . . . secretly organized by the employer") denounced the Board and said its conclusions were based on the false statements of disgruntled ex-employees. And Remington Rand, which had not called witnesses at the Labor Board hearings, called the Board's charges a slander.

In the history of the Wagner Act, and in the Remington Rand strike itself, these charges and countercharges are of primary significance. But in the wave of 10,000 strikes, of which the Remington Rand strike was only a part, they are of less importance than the trends the strike revealed. For the Remington Rand strike shows quite clearly what other strikes barely suggest — the mechanics of a modern back-to-work movement.

Rubber, 1936: The Sitdown Begins

Some observer poised high above the class struggle about that time might have thought that capital now had all the advantage, with labor's enthusiasm for the

NRA ended and the spectacular, coördinated, theatrical Mohawk Valley Formula presently to come into being as an instrument for breaking strikes almost as soon as they got under way. And it might have seemed that with some of the mushroom unions of the NRA period smashed in their attempt to achieve recognition (as in the textile industry) and others broken after they had achieved it (as in the Remington Rand strike), the strike wave was now due to shrink to the proportions of an episode in labor's uneven history.

Instead, out in Akron, Ohio, at three in the morning of February 14, 1936, something happened that sent the strike wave surging to a new high — although its results were not immediately apparent. A major strike began in the rubber industry, growing out of a tangle of accumulated grievances, but taking a form that gave it historical importance. The form it took may have been a natural development in a long chain of brief stay-in and slow-down strikes. But whatever the reason, on that night a group of tire builders in Goodyear Tire & Rubber Co.'s Plant II sat down on the job. Theirs was not the first sitdown. But theirs grew into the Goodyear rubber strike that lasted five weeks, involved 14,000 employees, saw an eleven-mile picket line, and was described by the Department of Labor as "characterized by a lack of violence." It gave the sitdown nationwide publicity, ended with partial recognition of the union, and launched a drive that swept Akron's rubber union membership from less than 2,000 to approximately 37,000, the United Rubber Workers of America from about 3,000 to an organization of 75,000 with 136 locals and the reputation of never having lost a strike.

But it did not begin impressively. On that stormy St. Valentine's day in Akron, Goodyear's management distributed some unwelcome valentines to sixty-nine tire builders of Plant II — the pink slips that meant a layoff. (February sales had been bad, said the management.) The first three men who got them, according to the story, "swore and sat down." They and many others remained sitting down while production heads hurried to the factory. The later shifts coming to work elected committees to support them, and — most important — the conveyers leading to the department were filled and the hot and steamy curing department immediately beyond had no tires to prepare. At nine in the morning the first sitdowners left the plant. Later shifts intermittently worked and sat down. At nine-forty that night Goodyear's outraged management gave notice that anyone not back at work in forty minutes would be dropped from the payroll. At ten-thirty the foremen began handing out notices. One hundred and thirty-seven men were dismissed. Thereafter the progress of the strike became confused — over the issues involved (it grew out of the union's opposition to increased hours and the threat of a wage cut); over union politics (since the union was one of the mushroom unions of the A.F. of L. involved in the split with the C.I.O.); over a back-to-work movement that flourished briefly and died; and over the numerous settlements proposed to end the strike. In the rubber strike itself, in Akron politics, and in the struggle between the A.F. of L. and the C.I.O., these subtleties were of first importance. But in the wave of strikes the sitdowns in Goodyear rubber were consequential because they introduced one of labor's answers to the Mohawk Valley Formula or the less highly organized back-to-work movements of the other side. In the auto strikes that came soon after the sitdown it was to make history on a grand scale. And in the strike in Little Steel, the Mohawk Valley Formula was (perhaps) to be applied on a scale no less sweeping.

Autos, 1936–37: The Sitdown

By November, 1936, the strike wave we have been describing had added up to over 7,000 strikes. It had included at least six general strikes, the great maritime strikes of the East and West Coast, a nationwide miners' strike, and a multitude of small strikes that followed in the wake of the big ones. It had passed through two distinct stages, suggested by our accounts of the textile strike and the strike at Remington Rand. And it looked as if it were going to decline. The number of strikes had increased slightly through 1936 but the number of men involved had gone down — which meant that the strike wave was now reaching smaller plants, and the figures were swollen by the inclusion of later strikes, strikes of grocery clerks, even by a strike of the graveyard workers of Minneapolis.

Then — to set an arbitrary date for the beginning of the next surge — at eight-twenty-five on the sunny morning of November 18, 1936, five men in the trim department of General Motors' Fisher Body plant in Atlanta were laid off because they came to work wearing union buttons. To General Motors that was a violation of company rules. To the union their dismissal was part of a general attempt to smash the United Automobile Workers, and a sitdown strike occurred. If you were a member of the union and had observed it rise and fall, you probably believed that the systematic firing of union men was part of General Motors policy. You may have joined the auto workers union in 1934 when, as a skyrocketing federal union of the A.F. of L., it claimed 200,000, with 60,000 members in Detroit. You may have been with it in 1935 when it plummeted down to the point where William Green could complain: "Today, I am sorry to say, we have 35,000. A year ago there were more, but for different reasons they are not with us now." Among those reasons was one later revealed by the La Follette Committee: that General Motors had spent $839,000 in two and a half years on detective services, that a Lansing local had five members, all officers and all stool pigeons provided by a spy agency hired by the company.

If you were a rank-and-file union man among General Motors' 135,000 employees, your biggest grievance was the "speedup" — the most likely cause for "a conflagration in the automobile industry," the NRA's Research and Planning Division had reported. And as a union man, the subsequent months of that conflagration were the most important of your union experience. There was a strike at the Kansas City Fisher Body plant when a union man was fired for jumping over the assembly line. There were three sitdown strikes in the auto-parts industry: at Bendix in South Bend and at Midland Steel and Kelsey-Hayes in Detroit. In Cleveland and Norwood, Ohio, there were General Motors walkouts; at the General Motors Guide Lamp Plant in Anderson, Indiana, there was a sitdown involving 2,400; and in the long, rectangular, brick factories that house the Fisher Body plants of Flint, the strike was touching the heart of the General Motors empire.

Deep in the interior of Fisher I, about a mile away from the imposing group of factories in the central General Motors plant, a sitdown started on December 30. The union had presented a contract to the company a few days before, and now the strikers saw (or thought they saw, for the company says it never happened) preparations being made for removing the big dies from which turret-top bodies are made. Which, they assumed, must mean that the plant was being abandoned. Or that a scare was being thrown into Flint, 45,000 of whose 150,000 work for General Motors. At Fisher II, across Chevrolet Avenue from Chevrolet II, three inspectors who were union men were demoted to the assembly line. (Because they were union men, said the union; because they were supervisors, said the company, and supervisors could not belong to the union.) Workers sat down in both Fisher plants. During the rubber strike, the sitdowners left the plant, formed their picket lines outside. But at Flint several hundred strikers remained in Fisher I and II. The union listed eight demands, including a thirty-hour week, seniority rights, a national agreement, and joint determination of the speed of the line. The company replied that the plants had to be vacated before there could be any discussion. The stage was set for what motor makers still call Detroit's sociological nightmare.

Seen only in relation to Detroit, or to the state of Michigan (where for a period one person in every thirty-three was on strike), or to the automobile industry, the sitdown certainly assumed nightmarish proportions. And because during the General Motors strike there was dancing twenty-four hours a day in Flint at the strike head-quarters at Pengelly Hall, plus ball games in the struck plants, plus food prepared for the strikers by a union chef formerly of Detroit's swank Athletic Club, the sitdowns seemed to take place in a nightmare world where the laws of capitalism, if they operated at all, worked the way the laws of gravity do in a dream. But if viewed in relation to the 1933–37 strike wave, the General Motors strike becomes part of a great pattern. It saw, for example, a back-to-work movement, as well as an injunction against the strikers. The injunction was defied, and the back-to-work movement collapsed, for reasons connected not only with the sitdown, but with the change in labor's tactics in general.

During the strike General Motors got an injunction to evict the sitdowners. But the injunction lost some of its authority when the union promptly disclosed that Judge Edward Black, who issued it, owned 1,000 shares of General Motors stock. Whereupon General Motors got another injunction from another judge. But the sheriff who went inside the plant to read it to the strikers was greeted with boos and catcalls. And Governor Murphy refused to order the National Guard to enforce the injunction until all peaceful means of settlement had been exhausted.

As for the back-to-work movement, in this case called the "Flint Alliance for Security of Our Jobs, Our Homes, and Our Community," it came to its own peculiar kind of grief. While it was growing to claim 12,000 and making preparations for a mass meeting, Governor Murphy was holding conferences with General Motors and the union. On January 11 there was an unexpected crisis: the sitdowners remaining in Fisher II thought an attempt was going to be made to evict them. Heat was cut down; the company guards who had previously handed food into the factory now refused to let it enter. But according to General Motors the strikers had for the first time prevented the office force from going to work, which was why the heat was turned off, and although the company guards would no longer hand food into the plant, they would permit it to be handed through the windows. Whatever the reason, the situation suddenly became ominous. By nightfall police had assembled around the plant. In the beginning of a battle that lasted for seven hours, the police broke a window in the plant and fired a tear-gas shell inside; the strikers built a barricade of autos in the street, doused the tear-gas bombs with water from a fire hose, and held their ground. On the third rush the police fired, and fourteen strikers were wounded. And the next day militia massed at Flint, the Fleetwood plant went on strike, while from Washington John Lewis announced that the auto strikers would have the full support of the C.I.O. and Homer Martin hurried to Washington to confer with him.

During the forty-eight crowded hours after the riot in Flint, the ascetic Governor Murphy (whose picture, labeled "Our Friend," looked sternly down on several hundred sitdowners) arranged the famous "Lansing Truce." By its terms the union agreed to evacuate the plants, General Motors agreed not to resume operations in the struck plants, and the union temporarily waived its sole bargaining demand. So it came about that on Saturday, January 16, the sitdowners left the Guide Lamp plant in Anderson, Cadillac and Fleetwood in Detroit. But in Flint a hitch occurred. Talkative ex-Mayor George Boysen, once a Buick paymaster, organizer of the Flint Alliance, told a reporter that at four o'clock Sunday afternoon General Motors would announce that it was going to deal with the Alliance. The sitdowners were scheduled to leave the plants at one o'clock. Informed of this, the union refused to evacuate Fisher I and Fisher II in Flint, and the General Motors strike flared up again.

Such happenings gave a good share of Michigan's population its conviction that law and order had collapsed. But seen in perspective against the strike wave, they illustrated how profoundly union tactics, as well as unions themselves, had changed in the period since the textile strike. Unlike the Remington Rand strikers, the auto strikers had successfully countered a back-to-work movement. They had developed a new organizing technique and a new strike strategy. But more profoundly, they had developed a new concept of strike action, which is nowhere better illustrated than in the story of the seizure of Chevvy IV. By the end of the first month of the strike union leaders wanted a bold stroke to bolster union morale. Half a dozen of them went to the bluff overlooking the seven plants on Chevrolet's eighty-acre tract and decided that they had to capture Plant IV, which assembles motors for all Chevrolet automobiles. If the union could get and hold that plant, they could give General Motors all the rest of its establishment and still stop enough production to count.

But a direct attack on Chevvy IV was out of the question. Hardly a hundred feet from this plant was the personnel building, which served as the headquarters and arsenal for the company police. It was too well guarded. Furthermore, the union was not very strong there. They decided to make a false attempt to take Chevrolet IX, a bearing plant on the other end of the tract. Not more than eight strike leaders knew the full details of the plan.

First, thirty-five shop stewards were called to a meeting. It was held after midnight in Fisher I, where the sitdown was in progress, to impress them with its importance and secrecy. Among them, by design, were men known by the organizers to be informers. They were told that an effort would be made to capture Chevrolet IX. This plan met with strong objection because the men knew that the bearing plant would be hard to take — and also that it was relatively unimportant to production because General Motors could get bearings elsewhere. Nevertheless, the program was decided on.

At 3:00 P.M. on February 1, a mass meeting was held in Pengelly Hall. At 3:20 a note was handed up to Bob Travis, chairman of the meeting, who then announced that there was trouble at Chevrolet IX and that everybody should go down there at once. Actually, nothing had yet happened at Chevrolet IX, but promptly at three-thirty at the change of shift the men refused to work, refused to leave the plant, and set up a terrific din. When the strikers from Pengelly Hall arrived at three-thirty-five the "trouble" at Chevrolet IX was in progress.

As had been expected, guards rushed to the plant. Meanwhile, at Chevrolet VI, far from the scene of the trouble, promptly at three-thirty-five a union steward named Ed Cronk sounded a siren, picked up an American flag, and started marching around the factory. He led the march to Chevrolet IV. But in his excitement he forgot to look around, discovering when he got to Chevrolet IV that he had only twenty-five men with him. He rushed back and marched around the factory again, carrying the flag, and this time collected more followers. Once in Chevy IV the strikers quickly ejected foremen, plant officials, and non-union workers and began to barricade all the doors. Fourteen minutes had elapsed between the time the commotion had started at Chevrolet IX and the time Chevrolet IV was barricaded.

Out of all the sensational news of the auto strike, the seizing of Chevvy IV was the high point. In terms of the auto strike alone it was either the final indignity offered outraged property rights — if you were on the side of the employers — or an illustration of labor's growing initiative — if you were not. But in terms of the 1933–37 strike wave its significance is of a different order. When you compare it with the moves made during the textile strike it serves as a landmark, measuring how far labor had traveled in less than three years and through some 4,000 strikes.

Little Steel, 1937: Back to Work Again

The strike in the twenty-seven plants of Republic, Youngstown Sheet & Tube, and Inland Steel broke under circumstances that will probably make discussion of it one of the classic problems of union shoptalk, like the seizing of Chevvy IV in the auto strike. It broke less than three months after U.S. Steel signed its agreement with the Steel Workers' Organizing Committee of the C.I.O., six weeks after the Supreme Court declared the Wagner Act constitutional, and five days after the union won a consent election, conducted by the NLRB, at the two great plants of Jones & Laughlin. Because of these facts (and because it was lost) the strike in Little Steel posed its questions for the innumerable grandstand quarterbacks of the labor movement: could it have been won if held back a little longer, until the S.W.O.C.'s organizing campaign had advanced more? Or, could it have been won if more care had been paid public opinion and less reliance placed on public officials? And, finally, what does its loss mean to the C.I.O., and the immediate future of American labor?

Before you can consider these posers in detail, it is necessary to look back on the great steel organizing drive of the C.I.O., begun last year and described in FORTUNE of October, 1936. Forearmed with exhaustive economic studies of the steel industry, financed with a $500,000 war chest contributed by the ten original unions of the C.I.O., manned with skilled old-line organizers of the United Mine Workers (as well as with young recruits from the mushroom NRA unions and a few from the insurgent company unions), that drive was directed primarily at the traditional anti-union fortress of U.S. Steel. In November, 1936 (when the General Motors strike was beginning in Atlanta), the S.W.O.C. held a convention of organizers and announced that 82,000 of the steel industry's 500,000 employees had been signed up. And on March 2, 1937, the quiet of the S.W.O.C.'s office on the thirty-sixth floor of the Grant Building in Pittsburgh was shattered by the most sensational news in the history of steel labor: John L. Lewis and Myron C. Taylor had come to an agreement by whose terms U.S. Steel recognized the S.W.O.C. as the agency for collective bargaining. Thirty-five thousand members, the union claimed, were signed up in the next two weeks. Before the outbreak of the strike in Little Steel, the S.W.O.C. could boast that it had negotiated 140² agreements, established fifty-two administrative offices, and brought 400,000 workers into 797 local lodges.

All of which had brought an answer from the masters of Little Steel. Their argument against unions in general and the S.W.O.C. in particular, distilled from opinions in steel journals, the speeches and writings of steel men, would run about like this: if the proportion of union members to total nonagricultural workers in the U.S. has remained below that of the European democracies, it has not been because collective bargaining has been resisted more strenuously by American employers. It has been because American workmen are not greatly interested in national labor unions. From this it follows that national unions are foreign importations, the outgrowth of the rigid class divisions of Europe. From this point of view the issue of collective bargaining is false, since these people maintain that local unions, independent unions, employee-representation plans, and the like provide collective bargaining. Where the Labor Board has decided in a number of cases that such organizations are simply the old-fashioned company unions, revamped to comply with the Wagner Act, the answer is that the Labor Board is prejudiced and unfair. The figures on the increase of union membership are answered by the assertion that the figures are exaggerated, that most members do not pay their dues, and that the labor advance we have described is less a mass movement than the result of a political alliance between the Administration and the leaders of organized labor — who, even if their claims are granted, represent only a small percentage of the total industrial population. This point of view, to be sure, is found in other circles than in steel, but in no other industry has it been so vehemently advanced. "I won't have a contract, verbal or written," said Mr. Girdler, "with an irresponsible, racketeering, violent, communistic body like the C.I.O., and until they pass a law making me do it, I am not going to do it."

The density of union membership in all branches of an industry during a union drive is one of labor's essential secrets. But it was no secret, before the strike in Little Steel, that most of the S.W.O.C.'s organizing effort had gone into the campaign against Big Steel. (In Monroe, Michigan, for example, which was to be a crucial outpost in the strike, the S.W.O.C. office was not opened until late in February.) Nor was it a secret that many of the organizers in the Little Steel area were old-line officials of the United Mine Workers, accustomed to handling strikes in the intensely pro-union mine country; or that the 360 strike functionaries — relief directors, clerical force, organizers — were largely directed by men whose experience had been in other lines than steel. All of which, in the opinion of the hot-stove-league experts of labor, pointed to inadequate preparation in the critical pre-strike months. But to answer that, the S.W.O.C. had been organizing in Youngstown a year before the strike and had two groups, each of 500 picked men, called the organizing committee, in Youngstown Sheet & Tube alone. It had prepared a list of 200 lawyers in spots where trouble was expected, and had investigated 100 of these; an exhaustive study of state laws had been made; and an intricate, foolproof, revolving-fund strike-relief system, making possible cash payment for all supplies, had been laid out. "The S.W.O.C. was ready," said one observer, "but not for what happened."

For what happened began outside the area of Little Steel. It began when the Supreme Court on April 12 upheld the constitutionality of the Wagner Act in five cases dealing with discriminatory discharge for union activity — among them the case of ten employees of Jones & Laughlin Steel Corp., who were ordered reinstated with full back pay. It was carried forward the next month when a strike was voted at the two Jones & Laughlin plants, when S.W.O.C. organizers met in Pittsburgh, and, in anticipation of trouble with Republic Steel and Youngstown Sheet & Tube, authorized Chairman Philip Murray to call a strike at his discretion. On the day before the Jones & Laughlin strike began, the C.I.O.'s regional director Clinton S. Golden met Republic Steel's director of industrial relations, Mr. J. A. Voss, in Cleveland, there to define, with that mixture of politeness, strain, diplomacy, and plain speaking that distinguishes big-time union negotiations, the position of both sides. To Republic as well as to the other independent steel companies, agreements had previously been submitted identical with those U.S. Steel had signed. The companies refused to sign, giving as reason their unalterable opposition to the closed shop and the check-off. The union replied simply that it was not asking for the closed shop and the check-off. Wages and hours were not an immediate issue — although the stability of wages was. But the issue became identified in the public mind as solely over a signed contract — which, in the opinion of the S.W.O.C.'s critics, meant that the union was going into battle with two strikes against it.

Meanwhile at Jones & Laughlin the forty-hour strike ended peacefully with a consent election conducted by the Labor Board, the union winning a sensational 70 per cent of the votes cast. There was a premonitory clash between Republic and the S.W.O.C. on the night before the balloting began: the union asked warrants for the arrest of eight Republic employees who appeared in Aliquippa, charging they were there to create a disturbance that would disrupt the voting. Republic asserted they were there only as observers. In this period at least seventy-five cases of discharge for union activity in Republic plants were filed with the Labor Board, as well as more cases of threatened discharge; Republic's tinplate mill at Canton was closed and its Massillon plant, where the union was strong, suspended operations. The Massillon local, without authorization of S.W.O.C.'s headquarters, took a strike vote. After signing an agreement with Jones & Laughlin, which made the S.W.O.C. the sole bargaining agency, Philip Murray rushed to a meeting of 200 delegates in Youngstown. It had been hastily called to forestall runaway strike action. It voted a strike in three of the five companies of Little Steel. "Our membership had to be protected," Philip Murray said, making the question of whether the strike was called prematurely largely an academic one.

From the bridges over the Mahoning at Youngstown you can look down upon the giant byproduct coke ovens, the blast furnaces, the open-hearth furnaces, the Bessemer converters, the blooming mills, the billet and bar mills, the skelp mills, and the spike plant of Republic's Youngstown works; on the smaller mills of Youngstown Sheet & Tube, set almost in the center of the city. You can look down too upon a stretch of grim and smoke-darkened streets, on the section given over to its lurid night life, beside the fence surrounding the Youngstown Sheet & Tube Works. You can see the Bessemer converter that stands like a howitzer beside the red-light district, and from which flames periodically shoot skyward with a volcanic roar, blanching the street with a sulphurous light. You can look down upon a section of gray wooden houses where live a good share of Youngstown's 32,938 foreign-born, alongside her 14,552 Negroes. And on the far side you can see the tree-shaded residential streets, equally remote from the mills and the slums, so closely knit that dwellers there insist that Youngstown, for all its 170,000, is essentially a small town.

Up and down the Mahoning, as the strike got under way, the picket lines formed. They were established at mill gates and along the railroad embankments, organized into groups of five doing six-hour turns, with one leader for each group, four division captains (one for each turn), and a head picket. Forty-two cars patrolled the

Campbell picket line. In Warren the line stretched over the eight-mile circuit around the Republic plant. In Monroe it crossed the road beside the Raisin River that led to the main gate. In South Chicago, on the first day of the strike, it formed near the plant entrance at 116th Street and Burley Avenue, but was dispersed by the police, and twenty-three pickets were arrested. Within Republic's plants, by the company's count, a large number of men were still at work — 2,400 in Warren, 1,400 in South Chicago, "several hundred" at Niles, 2,900 at Buffalo — and food was brought in to them by airplane and sent parcel post. At Youngstown a train, crashing through the picket line at Youngstown Sheet & Tube, led to violence in the first days of the strike. The planes were fired on, the mails were stopped, and after the train at Youngstown crashed through the picket line pickets cut the rails with acetylene torches.

In every strike the men who remain at work — the loyal workers of embattled management, the scabs of strikers — draw on themselves the accumulated resentment of the picket lines. But in the strike in Little Steel, for reasons that will presently become apparent, the status of nonstriking employees decidedly changed, and with it there was an equally momentous change in the attitude of the union toward them. It was to protect these loyal workers, Republic Steel claimed, that it armed its plants. (Ninety-two riot guns, 2,295 long-range projectiles — tear and sickening gas — 326 short-range gas cartridges, and 2,029 gas grenades were purchased by Republic and its subsidiaries in May and June — a total expenditure of $43,901.) And the police of Chicago claimed that it was while protecting the 1,400 (company's figure) workers who remained in the South Chicago works of Republic Steel, on Memorial Day, when the strike was four days old, that the pickets were dispersed, with four killed outright, six fatally injured, and ninety wounded, some thirty of them by gunfire.

Read the report of the La Follette Committee on what it calls the Memorial Day incident and you will find a story as savage as any in the dark annals of American labor struggles. You will read of the strike starting on the day of the general strike call, of gas costing $3,300 stored in the plant, of how the first picket line was dispersed, with twenty-three arrested, and how, afterward, Mayor Kelly stated that peaceful picketing would be permitted. You will read of the increased police force around the plant, of a mass meeting called near the factory, followed by a march toward it to establish the picket lines over "a stretch of flat waste sparsely-inhabited prairie land east of and adjacent to the South Chicago plant of the steel corporation — the plant itself is bounded on the west by the Calumet River, on the north by steel scrap piles, the south by low prairie land, and on the east by a barbed-wire-topped fence and the tracks of the Pennsylvania Railroad." You will read also of the marchers approaching the line of 264 police, of a discussion about picketing suddenly interrupted by a stick thrown by the inevitable unknown, a tear-gas bomb tossed at the moment the cameraman was changing his lenses, and, after a graphic report of the subsequent gunfire, the brutal treatment of the injured, and the sixty-seven arrests, the grim conclusion that "the consequences of the Memorial Day encounter were clearly avoidable by the police." [3]

As has been pointed out in the Remington Rand strike, the back-to-work movement of contemporary strikes occupies the center of the stage. Early in the Little Steel strike Philip Murray charged that the Mohawk Valley Formula was being followed step by step, and when the strike spread to Johnstown the New York *Times* correspondent, F. Raymond Daniell, found its pattern repeated in the events that led to the formation of a Citizens' Committee and a demand for the reopening of Bethlehem's Cambria plant. But a strike involving 83,000 and extending over seven states is a vastly different affair from one in a small city dependent upon a single industry, and only at Monroe, Michigan (where the small Republic-owned Newton Steel Co.'s plant was an unimportant unit in Republic's production, but of vital consequence to the community), did events correspond to those in Ilion.

There the mayor polled the employees to determine how many wanted to return to work. Out of a total of 1,350, it was officially claimed 826 voted for, 20 against, and 504 didn't vote. After some 300 men had been deputized, a date was set for opening the plant. It was postponed at Governor Murphy's request. He called a conference in Lansing, to be attended by the mayor, the union organizer, and representatives of the back-to-work movement. While the conference was on, at three in the afternoon of June 10, some 200 deputies marched to the picket line, ahead of the members of the back-to-work movement, organized into an independent union. Given two minutes to open the road, the picket captain gained twenty minutes more in order to telephone Governor Murphy. But while negotiations were going on the ubiquitous tear-gas bomb was thrown toward the pickets while a stone simultaneously sailed toward the deputies, and within ten minutes the pickets were in flight, at least nine automobiles were dumped into the Raisin River by the deputies, and the nonstriking employees returned to work.

At Massillon the back-to-work movement ran into greater difficulties and led to a more tragic ending. There the chief of Massillon's police force of eighteen men refused to permit a poll to be taken because, he said, it would cause trouble unless conducted by the Labor Board. But after a month in which, he testified, he was warned by Republic officials that if the mills closed Massillon would be "just a junction with no need for a mayor or a chief of police," and during which he was urged to deputize special policemen and guards, he blew up: "I said all right I would appoint the whole damn outfit. I would give them everything they wanted." The deputies were sworn in and armed. In spite of the unwillingness of the officials to take this course on the grounds that violence would follow, nothing happened until the night of Sunday, July 11, when Police Chief Switter took "a little drive in the country for a glass of beer." When he returned he found that in his absence a riot in front of union headquarters had cost the life of a union member, that thirteen had been injured, and 160 arrested.

But for observing the process by which a full-grown back-to-work movement comes into being (as well as the tension it may create), Youngstown provides a better specimen for study than smaller communities. In the first days of the strike the Independent Association of Republic Employees and the Independent Society of Workers of Youngstown Sheet & Tube opened adjoining offices in the Dollar Savings & Trust Co. ("paying no rent," said the Labor Board's investigator sourly) and began collecting signatures of employees who wanted to return to work. While Governor Davey was calling peace conferences, airplanes were dropping food into the plants and the back-to-work movement spread among the pleasant homes of Norwood Avenue and Poland Manor — an intense drive, made up of employees who did not support the strike, of businessmen who believed that a minority of pickets was preventing the majority of employees from working, of clubwomen who telephoned their resolutions to Boake Carter, wrote letters to the President, and sent a delegation to Governor Davey at three in the morning.

The strike was in its third week when Secretary of Labor Perkins appointed a Steel Mediation Board, President Roosevelt declared that companies willing to make oral agreements should put them into writing, and another night riot left two dead and some thirty to fifty injured in Youngstown. The Steel Mediation Board negotiations soon broke down, not over the question of a signed agreement, but over a proposal that the companies recognize the S.W.O.C. pending Labor Board election, the agreements to be torn up in plants where the union lost. The Senate Post Office inquiry was proceeding. That inquiry resembled a La Follette Committee hearing turned around, for in place of reports of violence against strikers by police or company guards, it was filled with reports of violence by pickets against nonstriking workers — stories of men beaten, stripped, or driven from home. In Youngstown the sheriff deputized a hundred men, and Republic Steel and Youngstown Sheet & Tube had already announced that their plants would be reopened on Tuesday morning, June 22. "In the name of God and the overwhelming majority of steel workers of Youngstown," the union wired the President, ". . . we urge you to immediately intervene in this critical hour and avoid a calamity and disaster that Ohio may remember for decades to come." The United Labor Congress threatened a general strike, the truck drivers struck, union sympathizers streamed into town. Word came at midnight that the mediation conference had broken down, and in the office building of Youngstown Sheet & Tube reporters crowded into two rooms overlooking Shop 14, where the heaviest concentration of pickets was massed before the gates. After midnight word came that by the President's request the mills would not reopen. At Governor Davey's order 5,000 National Guardsmen marched in, and in the morning to the accompaniment of cheers from the picket lines, the tension was broken. And, although it was not apparent until later, so was the strike.

Three days later on June 25 Governor Davey completely reversed his position and, issuing a statement, "the right to work is sacred," ordered National Guardsmen to protect returning workers. The picket lines had been withdrawn, and the Guard now made the reëstablishment of the picket line impossible. Attempts to bring in supplementary pickets from Akron and elsewhere were thwarted and simultaneously arrests of strikers and sympathizers began — 225 were arrested in Youngstown alone.

In terms of its immediate importance, the Little Steel strike is consequently involved with politics — with the union's belief that it had Governor Davey's support no less than with the labor policy of the Administration, and with whatever decisions were forming in Franklin D. Roosevelt's mind when he wished a plague on the house of John L. Lewis and on the house of Tom Girdler. But in terms of the wave of 10,000 strikes that swept higher while the Little Steel strike was in progress, it marked the first big strike after the Supreme Court decision upholding the constitutionality of the Wagner Act. In the five strikes described (although it was more complex than any except the auto strike) it most nearly resembled the textile strike of 1934.

But its outcome was less clear. . . . At present the C.I.O.'s partisans insist that, although the union lost the strike, the companies did not win. If the employers believe that the strike turned public opinion against the C.I.O., the union believes just as strongly that public opinion was turned against the companies because of Girdler's refusal to settle. There is a general agreement that in the strike-bound communities themselves only careful publicity could have forestalled the growth of back-to-work movements, and that the union's reliance on Governors Earle and

Davey to intervene constituted the main weakness of the strike. But union officials are also careful to point out that the loss of the strike in Little Steel bears no relation to the loss of the steel strike of 1919, which stopped organizing efforts in steel for twelve years.

They further point out that the Labor Board hearings in the steel companies are still proceeding. Eventually, they expect, elections will be ordered in the plants. Which leads to the profound change in contemporary strikes that the steel strike demonstrated. When it became apparent that the strike could not succeed, the union's attitude toward the men remaining at work underwent a transformation. The nonstriking workers, the historic object of resentment in labor disputes, became the voters of the future, to be appealed to as potential supporters rather than denounced as scabs. This development occurred too late in the steel strike to be of great importance. What it means for the future conduct of unions depends on the next stage in the evolution of the National Labor Relations Board. . . . In the wave of strikes the pattern of labor disputes has begun to change since the signing of the Wagner Act.

Or, more exactly, since the Supreme Court decision upholding the constitutionality of the act. In the eighteen months of its existence before April 12, 1937, some 2,425 complaints were filed with the Board. In the seventy-five days after the decision there were 3,137. Even that increase does not suggest how large the Board now looms over every threatening strike situation and every organizing drive, how greatly it figures in the plans of organizers and the literature of trade associations. In the Little Steel strike, when witnesses at its hearings testified that the steel companies had brought pressure to bear on public officials, or in the National Electric Products situation, where it declared void a contract upheld by the district court, the Board has taken steps whose significance cannot be measured by statistics. But statistics will show how deeply a part of the strike pattern the Board now is: during the past year (October 1936–37) the A.F. of L. and the C.I.O. have each filed more than 2,000 complaints, the Board settling slightly more than 700 for the A.F. of L. and slightly less than 700 for the C.I.O. The A.F. of L. has lost as many plant elections as it has won; the C.I.O. has won three times as many elections as it has lost.

The Labor Board is the most recent figure added to the pattern of labor disputes, and with its appearance the positions of the other figures in that pattern have changed. Before the Supreme Court decision, for example, there was a bombardment of injunction suits against the Board (eighty-three up to the time of the Remington Rand strike), and twenty of them resulted in temporary injunctions granted by federal district courts. "The process was like a rolling snowball," the Board complained. "Employers were never complying with our orders . . . They always challenged us to take them into court." Since the decision the Board, no less than the Federal Trade Commission or the Interstate Commerce Commission in their early days, faces the period that every regulatory body goes through, of innumerable court fights on its intricate issues, fought through until a series of Supreme Court rulings defines its powers.

It is no secret that one reason why the close advisers of the President were vitally concerned that his Supreme Court proposal should be vigorously pressed was that they anticipated — and on good precedent — the Court's rejection of the Wagner Act, and the consequent impotence of the Labor Board. It is also no secret that Mr. Justice Roberts reads the newspapers; and it was his vote that validated the act. Without that validation, said many a Washington observer partisan to the President, the labor situation in the U.S. might swiftly have become blood and chaos. Now that the act exists and has been pronounced to conform to the Constitution, Washington breathes more easily. But industry's breathing is still labored — and whether it will become softer or harsher because of the act of 1938, is anybody's guess. The doctors disagree.

NOTES

1. This was the high for number of strikes, but 1919 constituted the high for the number of workers involved. Nationwide steel and coal strikes, calling out 800,000 workers, helped the total to 4,100,000.
2. Of these, however, the greater number were in smaller fabricating plants. In steel production, the S.W.O.C., with agreements with U.S. Steel, Wheeling, Jones & Laughlin, and some forty others, could claim to have agreements in plants employing about 50 per cent of the workers.
3. The verdict of the coroner's jury was made public the day before the report of the La Follette Committee. The shootings were termed "justifiable homicide."

The Social Significance of Organized Crime

"Crime, in many ways, is a Coney Island mirror, caricaturing the morals and manners of a society," Daniel Bell remarks in the following essay. In the case of American organized crime, the mirror does more than caricature: it accurately reflects some of the basic characteristics of society. No less than any other businessmen on the make, for example, the entrepreneurs of organized crime have been driven by a thirst for economic opportunity and social mobility. It has been no accident that the low man on the ethnic ladder — the Irish, the Jews, then the Italians — have, at various times, dominated the illicit activities of America's cities. For the able and the ambitious in the ghettos, striving to break out and finding no ready access to the normal avenues of economic advancement, crime has offered one road to fame and fortune.

Organized crime has paralleled legitimate business not only in motivation, but also in structure. Just as conventional enterprise progressed from cut-throat competition in a production-oriented economy to large-scale organization and control in a consumer-oriented economy, so has American crime. There is, too, an important link with urban politics, ironically made tighter because the New Deal dried up earlier sources of financial support. The Italian-American success in local politics since the 1930s, Bell suggests, has partly been bankrolled by the underworld, evidently as much out of ethnic pride as from any expectation of a payoff. There is, finally, the reaction of respectable America to its periodic rediscovery of organized crime in its midst. The shocked response to the revelations of the Lexow Committee of the 1890s, the Seabury Committee of the early 1930s, the Kefauver Committee of the early 1950s, tell as much about the reform mind as they do about American criminality.

So Daniel Bell's essay is doubly revealing. Not only does it describe an important phase of American life (gambling, Elmo Roper has estimated, is the sixth largest industry by volume of business) but, curiously, it is equally revealing about the larger society in which organized crime flourishes.

FOR FURTHER READING:

COOK, FRED J. *Secret Rulers: Criminal Syndicates and How They Control the U.S. Underworld.* New York: Duell, Sloan and Pearce, 1966.*

GLAZER, NATHAN, and MOYNIHAN, PATRICK. *Beyond the Melting Pot.* Cambridge, Mass.: MIT Press, 1963.*

WHYTE, WILLIAM. *Street Corner Society.* Chicago: University of Chicago Press, 1955.*

Asterisk denotes paperback edition.

Crime as an American Way of Life   DANIEL BELL

In the 1890's the Reverend Dr. Charles Parkhurst, shocked at the open police protection afforded New York's bordellos, demanded a state inquiry. In the Lexow investigation that followed, the young and dashing William Travers Jerome staged a set of public hearings that created sensation after sensation. He badgered "Clubber" Williams, First Inspector of the Police Department, to account for wealth and property far greater than could have been saved on his salary; it was earned, the Clubber explained laconically, through land speculation "in Japan." Heavy-set Captain Schmittberger, the "collector" for the "Tenderloin precincts" — Broadway's fabulous concentration of hotels, theaters, restaurants, gaming houses, and saloons — related in detail how protection money was distributed among the police force. Crooks, policemen, public officials, businessmen, all paraded across the stage, each adding his chapter to a sordid story of corruption and crime. The upshot of these revelations was reform — the election of William L. Strong, a stalwart businessman, as mayor, and the naming of Theodore Roosevelt as police commissioner.

It did not last, of course, just as previous reform victories had not lasted. Yet the ritual drama was re-enacted. Thirty years ago the Seabury investigation in New York uncovered the tin-box brigade and the thirty-three little McQuades. Jimmy Walker was ousted as Mayor and in came Fiorello LaGuardia. Tom Dewey became district attorney, broke the industrial rackets, sent Lucky Luciano to jail, and went to the governor's chair in Albany. Then reform was again swallowed up in the insatiable maw of corruption until in 1950 Kefauver and his committee counsel Rudolph Halley threw a new beam of light into the seemingly bottomless pit.

How explain this repetitious cycle? Obviously the simple moralistic distinction between "good guys" and "bad guys," so deep at the root of the reform impulse, bears little relation to the role of organized crime in American society. What, then, does?

The Queer Ladder

Americans have had an extraordinary talent for compromise in politics and extremism in morality. The most shameless political deals (and "steals") have been rationalized as expedient and realistically necessary. Yet in no other country have there been such spectacular attempts to curb human appetites and brand them as illicit, and nowhere else such glaring failures. From the start America was at one and the same time a frontier community where "everything goes," and the fair country of the Blue Laws. At the turn of the century the cleavage developed between the Big City and the small-town conscience. Crime as a growing business was fed by the revenues from prostitution, liquor, and gambling that a wide-open urban society encouraged and that a middle-class Protestant ethos tried to suppress with a ferocity unmatched in any other civilized country. Catholic cultures have rarely imposed such restrictions and have rarely suffered such excesses. Even in prim and proper

---

Source: Daniel Bell, "Crime as an American Way of Life," *Antioch Review,* vol. 13 (Summer 1953), pp. 131–154.

Anglican England, prostitution is a commonplace of Piccadilly night life, and gambling is one of the largest and most popular industries. In America the enforcement of public morals has been a continuing feature of our history.

Some truth may lie in Max Scheler's generalization that moral indignation is a peculiar fact of middle-class psychology and represents a disguised form of repressed envy. The larger truth lies perhaps in the brawling nature of American development and in the social character of crime. Crime, in many ways, is a Coney Island mirror, caricaturing the morals and manners of a society. The jungle quality of the American business community, particularly at the turn of the century, was reflected in the mode of "business" practiced by the coarse gangster elements, most of them from new immigrant families, who were "getting ahead," just as Horatio Alger had urged. In the older, Protestant tradition the intensive acquisitiveness, such as that of Daniel Drew, was rationalized by a compulsive moral fervor. But the formal obeisance of the ruthless businessman in the workday world to the church-going pieties of the Sabbath was one that the gangster could not make. Moreover, for the young criminal, hunting in the asphalt jungle of the crowded city, it was not the businessman with his wily manipulation of numbers but the "man with the gun" who was the American hero. "No amount of commercial prosperity," once wrote Teddy Roosevelt, "can supply the lack of the heroic virtues." The American was "the hunter, cowboy, frontiersman, the soldier, the naval hero" — and in the crowded slums, the gangster. He was a man with a gun, acquiring by personal merit what was denied him by complex orderings of stratified society. And the duel with the law was the morality play par excellence: the gangster, with whom ride our own illicit desires, and the prosecutor, representing final judgment and the force of the law.

Yet all this was acted out in a wider context. The desires satisfied in extra-legal fashion were more than a hunger for the "forbidden fruits" of conventional morality. They also involved, in the complex and ever shifting structure of group, class, and ethnic stratification, which is the warp and woof of America's "open" society, such "normal" goals as independence through a business of one's own, and such "moral" aspirations as the desire for social advancement and social prestige. For crime, in the language of the sociologists, has a "functional" role in the society, and the urban rackets — the illicit activity organized for continuing profit, rather than individual illegal acts — is one of the queer ladders of social mobility in American life. Indeed, it is not too much to say that the whole question of organized crime in America cannot be understood unless one appreciates (1) the distinctive role of organized gambling as a function of a mass-consumption economy; (2) the specific role of various immigrant groups as they, one after another, became involved in marginal business and crime; and (3) the relation of crime to the changing character of the urban political machines.

Gatsby's Model

As a society changes, so does, in lagging fashion, its type of crime. As American society became more "organized," as the American businessman became more "civilized" and less "buccaneering," so did the American racketeer. And just as there were important changes in the structure of business enterprise, so the "institutionalized" criminal enterprise was transformed too.

In the America of the last fifty years the main drift of society has been toward the rationalization of industry, the domestication of the crude self-made captain of industry into the respectable man of manners, and the emergence of a mass-consumption economy. The most significant transformation in the field of "institutionalized" crime in the 1940's was the increasing importance of gambling as against other kinds of illegal activity. And, as a multi-billion-dollar business, gambling underwent a transition parallel to the changes in American enterprise as a whole. This parallel was exemplified in many ways: in gambling's industrial organization (e.g., the growth of a complex technology such as the national racing-wire service and the minimization of risks by such techniques as lay-off betting); in its respectability, as was evidenced in the opening of smart and popular gambling casinos in resort towns and in "satellite" adjuncts to metropolitan areas; in its functional role in a mass-consumption economy (for sheer volume of money changing hands, nothing has ever surpassed this feverish activity of fifty million American adults); in the social acceptance of the gamblers in the important status world of sport and entertainment, i.e., "café society."

In seeking to "legitimize" itself, gambling had quite often actually become a force against older and more vicious forms of illegal activity. In 1946, for example, when a Chicago mobster, Pat Manno, went down to Dallas, Texas, to take over gambling in the area for the Accardo-Guzik combine, he reassured the sheriff as follows: "Something I'm against, that's dope peddlers, pickpockets, hired killers. That's one thing I can't stomach, and that's one thing the fellows up there — the group won't stand for, things like that. They discourage it, they even go to headquarters and ask them why they don't do something about it."

Jimmy Cannon once reported that when the gambling raids started in Chicago the "combine" protested that, in upsetting existing stable relations, the police were only opening the way for ambitious young punks and hoodlums to start trouble. Nor is there today, as there was twenty or even forty years ago, prostitution of major organized scope in the United States. Aside from the fact that manners and morals have changed, prostitution *as an industry* doesn't pay as well as gambling. Besides, its existence threatened the tacit moral acceptance and quasi-respectability that gamblers and gambling have secured in the American way of life. It was, as any operator in the field might tell you, "bad for business."

The criminal world of the 1940's, its tone set by the captains of the gambling industry, is in startling contrast to the state of affairs in the decade before. If a Kefauver report had been written then, the main "names" would have been Lepke and Gurrah, Dutch Schultz, Jack "Legs" Diamond, Lucky Luciano, and, reaching back a little further, Arnold Rothstein, the czar of the underworld. These men (with the exception of Luciano, who was involved in narcotics and prostitution) were in the main "industrial racketeers." Rothstein, the model for Wolfsheim the gambler in F. Scott Fitzgerald's *The Great Gatsby*, had a larger function: he was, as Frank Costello became later, the financier of the underworld, the pioneer big businessman of crime who, understanding the logic of coordination, sought to *organize* crime as a source of regular income. His main interest in this direction was in industrial racketeering, and his entry was through labor disputes. At one time, employers in the garment trades hired Legs Diamond and his sluggers to break strikes, and the Communists, then in control of the cloakmakers union, hired one Little Orgie to protect the pickets and beat up the scabs; only later did both sides learn that Legs Diamond and Little Orgie were working for the same man, Rothstein.

Rothstein's chief successors, Lepke Buchalter and Gurrah Shapiro, were able, in the early thirties, to dominate sections of the men's and women's clothing industries, of painting, fur dressing, flour trucking, and other fields. In a highly chaotic and cutthroat industry such as clothing, the racketeer, paradoxically, played a stabilizing role by regulating competition and fixing prices. When the NRA came in and assumed this function, the businessman found that what had once been a quasi-economic service was now pure extortion, and he began to demand police action. In other types of racketeering, such as the trucking of perishable foods and waterfront loading, where the racketeers entrenched themselves as middlemen — taking up, by default, a service that neither shippers nor truckers wanted to assume — a pattern of accommodation was roughly worked out, and the rackets assumed a quasi-legal veneer. On the waterfront, old-time racketeers perform the necessary function of loading — but at an exorbitant price — and this monopoly was recognized by both the union and the shippers, and tacitly by the government.

But in the last decade and a half, industrial racketeering has not offered much in the way of opportunity. *Like American capitalism itself, crime shifted its emphasis from production to consumption.* The focus of crime became the direct exploitation of the citizen as consumer, largely through gambling. And while the protection of these huge revenues was inextricably linked to politics, the relation between gambling and "the mobs" became more complicated.

Big-Business Bookies

Although it never showed up in the gross national product, gambling in the last decade was one of the largest industries in the United States. The Kefauver Committee estimated it as a $20 billion business. This figure has been picked up and widely quoted, but in truth no one knows what the gambling "turnover" and "take" actually is, nor how much is bet legally (parimutuel, etc.) and how much illegally. In fact, the figure cited by the committee was arbitrary and was arrived at quite sloppily. As one staff member said: "We had no real idea of the money spent. . . . The California crime commission said twelve billion. Virgil Peterson of Chicago estimated thirty billion. We picked twenty billion as a balance between the two."

If comprehensive data are not available, we do know, from specific instances, the magnitude of many of the operations. Some indication can be seen from these items called at random:

James Carroll and the M & G syndicate did a $20 million annual business in St. Louis. This was one of the two large books in the city.

The S & G syndicate in Miami did a $26 million volume yearly; the total for all books in the Florida resort reached $40 million.

Slot machines were present in 69,786 establishments in 1951 (each paid $100 for a license to the Bureau of Internal Revenue); the usual average is three machines to a license, which would add up to 210,000 slot machines in operation in the United States. In legalized areas, where the betting is higher and more regular, the average gross "take" per machine is $50 a week.

The largest policy wheel (i.e., "numbers") in Chicago's "Black Belt" reported taxable net profits for the four-year period from 1946 through 1949, after sizable deductions for "overhead," of $3,656,968. One of the large "white" wheels reported in 1947 a gross income of $2,317,000 and a net profit of $205,000. One CIO official estimated that perhaps 15 percent of his union's lower-echelon officials are involved in the numbers racket (a steward, free to roam a plant, is in a perfect situation for organizing bets).

If one considers the amount of dollars bet on sports alone — an estimated six billion on baseball, a billion on football pools, another billion on basketball, six billion on horse racing — then Elmo Roper's judgment that "only the food, steel, auto, chemical, and machine-tool industries have a greater volume of business" does not seem too farfetched.

While gambling has long flourished in the United States, the influx of the big mobsters into the industry — and its expansion — started in the thirties, when repeal of Prohibition forced them to look about for new avenues of enterprise. (The change, one might say crudely, was in the "democratization" of gambling. In New York of the 1860's 1870's, and 1880's one found elegant establishments where the wealthy men of the city, bankers and sportsmen gambled. The saloon was the home of the worker. The middle class of the time did not gamble. In the changing mores of America, the rise of gambling in the 1930's and 1940's meant the introduction of the middle class to gambling and casinos as a way of life.) Gambling, which had begun to flower under the nourishment of rising incomes, was the most lucrative field in sight. To a large extent the shift from bootlegging to gambling was a mere transfer of business operations. In the East, Frank Costello went into slot machines and the operation of a number of ritzy gambling casinos. He also became the "banker" for the Erickson "book," which "laid off" bets for other bookies. Joe Adonis, similarly, opened up a number of casinos, principally in New Jersey. Across the country, many other mobsters went into bookmaking. As other rackets diminished and gambling, particularly horse-race betting, flourished in the forties, a struggle erupted over the control of racing information.

Horse-race betting requires a peculiar industrial organization. The essential component is time. A bookie can operate only if he can get information on odds up to the very last minute before the race, so that he can "hedge" or "lay off" bets. With racing going on simultaneously on many tracks throughout the country, this information has to be obtained speedily and accurately. Thus, the racing wire is the nerve ganglion of race betting.

The racing-wire news service got started in the twenties through the genius of the late Moe Annenberg, who had made a fearful reputation for himself as Hearst's circulation manager in the rough-and-tough Chicago newspaper wars. Annenberg conceived the idea of a telegraphic news service which would gather information from tracks and shoot it immediately to scratch sheets, horse parlors, and bookie joints. In some instances, track owners gave Annenberg the right to send news from tracks; more often, the news was simply "stolen" by crews operating inside or near the tracks. So efficient did this news distribution system become, that in 1942, when a plane knocked out a vital telegraph circuit which served an Air Force field as well as the gamblers, the Continental Press managed to get its racing wire service for gamblers resumed in fifteen minutes, while it took the Fourth Army, which was responsible for the defense of the entire West Coast, something like three hours.

Annenberg built up a nationwide racing information chain that not only distributed wire news but controlled sub-outlets as well. In 1939, harassed by the Internal Revenue Bureau on income tax and chivvied by the Justice Department for "monopolistic" control of the wire service, the tired and aging Annenberg simply walked out of the business. He did not sell his interest or even seek to salvage some profit;

he simply gave up. Yet, like any established and thriving institution, the enterprise continued, though on a decentralized basis. James Ragen, Annenberg's operation manager and likewise a veteran of the old Chicago circulation wars, took over the national wire service through a dummy friend and renamed it the Continental Press Service.

The salient fact is that in the operation of the Annenberg and Ragen wire service, formally illegal as many of its subsidiary operations may have been (i.e., in "stealing" news, supplying information to bookies, etc.), gangsters played no part. It was a business, illicit, true, but primarily a business. The distinction between gamblers and gangsters, as we shall see, is a relevant one.

In 1946, the Chicago mob, whose main interest was in bookmaking rather than in gambling casinos, began to move in on the wire monopoly. Following repeal, the Capone lieutenants had turned, like Lepke, to labor racketeering. Murray ("The Camel") Humphries muscled in on the teamsters, the operating engineers, and the cleaning-and-dyeing, laundry, and linen-supply industries. Through a small-time punk, Willie Bioff, and union official George Browne, Capone's chief successors, Frank ("The Enforcer") Nitti and Paul Ricca, came into control of the motion-picture union and proceeded to shake down the movie industry for fabulous sums in order to "avert strikes." In 1943, when the government moved in and smashed the industrial rackets, the remaining big shots, Charley Fischetti, Jake Guzik, and Tony Accardo, decided to concentrate on gambling, and in particular began a drive to take over the racing wire.

In Chicago, the Guzik-Accardo gang, controlling a subdistributor of the racing-news service, began tapping Continental's wires. In Los Angeles, the head of the local distribution agency for Continental was beaten up by hoodlums working for Mickey Cohen and Joe Sica. Out of the blue appeared a new and competitive nationwide racing information and distribution service, known as Trans-American Publishing, the money for which was advanced by the Chicago mobs and Bugsy Siegel, who, at the time, held a monopoly of the bookmaking and wire-news service in Las Vegas. Many books pulled out of Continental and bought information from the new outfit; many hedged by buying from both. At the end of a year, however, the Capone mob's wire had lost about $200,000. Ragen felt that violence would erupt and went to the Cook County district attorney and told him that his life had been threatened by his rivals. Ragen knew his competitors. In June, 1946, he was killed by a blast from a shotgun.

Thereafter, the Capone mob abandoned Trans-American and got a "piece" of Continental. Through their new control of the national racing-wire monopoly, the Capone mob began to muscle in on the lucrative Miami gambling business run by the so-called S & G syndicate. For a long time S & G's monopoly over bookmaking had been so complete that when New York gambler Frank Erickson bought a three months' bookmaking concession at the expensive Roney Plaza Hotel, for $45,000, the local police, in a highly publicized raid, swooped down on the hotel; the next year the Roney Plaza was again using local talent. The Capone group, however, was tougher. They demanded an interest in Miami bookmaking and, when refused, began organizing a syndicate of their own, persuading some bookies at the big hotels to join them. Florida Governor Warren's crime investigator appeared — a friend, it seemed, of old Chicago dog-track operator William Johnston, who had contributed $100,000 to the Governor's campaign fund — and began raiding bookie joints, but only those that were affiliated with S & G. Then S & G, which had been buying its racing news from the local distributor of Continental Press, found its service abruptly shut off. For a few days the syndicate sought to bootleg information from New Orleans, but found itself limping along. After ten days' war of attrition, the five S & G partners found themselves with a sixth partner, who, for a token "investment" of $20,000, entered a Miami business that grossed $26,000,000 in one year.

Gamblers and Guys

While Americans made gambling illegal, they did not in their hearts think of it as wicked — even the churches benefited from the Bingo and lottery crazes. So they gambled — and gamblers flourished. Against this open canvas, the indignant tones of Senator Wiley and the shocked righteousness of Senator Tobey during the Kefauver investigation rang oddly. Yet it was probably this very tone of surprise that gave the activity of the Kefauver Committee its piquant quality. Here were some senators who seemingly did not know the facts of life, as most Americans did. Here, in the person of Senator Tobey, was the old New England Puritan conscience poking around in industrial America, in a world it had made but never seen. Here was old-fashioned moral indignation, at a time when cynicism was rampant in public life.

Commendable as such moralistic fervor was, it did not make for intelligent discrimination of fact. Throughout the Kefauver hearings, for example, there ran the presumption that all gamblers were invariably gangsters. This was true of Chicago's Accardo-Guzik combine, which in the past had its fingers in many kinds of rackets. It was not nearly so true of many of the large gamblers in America, most of whom had the feeling that they were satisfying a basic American urge for sport and looked upon their calling with no greater sense of guilt than did many bootleggers. After all, Sherman Billingsley did start out as a speakeasy proprietor, as did the Kriendlers of the "21" Club; and today the Stork Club and the former Jack and Charlie's are the most fashionable night and dining spots in America (one prominent patron of the Stork Club: J. Edgar Hoover).

The S & G syndicate in Miami, for example (led by Harold Salvey, Jules Levitt, Charles Friedman, Sam Cohen, and Edward [Eddie Luckey] Rosenbaum), was simply a master pool of some two hundred bookies that arranged for telephone service, handled "protection," acted as bankers for those who needed ready cash on hard-hit books, and, in short, functioned somewhat analogously to the large factoring corporations in the textile field or the credit companies in the auto industry. Yet to Kefauver, the S & G men were "slippery and arrogant characters. . . . Salvey, for instance, was an old-time bookie who told us he had done nothing except engage in bookmaking or finance other bookmakers for twenty years." When, as a result of committee publicity and the newly found purity of the Miami police, the S & G syndicate went out of business, it was, as the combine's lawyer told Kefauver, because the "boys" were weary of being painted "the worst monsters in the world." "It is true," Cohen acknowledged, "that they had been law violators." But they had never done anything worse than gambling, and "to fight the world isn't worth it."

Most intriguing of all were the opinions of James J. Carroll, the St. Louis "betting commissioner," who for years had been widely quoted on the sports pages of the country as setting odds on the Kentucky Derby winter book and the baseball pennant races. Senator Wiley, speaking like the prosecutor in Camus's novel, *The Stranger,* became the voice of official morality:

SENATOR WILEY: Have you any children?

MR. CARROLL: Yes, I have a boy.

SENATOR WILEY: How old is he?

MR. CARROLL: Thirty-three.

SENATOR WILEY: Does he gamble?

MR. CARROLL: No.

SENATOR WILEY: Would you like to see him grow up and become a gambler, either professional or amateur?

MR. CARROLL: No. . . .

SENATOR WILEY: All right. Is your son interested in your business?

MR. CARROLL: No, he is a manufacturer.

SENATOR WILEY: Why do you not get him into the business?

MR. CARROLL: Well, psychologically a great many people are unsuited for gambling.

Retreating from this gambit, the Senator sought to pin Carroll down on his contributions to political campaigns:

SENATOR WILEY: Now this morning I asked you whether you contributed any money for political candidates or parties, and you said not more than $200 at one time. I presume that does not indicate the total of your contributions in any one campaign, does it?

MR. CARROLL: Well, it might, might not, Senator. I have been an "againster" in many instances. I am a reader of *The Nation* for fifty years and they have advertisements calling for contributions for different candidates, different causes. . . . They carried an advertisement for George Norris; I contributed, I think, to that, and to the elder LaFollette.

Carroll, who admitted to having been in the betting business since 1899, was the sophisticated — but not immoral! — counterpoint to moralist Wiley. Here was a man without the stigmata of the underworld or underground; he was worldly, cynical of official rhetoric, jaundiced about people's motives; he was an "againster" who believed that "all gambling legislation originates or stems from some group or some individual seeking special interests for himself or his cause."

Asked why people gamble, Carroll distilled his experiences of fifty years with a remark that deserves a place in American social history: "I really don't know how to answer the question," he said, "I think gambling is a biological necessity for certain types. I think it is the quality that gives substance to their daydreams."

In a sense, the entire Kefauver materials, unintentionally, seem to document that remark. For what the committee revealed time and time again was a picture of gambling as a basic institution in American life, flourishing openly and accepted widely. In many of the small towns, the gambling joint is as open as a liquor establishment. The town of Havana, in Mason County, Illinois, felt miffed when Governor Adlai Stevenson intervened against local gambling. In 1950, the town had raised $15,000 of its $50,000 budget by making friendly raids on the gambling houses every month and having the owners pay fines. "With the gambling fines cut off," grumbled Mayor Clarence Chester, "the next year is going to be tough."

Apart from the gamblers, there were the mobsters. But what Senator Kefauver and company failed to understand was that the mobsters, like the gamblers, and like the entire gangdom generally, were seeking to become quasi-respectable and establish a place for themselves in American life. For the mobsters, by and large, had immigrant roots, and crime, as the pattern showed, was a route of social ascent and place in American life.

The Myth of the Mafia

The mobsters were able, where they wished, to "muscle in" on the gambling business because the established gamblers were wholly vulnerable, not being able to call on the law for protection. The senators, however, refusing to make any distinction between a gambler and a gangster, found it convenient to talk loosely of a nationwide conspiracy of "illegal" elements. Senator Kefauver asserted that a "nationwide crime syndicate does exist in the United States, despite the protestations of a strangely assorted company of criminals, self-serving politicians, plain blind fools, and others who may be honestly misguided, that there is no such combine." The Senate committee report states the matter more dogmatically: "There is a nationwide crime syndicate known as the Mafia. . . . Its leaders are usually found in control of the most lucrative rackets in their cities. There are indications of a centralized direction and control of these rackets. . . . The Mafia is the cement that helps to bind the Costello-Adonis-Lansky syndicate of New York and the Accardo-Guzik-Fischetti syndicate of Chicago. . . . These groups have kept in touch with Luciano since his deportation from the country."

Unfortunately for a good story — and the existence of the Mafia would be a whale of a story — neither the Senate Crime Committee in its testimony, nor Kefauver in his book, presented any real evidence that the Mafia exists as a functioning organization. One finds police officials asserting before the Kefauver committee their *belief* in the Mafia: the Narcotics Bureau *thinks* that a world-wide dope ring allegedly run by Luciano is part of the Mafia; but the only other "evidence" presented — aside from the incredulous responses both of Senator Kefauver and Rudolph Halley when nearly all the Italian gangsters asserted that they didn't know about the Mafia — is that certain crimes bear "the earmarks of the Mafia."

The legend of the Mafia has been fostered in recent years largely by the peephole writing team of Jack Lait and Lee Mortimer. In their *Chicago Confidential*, they rattled off a series of names and titles that made the organization sound like a rival to an Amos and Andy Kingfish society. Few serious reporters, however, give it much credence. Burton Turkus, the Brooklyn prosecutor who broke up the "Murder, Inc." ring, denies the existence of the Mafia. Nor could Senator Kefauver even make out much of a case for his picture of a national crime syndicate. He is forced to admit that "as it exists today [it] is an elusive and furtive but nonetheless tangible thing," and that "its organization and machinations are not always easy to pinpoint." [1] His "evidence" that many gangsters congregate at certain times of the year in such places as Hot Springs, Arkansas, in itself does not prove much; people "in the trade" usually do, and as the loquacious late Willie Moretti of New Jersey said, in explaining how he had met the late Al Capone at a race track, "Listen, well-charactered people you don't need introductions to; you just meet automatically."

Why did the Senate Crime Committee plumb so hard for its theory of a Mafia and a national crime syndicate? In part, they may have been misled by their own hearsay. The Senate committee was not in the position to do original research, and its staff, both legal and investigative, was incredibly small. Senator Kefauver had begun the investigation with the attitude that with so much smoke there must be a raging fire. But smoke can also mean a smoke screen. Mob activities is a field in which busy gossip and exaggeration flourish even more readily than in a radical political sect.

There is, as well, in the American temper, a feeling that "somewhere," "somebody" is pulling all the complicated strings to which this jumbled world dances. In politics the labor image is "Wall Street" or "Big Business"; while the business stereotype was the "New Dealers." In the field of crime, the side-of-the-mouth lowdown was "Costello."

The salient reason, perhaps, why the Kefauver Committee was taken in by its own myth of an omnipotent Mafia and a despotic Costello was its failure to assimilate and understand three of the more relevant sociological facts about institutionalized crime in its relation to the political life of large urban communities in America, namely: (1) the rise of the American Italian community, as part of the inevitable process of ethnic succession, to positions of importance in politics, a process that has been occurring independently but also simultaneously in most cities with large Italian constituencies — New York, Chicago, Kansas City, Los Angeles; (2) the fact that there are individual Italians who play prominent, often leading roles today in gambling and in the mobs; and (3) the fact that Italian gamblers and mobsters often possessed "status" within the Italian community itself and a "pull" in city politics. These three items are indeed related — but not so as to form a "plot."

The Jews . . . The Irish . . . The Italians

The Italian community has achieved wealth and political influence much later and in a harder way than previous immigrant groups. Early Jewish wealth, that of the German Jews of the late nineteenth century, was made largely in banking and merchandising. To that extent, the dominant group in the Jewish community was outside of, and independent of, the urban political machines. Later Jewish wealth, among the East European immigrants, was built in the garment trades, though with some involvement with the Jewish gangster, who was typically an industrial racketeer (Arnold Rothstein, Lepke and Gurrah, etc.). Among Jewish lawyers, a small minority, such as the "Tammany lawyer" (like the protagonist of Sam Ornitz's *Haunch, Paunch and Jowl*), rose through politics and occasionally touched the fringes of crime. Most of the Jewish lawyers, by and large the communal leaders, climbed rapidly, however, in the opportunities that established and legitimate Jewish wealth provided. Irish immigrant wealth in the northern urban centers, concentrated largely in construction, trucking, and the waterfront, has, to a substantial extent, been wealth accumulated in and through political alliance, e.g., favoritism in city contracts.

Control of the politics of the city thus has been crucial for the continuance of Irish political wealth. This alliance of Irish immigrant wealth and politics has been reciprocal; many noted Irish political figures lent their names as important window-dressing for business corporations (Al Smith, for example, who helped form the U.S. Trucking Corporation, whose executive head for many years was William J. McCormack, the alleged "Mr. Big" of the New York waterfront), while Irish businessmen have lent their wealth to further the careers of Irish politicians. Irish mobsters have rarely achieved status in the Irish community, but have served as integral arms of the politicians, as strong-arm men on election day.

The Italians found the more obvious big-city paths from rags to riches preempted. In part this was due to the character of the early Italian immigrant. Most of them were unskilled and from rural stock. Jacob Riis could remark on the nineties, "the Italian comes in at the bottom and stays there." These dispossessed agricultural laborers found jobs as ditch-diggers, on the railroads as section hands, along the docks, in the service occupations, as shoemakers, barbers, garment workers, and stayed there. Many were fleeced by the "padrone" system; a few achieved wealth from truck farming, wine growing, and marketing produce, but this "marginal wealth" was not the source of coherent and stable political power.

Significantly, although the number of Italians in the United States is about a third as high as the number of Irish, and of the thirty million Catholic communicants in the United States, about half are of Irish descent and a sixth of Italian, there is not one Italian bishop among the hundred Catholic bishops in this country or one Italian archbishop among the 21 archbishops. The Irish have a virtual monopoly. This is a factor related to the politics of the American church; but the condition also is possible because there is not significant or sufficient wealth among Italian Americans to force some parity.

The children of the immigrants, the second and third generations, became wise in the ways of urban slums. Excluded from the political ladder — in the early thirties there were almost no Italians on the city payroll in top jobs, nor in books of the period can one find discussion of Italian political leaders — and finding few open routes to wealth, some turned to illicit ways. In the children's court statistics of the 1930's, the largest group of delinquents were the Italian; nor were there any Italian communal or social agencies to cope with these problems. Yet it was oddly enough, the quondam racketeer, seeking to become respectable, who provided one of the major supports for the drive to win a political voice for Italians in the power structure of the urban political machines.

This rise of the Italian political bloc was connected, at least in the major northern urban centers, with another important development which tended to make the traditional relation between the politician and the protected or tolerated illicit operator more close than it had been in the past. This is the fact that the urban political machines had to evolve new forms of fund-raising, since the big business contributions, which once went heavily into municipal politics, now — with the shift in the locus of power — go largely into national affairs. (The ensuing corruption in national politics, as recent Congressional investigations show, is no petty matter; the scruples of businessmen do not seem much superior to those of the gamblers.) One way that urban political machines raised their money resembled that of the large corporations which are no longer dependent on Wall Street: by self-financing — that is, by "taxing" the large number of municipal employees who bargain collectively with City Hall for their wage increases. So the firemen's union contributed money to O'Dwyer's campaign.

A second method was taxing the gamblers. The classic example, as *Life* reported, was Jersey City, where a top lieutenant of the Hague machine spent his full time screening applicants for unofficial bookmaking licenses. If found acceptable, the applicant was given a "location," usually the house or store of a loyal precinct worker, who kicked into the machine treasury a high proportion of the large rent exacted. The one thousand bookies and their one thousand landlords in Jersey City formed the hard core of the political machine that sweated and bled to get out the votes for Hague.

A third source for the financing of these machines was the new, and often illegally earned, Italian wealth. This is well illustrated by the career of Costello and his emergence as a political power in New York. Here the ruling motive has been the search for an entree — for oneself and one's ethnic group — into the ruling circles of the big city.

Frank Costello made his money originally in bootlegging. After repeal, his big break came when Huey Long, desperate for ready cash to fight the old-line political machines, invited Costello to install slot machines in Louisiana. Costello did, and he flourished. Together with Dandy Phil Kastel, he also opened the Beverly Club, an elegant gambling establishment just outside New Orleans, at which have appeared some of the top entertainers in America. Subsequently, Costello invested his money in New York real estate (including 79 Wall Street, which he later sold), the Copacabana night club, and a leading brand of Scotch whiskey.

Costello's political opportunity came when a money-hungry Tammany, starved by lack of patronage from Roosevelt and LaGuardia, turned to him for financial support. The Italian community in New York has for years nursed a grievance against the Irish and, to a lesser extent, the Jewish political groups for monopolizing political power. They complained about the lack of judicial jobs, the small number — usually one — of Italian congressmen, the lack of representation on the state tickets. But the Italians lacked the means to make their ambition a reality. Although they formed a large voting bloc, there was rarely sufficient wealth to finance political clubs. Italian immigrants, largely poor peasants from southern Italy and Sicily, lacked the mercantile experience of the Jews and the political experience gained in the seventy-five-year history of Irish immigration.

During the Prohibition years, the Italian racketeers had made certain political contracts in order to gain protection. Costello, always the compromiser and fixer rather than the muscle-man, was the first to establish relations with Jimmy Hines, the powerful leader of the West Side in Tammany Hall. But his rival, Lucky Luciano, suspicious of the Irish and seeking more direct power, backed and elected Al Marinelli for district leader of the Lower West Side. Marinelli in 1932 was the only Italian leader inside Tammany Hall. Later, he was joined by Dr. Paul Sarubbi, a partner of gangster Johnny Torrio in a large, legitimate liquor concern. Certainly, Costello and Luciano represented no "unified" move by the Italians as a whole for power; within the Italian community there are as many divisions as in any other group. What is significant is that different Italians, for different reasons and in various fashions, were achieving influence for the first time. Marinelli became county clerk of New York and a leading power in Tammany. In 1937, after being blasted by Tom Dewey, then running for district attorney, as a "political ally of thieves . . . and big-shot racketeers," Marinelli was removed from office by Governor Lehman. The subsequent conviction by Dewey of Luciano and Hines, and the election of LaGuardia, left most of the Tammany clubs finacially weak and foundering. This was the moment Costello made his move. In a few years, by judicious financing, he controlled a bloc of "Italian" leaders in the Hall — as well as some Irish on the upper West Side and some Jewish leaders on the East Side — and was able to influence the selection of a number of Italian judges. The most notable incident, revealed by a wire tap on Costello's phone, was the "Thank you, Francisco" call in 1943 by Supreme Court judge nominee Thomas Aurelio, who gave Costello full credit for his nomination.

It was not only Tammany that was eager to accept campaign contributions from newly rich Italians, even though some of these *nouveaux riches* had "arrived" through bootlegging and gambling. Fiorello LaGuardia, the wiliest mind that melting-pot politics has ever produced, understood in the early thirties where much of his covert support came from. (So too, did Vito Marcantonio, an apt pupil of the master: Marcantonio has consistently made deals with the Italian leaders of Tammany Hall — in 1943 he supported Aurelio and refused to repudiate him even when the Democratic party formally did.) Joe Adonis, who had built a political following during the late twenties, when he ran a popular speakeasy, aided LaGuardia financially to a considerable extent in 1933. "The Democrats haven't recognized the Italians," Adonis told a friend. "There is no reason for the Italians to support anybody but LaGuardia; the Jews have played ball with the Democrats and haven't gotten much out of it. They know it now. They will vote for LaGuardia. So will the Italians."

Adonis played his cards shrewdly. He supported LaGuardia, but also a number of Democrats for local and judicial posts, and became a power in the Brooklyn area. His restaurant was frequented by Kenny Sutherland, the Coney Island Democratic leader; Irwin Steingut, the Democratic minority leader in Albany; Anthony DiGiovanni, later a councilman; William O'Dwyer, and Jim Moran. But, in 1937, Adonis made the mistake of supporting Royal Copeland against LaGuardia, and the irate Fiorello finally drove Adonis out of New York.

LaGuardia later turned his ire against Costello, too. Yet Costello survived and reached the peak of his influence in 1942, when he was instrumental in electing Michael Kennedy leader of Tammany Hall. Despite the Aurelio fiasco, which brought Costello into notoriety, he still had sufficient power in the Hall to swing votes for Hugo Rogers as Tammany leader in 1948. In those years many a Tammany leader came hat-in-hand to Costello's apartment or sought him out on the golf links to obtain the nomination for a judicial post.

During this period, other Italian political leaders were also coming to the fore. Generoso Pope, whose Colonial Sand and Stone Company began to prosper through political contacts, became an important political figure, especially when his purchase of the two largest Italian-language dailies (later merged into one), and of a radio station, gave him almost a monopoly of channels to Italian-speaking opinion of the city. Through Generoso Pope, and through Costello, the Italians became a major political force in New York.

That the urban machines, largely Democratic, have financed their heavy campaign costs in this fashion rather than having to turn to the "moneyed interests" explains in some part why these machines were able, in part, to support the New and Fair Deals without suffering the pressures they might have been subjected to had their source of money supply been the business groups.[2] Although he has never publicly revealed his political convictions, it is likely that Frank Costello was a fervent admirer of Franklin D. Roosevelt and his efforts to aid the common man. The basic measures of the New Deal, which most Americans today agree were necessary for the public good, would not have been possible without the support of the "corrupt" big-city machines.

The "New" Money — and the Old

There is little question that men of Italian origin appeared in most of the leading roles in the high drama of gambling and mobs, just as twenty years ago the children of East European Jews were the most prominent figures in organized crime, and before that individuals of Irish descent were similarly prominent. To some extent statistical accident and the tendency of newspapers to emphasize the few sensational figures give a greater illusion about the domination of illicit activities by a single ethnic group than all the facts warrant. In many cities, particularly in the South and on the West Coast, the mob and gambling fraternity consisted of many other groups, and often, predominantly, of native white Protestants. Yet it is clear that in the major northern urban centers there was a distinct ethnic sequence in the modes of obtaining illicit wealth and that, uniquely in the case of the recent Italian elements, the former bootleggers and gamblers provided considerable leverage for the growth of political influence as well. A substantial number of Italian judges sitting on the bench in New York today are indebted in one fashion or another to Costello; so too are many Italian district leaders — as well as some Jewish and Irish politicians. And the motive in establishing Italian political prestige in New York was generous rather than scheming for personal advantage. For Costello it was largely a case of ethnic pride. As in earlier American eras, organized illegality became a stepladder of social ascent.

To the world at large, the news and pictures of Frank Sinatra, for example, mingled with former Italian mobsters could come somewhat as a shock. Yet to Sinatra, and to many Italians, these were men who had grown up in their neighborhoods and who were, in some instances, by-words in the community for their helpfulness and their charities. The early Italian gangsters were hoodlums — rough, unlettered, and young (Al Capone was only twenty-nine at the height of his power). Those who survived learned to adapt. By now they are men of middle age or older. They learned to dress conservatively. Their homes are in respectable suburbs. They sent their children to good schools and sought to avoid publicity.[3] Costello even went to a psychiatrist in his efforts to overcome a painful feeling of inferiority in the world of manners.

As happens with all "new" money in American society, the rough and ready contractors, the construction people, trucking entrepreneurs, as well as racketeers, polished up their manners and sought recognition and respectability in their own ethnic as well as in the general community. The "shanty" Irish became the "lace curtain" Irish, and then moved out for wider recognition. Sometimes acceptance came first in established "American" society, and this was a certificate for later recognition by the ethnic community, a process well illustrated by the belated acceptance in established Negro society of such figures as Sugar Ray Robinson and Joe Louis, as well as leading popular entertainers.

Yet, after all, the foundation of many a distinguished older American fortune was laid by sharp practices and morally reprehensible methods. The pioneers of American capitalism were not graduated from Harvard's School of Business Administration. The early settlers and foundings fathers, as well as those who "won the West" and built up cattle, mining, and other fortunes, often did so by shady speculations and a not inconsiderable amount of violence. They ignored, circumvented, or stretched the law when it stood in the way of America's destiny and their own — or were themselves the law when it served their purposes. This has not prevented them and their descendants from feeling proper moral outrage when, under the changed circumstances of the crowded urban environments, latecomers pursued equally ruthless tactics.

The Embourgeoisement of Crime

Ironically, the social development which made possible the rise to political influence sounds, too, the knell of the rough Italian gangster. For it is the growing number of Italians with professional training and legitimate business success that both prompts and permits the Italian group to wield increasing political influence; and increasingly it is the professionals and businessmen who provide models for Italian youth today, models that hardly existed twenty years ago. Ironically, the headlines and exposés of "crime" of the Italian "gangsters" came years after the fact. Many of the top "crime" figures had long ago forsworn violence, and even their income, in large part, was derived from legitimate investments (real estate in the case of Costello, motor haulage and auto dealer franchises in the case of Adonis) or from such quasi-legitimate but socially respectable sources as gambling casinos. Hence society's "retribution" in the jail sentences for Costello and Adonis was little more than a trumped-up morality that disguised a social hypocrisy.

Apart from these considerations, what of the larger context of crime and the American way of life? The passing of the Fair Deal signalizes, oddly, the passing of an older pattern of illicit activities. The gambling fever of the past decade and a half was part of the flush and exuberance of rising incomes, and was characteristic largely of new upper-middle-class rich having a first fling at conspicuous consumption. These upper-middle-class rich, a significant new stratum in American life (not rich in the nineteenth-century sense of enormous wealth, but largely middle-sized businessmen and entrepreneurs of the service and luxury trades — the "tertiary economy" in Colin Clark's phrase — who by the tax laws have achieved sizable incomes often much higher than the managers of the super-giant corporations), were the chief patrons of the munificent gambling casinos. During the war decade when travel was difficult, gambling and the lush resorts provided important outlets for this social class. Now they are settling down, learning about Europe and culture. The petty gambling, the betting and bingo which relieve the tedium of small-town life, or the expectation among the urban slum dwellers of winning a sizable sum by a "lucky number" or a "lucky horse," goes on. To quote Bernard Baruch: "You can't stop people from gambling on horses. And why should you prohibit a man from backing his own judgment? It's another form of personal initiative." But the lush profits are passing from gambling as the costs of coordination rise. And in the future it is likely that gambling, like prostitution, winning tacit acceptance as a necessary fact, will continue on a decentralized, small entrepreneur basis.

But passing, too, is a political pattern, the system of political "bosses" which in its reciprocal relation provided "protection" for, was fed revenue from, crime. The collapse of the "boss" system was a product of the Roosevelt era. Twenty years ago Jim Farley's task was simple; he had to work only on some key state bosses. Now there is no longer such an animal. New Jersey Democracy was once ruled by Frank Hague; now there are five or six men, each "top dog," for the moment, in his part of the state or faction of the party. Within the urban centers, the old Irish-dominated political machines in New York, Boston, Newark, and Chicago, have fallen apart. The decentralization of the metropolitan centers, the growth of suburbs and satellite towns, the breakup of the old ecological patterns of slum and transient belts, the rise of functional groups, the increasing middle-class character of American life, all contribute to this decline.

With the rationalization and absorption of some illicit activities into the structure of the economy, the passing of an older generation that had established a hegemony over crime, the general rise of minority groups to social position, and the breakup of the urban boss system, the pattern of crime we have discussed is passing as well. Crime, of course, remains as long as passion and the desire for gain remain. But the kind of big, organized city crime, as we have known it for the past seventy-five years, was based on more than these universal motives. It was based on certain characteristics of the American economy, American ethnic groups, and American politics. The changes in all these areas mean that, in the form we have known it, it too will change.

NOTES

1. The accidental police discovery of a conference of Italian figures, most of them with underworld and police records, in Apalachin, New York, in November 1957, revived the talk of a Mafia. *Time* magazine assigned a reporter, Serrell Hillman, to check the story, and this is what he reported: "I spent some two weeks in New York, Washington and Chicago running down every clue to the so-called Mafia that I could find. I talked to a large number of Federal, state and local law enforcement authorities; to police, reporters, attorneys, detectives, non-profit civic groups such as the Chicago Crime Commission. Nobody from the F.B.I. and Justice Department officials on down, with the exception of a couple of Hearst crime reporters — always happy for the sake of a street sale to associate the 'Mafia' with the most routine barroom shooting — and the Narcotics Bureau believed that a Mafia exists as such. The Narcotics Bureau, which has to contend with a big problem in dope-trafficking, contends that a working alliance operates between an organized Mafia in Italy and Sicily and a U.S. Mafia. But the Bureau has never been able to submit proof of this, and the F.B.I. is skeptical. The generally held belief is that there is no tightly knit syndicate, but instead a loose "trade association" of criminals in various cities and areas, who run their own shows in their own fields but have matters of mutual interest to take up (as at the Apalachin conference). At any rate, nobody has ever been able to produce specific evidence that a Mafia is functioning."
   In early 1959, Fredric Sondern, Jr., an editor of the *Reader's Digest,* published a best-selling book on the Mafia, *Brotherhood of Evil,* but a close reading of Mr. Sondern's text indicates that his sources are largely the files of the Narcotics Bureau, and his findings little more than a rehash of previously published material. (For a devastating review of the book, see the *Times Literary Supplement,* London, June 12, 1959, p. 351.) Interestingly enough, in May, 1959, Alvin Goldstein, a former assistant district attorney in New York, who had prosecuted racketeer Johnny Dio, conducted a crime survey of California for Governor Pat Brown and reported that he found no evidence of the existence of a Mafia in California.
2. This is an old story in American politics. Theodore Allen, a gambler and saloon keeper, whose American Mabille was an elegant music hall and bordello (he once told a Congressional investigating committee that he was the wickedest man in New York), gave Republican Boss Thurlow Weed a campaign contribution of $25,000 for the re-election of Abraham Lincoln in 1864.
3. Except at times by being overly neighborly, like Tony Accardo, who, at Yuletide 1949, in his elegant River Forest home, decorated a 40-foot tree on his lawn and beneath it set a wooden Santa and reindeer, while around the yard, on tracks, electrically operated skating figures zipped merrily around while a loudspeaker poured out Christmas carols. The next Christmas, the Accardo lawn was darkened; Tony was on the lam from Kefauver.

The Social Role of Religion

Within this mass society, how do Americans identify themselves? In other societies, a clear class structure serves to locate people socially and to generate their institutions. Extreme economic differentials and varying styles of life assuredly do exist in America, but not a feeling of class. A man may work in a factory or operate a small farm, but he does not think of himself as a worker or peasant; neither does a man of wealth and leisure identify himself as a gentleman. Physical place provides no better basis for social identity, given the high degree of geographical mobility, the dominance of city and suburb, and the disappearance of distinctive regions or localities. In a nation of immigrants, Oscar Handlin has suggested, ethnic lines have moved into the vacuum to serve as a basis for social identity and voluntary organization. Tenuous as might be the actual ethnic content derived from peasant grandparents in the life of, say, a third-generation Italian-American, that connection nevertheless serves an important and continuing social function for him. In their book, *Beyond the Melting Pot,* Nathan Glazer and Patrick Moynihan demonstrated this persuasively for the ethnic groups of New York.

In the following essay, Will Herberg redirects this analysis to the specifically religious factor. This is the part of the ethnic makeup that provides the link from generation to generation. It is the element whose continuance is most favored by American values and which is most readily adaptable by the children who have lost the cultural content of their ethnic origins. The religious factor, too, makes it possible to explain the process of social identification among Anglo-Saxon Americans, who have little sense of their European origins. Just as descendants of Italian and Russian-Yiddish immigrants think of themselves in America as Catholics and Jews, Anglo-Saxons identify themselves as Protestants. Herberg's analysis has the further virtue of explaining a major paradox about religion in modern America: that church affiliation and membership should be high (although the religious boom that was underway in 1960 when Herberg wrote his essay evidently has not been sustained), while religious belief and piety have clearly lost vitality. The process of secularization, it would seem, need not kill the churches; it may instead put them to essentially nonreligious uses.

FOR FURTHER READING:

HANDLIN, OSCAR. *The American People in the Twentieth Century.* Boston: Beacon Press, 1963.*
HERBERG, WILL. *Protestant, Catholic, Jew.* New York: Doubleday & Company, Anchor Books, 1955.*
LIPSET, SEYMOUR M. *The First New Nation.* New York: Doubleday & Company, Anchor Books, 1963.*

Asterisk denotes paperback edition.

Religion and Culture in Present-Day America   WILL HERBERG

Whatever may be true about the religious situation, it certainly cannot be doubted that religion is enjoying a boom of unprecedented proportions in America today. Well over 95 per cent of the American people identify themselves religiously, as Protestants, Catholics, or Jews — an incredibly high figure by all available standards of comparison. The proportion of Americans who are church members — that is, actually on the rolls of the churches — has nearly doubled in the past half century; in the last twenty years indeed, church membership has been increasing twice as fast as population. Church and synagogue attendance is rising rapidly, Sunday school enrollment is rising even more rapidly, and religious giving has reached a formidable figure, even allowing for the inflationary devaluation of the dollar. Interest in religion and religious thinking is widespread on all cultural levels. Whatever the criterion of religiousness we take — and by religiousness I mean the "externals" of religion, using this term in a neutral sense, without prejudice — we cannot escape the conclusion that we are today witnessing an upsurge of religion without precedent in recent times.

But it is a curious kind of religion. The very same people who are so unanimous in identifying themselves religiously, who are joining churches at an accelerating rate, and who take it for granted that religion is a "very important" thing, do not hesitate to acknowledge that religion is quite peripheral to their everyday lives: more than half of them quite frankly admit that their religious beliefs have no influence whatever on their ideas in economics and politics, and a good proportion of the remainder are obviously uncertain. The very same people who distribute the Bible in vast quantities, largely by voluntary effort, are unable in their majority to give the name of one single book of the New Testament, and the showing is not very different when you take the Bible as a whole. The very same people who, four out of five, say they regard Jesus as divine, when asked to name the most important event in all universal history, place the Christ-event — the birth or crucifixion of Christ — fourteenth on the list, tied with the Wright brothers' invention of the airplane: the Number 1 event, almost without exception, is given as Columbus' discovery of America.

This is the problem: America is in the grip of a great religious boom, that is obvious; yet equally obvious, though not so easy to establish by facts and figures, is the continuing "trend toward secularism in ideas," to use Professor Handlin's phrase — it is really a trend toward secularism not only in ideas, but in attitudes and values as well. This is the problem: the religiousness of a secularist society, the "strengthening of the religious structure in spite of increasing secularization." Thinking through this paradox will take us a long way toward understanding the present religious situation in this country.

The best approach to the problem, I think, is to try to understand something of the role that religious belonging plays in the social structure and functioning of con-

Source: Will Herberg, "Religion and Culture in Present-Day America," in *Roman Catholicism and the American Way of Life,* ed. Thomas McAvoy (South Bend, Ind.: University of Notre Dame Press, 1960), pp. 113–127.

temporary America. I well recognize that religion has its transcendent dimension, which escapes all external scrutiny and analysis; but I am deliberately limiting my inquiry at this point to those aspects that are subject to such scrutiny and analysis, and I think that these aspects are significant in the total picture. What, then, is it that strikes one about the new function of religion in the life of the American people today? It is, I think, that religion, in its tripartite form of Protestant-Catholic-Jew, is rapidly becoming the primary context of self-identification and social location in present-day America. Let us see what this really means.

By and large, since the latter part of the nineteenth century at any rate, Americans have tended to identify and locate themselves in terms of race, ethnicity, and religion. "When asked the simple question, 'What are you?,' " Gordon W. Allport has noted, referring to certain recent researches, "only ten per cent of four-year-olds answer in terms of racial, ethnic, or religious membership, but 75 per cent of nine-year-olds do so" — and the percentage is even higher for adults. "Race" in America today means color, white *vs.* non-white, and racial stigmatization has introduced an element of caste-like stratification into American life. For white Americans, ethnicity (immigrant origin) and religion have been, and remain, the major sources of pluralistic diversity, and therefore the major forms of self-identification and social location. But the relation between the two has changed drastically in the course of the past generation, and it is this change that provides a clue to the new role of religion in American life.

As long as large-scale immigration continued, and America was predominantly a land of immigrants, in the days when "the immigrants were American history," as Handlin puts it, the dominant form of diversity, and therefore the dominant form of self-identification, was immigrant ethnicity. The always interesting question about a new family moving into the neighborhood — "What are they?" — was regularly answered in terms of ethnic-immigrant origin. Religion was felt to be an aspect of ethnicity, a part of the ethnic heritage, recent or remote. The enthusiasts of the "melting pot" were eager to eliminate these diverse heritages as quickly as possible; the "cultural pluralists" were determined to perpetuate them; but both alike moved within a pluralism based substantially on ethnicity, ethnic culture, and ethnic religion.

Within the past generation, the picture has been radically transformed. The stoppage of mass immigration during the First World War, followed by the anti-immigration legislation of the 1920's, undermined the foundations of immigrant ethnicity and the immigrant ethnic group with amazing rapidity; what it did was to facilitate the emergence of third and post-third generations, with their characteristic responses and attitudes, as a decisive influence on American life, no longer threatened with submergence by the next new wave of immigration. Within the threefold American scheme of race, ethnicity, and religion, a shift took place, a shift is taking place, from ethnicity to religion as the dominant form of self-identification — as the dominant way of answering the question, What am I? How do I differ from 'one man's family'? Where do I fit in in the totality of American society?" Ethnic identifications and traditions have not disappeared; on the contrary, with the third generation, they are enjoying a lively popularity as symbols of "heritage." But now the relation between ethnicity and religion has been reversed: religion is no longer an aspect of ethnicity; it is ethnicity, or rather what remains of it, that is taken up, redefined, and expressed through religious identifications and institutions. Religion, or at least the tripartite differentiation of Protestant, Catholic, and Jew has (aside from race) become the prevailing form of defining one's identity as an American in contemporary American society.

Keeping this in mind, we can begin to understand one of the most striking facts in the religious history of this country during the past half century — the transformation of America from a *Protestant* country into a *three-religion* country.

Writing just thirty years ago, André Siegfried described Protestantism as America's "national religion," and he was largely right, despite the ban on religious establishment in the Constitution. Normally, to be born an American meant to be a Protestant; this was the religious identification that in the American mind quite naturally went along with being an American. Non-Protestants felt the force of this conviction almost as strongly as did the Protestants; Catholics and Jews, despite their vastly increasing numbers, experienced their non-Protestant religion as a problem, even as an obstacle, to their becoming full-fledged Americans: it was a mark of their foreignness. (This was true despite the much esteemed colonial heritage of both Jews and Catholics, since it was not the "old American" elements in these two groups that influenced American attitudes, but the newer immigrant masses.) In the familiar Troeltschean sense, Protestantism — not any one of the multiplying denominations, but Protestantism as a whole — constituted America's "established church."

This is no longer the case. Today, to be born an American is no longer taken to mean that one is necessarily a Protestant; Protestantism is no longer the obvious and "natural" religious identification of the American. Today, the evidence strongly indicates, America has become a three-religion country: the normal religious implication of being an American today is that one is either a Protestant, a Catholic, or a Jew. These three are felt to be, by and large, three different forms of being religious in the American way; they are the three "religions of democracy," the "three great faiths" of America. Today, unlike fifty years ago, not only Protestants, but increasingly Catholics and Jews as well, feel themselves, and are recognized to be, Americans not apart from, or in spite of, their religion, but because of it. If America today possesses a "church" in the Troeltschean sense — that is, a form of religious belonging which is felt to be involved in one's belonging to the national community — it is the tripartite religious system of Protestant-Catholic-Jew.

This transformation of America from a Protestant into a three-religion country has come about not because of any marked increase in Catholics or Jews — the Protestant-Catholic ratio has remained pretty well the same for the past thirty years, and the proportion of Jews in the general population has probably been declining. It has come about, as I have suggested, through the emergence of a stabilized American third generation, which is able to set its mark on American life because it is no longer threatened with dissolution by recurrent waves of mass immigration.

The immigrant generation, and this is true of all immigrant nationalities, established itself in America as an ethnic group with an ethnic culture, of which the ethnic language and the ethnic religion were generally the most significant elements. For the first, the immigrant generation, religion was part of ethnicity; for the Italian immigrant, in other words, his Catholicness was part of his Italianness; for the Jewish immigrant, his Judaism, his Jewish religion, was part of his *Yiddishkait,* his ethnic culture. You remember the movie "Marty." You remember how Marty brings home the girl Clara to introduce her to his mother. His mother is a good church-going Catholic, but what is the question she asks about Clara? Not "Is she Catholic?" but "Is she Italian?" Why? Because to the mother, the first-generation immigrant, if she's Italian, then she's Catholic, and if she's Catholic without being Italian, it doesn't do any good anyway! This is the outlook on ethnicity and religion characteristic of the immigrant generation.

The second generation is in a very different position. The second generation is marginal — "too American for the home and too foreign for the school," in Marcus Hansen's celebrated phrase. It is doubly alienated, belonging to two communities but at home in neither, torn away from the old moorings and not yet anchored in the new reality. The second generation responds to its marginality in a number of ways, but by and large it may be said that what the second generation wants most of all is to get rid of its foreignness and become American. This obviously influences its attitude to religion. Just because in the immigrant home, in which the second generation grows up, religion is understood to be a part of ethnicity, to be a part of the immigrant foreignness, the second generation takes a negative view of religion, sometimes breaking with it entirely, usually retaining an uneasy connection, mixed with hostility and embarrassment. The second generation — and that holds true for every immigrant group in America — is characteristically the least religious of American generations.

But now comes the third generation. The third generation — and with it we must include the post-third generations that have arisen on American soil — is again in a very different position. It is at last American, securely American, secure as any American is in his Americanness. But it is faced with a new problem, the problem of defining its identity. Ethnic identifications will no longer serve, as in one way or another they served the first and second generations. What then? — how is the third generation to answer the question, "What am I? How do I differ from 'one man's family'? Where do I fit in the totality of American society?" In an effort to define its social identity — without which no tolerable life is possible — the American third generation goes in search of a "heritage." In a sensational reversal of earlier attitudes, the third generation seeks a "return." Some two decades ago, Marcus Lee Hansen, studying not Italians or Jews on the east coast, but Scandinavian Lutherans in the Midwest in the twenties and thirties, expressed this reversal in a classic formula: "What the son wishes to forget, the grandson wishes to remember." The "son," constituting the second generation, wishes to "forget" because he wants so passionately to get rid of his foreignness; the "grandson," belonging to the third generation, wishes to "remember" because he needs a "heritage." But what of the grandfather can the grandson "remember"? — what of his grandfather's legacy can he take over and use for the purpose of giving himself a "heritage" and defining his identity? Not his grandfather's nationality, language, or culture; the American pattern of assimilative acculturation obviously makes that impossible. But the grandfather's religion is a very different thing: America not only permits, it even encourages, the perpetuation of one's religious diversity and distinctiveness without danger to one's Americanness. Of course, it is not the grandfather's religion as the grandfather would have recognized it; it is the grandfather's religion brought up to date and Americanized. But it serves; and so religion becomes the characteristic symbol of "heritage" for the third generation, and its return to its heritage becomes a return to religion. With Catholics and Jews, the process, however complex, is relatively unambiguous. With Protestants, however, there is a double movement: on the one side, a return to ethnically associated religion, as among Lutherans; on the other side, because of the confusion, blurring, and growing meaninglessness of denominational lines, a "return" to Protestantism rather than to any particular group within it as a form of religious identification. William H. Whyte's account, in *The Organization Man,* of the emergence of the United Protestant Church in Park Forest, Ill., a story which could be duplicated in so many other suburban communities, well illustrates this pattern of development; but even where denominational affiliations are still maintained, the basic identification is still Protestant, especially among the younger people. And so a three-religion America has emerged, an America in which being a Protestant, being a Catholic, and being a Jew are the three recognized alternative ways of being an American.

A word of caution is necessary. It should not be imagined that just because America has become, or is becoming, a three-religion country, all ethnic or religious group tensions are at an end. Anti-Semitism runs deeper than any merely sociological analysis can penetrate, and even on the sociological level, the new tripartite system would, for the time being at least, seem to make almost as much for the exacerbation as for the alleviation of intergroup tensions. Anti-Jewish manifestations are, for the moment, at a low ebb, but Protestant-Catholic antagonisms appear to be growing sharper. This accentuation of Protestant-Catholic tensions seems to me to be very largely a reflection of the painful transition period through which we are passing; there is every reason to hope that with the stabilization of the new situation, these hostilities too will abate. Yet we should not overlook the fact that the new system of tripartite coexistence is bound to raise its own problems and breed its own tensions with which we will have to cope in the time to come.

What has the transformation of America from an ethnic into a religious pluralism, and concomitantly from a Protestant into a three-religion country, meant so far as the status and character of religion in this country are concerned?

Very obviously, it has made for a boom in religious belonging. To have a "name" in American society today — to have an identity, to be able to answer the question "What am I? Where do I belong?" — means increasingly to identify oneself in religious terms, as Protestant, Catholic, or Jew. These are three alternative ways of being an American. This is eminently true of the burgeoning suburban sector of American society, least true in the rural areas, and measurably true in the older urban centers. It is certainly the over-all pattern of American life. Obviously, such self-identification in religious terms engenders a new sense of belonging to one's community; obviously, too, it impels to institutional affiliation, characteristically expressed in terms of concern for the children: "We have to join a church (or a temple) for the sake of the children." There is profound sociological wisdom in this remark, though its theological implications may be dubious. "The church," Oscar Handlin points out, "supplies a place where the children come to learn what they are" — what kind of Americans they are. The mechanisms of other-directed conformity to which David Riesman has called attention serve to give religious belonging the compelling power it is acquiring in the pattern of suburban "sociability," but the new role of religion in this process is the result of the more basic factors I have tried to indicate in my remarks on the third generation and the transformation of America into a three-religion country.

Just as Americans are coming more and more to think of being a Protestant, being a Catholic, and being a Jew as three alternative ways of being an American, so they are coming to regard Protestantism, Catholicism, and Judaism, the "three great faiths," as three alternative (though not necessarily equal) expressions of a great overarching commitment which they all share by virtue of being Americans. This commitment is, of course, democracy or the American Way of Life. It is the common allegiance which (to use Professor Williams' phrase) provides Americans with the "common set of ideas, rituals, and symbols" through which an "overarching sense of unity" is achieved amidst diversity and conflict." It is, in a sense far more real than John Dewey ever dreamed of, the "common religion" of Americans.

Let me illustrate this point with two texts borrowed from President Eisenhower, who may, I think, be taken as a representative American really serious about religion. "Our government," Mr. Eisenhower declared shortly after his election in 1952, "makes no sense unless it is founded in a deeply felt religious faith, *and I don't care what it is.*" It is the last phrase which I have emphasized — "and I don't care what it is" — to which I want to call your attention. Of course, President Eisenhower did not mean that literally; he would have been much disturbed had any sizable proportion of Americans become Buddhists, or Shintoists, or Confucianists — but of course that never entered his mind. When he said "I don't care what it is," he obviously meant "I don't care which of the three it is — Protestantism, Catholicism, or Judaism." And why didn't he care which it was? Because, in his view, as in the view of all normal Americans, they "all say the same thing." And what is the "same thing" which they all say? The answer is given to us from the current vocabulary: "the moral and spiritual values of democracy." These, for the typical American, are in a real sense final and ultimate; the three conventional religions are approved of and validated primarily because they embody and express these "moral and spiritual values of democracy."

Let me drive this home with the second text from President Eisenhower. In 1948, four years before his election, just before he became president of Columbia, Mr. Eisenhower made another important pronouncement on religion. "I am the most intensely religious man I know," he declared. "Nobody goes through six years of war without faith. That does not mean that I adhere to any sect. [Incidentally, following the way of all flesh, he was soon to join a "sect," the Presbyterian.] A democracy cannot exist without a religious base. I believe in democracy." Here we have the entire story in a single phrase: I believe in religion because I believe in democracy! Precisely the same conviction, though expressed in a rather more sophisticated manner, was affirmed by an eminent New York rabbi not long ago. "The spiritual meaning of American democracy," he declared, "is realized in its three great faiths." Similar statements, I assure you, could be found in the pronouncements of spokesmen of the other two religious groups.

What I am describing is essentially the "Americanization" of religion in America, and therefore also its thorough-going secularization. This process is not a recent one. It began for Protestantism some time after the Civil War and proceeded apace in the latter decades of the nineteenth century. Sidney Mead's brilliant description of this trend is particularly relevant.

> What was not so obvious at the time [he writes] was that the United States, in effect, had two religions, or at least two different forms of the same religion, and that the prevailing Protestant ideology represented a syncretistic mingling of the two. The first was the religion of the [Protestant] denominations which was commonly articulated in terms

of scholastic Protestant orthodoxy and almost universally practised in terms of the experimental religion of pietistic revivalism. . . . The second was the religion of the democratic society and nation. This . . . was articulated in terms of the destiny of America, under God, to be fulfilled by perfecting the democratic way of life for the example and betterment of mankind.

With remarkably little change — something would have to be said about the waning of scholastic orthodoxy and the new forms of pietistic revivalism — these words could stand as a description of the current situation. What is new, what is crucially new, is that this is no longer true merely of Protestantism; it is becoming more and more true of Catholicism and Judaism as well, precisely because Catholicism and Judaism have become American, integral parts of the three-religion America. In this, as in so many other respects, their Americanization has meant their "Protestantization," using this term to describe the American Protestant ethos, so at variance with classical Protestant Christian faith. With the loss of their foreignness, of their immigrant marginality, these two religious groups seem to be losing their capacity to resist dissolution in the culture. In becoming American, they have apparently become American all the way.

We are now, I think, in a position to penetrate the apparent paradox with which we initiated this discussion, the paradox of the religiousness of a secularist society. How can Americans be so religious and so secularistic at the same time? The answer is that for increasing numbers of Americans religion serves a function largely unrelated to the content of faith, the function of defining their identity and providing them with a context of belonging in the great wilderness of a mobile American society. Indeed, for such a purpose, the authentic content of faith may even prove a serious handicap, for if it is Jewish or Christian faith, it carries a prophetic impact which serves rather to unadjust than to adjust, to emphasize the ambiguity of every earthly form of belonging rather than to let the individual rest secure in his "sociability." For this reason, the typical American has developed a remarkable capacity for being serious about religion without taking religion seriously — in which respect he is not unlike sinful human beings of all ages. His ideas, values, and standards he takes from what is so often really his ultimate commitment, the American Way of Life. He combines the two — his religion and his culture — by making the former an expression of the latter, his religion an expression of the "moral and spiritual values of democracy." Hence his puzzling proreligious secularism, his secularistic religionism, which, looked at more closely, does not seem so puzzling after all. . . .

Black Power: Two Views

The cry for "Black Power," first heard in the land in June 1966, signaled a major turning point in the Negro's struggle for equality in America. Until then, the essential thrust had aimed at civil rights objectives: the elimination of segregation and discrimination and the protection of the right to vote. When the Supreme Court, in 1954, declared unconstitutional laws requiring segregated public schools, the civil rights movement received a powerful boost. This, clearly, marked the opening of a decisive shift in public policy, the precedent for ending the legal barriers to equal treatment and integration. Blacks, for their part, mobilized to help accomplish those objectives. Beginning with the Montgomery bus boycott of 1955, Martin Luther King's doctrine of nonviolent resistance was employed persistently and courageously in the hostile South.

But, despite a record of considerable surface success as measured by its original aims, the civil rights movement suffered a loss of hope by the mid-1960s, especially among its younger adherents. For one thing, nonviolence in the violent South took a terrific psychological toll on civil rights workers. For another, they discovered that formal rights did not lead automatically to actual equality; nor did it seem that the North was any more willing in practice to accept integrated schooling and open housing than the South. There was, too, a growing disillusionment with liberal white allies whose rhetoric often outstripped their actions: the Democratic convention of 1964 was a case in point. Finally, there was the growing realization that civil rights had little relevance to the problems of the poor blacks anyway. Ghetto unrest was mounting in the early 1960s; in the summer of 1965 Watts exploded in riot. The following May, the Student Nonviolent Coordinating Committee called on "black Americans to begin building independent political, economic, and cultural institutions that they will control and use as instruments of social change in this country." The following month, during the tense march to Jackson, Mississippi, after the shooting of James Meredith, Stokely Carmichael, the new SNCC chairman, denounced nonviolent tactics and issued the call for Black Power.

At first merely a slogan used in anger, Black Power quickly came to designate the militants' search for an authentic alternative to the civil rights movement. In the following months, Stokely Carmichael and others attempted to define, in a thoroughgoing way, the meaning of Black Power. The following essay is one such effort. Starting with the assumption that groups in America have always advanced by developing collective power, Carmichael argues that this has been the fundamental failing of black Americans. In trying to trace the reasons, Carmichael finds one in integrationism, which siphons off some blacks into middle-class America, leaving the black community the poorer and, by this form of tokenism, assuaging white guilt.

For their part, many white liberals deplored this turn in black thinking. As Milton Mayer observed in his response to Carmichael's essay, Black Power sacrificed the redemptive nature of the civil rights movement; instead of rejecting America's emphasis on power, as Martin Luther King had attempted to do, the Black Power advocates merely wanted to join the power system. Nor, Mayer feared, were they likely to succeed, for the black man confronted obstacles faced by no other American.

Since 1966, the Black Power issue has not become clearer; indeed, the ambiguities and unanswered questions have increased. Given their economic marginality, how are the black ghettos to develop viable economic institutions? Is it possible to reconcile the tendencies toward class action, which advocates an alliance with poor whites, with black nationalism and separatism? Does Black Power accept the system, as Carmichael seems to say in the following essay, or does it aim for revolution, as his public rhetoric and identification with Maoism would seem to indicate? And what of violence? Is it to be an instrument of defense or, as seems more and more the case, or attack? The lack of clear answers in part reflects insufficiently hard thinking by Black Power advocates, but in part too it reflects the unyielding dilemmas they face. But, if so much about Black Power remains cloudy, the underlying import seems clear enough: the civil rights movement, with its tactics of nonviolence, its focus on legal barriers, its integrationist ends, has fallen short and is being replaced by new forms of black protest.

FOR FURTHER READING:

CARMICHAEL, STOKELY, and HAMILTON, CHARLES V. *Black Power*. New York: Random House, Vintage Books, 1967.*
Report of the National Advisory Commission on Civil Disorders. New York: Bantam Books, 1968.*
SILBERMAN, CHARLES E. *Crisis in Black and White.* New York: Random House, Vintage Books, 1964.*
Asterisk denotes paperback edition.

Toward Black Liberation

STOKELY CARMICHAEL

One of the most pointed illustrations of the need for Black Power, as a positive and redemptive force in a society degenerating into a form of totalitarianism, is to be made by examining the history of distortion that the concept has received in national media of publicity. In this "debate," as in everything else that affects our lives, Negroes are dependent on, and at the discretion of, forces and institutions within the white society which have little interest in representing us honestly. Our experience with the national press has been that where they have managed to escape a meretricious special interest in "Git Whitey" sensationalism and race-war-mongering, individual reporters and commentators have been conditioned by the enveloping racism of the society to the point where they are incapable even of objective observation and reporting of racial *incidents*, much less the analysis of *ideas*. But this limitation of vision and perceptions is an inevitable consequence of the dictatorship of definition, interpretation, and consciousness, along with the censorship of history that the society has inflicted upon the Negro — and itself.

Our concern for the black power addresses itself directly to this problem, the ne-

Source: Stokely Carmichael, "Toward Black Liberation," in *Black and White in American Culture*, eds. Jules Chametsky and Sidney Kaplan (Amherst, Mass.: University of Massachusetts Press, 1969), pp. 76–87.

cessity to reclaim our history and our identity from the cultural terrorism and depredation of self-justifying white guilt.

To do this we shall have to struggle for the right to create our own terms through which to define ourselves and our relationship to the society, and to have these terms recognized. This is the first necessity of a free people, and the first right that any oppressor must suspend. The white fathers of American racism knew this — instinctively it seems — as is indicated by the continuous record of the distortion and omission in their dealings with the red and black men. In the same way that Southern apologists for the "Jim Crow" society have so obscured, muddied, and misrepresented the record of the reconstruction period, until it is almost impossible to tell what really happened, their contemporary counterparts are busy doing the same thing with the recent history of the civil rights movement.

In 1964, for example, the National Democratic party, led by L. B. Johnson and Hubert H. Humphrey, cynically undermined the efforts of Mississippi's black population to achieve some degree of political representation. Yet, whenever the events of that convention are recalled by the press, one sees only that aversion fabricated by the press agents of the Democratic party. A year later the House of Representatives, in an even more vulgar display of political racism, made a mockery of the political rights of Mississippi's Negroes when it failed to unseat the Mississippi Delegation to the House which had been elected through a process which methodically and systematically excluded over 450,000 voting-age Negroes, almost one half of the total electorate of the state. Whenever this event is mentioned in print it is in terms which leave one with the rather curious impression that somehow the oppressed Negro people of Mississippi are at fault for confronting the Congress with a situation in which they had no alternative but to endorse Mississippi's racist political practices.

I mention these two examples because, having been directly involved in them, I can see very clearly the discrepancies between what happened and the versions that are finding their way into general acceptance as a kind of popular mythology. Thus the victimization of the Negro takes place in two phases — first it occurs in fact and deed, then, and this is equally sinister, in the official recording of those facts.

The "Black Power" program and concept which is being articulated by SNCC, CORE, and a host of community organizations in the ghettoes of the North and South has not escaped that process. The white press has been busy articulating their own analyses, their own interpretations, and criticisms of their own creations. For example, while the press had given wide and sensational dissemination to attacks made by figures in the civil rights movement — foremost among which are Roy Wilkins of the NAACP and Whitney Young of the Urban League — and to the hysterical ranting about black racism made by the political chameleon that now serves as vice-president, it has generally failed to give accounts of the reasonable and productive dialogue which is taking place in the Negro community, and in certain important areas in the white religious and intellectual community. A national committee of influential Negro churchmen affiliated with the National Council of Churches, despite their obvious respectability and responsibility, had to resort to a paid advertisement to articulate their position, while anyone shouting the hysterical yappings of "Black Racism" got ample space. Thus the American people have gotten at best a superficial and misleading account of the very terms and tenor of this debate. I wish to quote briefly from the statement by the national committee of churchmen which I suspect that the majority of Americans will not have seen. This statement appeared in *The New York Times* of July 31, 1966.

We an informal group of Negro Churchmen in America are deeply disturbed about the crisis brought upon our country by historic distortions of important human realities in the controversy about "black power." What we see shining through the variety of rhetoric is not anything new but the same old problem of power and race which has faced our beloved country since 1619.

. . . The conscience of black men is corrupted because, having no power to implement the demands of conscience, the concern for justice in the absence of justice becomes a chaotic self-surrender. Powerlessness breeds a race of beggars. We are faced now with a situation where powerless conscience meets conscience-less power, threatening the very foundation of our Nation.

. . . We deplore the overt violence of riots, but we feel it is more important to focus on the real sources of these eruptions. These sources may be abetted inside the Ghetto, but their basic cause lies in the silent and covert violence which white middleclass America inflicts upon the victims of the inner city.

. . . In short; the failure of American leaders to use American power to create equal opportunity *in life* as well as *law,* this is the real problem and not the anguished cry for black power.

. . . Without the capacity to *participate with power, i.e.,* to have some organized political and economic strength to really influence people with whom one interacts — integration is not meaningful.

. . . America has asked its Negro citizens to fight for opportunity as *individuals,* whereas at certain points in our history what we have needed most has been opportunity for the *whole group,* not just for selected and approved Negroes.

. . . We must not apologize for the existence of this form of group power, for we have been oppressed as a group and not as individuals. We will not find our way out of that oppression until both we and America accept the need for Negro Americans, as well as for Jews, Italians, Poles, and white Anglo-Saxon Protestants, among others to have and to wield group power.

Traditionally, for each new ethnic group, the route to social and political integration into America's pluralistic society has been through the organization of their own institutions with which to represent their communal needs within the larger society. This is simply stating what the advocates of black power are saying. The strident outcry, *particularly* from the liberal community, that has been evoked by this proposal can only be understood by examining the historic relationship between Negro and white power in this country.

Negroes are defined by two forces, their blackness and their powerlessness. There have been traditionally two communities in America. The white community, which controlled and defined the forms that all institutions within the society would take, and the Negro community which has been excluded from participation in the power decisions that shaped the society, and has traditionally been dependent upon, and subservient to, the white community.

This has not been accidental. The history of every institution of this society indicates that a major concern in the ordering and structuring of the society has been the maintaining of the Negro community in its condition of dependence and oppression. This has not been on the level of individual acts of discrimination between individual whites against individual Negroes, but as total acts by the white community against the Negro community. This fact cannot be too strongly emphasized — that racist assumtpions of white superiority have been so deeply ingrained in the structure of the society that it infuses its entire functioning, and is so much a part of the national subconscious that it is taken for granted and is frequently not even recognized.

Let me give an example of the difference between individual racism and institutionalized racism, and the society's response to both. When unidentified white terrorists bomb a Negro church and kill five children, that is an act of individual racism, widely deplored by most segments of the society. But when in that same city, Birmingham, Alabama, not five but five hundred Negro babies die each year because of a lack of proper food, shelter, and medical facilities, and thousands more are destroyed and maimed physically, emotionally, and intellectually because of conditions of poverty and deprivation in the ghetto, that is a function of institutionalized racism. But the society either pretends it doesn't know of this situation, or is incapable of doing anything meaningful about it. And this resistance to doing anything meaningful about conditions in that ghetto comes from the fact that the ghetto is itself a product of a combination of forces and special interests in the white community, and the groups that have access to the resources and power to change that situation benefit, politically and economically, from the existence of that ghetto.

It is more than a figure of speech to say that the Negro community in America is the victim of white imperialism and colonial exploitation. This is in practical economic and political terms true. There are over twenty million black people comprising ten per cent of this nation. They for the most part live in well-defined areas of the country — in the shanty-towns and rural black belt areas of the South, and increasingly in the slums of northern and western industrial cities. If one goes into any Negro community, whether it be in Jackson, Mississippi, Cambridge, Maryland, or Harlem, New York, one will find that the same combination of political, economic, and social forces are at work. The people in the Negro community do not control the resources of that community, its political decisions, its law enforcement, its housing standards; and even the physical ownership of the land, houses, and stores *lie outside that community.*

It is white power that makes the laws, and it is violent white power in the form of armed white cops that enforces those laws with guns and nightsticks. The vast majority of Negroes in this country live in these captive communities and must endure these conditions of oppression because, and only because, *they are black and powerless.* I do not suppose that at any point the men who control the power and resources of this country ever sat down and designed these black enclaves and formally articulated the terms of their colonial and dependent status, as was done, for example, by the apartheid government of South Africa. Yet, one can not distinguish between one ghetto and another. As one moves from city to city it is as though some malignant racist planning unit had done precisely this — designed each one from the same master blueprint. And indeed, if the ghetto had been formally and deliberately planned, instead of growing spontaneously and inevitably from the racist functioning of the various institutions that combine to make the society, it would be somehow less frightening. The situation would be less frightening because, if these ghettoes were the result of design and conspiracy, one could understand their similarity as being artificial and consciously imposed, rather than the result of identical patterns of white racism which repeat themselves in cities as distant as Boston and Birmingham. Without bothering to list the historic factors which contribute to this pattern — economic exploitation, political impotence, discrimination in employment and education — one can see that to correct this pattern will require far-reaching changes in the basic power relationships and the ingrained social patterns within the society. The question is, of course, what kinds of changes are necessary, and how is it possible to bring them about?

In recent years, the answer to these questions which has been given by most articulate groups of Negroes and their white allies, the "liberals" of all stripes, has been in terms of something called "integration." According to the advocates of integration, social justice will be accomplished by "integrating the Negro into the mainstream institutions of the society from which he has been traditionally excluded." It is very significant that each time I have heard this formulation it has been in terms of "the Negro," the individual Negro, rather than in terms of the community.

This concept of integration had to be based on the assumption that there was nothing of value in the Negro community and that little of value could be created among Negroes, so the thing to do was to siphon off the "acceptable" Negroes into the surrounding middle-class white community. Thus the goal of the movement for integration was simply to loosen up the restrictions barring the entry of Negroes into the white community. Goals around which the struggle took place, such as public accommodation, open housing, job opportunity on the executive level (which is easier to deal with than the problem of semi-skilled and blue-collar jobs which involve more far-reaching economic adjustments), are quite simply middle-class goals, articulated by a tiny group of Negroes who had middle-class aspirations. It is true that the student demonstrations in the South during the early sixties, out of which SNCC came, had a similar orientation. But while it is hardly a concern of a black sharecropper, dishwasher, or welfare recipient whether a certain fifteen-dollar-a-day motel offers accommodations to Negroes, the overt symbols of white superiority and the imposed limitations on the Negro community had to be destroyed. Now, black people must look beyond these goals, to the issue of collective power.

Such a limited class orientation was reflected not only in the program and goals of the civil rights movement, but in its tactics and organization. It is very significant that the two oldest and most "respectable" civil rights organizations have constitutions which *specifically* prohibit partisan political activity. CORE once did, but changed that clause when it changed its orientation toward black power. But this is perfectly understandable in terms of the strategy and goals of the older organizations. The civil rights movement saw its role as a kind of liaison between the powerful white community and the dependent Negro one. The dependent status of the black community apparently was unimportant since — if the movement were successful — it would blend into the white community anyway. We made no pretense of organizing and developing institutions of community power in the Negro community, but appealed to the conscience of white institutions of power. The posture of the civil rights movement was that of the dependent, the suppliant. The theory was that without attempting to create any organized base of political strength itself, the civil rights movement could, by forming coalitions with various "liberal" pressure organizations in the white community — liberal reform clubs, labor unions, church groups, progressive civic groups — and at times one or other of the major political parties — influence national legislation and national social patterns.

I think we all have seen the limitations of this approach. We have repeatedly seen that political alliances based on appeals to conscience and decency are chancy things, simply because institutions and political organizations have no consciences, outside their own special interests. The political and social rights of Negroes have been and always will be negotiable and expendable the moment they conflict with the interests of our "allies." If we do not learn from history, we are doomed to repeat it, and that is precisely the lesson of the Reconstruction. Black people were allowed to register, vote, and participate in politics because it was to the advantage of powerful white allies to promote this. But this was the result of white decision, and it was ended by other white men's decision before any political base powerful enough to challenge that decision could be established in the Southern Negro community. (Thus at this point in the struggle Negroes have no assurance — save a kind of idiot optimism and faith in a society whose history is one of racism — that if it were to become necessary, even the painfully limited gains thrown to the civil rights movement by the Congress would not be revoked as soon as a shift in political sentiments should occur.)

The major limitation of this approach was that it tended to maintain the traditional dependence of Negroes and of the movement. We depended upon the goodwill and support of various groups within the white community whose interests were not always compatible with ours. To the extent that we depended on the financial support of other groups, we were vulnerable to their influence and domination.

Also, the program that evolved out of this coalition was really limited and inadequate in the long term and one which affected only a small select group of Negroes. Its goal was to make the white community accessible to "qualified" Negroes, and presumably each year a few more Negroes armed with their passports — a couple of university degrees — would escape into middle-class America and adopt the attitudes and life styles of that group; and one day the Harlems and the Wattses would stand empty, a tribute to the success of integration. This is simply neither realistic nor particularly desirable. You can integrate communities, but you assimilate individuals. Even if such a program were possible, its result would be, not to develop the black community as a functional and honorable segment of the total society, with its own cultural identity, life patterns, and institutions, but to abolish it — the final solution to the Negro problem. Marx said that the working class is the first class in history that ever wanted to abolish itself. If one listens to some of our "moderate" leaders, it appears that the American Negro is the first race that ever wished to abolish itself. The fact is that what must be abolished is not the black community, but the dependent colonial status that has been inflicted upon it. The racial and cultural personality of the black community must be preserved and the community must win its freedom while preserving its cultural integrity. This is the essential difference between integration as it is currently practised and the concept of black power.

What has the movement for integration accomplished to date? The Negro graduating from M.I.T. with a doctorate will have better job opportunities available to him than to Lynda Bird Johnson. But the rate of unemployment in the Negro community is steadily increasing, while that in the white community decreases. More educated Negroes hold executive jobs in major corporations and federal agencies than ever before, but the gap between white income and Negro income has almost doubled in the last twenty years. More suburban housing is available to Negroes, but housing conditions in the ghetto are steadily declining. While the infant mortality rate of New York City is at its lowest rate ever in the city's history, the infant mortality rate of Harlem is steadily climbing. There has been an organized national resistance to the Supreme Court's order to integrate the schools, and the federal government has not acted to enforce that order. Less than fifteen per cent of black children in the South attend integrated schools, and Negro schools, which the vast majority of black children still attend, are increasingly decrepit, overcrowded, under-staffed, inadequately equipped and funded.

This explains why the rate of school dropouts is increasing among Negro teenagers, who then express their bitterness, hopelessness, and alienation by the only means they have — rebellion. As long as people in the ghettoes of our large cities feel that they are victims of the misuse of white power without any way to have their needs represented — and these are frequently simple needs: to get the welfare inspectors to stop kicking down your doors in the middle of the night, the cops from beating your children, the landlord to exterminate the vermin in your home, the city to collect your garbage — we will continue to have riots. These are not the products of "black power," but of the absence of any organization capable of giving the community the power, the black power, to deal with its problems.

SNCC proposes that it is now time for the black freedom movement to stop pandering to the fears and anxieties of the white middle class in the attempt to earn its "good-will," and to return to the ghetto to organize these communities to control themselves. This organization must be attempted in northern and southern urban areas as well as in the rural black belt counties of the South. The chief antagonist to this organization is, in the South, the overtly racist Democratic party, and in the North, the equally corrupt big city machines.

The standard argument presented against independent political organization is "But you are only ten per cent." I cannot see the relevance of this observation, since no one is talking about taking over the country, but taking control over our own communities.

The fact is that the Negro population, ten per cent or not, is very strategically placed because — ironically — of segregation. What is also true is that Negroes have never been able to utilize the full voting potential of our numbers. Where we could vote, the case has always been that the white political machine stacks and gerrymanders the political subdivisions in Negro neighborhoods so the true voting strength is never reflected in political strength. Would anyone looking at the distribution of political power in Manhattan, ever think that Negroes represented sixty per cent of the population there?

Just as often the effective political organization in Negro communities is absorbed by tokenism and patronage — the time honored practice of "giving" certain offices to selected Negroes. The machine thus creates a "little machine," which is subordinate and responsive to it, in the Negro community. These Negro political "leaders" are really vote deliverers, more responsible to the white machine and the white power structure than to the community they allegedly represent. Thus the white community is able to substitute patronage control for audacious black power in the Negro community. This is precisely what Johnson tried to do even before the Voting Rights Act of 1966 was passed. The National Democrats made it very clear that the measure was intended to register Democrats, not Negroes. The President and top officials of the Democratic party called in almost one hundred selected Negro "leaders" from the Deep South. Nothing was said about changing the policies of the racist state parties, nothing was said about repudiating such leadership figures as James Eastland and Ross Barnett in Mississippi or George Wallace in Alabama. What was said was simply "Go home and organize your people into the local Democratic party — *then* we'll see about poverty money and appointments." (Incidentally, for the most part the War on Poverty in the South is controlled by local Democratic ward heelers — and outspoken racists who have used the program to change the form of the Negroes' dependence. People who were afraid to register for fear of being thrown off the farm are now afraid to register for fear of losing their Head Start jobs.)

We must organize black community power to end these abuses, and to give the Negro community a chance to have its needs expressed. A leadership which is truly "responsible" — not to the white press and power structure, but to the community — must be developed. Such leadership will recognize that its power lies in the unified and collective strength of that community. This will make it difficult for the white leadership group to conduct its dialogue with individuals in terms of patronage and prestige, and will force them to talk to the community's representatives in terms of real power.

The single aspect of the black power program that has encountered most criticism is this concept of independent organization. This is presented as third-partyism, which has never worked, or a withdrawal into black nationalism and isolationism. If such a program is developed it will not have the effect of isolating the Negro community but the reverse. When the Negro community is able to control local office and negotiate with other groups from a position of organized strength, the possibility of meaningful political alliances on specific issues will be increased. That is a rule of politics and there is no reason why it should not operate here. The only difference is that we will have the power to define the terms of these alliances.

The next question usually is: "So — can it work, can the ghettoes in fact be organized?" The answer is that this organization must be successful, because there are no viable alternatives — not the War on Poverty, which was at its inception limited to dealing with effects rather than causes, and has become simply another source of machine patronage. And "Integration" is meaningful only to a small chosen class within the community.

The revolution in agricultural technology in the South is displacing the rural Negro community into northern urban areas. Both Washington, D.C. and Newark, New Jersey, have Negro majorities. One third of Philadelphia's population of two million people is black. "Inner city" in most major urban areas is already predominantly Negro, and, with the white rush to suburbia, Negroes will in the next three decades control the hearts of our great cities. These areas can become either concentration camps with a bitter and volatile population whose only power is the power to destroy, or organized and powerful communities able to make constructive contributions to the total society. Without the power to control their lives and their communities, without effective political institutions through which to relate to the total society, these communities will exist in a constant state of insurrection. This is a choice that the country will have to make.

By Power Possessed   MILTON MAYER

Morris Cohen of C.C.N.Y. was lecturing at Chicago in 1941 (prior to December 7), and his old friend Irving Salmon (like Cohen a Jew) was giving a reception for

Source: Milton Mayer, "By Power Possessed," in *Black and White in American Culture*, eds. Jules Chametsky and Sidney Kaplan (Amherst, Mass.: University of Massachusetts Press, 1969), pp. 88–93.

him at the University. The small talk was large and loud with the European war. Salmon, a rabid interventionist, was saying, "I just want to bash in a few Nazi heads before I die." "It seems to me, Irving," said Cohen, "that bashing heads is for the ninety-six per cent — not for the four per cent."

Now Stokely Carmichael is not for bashing in heads — though I don't suppose it's excluded, since White Power doesn't exclude it. And I think I comprehend what he means by Black Power. What I don't apprehend is how he thinks Black Power will be come by and what he thinks it will do. His counsel of desperation is no better counsel for being a reflexive response to a condition he and I find unendurable; any more than the starving man's theft of bread is a meaningful attack on *his* condition.

Nor do Stokely Carmichael's references (outside his essay) to Irish Power enlighten me. The Kennedys could shuck their Irish skins — even their Catholic skins, which, incidentally, put them into the twenty-five to thirty per cent Power bracket — and emerge as rich and beautiful young Americans with plenty of everything. Rich, young, beautiful — and white. The Negro has plenty of nothing, and when he has plenty of everything — jobs, houses, schools, votes — he will still be black: the one discernible *other* in a society whose Know-Nothings were never able to close the door altogether against the "Irish." The discriminable Negro is the uniquely irresistible object of discrimination.

The Kennedys represent a majority amalgam of special interests. The Carmichaels represent the Negro (who is poor) and nobody else; least of all the poor white. The Negro's is a special interest in which nobody else is interested. His special interest is, to be sure, *intelligible* to a rich society which rocks along without any consuming concern for the common good, but the small special interest (like the corner grocer's) is increasingly inconsequential in the age of amalgamation.

Irish Power never mobilized the white Anglo-Saxon Protestants, except sectionally and sporadically; and they were so sharply divided among themselves that they could not focus their hostility on the Irish. But Black Power mobilizes the whites in an ad hoc alliance in which (as is usual in such situations) they sink their differences and gang up. If Stokely Carmichael means to pit the ten per cent's Power against the ninety per cent's, the ninety per cent will be delighted to accommodate him and see what it can do against the ten in a fair and free contest. "It is white power that makes the laws," he says, as if he were somehow arguing *for* his position, "and it is violent white power in the form of armed white cops that enforces those laws with guns and nightsticks."

Let us suppose, contrary to likelihood, that the ten per cent comes out on top in the contest. What will it be and do then? It is not beyond a reasonable doubt that coercive triumph, over the centuries, has improved the triumphant Wasps. Nor has modern triumph over the Wasps much improved the Irish beyond putting lace curtains in their windows. Whatever the Wasps did in their day, the Irish (and the Portuguese, the Poles, and the Patagonians) do in theirs; and this is not necessarily improvement. Socrates, Acton, and Fulbright all seem to be saying that Power is not an unmixed blessing, and the statesman of ancient days said of the horrors of his triumphant Rome, "All that we do, we do because Power compels us."

What makes Stokely Carmichael think that the Negroes will use Power to better advantage than the whites have been able to use it? I know there is no great point in describing the disappointments of freedom to the untutored slave. But Stokely Carmichael is a tutored slave. He may hope that the Negro would master Power rather than be mastered by it, but his tutoring must have acquainted him with the dictum of Confucius: "He who says, 'Rich men are fools, but when I am rich I will not be a fool,' is already a fool."

I say "would," rather than "will," because I cannot see how Black Power, as I understand it, will come into its own until blacks are thirty, or forty, or fifty-one per cent of the whole society. It will elect a sheriff where it is fifty-one per cent of the electorate; but there are not many such counties, and still fewer states. White Power will fight for its commercial control of the "inner city" — where the Negro already has fifty-one (or eighty-five) per cent of the overnight populace; and when it surrenders what will we have then, except the ghetto unpolluted, with the Negro completing the wall the white began?

The exploitation of the huddled "nationality" neighborhoods, Irish, Italian, Jewish, German, Polish, Swedish, and Bohemian, tore our metropolitan communities to pieces three-quarters of a century ago. Their "leaders" delivered them en bloc to the boodlers and got them a statue of Kosciusko in exchange. Stokely Carmichael has to convince us that his high hope will be realized; that the Negroes will be an exception to the upper class pattern and their inner city serve the welfare of its inhabitants and the general welfare on which the particular ultimately depends. It will not be radical idealists like Stokely Carmichael or Martin King who will do what has always had to be done to win American elections. It is much more likely that the present congressman from Harlem will be the mayor of Stokely Carmichael's *new* New York.

Stokely Carmichael is righter than he is wrong. Integration does mean what he says it means — the assimilation of the psychologically suicidal Negro into the white man's society on the white man's intolerable and unenviable terms. And he is right in suggesting that the white's guilt is collective — I and all the other "friends of the Negro" have exploited him; and not through our grandfathers, either. We travel as effortlessly as we do because we, not our grandfathers, are riding on the black man's back.

Stokely Carmichael is righter than he is wrong; but he is mortally wrong. He is mortally wrong because he accepts the white definition of Power and ignores the demonstrable (if mystifying) fact that there is a kind of power that a majority (be it all men but one) cannot handily dispose of. I speak of nonviolent noncooperation, nonviolent resistance, and nonviolent action undertaken in a nonviolent spirit.

Even on the white man's view of power, the Negro may get some mileage out of nonviolence. American society can live easier every year without menial labor, but for a few years or decades yet it cannot live in the manner to which it is accustomed without the Negro ten per cent. They perform its filthiest jobs and return the profit on its filthiest property. At excruciating cost to themselves, but in solid self-interest, they can leave some of its filth unswept and unprofitable. They still have a small margin of muscle in noncooperation, and by muscle I mean nothing more exalted than Stokely Carmichael or the white man means.

But the margin, in a society which cannot employ its whites, and does not need to, is shrinking. It is the powerlessness inherent in nonviolent noncooperation that the Negro can, perhaps — I say only "perhaps" — turn to account as a peculiar form of power. The whites are guilty. And they would rather fight than switch to expiation. If the Negro can find a weapon that will take the fight out of them, the whites' only remaining course may be justice, not only for the Negro but for every other oppressed minority.

In his *Massachusetts Review* statement, where he purports to present the essentials of the matter, Stokely Carmichael seems never to have heard of Martin King, or of Greensboro. Or of Rosa Parks — who brought Martin King and Greensboro *and Stokely Carmichael* into being. Rosa Parks had something less than ten per cent of the Power (as Stokely Carmichael reckons it) when she could not bring herself to move to the back of the bus in Montgomery. But without the strange power she exercised that day in 1955, Stokely Carmichael would not have the familiar power he has now.

Her power wasn't black. It was human (and, for all any of us know, divine by virtue of its being human). It was the power to heap coals of fire on the heads of the Powerful until they would *want* to do differently than they were doing. It was the power of redemption, and it came out of the most impotent segment of American society, the psalm-singing Southern Negro with his childlike power to believe that he would overcome some day. Out of that power came the Movement; out of the Movement came all that came in the next decade; and out of the deliquescence of the Movement, as it went North to the unbelieving Negro, comes the present vacuum into which Stokely Carmichael would proceed with hopeless weapons instead of none. The analogy with India is colossally imperfect, but it has this much application: We do not *know* that the American white man is less susceptible of being civilized than the British were at Amritsar.

Stokely Carmichael pointedly ignores the power that gave him birth, and he divides the Negroes into the unaccepting (like himself) and the acceptable "passers." He cannot possibly be unconscious of the singular phenomenon of our time and of all time — the power of one powerless person, neither murderer nor victim, neither combatant nor suppliant, to overcome; and, what is more, to win supporters from the ranks of the enemy. Until Montgomery nothing else had ever moved the white man's church at all. And without moved and uncoerced allies the ten per cent will never make it in the halls of Congress or the streets of Selma or any other center of Stokely Carmichael's kind of power.

The Movement is failing, if it is failing, because it has gone North, where the Negro is who doesn't see why he, of all people, should have to be better than the White man. The primitive Negro of the South sees why. Washed in the blood of the Lamb, he sees why he has to be responsible, not for the Negro, not for the white man, but for Man and the salvation of Man through sorrow and suffering and endurance to the end. But moving mountains is slow going, and Stokely Carmichael sounds like Marx's London businessman who would cut off his own right arm for a short-term profit. The short-term Negro will not even get the profit; he hasn't enough to invest.

The redemptive love to which men are called — and to which the psalm-singing Negro responded — is not assured of a profit either. Its prospect of short-term success is slight, but the slightest prospect is better than no prospect at all, and Stokely Carmichael's way has been tried (by the white man) again and again and again. It has failed.

Its very failure may be a sign that men are not bad, and that treating them (and oneself) as if they were is therefore inefficacious. "We have repeatedly seen," says Stokely Carmichael, "that political alliances based on appeals to conscience and decency are chancy things, simply because institutions and political organizations have no consciences outside their own special interests." ("Men are bad," says Machiavelli, "and if you do not break faith with them, they will break faith with you.")

If Stokely Carmichael is right, his way is no worse than Martin King's, only more tiresome as a spectacle; except that Martin King's is directed to the refinement of our sensibilities and Stokely Carmichael's is not.

The issue between them is the issue of knowing. Stokely Carmichael knows, and Martin King doesn't. Martin King doesn't know what power may be within us, or working through us, or what we can and cannot do. William Penn was the first white man the Indians had ever seen without a gun. He went to them, saying to his followers, "Let us try what love will do, for if they see that we love them they will not want to injure us," and on that occasion, and as long as Penn and his successors governed Pennsylvania, and in Pennsylvania alone, the prospect proved to have been splendidly justified. But it was so slight that it took faith above all knowing.

Stokely Carmichael does not display that faith. For all the good his having become a Southern Negro has done him, he might as well have been a white man. He appropriates the white man's racism as the black's and adopts the white man's Power without either God *or* the big battalions. So far is he from supposing that there may be an omnipotence which empowers its votaries, that he has got to settle in the end, not for God, or even for man, but for brute. Count clubs or noses — and if men are brutes, it matters not which — coercion carries the day in the jungle. Whoever chooses the jungle had better be a lion.

The Changing Place of Women in America

Feminism is again on the march in America. Spurred in part by the example of black activism, female militants have issued the call for "Women's Liberation." With the legal barriers to full equality long since dismantled and overt social equality largely achieved, modern feminists have focused more attention on the underlying obstacles — sexual attitudes, conceptions of the family, the social roles accorded men and women — that hem the American female in and limit her chances for full self-development. If the strident voice of Women's Liberation tends to be deprecated, as militant feminists always have been in the American past, clearly the claim to equality is taken with greater seriousness today than ever before in our history. Even the prohibition against job discrimination on account of sex in civil rights legislation — hitherto a dead letter — seems about to receive some measure of enforcement.

In the following essay, Carl N. Degler traces the changing status of women in America. He attempts to answer two questions. What has been the nature and extent of women's advancement in our society? What accounts for such progress as has been made? On neither count can today's feminists take much comfort. Immense progress, of course, there has been since the first half of the nineteenth century in legal status, social roles, and economic activity. But women today have far inferior job opportunities: they have little access to high-status occupations, and their average income is only two-thirds that of men. The central barrier to meaningful careers — how to reconcile career and marriage — remains immovable. As for the reasons for change, Degler locates them not in self-conscious feminism, but in the larger social conditions of the country. The frontier, with its perennial shortage of women, provided a long-term feminist bias; industrialization helped liberate women from the bondage of farm and kitchen; and in the twentieth century a variety of factors — affluence, contraception, expanding job opportunities in the white-collar world, and, of course, war — have favored women's progress. Those achievements won by feminists — for example, prohibition and voting rights — have not lived up to the hopes of female advocates. The point is, Degler argues, that American society, male and female, is resistant to ideological change, but responsive to the dictate of practical conditions. Degler's thesis does not bode well for Women's Liberation, in a sectarian sense, but given the rapidity of social change in present-day America, it does hold out some hope for American women.

FOR FURTHER READING:

FLEXNER, ELEANOR. *A Century of Struggle: Woman's Rights Movement in the U.S.* New York: Atheneum Publishers, 1959.*
FRIEDAN, BETTY. *The Feminine Mystique.* New York: Dell Publishing Company, 1963.*
O'NEILL, WILLIAM L. *Everyone Was Brave: The Rise and Fall of Feminism in America.* Chicago: Quadrangle Books, 1969.*

Asterisk denotes paperback edition.

Revolution Without Ideology: The Changing Place of Women in America

CARL N. DEGLER

If feminism is defined as the belief that women are human beings and entitled to the same opportunities for self-expression as men, then America has harbored a feminist bias from the beginning. In both the eighteenth and nineteenth centuries foreign travelers remarked on the freedom for women in America. "A paradise for women," one eighteenth-century German called America, and toward the close of the nineteenth century Lord Bryce wrote that in the United States "it is easier for women to find a career, to obtain work of an intellectual as of a commercial kind, than in any part of Europe."

Certainly the long history of a frontier in America helps to account for this feminist bias. In a society being carved out of a wilderness, women were active and important contributors to the process of settlement and civilization. Moreover, because women have been scarce in America they have been highly valued. During almost the whole of the colonial period men outnumbered women, and even in the nineteenth century women remained scarce in the West. As late as 1865, for example, there were three men for each woman in California; in Colorado the ratio was as high as 20 to 1. Such disparities in the sex ratio undoubtedly account for the West's favorable attitude toward women as in an Oregon law of 1850 that granted land to single women and, even more significant for the time, to married women; or in the willingness of western territories like Wyoming (1869) and Utah (1870) to grant the suffrage to women long before other regions where the sex ratio was more nearly equal.

Another measure of women's high esteem in American society was the rapidity with which the doors of higher education opened to women. Even without counting forerunners like Oberlin College, which admitted women in 1837, the bars against women came down faster and earlier in America than anywhere. The breakthrough came during the Civil War era, when women's colleges like Elmira, Vassar and Smith were founded, and universities like Michigan and Cornell became coeducational. The process was later and slower in Europe. Girton College, Cambridge, for example, which opened in 1869, was the sole English institution of higher education available to women until London University accorded women full privileges in 1879. Heidelberg, which was the first German university to accept women, did not do so until 1900. More striking was the fact that at its opening Girton provided six places for young women; Vassar alone, when it opened in 1865, counted some 350 students in residence. Another indication of the American feminist bias was that at the end of the century girls outnumbered boys among high school graduates.

But if the frontier experience of America helped to create a vague feminist bias that accorded women more privileges than in settled Europe, the really potent force changing women's place had little to do with the frontier or the newness of the

Source: Carl N. Degler, "Revolution Without Ideology: The Changing Place of Women in America," *Daedalus*, vol. 93 (1964), pp. 653–670.

country. It was the industrial revolution that provided the impetus to women's aspirations for equality of opportunity; it was the industrial revolution that carried through the first stage in the changing position of women — the removal of legal and customary barriers to women's full participation in the activities of the world.

Today it is axiomatic that men work outside the home. But before the industrial revolution of the nineteenth century, the great majority of men and women were co-workers on the land and in the home. Women worked in the fields when the chores of the home and child-rearing permitted, so that there was not only close association between work and home for both sexes, but even a certain amount of overlap in the sexual division of labor. The coming of machine production changed all that. For a time, it is true, many unmarried women and children — the surplus labor of the day — were the mainstay of the new factory system, but that was only temporary. By the middle of the nineteenth century the bulk of industrial labor was male. The coming of the factory and the city thus wholly changed the nature of men's work. For the first time in history, work for most men was something done outside the family, psychologically as well as physically separated from the home.

The same industrial process that separated work and home also provided the opportunities for women to follow men out of the home. For that reason the feminist movement, both socially and intellectually, was a direct consequence of the industrial changes of the nineteenth century. Furthermore, just as the new industrial system was reshaping the rural men who came under its influence, so it reshaped the nature of women.

The process began with the home, which, in the early years of industrialization, was still the site of most women's work. Because of high land values, the city home was smaller than the farm house, and with less work for children, the size of the urban family was smaller than the rural. Moreover, in the city work in the home changed. Machines in factories now performed many of the tasks that had long been women's. In truth, the feminist movement began not when women felt a desire for men's jobs, but when men in factories began to take away women's traditional work. Factory-produced clothing, commercial laundries, prepared foods (e.g., prepared cereals, canned vegetables, condensed milk, bakery bread) were already available in the years after the Civil War. Toward the end of the century an advanced feminist like Charlotte Perkins Gilman, impressed by the accelerating exodus of women's chores from the middle-class home, predicted that the whole kitchen would soon be gone. She was wrong there, but even today the flight continues with pre-cooked and frozen foods, TV dinners, cake mixes, special packaging for easy disposal, diaper services and the like.

Middle-class women were the main beneficiaries of the lightening of the chores of the home; few working-class or immigrant women could as yet take advantage of the new services and products. These middle-class women became the bone and sinew of the feminist movement, which was almost entirely an urban affair. They joined the women's clubs, organized the temperance crusades and marched in the suffrage parades. With an increasing amount of time available to them in the city, and imbued with the historic American value of work, they sought to do good. And there was much to be done in the raw, sometimes savage, urban environment of the late nineteenth century. For example, public playgrounds in the United States began in Boston only in the 1880's, when two public-spirited middle-class women caused a cartload of sand to be piled on an empty lot and set the neighborhood children loose upon it. Many a city and small town at the turn of the century owed its public library or its park to the dedicated work of women's clubs. The venerable giant redwood trees of northern California survive today because clubwomen of San Francisco and nearby towns successfully campaigned in 1900 to save them from being cut down for lumber. The saloon and prostitution were two other prevalent urban blights that prompted study and action by women's organizations.

More important than women's opposition to social evils was the widening of women's knowledge and concerns that inevitably accompanied it. What began as a simple effort to rid the community of a threat to its purity often turned into a discovery of the economic exploitation that drove young working girls into brothels and harried working men into saloons. Frances Willard, for example, while head of the Women's Christian Temperance Union, broadened the WCTU's reform interests far beyond the liquor question, causing it to advocate protective legislation for working women, kindergartens and training programs for young working girls. Jane Addams, at Hull-House in Chicago's slums, quickly learned what historians have only recently discovered, that it was the urban boss's undeniable services to the immigrants that were the true sources of his great political power and the real secret of his successful survival of municipal reform campaigns.

The most direct way in which industrialization altered the social function of women was by providing work for women outside the home. Production by machine, of course, widened enormously the uses to which women's labor could be put once physical strength was no longer a consideration. And toward the end of the century, as business enterprises grew and record-keeping, communications and public relations expanded, new opportunities for women opened up in business offices. The telephone operator, the typist, the clerical worker and the stenographer now took places beside the seamstress, the cotton mill operator and the teacher.

As workers outside the home, women buried the Victorian stereotype of the lady under a mountain of reality. After all, it was difficult to argue that women as a sex were weak, timid, incompetent, fragile vessels of spirituality when thousands of them could be seen trudging to work in the early hours of the day in any city of the nation. Nor could a girl who worked in a factory or office help but become more worldly. A young woman new to a shop might have been embarrassed to ask a male foreman for the ladies' room, as some working girls' autobiographies report, but such maidenly reticence could hardly survive very long. Even gentle, naïve farm girls soon found out how to handle the inevitable, improper advances of foremen. They also learned the discipline of the clock, the managing of their own money, the excitement of life outside the home, the exhilaration of financial independence along with the drudgery of machine labor. Having learned something of the ways of the world, women could not be treated then, nor later in marriage, as the hopeless dependents Victorian ideals prescribed.

In time work transformed the outer woman, too. First to go were the hobbling, trailing skirts, which in a factory were a hazard and a nuisance. Even before the Civil War, Amelia Bloomer and other feminists had pointed out that women, if they were to work in the world as human beings, needed looser and lighter garments than those then in fashion. Until working women were numbered in the millions, no change took place. After 1890 women's skirts gradually crept up from the floor, and the neat and simple shirtwaist became the uniform of the working girl. A costume very like the original bloomer was widely worn by women factory workers during the First World War. Later the overall and the coverall continued the adaptation of women's clothes to the machine.

The most dramatic alteration in the image of woman came after the First World War, when there was a new upsurge in women's employment. The twenties witnessed the emergence of the white-collar class, and women were a large part of it. Over twice as many women entered the labor force that decade as in the previous one; the number of typists alone in 1930 was three-quarters of a million, a tenfold increase since 1900. And woman's appearance reflected the requirements of work. Except for some of the extreme flapper fashions, which were transient, the contemporary woman still dresses much as the woman of the 1920's did. In the 1920's women threw out the corset and the numerous petticoats in favor of light undergarments, a single slip, silk or rayon stockings, short skirts and bobbed hair. So rapid and widespread was the change that an investigation in the 1920's revealed that even most working-class girls no longer wore corsets, and the new interest in bobbed hair resulted between 1920 and 1930 in an increase of 400 per cent in the number of women hair dressers.

The physical freedom of dress that women acquired during the 1920's was but the superficial mark of a new social equality. The social forces behind this new equality are several. Some of these forces, like the growing number of college-trained women and the increasing number of women in the working force, go back far into the past; others, like the impact of the war and the arduous campaign for women's suffrage, were more recent. But whatever the causes, the consequences were obvious. Indeed, what is generally spoken of as the revolution in morals of the 1920's is more accurately a revolution in the position of women. Within a few short years a spectrum of taboos was shed. For the first time women began to smoke and drink in public; cigarette manufacturers discovered and exploited in advertising a virtually untouched market. As recently as 1918 it was considered daring for a New York hotel to permit women to sit at a bar. In the twenties, despite prohibition, both sexes drank in public.

Perhaps most significant, as well as symbolic, of the new stage in the position of women was their new sexual freedom. The twenties have long been associated with the discovery of Freud and a fresh, publicly acknowledged interest in sex. But insofar as these attitudes were new they represented changes in women, particularly those of the middle and upper classes. Premarital and extramarital sexuality by men had never been severely criticized, and discussion of sexual matters was commonplace wherever men gathered. Now, though, middle-class women also enjoyed that freedom. For the first time, it has been said, middle-class men carried on their extramarital affairs with women of their own social class instead of with cooks, maids and prostitutes.

An easier sexuality outside of marriage was only the most sensational side of the revolution in morals; more important, if only because more broadly based, was a new, informal, equal relationship between the sexes, culminating in a new conception of marriage. The day was long since past when Jennie June Croly could be barred, as she was in 1868, from a dinner in honor of Charles Dickens at a men's club even though her husband was a member and she was a professional writer. (Indeed, so thoroughly has such separation of the sexes been abandoned that the New Princeton Club in New York City has closed all but one of its public rooms to any man who is not accompanied by a woman!) And at least in the gatherings of the educated middle class, talk between the sexes was often free, frank and wide-ranging. The same mutual acceptance of the sexes was visible in the prevalent talk about the "new marriage," in which the woman was a partner and a companion, not simply a mother, social convenience and a housekeeper.

The reality of the new conception of marriage was reflected in the sharp increase in the divorce rate. Because marriage, legally as well as socially, in the nineteenth century was more confining for women than for men, the early feminists had often advocated more liberal divorce laws. And even though divorce in the nineteenth century was more common in the United States than in any European country, the divorce rate in the 1920's shot up 50 per cent over what it had been only ten years before. One sign that women in the 1920's were seeking freedom from marriage if they could not secure equality in marriage was that two thirds of the divorces in that decade were instituted by women.

By the close of the twenties the ordinary woman in America was closer to a man in the social behavior expected of her, in the economic opportunities open to her and in the intellectual freedom enjoyed by her than at any time in history. To be sure there still was a double standard, but now its existence was neither taken for granted nor confidently asserted by men.

In truth, the years since the twenties have witnessed few alterations in the position of women that were not first evident in that crucial decade. The changes have penetrated more deeply and spread more widely through the social structure, but their central tendency was then already spelled out. Even the upsurge in women's employment, which was so striking in the twenties, continued in subsequent years. Each decade thereafter has counted a larger number of working women than the previous one. During the depression decade of the 1930's, even, half a million more women entered the labor force than in the prosperous twenties. By 1960 some 38 per cent of all women of working age — almost two out of five women — were employed outside the home.

The movement of women out of the home into remunerative work, however, has been neither steady nor unopposed. Undoubtedly one of the underlying conditions is an expanding economy's need for labor. But something more than that is needed to break society's traditional habits of mind about the proper work for women. Certainly here the feminist demands for equality for women played a part. But a social factor of equal importance was war. By their very disruption of the steady pulse of everyday living, wars break the cake of custom, shake up society and compel people to look afresh at old habits and attitudes. It is not accidental, for instance, that women's suffrage in England, Russia and Germany, as well as the United States, was achieved immediately after the First World War and in France and Italy after the Second.

At the very least, by making large and new demands upon the established work force, war draws hitherto unused labor into the economic process. During the Civil War, for example, young women assumed new roles in the economy as workers in metal and munitions factories, as clerks in the expanded bureaucracy in Washington and as nurses in war hospitals. Moreover, when the war was over women had permanently replaced men as the dominant sex in the teaching profession. Furthermore, since many women found a new usefulness in the Sanitary Fairs and other volunteer work, the end of hostilities left many women unwilling to slip back into the seclusion of the Victorian home. It is not simply coincidental that the women's club movement began very soon after the war.

When the First World War came to the United States, feminist leaders, perhaps recalling the gains of the Civil War, anticipated new and broad advances for their sex. And the demand for labor, especially after the United States entered the war, did open many jobs to women, just as it was doing in contemporary Great Britain and Germany. All over the United States during the war customary and legal restrictions on the employment of women fell away. Women could be seen doing everything from laying railroad ties to working in airplane factories. The war also brought to a successful climax the struggle for the suffrage. Pointedly women had argued that a war for democracy abroad should at least remedy the deficiencies of democracy at home.

If politically the war was a boon to women, economically it failed to live up to feminist anticipations. The First World War, unlike the Civil War, did not result in a large permanent increase in the number of working women. Indeed, by 1920 there were only 800,000 more women working than in 1910. But as a result of wartime demands, women did get permanent places in new job categories, like elevator operators and theater ushers. (But women street car conductors disappeared soon after the armistice.) Certain traditional professions for women, like music teaching, lost members between 1910 and 1920, while professions that required more training and provided steadier income, like library and social work and college teaching, doubled or tripled their numbers in the same period.

The Second World War, with its even more massive demands for labor and skills, brought almost four million new women workers into the nation's factories and offices. Once again jobs usually not filled by women were opened to them. For example, the number of women bank officers rose 40 per cent during the four years of the war and the number of women employees in finance has continued to rise ever since. Furthermore, unlike the situation after the First World War, the female work force after 1945 not only stayed up but then went higher.

Measured in the number of women working, the changes in the economic position of women add up to a feminist success. Twenty-four million working women cannot be ignored. But weighed in the scales of quality instead of quantity, the change in women's economic status is not so striking. It is true that women now work in virtually every job listed by the Bureau of the Census. Moreover, the popular press repeatedly tells of the inroads women are making into what used to be thought of as men's jobs. Three years ago, for example, a woman won a prize as the mutual fund salesman of the year. Women are widely represented in advertising and in real estate, and even women taxicab drivers are no longer rare. Yet the fact remains that the occupations in which the vast majority of women actually engage are remarkably similar to those historically held by women. In 1950 almost three quarters of all employed women fell into twenty occupational categories, of which the largest was stenographers, typists and secretaries — a category that first became prominent as a woman's occupation over a half century ago. Other occupations which have traditionally been women's, like domestic service, teaching, clerical work, nursing and telephone service, are also conspicuous among the twenty categories. Further than that, the great majority of women are employed in occupations in which they predominate. This sexual division of labor is clearly evident in the professions, even though women are only a small proportion of total professional workers. Two thirds of all professional women are either nurses or teachers; and even in teaching there is a division between the sexes. Most women teach in the primary grades; most men teach in high school. Women are notoriously underrepresented in the top professions like law, medicine, engineering and scientific research. No more than 7 per cent of all professional women in 1950 were in the four of these categories together. Only 6 per cent of medical doctors and 4 per cent of lawyers and judges were women. In contrast, almost three quarters of medical doctors are women in the Soviet Union; in England the figure is 16 per cent. In both France and Sweden women make up a high proportion of pharmacists and dentists; neither of those professions attracts many women in the United States.

One consequence as well as manifestation of the sexual division of labor in the United States has been the differences in pay for men and women. That difference has been a historical complaint of feminist leaders. In 1900 one study found women's wages to be, on the average, only 53 per cent of men's. The reason was, of course, that women were concentrated in the poorer paying jobs and industries of the economy. The disparity in pay between the sexes has been somewhat reduced today, but not very much. In 1955 among full-time women workers of all types the median wage was about two thirds of that for men. In short, women are still supplying the low-paid labor in the economy just as they were in the last century. (In substance, women workers and Negroes of both sexes perform a similar function in the economy.) The willingness of women to supply cheap labor may well account for their getting the large number of jobs they do; men often will not work for the wages that women will accept.

Today, there does not seem to be very much disparity between men's and women's wages for the same work, though the sexual division of labor is so nearly complete that it is difficult to find comparable jobs of the two sexes to make a definitive study.

There has been no improvement in women's position in higher education; indeed, it can be argued that women have failed to maintain the place reached much earlier. As we have seen, the United States led the world in opening higher education to women. This country also led in broadening the social base of education for women. No other country educated such a large proportion of women in its universities and colleges as did the United States. At the close of the nineteenth century, one third of American college students were women; by 1937 women made up almost 40 per cent of the students in American institutions of higher learning. In Germany, just before Hitler took power, no more than one out of ten university students was a woman; in Swedish universities in 1937 only 17 per cent of the students were women; in British universities the ratio was 22 per cent.

But since the Second World War the gap between American and European proportions of women in higher education has narrowed considerably. In 1952–1953 women constituted only 35 per cent of the American college population, while France counted women as 36 per cent of its university students and Sweden 26 per cent. The *number* of women in American colleges, of course, is considerably greater than it was in the 1920's and 1930's, but in proportion to men, women have lost ground in America while gaining it in Europe.

A further sign of the regression in the educational position of women in the United States is that in the early 1950's women earned about 10 per cent of the doctoral degrees in this country as compared with almost 15 per cent in the 1920's.

How is one to explain this uneven, almost contradictory record of women in America? How does it happen that a country with a kind of built-in feminism from the frontier falls behind more traditional countries in its training of college women; that a country with one of the highest proportions of working women in the world ends up with such a small proportion of its women in medicine, in law and in the sciences? Perhaps the correct answer is that the question should not be asked — at least not by Americans. For like so much else in American society, such contradictions are a manifestation of the national avoidance of any ideological principle, whether it be in feminist reform or in anything else. To be sure there has been no lack of feminist argument or rationale for women's work outside the home, for women's education and for other activities by women. But American women, like American society in general, have been more concerned with individual practice than with a consistent feminist ideology. If women have entered the labor force or taken jobs during a war they have done so for reasons related to the immediate individual or social circumstances and not for reasons of feminist ideology. The women who have been concerned about showing that women's capabilities can match men's have been the exception. As the limited, and low-paying, kinds of jobs women occupy demonstrate, there is not now and never has been any strong feminist push behind the massive and continuing movement of women into jobs. Most American women have been interested in jobs, not careers. To say, as many feminists have, that men have opposed and resisted the opening of opportunities to women is to utter only a half truth. The whole truth is that American society in general, which includes women, shuns like a disease any feminist ideology.

Another way of showing that the historical changes in the status of women in America bear little relation to a feminist ideology is to examine one of those rare instances when women did effect a social improvement through an appeal to ideology, for instance, the struggle for the suffrage. By the early twentieth century the feminist demand for the vote overrode every other feminist goal. Once women achieved the vote, it was argued, the evils of society would be routed, for women, because of their peculiar attributes, would bring a fresh, needed and wholesome element into political life. In form, and in the minds of many women leaders, the arguments for the suffrage came close to being a full-blown ideology of feminism.

In point of fact, of course, the Nineteenth Amendment ushered in no millennium. But that fact is of less importance than the reason why it did not. When American women obtained the vote they simply did not use it ideologically; they voted not as women but as individuals. Evidence of this was the failure of many women to vote at all. At the end of the first decade of national suffrage women still did not exercise the franchise to the extent that men did. Nor did many women run for or hold political offices. The first woman to serve in Congress was elected in 1916; in 1920, the first year of national women's suffrage, four women were elected to Congress, but until 1940 no more than nine women served at one time in the House of Representatives and the Senate together. That we are here observing an American and not simply a sexual phenomenon is shown by a comparison with European countries. In nonfeminist Germany, where the ballot came to women at about the same time as in the United States, the first Reichstag after suffrage counted forty-one women as members. In 1951 seventeen women sat in the British House of Commons as compared with ten in the United States House of Representatives. Twice the number of women have served as cabinet ministers in Britain between 1928 and 1951 as have served in the United States down to the present.

Another instance in which social change was effected by feminist ideology was prohibition. The achievement of national prohibition ran second only to the suffrage movement as a prime goal of the organized women's movement; the Eighteenth Amendment was as much a product of feminist ideology as the Nineteenth. Yet like the suffrage movement, prohibition, despite its feminist backing, failed to receive the support of women. It was *after* prohibition was enacted, after all, that women drank in public.

In the cases of both suffrage and prohibition, women acted as individuals, not as members of a sex. And so they have continued to act. It is not without relevance that the women's political organization that is most respected — the League of Women Voters — is not only nonpartisan but studiously avoids questions pertaining only to women. To do otherwise would be feminist and therefore ideological.

One further conclusion might be drawn from this examination of the non-ideological character of American women. That the changes that have come to the position of women have been devoid of ideological intent may well explain why there has been so little opposition to them. The most successful of American reforms have always been those of an impromptu and practical nature. The great revolution of the New Deal is a classic example. The American people, like F. D. R. himself, simply tried one thing after another, looking for something — anything — that would get the nation out of the depression. If lasting reforms took place too, so much the better. On the other hand, reforms that have been justified by an elaborate rationale or ideology, like abolition, have aroused strong and long-drawn-out opposition. By the same token, when women became ideological in support of suffrage and prohibition, they faced their greatest opposition and scored their most disappointing triumphs.

The achievement of the suffrage in 1920 is a convenient date for marking the end of the first phase in the changing position of women, for by then women were accorded virtually the same rights as men even if they did not always exercise them. The second phase began at about the same time. It was the participation of married women in the work force. During the nineteenth century few married women worked; when they did it was because they were childless or because their husbands were inadequate providers. Even among the poor, married women normally did not work. A survey of the slum districts in five large cities in 1893 revealed that no more than 5 per cent of the wives were employed. Only Negro wives in the South and immigrant wives in big northern cities provided any significant exceptions to this generalization.

Before the First World War, the movement of wives into the working force was barely noticeable. During the 1920's there was an acceleration, but as late as 1940 less than 17 per cent of all married women were working. Among working women in 1940, 48 per cent were single and only 31 per cent were married. The Second World War dramatically reversed these proportions — another instance of the influence of war on the position of women. By 1950 the proportion of married women living with their husbands had risen to 48 per cent of all working women while that of single women had fallen to 32 per cent. In 1960 the Census reported that almost 32 per cent of all married women were employed outside the home and that they comprised 54 per cent of all working women. No industrial country of Europe, with the exception of the Soviet Union, counted such a high proportion. Today, married women are the greatest source of new labor in the American economy. Between 1949 and 1959, for example, over four million married women entered the labor force, some 60 per cent of *all* additions, male and female.

Such a massive movement of married women out of the home was a development few of the early feminists could have anticipated. That it has taken place is at once a sign and a yardstick of the enormous change in women's position in society and in the family. In the nineteenth century work outside the home was unthinkable for the married woman. Not only were there children to care for, but there were objections from husbands and society to consider. That is why the convinced feminist of the nineteenth century often spurned marriage. Indeed, it is often forgotten that the feminist movement was a form of revolt against marriage. For it was through marriage, with the legal and social dominance of the husband, that women were most obviously denied opportunities for self-expression. Even after the legal superiority of the husband had been largely eliminated from the law, middle-class social conventions could still scarcely accommodate the working wife. To the woman interested in realizing her human capabilities, marriage in the nineteenth century was not an opportunity but a dead end. And it was indeed a minor scandal of the time that many of the "new women" did in fact reject marriage. The tendency was most pronounced, as was to be expected, among highly educated women, many of whom felt strongly their obligation to serve society through careers. Around 1900 more than one fourth of women who graduated from college never married; more than half of the women medical doctors in 1890 were single.

Like other changes in the position of women, the movement of married women into the work force — the reconciliation of marriage and work — must be related to the social changes of the last three decades. One of these social changes was the increase in contraceptive knowledge, for until married women could limit their families they could not become steady and reliable industrial workers. Information about contraceptive techniques which had been known for a generation or more to educated middle-class women did not seep down to the working class until the years of the Great Depression. In 1931, for instance, there were only 81 clinics disseminating birth control information in the United States; in 1943 there were 549, of which 166 were under public auspices. As the number of public clinics suggest, by the end of the 1930's birth control was both socially and religiously acceptable, at least among Protestants. And a method was also available then to Roman Catholics, since it was in the same decade that the rhythm method, the only one acceptable to the Roman Catholic Church, was first brought to popular attention with the approval of ecclesiastical authorities.

Another social force underlying the movement of wives and mothers in the work force was the growing affluence of an industrial society, especially after 1940. Higher health standards, enlarged incomes of husbands and a better standard of living in general permitted a marked alteration in the temporal cycle of women's lives. Women now lived longer, stayed in school later and married earlier. In 1890 half the girls left school at 14 or before — that is, when they finished grammar school; in 1957 the median age was 18 — after graduation from high school. The girl of 1890, typically, did not marry until she was 22; the age of her counterpart in 1957 was 20, leaving no more than two years for work between the end of school and marriage. Among other things this fact explains the fall in the proportion of single women in the work force in the United States as compared with other industrial societies. Few other countries have such an early median age of marriage for girls.

Early marriages for women produce another effect. With knowledge of contraceptive techniques providing a measure of control over child-bearing, women are now having their children early and rapidly. When this tendency is combined with a younger age of marriage, the result is an early end to child-bearing. In 1890 the median age of a mother when her last child was born was 32; in 1957 it was 26. A modern mother thus has her children off to school by the time she is in her middle thirties, leaving her as much as thirty-five years free for work outside the home. And the fact is that almost half of working women today are over forty years of age. Put another way, 34 per cent of married women between the ages of thirty-five and forty-four years are gainfully employed.

Unquestionably, as the practical character of the woman's movement would lead us to expect, an important force behind the influx of married women into the work force is economic need. But simple poverty is not the only force. Several studies, for example, have documented the conclusion that many women who work are married to men who earn salaries in the upper income brackets, suggesting that poverty is not the controlling factor in the wife's decision to work. A similar conclusion is to be drawn from the positive correlation between education and work for married women. The more education a wife has (and therefore the better salary her husband is likely to earn) the more likely she is to be working herself. Many of these women work undoubtedly in order to raise an adequate standard of living to a comfortable one. Many others work probably because they want to realize their potentialities in the world. But that women are so poorly represented in the professions and other careers suggests that most married women who work are realizing their full capabilities neither for themselves nor for society.

Over sixty years ago, in *Women and Economics,* the feminist Charlotte Perkins Gilman cogently traced the connection between work and the fulfillment of women as human beings. In subsequent writings she grappled with the problem of how this aim might be realized for married women. As a mother herself, raising a child under the trying circumstances of divorce, Gilman knew first hand that work outside the home and child-rearing constituted *two* full-time jobs. No man, she knew, was expected or required to shoulder such a double burden. Gilman's remedies of professional domestic service and kitchenless apartments never received much of a hearing, and considering the utopian if not bizarre character of her solutions, that is not surprising. Yet the problem she raised remained without any solution other than the eminently individualistic and inadequate one of permitting a woman to assume the double burden if she was so minded. Meanwhile, as the economy has grown, the problem has entered the lives of an ever increasing number of women. Unlike most of her feminist contemporaries, who were mainly concerned with the suffrage and the final elimination of legal and customary barriers to women's opportunities, Gilman recognized that the logic of feminism led unavoidably to the working mother as the typical woman. For if women were to be free to express themselves, then they should be able to marry as well as to work. Women should not have to make a choice any more than men. To make that possible, though, would require that some way be found to mitigate the double burden which biology and society had combined to place only on women.

As women moved into the second stage of their development — the reconciliation of work and marriage — the problem which Gilman saw so early was increasingly recognized as the central issue. Virginia Collier, for example, in a book *Marriage and Careers,* published in 1926, wrote that since so many married women were working, "The question therefore is no longer should women combine marriage with careers, but how do they manage it and how does it work." Interestingly enough, her study shows that what today Betty Friedan, in *The Feminine Mystique,* has called the "problem that has no name," was already apparent in the 1920's. One working wife explained her reasons for taking a job in these words, "I am burning up with energy and it is rather hard on the family to use it up in angry frustration." Another said, "I had done everything for Polly for six years. Suddenly she was in school all day and I had nothing to do. My engine was running just as hard as ever, but my car was standing still." A year after Collier's book appeared, President William A. Neilson of Smith College observed "that the outstanding problem confronting women is how to reconcile a normal life of marriage and motherhood with intellectual activity such as her college education has fitted her for." That the issue was taken seriously is attested by an action of the Board of Trustees of Barnard College in 1932. The board voted to grant six months' maternity leave with pay to members of the staff and faculty. In announcing the decision, Dean Virginia Gildersleeve clearly voiced its import. "Neither the men nor the women of our staff," she said, "should be forced into celibacy, and cut off from that great source of experience of joy, sorrow and wisdom which marriage and parenthood offer."

With one out of three married women working today, the problem of reconciling marriage and work for women is of a social dimension considerably larger than in the days of Charlotte Gilman or even in the 1930's. But the fundamental issue is still the same: how to make it possible, as Dean Gildersleeve said, to pursue a career or hold a job while enjoying the "experience . . . joy, sorrow and wisdom" of marriage and parenthood. The practical solutions to this central problem of the second stage in the changing position of women seem mainly collective or governmental, not individual. Child-care centers, efficient and readily available house-keeping services, and emergency child-care service such as the Swedes have instituted are obviously a minimal requirement if women are to have the double burdens of homemaking and employment lightened. The individual working woman cannot be expected to compensate for the temporary disabilities consequent upon her role as mother any more than the individual farmer or industrial worker can be expected single-handedly to overcome the imbalance between himself and the market. Today both farmers and workers have government and their own organizations to assist them in righting the balance.

But as the history of farmers and industrial labor makes evident, to enact legislation or to change mores requires persuasion of those who do not appreciate the necessity for change. Those who would do so must organize the like-minded and mobilize power, which is to say they need a rationale, an ideology. And here is the rub; in pragmatic America, as we have seen, any ideology must leap high hurdles. And one in support of working wives is additionally handicapped because women themselves, despite the profound changes in their status in the last century, do not acknowledge such an ideology. Most American women simply do not want work outside the home to be justified as a normal activity for married women. Despite the counter-argument of overwhelming numbers of working wives, they like to think of it as special and exceptional. And so long as they do not advance such an ideology, American society surely will not do so, though other societies, like Israel's and the Soviet Union's, which are more ideological than ours, obviously have.

Perhaps the kind of gradual, piecemeal advance toward a feminist ideology that Mrs. Rossi proposes in other pages of this book may contain the seeds of change. But a reading of the past reminds us forcefully that in America the soil is thin and the climate uncongenial for the growth of any seedlings of ideology.

Deprivation in an Affluent Society

In the years after World War II, the American economy performed with immense success. The terrible shadow of depression, which had hung over the country during the 1930s, seemed permanently dissipated. But the level of economic activity was not the only measure of economic performance. Who had benefited from the quadrupling of the Gross National Product between 1945 and 1965? For a decade and more following the war, a genuine redistribution of income seemed to be in process. Existing data indicated that, since 1929, the share going to the top 5 percent had been shrinking, while the bottom 20 percent had been gaining a larger share. With total income growing and redistribution taking place, it seemed in the 1950s as if America was reaching the economic millennium — the point at which poverty would become unknown. It came, therefore, as a rude shock to discover that poverty, even if invisible to affluent Americans, was not disappearing, that it in fact was persistent and that it covered fully a quarter of the population. That was the dismal message of Michael Harrington's *The Other America,* and other investigators following him. The "rediscovery" of America's poor, plus the eruption of the black ghettos, had a powerful effect on the nation's politics: it made "the war on poverty" the primary domestic issue of the 1960s.

In the following essay Richard Parker, a Junior Fellow at the Center for the Study of Democratic Institutions, examines the subject from the perspective of the decade's end. He takes a far dimmer view of income redistribution than had his predecessors in the 1950s. The share of the poverty-stricken bottom has not changed significantly since 1910, Parker concludes. The share of the top 5 percent may have fallen slightly but, for reasons Parker explains, it fell a good deal less than earlier statistics had indicated. More striking yet are Parker's conclusions regarding the economic middle. Long-term redistribution of income has actually favored the upper-middle income group — the technocratic elite. As one goes down the economic ladder, distribution gains consistently lessen. And, what is more, the lower-middle class, a full third of the population, lives in a state of deprivation, lacking an income that is adequate for a standard of decent comfort.

Why has the nation so persistently blinded itself to these harsh realities? Why have its efforts at reform so consistently fallen short? Parker addresses himself to these questions in a thoughtful and imaginative way. If his answers seem to foreclose too definitely the possibility of change, assuredly they do express the pessimism of the intellectual generation now coming of age.

FOR FURTHER READING:

CAUDILL, HARRY M. *Night Comes to the Cumberlands.* Boston: Little, Brown & Company, Atlantic Monthly Press, 1963.*
GALBRAITH, JOHN K. *The Affluent Society.* New York: New American Library, Mentor Books, 1959.*
HARRINGTON, MICHAEL. *The Other America.* Baltimore: Penguin Books, Pelican Books, 1962.*

Asterisk denotes paperback edition.

The Myth of Middle America

RICHARD PARKER

It was a tenet of both liberal and conservative dogmas following World War II that, economically, life in America was getting better all the time. Aside from the political flurry of McCarthyism in the early nineteen-fifties, the economy was everyone's favorite topic of discussion. After economists had predicted a major postwar recession, the American economy fooled them and began what seemed like a skyrocket burst. Between 1945 and 1965, the Gross National Product quadrupled, and disposable personal income increased two-and-a-half-fold. Postulating a "trickle-down" theory of income distribution, economists assumed that it was only a question of time before poverty was eliminated in America.

Suckled on the Horatio Alger myth and teethed on depression and war, the American public was glad to hear the news. Madison Avenue blared the New Affluence across front pages, and invited all of us to join the feast of consumption. The new symbol of America was the suburb, the grassy, tree-shaded Eden of responsible Americans. There a family was safe and happy with its two cars, two children, dog, and barbeque pit. Social science and the academy in general took over the affluence myth virtually *in toto,* declaring the end of scarcity, and with it the end of ideology, and the dawn of a new technocratic age where abundance, rather than scarcity, would be our bane. A Gallup Poll would most likely have found wide acceptance of David Lilienthal's views that "one finds the physical benefits of our society distributed widely, to almost everyone, with scant regard to status, class, or origin of the individual."

But the myth of the New Affluence was a cruel distortion of reality. Composed of half-truths, it closed our eyes, cut us off from a recognition of America, and blocked off political and social alternatives. Today, poverty in the midst of prosperity seems almost characteristic of mature capitalism. Moreover, deprivation also seems characteristic and, together with poverty, describes the living conditions of nearly half the American people. What once appeared to be a New Affluence, I contend, is in fact an expansion of the economy which has disproportionately benefited the upper and upper-middle classes, while it has left the poor and the deprived to gather what crumbs fall from the table.

Marx contended in *Das Kapital* and elsewhere that poverty was a normal condition of capitalism even in the best of times. He argued that even if workers' actual wages rose, the differential between their wages and the income of the rich would continue to increase. The issue was settled to the satisfaction of most American economists by the performance of their own economy after the Second World War. A number of them had their faith in capitalism shaken by the Depression, but the postwar boom quickly allayed most of their doubts. The original Marxian criticism that wages might rise but differentials between classes grow larger was lost sight of in the general euphoria of the nineteen-fifties.

The euphoria, moreover, was not limited to the traditional, or laissez-faire, economists. Liberal interventionists and Keynesians alike joined with conservatives to announce the death of poverty in mature capitalism. John Kenneth Galbraith, for

Source: Richard Parker, "The Myth of Middle America," *The Center Magazine* (March 1970), pp. 61–70.

example, claimed that by the late fifties American poverty was limited to "the insular poor" and "the case poor." The former were the inhabitants of areas like Appalachia and the rural South, where shifting employment patterns were causing "painful, but temporary hardship." The "case poor" were the alcoholics, invalids, and elderly who could not, or would not, get ahead. Keynes himself (like Marx) had, of course, foreseen no such amelioration, even in Keynesian capitalism. As Paul Mattick notes in his book *Marx and Keynes,* "Keynesian interventions in the economy necessarily adjust production and consumption in favor of investments. Such adjustments cannot end the paradox of poverty in the midst of plenty, and are not designed to do so." The problem of economists was to explain *why* poverty was disappearing at such a rapid rate. Census statistics indicated that families with incomes below three thousand dollars had declined from twenty-eight to fourteen per cent between 1947 and 1966. But why? Obviously prosperity in general, and unionization in particular, had improved the lot of the workingman. But raw data, as well as a few highly sophisticated studies, indicated not only that the economic pie was getting bigger but that a significant reallocation was taking place. It appeared that, for some poorly understood reasons, a real change was taking place in the economy. Arthur Burns, then an Eisenhower adviser, rejoiced: "The transformation in the distribution of our national income . . . may already be counted as one of the great social revolutions of history." Paul Samuelson spoke for the liberals when he said,"The American income pyramid is becoming less unequal."

Though still lacking an explanation, the economists' statistical foundations seemed eminently solid. Simon Kuznets' massive study, *Shares of Upper Income Groups in Income and Savings,* indicated a major decline in the percentage of personal income controlled by the upper strata of the society, a decline that "would continue." The late Selma Goldsmith and her associates showed that the share of personal income received by the top five per cent declined from thirty per cent in 1929 to 26.5 per cent in 1936–37, and to 20.7 per cent by 1944. Similarly, she showed that the share of the top twenty per cent declined from 54.4 to 51.7 to 45.8 per cent in the same periods. At the other end of the spectrum, the bottom twenty per cent began to show some, if sizably smaller, gains.

Using these data, plus rawer data collected by the Bureau of the Census and other government agencies, economists postulated a theory for income distribution. According to the theory, income was slowly but irreversibly "trickling down" the income scale from the rich to the poor, to result finally in Samuelson's "flattened pyramid." It was presumed to be only a question of time before the last vestiges of poverty would disappear entirely; by the late fifties, Galbraith declared calmly, poverty in America was no longer "a massive affliction but more nearly an afterthought."

As a consequence, the study of income distribution as an economic discipline rapidly declined throughout the fifties. The university, like the nation at large, mesmerized by the new Affluent Society, was content to rest its discussions of poverty on clichés and rudimentary data. In economics, the new interest was in "value-free" econometrics; in the popular consciousness, it was in *The Organization Man* and *The Man in the Gray Flannel Suit.* Affluence was the presumed condition of almost all, and discussion centered on suburbia, Martinis, and psychoanalysis. Maladies were the result of too much rather than too little.

The "rediscovery" of poverty in America, then, came as a rude awakening to most. Michael Harrington's *The Other America,* which got widespread attention in the early sixties, provided graphic portrayals of the personal impact as well as the extent of poverty. It inspired a major reëxamination of the country's goals. Harrington's estimation that one-quarter of the American people lived in poverty shattered not only national pride but also the sublime self-confidence of the economics establishment. To them, his words were heresy.

Discomfiture was not limited to economists. It spread through the social sciences. Two sociologists, S. M. Miller and Martin Rein, looking back on their colleagues' embarrassing mistakes, described the general theory that had governed sociological thinking in the fifties: "The expansion of production and productivity resulted in a much greater economic pie. The graduated income tax, expanded welfare services, and education were more equitably distributing this larger pie. Continued increase in aggregate economic wealth would invariably filter down, more or less equitably, to all income groupings. Marginal economic groups, it was assumed, would in time 'gracefully succumb' to continued economic growth and that small residual group not covered by expanded welfare and social security programs would be handily cared for by the public dole."

But even after Harrington pricked the popular balloon, air leaked out with surprising slowness. Those running the federal government's War on Poverty (and many social scientists) agreed to define as poor only those families with annual incomes below three thousand dollars. This swift bit of statistical legerdemain immediately shrank Harrington's one-quarter to a less frightening one-fifth. The effect was not only to minimize the poverty in America but to ignore the basic contradictions in the myth of prosperity.

A reëvaluation of postwar prosperity leads to major second thoughts about "trickle down" theories of income distribution. As early as 1957, Robert Lampman, of the University of Michigan, noted that initial gains by the poor to increase their share of the wealth had not only stopped but were reversing. By the early sixties, the rich were again increasing their control of the lion's share of personal income.

The premature optimism of economists like Burns lay in statistics that took no official notice of their unusual circumstances. During the war and shortly thereafter, the income of laborers and service workers increased almost twice as fast as that of professionals and managerial workers. But this was due chiefly to war-related factors that would be unlikely in a peacetime economy, such as full employment mixed with a shortage of non-skilled labor. By the late fifties, the lower categories no longer showed high-rate gains: laborers' and service workers' income increased only forty-eight per cent while managerial income increased seventy-five per cent. Joseph Pechman concluded in 1969 that "the distribution of income in the nineteen-fifties period may not have been very different from what it was in the early nineteen-twenties."

These gross figures, some would argue, are misleading because of shifts in the labor market. Thus the small gains for laborers might be offset by the diminishing number of common laborers, or the high incidence of poverty among farmers offset by decreasing numbers of farmers. But Herman Miller, an economist with the Census Bureau, disagreed. Writing in a Bureau monograph, *Income Distribution in the United States,* he concluded that shifts in job distribution did not substantially affect patterns of income distribution. "Of course it could still be argued that the over-all stability of income distribution for the urban population masks important changes which have taken place for various subgroups within the population. But this hypothesis . . . does not appear to be supported by the facts. Income distribution within the urban population has not shifted even when that population is further classified by labor force status of wife, age of head, or size of family."

Miller, however, does underline one important trend: the increasing number of families in which both husband and wife work. "It should be noted that incomes are much more equally distributed among families where the wife is working than where she is not working; the sizable increase in the proportion of families with working wives has therefore tended to decrease income inequality during the past decade." Moreover, Census projections show that the proportion of women in the labor force will continue to grow over the next two decades.

Yet even the increased family income provided by a second earner was unable to offset the gains by upper and upper-middle classes in control of personal income. Using Census data as well as studies by various economic agencies, Joseph Pechman acknowledged that the rich, but not the poor, had prospered in the postwar era. He pointed out that the simplest Census tables, those most often cited, exclude capital gains and therefore grossly misrepresent income trends in the upper fifth of the economy. For example, the following table shows the standard before-tax income shares of the rich, according to Census data:

Year	Top 5% of Families	Top 20% of Families
1952	18%	42%
1957	16	40
1962	16	42
1967	15	41

What this table indicates obviously is confirmation of Burns' "great revolution." But are the figures accurate?

Tax data are needed to push the analysis further. These data are more useful, because they show the realized capital gains of these families and net income after federal taxes. The salient observation here is that, contrary to another popular myth now also on the wane, the federal income tax is *not* progressive in its effect. Computing total disposable (i.e. after-tax) income, we find the following:

Year	Tax Units Top 5%	Tax Units Top 15%
1952	16%	30%
1963	17	33
1967	17	34

However, this table itself can only be considered an estimate that falls to the low side. Since the Second World War, innumerable tax benefits and payment forms have grown up which benefit only the rich. Pechman names tax-exempt interest and depletion allowances as sources of income, then adds: "During World War II, methods of compensation were devised to funnel income to business executives in non-taxable forms. The devices used are well known: deferred compensation and pen-sion plans, stock option arrangements, and direct payment of personal consumption expenditures through expense accounts." Having listed these varieties of unreported income, he prefers caution, and concludes, "Little is known about the impact on the distribution of income."

Gabriel Kolko is not so timorous. In *Wealth and Power in America,* Kolko announced that "the impact of the federal income tax on the actual distribution of income has been minimal, if not negligible." Drawing on a number of sources for his data, he deduced that adding the uncomputed income of the upper classes would raise their total disposable income two or three percentage points above Pechman's own figures. (Thus the top five per cent received about twenty per cent of the personal income, and the top one per cent about ten per cent of that income.) Since 1952, the effective federal tax rate on the upper one per cent of the population has *dropped* from thirty-three to twenty-six per cent.

What may be said of the federal tax structure can be repeated *ad nauseam* for state and local tax structures. The impact of property and sales taxes is clearly regressive, and, as one economist put it, this is "disturbing because the state-local tax system is the growing element of the national system." Federal tax revenues have remained fairly constant as a proportion of Gross National Product, hovering around twenty per cent since 1951. State and local taxes, by contrast, have risen from 7.1 per cent of the Gross National Product in 1951 to 11.9 per cent in 1968. "Assuming that state-local taxes respond more or less proportionately to the rise in the national product . . . the states and local governments must have increased rates by sixty-eight per cent in these seventeen years to push up their tax yields to current levels." The motivation is obviously not simple greed, but a reflection of increased demand on public services and increasing population concentration in metropolitan areas. Nonetheless, the burden of these social changes falls most heavily on those least able to pay.

The Economic Report of the President, 1969 shows the following:

Income Classes	State and Local Taxes (Percentage of Income)
Under $2,000	25%
2,000–4,000	11
4,000–6,000	10
6,000–8,000	9
8,000–10,000	9
10,000–15,000	9
15,000 and over	7

Analysis of income alone, in the case of the rich, obviously also misrepresents the actual concentration of economic well-being in the country. Affluence for the rich, unlike income for the middle and lower classes, is rarely limited to wages and salaries. Rents, dividends, interest, all go into the total wealth of the upper class. James D. Smith, of the Office of Economic Opportunity, in analyzing data of persons with gross assets in excess of sixty thousand dollars, found a highly concentrated wealth structure. This group, representing the top 1.5 per cent of the wealth-holders in the country, received the following amounts of income:

Type	Billions	Per Cent of Total (Each Type)
Wages and salaries	$25.9	10.8%
Dividends	8.0	74.8
Interest	3.1	27.9
Rent	6.4	52.5
Capital gains	57.6	71.4

Furthermore, this table is an understatement of concentration. It excludes $1.7 billion in dividends paid to trust funds and non-profit foundations; it assumes only average yields on assets, rather than optimum figures to be obtained through the advice of investment counselors; finally, its data are for 1958, and all subsequent information shows increasing pyramiding of the wealth structure.

Gabriel Kolko also contributes significant figures on the concentration of total wealth in the upper brackets which supplement Smith's own research. For example, in 1960 the top ten per cent controlled two-thirds of all liquid assets, while fifty-one per cent of the spending units headed by unskilled or service workers had no assets. Other, more shocking data suggest that between .2 and .3 of one per cent of the population control twenty-two per cent of the personal wealth and sixty to seventy per cent of all privately held corporate wealth.

What in fact was the condition of the poor through the fifties and into the sixties? First of all, we must have a definition of poverty. The federal government has chosen the income-line method, with all families falling below three thousand dollars (now thirty-seven hundred, because of inflation) defined as poor, and therefore eligible for charitable assistance. Before 1962, little was known about this group; since then, a veritable anti-poverty industry has dredged up quantities of information about these people, from their illiteracy rates to their reproduction out of wedlock.

Given all this information, what have we learned? First of all, the income-line method is misleading. It fails to account for assets, temporary impoverishment, and several other factors. Second, and more important, the three thousand dollars has been recognized as ridiculously, if not criminally, low.

How in fact was the government's poverty budget originally arrived at? Politically, several factors interacted; methodologically, the explanation is simple. An annual food budget was prepared, and then that figure was tripled. The budget followed Department of Agriculture guidelines that included the notion that food occupies about one-third of normal expenditures. But simple methodology belied the gross underestimation of need. Oscar Ornati, in *Poverty Amid Affluence,* summarized a typical 1960 "adequate minimum" budget for a family of four:

"It provides for simple clothing to protect against the weather and maintain cleanliness. A woman's coat, for instance, must last five years. Leftover food must be retrieved. A cup of flour spilled means no thickening that week; a blown bulb, no light for that month; and a chair broken in anger cannot be replaced for a year. The meat budget allows for stewing lamb, beef liver, or heart, picnic shoulder, fillet of haddock, or perhaps a boned veal roast. No frozen foods are provided for. It allows nothing for an occasional glass of beer, tobacco, or telephone calls. The budget assumes a small rented five-room flat. The family living room might have two chairs. A mattress and spring on legs may serve as a couch, a dropleaf table for eating; two straight chairs may also be there. Linoleum may cover the floor, and there can be a lamp or two. An electric refrigerator and iron are allowed. The family may listen to the radio an hour a day, but television is not included in the budget. There will be money to buy aspirin but none for 'miracle' drugs. The husband may get a haircut once a month, and the wife a home permanent once a year. She can use a self-service launderette. There will be no money to buy the children candy or ice cream, or to go to the movies, or to offer a visitor a cup of coffee."

The government's budget is unrealistic on other scores. It fails to take account of the overpricing and shoddy quality of food in poor areas, as documented in books like David Caplovitz' *The Poor Pay More.* It ignores the high cost of other items such as housing and furniture, etc. (usually ten to twenty-five per cent overpriced, according to one Bureau of the Census economist) that drives up maintenance costs in the other two-thirds of its budget. In farm areas, it still relies heavily on the presumption that the rural families produce much of their own food, although as a percentage of the total food consumed, home-grown items have fallen from seventy to thirty-six per cent in the past twenty years. It makes no allowances for the higher education of the children, unless one presumes they will receive full scholarship aid, which is highly unlikely. Finally, it assumes no major medical expenses in the family, although over half of the poor are not covered by medical insurance.

The actual meals upon which the entire budget is based inspire greater disbelief. The words of the Census that "assuming the homemaker is a good manager and has the time and skill to shop wisely, she may prepare nutritious, palatable meals . . . for herself, a husband, and two young children" on a budget of seventy cents per day per person inspired one pundit to comment that "Betty Crocker herself would starve." A statistician for H.E.W. describes how a housewife must spend her money:

"For a meal all four of them ate together, she could spend on the average only ninety-five cents, and to stay within her budget she must allow no more a day than a pound of meat, poultry, or fish altogether, barely enough for one small serving for each family member at one of the three meals. Eggs could fill out her family fare only to a limited degree because the plan allows less than two dozen a week for all uses in cooking and at the table, not even one to a person a day. And any food extras, such as milk at school for the children or the coffee her husband might buy to supplement the lunch he carries to work, have to come out of the same food money or compete with the limited funds available for rent, clothing, medical care, and all other expenses. Studies indicate that, on the average, family members eating a meal away from home spend twice as much as the homemaker would spend for preparing one for them at home. The twenty-five cents allowed for a meal at home in the economy plan would not buy much even in the way of supplementation."

Despite the obvious sub-minimal character of this "minimum budget," some optimism has been generated by the War on Poverty and a booming economy, inducing people to believe that the poor are "disappearing." But this optimism needs closer scrutiny. First of all, a three-thousand-dollar limit is a ridiculously low level separating the poor from the non-poor. Second, the government has continued to play games with its own figures ever since the War on Poverty began. For example, the cutoff limit of poverty is measured by pre-tax income figures, although the poverty budget was constructed on an after-tax basis. Third, politics has taken a heavy toll on the poor. According to the McGovern Committee: "In 1968, government statisticians estimated there were between twenty-two and twenty-seven million Americans living in poverty." But at the beginning of 1969 "the higher of these two figures was dropped without explanation" and the twenty-two million used as the official estimate. Finally, government economists have consistently underestimated the effect of taxes and inflation on the poor, or so say a group of non-government economists (writing in *Life,* August 15, 1969). Since fixture of the three-thousand-dollar figure in 1960–61 dollars, inflation and taxes have required a gain of forty-one per cent in actual income to maintain a real income equivalent. This would require a present definition of the poverty level at $4,240, or $540 more than the government now allows. Such an adjustment would add several million more families to the rolls of the poor.

For the extremely poor, times are now even harder. As the Southern Rural Research Project reported: "The poor and the hungry had their brief moment in the sun: America may lionize its victims, but the vogue of compassion passes quickly on; the hungry have now become somewhat passé. Americans seem to take it for granted that once such alarming conditions are publicly known, the appropriate authorities will automatically step in and clear the matter up." Dr. Arnold Schaefer, who headed the Public Health Service's National Nutrition Survey, had been among the first to document malnutrition in sample counties in Texas and Louisiana; now the survey has been discontinued, and Dr. Schaefer has passed quietly from the scene. One wonders if the fifteen million malnourished have disappeared as quietly.

The Nixon Administration's response to the crisis of poverty remains to be seen, since its proposed revamping of the welfare system has yet to pass Congress. The central feature of minimum income is an advance over existing programs, since it recognizes working as well as non-working poor; but its own ceilings of aid are so low as to offset the extension in coverage. His proposals to tie Social Security to cost-of-living indices also seem designed to benefit one segment of the poor, but this was rejected in favor of a one-shot fifteen-per-cent bonus.

The central fallacy, or perhaps the central design, in the government's designation of the poor is its narrowness. Given the present definition of the poor, we avoid the larger contours of our social reality. Compared with the wealthy or near-wealthy, the gains of the poor have been almost immaterial. In 1946, the bottom twenty per cent of all families (the government estimate of the "poor" hovers around sixteen per cent) received five per cent of the income; by 1967, the same fifth — now forty million people — received 5.4 per cent. In other words, the intonations of "trickle down" by economists of the fifties now sound hollow indeed.

Crucial to the isolation of the poor is not only the government's action, but the basic American myth. We are people of the *middle* class, bourgeois, home folks, people who still like Norman Rockwell and live decent, unextravagant lives. De Tocqueville did not instigate the myth, but *Democracy in America* certainly strengthened it. His comments on the "tendencies toward the equalization of the conditions of life" set the pattern for all later social scientists and historians who sought to capture the fundamental character of the country. Louis Hartz, as recently as the middle nineteen-fifties, still wrote of "irrational Lockeanism" as the controlling factor in American political life, and saw this as a reflection of the dominant "middle class."

The belief in progress has always caused Americans to see their past in an ambivalent light. They have viewed the past romantically, choosing to see our problems as smaller and our victories larger than life. What is imperialism to some has been Manifest Destiny in America. What for some was genocide directed toward the Indian was only "resettlement" of the natives. Even when we made mistakes, there was seldom an accusation of guile or willfulness on our part. The Spanish-American War was "misguided," but it was fought with the best of intentions.

By this kind of logic, our poor today are still better off than ninety per cent of the world, and certainly in a better state than they were fifty years ago. The discomfort that greeted disclosures by the muckrakers and writers of the naturalist school at the turn of the century has been replaced today by a comfortable agreement that "things were bad then, but just look at them now." After all, the middle class has always been America's strength and salvation. If we do have poor, well, either they are lazy and inefficient (the conservative view) or they are victimized minorities — blacks, the old, unwed welfare mothers (the liberal view). In any case, nobody opposes welfare anymore — Nixon is pushing the guaranteed income — and besides, as liberal economist Alan Batchelder has assured us, "the poor will continue to disappear as the economy expands."

The fundamental misdirection of all this is away from analysis of the "middle class" to a blind invocation of the myth itself. As recently as October, 1969, *Newsweek*, for example, ran an otherwise perceptive article entitled simplistically: *The Troubled American — A Special Report on the White Majority*. Studded with references to "America's vast white middle-class majority," it intoned the familiar lauds: "America has always been the most middle class of nations, the most generous and the most optimistic." But what in fact the article showed most clearly is that for an enormous proportion of the "middle class," embourgeoisement has been a half-filled dream, a set of unsatisfied hopes. These are the people Leon Keyserling has called not the poor but "the deprived Americans" — "above poverty but short of the minimum requirements for a modestly comfortable level of living." In 1964, Keyserling estimated their number at seventy-seven million men, women, and children.

Keyserling's distinction between a family income of thirty-five hundred dollars ("poverty") and forty-five hundred ("deprivation") should be clear to an economist: the "deprived" all work. Unlike the poor, whose ranks are swelled by the elderly, the infirm, and the blacks, the "deprived" cannot be dismissed as victims of "nonmarket forces." The "deprived" are functioning, productive members of our economic system: the manual laborers, the clerks, the launderers, the hospital workers of our society. They may have their own home, but it is heavily mortgaged; they may have a late-model car, but it has been financed at steep rates. Their savings, which form a family's cushion against disaster, are marginal: forty per cent are either in debt or have savings of less than one hundred dollars. Liquid assets show even less room for error: twenty per cent of all families own no assets, and forty-eight per cent own less than five hundred dollars' worth. Yet, as Kolko rightly points out: "Liquid assets — such as checking and savings accounts, shares in savings-and-loan associations and credit unions, and government savings bonds — are of decisive importance to low- and even middle-income families exposed to layoffs, unemployment, or medical and other emergencies. Often they represent the entire margin between security and the relief rolls."

The myth of the middle class serves as a permanent leash on the deprived. Lacking the income, they are still expected to provide their families with the amenities that advertising, television, and the academic mythmakers have told them the "middle class" enjoys. Constantly under pressure, they retain all the old American virtues as a desperate bulwark against the encroachment of the "shiftless poor."

They, like the poor, bear a heavy burden of the taxation because of regressive tax structures. They aspire to better education for their children, their own home, and more leisure. Yet, in a great many cases, both father and mother must work simply to maintain their present condition.

The disparities within the "middle class" and the number of the "deprived" are brought out most clearly when one examines the data of income growth over the past half-century. The accompanying table shows control of the income shares by population tenths since 1910. Omitting the top tenth as "upper class" and the bottom two-tenths as "poor," analysis of the remaining "middle class" yields striking results.

Percentage of National Personal Income, Before Taxes,
Received by Each Income-Tenth*

	Highest Tenth	2nd	3rd	4th	5th	6th	7th	8th	9th	Lowest Tenth
1910	33.9	12.3	10.2	8.8	8.0	7.0	6.0	5.5	4.9	3.4
1918	34.5	12.9	9.6	8.7	7.7	7.2	6.9	5.7	4.4	2.4
1921	38.2	12.8	10.5	8.9	7.4	6.5	5.9	4.6	3.2	2.0
1929	39.0	12.3	9.8	9.0	7.9	6.5	5.5	4.6	3.6	1.8
1934	33.6	13.1	11.0	9.4	8.2	7.3	6.2	5.3	3.8	2.1
1937	34.4	14.1	11.7	10.1	8.5	7.2	6.0	4.4	2.6	1.0
1941	34.0	16.0	12.0	10.0	9.0	7.0	5.0	4.0	2.0	1.0
1945	29.0	16.0	13.0	11.0	9.0	7.0	6.0	5.0	3.0	1.0
1946	32.0	15.0	12.0	10.0	9.0	7.0	6.0	5.0	3.0	1.0
1947	33.5	14.8	11.7	9.9	8.5	7.1	5.8	4.4	3.1	1.2
1948	30.9	14.7	11.9	10.1	8.8	7.5	6.3	5.0	3.3	1.4
1949	29.8	15.5	12.5	10.6	9.1	7.7	6.2	4.7	3.1	0.8
1950	28.7	15.4	12.7	10.8	9.3	7.8	6.3	4.9	3.2	0.9
1951	30.9	15.0	12.3	10.6	8.9	7.6	6.3	4.7	2.9	0.8
1952	29.5	15.3	12.4	10.6	9.1	7.7	6.4	4.9	3.1	1.0
1953	31.4	14.8	11.9	10.3	8.9	7.6	6.2	4.7	3.0	1.2
1954	29.3	15.3	12.4	10.7	9.1	7.7	6.4	4.8	3.1	1.2
1955	29.7	15.7	12.7	10.8	9.1	7.7	6.1	4.5	2.7	1.0
1956	30.6	15.3	12.3	10.5	9.0	7.6	6.1	4.5	2.8	1.3
1957	29.4	15.5	12.7	10.8	9.2	7.7	6.1	4.5	2.9	1.3
1958	27.1	16.3	13.2	11.0	9.4	7.8	6.2	4.6	3.1	1.3
1959	28.9	15.8	12.7	10.7	9.2	7.8	6.3	4.6	2.9	1.1

* In terms of "recipients" for 1910–37 and "spending units" for 1941–59.

SOURCE: Data for 1910–37 are from National Industrial Conference Board, *Studies in Enterprise and Social Progress* (New York: National Industrial Conference Board, 1939), p. 125. Data for 1941–59 were calculated by the Survey Research Center. Figures for 1941–46 are available in rounded form only.

The most interesting observation is that there are two distinct strata in the "middle class," the upper of the two having gained markedly greater control of income. Between 1910 and 1959, the second, third, and fourth deciles increased their percentage of the total income more than one-quarter, while the fifth, sixth, seventh, and eighth deciles were able to advance only from 26.5 per cent to 27.9 per cent in the same period.

This information sheds light on much of the writing over the past two decades on the Affluent Society. The "middle class," as a homogeneous group, has done well; but closer examination reveals that that success becomes smaller and smaller as one moves down the income scale within that class. The astigmatic concern of the social scientists for suburbia, executive anomy, and the crises of "the abundant society" has proceeded from myths that now seem badly worn — from the myth of the New Affluence, from the myth of "trickle-down" income and wealth redistribution and the omnipotence of Keynes, and from the capstone myth of them all — the myth of the American middle class.

As a matter of fact, the "middle class" may have escaped the grasp of more than the poor and the deprived. If by "middle class" one means a decent, modest standard of living, it seems that perhaps sixty to seventy per cent of the country have difficulty in reaching it. In 1966, the Bureau of Labor Statistics announced that the average urban family required $9,191 per year to live comfortably; yet the median income that same year was fourteen hundred dollars less than that figure.

At this point, it seems wise to stop and make two observations: the first an estimation of some present and possibly future realities; the second, an historical speculation.

The first observation is about the "unmentioned middle class," the professional, technical elite and its immediate support structure. These people are the true beneficiaries of the Affluent Society, and are the class which has sought to reshape the American myths in its image. College-educated, employed as lawyers, engineers, advertisers, and real-estate dealers, these people are the upper strata of the middle class that experienced the greatest gains in postwar years. The suburban crises of the fifties were *their* crises, the suburban malaise was drowned in *their* Martini glasses. If one were to seek a paradigm for their group, one would find it during the Kennedy era, in the bright young men around the seat of power; but one could also find it in the older and younger men, in corporations and universities. They are those whom Daniel Bell described as the "technocratic elite."

An attack on this group here is not immediately relevant. The Vietnam war has already prompted a number of incisive critiques of them, particularly on the university level. However, critique and solution are not synonymous. It seems likely that the import of young people's radicalism will be diffused and co-opted back into electoral party politics, and the thrust of radical restructuring lost, as it was in the New Deal. Already the "beautiful people" seem to be emerging as the new archetype of this social caste . . . human beings who span Establishment and anti-Establishment factionalism, who work for corporations by day, yet smoke dope by night.

The problem is that their amorality is more difficult to detect because it so often hides behind a veil of rhetorical concern. Unlike the industrial captains of the last century, their contemporary lieutenants feign not indifference but impotence. After all, they *are* concerned, God knows, but they are only vice-presidents or mere managers. They may give occasionally to the political *outré* or talk of "repressive tolerance" at cocktail parties, but those gestures mark the boundaries of their social concern.

One index of that social indifference emerges in an ironic place: Michael Harrington in January had an article in *The Atlantic* entitled "The Betrayal of the Poor." The irony is that *The Atlantic*, for all its enlightenment, is still an organ of that upper-middle class who have not so much resisted, as they have ignored, social change.

The article begins: "For all the rhetoric of recent years about the war on poverty, the poor in America are almost as numerous as ever. . . . Unless the government makes immensely greater commitments of resources and planning, the country is doomed to a social explosion in the seventies that will make the turbulent sixties seem tranquil by comparison." The article, like articles on the malnourished, on housing conditions, on the quality of education in the ghetto, will be read and then lost in the comfortable notion that once federal programs are established, everything will be taken care of. Enter the New Deal, Phase II.

The error in this remains the presumption of the liberal upper-middle class since the first decade of this century: that social legislation by the federal government will cure what ails us. Jane Addams suggested it; Ralph Hunter, one of the nation's first social welfare workers, endorsed it; the New Deal itself put the seal of approval on it; and now even Republicans have begun to see merit in the idea. Unfortunately, the theory has never worked.

The critical assumption behind liberal optimism about coalition between the federal government and corporate capitalism has been that things keep getting better all the time. There are more cars, more homes, better schools, etc., than ever before and, in the midst of this prosperity, the distribution of all this largesse has been getting better as well.

Taking the first half of this claim — that the total quantity of goods has increased — there is no dispute. But one *can* make some comparisons between the United States and other industrialized nations. Fifteen nations have higher literacy rates. Ten nations have lower infant mortality rates. To my knowledge, the United States is the only industrialized nation that does not offer comprehensive medical insurance for all its people. It offers perhaps the worst unemployment protection and the worst welfare system among the developed countries. It has fifteen million malnourished. It has thirty million poor. It has seventy-seven million deprived. Few other nations can claim such tawdry conditions amid such phenomenal growth.

On the second half of the comfortable liberal optimism — that distribution has been getting better and better — there is a fundamental error in the assumption. Since the Second World War, the only significant redistribution of income in the United States has been between the upper and the upper-middle classes. Overall, distribution has remained essentially stable not only over the past twenty years but over the entire twentieth century.

There are three sources for this statement. The first is the chart on income distribution (see p. 491) that shows the limits of change. The second is from Joseph Pechman, a conventionally liberal economist, writing in *The Public Interest*, who states: "The year 1929 must have been the high point of inequality during the nineteen-twenties, so that distribution of income in the more recent period may not have been very different from what it was in the early twenties if account is taken of undistributed profits." The third is a much earlier source. Published in 1904, Robert Hunter's *Poverty* is probably the first attempt made to estimate the number of poor in America. Highly sympathetic to the poor, it uses the data of state and private welfare agencies (since federal data were nonexistent). While emphasizing the wretched conditions of the poor, Hunter limits their number to only twelve per cent of the population. Today economic historians agree that Hunter's estimate was off the mark by six per cent, thus leaving at the turn of the century a minority poor of eighteen per cent. Yet eighteen per cent was the government's estimate of the poor sixty years later!

None of these three estimates is perfect (none ever can be, because crucial data are lacking); but they can give a newer and perhaps more accurate contour of poverty and affluence in America. We are, as De Toqueville said, and as American social scientists have reaffirmed ever since, "a people of the middle class." But to be middle class is both a social-psychological and economic problem. Among those who call themselves "middle class," perhaps a majority have always lacked the money to be in fact what they believe they are. Not only are the poor still with us, but they have been there for years. Michael Harrington's announcement that our poor are the "first minority poor in history" has been misunderstood; the poor have always been a minority in America, but a stubborn minority that refuses to decrease and disappear. The rich in America just keep getting richer. All the talk of income distribution, of flattening pyramids, and of peaceful economic revolutions has been nonsense, fabricated in part out of optimism, in part out of a myopia in the professional classes who themselves gained so rapidly after the Second World War.

At the end of an account such as this, it is usually expected that the author will offer remedies, specific reforms such as tax legislation or welfare payments — or at least see reason for hope on the horizon. I cannot. First, because "reform" has become the province of politicians and electoral platforms, and deals with our needs about as realistically as someone using a Band-Aid on a compound fracture. Yet, even liberals accept reformism, as they did when they quietly applauded the Nixon proposal of a guaranteed annual income for the poor, despite the dire (and probably accurate) warning of Michael Harrington that "a guaranteed annual income could be a way to institutionalize poverty at the subsistence level in the United States."

Second, and more important, I do not seek "reform" because, at age twenty-three, I have lost faith in the willingness of America to "reform." I have lived with the poor, eaten their food, slept in their beds, and taught their children, in Alabama, in Vermont, in Watts. I know their bitterness, and I share it. John Kenneth Galbraith observed recently that "liberalism has been excessively tender toward the rich." A surprise to liberals, but a fact of life for the poor. Attempts at reform have delivered to the poor nothing but promises. They have watched the War on Poverty beaten into ineffectual irrelevance. They have listened to America's liberal politicians promise food as they stare at empty plates. They know the sham of reform.

A College Generation in Rebellion

The nation's campuses have never quite matched the fond stereotypes of old grads and TV writers. Varying from college generation to generation, there has always been student engagement with the issues agitating the larger society. The 1950s marked a low point of student activism; it was the "silent" generation. The 1930s, on the other hand, saw intense student militancy on many campuses. Then as now, vocal radicals took the lead and, antiwar sentiment was powerful — in 1937 students took a pledge nationwide not to participate in any future war. Then as now, demonstrating students attracted national attention and infuriated their elders. But the similarities should not be permitted to mask what is new in the current unrest. Never before has an American student movement been so widespread and deeply felt, never has it confronted in so fundamental a way the shortcomings of the society, never has it been so violent and disruptive. From rather modest beginnings, as it now seems, in the Free Speech Movement at Berkeley in 1964, student activism gathered force until, triggered by the invasion of Cambodia and the killing of six students at Kent State University and Jackson State College, it paralyzed virtually the entire system of higher education in May 1970 and had profound repercussions throughout the nation. Something seems to be happening that has never before occurred in our history: college students are becoming a force for social change in America.

In the following essay, Yale psychologist Kenneth Keniston examines the roots of contemporary student unrest. The primary source he locates in the "postindustrial" stage of our development, that is, the point at which the objectives of industrialism have essentially been accomplished. This has served, first, to undermine the very values — industrial ethic — that brought about that success; and, second, to create a student population unique in numbers and development and by definition idealistic and questioning in its view of the world. So, paradoxically, student activism arises more from the successes of the system than from its failures. (The specific evils under student attack, Keniston notes, are not any worse than in the past, and some are hardly as bad.) From the two above conditions, the characteristics of student unrest follow: fury at the shortcomings in the old order — judged by its own standards — and, at once, an insistence on an educational system and style of life that rejects the ethic of the old order.

The thrust of Keniston's analysis is to emphasize the significance of student activism as a social phenomenon rather than merely as a response to specific provocations or as an expression of personal disorders. By so doing, Keniston gives new importance to the rebellion of youth. It is likely to endure and to leave a permanent mark on contemporary America.

FOR FURTHER READING:

FEUER, LEWIS. *Conflict of Generations.* New York: Basic Books, 1969.

KENISTON, KENNETH. *The Uncommitted: Alienated Youth in American Society.* New York, Dell Publishing Company, Delta Books, 1967.*

———. *Young Radicals.* New York: Harcourt, Brace & World, 1968.

KUNEN, JAMES S. *Strawberry Statement: Notes of a College Revolutionary.* New York: Random House, 1969.*

Asterisk denotes paperback edition.

You Have to Grow Up in Scarsdale to Know How Bad It Is

KENNETH KENISTON

The recent events at Harvard are the culmination of a long year of unprecedented student unrest in the advanced nations of the world. We have learned to expect students in underdeveloped countries to lead unruly demonstrations against the status quo, but what is new, unexpected and upsetting to many is that an apparently similar mood is sweeping across America, France, Germany, Italy and even Eastern European nations like Czechoslovakia and Poland. Furthermore, the revolts occur, not at the most backward universities, but at the most distinguished, liberal and enlightened — Berkeley, the Sorbonne, Tokyo, Columbia, the Free University of Berlin, Rome and now Harvard.

This development has taken almost everyone by surprise. The American public is clearly puzzled, frightened and often outraged by the behavior of its most privileged youth. The scholarly world, including many who have devoted their lives to the study of student protest, has been caught off guard as well. For many years, American analysts of student movements have been busy demonstrating that "it can't happen here." Student political activity abroad has been seen as a reaction to modernization, industrialization and the demise of traditional or tribal societies. In an already modern, industrialized, detribalized and "stable" nation like America, it was argued, student protests are naturally absent.

Another explanation has tied student protests abroad to bad living conditions in some universities and to the unemployability of their graduates. Student revolts, it was argued, spring partly from the misery of student life in countries like India and Indonesia. Students who must live in penury and squalor naturally turn against their universities and societies. And if, as in many developing nations, hundreds of thousands of university graduates can find no work commensurate with their skills, the chances for student militancy are further increased.

These arguments helped explain the "silent generation" of the nineteen-fifties and the absence of protest, during that period, in American universities, where students are often "indulged" with good living conditions, close student-faculty contact and considerable freedom of speech. And they helped explain why "super-employable" American college graduates, especially the much-sought-after ones from colleges like Columbia and Harvard, seemed so contented with their lot.

But such arguments do not help us understand today's noisy, angry and militant students in the advanced countries. Nor do they explain why students who enjoy the greatest advantages — those at the leading universities — are often found in the revolts. As a result, several new interpretations of student protest are currently being put forward, interpretations that ultimately form part of what Richard Poirier has termed "the war against the young."

Many reactions to student unrest, of course, spring primarily from fear, anger,

---

Source: Kenneth Keniston, "You Have to Grow Up in Scarsdale to Know How Bad It Is," *The New York Times Magazine* (April 27, 1969), pp. 27–28, 122–129.

confusion or envy, rather than from theoretical analysis. Governor Wallace's attacks on student "anarchists" and other "pin-headed intellectuals;" for example, were hardly coherent explanations of protest. Many of the bills aimed at punishing student protesters being proposed in Congress and state legislatures reflect similar feelings of anger and outrage. Similarly, the presumption that student unrest *must* be part of an international conspiracy is based on emotion rather than fact. Even George F. Kennan's recent discussion of the American student left is essentially a moral condemnation of "revolting students," rather than an effort to explain their behavior.

If we turn to more thoughtful analyses of the current student mood we find two general theories gaining widespread acceptance. The first, articulately expressed by Lewis S. Feuer in his recent book on student movements, "The Conflict of Generations," might be termed the "Oedipal Rebellion" interpretation. The second, cogently stated by Zbigniew Brzezinski and Daniel Bell, can be called the theory of "Historical Irrelevance."

The explanation of Oedipal Rebellion sees the underlying force in all student revolts as blind, unconscious Oedipal hatred of fathers and the older generation. Feuer, for example, finds in all student movements an inevitable tendency toward violence and a combination of "regicide, parricide and suicide." A decline in respect for the authority of the older generation is needed to trigger a student movement, but the force behind it comes from "obscure" and "unconscious" forces in the child's early life, including both intense death wishes against his father and the enormous guilt and self-hatred that such wishes inspire in the child.

The idealism of student movements is thus, in many respects, only a "front" for the latent unconscious destructiveness and self-destructiveness of underlying motivations. Even the expressed desire of these movements to help the poor and exploited is explained psychoanalytically by Feuer: Empathy for the disadvantaged is traced to "traumatic" encounters with parental bigotry in the students' childhoods, when their parents forbade them to play with children of other races or lower social classes. The identification of today's new left with blacks is thus interpreted as an unconscious effort to "abreact and undo this original trauma."

There are two basic problems with the Oedipal Rebellion theory, however. First, although it uses psychoanalytic terms, it is bad psychoanalysis. The real psychoanalytic account insists that the Oedipus complex is universal in all normally developing children. To point to this complex in explaining student rebellion is, therefore, like pointing to the fact that all children learn to walk. Since both characteristics are said to be universal, neither helps us understand why, at some historical moments, students are restive and rebellious, while at others they are not. Second, the theory does not help us explain why some students (especially those from middle-class, affluent and idealistic families) are most inclined to rebel, while others (especially those from working-class and deprived families) are less so.

In order really to explain anything, the Oedipal Rebellion hypothesis would have to be modified to point to an unusually *severe* Oedipus complex, involving especially *intense* and unresolved unconscious feelings of father-hatred in student rebels. But much is now known about the lives and backgrounds of these rebels — at least those in the United States — and this evidence does not support even the modified theory. On the contrary, it indicates that most student protesters are relatively *close* to their parents, that the values they profess are usually the ones they learned at the family dinner table, and that their parents tend to be highly educated, liberal or left-wing and politically active.

Furthermore, psychological studies of student radicals indicate that they are no more neurotic, suicidal, enraged or disturbed than are non-radicals. Indeed, most studies find them to be rather more integrated, self-accepting and "advanced," in a psychological sense, than their politically inactive contemporaries. In general, research on American student rebels supports a "Generational Solidarity" (or chip-off-the-old-block) theory, rather than one of Oedipal Rebellion.

The second theory of student revolts now being advanced asserts that they are a reaction against "historical irrelevance." Rebellion springs from the unconscious awareness of some students that society has left them and their values behind. According to this view, the ultimate causes of student dissent are sociological rather than psychological. They lie in fundamental changes in the nature of the advanced societies — especially, in the change from industrial to post-industrial society. The student revolution is seen not as a true revolution, but as a counterrevolution — what Daniel Bell has called "the guttering last gasp of a romanticism soured by rancor and impotence."

This theory assumes that we are moving rapidly into a new age in which technology will dominate, an age whose real rulers will be men like computer experts, systems analysts and technobureaucrats. Students who are attached to outmoded and obsolescent values like humanism and romanticism unconsciously feel they have no place in this post-industrial world. When they rebel they are like the Luddites of the past — workers who smashed machines to protest the inevitable industrial revolution. Today's student revolt reflects what Brzezinski terms "an unconscious realization that they [the rebels] are themselves becoming historically obsolete"; it is nothing but the "death rattle of the historical irrelevants."

This theory is also inadequate. It assumes that the shape of the future is already technologically determined, and that protesting students unconsciously "know" that it will offer them no real reward, honor or power. But the idea that the future can be accurately predicted is open to fundamental objection. Every past attempt at prophecy has turned out to be grievously incorrect. Extrapolations from the past, while sometimes useful in the short run, are usually fundamentally wrong in the long run, especially when they attempt to predict the quality of human life, the nature of political and social organization, international relations or the shape of future culture.

The future is, of course, made by men. Technology is not an inevitable master of man and history, but merely provides the possibility of applying scientific knowledge to specific problems. Men may identify with it or refuse to, use it or be used by it for good or evil, apply it humanely or destructively. Thus, there is no real evidence that student protest will emerge as the "death rattle of the historical irrelevants." It could equally well be the "first spark of a new historical era." No one today can be sure of the outcome, and people who feel certain that the future will bring the obsolescence and death of those whom they dislike are often merely expressing their fond hope.

The fact that today's students invoke "old" humanistic and romantic ideas in no way proves that student protests are a "last gasp" of a dying order. Quite the contrary: *All* revolutions draw upon older values and visions. Many of the ideals of the

French Revolution, for example, originated in Periclean Athens. Revolutions do not occur because new ideas suddenly develop, but because a new generation begins to take *old* ideas seriously — not merely as interesting theoretical views, but as the basis for political action and social change. Until recently, the humanistic vision of human fulfillment and the romantic vision of an expressive, imaginative and passionate life were taken seriously only by small aristocratic or Bohemian groups. The fact that they are today taken as real goals by millions of students in many nations does not mean that these students are "counterrevolutionaries," but merely that their ideas follow the pattern of every major revolution.

Indeed, today's student rebels are rarely opposed to technology *per se*. On the contrary, they take the high technology of their societies completely for granted, and concern themselves with it very little. What they *are* opposed to is, in essence, the worship of Technology, the tendency to treat people as "inputs" or "outputs" of a technological system, the subordination of human needs to technological programs. The essential conflict between the minority of students who make up the student revolt and the existing order is a conflict over the future direction of technological society, not a counterrevolutionary protest against technology.

In short, both the Oedipal Rebellion and the Historical Irrelevance theories are what students would call "put-downs." If we accept either, we are encouraged not to listen to protests, or to explain them away or reject them as either the "acting out" of destructive Oedipal feelings or the blind reaction of an obsolescent group to the awareness of its obsolescence. But if, as I have argued, neither of these theories is adequate to explain the current "wave" of student protest here and abroad, how can we understand it?

One factor often cited to explain student unrest is the large number of people in the world under 30 — today the critical dividing line between generations. But this explanation alone, like the theories just discussed, is not adequate, for in all historical eras the vast portion of the population has always been under 30. Indeed, in primitive societies most people die before they reach that age. If chronological youth alone was enough to insure rebellion, the advanced societies — where a greater proportion of the population reaches old age than ever before in history — should be the *least* revolutionary, and primitive societies the *most*. This is not the case.

Most relevant factors are the relationship of those under 30 to the established institutions of society (that is, whether they are engaged in them or not); and the opportunities that society provides for their continuing intellectual, ethical and emotional development. In both cases the present situation in the advanced nations is without precedent.

Philippe Aries, in his remarkable book, "Centuries of Childhood," points out that, until the end of the Middle Ages, no separate stage of childhood was recognized in Western societies. Infancy ended at approximately 6 or 7, whereupon most children were integrated into adult life, treated as small men and women and expected to work as junior partners of the adult world. Only later was childhood recognized as a separate stage of life, and our own century is the first to "guarantee" it by requiring universal primary education.

The recognition of adolescence as a stage of life is of even more recent origin, the product of the nineteenth and twentieth centuries. Only as industrial societies became prosperous enough to defer adult work until after puberty could they create institutions — like widespread secondary-school education — that would extend adolescence to virtually all young people. Recognition of adolescence also arose from the vocational and psychological requirements of these societies, which needed much higher levels of training and psychological development than could be guaranteed through primary education alone. There is, in general, an intimate relationship between the way a society defines the stages of life and its economic, political and social characteristics.

Today, in more developed nations, we are beginning to witness the recognition of still another stage of life. Like childhood and adolescence, it was initially granted only to a small minority, but is now being rapidly extended to an ever-larger group. I will call this the stage of "youth," and by that I mean both a further phase of disengagement from society and the period of psychological development that intervenes between adolescence and adulthood. This stage, which continues into the 20s and sometimes into the 30s, provides opportunities for intellectual, emotional and moral development that were never afforded to any other large group in history. In the student revolts we are seeing one result of this advance.

I call the extension of youth an advance advisedly. Attendance at a college or university is a major part of this extension, and there is growing evidence that this is, other things being equal, a good thing for the student. Put in an oversimplified phrase, it tends to free him — to free him from swallowing unexamined the assumptions of the past, to free him from the superstitions of his childhood, to free him to express his feelings more openly and to free him from irrational bondage to authority.

I do not mean to suggest, of course, that all college graduates are free and liberated spirits, unencumbered by irrationality, superstition, authoritarianism or blind adherence to tradition. But these findings do indicate that our colleges, far from cranking out only machinelike robots who will provide skilled manpower for the economy, are also producing an increasing number of highly critical citizens — young men and women who have the opportunity, the leisure, the affluence and the educational resources to continue their development beyond the point where most people in the past were required to stop it.

So, one part of what we are seeing on campuses throughout the world is not a reflection of how bad higher education is, but rather of its extraordinary accomplishments. Even the moral righteousness of the student rebels, a quality both endearing and infuriating to their elders, must be judged at least partially a consequence of the privilege of an extended youth; for a prolonged development, we know, encourages the individual to elaborate a more personal, less purely conventional sense of ethics.

What the advanced nations have done is to create their own critics on a mass basis — that is, to create an ever-larger group of young people who take the highest values of their societies as their own, who internalize these values and identify them with their own best selves, and who are willing to struggle to implement them. At the same time, the extension of youth has lessened the personal risks of dissent: These young people have been freed from the requirements of work, gainful employment and even marriage, which permits them to criticize their society from a protected position of disengagement.

But the mere prolongation of development need not automatically lead to unrest. To be sure, we have granted to millions the opportunity to examine their societies, to compare them with their values and to come to a reasoned judgment of the existing order. But why should their judgment today be so unenthusiastic?

What protesting students throughout the world share is a mood more than an ideology or a program, a mood that says the existing system — the power structure — is hypocritical, unworthy of respect, outmoded and in urgent need of reform. In addition, students everywhere speak of repression, manipulation and authoritarianism. (This is paradoxical, considering the apparently great freedoms given them in many nations. In America, for example, those who complain most loudly about being suffocated by the subtle tyranny of the Establishment usually attend the institutions where student freedom is greatest.) Around this general mood, specific complaints arrange themselves as symptoms of what students often call the "exhaustion of the existing society."

To understand this phenomenon we must recognize that, since the Second World War, some societies have indeed begun to move past the industrial era into a new world that is post-industrial, technological, post-modern, post-historic or, in Brzezinski's term, "technectronic." In Western Europe, the United States, Canada and Japan, the first contours of this new society are already apparent. And, in many other less-developed countries, middle-class professionals (whose children become activists) often live in post-industrial enclaves within pre-industrial societies. Whatever we call the post-industrial world, it has demonstrated that, for the first time, man can produce more than enough to meet his material needs.

This accomplishment is admittedly blemished by enormous problems of economic distribution in the advanced nations, and it is in terrifying contrast to the overwhelming poverty of the Third World. Nevertheless, it is clear that what might be called "the problem of production" *can,* in principle, be solved. If all members of American society, for example, do not have enough material goods, it is because the system of distribution is flawed. The same is true, or will soon be true, in many other nations that are approaching advanced states of industrialization. Characteristically, these nations, along with the most technological, are those where student unrest has recently been most prominent.

The transition from industrial to post-industrial society brings with it a major shift in social emphases and values. Industrializing and industrial societies tend to be oriented toward solving the problem of production. An industrial ethic — sometimes Protestant, sometimes Socialist, sometimes Communist — tends to emphasize psychological qualities like self-discipline, delay of gratification, achievement-orientation and a strong emphasis on economic success and productivity. The social, political and economic institutions of these societies tend to be organized in a way that is consistent with the goal of increasing production. And industrial societies tend to apply relatively uniform standards, to reward achievement rather than status acquired by birth, to emphasize emotional neutrality ("coolness") and rationality in work and public life.

The emergence of post-industrial societies, however, means that growing numbers of the young are brought up in family environments where abundance, relative economic security, political freedom and affluence are simply facts of life, not goals to be striven for. To such people the psychological imperatives, social institutions and cultural values of the industrial ethic seem largely outdated and irrelevant to their own lives.

Once it has been demonstrated that a society *can* produce enough for all of its members, at least some of the young turn to other goals: for example, trying to make sure that society *does* produce enough and distributes it fairly, or searching for ways to live meaningfully with the goods and the leisure they *already* have. The problem is that our society has, in some realms, exceeded its earlier targets. Lacking new ones, it has become exhausted by its success.

When the values of industrial society become devitalized, the élite sectors of youth — the most affluent, intelligent, privileged and so on — come to feel that they live in institutions whose demands lack moral authority or, in the current jargon, "credibility." Today, the moral imperative and urgency behind production, acquisition, materialism and abundance has been lost.

Furthermore, with the lack of moral legitimacy felt in "the System," the least request for loyalty, restraint or conformity by its representatives — for example, by college presidents and deans — can easily be seen as a moral outrage, an authoritarian repression, a manipulative effort to "co-opt" students into joining the Establishment and an exercise in "illegitimate authority" that must be resisted. From this conception springs at least part of the students' vague sense of oppression. And, indeed, perhaps their peculiar feeling of suffocation arises ultimately from living in societies without vital ethical claims.

Given such a situation, it does not take a clear-cut issue to trigger a major protest. I doubt, for example, that college and university administrators are in fact *more* hypocritical and dishonest than they were in the past. American intervention in Vietnam, while many of us find it unjust and cruel, is not inherently *more* outrageous than other similar imperialistic interventions by America and other nations within the last century. And the position of blacks in this country, although disastrously and unjustifiably disadvantaged, is, in some economic and legal respects, better than ever before. Similarly, the conditions for students in America have never been as good, especially, as I have noted, at those élite colleges where student protests are most common.

But this is *precisely* the point: It is *because* so many of the *other* problems of American society seem to have been resolved, or to be resolvable in principle, that students now react with new indignation to old problems, turn to new goals and propose radical reforms.

So far I have emphasized the moral exhaustion of the old order and the fact that, for the children of post-industrial affluence, the once-revolutionary claims of the industrial society have lost much of their validity. I now want to argue that we are witnessing on the campuses of the world a fusion of *two revolutions* with distinct historical origins. One is a continuation of the old and familiar revolution of the industrial society, the liberal-democratic-egalitarian revolution that started in America and France at the turn of the 18th century and spread to virtually every nation in the world. (Not completed in any of them, its contemporary American form is, above all, to be found in the increased militancy of blacks.) The other is the new revolution, the post-industrial one, which seeks to define new goals relevant to the 20th and 21st centuries.

In its social and political aspects, the first revolution has been one of universalization, to use the sociologist's awkward term. It has involved the progressive extension to more and more people of economic, political and social rights, privileges and opportunities originally available only to the aristocracy, then to the middle class, and now in America to the relatively affluent white working class. It is, in many respects, a *quantitative* revolution. That is, it concerns itself less with the quality of life than with the amount of political freedom, the quantity and distribution of goods or the amount and level of injustice.

As the United States approaches the targets of the first revolution, on which this society was built, to be poor shifts from being an unfortunate fact of life to being an outrage. And, for the many who have never experienced poverty, discrimination, exploitation or oppression, even to *witness* the existence of these evils in the lives of others suddenly becomes intolerable. In our own time the impatience to complete the first revolution has grown apace, and we find less willingness to compromise, wait and forgive among the young, especially among those who now take the values of the old revolution for granted — seeing them not as goals, but as *rights.*

A subtle change has thus occurred. What used to be utopian ideals — like equality, abundance and freedom from discrimination — have now become demands, inalienable rights upon which one can insist without brooking any compromise. It is noteworthy that, in today's student confrontations, no one requests anything. Students present their "demands."

So, on the one hand, we see a growing impatience to complete the first revolution. But, on the other, there is a newer revolution concerned with newer issues, a revolution that is less social, economic or political than psychological, historical and cultural. It is less concerned with the quantities of things than with their qualities, and it judges the virtually complete liberal revolution and finds it still wanting.

"You have to have grown up in Scarsdale to know how bad things really are," said one radical student. This comment would probably sound arrogant, heartless and insensitive to a poor black, much less to a citizen of the Third World. But he meant something important by it. He meant that *even* in the Scarsdales of America, with their affluence, their upper-middle-class security and abundance, their well-fed, well-heeled children and their excellent schools, something is wrong. Economic affluence does not guarantee a feeling of personal fulfillment; political freedom does not always yield an inner sense of liberation and cultural freedom; social justice and equality may leave one with a feeling that something else is missing in life. "No to the consumer society!" shouted the bourgeois students of the Sorbonne during May and June of 1968 — a cry that understandably alienated French workers, for whom affluence and the consumer society are still central goals.

What, then, are the targets of the new revolution? As is often noted, students themselves don't know. They speak vaguely of "a society that has never existed," of "new values," of a "more humane world," of "liberation" in some psychological, cultural and historical sense. Their rhetoric is largely negative; they are stronger in opposition than in proposals for reform; their diagnoses often seem accurate, but their prescriptions are vague; and they are far more articulate in urging the immediate completion of the first revolution than in defining the goals of the second. Thus, we can only indirectly discern trends that point to the still-undefined targets of the new revolution.

What are these trends and targets?

First, there is a revulsion against the notion of quantity, particularly economic quantity and materialism, and a turn toward concepts of quality. One of the most delightful slogans of the French student revolt was, "Long live the passionate revolution of creative intelligence!" In a sense, the achievement of abundance may allow millions of contemporary men and women to examine, as only a few artists and madmen have examined in the past, the quality, joyfulness and zestfulness of experience. The "expansion of consciousness"; the stress on the expressive, the aesthetic and the creative; the emphasis on imagination, direct perception and fantasy — all are part of the effort to enhance the quality of this experience.

Another goal of the new revolution involves a revolt against uniformity, equalization, standardization and homogenization — not against technology itself, but against the "technologization of man." At times, this revolt approaches anarchic quaintness, but it has a positive core as well — the demand that individuals be appreciated, not because of their similarities or despite their differences, but because they *are* different, diverse, unique and noninterchangeable. This attitude is evident in many areas: for example, the insistence upon a cultivation of personal idiosyncrasy, mannerism and unique aptitude. Intellectually, it is expressed in the rejection of the melting-pot and consensus-politics view of American life in favor of a post-homogeneous America in which cultural diversity and conflict are underlined rather than denied.

The new revolution also involves a continuing struggle against psychological or institutional closure or rigidity in any form, even the rigidity of a definite adult role. Positively, it extols the virtues of openness, motion and continuing human development. What Robert J. Lifton has termed the protean style is clearly in evidence. There is emerging a concept of a lifetime of personal change, of an adulthood of continuing self-transformation of an adaptability and an openness to the revolutionary modern world that will enable the individual to remain "with it" — psychologically youthful and on top of the present.

Another characteristic is the revolt against centralized power and the complementary demand for participation. What is demanded is not merely the consent of the governed, but the involvement of the governed. "Participatory democracy" summarizes this aspiration, but it extends far beyond the phrase and the rudimentary social forms that have sprung up around it. It extends to the demand for relevance in education — that is, for a chance for the student to participate in his own educational experience in a way that involves all of his faculties, emotional and moral as well as intellectual. The demand for "student power" (or, in Europe, "co-determination") is an aspect of the same theme: At Nanterre, Columbia, Frankfurt and Harvard, students increasingly seek to participate in making the policies of their universities.

This demand for participation is also embodied in the new ethic of "meaningful human relationships," in which individuals confront each other without masks, pretenses and games. They "relate" to each other as unique and irreplaceable human beings, and develop new forms of relationships from which all participants will grow.

In distinguishing between the old and the new revolutions, and in attempting to define the targets of the new, I am, of course, making distinctions that students themselves rarely make. In any one situation the two revolutions are joined and fused, if not confused. For example, the Harvard students' demand for "restructuring the university" is essentially the second revolution's demand for participation; but their demand for an end to university "exploitation" of the surrounding community is tied to the more traditional goals of the first revolution. In most radical groups there is a range of opinion that starts with the issues of the first (racism, imperialism, exploitation, war) and runs to the concerns of the second (experiential education, new life styles, meaningful participation, consciousness-expansion, relatedness, encounter and community). The first revolution is personified by Maoist-oriented Progressive Labor party factions within the student left, while the second is represented by hippies, the "acid left," and the Yippies. In any individual, and in all student movements, these revolutions coexist in uneasy and often abrasive tension.

Furthermore, one of the central problems for student movements today is the absence of any theory of society that does justice to the new world in which we of the most industrialized nations live. In their search for rational critiques of present societies, students turn to theories like Marxism that are intricately bound up with the old revolution.

Such theories make the ending of economic exploitation, the achievement of social justice, the abolition of racial discrimination and the development of political participation and freedom central, but they rarely deal adequately with the issues of the second revolution. Students inevitably try to adapt the rhetoric of the first to the problems of the second, using concepts that are often blatantly inadequate to today's world.

Even the concept of "revolution" itself is so heavily laden with images of political, economic and social upheaval that it hardly seems to characterize the equally radical but more social-psychological and cultural transformations involved in the new revolution. One student, recognizing this, called the changes occurring in his California student group, "too radical to be called a revolution." Students are thus often misled by their borrowed vocabulary, but most adults are even more confused, and many are quickly led to the mistaken conclusion that today's student revolt is nothing more than a repetition of Communism's in the past.

Failure to distinguish between the old and new revolutions also makes it impossible to consider the critical question of how compatible they are with each other. Does it make sense — or is it morally right — for today's affluent American students to seek imagination, self-actualization, individuality, openness and relevance when most of the world and many in America live in deprivation, oppression and misery?

The fact that the first revolution is "completed" in Scarsdale does not mean that it is (or soon will be) in Harlem or Appalachia — to say nothing of Bogotá or Calcutta. For many children of the second revolution, the meaning of life may be found in completing the first — that is, in extending to others the "rights" they have always taken for granted.

For others the second revolution will not wait; the question. "What lies beyond affluence?" demands an answer now. Thus, although we may deem it self-indulgent to pursue the goals of the new revolution in a world where so much misery exists, the fact is that in the advanced nations it is upon us, and we must at least learn to recognize it.

Finally, beneath my analysis lies an assumption I had best make explicit. Many student critics argue that their societies have failed miserably. My argument, a more historical one perhaps, suggests that our problem is not only that industrial societies have failed to keep all their promises, but that they have succeeded in some ways beyond all expectations. Abundance was once a distant dream, to be postponed to a hereafter of milk and honey; today, most Americans are affluent. Universal mass education was once a Utopian goal; today in America almost the entire population completes high school, and almost half enters colleges and universities.

The notion that individuals might be free, en masse, to continue their psychological, intellectual, moral and cognitive development through their teens and into their 20's would have been laughed out of court in any century other than our own; today, that opportunity is open to millions of young Americans. Student unrest is a reflection not only of the failures, but of the extraordinary successes of the liberal-industrial revolution. It therefore occurs in the nations and in the colleges where, according to traditional standards, conditions are best.

But for many of today's students who have never experienced anything but affluence, political freedom and social equality, the old vision is dead or dying. It may inspire bitterness and outrage when it is not achieved, but it no longer animates or guides. In place of it, students (and many who are not students) are searching for a new vision, a new set of values, a new set of targets appropriate to the post-industrial era — a myth, an ideology or a set of goals that will concern itself with the quality of life and answer the question, "Beyond freedom and affluence, what?"

What characterizes student unrest in the developed nations is this peculiar mixture of the old and the new, the urgent need to fulfill the promises of the past and, at the same time, to define the possibilities of the future.

A B C D E F G H I J   9 8 7 6 5 4 3 2 1